# Professional Resumes *for* Executives, Managers, and Other Administrators

A New Gallery of Best Resumes by Professional Resume Writers

*by David F. Noble, Ph.D.*

jist

*Professional Resumes for Executives, Managers, and Other Administrators*



Published by JIST Works, an imprint of JIST Publishing, Inc.
8902 Otis Avenue
Indianapolis, IN 46216-1033
Phone: 1-800-648-JIST Fax: 1-800-JIST-FAX E-mail: editorial@jist.com

Interior Design: Debbie Berman

Printed in the United States of America

03 02 01 00 5 4 3 2

Library of Congress Cataloging-in-Publication Data

Noble, David F. (David Franklin), 1935–
Professional resumes for executives, managers, and other administrators : a new gallery of best resumes by professional resume writers / by David F. Noble.
p. cm.
Includes bibliographical references and index.
ISBN 1-56370-483-8
1. Résumés (Employment) 2. Executives. 3. Cover letters.
I. Title.
HF5383.N623 1998 98-20676
650.14'024658--dc21 CIP



We have been careful to provide accurate and authoritative information throughout this book, but it is possible that errors and omissions have been introduced. Please consider this in making any career plans or other important decisions. Trust your own judgment above all else and in all things.

ISBN 1-56370-483-8

*To Kari, Lance, Mary, and Sarah*

# Acknowledgments

This new collection of professionally written resumes would not have been possible without the resume submissions of the writers featured in this book. When I compiled the first Gallery (*Gallery of Best Resumes,* Indianapolis: JIST Works, Inc., 1994), I knew these writers only as names on a mailing list from the Professional Association of Résumé Writers, which I had recently joined. Since the publication of that first Gallery and its sequel (*Gallery of Best Resumes for Two-Year Degree Graduates,* Indianapolis: JIST Works, Inc., 1996), I have met personally many of these writers at annual meetings of the PARW—first at Scottsdale, Arizona, in 1996 and then in Boston in 1997. I continue to marvel at the creativity of these writers in exploring new ways to display the strengths of their clients to prospective employers. I am happy to showcase the exceptional work of these professional writers in this new Gallery.

Some of the contributing writers are members also of another group of resume writers that came into being early in 1997: the National Résumé Writers' Association (NRWA). I have joined that group as well and, like some PARW members, belong to both groups. Resumes by some NRWA members are included as well in this new Gallery since both groups are dedicated to elevating the level of resume writing in the United States.

Once again, I want to thank Jim Irizarry at JIST for putting another Gallery in the "Works." New thanks go to JIST's new Associate Publisher, Marta Partington, for her professional editing skills, book development skills, book design sense, and can-do approach to projects. I am grateful also to Amy Goodwin, Karin Ostrom, and Thelma Silvola for their many hours of help in recording, copying, filing, and managing in other ways the submitted resumes and cover letters. Carolyn Newland was always willing to answer some new question about design and layout. Amy and Marta also helped to verify List of Contributors information in the final stage of the project. Many thanks to Debbie Berman for her final desktop publishing of the book. I am especially grateful to Marta Partington and Susan Pines for proofing the desktop published copy of the book and catching any remaining errors.

Finally, I am indebted to my wife, Ginny, a professional editor, who had the foresight and the expertise to create from the preceding Gallery a set of Word templates for this new Gallery. Her editorial touch carries over into this new work through her edited files that were updated for this new Gallery.

# Contents

**Best Resume Design and Layout Tips** .......... 11

This section shows you effective design techniques, such as how to use white space for an uncluttered look; how to use choice phrases from reference letters as testimonials in a resume; how to make decisions about fonts and typefaces; how to handle capital letters, underlining, italic, and boldfacing; and how to use graphic elements such as bullets, horizontal lines, vertical lines, and boxes.

**Best Resume Writing Style Tips** .......... 16

To help you make your resume error-free, you learn practical writing tips, such as how to use capital letters in computer terms; how to use hyphens in words and phrases; and how to use commas, semicolons, dashes, and colons correctly.

# Part 2: The Gallery .......... 21

## The Gallery at a Glance .......... 22

**How to Use the Gallery** .......... 23

This Gallery has three sections of professional resumes for executives, managers, and other administrators, respectively; but, whatever the title of your position, you should check out all the resumes throughout the Gallery for design tips, ways to express ideas, impressive formats, and so forth. At the bottom of each resume and cover letter page are mini-reviews that call your attention to noteworthy features or solutions to problems.

**Professional Resumes for Executives** .......... 27

Account Executives .......... 29
Chief Executive Officer .......... 32
Consultants .......... 34
Controllers .......... 52
Executive Chefs .......... 55
Executive Directors .......... 60
Owners .......... 72
Partners .......... 86
Presidents .......... 94
Vice Presidents .......... 108

**Professional Resumes for Managers** .......... 143

Accounting/Finance Managers .......... 145
Auto Body Shop Managers .......... 152
Branch Managers .......... 154
Case Managers .......... 157
City Managers .......... 160
Computer Systems Managers .......... 163
General Managers .......... 167
Hospitality Managers .......... 174
Human Resources Managers .......... 186
Inventory Managers .......... 194
Maintenance Managers .......... 197
Manufacturing Managers .......... 204

A quality resume can make a great impression, but it can be ruined quickly by a poorly written cover letter. This section shows you how to eliminate common errors in cover letters. It amounts to a crash writing course that you won't find in any other resume book. After you read the following sections, you will be better able to write and polish any letters you create for your job search.

**Using Good Strategies for Letters** .......... **558**

**Using Pronouns Correctly** .......... **559**

**Using Verb Forms Correctly** .......... **560**

**Using Punctuation Correctly** .......... **561**

**Using Words Correctly** .......... **565**

**Exhibit of Cover Letters** .......... **567**

In this section, you learn how to evaluate 18 sample cover letters, which actually accompanied resumes that were submitted for use in the Gallery. After you study this exhibit, you will have a better feel for designing your own cover letters to make them distinctive and effective.

## Appendix: List of Contributors .......... 587

Use this Appendix to locate or contact a professional resume writer whose resume styles you admire. Besides working with clients locally, a number of the writers work with clients by phone, fax, or e-mail, or on the World Wide Web.

## Occupational Index (Current or Last Job) .......... 601

New with this Gallery, this Index enables you to find quickly sample resumes for current or recent job positions. They are listed alphabetically and cross-referenced. For example, if you want to see resumes for current or past store managers, look up either Store Manager or Manager, Store, in the Index. The numbers are resume numbers, not page numbers.

# Introduction

Like the *Gallery of Best Resumes* and the *Gallery of Best Resumes for Two-Year Degree Graduates, Professional Resumes for Executives, Managers, and Other Administrators* is a collection of quality resumes from professional resume writers, each with individual views about resumes and resume writing. Unlike many resume books whose selections "look the same," this book contains resumes that look different because they are scanned representations of *real* resumes prepared by different professionals for actual job searchers throughout the country. (Certain information on the resumes has been fictionalized by the writers to protect, where necessary, each client's right to privacy.) Even when several resumes from the same writer appear in the book, most of these resumes are different because the writer has customized each resume according to the background information and career goals of the client for whom the resume was prepared.

Instead of assuming that "one resume style fits all," the writers featured here believe that a client's past experiences and next job target should determine the resume's type, design, and content. The writers interacted with clients to fashion resumes that seemed best for each client's situation at the time.

This book features resumes from writers who share several important qualities: good listening skills, a sense of what details are appropriate for a particular resume, and flexibility in selecting and arranging the resume's sections. By "hearing between" a client's statements, the perceptive resume writer can detect what kind of job the client really wants. The writer then chooses the information that will best represent the client for the job being sought. Finally, the writer decides on the best arrangement of the information, usually from the most important to the least important, for that job. With the help of this book, you can create this kind of resume yourself or know how to contact a professional writer who can create a custom resume for you.

Most of the writers of the resumes in this Gallery are members of the Professional Association of Résumé Writers (PARW). Some of these writers are members also of the National Résumé Writers' Association (NRWA), which was established by a regional PARW chapter in February, 1997. Those who have CPRW certification, for Certified Professional Résumé Writer (see the Appendix, "List of Contributors"), received this designation from PARW after they studied specified course materials and demonstrated proficiency in an examination. Those who have NCRW certification, for National Certified Résumé Writer, received this designation from NRWA after a different course of study and a different examination. A few contributors are not members of either organization but are either past PARW members or are professional writers in Indiana, Michigan, and Ohio who were invited by the author to submit works for possible selection for this special Gallery for executives, managers, and other administrators.

## Why a Gallery for Executives, Managers, and Other Administrators?

This new Gallery of best resumes was devoted just to business leaders because they have special resume needs that "lower level" workers don't tend to have. Company officers, managers, and other administrators usually have accumulated leadership experiences over a relatively longer work life. This greater amount of managerial experience may be from work for different companies or from different positions within the same company as the worker climbed the company ladder and received more responsibility with each new job title. A challenge in writing a resume for an experienced company officer is selecting from an abundance of experience the right information to display in a resume for a person's career goals, particularly when the appearance of "being overqualified" can be a handicap in a competitive job market.

A trade-off of greater experience is older age. A legitimate concern in resume writing for executives is finding ways to play down a person's age while calling attention to the individual's experience and achievements.

Company leaders not only have more career-related experience but also tend to have multiple skills that have been put to work in a greater range of experience. For example, a person who is currently an entrepreneur as the owner and president of a new company might have been a regional sales manager who was also a vice president and who started out not in sales but as an engineer or as an accountant. The resume writing challenge here is determining which experiences to emphasize and which to downplay. A related task is knowing what to exclude. Some clients of professional resume writers want to include "everything," but the writers prefer to present only the most important information on one or two pages.

## How This Book Is Organized

*Professional Resumes for Executives, Managers, and Other Administrators*, like the preceding two Galleries, consists of three parts. Part 1, "Best Resume Tips," presents resume writing strategies, design and layout tips, and resume writing style tips for making resumes visually impressive. Some of these strategies and tips were suggested by resume writers who contributed resumes to *Gallery of Best Resumes* (Indianapolis: JIST Works, Inc., 1994). When one of the writers is the known source of a strategy or tip, the writer's name appears in brackets. A reference is given also to one or more Gallery resumes that illustrate the strategy or tip. These reference are not exhaustive. If you browse through the Gallery, you may see other resumes that exhibit the same strategy or tip.

Part 2 is the Gallery itself, containing 342 resumes from 84 resume writers. These resumes are grouped according to three broad categories: Resumes for Executives, Resumes for Managers, and Resumes for Other Administrators. These categories are nominal distinctions (that is, in name only) that were useful for sorting resumes and should not be used to make functional judgments about the duties or responsibilities of any particular job title. Many executives have managerial responsibilities. Many managers are considered executives within their own corporate structures. Many other administrators, like coordinators, directors, and superintendents, have executive or managerial roles.

Because of this overlapping in responsibilities from executives to managers to other administrators, and from position to position within each of the three broad categories, you should look at all of the resumes in this collection and not just at those of your particular position. All of the resumes form a hunting ground for ideas that may prove useful to you for developing your own resume.

Resume writers commonly distinguish between chronological resumes and functional (or skills) resumes. A *chronological resume* is a photo—a snapshot history of what you did and when you did it. A *functional resume* is a painting—an interpretive sketch of what you can do for a future employer. A third kind of resume, known as a *combination resume*, is a mix of recalled history and self-assessment. Besides recollecting "the facts," a combination resume contains self-interpretation and is therefore more like dramatic history than news coverage. A chronological resume and a functional resume are not always that different; often, all that is needed for a functional resume to qualify as a combination resume is the inclusion of some dates, such as those for positions held. All three kinds of resumes are illustrated in the Gallery.

When there are a number of resumes for a particular job title, the resumes are generally arranged from the simple to the complex, and from the most recent to the least recent. That is, a resume for a district manager who has had that title for five years will appear before a resume for a district manager who has been in that role for seven years. Generally, as the number of years of service increases, the resumes become more complex. Many of the resumes are one page, but a number of them are two pages. A few are more than two pages.

The Gallery offers a wide range of resumes whose features you can use in creating and improving your own resumes. Notice the plural. An important premise of an active job search is that you will not have just one "perfect" resume for all potential employers, but different versions of your resume for different interviews. The Gallery is therefore not a showroom where you say, "I'll take that one." It is a valuable resource of design ideas, expressions, and organizational patterns that can help make your own resume a "best resume" for your next interview.

Creating multiple versions of a resume may seem difficult, but it is easy to do if you have (or have access to) a personal computer and a laser printer or some other kind of printer that can produce quality output. You will also need word processing, desktop publishing, or resume software. If you don't have a computer or a friend who does, don't despair. Most professional resume writers have the hardware and software, and they can make your resume look like those in the Gallery. A local fast-print shop can make your resume look good, but you will probably not get there the kind of advice and service the professional resume writer provides. Of course, if all you have is a typewriter, you can still produce versions of your resume, but you will have to retype the resume for each new version.

Part 3, "Best Cover Letter Tips," contains a discussion of some myths about cover letters, plus tips for polishing cover letters. Much of the advice offered here applies also to writing resumes. Included in this part is an exhibit of 18 cover letters. All of these letters accompanied resumes that appear in the Gallery.

The Appendix is a "List of Contributors," which contains the names, addresses, phone numbers, and other information of those who contributed resumes and cover letters for this book. The list is arranged alphabetically by state and city. Although most of these resume writers work with local clients, some of the writers work with clients by phone, e-mail, and the World Wide Web from anywhere in the United States.

New with this book is an Occupational Index for looking up resumes by current or most recent job title. Many professional writers have asked for some kind of an index. This addition to the Gallery should prove useful. The Occupational Index, however, should not replace careful examination of all of the resumes. Too many resumes for some other occupation may have features adaptable to your own occupation. Limiting your search to the Occupational Index pond may cause you to miss some of the awesome creatures swimming in the entire Gallery ocean.

## Who This Book Is For

Anyone who wants ideas for creating or improving a resume can benefit from this book. It is especially useful for active job seekers—those who understand the difference between active and passive job searching. A *passive* job seeker waits until jobs are advertised and then mails copies of the same resume, along with a standard cover letter, to a number of Help Wanted ads. An *active* job seeker believes that a resume should be modified for a specific job target *after* having talked in person or by phone to a prospective interviewer *before* a job is announced. To schedule such an interview is to penetrate the "hidden job market." Active job seekers can find in the Gallery's focused resumes a wealth of strategies for targeting a resume for a particular interview. The section "How to Use the Gallery" at the beginning of Part 2 shows you how to do this.

## What This Book Can Do for You

Besides providing you with a treasury of quality resumes whose features you can use in your own resumes, this book can help transform your thinking about resumes. If you think that there is one "best" way to create a resume, this book will help you learn how to shape a resume that is best for you as you try to get an interview with a particular person for a specific job.

If you have been told that resumes should be only one page long, the examples of multiple-page resumes in the Gallery will help you see how to distribute information effectively across two or more pages. If you believe that the way to update a resume is to add your latest work experiences to your last resume, this book will show you how to rearrange your resume so that you can highlight the most important information about your experience and skills.

After you have studied "Best Resume Tips" in Part 1, examined the professionally written resumes in the Gallery in Part 2, and reviewed "Tips for Polishing Cover Letters" in Part 3, you should be able to create your own resumes worthy of inclusion in any gallery of best resumes.

If you want to ensure that your resume is top-notch and makes a powerful impression, you might contact one of the professional resume writers featured in this book and included in the List of Contributors in the Appendix. These writers earn a living preparing resumes for job candidates and are dedicated to representing their clients at their best. These writers are savvy about job searching and, besides preparing resumes and cover letters, might offer advice about networking, interviewing, and managing your job search in other ways. The writers charge a fee depending on the kind and amount of services you need. Average fees range from under $100 to $500. Many writers offer flexible packages within that range so that you can find an affordable mix of services for your particular job search. Most writers keep your work on file so that you can later update your resume for a modest additional fee.

# 1
P • A • R • T

# Best Resume Tips

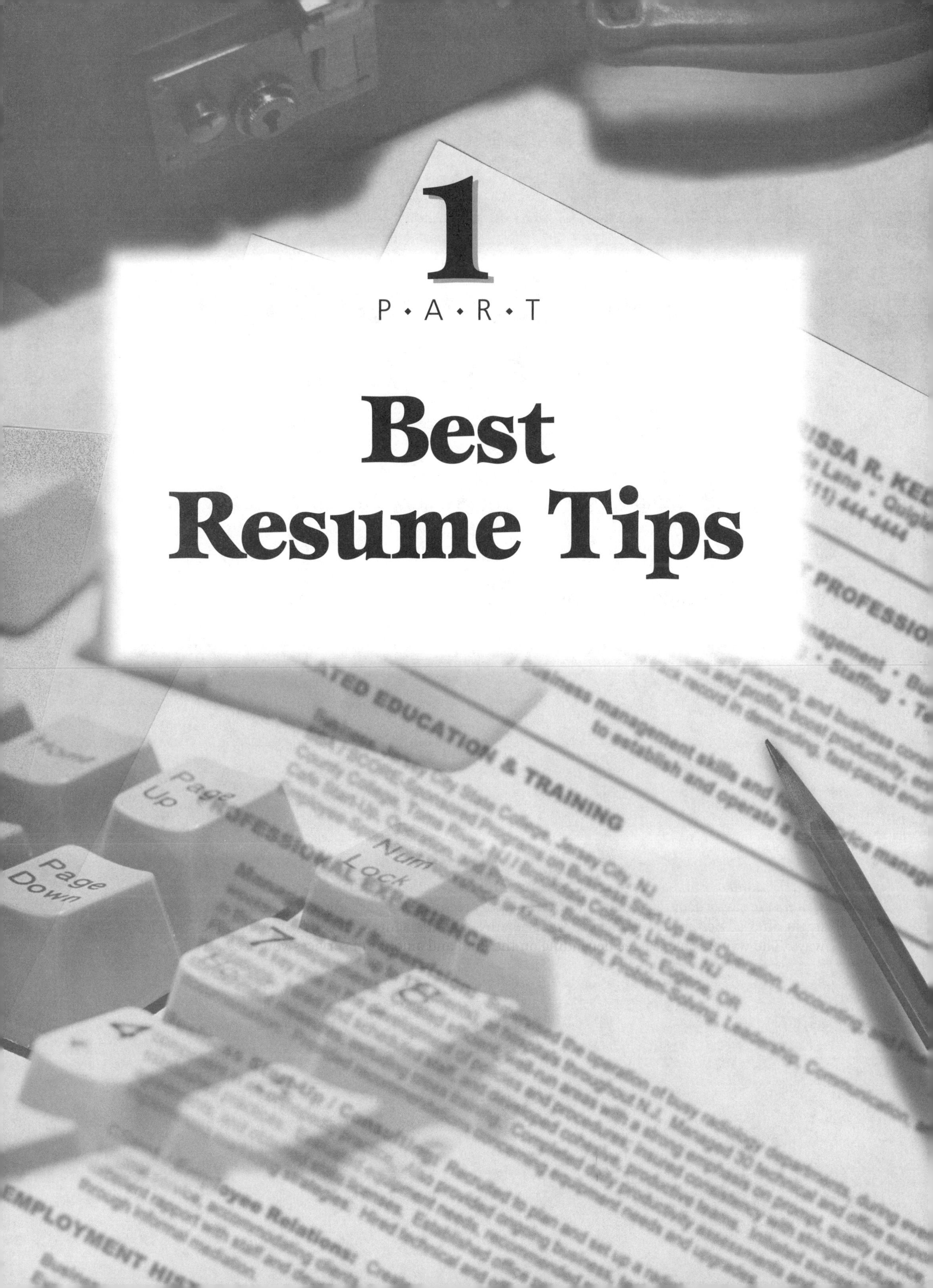

# Best Resume Tips at a Glance

# Best Resume Tips

In a passive job search, you rely on your resume to do most of the work for you. An eye-catching resume that stands out above all the others may be your best shot at getting noticed by a prospective employer. If your resume is only average and looks like most of the others in the pile, the chances are great that you won't be noticed and called for an interview. If you want to be singled out because of your resume, it should be somewhere between spectacular and award-winning.

In an active job search, however, your resume complements your efforts at being known to a prospective employer *before* that person receives it. For this reason, you can rely less on your resume for getting someone's attention. Nevertheless, your resume has an important role in an active job search that may include the following activities:

- Talking to relatives, friends, and other acquaintances to meet people who can hire you before a job is available
- Contacting employers directly, using the *Yellow Pages* to identify types of organizations that could use a person with your skills
- Creating phone scripts to speak with the person who is most likely to hire someone with your background and skills
- Walking into a business in person to talk directly to the one who is most likely to hire someone like you
- Using a schedule to keep track of your appointments and callbacks
- Working at least 25 hours a week to search for a job

When you are this active in searching for a job, the quality of your resume confirms the quality of your efforts to get to know the person who might hire you, as well as your worth to the company whose workforce you want to join. An eye-catching resume makes it easier for you to sell yourself directly to a prospective employer. If your resume is mediocre or conspicuously flawed, it will work against you and may undo all of your good efforts in searching for a job.

The following list offers ideas for making resumes visually impressive. Many of the ideas are for making resumes pleasing to the eye, but a number of the ideas are strategies to use in resumes for special cases. Other ideas are for eliminating common writing mistakes and stylistic weaknesses.

A number of the ideas have come from comments of the professional resume writers who submitted resumes for *Gallery of Best Resumes* (Indianapolis: JIST Works, Inc., 1994). The name of the writer appears in brackets. Resumes in *Professional Resumes for Executives, Managers, and Other Administrators* that illustrate these ideas are referenced by resume number.

Some of these ideas can be used with any equipment, from a manual typewriter to a sophisticated computer with desktop publishing software. Other ideas make sense only if you have a computer system with word processing or desktop publishing. Even if you don't have a computer, take some time to read all of the ideas. Then, if you decide to use the services of a professional resume writer, you will be better informed about what the writer can do for you in producing your resume.

## Best Resume Writing Strategies

1. **Although many resume books say that you should spell out the name of the state in your address at the top of the resume, consider using the postal abbreviation instead.** The reason is simple: it's an address. Anyone wanting to contact you by mail will probably refer to your name and address on the resume. If they appear there as they should on an envelope, the writer or typist can simply copy the information you supply. If you spell out the name of your state in full, the writer will have to "translate" the name of the state to its postal abbreviation.

   Not everyone knows all the postal abbreviations, and some abbreviations are easily confused. For example, those for Alabama (AL), Alaska (AK), American Samoa (AS), Arizona (AZ), and Arkansas (AR) are easy to mix up. You can prevent confusion and delay simply by using the correct postal abbreviation. As resumes become more "scannable," the use of postal abbreviations in addresses will become a requirement.

   If you decide to use postal abbreviations in addresses, make certain that you do not add a period after the abbreviations, even before ZIP codes. This applies also to postal abbreviations in the addresses of references, if provided.

   Do not, however, use the state postal abbreviation when you are indicating only the city and state (not the mailing address) of a school you attended or a business where you worked. In these cases, it makes sense to write out the name of the state in full.

2. **Adopt a sensible form for phone numbers in the contact information and then use that form consistently.** Do this in your resume and in all of the documents you use in your job search. Some forms for phone numbers make more sense than others. Compare the following forms:

| | |
|---|---|
| 123-4567 | This form is best for a resume circulated locally, within a region where all the phone numbers have the same area code. |
| (222) 123-4567 | This form is best for a resume circulated in areas with different area codes. |
| 222-123-4567 | This form suggests that the area code should be dialed in all cases. But that won't be necessary for prospective employers whose area code is 222. This form should be avoided. |

| | |
|---|---|
| 222/123-4567 | This form is illogical and should be avoided also. The slash can mean an alternate option, as in ON/OFF. In a phone number, this meaning of a slash makes little sense. |
| 1 (222) 123-4567 | This form is long, and the digit 1 isn't necessary. Almost everyone will know that 1 should be used before the area code to dial a long-distance number. |

*Note:* For resumes directed to prospective employers *outside* the United States, be sure to include the correct international prefixes in all phone numbers so that you and your references can be reached easily by phone.

3. **If your resume has an Objective statement, make it focused, interesting, and unique so that it grabs the reader's attention.** See, for example, Resume 23. If your Objective statement fails to do this, the reader might discard the resume without reading further. An Objective statement can be your first opportunity to sell yourself.

4. **If you can sell yourself better with some other kind of section, consider omitting an Objective statement and putting a Summary of Qualifications, a Profile, or an Areas of Expertise section just after the contact information.** See, for example, Resumes 3, 4, 5, 6, and most of the other resumes in the Gallery.

5. **A Profile can replace an Objective statement if you mention the target field in a subheading for the Profile.** [Schuster] See, for example, Resume 296.

6. **Making a Qualifications Summary long helps to position important information at the top of the first page.** See, for example, Resume 12.

7. **Listing Qualifications (or Areas of Expertise, or Skills) in columns makes them easy to alter (by deleting some and adding others) when your target is a different job or industry.** See, for example, Resumes 75, 88, 100, 146.

8. **Spend considerable time determining how you present your skills.** You might present them under one or more of the following headings:
   - **Areas of Expertise** (see, for example, Resumes 13, 31, 32, 41, 43, 45, 58, 62, 84, 87, 96, 115, 118, 131, 143, 169, 178, 217, and many others)
   - **Areas of Proficiency** (Resume 103)
   - **Certifications** (Resume 73)
   - **Computer Knowledge** (Resume 104)
   - **Computer Skills** (Resume 11)
   - **Demonstrated Skills** (Resume 140)
   - **Demonstrated Strengths** (Resume 112)
   - **Key Skills** (Resumes 44, 150)
   - **A Key Skills Profile** (Resume 90)
   - **Key Strengths** (Resumes 94, 111, 112)
   - **Leadership Abilities** (Resume 104)

- **Primary Areas of Emphasis** (Resume 98)
- **Professional Capabilities** (Resume 100)
- **Qualifications** (Resume 75)
- **Skill Areas** (Resumes 106, 123)
- **Skills** (Resume 125)
- **Skills and Accomplishments** (Resume 69)
- **Specialties** (Resume 92)
- **A Summary of Attributes** (Resume 49)
- **Technical Proficiency/Certification** (Resume 72)
- **Technical Skills** (Resumes 104, 141)
- **Unspecified** (Resume 145)

9. **In the Experience section or elsewhere, state achievements, not just duties or responsibilities.** Duties and responsibilities for a given position are often already known by the reader. Achievements, however, can be attention-getting. The reader probably considers life too short to be bored by lists of duties and responsibilities in a stack of resumes.

10. **In the Experience section and for each position held, consider explaining responsibilities in a brief paragraph and using bullets to point to achievements.** See, for example, Resumes 82, 85, 150, 164.

11. **When you indicate achievements, consider boldfacing them** (Resumes 2, 8), **quantifying them** (for example, Resumes 2, 6, 8, 9, 10, and many others), **or providing a separate heading for them** (Resumes 2, 8, and others).

12. **When skills, abilities, and qualifications are varied, group them according to categories for easier comprehension.** See, for example, Resumes 1, 12, 24, 28, 34, 35, and many others as you browse through the Gallery.

13. **To tell something about a company where you have worked, try explaining the company name.** See, for example, Resumes 15, 111.

14. **Group positions to avoid repetition in a description of duties.** See, for example, Resumes 175, 181, 329.

15. **As a general strategy, emphasize the important but withhold the irrelevant.** See, for example, Resume 33.

16. **To diminish the negative impact of a gap in your employment, omit the dates of employment and consider listing employment in some order other than chronological.** [Lawrence]

17. **Play up experience and on-the-job training to offset a lack of higher education.** See, for example, Resume 23.

18. **If you have no formal education, omit an Education section in your resume.** No section is better than a weak one. See, for example, Resume 86.

19. **If age is a problem and you want to show that you are in good health, consider providing a personal section at the end of the resume.** See, for example, Resume 44.

20. **Contact information given also at the end of a resume makes it easier for the reader to phone the applicant.** See, for example, Resume 15.

## Best Resume Design and Layout Tips

21. **Use quality paper correctly.** If you use quality watermarked paper for your resume, be sure to use the right side of the paper. To know which side is the right side, hold a blank sheet of paper up to a light source. If you can see a watermark and "read" it, the right side of the paper is facing you. This is the surface for typing or printing. If the watermark is unreadable or if any characters look backward, you are looking at the "underside" of a sheet of paper—the side that should be left blank if you use only one side of the sheet.

22. **Use adequate "white space."** A sheet of white paper with no words on it is impossible to read. Likewise, a sheet of white paper with words all over it is impossible to read. The goal is to have a comfortable mix of white space and words. If your resume has too many words and not enough white space, the resume looks cluttered and unfriendly. If it has too much white space and too few words, the resume looks skimpy and unimportant. Make certain that adequate white space exists between the main sections. For a resume with a satisfying amount of white space, see Resume 209. For a resume with adequate white space even with a small font size, see Resume 51. For white space provided through blank lines, see Resumes 1, 9, 11, 12, 13, 27, 65, and many others. For white space accomplished through center-alignment, see Resume 32.

23. **Margins in resumes for executives, managers, and other administrators tend to be narrower than margins in other resumes.** See, for example, Resume 11. Narrower margins are often used in connection with smaller type to get more information on a one- or two-page resume.

24. **Be consistent in your use of line spacing.** How you handle line spacing can tell the reader how good you are at details and how consistent you are in your use of them. If, near the beginning of your resume, you insert two line spaces (two hard returns in a word processing program) between two main sections, be sure to put two line spaces between main sections throughout the resume.

25. **Be consistent in your use of horizontal spacing.** If you usually put one character space after a period at the end of a sentence, make certain that you do so consistently. The same is true for colons. If you put one space after a colon, do so consistently.

    Note that an em dash—a dash the width of the letter *m*—does not require spaces before or after it. No space should go between the *P* and *O* of P.O. Box. Only one space is needed between the postal abbreviation of a state and the ZIP code. You should insert a space between the first and second initials of a person's name, as in I. M. Jobseeker (not I.M. Jobseeker). These conventions have become widely adopted in English and business communications. If, however, you use other conventions, be sure to be consistent. In resumes, as in grammar, consistency is more important than conformity.

26. **Make certain that characters, lines, and images contrast well with the paper.** The quality of "ink" depends on the device used to type or print your resume. If you use a typewriter or a dot-matrix printer with a cloth ribbon,

check that the ribbon is fresh enough to make a dark impression. If you use a typewriter or a printer with a carbon tape, make certain that your paper has a texture that allows the characters to adhere permanently. (For a test, send yourself a copy of your resume and see how it makes the trip through the mail.) If you use an inkjet or laser printer, check that the characters are sharp and clean, without ink smudges or traces of extra toner. Mail yourself also a laser-printed envelope to make sure that it looks good after a trip through the mail. A cover letter with a flaking impression for the address does not make a good impression.

After much use, a cloth ribbon in a typewriter or a daisywheel printer may cause some characters (especially *a*, *e*, *o*, *g*, and *p*) to look darker than others. The reason probably is that ink has collected in the characters on the type bars or print wheel. To fix this problem, use a toothbrush and a safe solvent to clean the type.

27. **Use vertical alignment in stacked text.** Resumes usually contain tabbed or indented text. Make certain that this "stacked" material is aligned vertically. Misalignment can ruin the appearance of a well-written resume. Try to set tabs or indents that control this text throughout a resume instead of having a mix of tab stops in different sections. If you use a word processor, make certain that you understand the difference between tabbed text and indented text, as in the following examples:

| | |
|---|---|
| Tabbed text: | This text was tabbed over one tab stop before the writer started to write the sentence. |
| Indented text: | This text was indented once before the writer started to write the sentence. |

*Note:* In a number of word processing programs, the Indent command is useful for ensuring the correct vertical alignment of proportionally spaced, stacked text. After you issue the Indent command, lines of wrapped text are vertically aligned automatically until you terminate the command by pressing Enter.

28. **For the vertical alignment of dates, try left- or right-aligning the dates.** This technique is especially useful in chronological resumes and combination resumes. For examples of left-aligned dates, see Resumes 16, 20, 24, and others. For right-aligned dates, look at Resumes 3, 6, 7, 8, 9, 15, and many others. See Resume 296 in which dates of overall employment are put in the left column, while dates for each position are put after it to avoid the appearance of job hopping [Schuster].

29. **Use as many pages as you need for portraying yourself adequately to a specific interviewer about a particular job.** Try to limit your resume to one page or two pages, but set the upper limit at four pages. No rule about the number of pages makes sense in all cases. The determining factors are a person's qualifications and experiences, the requirements of the job, and the interests and pet peeves of the interviewer. If you know that an interviewer refuses to look at a resume longer than a page, that says it all. You need to deliver a one-page resume if you want to get past the first gate.

More important than the question of how many pages is the issue of complete pages. A full page sends a better message than a partial page (which says "not enough to fill"). Therefore, one full page is better than 1.25 pages, and two full pages are better than 1.75 pages.

30. **When you have letters of recommendation, use quotations from them as testimonials in the first column of a two-column format or somewhere else in the resume.** Devoting a column to the positive opinions of "external authorities" helps to make a resume convincing as well as impressive. See, for example, Resume 81, which shows that a gifted amateur has merits. See Resume 93, which uses testimonials to show that an ex-military person has skills for a successful civilian job performance. See also Resume 303, which uses testimonials to show that an elementary school teacher has what it takes to be a school principal.

31. **Unless you enlist the services of a professional printer or skilled desktop publisher, resist the temptation to use full justification for text.** The price that you pay for a straight right margin is uneven word spacing. Words may appear too close together on some lines and too spread out on others. Although the resume might look like typeset text, you lose readability. See also Tip 4 in Part 3 of this book.

32. **If you can choose a typeface for your resume, use a serif font for greater readability.** Serif fonts have little lines extending from the top, bottom, and end of a character. These fonts tend to be easier to read than sans serif (without serif) fonts, especially in low-light conditions. Compare the following font examples:

| Serif | Sans Serif |
|---|---|
| Century Old Style | Gill Sans |
| Courier | Futura |
| Times Roman | Helvetica |

Words like *minimum* and *abilities* are more readable in a serif font.

33. **If possible, avoid using monospaced type like this Courier type.** Courier was a standard of business communications during the 1960s and 1970s. Because of its widespread use, it is now considered "common." It also takes up a lot of space, so you can't pack as much information on a page with Courier type as you can with a proportionally spaced type like Times Roman.

34. **Think twice before using all uppercase letters in parts of your resume.** A common misconception is that uppercase letters are easier to read than lowercase letters. Actually, the ascenders and descenders of lowercase letters make them more distinguishable from each other and therefore more recognizable than uppercase letters. For a test, look at a string of uppercase letters and throw them gradually out of focus by squinting. The uppercase letters become a blur sooner than lowercase letters.

35. **Think twice about underlining some words in your resume.** Underlining defeats the purpose of serifs at the bottom of characters by blending with the serifs. In trying to emphasize words, you lose some visual clarity. This is especially true if you use underlining with uppercase letters in centered or side headings.

36. **If you have access to many fonts through word processing or desktop publishing, beware of becoming "font happy" and turning your resume into a font circus.** *Frequent* font changes *can distract* the reader **adversely,** **AND SO CAN GAUDY DISPLAY TYPE.**

37. **To make your resume stand out, consider using a nonstandard format with the headings in unconventional display type.** See, for example, Resume 92, which casts the resume as a menu. When you compare this idea with the preceding idea, you can see that one of the basic rules of resume making is, "Anything goes." What is usually fitting for resumes for some prospective jobs, however, is not always the most appropriate resume strategy for executive positions. Try to match the style of your resume to the target company's "corporate image" if it has one.

38. **Be aware of the value differences of black type.** Some typefaces are light; others are dark. Notice the following lines:

    A quick brown fox jumps over the lazy dog.

    **A quick brown fox jumps over the lazy dog.**

    Most typefaces fall somewhere in-between. With the variables of height, width, thickness, serifs, angles, curves, spacing, ink color, ink density, boldfacing, and typewriter double-striking, type offers an infinite range of values from light to dark. Try to make your resume more visually interesting by offering stronger contrasts between light type and dark type. Browse through the Gallery and notice the differences in light and dark type.

39. **Use italic characters carefully.** Whenever possible, use italic characters instead of underlining when you need to call attention to a word or phrase. You might consider using italic for duties or achievements. Think twice, however, about using italic throughout your resume. The reason is that italic (slanted) characters are less readable than normal (vertical) characters. You might have to hold the resume at an angle to make an all-italic resume more readable. Such a maneuver can irritate a reader.

40. **Use boldfacing to make different job titles more evident.** See, for example, Resumes 1, 3, 4, 5, and many others.

41. **For getting attention, make a heading white on black if you use software that has this capability.** See, for example, Resume 121.

42. **If you use word processing or desktop publishing and have a suitable printer, use special characters to enhance the look of your resume.** For example, use enhanced quotations marks (" ") instead of their typewriter equivalents (" "). Use an em dash (—) instead of two hyphens (--) for a dash. To separate dates, try using an en dash (a dash the width of the letter *n*) instead of a hyphen, as in 1998–1999.

43. **To call attention to an item in a list, use a bullet (•) or a box (■) instead of a hyphen (-).** Browse through the Gallery and notice how bullets are used effectively as attention getters.

44. **For variety, try using bullets of a different style, such as diamond (◆) bullets, rather than the usual round or square bullets.** Examples with diamonds are Resumes 1, 8, 12, 31, 82, 124, and many others. For other kinds of "bullets," see Resumes 99 (arrow tips); 88 (check marks); 125 (chevrons); 128 (decorative); 15 (ellipses); 4, 6, 7, 26, 27, 29, 52, 66, 87, and many others (filled squares); 52, 69 (five-pointed stars); 45 (pairs of sixteenth notes); 1, 15,

28, 95 (right-pointing arrow tips); 21, 30 (shadowed circles); and 6, 25, 55, 150 (shadowed squares). This list is not exhaustive. You will see more if you browse through the entire Gallery.

45. **Make a bullet a little smaller than the lowercase letters that appear after it.** Disregard any ascenders or descenders on the letters. Compare the following bullet sizes:

    • Too small ● Too large • Better • Just right

46. **When you use bullets, make certain that the bulleted items go beyond the superficial and contain information that employers really want to know.** Many short bulleted statements that say nothing special can affect the reader negatively. Brevity is not always the best strategy with bullets [Noonan].

47. **When the amount of information justifies a longer resume, repeat a particular graphic, such as a filled square bullet (■) or a shadowed circle (❍), to unify the entire resume.** See, for example, Resumes 7 and 21.

48. **If possible, visually coordinate the resume and the cover letter with the same graphic to catch the attention of the reader.** See, for example, Resume 204 and Cover Letter 7.

49. **Use a horizontal line or a combination of lines to separate the contact information from the rest of the resume.** See, for example, Resumes 2, 6, 11, 12, 16, 67, 77, and many others.

50. **Use horizontal lines to separate the different sections of the resume and to make them visible at a glance.** See, for example, Resumes 7, 22, 27 (Education included with Career Development), 30, 52, 59, 64, 129, and many others.

51. **To call attention to a resume section or certain information, use horizontal lines to enclose it.** See, for example, Resumes 9, 14, 19, 124, 138, 140, 149, 277, 278, and many others.

52. **Change the thickness of part of a horizontal line to call attention to a section heading below the line.** See, for example, Resumes 95, 209.

53. **Use a vertical line (or lines) to spice up your resume.** See, for example, Resumes 4, 13.

54. **Use a box to make a page visually more interesting.** See, for example, Resumes 30, 282.

55. **Use a page border to make a page visually more interesting.** See, for example, Resumes 8, 31, 42, 45, 70, 82, 268.

56. **Consider using center-alignment to make short statements look better than if they were left-aligned.** See, for example, Resume 300.

57. **Consider using double indentation to make a Profile or some other section stand out.** See, for example, Resume 38.

58. **Consider using hanging indentation of section headings to make them stand out.** See, for example, Resume 79.

59. **Consider centering headings to make them easy to read down a page.** See, for example, Resume 147.

60. **Notice that a thick bold line above a name in boldface makes it the first item to be seen.** See, for example, Resumes 15, 209.

61. **For a scannable resume, add extra letter spacing to make bold characters scannable, and with that make a scanned resume more appealing.** See, for example, Resume 330.

## Best Resume Writing Style Tips

62. **Check that words or phrases in lists are parallel.** For example, notice the bulleted achievements in the Achievements section of Resume 3. All the verbs are in the past tense. Notice also the list in the Profile section of Resume 21. Here all the entries contain nouns.

63. **Use capital letters correctly.** Resumes usually contain many of the following:

    - Names of people, companies, organizations, government agencies, awards, and prizes
    - Titles of job positions and publications
    - References to academic fields (such as chemistry, English, and mathematics)
    - Geographic regions (such as the Midwest, the East, the state of California, Oregon State, and northern Florida)

    Because of such words, resumes are minefields for the misuse of uppercase letters. When you don't know whether a word should have an initial capital letter, don't guess. Consult a dictionary, a handbook on style, or some other authoritative source. Often a reference librarian can provide the information you need. If so, you are only a phone call away from an accurate answer.

64. **Check that capital letters and hyphens are used correctly in computer terms.** If you want to show in a Computer Experience section that you have used certain hardware and software, you may give the opposite impression if you don't use uppercase letters and hyphens correctly. Note the correct use of capitals and hyphens in the following names of hardware, software, and computer companies:

| | | |
|---|---|---|
| LaserJet III | Hewlett-Packard | dBASE |
| PageMaker | MS-DOS | Microsoft |
| WordPerfect | PC DOS | Microsoft Word |
| NetWare | PostScript | |

The reason that many computer product names have an internal uppercase letter is for the sake of a trademark. A word with unusual spelling or capitalization is trademarkable. When you use the correct forms of these words, you are honoring trademarks and registered trademarks.

65. **Use all uppercase letters for most acronyms.** An *acronym* is a pronounceable word usually formed from the initial letters of the words in a compound term, or sometimes from multiple letters in those words. Note the following examples:

| | |
|---|---|
| BASIC | Beginner's All-purpose Symbolic Instruction Code |
| COBOL | COmmon Business-Oriented Language |
| DOS | Disk Operating System |
| FORTRAN | FORmula TRANslator |

An acronym like *radar* (*ra*dio *d*etecting *a*nd *r*anging) has become so common that it is no longer all uppercase.

66. **Be aware that you may need to use a period with some abbreviations.** An *abbreviation* is a word shortened by removing the latter part of the word or by deleting some letters within the word. Here are some examples:

| | |
|---|---|
| *adj.* for *adjective* | *amt.* for *amount* |
| *adv.* for *adverb* | *dept.* for *department* |

Usually, you can't pronounce an abbreviation as a word. Sometimes, however, an abbreviation is a set of uppercase letters (without periods) that you can pronounce as letters. AFL-CIO, CBS, NFL, and YMCA are examples.

67. **Be sure to spell every word correctly.** A resume with just one misspelling is not impressive and may undermine all the hours you spent putting it together. Worse than that, one misspelling may be what the reader is looking for to screen you out, particularly if you are applying for a position that requires accuracy with words. If you multiply the annual salary you don't get times the number of years you might have worked for that company, that's an expensive misspelling!

If you use word processing and have a spelling checker, you may be able to catch any misspellings. Be wary of spelling checkers, however. They can detect a misspelled word but cannot detect when you have inadvertently used a wrong word (*to* for *too*, for example). Be wary also of letting someone else check your resume. If the other person is not a good speller, you may not get any real help. The best authority is a good, *current* dictionary.

68. **For words that have a couple of correct spellings, use the preferred form.** This form is the one that appears first in a dictionary. For example, if you see the entry **trav•el•ing** *or* **trav•el•ling**, the first form (with one *l*) is the preferred spelling. If you make it a practice to use the preferred spelling, you will build consistency in your resumes and cover letters.

69. **Avoid British spellings.** These slip into American usage through books published in Great Britain. Note the following words:

| **British Spelling** | **American Spelling** |
|---|---|
| acknowledgement | acknowledgment |
| centre | center |
| judgement | judgment |
| towards | toward |

**70. Avoid hyphenating words with such prefixes as *co-*, *micro-*, *mid-*, *mini-*, *multi-*, *non-*, *pre-*, *re-*, and *sub-*.** Many people think that words with these prefixes should have a hyphen after the prefix, but most of these words should not. The following words are spelled correctly:

| | | |
|---|---|---|
| coauthor | microcomputer | minicomputer |
| coworker | midpoint | multicultural |
| cowriter | midway | multilevel |
| nondisclosure | prearrange | reenter |
| nonfunctional | prequalify | subdirectory |

*Tip:* If you look in a dictionary for a word with a prefix and can't find the word, look for the prefix itself in the dictionary. You might find there a small-print listing of a number of words that have the prefix.

**71. Be aware that compounds (combinations of words) present special problems for hyphenation.** Writers' handbooks and books on style do not always agree on how compounds should be hyphenated. Many compounds are evolving from *open* compounds to *hyphenated* compounds to *closed* compounds. In different dictionaries, you can therefore find the words *copy editor*, *copy-editor*, and *copyeditor*. No wonder the issue is confusing! Most style books do agree, however, that when some compounds appear as an adjective before a noun, the compound should be hyphenated. When the same compound appears after a noun, hyphenation is unnecessary. Compare the following two sentences:

I scheduled well-attended conferences.

The conferences I scheduled were well attended.

For detailed information about hyphenation, see a recent edition of *The Chicago Manual of Style*. You should be able to find a copy at a local library.

**72. Be sure to hyphenate so-called *permanent* hyphenated compounds.** Usually, you can find these by looking them up in a dictionary. You can spot them easily because they have a "long hyphen" (—) for visibility in the dictionary. Hyphenate these words (with a standard hyphen) wherever they appear, before or after a noun. Here are some examples:

| | |
|---|---|
| all-important | self-employed |
| day-to-day | step-by-step |
| full-blown | time-consuming |

**73. Use the correct form for certain verbs and nouns combined with prepositions.** You may need to consult a dictionary for correct spelling and hyphenation. Compare the following examples:

| | |
|---|---|
| start up | (verb) |
| start-up | (noun) |
| start-up | (adj.) |
| startup | (noun, computer industry) |
| startup | (adj., computer industry) |

74. **Avoid using shortcut words, such as abbreviations like *thru* or foreign words like *via*.** Spell out *through* and use *by* for *via*.

75. **Use the right words.** The issue here is correct *usage*, which often means the choice of the right word or phrase from a group of two or more possibilities. The following words and phrases are often used incorrectly:

| | |
|---|---|
| **alternate** (adj.) | Refers to an option used every other time. OFF is the alternate option to ON in an ON/OFF switch. |
| **alternative** | Refers to an option that can be used at any time. If cake and pie are alternative desserts for dinner, you can have cake three days in a row if you like. The common mistake is to use *alternate* when the correct word is *alternative*. |
| **center around** | A common illogical expression. Draw a circle and then try to draw its center around it. You can't. Use *center in* or *center on* as logical alternatives to *center around*. |

For information about the correct *usage* of words, consult a usage dictionary or the usage section of a writer's handbook.

76. **Use numbers consistently.** Numbers are often used inconsistently with text. Should you present a number as a numeral or spell out the number as a word? One approach is to spell out numbers *one* through *nine* but present numbers 10 and above as numerals. Different approaches are taught in different schools, colleges, and universities. Use the approach you have learned, but be consistent.

77. **Use (or don't use) the serial comma consistently.** How should you punctuate a series of three or more items? If, for example, you say in your resume that you increased sales by 100 percent, opened two new territories, and trained four new salespersons, the comma before *and* is called the *serial comma*. It is commonly omitted in newspapers, magazine articles, advertisements, and business documents; but it is often used for precision in technical documents or for stylistic reasons in academic text, particularly in the Humanities.

78. **Use semicolons correctly.** Semicolons are useful because they help to distinguish visually the items in a series when the items themselves contain commas. Suppose that you have the following entry in your resume:

> Increased sales by 100 percent, opened two new territories, which were in the Midwest, trained four new salespersons, who were from Georgia, and increased sales by 250 percent.

The extra commas (before *which* and *who*) throw the main items of the series out of focus. By separating the main items with semicolons, you can bring them back into focus:

> Increased sales by 100 percent; opened two new territories, which were in the Midwest; trained four new salespersons, who were from Georgia; and increased sales by 250 percent.

Use this kind of high-rise punctuation even if just one item in the series has an internal comma.

79. **Avoid using colons after headings.** A colon indicates that something is to follow. A heading indicates that something is to follow. A colon after a heading is therefore redundant.

80. **Use dashes correctly.** One of the purposes of a dash (an em dash or two hyphens) is to introduce a comment or afterthought about preceding information. A colon *anticipates* something to follow, but a dash *looks back* to something already said. Two dashes are sometimes used before and after a parenthetical remark a related but nonessential remark—such as this—within a sentence. In this case, the dashes are like parentheses, but more formal.

81. **Avoid using the archaic word *upon* in the References section.** The common statement "References available upon request" needs to be simplified, updated, or even deleted in resume writing. The word *upon* is one of the finest words of the 13th century, but it's a stuffy word on the eve of the next century. Usually, *on* will do for *upon*. Other possibilities are "References available by request" and "References available." Because most readers of resumes know that applicants can usually provide several reference letters, this statement is probably unnecessary. A reader who is seriously interested in you will ask about reference letters.

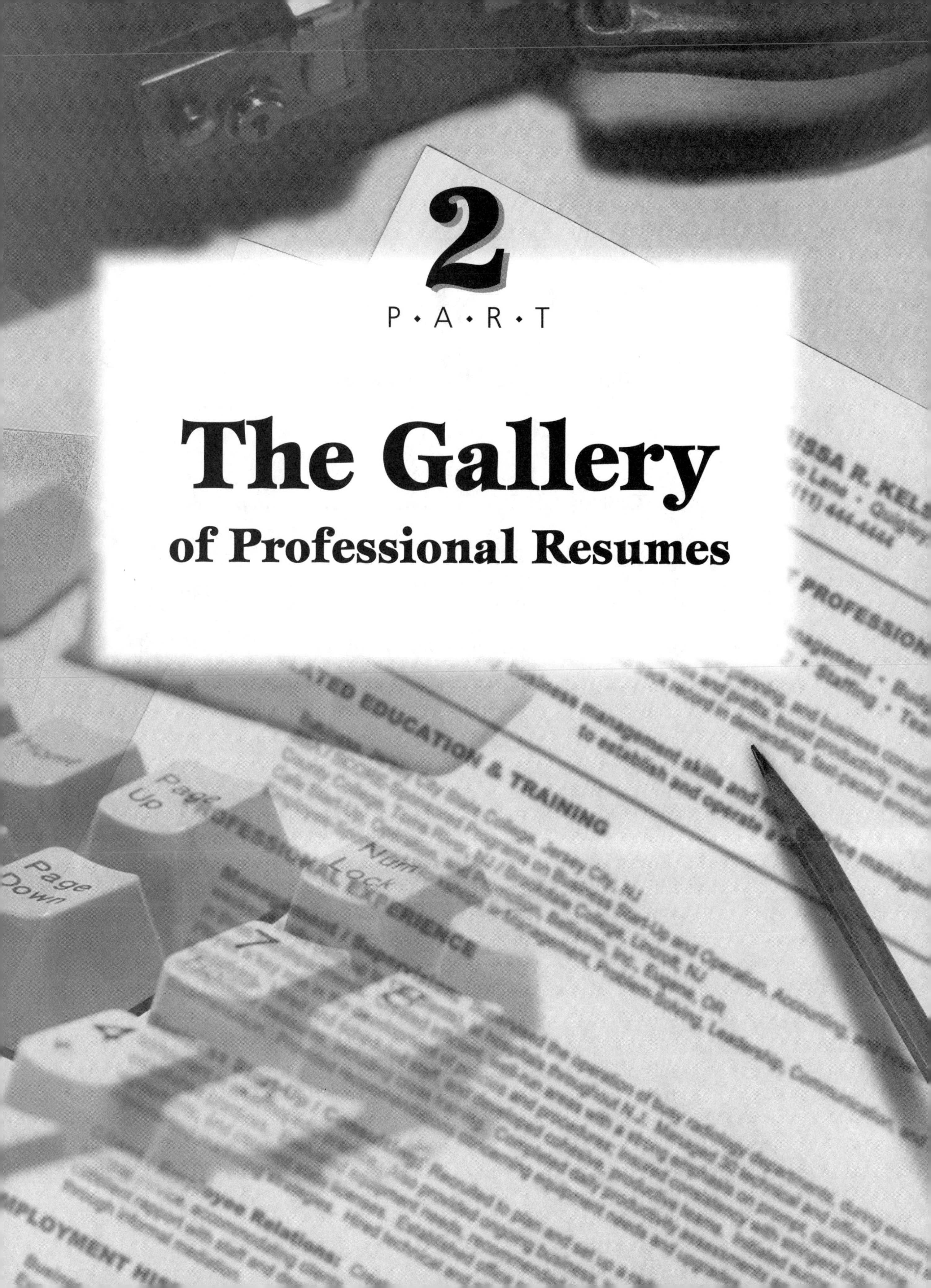

2

P·A·R·T

# The Gallery

## of Professional Resumes

# The Gallery at a Glance

# How to Use the Gallery

You can learn much from the Gallery just by browsing through it. This new collection contains resumes for executives, managers, and other administrators—in that order. The resumes are grouped by current or recent job position. To make the best use of this resource, however, read the following suggestions before you begin.

**Look at the resumes in the category containing your field, related fields, or your target occupation.** Use the Occupational Index to find a resume by job title if a resume for that position is included in the Gallery. Notice what kinds of resumes other people have used to find similar jobs. Always remember, though, that your resume should not be "canned." It should not look just like someone else's resume but should reflect your own background, unique experiences, and goals.

**Use the Gallery primarily as an "idea book."** Even if you don't find a resume for your specific occupation or job, be sure to look at all the resumes for ideas you can borrow or adapt. You may be able to modify some of the sections or statements with information that applies to your own situation or job target.

**Study the ways professional resume writers have formatted the names, addresses, and phone numbers of the subjects.** In most instances, this contact information appears at the top of the first page of the resume. Look at type styles, size of type, and use of boldface. See whether the personal information is centered on lines, spread across a line, or located near the margin on one side of a page. Look for the use of horizontal lines to separate this information from the rest of the resume, or to separate the address and phone number from the person's name.

**Look at each resume to see what section appears first after the personal information.** Then compare those same sections across the Gallery. For example, look just at the resumes that have a Goal or an Objective statement as the first section. Compare the length, clarity, and use of words. Do these statements contain complete sentences, or one or more partial lines of thought? Are some statements better than others from your point of view? Do you see one or more Objective statements that come close to matching your own objective? After you have compared these statements, try expressing *in your own words* your goal or objective.

**Repeat this "horizontal comparison" for each of the sections across the Gallery.** Compare all of the Summary of Qualifications sections, Profiles, Areas of Expertise sections, and so on. As you make these comparisons, continue to note differences in length, the kinds of words and phrases used, and the effectiveness of the content. Jot down any ideas that might be true for you. Then put together similar sections for your own resume.

As you compare sections across the Gallery, pay special attention to the statements about a person's skills and knowledge. Notice in Work Experience sections how responsibilities and achievements are worked into these sections. Skills, knowledge, and achievements are *variables* that you can select to put a certain "spin" on your resume as you pitch it toward a particular interviewer or job. Your observations here should be especially valuable for your own resume versions.

**After you have examined the resumes "horizontally" (section by section), compare them "vertically" (design by design).** To do this, you need to determine which resumes have the same sections in the same order and then compare just those resumes. For example, look for resumes that have contact information at the top, an Objective statement, a Summary of Qualifications, an Experience section, an Education section, and finally a line about references. (Notice that the actual words in section headings may differ slightly. Instead of the word *Experience*, you might find *Work Experience, Professional Experience,* or *Employment.*) When you examine the resumes in this way, you are looking at their *structural design*, which means the order in which the various sections appear. The same order can appear in resumes of different fields or jobs, so it is important to explore the *whole* Gallery and not limit your investigation to resumes in your field or related fields.

Developing a sense of resume structure is extremely important because it enables you to emphasize the most important information about yourself. A resume is a little like a newspaper article read quickly and usually discarded before the reader finishes. That is why the information in newspaper articles often dwindles in significance toward the end. For the same reason, the most important, attention-getting information about you should be at or near the top of your resume. What follows should appear in order of descending significance.

If you know that the reader will be more interested in your work experience than your Education information, put your Education section toward the end of the resume. If you know that the reader will be interested in your skills regardless of your education and work experience, put your Skills section at or near the beginning of your resume. In this way, you can help to ensure that anyone who reads only *part* of your resume will read the "best about you." Your hope is that this information will encourage the reader to read on to the end of the resume and, above all, take an interest in you.

Compare the resumes according to visual design features, such as the use of horizontal and vertical lines, borders, boxes, bullets, white space, graphics, and inverse type (light characters on a dark background). Notice which resumes have more visual impact at first glance and which ones make no initial impression. Do some of the resumes seem more inviting to read than others? Which ones are less appealing because they have too much information, or too little? Which ones seem to have the right balance of information and white space?

**After comparing the visual design features, choose the design ideas that might improve your own resume.** You will want to be selective here and not try to work every design possibility into your resume. As in writing, "less is more" in resume making, especially when you integrate design features with content.

The indication of whether a resume is a chronological, functional (skills), or combination resume is only a quick and personal assessment. Generally, a resume is labeled *chronological* if it displays a list of jobs in chronological order (from current or most recent to least recent) but has no skills, qualifications, or profile section. A resume is designated *functional* if it has an evident skills, qualifications, or profile section but no historical list of jobs and no work history near the end of the resume. A resume is judged to be a *combination* resume if it has at least a skills, qualifications, or profile section and also a historical list of jobs or a work history. The category most debatable in this assessment is the combination category. Some may prefer to label as functional a resume that has a brief work history near the end of the resume but elsewhere stresses the candidate's skills and qualifications. That kind of assessment is defensible, and readers, of course, are free to classify a resume in some other way.

Another method of arrangement in this Gallery is to arrange resumes for one occupation from the most recently attained to the longest held. For example, a resume for an individual who has been a company president from 1994 to the present is placed before a resume for a person who has been a company president from 1992 to the present. You can then view together resumes displaying comparable years of experience.

**Note:** Words in quotation marks in the captions below the resumes are from the resume writer's written comments about the resume.

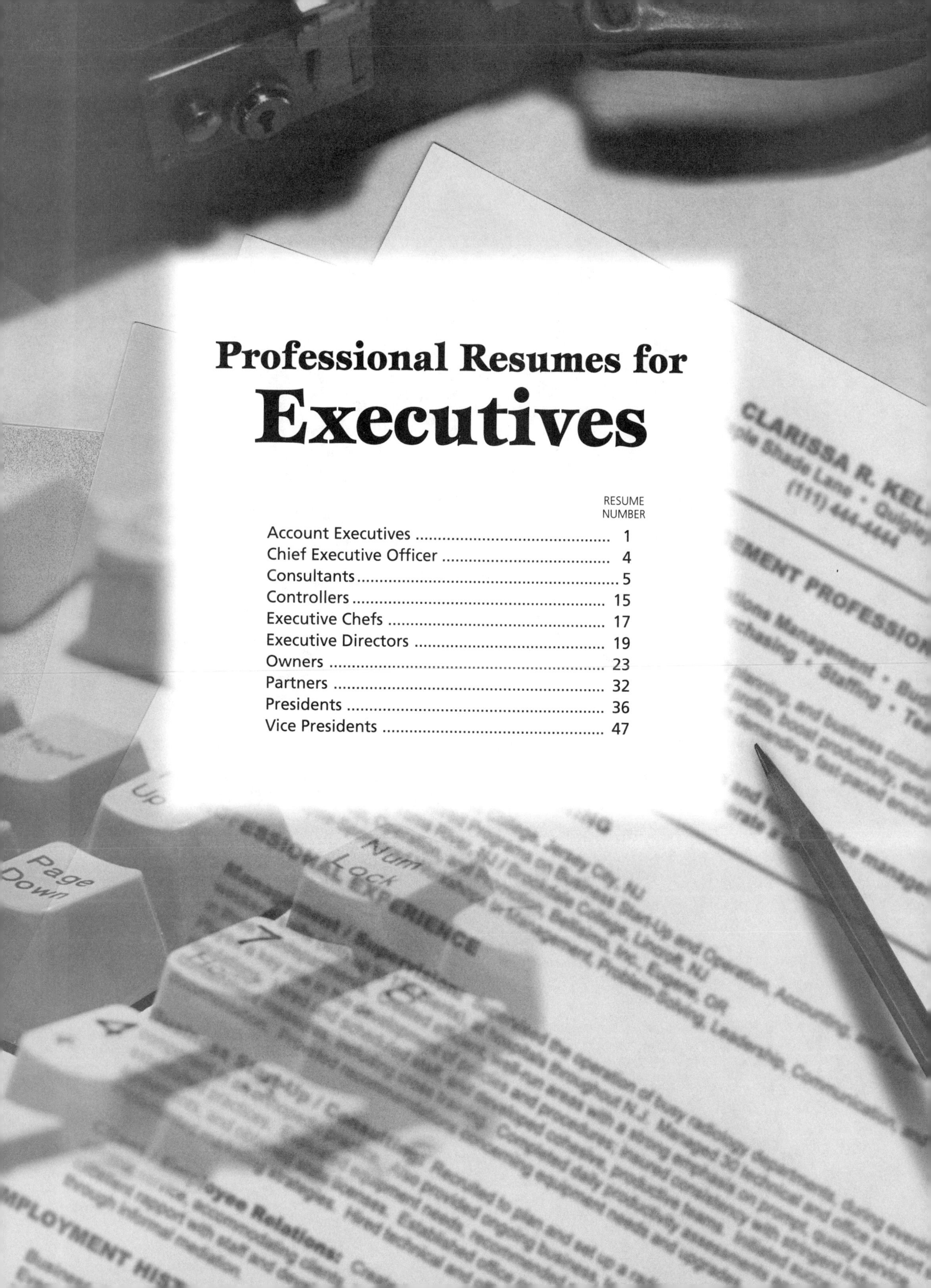

# Professional Resumes for
# Executives

## Emmett A. Doumaliay

0000 N. West ♦ Anywhere, USA
(000) 000-0000

### Objective

Continued career growth in the Securities Industry with a brokerage that will benefit from my ability to generate new business, service and develop existing accounts, and earn bottom-line profits for investors and management.

### Qualifications

- **Sales/Business Development** -- Consistently exceeded goals for revenue attainment in customer-driven sales environments ... excellent human relations and communications skills for effective presentations, evaluation of client needs, and client service.
- **Management** -- Prior background in management includes business operations, employee training and supervision, customer service, purchasing, and records management. As Securities Broker, proactively managed established accounts to sustain diversity and growth.
- **Profile** -- Regard integrity, consistency, and the establishment of long-term business relationships as critical components of my sales philosophy. Self-directed and committed to success--regularly work 60+ hours per week, committing part-time hours to establish new brokerage career while maintaining full-time responsibilities with second employer.

### Education and Licensure

Series 7 and Series 63 Licenses
State of Nevada, Department of Insurance -- Life License (qualified to sell annuities)
Business Major: Nevada State University

### Professional Experience

- **Account Executive** -- Unlimited Securities, Anywhere, USA 3/94-Present
  Generate sales of securities and investment products for full-service brokerage. Open and manage brokerage accounts.
  - Achieving strong growth in assets under management utilizing networking sources to develop accounts.
- **Manager/Bartender** -- The Best Bar, Anywhere, USA 8/85-4/92 and 6/94-Present
  Held P&L accountability for well-established restauranteur catering to upscale clientele in a prime business district. Hired and trained employees. Purchased stock. Monitored and controlled expenses.
  - Built day business to more than double original volume through focus on customer service.
  - Reduced pour costs to well below industry average, positively impacting profits.
- **Assistant Manager/Bartender** -- The Second Best Bar, Anywhere, USA 10/78-8/85 and 4/92-5/94
  Performed management and service responsibilities for popular sports bar.
  - Consistently met company objectives for sales and cost controls.
  - Organized promotional activity to benefit charity, generating second highest donations citywide.

### Interests

Gourmet cooking (Armenian, Filipino, Japanese, Italian cuisine) ... Travel (explored over 40 states as well as Mexico and Canada) ... Reading (investment magazines, Prodigy on-line services) ... Fly Fishing.

♦ ♦ ♦

1

**Combination.** *Susan Britton Whitcomb, Fresno, California*

The overall design of this resume is easy to size up at a glance because of flush-left side headings, boldfacing, distinctive bullets, and white space between paragraphs and sections.

## CHRIS A. SMITH

400 Anywhere Street, Anywhere, USA 00000 (555) 555-5555

**OBJECTIVE**

Dynamic, energetic professional seeks position where advancement potential is based on initiative and skills. Background focused on effectively developing skills to enhance company's "bottom line" and enable me to compete and excel in the telecommunication sales/marketing field.

**SUMMARY OF QUALIFICATIONS**

- Proven track record in telecommunication sales and management
- Positive and enthusiastic, highly motivated, excellent leadership techniques, and professional attention to detail supplemented by the ability to influence and stimulate others
- Communicate well with business professionals, easily establishing rapport and gaining client confidence; extremely sociable, articulate; professional in appearance and manner

**WORK EXPERIENCE**

THE COMPANY, Anywhere, USA 0000 - Present

*Account Executive*

- Outside sales - selling commercial systems to medium-sized businesses
- Set up office in Anytown including training of 25 sales representatives; promoted to supervisor
- Wrote and presented program on selling and closing sales
- Motivational and technical speaker at weekly meetings
- Conducted Sales Training seminars
- Transferred to Anywhere July 0000

**Achievements:**

- **The Company Achiever's Club** (awarded to only 5% of all personnel)
- **Met 100% of quota in first year**
- **Accommodation Plaque/Monetary bonus for successful Anytown operation**

BEST COMPANY, INC., Anywhere, USA 0000 - 0000

*Sales Representative*

- Cold calling, canvassing and creating leads.
- Closed sales, maintained accounts and kept detailed records of all contacts

ANY COMPANY, INC., Anytown, USA 0000 - 0000

*Owner/Manager*

- Overall operation of custom golf store
- Repairs, sales, merchandising/marketing, purchasing and record keeping

ANY STORE, Anywhere, USA 0000 - 0000

*Sales Representative*

- Cold calls, direct customer contact, negotiated and closed sales for peripheral equipment
- Installed equipment and followed-up to ensure customer satisfaction; maintained accounts and expedited orders

**Achievements:**

- **One of the top two salesman throughout the tri-state area**
- **Top salesman of branch office**

**EDUCATION**

Any College, Anywhere, USA 0000

Major: Business Management, Computers and Marketing

*References Available Upon Request*

2

**Combination.** *M. Carol Heider, Tampa, Florida*

Originally on decorative paper, this resume has flush-left side headings and job positions in italic. Separate Achievements sections in boldface strengthen the pitch for a strong candidate.

# ROBERT J. DICKINSON

1839 Miller Avenue • Chelsea, Michigan 48555 • (810) 555-9886

## PROFILE

Experienced, motivated professional with background in sales, customer service and public relations. Consistently promoted to positions of increasing responsibility. Highly organized.

## ACHIEVEMENTS

- Met goals of *Management Incentive Plan* resulting in stock bonus during first year of eligibility.
- Recruited to handle demanding *peak assignments* while concurrently maintaining existing responsibilities.
- Awarded Federal Express's *Pursuit of Excellence* commendation three consecutive years.
- Led team of seasonal workers who won first place in two of three categories during holiday sales contest.
- Requested by management to represent Business Development division at state-wide meeting of *Customer Evaluation Response Team* (CERT).

## EMPLOYMENT HISTORY

FEDERAL EXPRESS (Fed Ex) • Flint and Lansing, MI — 1990-Present

**Account Executive** (1993-Present) - Provide sales, customer liaison and logistical support to 700 accounts each generating $75,000-$200,000 in Fed Ex sales annually. Collaborate with other Fed Ex professionals to consult with customers and offer solutions to their shipping needs. Cold call on prospective customers.

**Operations Coordinator** (*Special assignment* 11/94-1/95) - Supervised 30 seasonal employees assigned to 40 routes supplementing permanent drivers. Planned schedules which varied daily based on actual volume each morning.

**Operations Coordinator** (*Special assignment* 11/93-1/94) - Motivated and supervised 15 seasonal customer counter clerks. Planned daily activities based on volume projections; generated daily reports for future projections. Conducted random customer sampling. Responded to customer concerns.

**Sales Associate** (1991-1993) - Conducted telemarketing and generated inside sales. Provided sales and administrative support for account executives.

**Customer Service Telephone Representative** (1990-1991) - Responded to customer telephone inquiries and performed general office duties.

TRIPLE-A ELECTRONICS • Flint, MI — 1988-1989

**Sales Representative** - Provided sales and customer support of computer, audio, video and electronic equipment.

## ADDITIONAL EXPERIENCE

DELTA COLLEGE • Saginaw, MI — Summer 1987

**Human Resources Intern** - Recruited, tested and processed applicants.

FORD MOTOR CORPORATION • Ypsilanti, MI — Summer 1986

**Labor Coordinator/Intern** - Coordinated activity between union representatives and employees; processed documentation relating to grievances.

## EDUCATION

MICHIGAN STATE UNIVERSITY • East Lansing, MI — *Anticipated Completion:* June 1998
**Master of Public Administration**

EASTERN MICHIGAN UNIVERSITY • Ypsilanti, MI
**Bachelor of Arts in Merchandising Management** — 1992

## SKILLS ENHANCEMENT

- Supervisor Leadership (three week course)
- Peak Selling
- Valuing Diversity
- People's Workshop (sensitivity with co-workers)
- Trust & Teamwork (with managerial co-workers)
- Speak Easy (presentation skills)

*References available on request.*

3

**Combination.** *Janet L. Beckstrom, Flint, Michigan*

A resume for a "high-achieving sales/account executive" who would like to "expand into Human Resources." Job positions in boldface show personal growth within one company since 1990.

# VICTOR L. STEPHENS

1234 Lynwood Court • Deltona, Florida 40100 • (407) 333-0000

## SUMMARY OF QUALIFICATIONS

- Strong background in managing automated data processing systems, effectively budgeting resources, coordinating and planning diverse projects, negotiating mutually beneficial agreements, and interfacing with community agencies, departments, and individuals to complete objectives.
- Proven record of developing and implementing solutions to multidimensional, complex operational problems.
- Outstanding interpersonal and communications skills.
- High-energy self-starter with the ability to develop and maintain an efficient, highly productive work force.

## HIGHLIGHTS OF MANAGEMENT EXPERIENCE

### Automated Data Processing Systems

- CEO of the Telecommunications Preparation Center, the world's largest simulator center. Managed this $50 million computer and telecommunications complex which provided simulator support worldwide by both terrestrial and satellite communications utilizing the most advanced state-of-the-art systems, including 13 mainframe digital computers and more than 700 stand-alone computers.
- Directed advanced and conventional communications systems. Developed and supervised training exercises which dealt with simulations of air, space, land, and sea operations. Established an interface between simulators and real world command and control systems which significantly enhanced realism.
- Managed fielding and testing of new computer and satellite equipment. Directed the operation of a worldwide command and control system terminal to link the company to other organizations across the United States. Established an automated data processing system which enhanced organizational effectiveness.
- Established initial management, automated data processing systems, and logistic policies and procedures for Space and Telecommunications Systems (STS). Obtained the appropriate systems and equipment. Directed the acquisition of 220 vehicles with supporting communications systems.

### Human Resources & Financial Management

- Developed and directed a $95 million annual operating budget for STS. Hired and managed 468 employees. Coordinated employee training in various specialties to strengthen job performance and increase productivity. Planned and managed execution of funding and training for personnel at disparate locations throughout a nine-state area.
- Developed and executed an annual operating budget of $75 million for the Telecommunications Preparation Center. Coordinated technical and operational support for a staff of 185 personnel and 65 contractors from twelve national and international companies for this large automated data processing center.
- Managed more than 1,000 employees and supervisors, and 28 contractors in a highly mobile operation. Developed and administered a budget of more than $61 million. Developed internal control systems to more efficiently manage resources. Managed all facilities and

4

**Combination.** *Connie S. Stevens, Radcliff, Kentucky*

Bold vertical and horizontal lines, bold side headings, and two kinds of bold bullets give an impression of authority and confidence. Even right margins, made by full justification, match

**VICTOR L. STEPHENS**                                                                    **PAGE 2**

maintenance, including warehouses and office buildings, for this operation consisting of a $900 million inventory of equipment and vehicles.

### Negotiations & Communications

➡ Managed negotiation of plans for shipment of equipment, transportation of employees, and custom's clearance through international agencies for computer/satellite simulator training activities. Communicated with local management representatives and agencies to coordinate training facilities and lodging for employees and contractors.
➡ Directed complete start-up of a newly formed organization with main offices located in California and Florida and satellite facilities in nine states. Negotiated procurement and renovation of buildings and support agreements with the state and federal government. Interfaced with local community agencies and ensured that appropriate facilities were in place to adequately support the daily operations of the organization and to meet the needs of the employees and their families.
➡ Mediated between two distinctly different international organizations which had formed a coalition for joint actions to accomplish a common goal. Coordinated and established cooperative objectives, plans, and operations between the companies for all joint efforts. Ensured that close communications between all senior executives were maintained. Negotiated agreements between these organizations for use of major support facilities within Europe. Managed air transportation interface between the organizations and offices in Europe, Asia, and Africa.
➡ Coordinated security and life support for the visit of President Reagan.

## EDUCATION & TRAINING

**University of Southern California** ◆ Los Angeles, CA
Master of Science in Telecommunications ◆ Dec 76

**Massachusetts Institute of Technology** ◆ Cambridge, MA
Bachelor of Science in Engineering ◆ May 71

## CAREER PATH

Space and Telecommunications Systems ◆ Any City, CA
**Chief Executive Officer** ◆ Feb 90 - Present

Telecommunications Preparation Center ◆ Any City, USA
**Chief Executive Officer** ◆ Jan 87 - Feb 90
**Vice President** ◆ May 83 - Jan 87

Communications Liaison Group ◆ Any City, Europe
**Senior Director** ◆ Jan 78 - May 83

visually the vertical lines, which define the left margins. Boldfacing for the educational institutions and job positions makes their important names stand out. Management experience is described in a three-part Highlights section rather than in the Career Path (work history) section.

**John B. Smart**

666 Devil's Glen NW • Rapids, Montana 55555 • (888) 555-4012

PROFILE

**SENIOR FINANCE & ADMINISTRATION MANAGER**

*Corporate Planning ... Financial Analysis ... Capital & Operating Budgets*
*Credit Management ... Financial Reporting ... Employee Benefits Management*
*Operating Cost Reduction ... Productivity Maximization*

CAREER DEVELOPMENT

JOHN B. SMART—Financial Consultant, Rapids, Montana
**Independent Contractor (199x to Present)**

Guide operating management through introduction of HPWS, CPI and TQM programs designed to improve production output and control accelerating costs. Introduce strategic plans, financial controls, information technologies, and sales/marketing initiatives which improve revenues, strengthen administrative processes, and enhance reporting and forecasting capabilities.

*Representative Clients / Projects*

- Specific Works, Inc.—Interim Financial Analyst charged with monitoring inventory and production systems ($1 billion in finished goods) during corporate-wide transition to new financial management system.
- Major Cornmilling, Inc.—Recruited to manage financial aspects of a critical $22MM joint venture with Mega Foods, Inc. in developing new starch product.
- Bestmind College Publishing, Inc.—Engaged to assist with development of calculus, trigonometry, algebra and finite math textbooks for business, social science or liberal arts students.

SITE GLASS PRODUCTS, Rapids, Montana

*Privately-held $4 million company engaged in wholesale / retail sales and installation of glass products and serving primarily the Eastern Iowa region.*

**Controller** (198x to 199x)

Fast-track promotion to full responsibility for strategic planning, development and leadership of corporation's complete finance function. Scope of responsibility was diverse and included financial and strategic planning, financial analysis, quarterly and year-end reporting, corporate treasury, banking, debt management, corporate tax, cash management, and internal audit. Concurrent executive management responsibility for day-to-day operations, customer service and employee benefits administration. Directed 18 professionals and 15 support personnel.

- Reengineered critical accounting operations and initiated purchase of computerized accounting system which netted $30,000 in annual savings.
- Restructured insurance benefits and introduced corporation's first self-funded insurance plan resulting in annual savings of $20,000.

**Senior Accountant** (198x to 198x)

Worked cooperatively with executive management team, senior operating personnel and Board of Directors to establish and implement improved employee benefits program. Focused efforts on financial, economic, operational and human resource issues. Responsible for accurate accounting and reporting of over $3.8 million annual expenditures. Supervised 7 accounting department staff.

- Structured and negotiated independent corporate / union bargaining agreement ($35,000 savings).
- Spearheaded development and implementation of corporation's first 401k plan.

COOPERS & LYBRAND—Certified Public Accountants, Chicago, Illinois
**Staff Accountant / Auditor** (198x to 198x)

EDUCATION

ANY UNIVERSITY, Bigtown, State
**BS—Marketing** (198x)

5

**Combination.** *Elizabeth J. Axnix, Iowa City, Iowa*

"A resume for an individual who moved from the corporate environment to an independent management/finance consultant role." A Profile section to the right is a distinctive touch.

## JOHN B. BRITTON

1234 West Washoe ▪ Flagstaff, Arizona 80222 ▪ (202) 222-2345

### EXPERIENCE SUMMARY

SENIOR HEALTH CARE EXECUTIVE with 17 years management experience in acute care hospitals and freestanding outpatient facilities. Strengths include:

- **Administration** with emphasis in accounts receivable management, credit/collections, organizational structure, and personnel management.
- **Start-Up Operations** including budgeting, policy development, physician recruitment, operating systems, and acquisition of rural health clinic status.
- **Public Relations** with the medical community, governing agencies, management, and support staff.
- **MPA Degree and BA in Spanish/International Relations** (fluent in Spanish).

### PROFESSIONAL EXPERIENCE

RURAL HEALTH MANAGEMENT AND DEVELOPMENT, Kelsey, Arizona — 1990-Present

**Managed Care Consultant:** Manage consulting firm formulated to assist primary care physicians and acute care hospitals in acquiring Rural Health Clinic Services Act status. Prepare and submit applications to appropriate federal and state regulatory agencies. Research, prepare, and submit data for acquisition of shortage designation from Office of Shortage Designation, U.S. Dept. of Health and Human Services.

- ❑ Doubled outpatient revenues for four hospital-based and county facilities in Maricopa, Chula Vista, and Flagstaff.
- ❑ Increased stand-alone physician's receivables by $250-300,000 per year, with a reimbursement per patient increase of as much as 259%.
- ❑ Accomplished designation process for clients in 90-180 days, well under half the normal time.

SONOMA DISTRICT HOSPITAL, Sonoma, Colorado — 1982-1990

**Chief Executive Officer/Administrator:** Held direct accountability for full scope of operations in a 228-bed general acute care hospital. Prepared and administered $65 million operating budget. Made recommendations for cost controls and revenue enhancements. Reported to District Board of Directors.

- ❑ Negotiated an unprecedented pre-payment contract with Sonoma State Prison.
- ❑ Improved cash flow by more than one-third, or $750,000 monthly.

DAVENPORT COUNTY HOSPITAL, Davenport, Iowa — 1979-1982

**Assistant Administrator:** Recruited by Board of Directors to correct receivables problem and revitalize/ retool business office policy. Established and supervised Credit/Collections Department within hospital.

- ❑ Collected over $750,000 in bad debt and aging receivables, taking hospital from negative to positive cash position in less than six months.

### EDUCATION, LICENSURE

**Masters of Public Administration**, California State University, Long Beach (1974)
**Bachelor of Arts, Spanish / International Relations**, California State University, Long Beach (1972)
**Licensed Vocational Nurse,** State of California

▪ ▪ ▪

**6**

**Combination.** *Susan Britton Whitcomb, Fresno, California*

Thick-thin lines (referring first to the bottom line and then to the line above it) separate contact information from the rest of the resume. This person wanted to return to hospital work.

# James Olavira

237 River Road
Glens Falls, NY 55555

phone ■ (555) 555-5555
fax ■ (555) 555-5555
E-mail ■ medpro@aol.com

**■ product development and marketing**
**■ financial analysis and MIS administration**
**■ global commerce and relationship management**

## Career and Personal Profile

- Broad international business management experience in the areas of product development, marketing and financial analysis. Products include medical devices and consumer goods.
- Speak fluent Italian, Spanish and conversational French. Widely traveled in Europe, Central America and South America. Entirely conversant with business practices on both sides of the Atlantic.

## Professional Development

**Product Development, Patent and Start-up Consultant** **1996 to present**
Med Pro, Inc., Port Jervis, NY

Currently consulting with manufacturer to develop new product advertising, distribution and licensing.

- Invented improved nasal cannula. Developed prototypes, applied for patent protection (pending), and located ISO 9002 Italian manufacturer.
- Coordinated all 510(k) application procedures for Class I and Class II devices. Developed promotional strategies for new products. Negotiated exclusive distribution agreements with foreign manufacturers.

**Product Development and Marketing Specialist** **1994 to 1996**
Compmed Corp., New York, NY

International company distributing plastic components to manufacturers of disposable medical devices.

- Generated $1 million in new sales in Italian and Spanish markets through design and implementation of innovative direct marketing activities.
- Increased total revenue by 12% in 1996 through identification of an opportunity to expand company's product line to include complementary products.
- Identified new overseas vendors. Personally inspected prospective suppliers for ability to comply with GMPs, QC procedures, utilization of USP Class VI materials and Clean Room manufacturing.
- Built profitable European alliances by conducting business, in the European manner, through the building of sound professional relationships at the highest levels.
- Designed ad campaign and collateral materials specifically aimed at development of overseas customers. Developed and coordinated international and domestic trade show materials and activities.
- Conceived and developed customer retention program to identify and retain at-risk accounts.

7

**Combination.** *Deborah Wile Dib, Medford, New York*

This candidate had "a wide background in international business in diverse fields." The names of these fields are staggered near the top of the first page so that they extend from the left margin

## James Olavira

page two

### Professional Development (continued)

**Marketing Analyst, Assistant to the Controller, Assistant MIS Director** **1990 to 1994**
Home Furnishings Centers, New York, NY

New York Metro region chain of 70 stores.

- Designed innovative Spanish language promotional materials and ad campaign that generated 30% increase in neighborhood store sales. Independently produced business plan and advertising samples.
- Proposed and developed new radio and television advertising campaigns. Prepared market trend and condition reports to track company's marketing efforts.
- Generated all monthly financial reports. Performed general ledger analysis and lease analysis. Coordinated year-end inventory procedures for company's 70+ stores and 2 warehouses.
- Installed a chain-wide, computerized POS system. Initiated all system accounting changes, procedures, testing and de-bugging. Led training of all store and warehouse personnel.

**Operations Manager, Custom Furniture Manufacturing Division** **1982 to 1990**
La Sala Industries, locations in Florida, Guatemala and Honduras

High-end, custom furniture manufacturer with international clientele and operations.

- Implemented and managed transition of fine furniture manufacturing division from totally hand-made custom shop to full-line automated manufacturing facility with MRP and Synchronous manufacturing systems that increased production and reduced waste.
- Designed production-line profitability systems and cell manufacturing. Consistently pursued the use of technologies and the modernization of company's manufacturing equipment. Retrained custom craftspeople entrenched in old ways.
- Coordinated photo shoots, press releases and showroom set-ups for international clients—designers, architects, embassies, magazines and other media. Lived in Guatemala for twelve years.

### Technology

- MS-DOS, UNIX, Windows
- Daily user of Excel, Lotus, Word Perfect, MS Word, Internet and E-mail.
- Installed all hardware/communications equipment for 70 store POS system with IBM RISC 6000 server.
- Led training of personnel (for 70 stores) in a PICK "Promax" software application (UNIX).

### Education

**Master in Business Administration, concentration in Marketing, 1996**

**Bachelor of Science in Architectural Technology, 1993**

Fordham University, New York, NY. Earned degrees while holding full-time positions.

to the right margin. Bold horizontal lines separate the sections so that you can grasp the overall design of the resume at a glance. Square bullets appear in all sections except the Education section. Use of the same bullet style across sections helps to unify the resume visually.

**DAVID ORRICK**
298 Creek Drive • Atlanta, Georgia 00000
**(000) 000-0000**

**CORPORATE/MARKETING COMMUNICATIONS PROFESSIONAL**

*HIGH PROFILE* professional with a dynamic career and a proactive approach • Proven track record of creating and implementing successful corporate marketing/advertising strategies • Able to direct and motivate a diverse staff to achieve and exceed organizational goals • Possesses high-calibre presentation skills • Maintains an entrepreneurial approach to business with a proven willingness to anticipate and manage change • Proficient in computer applications.

- **ACHIEVED 300% REVENUE GROWTH THROUGH INNOVATIVE PROMOTION PROGRAMS**
- **EXPERTLY REDEFINES COMPANY'S CORPORATE IMAGE.**

**Achievements**

- **Delivered explosive sales leads growth of 350% by developing and implementing strategic corporate communication campaigns, including press releases, media relations and sales support programs.**
- **Revitalized the entire advertising strategy; developed and implemented co-op advertisement and direct mail support programs, increasing sales from $10 million to over $35 million in 4 years.**
- **Delivered strong and substantial revenue growth of $15 million within 2 years through the implementation of a national dealer yellow page program.**
- **Spearheaded industry's largest conference; increased annual conference attendance from 148 to 425. Revenue soared from less than $50,000 to over $280,000 in 3 years. Obtained and implemented sponsorship and improved national recognition.**

**Professional Experience**

MARKETING/COMMUNICATIONS CONSULTANT — 1994 - Present

- Consultant to corporate clients in a wide variety of industries including electronics, healthcare, petroleum and retail.
- Manages projects valued at over $100,000 including development of marketing communications plans, production of corporate videos, management of major industry trade shows and conferences and development of corporate communications/sales brochures.
- Challenged to write and implement a script to be presented live, on an ongoing basis during an industry's largest annual trade show.
- Develops and integrates innovative marketing principles into fast paced organizations to further support revenue growth including a development of a regional sales meeting resulting in projected revenues of $300,000 annually.
- Interfaces with key sales and marketing executives.

INTERNATIONAL ELECTRONIC INFORMATION, INC. — Atlanta, Georgia
*Director of Corporate Communications* — *1987 - 1994*

- High profile marketing position accountable for the development of strategic public relations, advertising and corporate image programs for a $38 million company providing electronic data exchange services for healthcare providers and payers.
- Directed and coordinated trade shows, conferences, sales promotions, co-op advertising and direct mail campaigns in support of corporate and sales objectives for direct and dealer sales force.
- Recruited, trained and supervised a team of professionals to peak levels of performance.
- Controlled an annual budget of $600,000.
- Positioned Company for fast track growth through innovative marketing programs.
- Repositioned Company to recognized industry leader.
- Liaison with media personnel.

8

**Combination.** *Alesia Benedict, Rochelle Park, New Jersey*

A page border appears on both pages to make the resume stand out. Partial, flush-right horizontal lines identify at a glance the side headings for the main sections. These lines are

**DAVID ORRICK** **(000) 000-0000** **- Page Two -**

**Professional Experience continued**

**RICOH CORP.** West Caldwell, New Jersey
*Director, Marketing Communications* *1982 - 1987*

- Recruited to lead corporate communications activities for an international leader in office products.
- Strategically managed and produced all public relations, direct mail, collateral materials, trade shows and sales incentive programs.
- Supervised Sales Training Department and staff.
- Division spokesperson to trade and business press; appeared on Wall Street Journal Reports and various business interview programs.
- Represented division's interest in pubic relations and advertising strategies.
- Planned, controlled and administered budgets.

**EXXON OFFICE SYSTEMS** Stamford, Connecticut
*Exhibits Manager* *1977 - 1982*

- Directed national exhibit and trade show program for the office products division of Exxon Corp.; managed participation in 30 - 40 shows annually and oversaw up to 5 trade shows in various stages of implementation concurrently.
- Fostered communications with suppliers, travel agencies and hotel/conference directors.
- Successfully integrated 3 division into a single marketing organization streamlining procedures and increasing productivity.
- Efforts pooled dealers' promotional money and increased market awareness.

**Educational Background**

St. Peter's College • Jersey City, New Jersey
Bachelor of Science in Economics

Regularly attends advanced training in:

- corporate communications
- public relations
- marketing
- sales support

**Professional Affiliations**

American Management Association
American Marketing Association
Public Relations Society of America

helpful since the upper- and lowercase side headings by themselves are less conspicuous than the all-uppercase position or company names in the Professional Experience section. The professional writer considers this use of borders and lines an "aggressive format." Achievements are in boldface.

**MAXWELL S. MANAGEMENT**
119 Old Stable Road
Lynchburg, Virginia U.S.A.
Phone (804) 384-4600 Fax (804) 384-4700

---

**SENIOR OPERATING & MANAGEMENT EXECUTIVE**
***Building & Leading Start-Up, Turnaround & Fast-Track Growth Corporations***

Talented, creative and profit-driven executive recognized nationally for pioneering efforts in product development and industry leadership. Expertise in sales/marketing, global business expansion, manufacturing, corporate finance and business process development. Harvard University Graduate. Distinguished honors and credentials include:

- "Person of the Year", *Magazine's* highest award in the Promotional Products Industry (1985). Honored as the Founder of a billion dollar consumer products market.
- U.S. Delegate to the 1987 People-To-People Economic Conference in Beijing, China. Long-term career in developing cooperative business ventures with Pacific Rim partners.
- Well-respected public speaking career at national and international trade associations, universities and professional industry conferences.
- Impressionist Painter with works in private and corporate collections in 15 countries worldwide. Earned prestigious designation as a Signature Member of the National Oil & Acrylics Painters Society (N.O.A.P.S.).
- State Masters Racquetball Champion. Ranked #6 in the U.S.

---

**CAREER HISTORY:**

**Executive Marketing & Management Consultant** 1991 to Present
**Senior Associates**, Lynchburg, Virginia

Consult with U.S. and Asian companies to provide top-flight expertise in strategic business planning, product development, global marketing, sales promotion and marketing communications.

- Identified joint venture partners and researched international trade/tariff regulations for diversified Asian manufacturer seeking expansion into the Latin American market.
- Guided insurance company in the preparation of 5-year business plan and capital funding request.
- Orchestrated successful introduction of well-established U.S. mail order company into the promotional products market. Developed budget, defined infrastructure requirements and designed product promotions (e.g., catalogs, literature, customer communications).
- Currently consulting with premier U.S. supplier of holographic products to provide situational analysis and market development strategies and for successful product positioning.

**Chief Executive Officer** 1972 to 1991
**Graphics International**, Lynchburg, Virginia

Senior Operating Executive of this printed apparel and textile manufacturing company supplying the promotional products, premium, department store and mass merchant markets nationwide. Initially directed operations from Lynchburg based headquarters. Subsequently directed company's start-up of subsidiaries in Columbus, Georgia and Kowloon, Hong Kong. Chaired the Board of Directors.

9

**Combination.** *Wendy S. Enelow, Lynchburg, Virginia*

Horizontal lines enclose the biographical summary near the top of the first page. Such lines call attention to the information between them. On page 2 another line separates the name at the

**MAXWELL S. MANAGEMENT - Page Two**

Held full P&L responsibility for the entire corporation, all design and production operations, key account sales and business development programs, human resource affairs (staff of 350), technology acquisition, capital improvement, materials sourcing and the complete finance/accounting function. Directed a four-person senior management team, on-site plant and production management staff, and Managing Director of Hong Kong trading company.

- Built company from $600,000 in annual revenues to $17.8 million and ranking as the fifth largest screen printer in the U.S. Produced over 22,000 orders annually.
- Pioneered development of industry-leading products, technologies and production methods currently the foundation for a multi-billion dollar industry. Achievements included development of the first 10-color textile printing presses in the U.S., introduction of original packaging standards for major activewear mills, and most significantly, the first multi-color textile apparel printing processes.
- Launched the successful introduction into the global market through development of both import and export operations (combined annual revenues of $1.5+ million).
- Identified tremendous market opportunity for the efficient design and production of small custom orders virtually ignored by major competitors. Developed innovative printing techniques, captured millions of dollars in sales, and won dominant market positioning nationwide.
- Built a nationwide network of 2200 distributors that generated over 50% of total company revenues. Personally directed and negotiated sales programs direct to major accounts including Sears ($2 million annually), Walmart, Target, J.C. Penney and Wards.
- Introduced sophisticated technologies into the manufacturing, administrative and financial departments that consistently enhanced quality, productivity and profit performance.

**President** 1968 to 1972
**Corporation (Subsidiary of Advertising Company)**, Lynchburg, Virginia

Senior Operating Executive of sales promotion firm servicing its parent advertising agency and major national accounts. Worked in cooperation with teams of advertising executives and creative staffs to plan, design and produce (via contracted manufacturing) theme-based promotional and internal incentive products in concert with national ad campaigns.

- Completed projects for major U.S. corporations including Anheuser-Busch, McDonald's, Cadillac, Ralston Purina and Southwestern Bell.

*(NOTE: Established Corporation in 1966 and sold to Advertising Company in 1968. Subsequently purchased it back in 1972 as the foundation upon which Graphics International was founded.)*

**EDUCATION:**

**HARVARD UNIVERSITY GRADUATE SCHOOL OF BUSINESS ADMINISTRATION**
**Graduate, OPM Program**

**UNIVERSITY SCHOOL OF FINE ARTS**

Three EURAM International Marketing Conferences (Amsterdam, London, Paris)
Five AMA President Association Programs
Certified Advertising Specialist (C.A.S.) Designation

top from the rest of the resume. The amount of information in this resume is easy to read because of white space—that is, the insertion of at least one blank line before and after (side headings, subheadings, paragraphs, and bulleted items) so that the design makes sense.

**Michael Executive, SPHR**
119 Old Stable Road
Lynchburg, Virginia
Home (804) 384-4600 Fax (804) 384-4700

**Human Resources & Organizational Development Executive**

***Providing HR Leadership to Start-Up, Turnaround and Fast-Track Growth Companies in the U.S., Europe, Pacific Rim & Former Soviet Union***

Strong and decisive HR Executive with expertise in all generalist HR functions including recruitment, training/development, wage and salary administration, benefits administration and succession planning. Pioneered successful organizational development initiatives that delivered consistent and sustainable operating, revenue, profit and quality improvements through dedicated efforts in:

- Corporate Change Management
- Participative Management
- Pay For Performance Incentives
- Performance Management Systems
- Cultural Diversity
- Team Building/Leadership
- Broadbanding
- HR Information Systems

**Certified Senior Professional Human Resources 1989 to Present**

**Career Summary:**

**Executive HR Consultant - Domestic & International** (1990 to Present)

***Domestic Assignments:***
- Manufacturing Company, Detroit, Michigan
- State Bank, New York, New York

***International Assignments:***
- Islamic Bank, Istanbul, Turkey
- The Bank of Budapest, Budapest, Hungary

**Director of HR** (516 employees), Consulting Group (1988 to 1990)
**Director of HR** (1100 employees), State Bank (1986 to 1988)
**Director of HR** (270 employees), Insurance Company (1979 to 1986)

**Career Highlights:**

***Corporate Change, Development, Reengineering & Consolidation***

- Led massive culture transition for The Bank of Budapest to refocus the mission of the organization and capitalize upon emerging opportunities for free enterprise in the unified European market.
- Consolidated the HR, compensation, employee relations, recruitment and benefits organizations of five separate companies into one centralized function following merger and creation of the Consulting Group.
- Restructured and integrated four newly acquired companies into the core business organization of State Bank.
- Facilitated corporate reengineering which positioned a Turkish company for World Bank accreditation and multi-million dollar loan guarantees for the development of manufacturing, mining, oil, gas and timber industries in the Turkish far east.

10

**Combination.** *Wendy S. Enelow, Lynchburg, Virginia*

Everything said about the preceding resume is true also for this resume by the same writer. What is different is the use of a series of bold italic subheads in the Career Highlights section to

**MICHAEL EXECUTIVE, SPHR** *Page Two*

**CAREER HIGHLIGHTS:**
*(Continued)*

***Compensation & Benefits***

- Spearheaded an innovative incentive compensation system at State Bank that delivered a 30% increase in productivity, reduced processing errors by 50% and captured $275,000 in annual cost savings.

- Recovered $400,000 cash from Consulting's over-funded pension plan, simplified administrative processes for 401(k) and pension reporting. Saved 25% in corporate insurance and employee benefit costs while maintaining or enhancing coverages.

- Redesigned benefits plans for State Bank that captured $275,000 in annual cost reductions for this $60 million corporation.

***Information Technology***

- Introduced leading edge HRIS technology into Consulting and Islamic Bank that delivered significant improvements in planning, analysis, reporting and database management.

***Employee Recruitment & Retention***

- Reduced turnover at State Bank from 43% to 28% through improved recruitment processes, team building and quality-based management.

***Training & Development***

- Created the first-ever training programs and/or dramatically expanded portfolio of training programs for each corporation (both as employee and consultant).

***Budget Administration***

- Developed and administered annual budgets for HR operations, benefits and compensation, and technology acquisition ranging from $3 million to $16 million.

***Regulatory Affairs & Negotiations***

- Personally negotiated and favorably resolved Civil Rights legal action, EEOC complaints and Affirmative Action cases.

**EDUCATION:**

**Certificates in EEO and Federal Wage & Hour**, University, 1994
**M.S., Community Health Administration**, College for Health Sciences, 1993
**M.S., Administration**, Central University, 1986
**B.A., Economics & Political Science**, State College, 1978

***References Provided Upon Request***

indicate areas of activity. Bulleted items in the different areas indicate achievements, many of which are quantified in percentages or dollars. The second page ends on a strong note with *two* master's degrees and recent certificates as evidence of continuing self-improvement.

15901 Timberland Road
Orlando, Florida 00000
(813) 000-0000

# PAUL C. GRAHAM

## CAREER PROFILE

***Senior-level Corporate Accounting/Management Professional*** with distinct record of accomplishments. Proactive leader recognized for ability to deliver strong, sustainable results. Seven-year tenure combines diverse scope of controllership-related experience with sales management and technical expertise. Outstanding performance in facilitating developmental strategies that led to gaining market share and growing revenue. Well-honed skills in automated accounting systems, maximizing operations, training, conducting presentations to large audiences and augmenting fiscal efficiency. Effective communicator, adept in public relations; demonstrated strengths in projecting high-level motivation, problem-solving and decision-making. ***Willing to relocate.***

## COMPUTER SKILLS

DOS/Windows-based programs; Microsoft Word, Excel, PowerPoint; Quickbooks; Real-T Pro; Windows 95; Internet

## EXPERIENCE SUMMARY

***Sales Management***

- **Business/Management Consultant** responsible for successfully directing and supporting managerial operations inclusive of P&L for 100 offices in 14 county area located throughout the south and central Florida region.
- **Dynamic record of accomplishments** stemming from ability to motivate people, conduct effective training seminars, achieve bottomline results and consistently out performing other regions.
- **Expertise in consultative sales management**, strategic business planning, sales forecasting and implementing developmental programs within high-growth, competitive markets.
- **Corporate leader,** accelerated sales volume and out performed other regions; chosen to serve as ownership's chief liaison at geographical council meetings communicating goals and assisting in developing cooperative advertising campaigns.
- **Conversant with performing due diligence**, market analyses, needs assessment and formulating short and long-term financial projections for start-up and conversion operations.
- **Thorough knowledge** of coordinating, structuring and negotiating company mergers focused on increasing revenues and expanding market share.

***Accounting/Financial Management***

- **Integral role as Financial Services Representative,** charged with providing consulting assistance to strategically plan, develop and execute fiscal directives for 100 independent companies.
- **Skilled in corporate accounting procedures**, budgeting, conducting financial/operational audits, presiding over accounts receivable process, preparing/analyzing financial statements and overseeing collections.
- **Orchestrated improvements** of automated accounting systems, documentation and internal controls to eliminate operational deficiencies and provide a monitoring system to ensure compliance with policies/procedures.
- **Spearheaded training** of accounting staff in automated accounting systems and financial statement preparation.

11

**Combination.** *Diane McGoldrick, Tampa, Florida*

This resume illustrates a tendency by some writers to use a smaller font size and narrower margins in order to include on a page more of the impressive information many executives can

**PAUL C. GRAHAM** **Page Two**

**EMPLOYMENT HISTORY**

**HFS, INC.** **1990 - 1997**

***(World's largest franchisor of hotels and residential real estate brokerage offices; acquired Century 21 Real Estate Corporation in 1996.)***

***Exceptional record of consistently exceeding corporate expectations resulted in successive promotions to visible, senior management positions and highly demanding, pivotal role amplified by the acquisition and restructuring of corporate parameters.***

**Business Consultant** (1996 - 1997)
Reported to Vice President/Director of Broker Services, Southern Division. Spearheaded development and growth of existing real estate franchises, start-up and conversion businesses in four dominant market areas comprised of 100 independent offices throughout central Florida. Provided leadership and consulting services delineating managerial policies/procedures, strategic business planning, market penetration and profitable financial management.

- **Expedited planning, negotiating and approval process for three separate affiliate franchise mergers that generated gain in market share and profitability for franchisor.**
- **Facilitated implementation of business operating systems.**
- **Key role in providing detailed analyses for expansion, marketing and return on investment for franchisee.**
- **Increased revenue 15% within first year following the acquisition.**
- **1996: Received bonus for increasing sales growth and volume.**

**Management Consultant** (1993 - 1996)
Served under direction of President. Charged with providing sales management training, comprehensive business plans and market analyses. Monitored compliance with franchise agreement and coordinated support for franchise businesses marketing the Century 21 name. Assisted in sale of franchises, presided over orientation programs for prospective buyers and conducted career-oriented presentations to recruit potential sales agents.

- **Designed profitability models to identify sales results and expense variances by category producing a more effective decision-making process for cost reductions.**
- **Pioneered benchmarking study of top franchises to initiate standardized corporate procedures focused on improving organizational structure, financial performance, sales training, recruiting methods and motivational team building techniques.**
- **Consistently out-performed other regions; grew territory sales 38% over three-year period.**
- **1993/1994/1995: Earned bonus for outstanding performance.**

**Auditor/Financial Services Representative** (1990 - 1993)
Worked in correlation with Controller. Extensively interacted with franchise members to provide financial consulting services involving all aspects of corporate accounting functions. Participated in preparation of documentation for year-end audit.

- **Wrote operational audit program incorporating follow-up procedures to increase franchise efficiency.**
- **Devised automated collection process that reduced active A/R by 50%.**
- **Created standardized chart of accounts implemented by corporate throughout the region.**
- **Instrumental in training accounting staff in automated accounting systems and financial statement preparation.**

**EDUCATION**

**B.A. - Accounting** UNIVERSITY OF WEST FLORIDA , 1990

**Certified Management Operations Facilitator** CENTURY 21

**PROFESSIONAL SEMINAR TRAINING**

Sales Management. . .Accounting. . .Automated Accounting Systems for Real Estate
Sales Training. . .Consultative Management. . .Recruiting Techniques. . .Computer Training

put in a resume. Adequate white space through blank lines helps to keep the resume from appearing overcrowded. The smaller type size, together with full justification for an even right margin, gives this resume a "printed" look. This downsized applicant found a new job quickly.

# WARREN ARMSTRONG

1234 N. West Street #123
Reno, Nevada 87654

(202) 222-2234
Available for Relocation

## QUALIFICATIONS SUMMARY

SENIOR MANAGEMENT EXECUTIVE with stellar track record in the restructuring, management, and growth of multi-unit, high-volume retail operations generating up to $90 million in annual sales. Highlights include:

- **Overview:** Characterized by senior management as a visionary in business ... successfully led corporations through critical start-up, reorganization, turnaround, and fast-track growth ... recognized as first specialty retailer to introduce "shop concepts", reversing one company's 10-year loss history to profits of $1.5 million in just two years.
- **Profit-Oriented:** Recruited to restructure and realign operations for under-capitalized West Coast chain ... conceived and launched an aggressive marketing and business development initiative which brought company's $21 million debt to zero. For Southwest retailer, achieved sales increases of more than 70%, catapulting stores to rank as a major profit contributor to parent corporation.
- **Operations:** Proactive corporate leader with comprehensive management skills in multiple disciplines: merchandising, marketing, financial analysis, MIS, central warehouse distribution systems, vendor and lease negotiations ... redesigned infrastructure to consolidate internal functions which reduced operating expenses by as much as 11%.
- **Finance:** Strengths include financial analysis, planning, and implementation ... skilled negotiator, managing Chapter 11 proceedings without loss of equity to ownership. Spearheaded successful effort to take Colorado-based company public.
- **International Orientation:** Opened new markets in Japan and Europe ... piloted "industry firsts" such as international retail joint ventures, applying the concept of licensing at the retail level and earning over $200,000 in additional revenues.

## EXPERIENCE HIGHLIGHTS

ARMSTRONG CONSULTING 1990-Present

**The Gentleman's Corner**, Reno, Nevada

Designed comprehensive financial and business operating plan for 13-store chain of upscale men's clothing. Created budgets and open-to-buy figures for all departments.

- Reduced 75% of $8 million excess inventory.
- Developed motivational goals for management and sales staff, resulting in a 1st year sales increase of 18%.
- Consolidated five small storage units into one large, efficient warehouse.
- Successfully completed implementation of new computer retail system.

**Club Wholesale**, Nampa, Idaho

Recruited by Board of Directors to turnaround and manage $90 million multi-unit general and office supply warehouse clubs.

- Reorganized existing business to eliminate company's multi-million dollar debt within first year.
- Managed negotiations in Chapter 11 bankruptcy which enabled principals to retain full equity position.
- Installed new merchandising, marketing, and financial systems to reposition company, resulting in profitable sale of company.

12

**Combination.** *Susan Britton Whitcomb, Fresno, California*

This is another resume with a printed look because of smaller type, narrower margins, and full justification. Careful use of blank lines ensures that the resume design will be easily grasped at a

# WARREN ARMSTRONG

Page Two

THE APPAREL COMPANY 1985-1990

**President:** Completely restructured company from partial apparel, partial sporting goods into a fine specialty retailer.

- Turned around multiple-year history of losses to profitability, resulting in a $1.5 million swing.
- Popularized the concept of manufacturer's shops within a store, negotiating contracts with vendors such as Burberry, Head Ski and Tennis, Boston Trader, and Timberland.
- Took company public on the New York Stock Exchange. Subsequently negotiated profitable sale to a Denver partnership.

RETAILCO CORPORATION

**Corporate Assignment** (1979-1985):

- Envisioned, organized, and opened 60 joint venture concept stores in the Orient and 12 stores in Europe.

Retail Specialist for divisions listed below, turning each company's losses into high profits. Highlights include:

**Casual Contempo** (1984-1985): Provided total direction for company while merging three separate entities (Casual Contempo, Finney's, and Anne Thielen) into a West Coast Division.

- Firmly established reputation of companies' 32 stores as the leading men's and women's quality apparel stores by providing new direction in advertising, merchandising, promotion, and sales motivation.
- Remodeled stores, recruited new executives, and retrained sales staff, resulting in return of West Coast Division to profitability.

**Thompson Clothing** (1979-1984): Held P&L accountability for 44 stores with history of declining market presence. Conceived and orchestrated new direction in advertising, merchandising, promotions, and sales motivation.

- Achieved 40 consecutive months of sales increases, generating $52 million in annual sales and returning company to flagship status that it had previously lost.
- Completed successful negotiations with unions and reorganized central warehouse and MIS systems, resulting in lower overall cost structure.

**Finney's Clothing Company** (1975-1979): Directed company's eight stores operating as a separate corporation from the parent company.

- Achieved profit first year (from large losses) and entrenched company as a major profit contributor to parent corporation.
- In three years, successfully led Finney's to exceed each year's goals in profit and R.O.N.A. with sales volume increasing by 72.8%.

**Sharpmore** (1972-1975): Supervised all buyers and provided complete fashion direction in merchandising and operations.

- Selected as Chairman of Corporate Executive Piece Goods Committee and guided corporate manufacturing in the purchase of piece goods.

## AFFILIATIONS

Served on Board of Directors for industry and community organizations (Chicago Apparel Club, Phoenix Convention Bureau, Valley Big Brothers, Men's and Boy's Apparel Club of Southern California, Better Business Bureau, Mercy Hospital, and more).

♦ ♦ **References Upon Request** ♦ ♦

glance and that the resume will be "friendly" to read in spite of the amount of information. This writer tries to present two pages for candidates who are looking for salaries of $100,000 or more. An extensive Qualifications Summary gets important information at the top of page one.

Specialty Foods Consulting and Management

*Dean and Deluca*

*Delmonico's Food Market*

*Murray's Cheese*

*Gourmet Garage*

*Wild by Nature*

*Lucy's Ravioli Kitchen*

*Eccola Gastronomia*

*Gourmet Buys*

*Amagansett Farmer's Market*

# Henri P. Flego

25 Third Avenue, Apt. 3B • New York, NY 55555 • (212) 555-5555

## Specialty Foods Consultant

Over twenty years experience providing comprehensive start-up, long-term and consultative management services for specialty food stores and departments as well as expert revitalization of existing operations. Broad background and strong skills in specialty foods merchandising, sales, management, purchasing, training, planning and budgeting. World traveled, with extensive network of domestic and international colleagues, contacts and vendors.

## Areas of Expertise

- Specialty Foods

Develop vendor structure; purchase specialty food items. Expertise includes charcuterie, pasta, cheese, packaged goods, smoked fish, prepared foods and espresso bar operations.

- Store Set-up and Display

Provide image and ambiance development, product merchandising, fixturing and window display for existing or start-up specialty departments or entire stores.

- Comprehensive Staff Training

Stress exceptional customer service techniques, comprehensive product knowledge, correct treatment of specialty foods and perishable foods, expert slicing and presentation procedures, and equipment handling and safety methods.

- Marketing and Advertising

Consult with marketing team for advertising vehicles, advise on signage and ad copy, develop promotional materials and events. Represent companies at trade shows.

## Summary of Qualifications

Design profitable gourmet programs and menus for shops, large stores and restaurants; known for creation of up-scale ambiance, exceptional product assortment and comprehensive staff training.

Reduce perishable waste and shortage by set up of efficient inventory and quality controls and by rigorous staff training in specialty foods handling.

Communicate effectively at all levels—staff and managers to principles and senior level executives.

Revive ailing businesses; revitalized lagging lunch business of upscale Pino Luongo/Piccola Cucina restaurants in Texas and California by introduction of popular luncheon menu.

Create imaginative and appealing windows; Pasta and Cheese window displays featured in The Village Voice and Time magazine.

**13**

**Combination.** *Deborah Wile Dib, Medford, New York*

This resume looks different because of a number of distinctive features. First of all, each page can be created as a one-row, three-column table without lines. Pressing Enter repeatedly in any

Specialty Foods Consulting and Management (continued)

North Country Market

Karabellas Food Store

Marché Madison

Fairway Market

Fay & Allen's Foodworks

Dino's Pasta Shops

Pino/Longo Cucina

Creative Cookery

Fairway Market

Pasta and Cheese

## Henri P. Flego

page 2

### Representative Consulting Projects

Provide comprehensive management and operations services for start-up and revitalization of large and small specialty food shops, full-line grocers, department stores and restaurants. (1980 to present)

Dean and Deluca, New York, NY
Headed espresso bar. Focused operation, reduced shrink/waste, added new lines. Area became store's most profitable per square foot department.

Gourmet Garage, New York, NY
Implemented pre-packed cheese department and expanded existing cheese business. Brought in all displays and machinery, trained staff, developed olive department. Retained as advisor after start-up.

Wild By Nature, (a division of King Kullen supermarkets), Setauket, NY
Designed, set-up, and implemented operation of cheese and pasta department. Concurrently advised and merchandised prepared foods and deli departments. Maintained consistent profit margin.

Eccola Gastronomia, Parsippany, NJ
Hired by restaurateur to save and revitalize fledgling food store division of restaurant mismanaged by original start-up team.

Lucy's Ravioli Kitchen, Princeton, NJ
Designed and set-up turn key operation for ravioli manufacturer's expansion to 1,000 square foot retail store.

Murray's Cheese, New York, NY
Consulted for owner's move and new set-up of this famous, fifty year old cheese shop in New York City's West Village.

Amagansett Farmers Market, Amagansett, NY
Revitalized perishable foods department, consulted for cheese department, and trained staff in food/financial operations.

Gourmet Buys, Glen Head, NY
Set-up turnkey operation. Determined sales philosophy, chose vendors, fixtures, set pricing and merchandising strategies, etc.

Karabellas, New York, NY
Headed complete start up operation for multi-faceted food store with café and espresso bar. Set up vendors, merchandising, pricing and training.

North Country Market, Setauket, NY
Planned and set-up specialty foods store/espresso bar. Owner was thriving meat wholesaler venturing into specialty foods market.

Pino/Longo Cucina Restaurants, TX and CA
Developed new, profitable lunch program in three restaurants.

column "pushes" the single row down to the bottom of the page. The same graphic is inserted as an image in the first column of each page. Text in the first column on pages 1 and 2 is right-aligned. A vertical line is inserted in the second column on all three pages. The main text of the resume is placed in the third

Henri P. Flego page 3

## Representative Consulting Projects (continued)

Delmonico's Food Market, New York, NY
Directed opening of store's first branch (49th St. and Lexington). Set up sandwich program and cheese, coffee and charcuterie departments.

Dino's Pasta Shops, New York, NY
Aided Dean Scadutto, grandson of the Bruno Ravioli family, in the development of operational plans for the turn-key opening of eight new pasta stores. Directed turn-key opening of two stores.

Marché Madison,
Store took over famous Fraser-Morris shop. Headed full line gourmet shop start-up operation.

## Employment in Specialty Foods

Owner/Manager, Aubergine Cafe
New York, NY 1984 to 1986
Conceived and directed the opening/running of popular East Village cafe.

Merchandising Manager and Buyer, Desi's Delights
Oklahoma City, OK 1983 to 1984
Designed and implemented policies/procedures to upgrade image, service and product. Redirected marketing, merchandising and sales strategies.

Manager, Greenway Market
New York, NY 1982 to 1983
Acting front-end manager. Coordinated merchandising/displays. Established contact with Valencay, France cheese cooperatives; visited Rungis to cultivate new importers.

Merchandising and Display Director, Bread and Cheese Board
New York, NY 1980 to 1982
Designed/set up window and in-store displays; conducted training seminars; planned/supervised opening of new locations. Represented company at Cologne Food Show and New York Fancy Food Show.

Cheese Department Designer, Felice's Foodworks
New York, NY 1979 to 1980

Manager, Dean and Deluca
New York, NY 1977 to 1979
One of founding employees. Managed charcuterie/smoked fish departments.

## Education

Bachelor of Arts in Philosophy
New York University, New York, NY

column on each page. A font resembling technical printing is used for the contact information and the headings. A sans serif font is used for the main text, and adequate white space is provided through blank lines throughout. The overall effect is striking.

**CLARISSA R. KELSTON**
**16 Maple Shade Lane • Quigley, NJ 55555**
**(111) 444-4444**

**MANAGEMENT PROFESSIONAL**

**Business Start-Up & Development • Operations Management • Budgeting & Financial Management**
**Customer Service • Marketing • Purchasing • Staffing • Team Building • Training**

"Hands-on" manager with extensive supervisory, strategic planning, and business consulting experience. Expertise in introducing systems and strategies that build revenues and profits, boost productivity, enhance customer service, and strengthen employee satisfaction. Successful track record in demanding, fast-paced environments requiring stamina, patience, and time management skills.

**Eager to apply business management skills and food service management training to establish and operate a cafe.**

**RELATED EDUCATION & TRAINING**

Business, Jersey City State College, Jersey City, NJ
SBA / SCORE-Sponsored Programs on Business Start-Up and Operation, Accounting, and Finance, Ocean County College, Toms River, NJ / Brookdale College, Lincroft, NJ
Cafe Start-Up, Operation, and Promotion, Bellisimo, Inc., Eugene, OR
Employee-Sponsored Workshops in Management, Problem-Solving, Leadership, Communication, and Productivity

**PROFESSIONAL EXPERIENCE**

**Management / Supervision:** Supervised the operation of busy radiology departments, during evening and weekend shifts (with up to 125 clients), at hospitals throughout N.J. Managed 30 technical and office support staff in three subdepartments. Created efficient, well-run areas with a strong emphasis on prompt, quality service. Played a key role in the development of policies and procedures; insured consistency with stringent industry regulations. Hired and scheduled staff, and developed cohesive, productive teams. Initiated successful cost-containment measures, including cross training. Completed daily productivity assessments and payroll documentation. Provided recommendations concerning equipment needs and upgrades.

**Business Start-Up / Consulting:** Recruited to plan and set up a radiology practice and the radiology component in an orthopedic practice. Also provided ongoing business, technical, and staffing support for established practices. Evaluated equipment needs, recommended products, negotiated lease and purchase agreements, and obtained state licenses. Established office procedures, systems, and guidelines. Developed and implemented marketing strategies. Hired technical and office support staff.

**Client / Employee Relations:** Created customer-centered environments; gained recognition for providing efficient service, accommodating clients, and interacting with them personably and professionally. Established excellent rapport with staff and developed goal-oriented teams. Promptly resolved employee relations problems through informal mediation.

**EMPLOYMENT HISTORY**

| | |
|---|---|
| **Business Consultant**, Radiology and Medical Practices, NJ | 1971 - Present |
| **Evening Radiology Supervisor**, Hope Medical Center, Hope, NJ | 1987 - Present |
| **Midnight Radiology Supervisor**, Lake Morris Hospital, Lake Morris, NJ | 1985 - 1987 |
| **Evening Radiology Supervisor**, Carlton Medical Center, Carlton, NJ | 1978 - 1985 |
| **Weekend Supervisor**, Riverside General Hospital, Secaucus, NJ | 1976 - 1978 |

**LICENSURE / EDUCATION**

License of Radiologic Technology • American Registry in Radiologic Technology • Fellowship in MRI
Jersey City Medical Center School of Radiologic Technology, Jersey City, NJ

14

**Combination.** *Rhoda Kopy, Toms River, New Jersey*

A resume whose design is easy to comprehend at a glance because of boldfacing and blank lines between resume elements. A pair of dual horizontal lines enclose important profile information.

# Luke R. Roberts

9201 Michigan Avenue
Chicago, Illinois 60606
212.555.9201

SENIOR FINANCE & ADMINISTRATION EXECUTIVE

***Financial Analysis / Corporate Planning / Credit Management***
***Strategic Marketing / Management Information Systems / Negotiations / Financial Reporting***

Qualified ***Financial Representative / Controller*** with a solid accounting background. Strong analytical skills, computer experience, and proven successful business development. Demonstrated excellent personal commitment with a high level of integrity, knowledge, and understanding.

## SUMMARY OF QUALIFICATIONS

*BUSINESS PLANNING*

- Experience with day-to-day operations of million-dollar corporations.
- Knowledge of percentage of completion accounting and system development life-cycle approach to MIS design.

*CUSTOMER RELATIONS/NEGOTIATIONS*

- Strong professional presence; ability to obtain confidence and trust.
- Effective negotiator, with experience managing annual corporate general liability, vendor terms and conditions.

*COMPUTER*

- IBM Systems 36/38; Windows; applications include: Lotus 1-2-3, Peachtree, AIMS Plus, Microsoft Word-Excel, Symix, RV-Soft, and industry specific programs.
- Experience converting from manual to computerized accounting, one mainframe to another, and replacing software applications.

*OTHER*

- Effective Human Resource manager/trainer.

## SELECTED ACHIEVEMENTS

- Led the successful financial software conversion of a manufacturing organization generating $55M in annual revenue.
- Wrote the entire record retention portion of the documentation process for QS9000 Certification.
- Reduced outstanding customer accounts from $150,000 to less than $30,000 in just four weeks after employment.
- Saved a company $90,000 a year in wholesale gas pricing with innovative concepts.

## EDUCATION AND PROFESSIONAL DEVELOPMENT

*STATE COLLEGE OF ILLINOIS*
**BACHELOR OF ARTS DEGREE** — Accounting, 1982

- Minor: *Management*

15

**Combination.** *Lorie Lebert, Novi, Michigan*

A thick bold line above the candidate's name in boldface makes that name the first item to be seen. Qualifications in the Summary of Qualifications are grouped according to four categories.

**EXPERIENCE**

*EVANSTON WIRE COMPANY INC.* Evanston, Illinois
*Manufacturer of wire and rod to tier 1 suppliers in the automotive industry.*
**CONTROLLER** 1997-current

- Manage all the financial activities of company generating $55M annually.
- Research and prepare budgets, forecasts, business activity, and financial position.
- Work with management team to determine economic objectives and policies.
- Oversee corporate insurance programs including property, liability, and workers' compensation; oversee leased vehicle program.
- Prepare all support schedules for annual state and federal income tax returns.
- Delineate monthly financial statements including journal entries, account analysis posting, and review *(computerized)*.
- Assist all departments with analysis as requested/required.

*SMYTHE INDUSTRIES, INC.* Chicago, Illinois
*Manufacturer of automotive products.*
**ASSISTANT CONTROLLER** 1995-97

- Directed the day-to-day activities of ten accounting, clerical, and administrative staff in company with $22M in annual revenues.
- Performed all Controller responsibilities during 1996-97.
- Managed AR/AP, audits; developed job cost analysis reports.
- Provided employee computer training, performance reviews/evaluations, and employee discipline/encouragement.

*MASTER MARINE CORPORATION* Northshore, Illinois
*Distributor of marine associated products.*
**CONTROLLER** 1990-94

- Directed the allocation of $20M annually; staff of one accountant and two clerical.
- Participated in strategic planning and operation analysis.
- Developed specific market-level financial reports.
- Positioned operations for maximum profitability; managed payroll, tax reports.
- Negotiated contracts, terms/conditions with vendors to maintain cash flow and reduce debt.
- Administered employee benefits programs.

*NETALL COMMUNICATION SERVICES, INC.* Bingham Farms, Illinois
*Long-distance telecommunications company.*
**BILLING SUPERVISOR** 1989-90

- Oversaw daily billing operation involving more than 10,000 accounts, five analysts.
- Researched/analyzed procedures to identify inefficient operations.
- Established and monitored computerized control systems and unit goals.

*Other experience:*
*VETERANS ADMIMISTRATION SERVICES* — **ACCOUNTING MANAGER**
*Non-profit organization for child placement.*
*CAROL BIRD & ASSOCIATES, INC.* — **ACCOUNTANT**
*CONCEPTS & CARS* — **GENERAL ACCOUNTANT**

**Luke R. Roberts** . . . . . . . . . . . . . . . . . . . . . . . . . . . . . . . 9201 Michigan Avenue, Chicago, Illinois 60606
212.555.9201

Most of the achievements are quantified in dollars earned or saved. Boldfacing makes the positions easily seen as you read down the second page. Each company is explained briefly. Contact information is presented both at the top of page one and at the end of the resume.

**MARSHA HARRIS**
**125 E. 15th Street**
**Brooklyn, New York 11228**
**(718) 765-9876**

---

**PROFESSIONAL SUMMARY**

... DEDICATED COMPTROLLER with women's apparel importing and manufacturing experience
... DEMONSTRATED EXPERTISE in all aspects of financial operations
... STRONG ABILITY to work well with bankers, brokers, factors, accounting staff, and management
... SUBSTANTIAL FAMILIARITY with computerized accounting systems
... PROVEN supervisory and management skills
... TALENT for prioritizing numerous financial and administrative projects

**EXPERIENCE**

1983 - 1996 **Separates Incorporated** New York, New York
*Comptroller*

- Reported directly to President and Vice-President of large apparel importer.

Advancement....
- Initially began as Full Charge Bookkeeper. Selected by top management to assume additional financial responsibilities as a result of company's rapid expansion.

MAJOR RESPONSIBILITIES

- Directed all financial aspects of blouse manufacturing subsidiary with $50 million in annual sales. Oversaw credit and collections. Worked with factors.
- Prepared monthly financial statements, cash flow, expenses, and inventory controls.
- Supervised and trained eleven employees in all accounting operations.
- Established productive working relationships with bankers, brokers, and freight forwarders.
- Facilitated opening and payment of letters of credit.
- Successfully managed substantial investment portfolio of company and its owners, including stocks, bonds, and real estate. Secured mortgages for owner and represented him at closing.

1978 - 1983 **Scarves Ltd.** New York, New York
*Full Charge Bookkeeper/Office Manager*

- Supervised a staff of 5 in accounting and office operations. Oversaw credit and collections, cash flow, cost accounting, duty, declarations, letters of credit, and foreign currency payments.

1973 - 1978 **Marissa Naples Inc.** New York, New York
*Full Charge Bookkeeper/Office Manager*

1970 - 1973 **Marion Stoller Company** New York, New York
*Full Charge Bookkeeper/Office Manager*

**REFERENCES** Furnished on request.

16

**Combination.** *David Feurst, New York, New York*

A full horizontal line separates the contact information from the rest of the resume. Small caps call attention to qualifications in the Professional Summary. Experience means growth in one company.

*Professional*

*Profile*

SANDY HARLLEY

Executive Chef/Instructor

**17**

**Combination.** *Fran Holsinger, Tempe, Arizona*

This writer likes to present a resume as a booklet with a graphic front cover that matches the candidate's occupation or job search goal. A characteristic feature of this writer's resumes is the

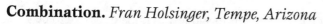

# SANDY HARLLEY

555 S. Benchside Dr. Tempe, AZ 55555 [555] 000-0000

## SUMMARY OF QUALIFICATIONS:

- Over 15 years experience as Executive/Corporate Chef/Consultant....
- Experienced culinary instructor at Scottsdale Culinary Institute....
- Developed recipes/menus restaurant concepts....
- Catered simultaneous functions for up to 25,000 people....
- Provided Executive Chef services/catering for Super Bowl XXX.... $375,000 in sales....
- Opened new properties employing seafood/Northern Italian Bistro concepts....
- Traveled through out the Eastern U.S. to establish services at hotel properties....
- Designed/developed culinary classes for school/retail outlet....
- Consulted with owners on opening new stores....
- Controlled costs/inventory/labor....
- Interviewed/hired/trained/supervised/evaluated employees....
- Prepared food service for numerous venues from parking lot events to Black Tie affairs....
- Excellent communication skills....creative....innovative....team leader... dedicated....organized....detail oriented....decision maker....problem solver....

## EDUCATION:

CULINARY INSTITUTE OF AMERICA - Hyde Park, NY
AOS Degree
UNIVERSITY OF GEORGIA EXTENSION PROGRAM - Atlanta, GA
Module Teaching Techniques: Completed 30 Modules
Externships: Hugo's West Hyatt Regency Hotel - Atlanta, GA
Alfredo's Restaurant - Myrtle Beach Hilton, SCA
Top of the Crown Restaurant, Crown Center Hotel - Kansas City , MO
Additional Course Work in Nutrition

use of ellipses (....) sometimes within but always after each statement to suggest that there is more to be said about the candidate than what is presented here. A list of qualifications that takes up almost a full page is impressive. The style of the headings calls attention to the candidate's name, which has the same style

professional profile

PROFESSIONAL HIGHLIGHTS:

**EXECUTIVE CHEF**

- Facilitated food/beverage service for NFL Arizona Cardinals/ASU football games....
- Directed food/beverage service for University Club/Gammage Theater/Sun Dome Theater/ASU Athletic Department: football/men & women's basketball/baseball training tables....
- Wrote/costed menus for 5,000 spectators/game....
- Catered special functions....
- Supervised 70 employees....
- Functioned as Corporate Chef....conceptualized/setup 15 different restaurants/hotel operations throughout Eastern US....
- Served as personal chef for CEO of Eastman-Kodak....
- Opened new properties with seafood/Fedora concept: Chequers Bar & Grill - Atlanta/Devon Seafood Grill - Washington, DC & Houston/ Bristol Bar & Grill - Minneapolis/Fedora Cafe - Miami/Tyson's Corner, VA

**INSTRUCTOR**

- Taught Basic/Intermediate/Advanced Classical Cuisine....
- Provided personalized approach through small classes....
- Developed/planned curriculum....
- Created culinary program for new training school....
- Set-up/instructed classes for retail kitchen outlet....
- Furnished services for Scottsdale Culinary Institute's enterprises: L'Ecole restaurant/banquets/catered events/saucier....

EMPLOYERS: ART INSTITUTE OF PHOENIX - Phoenix, AZ
***Chef/Instructor:*** 1996 to present
FINE HOST CORPORATION - Tempe, AZ
***Executive Chef:*** 1995 - 1996
SCOTTSDALE CULINARY INSTITUTE - Scottsdale, AZ
***Chef/Instructor:*** 1988 - 1995
B. F. SAUL - Chevy Chase, MD
GILBERT/ROBINSON - Kansas City, MO
***Corporate Chef:*** 1987 - 1988/1984 - 1988

AWARDS: CULINARY ART SHOWS:
- Tucson 1993
- Atlanta - 1983
- Houston - 1980
- South Carolina - 1978
- New York - 1977

but is slightly larger. In the Employer's section, positions are both bold and underlined to stand out. Bands of three horizontal lines at the top of the second and third pages are strong visually. The first band, enclosing the person's name, calls attention to it.

# Peter Francis — *Executive Chef*

22220 Laredo Court
Alamo, California 94000
Telephone (510) 000-000

- European training and experience in premiere restaurants with the highest ratings.
- Fully qualified in classic and innovative food preparation, menu planning, and kitchen management.
- Exceptional knowledge of fine wines.
- Experienced in hiring, training, scheduling and supervising of large staffs.
- Establish rapport easily with all levels of staff, senior management and guests.
- Consistently maintain excellent food and labor costs through planning, purchasing, production and inventory management control.
- Working knowledge of French.

BLACK HILLS GOLF & COUNTRY CLUB Alamo, California May 1992 - Present
**Executive Chef** — Joined this prestigious club during a multi-million renovation under the auspices of restaurant designer Dieter Haupt. Initiated a complete upgrade of the kitchen, 500-seat dining room, catering and wine services for the club's 600-plus members. Revitalized entire menu program emphasizing contemporary cuisine inspired by classical standards. Achieved 35% growth in food and beverage revenue.

CARLYLE PLACE Monterey, California 1991 - 92
☆☆☆☆ *Deluxe Hotel (120 rooms) • 15 Points Gault Millau. Recognized as one of the top 25 restaurants in the U.S. by Food & Wine magazine in 1991.*
**Sous Chef -** Awarded best breakfast, brunch and lunch in San Francisco Bay Area by Bay Food Magazine reader poll. Co-authored degustation menus for monthly vintner dinner events. Managed staff of 15 in this highly regarded fine-dining hotel restaurant.

THE BELAIR San Diego, California 1991
☆☆☆☆☆ *Deluxe Hotel (336 rooms) • Member: Leading Hotels of the World*
**Sous Chef Tournant -** Selected for opening staff. Multi-faceted supervisory position in extensive food and beverage operation. Represented hotel in charity wine auctions.

HÔTEL DU PALAIS Biarritz, France 1989 - 90
☆☆☆☆ *Deluxe Hotel (140 rooms) • Gault Millau Clef d'Or • Member: Leading Hotels of the World*
**Chef Tournant -** Prepared classical & contemporary French and Basque cuisine under Chef Gregoire Sein.

SWISSOTEL LTD. 1988 - 90

DRAKE HOTEL-RESTAURANT LAFAYETTE New York, New York
☆☆☆☆ *Deluxe Hotel (585 rooms) • One of New York City's five top restaurants by Zagats Guide and Gault Millau.*
**Chef de Partie -** Worked closely with Jean-George Vongerichten in formal dining setting.

HOTEL INTERNATIONAL Zurich, Switzerland
☆☆☆☆☆ *Deluxe Hotel (350 rooms) • Second largest hotel in Switzerland.*
**Chef de Partie -** Traditional French-Swiss cuisine in classical service environment.

Continues ...

**18**

**Combination.** *Ted Bache, Portola Valley, California*

Boldfacing and a larger font size make the applicant's name stand out in the upper-left corner of the resume. Because the positions held are in boldface, you can glance at both pages and see

Page Two

Peter Francis

HOTEL LE PLAZA Basel, Switzerland
☆☆☆☆☆ *Deluxe Hotel (243 rooms) • Part of the European World Trade Center • Convention capacity for 2,000.*
**Chef de Partie** - Designed the menu to reflect a California Cafe ambiance.

CALIFORNIA CAFE Sunnyvale, California 1988
*170-seat restaurant serving international and California cuisine*
**Executive Chef** - Assisted in the design and layout of restaurant renovation. Created and implemented menu. Established vendor and product sources, and selected staff of 30.

KULETO'S San Francisco, California 1986 - 87
*160-seat California/Italian style restaurant recognized by Focus Magazine for outstanding food, ambiance and decor.*
**Executive Chef** - Received recognition as a Grand Master Chef of America in the 1988 National Directory. Participated in the conception and design of the restaurant and kitchen. Hired and supervised staff of 38. Successfully planned and revised menus. Significantly reduced food cost to below 31 percent.

CAFE MARIPOSA Deer Valley Ski Resort, Utah 1985 - 86
*Fine cuisine in a luxury ski resort, and rated best restaurant in the state.*
**Sous Chef** - Supervised deluxe dining room, Sister hotel: Stanford Court in San Francisco.

MAX'S 888 CAFE San Francisco, California 1984 - 85
*High-volume restaurant in multi-use showroom and conference center.*
**Sous Chef** - Responsible for daily menu and kitchen staff for up to 400 lunches. Served as catering chef for events with up to 4,000 guests.

---

Stage Experience

| | | | |
|---|---|---|---|
| **Le Crocodile** | Strasbourg, France | ★★★ | (Michelin) |
| **Les Pyrenées** | St. Jean Pied de Port, France | ★★★ | |
| **Le Couronne** | Paris, France | ★★ | |
| **Grand Vefour** | Paris, France | ★★ | |
| **Pain Adour et Fantaisie** | Grenade-sur-l'Adour, France | ★★ | |
| **Buerehiesel** | Strasbourg, France | ★★ | |

---

**Cordon Rouge**
Sausalito, California 1983

**Bachelor of Arts - Psychology**
SONOMA STATE UNIVERSITY
Rohnert Park, California 1976

quickly the course of the candidate's career. A star system typically used to rate hotels lets the reader know that this executive chef has worked at some top places. Beyond the star symbols, an italic statement after each establishment's name gives further information about the place.

**RAYMOND P. TOWNSEND, P.H.M.**
12 Arnold Street • Yardley, NJ 00001 • Willing to Relocate
(555) 555-5555

**HOUSING INDUSTRY EXECUTIVE**

Dynamic management career in the public housing industry with a proven track record in operations management, program development and administration, financial management, labor relations, and negotiation. Comprehensive knowledge of H.U.D. standards, and government policies and regulations. Exceptional success in obtaining funding for construction and modernization projects. Solid business relationships with building department representatives, utilities authorities, law enforcement agencies, local officials, community groups, and tenant associations. Adept at overcoming obstacles; thrive on challenge.

***Committed to the provision of safe, sanitary, and affordable housing for individuals with limited finances.***

**PROFESSIONAL EXPERIENCE**

**Todden Township Housing Authority**, New Jersey 1994 - 1996
**EXECUTIVE DIRECTOR**

Selected to turn around this troubled agency plagued by problems related to operations and financial management, documentation and reporting, and board-staff relations. Oversaw the management of 70 family and senior units, and 95 new construction projects (Section 8). Administered a budget of $735,000 and a $2,401,000 modernization (MOD) program; supervised a staff of four. Responsibilities included program planning and coordination, program development, project supervision, financial management, and contract negotiations.

**Key Accomplishments**

- Brought the agency up to operating standards in five months; boosted PHMAP score from 50% to 68%.
- Within months, recouped $752,000 in modernization (MOD) funds from the federal government, which had been denied for eight years.
- Successfully demonstrated the need for a $1.5 million grant to renovate and modernize 14 seriously neglected buildings; competed for these funds with 21 Small Housing Authorities in N.J.
- Planned, coordinated, and oversaw renovations, which included roof replacements, new vinyl siding, replacement windows, wood sheathing, and insulation.
- Uncovered the need for additional housing; applied for and received 25 rental certificates ($350,000) to provide rental assistance funds to needy individuals.
- Initiated a successful after-school program, "Operation School House," for over 50 youngsters in a public housing project (Landemiere Gardens), in an area with serious drug-related problems; collaborated with the Wayne County Prosecutor's Office and the Todden Township Board of Education.
- Spearheaded a Head Start Program for 60 preschoolers at the same housing project, which provided social and academic opportunities for the children, while enabling parents to work. Obtained funding through A.B.C., Inc., and coordinated planning efforts with the township's mayor.
- Curtailed crime and drug abuse at Landemiere Gardens by obtaining funding for additional police foot patrols.

**Sanders Township Housing Authority**, New Jersey 1972 - 1994
**EXECUTIVE DIRECTOR** (1984 - 1994) • **COMMISSIONER** (1972 - 1984)

Directed an Authority responsible for the management of 269 senior units and the coordination of a Section 8 Rental Assistance Program for 40 units. Administered a budget of $1,200,000 and supervised a staff of eight employees. Scope of responsibilities included program / project planning and administration, procurement and management of government funds, policy enforcement, and staff recruitment.

19

**Combination.** *Rhoda Kopy, Toms River, New Jersey*

A pair of thin-thick lines enclose the profile-like section near the top of the first page. Bullets call attention to Key Accomplishments, most of which are quantified in dollars or percentages.

**RAYMOND P. TOWNSEND, P.H.M.**
**Page Two**

**Key Accomplishments** (continued)

- Designated as a "high performer" by the federal government and achieved PHMAP score of 95% in 1994; earned the Sanders Township Housing Authority a reputation as the "country club of public housing," as a reflection of the well-managed and well-maintained properties.
- Gained a high level of autonomy after being designated as one of 12 housing authorities out of 81 in N.J. to be decontrolled by the Dept. of H.U.D., based on exceptional performance.
- Played a key role in assessing the critical need for low-income housing for seniors, acquiring government funds, and overseeing three major construction projects.
- Instrumental in obtaining $7 million in H.U.D. funds, in 1979, for the construction of a four-story building with 125 single bedroom apartments, which was completed in 1981; obtained funding of $2,500,000 for construction of a 45-unit project, completed in 1983.
- Consistently evaluated renovation needs at all sites and applied for funds when necessary: Acquired $770,000 in MOD funds, in 1987, for extensive renovations on a 101 unit senior housing project. Received an annual comprehensive improvement grant (COMP) of $350,000, in 1993, to institute improvements and renovations on any of the facilities.

**RELATED EXPERIENCE**

**Alcott Mortgage Services, Inc.**, Clarksten, NJ — 1996 - Present
**LICENSED MORTGAGE BANKER**

**PROFESSIONAL DEVELOPMENT AND EDUCATION**

Completed numerous NAHRO (National Association of Housing and Redevelopment Officials) certification and training programs:

- N.J. Certification Courses for Executive Directors, 1995
- Family Self Sufficiency Program, 1994
- Section 8, 1989
- Financial Management, 1986
- Computer Workshop, 1985
- Occupancy Workshop, 1985
- Executive Management and Leadership, 1984
- Elderly Housing Management, 1984
- Certification as Public Housing Manager, 1980

Attended additional seminars in management, motivation, and customer relations.
Completed course work in Business Management at Wayne County Community College, Bailey, NJ.

**CIVIC AND PROFESSIONAL AFFILIATIONS**

- Public Housing Authority Directors Association
- National Association of Housing and Redevelopment Officials (N.A.H.R.O.)
- New Jersey Chapter of N.A.H.R.O.
- New Jersey Association of Housing and Redevelopment Officials
- National Housing Conference
- Ocean County C.H.A.S. Committee
- Chamber of Commerce
- Fraternal Order of Police, Lodge #10

**MILITARY SERVICE**

Honorable Discharge, United States Army

More bulleted Key Accomplishments appear on the second page. Blank lines and short entries in the last four sections on page two provide adequate white space and offer relief to the long lines elsewhere in the resume due to narrow margins and full justification.

**PATRICIA DARROW**
**ASSOCIATION DIRECTOR**

4343 South Adams Street
Windfall, Illinois 00000
(708) 555-5555

**PROFILE**

- Personable, versatile, and creative professional offering key competencies in **office administration, project management, public relations, and graphic design**.
- Over five years' experience as a community-minded association director.
- Adept at organizing groups to meet board goals; team-oriented.
- Demonstrated ability to direct and complete multiple projects while meeting strict deadlines.
- Well-developed writing skills: reports, newsletters, promotional pieces, ad copy, and press releases.

**PROFESSIONAL EXPERIENCE**

12/90 to Date **EXECUTIVE DIRECTOR**
12/89 to 12/90 **ASSOCIATE DIRECTOR**
*Southwest Business Association, Windfall, Illinois*

- Direct full range of association activities with a high degree of autonomy; report to the 25-member board. Control expenses to remain within $260,000 annual budget. Supervise three employees and work cooperatively with volunteers on committees and special projects.

- Plan events, schedule meetings, and take minutes. Perform all bookkeeping; prepare and publish all publicity. Write monthly newsletter for association members. In addition, create graphic artwork and write cable TV scripts to promote various events.

- **Project Manager** of the annual Southwest Arts & Crafts Festival. Redesigned and updated programs and artist entry forms; raised exhibitors from 95 to 135. Mapped layout of park for artists and the public. Expanded advertisements in newspapers to promote the event. As a result, association profit has increased and festival quality has improved.

- Also manage retail promotions for Windfall and Sharpsburg, such as the sidewalk sale, tent sale, Halloween parade, and Christmas walk. Coordinate logistics for $25,000 worth of Christmas decorations for the villages, including vendor bidding.

- **Project Manager** and sole producer of the annual *Southwest Business Directory*: Sell ads, do page layout, specify type, shoot and crop photos, proofread and edit, and prepare the financial report.

- Increased membership by 10% for 1995 by instituting a discount for first-year dues. Also gained new members by promoting a members-only advertising campaign. Boosted attendance and generated new interest at weekly luncheons by introducing guest speakers once or twice per month.

- Trained staff in office procedures and computer applications: Excel, Q & A, and Word for Windows.

*Continued...*

20

**Combination.** *Jennie Dowden, Flossmoor, Illinois*

Bulleted items in the Professional Experience section contain a mix of duties and achievements. The graphic at the bottom of the first page "is appropriate for this person, who uses graphic

**Patricia Darrow**...*Page 2*

3/87 to 12/89 **OFFICE MANAGER AND GRAPHIC ARTIST**
*Kawai Communications, Windfall, Illinois*

- Responsibilities ranged from creative (layout and design) to secretarial and light bookkeeping. Managed office and met with clients when owner was absent.

9/84 to 3/87 **CALLIGRAPHY TEACHER**
*Tipton College, Fox Grove, Illinois*

- Taught several off-campus, non-credit classes. Solely responsible for planning lessons and all class and lab preparation. Added two classes to meet the demand for advanced instruction.

Prior Positions **STAFF DESIGNER**
*University of Rochester Publications Department, Rochester, New York*

**EDITORIAL ASSISTANT**
*University of Detroit Alumni Department, Detroit, Michigan*

**SELECTED COMMUNITY VOLUNTEER EXPERIENCE**

1994 to Date **MEMBER**
*Windfall Economic Development Committee*

- Researched cooperation between village government and business/employer associations in five communities. Drafted report, which has been used as an informational tool for Windfall village government. Made recommendations to enhance the downtown's economic well-being.

1989 to 1994 **MEMBER**
*College of Madison Caucus*

- Helped select candidates for COM Board of Directors.

**EDUCATION**

**B.S., COMMUNICATIONS and ADVERTISING DESIGN** (dual major)
*University of Detroit, Detroit, Michigan*

- Dean's List; member of Delta Phi Delta, artistic scholastic honorary.

***References, writing samples, and graphic artwork furnished on request.***

design skills on the job." This individual is an "older job seeker, so no dates are listed" for Prior Positions or for information in the Education section. The second and third side headings extend across the resume's columns, tying them together visually. The resume has adequate white space.

CONFIDENTIAL

**Charles M. Downer**

2114 Pitt Street
Montgomery, Virginia 36117

✆ [703] 555-5555 (Home)
[703] 555-6666 (Office)

**Value to the Coleman County Board of Education:** As your Chief Executive Officer, lead your school district to be a national model of instructional, financial, and personnel leadership.

PROFILE:

- Seasoned school administrator with a demonstrated record of infusing excellence into entire school systems
- Sought after consultant in every aspect of educational leadership
- Noted presenter and workshop director before staff and leadership at every level from primary to post-secondary schools
- Capable businessman with a proven record of resource accountability

PROFESSIONAL EXPERIENCE AND SELECTED ACCOMPLISHMENTS:

| | |
|---|---|
| **Executive Director**<br>September 1998 - Present | Northern Virginia Council of School Administration and Supervision, Arlington, Virginia |
| **Independent Educational Leadership Consultant**<br>July 1997 - September 1998 | ❍ Perfected forty hour staff development program for 10 district consortium. Very well received.<br>❍ Researched and wrote the program all new school superintendents must complete starting in 1998. State Superintendent accepted my proposals without change.<br>❍ Continue to train scores of school principals as a certified LEADER 1-2-3 program facilitator. |
| **Assistant Superintendent of Education**<br>August 1988 - June 1997 | Lorton City Schools, Lorton, Virginia<br>❍ Transformed school system with no computer learning resources into state-of-the-art facilities. Applied Technology Labs recognized by American Vocational Association.<br>❍ Built our program with no internal funds by raising first $90,000, then $100,000, in grants from corporate partners.<br>❍ Organized Lorton High to become one of ten "Supercomputer Sites" in Virginia — with no additional staff.<br>❍ Tied school's computers to NASA's mainframe. Students 175 miles from nearest research library now undertaking projects with worldwide help.<br>❍ Helped boose SAT scores 10 percentile points.<br>❍ Brought our system to nearly 25 percentile points above state average. |

CONFIDENTIAL

21

**Combination.** *Donald P. Orlando, Montgomery, Alabama*

The writer had to write this four-page resume "to meet the special interests of diverse members of a county board of education." Instead of using the typical structure of a curriculum vitae (CV),

CONFIDENTIAL

**Charles M. Downer** | School System Chief Executive Officer | ✆ [703] 555-5555

**Director, Millburg University Regional In-service Education Center**
and
**Coordinator, Secondary Education Program**
June 1985 - August 1988

Millburg University, Millburg, Virginia

- Built first regional professional education development center in Virginia from a single, renovated classroom.
- Visited 22 school districts employing 6,500 teachers and administrators to complete the area's first integrated needs assessment. Done in three months. Highest participation of 11 similar efforts.
- Asked by National Council of States on In-service Education to explain our model center at their national convention.
- Got our four hour training blocks adapted for broadcast by Virginia Public Television.
- Organized first annual conference on the teaching of writing. Persuaded nation's top presenters to appear. Nearly doubled our goal of 200 attendees. Now teachers come from as far away as Alaska and England.

**Superintendent of Education**
September 1981 - June 1985

Renton City Board of Education, Renton, Virginia

- Guided my staff of seasoned professionals to abandon their reliance upon taskings. Productivity rose steadily. Our new basic skills criteria validated by Department of Education as "a model for the state."
- Made time to find what teachers needed to enhance instruction across the curricula, identified right programs and set guideline for contractors.
- Got entire community support for school tax measure. Parents called voters every night for six weeks, arranged for public service announcements, invited senior citizens to school. Measure passed by 98% in high turnout.

Nine years of increasingly responsible service to education from **Head Coach** to **Athletic Director to the Principal** at elementary, junior high and high school levels.

EDUCATION AND TRAINING:

- ABD, Educational Leadership, Auburn University, Auburn, Alabama
- "AA" Certification in Educational Leadership, Auburn University, Auburn, Virginia, 1980
- Master of Education in Educational Leadership, Georgia State University, Atlanta, Georgia, 1973
- B.S., Social Science, Livingston University, Livingston, Virginia, 1968

– 2 –

CONFIDENTIAL

the writer provided "hard-hitting examples of performance" and sought "to guide the search committee to hire" on the basis of "strong qualifications, not political considerations." Distinctive features in this resume include the phone symbol in the contact information "header" at the top of each page and the shadowed

RECENT SERVICE ON PROFESSIONAL COMMITTEES:

- Steering Committee of the Administrative Professional Development Task Force, Virginia State Board of Education. Appointed by State Superintendent of Education to help shape a comprehensive leadership development program for all practicing and prospective school administrators in the state, October, 1990 - Present.
- Student Instructional Services Advisory Committee. Appointed by State Superintendent of Education to advise the Department of Education's Division of Instructional Services on new issues in public education, October, 1990 - Present.
- Member, Board of Visitors. Appointed by the Southern Association of Colleges and Schools as a member of the team recommending accreditation for schools in grades K - 12, July 1994 - September 1995.
- Chair, Ten-year Reevaluation Committees. Appointed by the Southern Association of Colleges and Schools to coordinate the committee's site visit and compile and edit the final report for the following schools:
  - Norwood High School, Norwood, Virginia, April 1990
  - Callahan Middle School, Washington, Virginia, April 1989
  - Corners School, Covington County, Virginia, April 1989

RECENT KEYNOTE PRESENTATIONS:

- "If I had Known I Would Live This Long I Would Have Taken Better Care of Myself," The Virginia Community College Association Commission on Support, Staunton, Virginia, November 1993
- "The Instructional Focus," Kinston High School, Kinston, Virginia, February 1991
- "Self-Esteem: The Transferable Skill," Alexandria City Schools, Alexandria, Virginia, February 1991
- "The Strategies of Leadership," Northern State Community College, Lipton, Virginia, December 1990
- "Self-Esteem: The Educator's Mirror," Wall State University, Centerville, Virginia, August 1990
- "Effective Schools with an Instructional Focus," Hillcrest High School, Selton, Virginia, August 1990
- "Effective Schools: A Virginia Perspective," Virginia State Department of Education statewide Conference on Effective School Practices, Richmond, Virginia, July 1990

PUBLICATIONS AND PRODUCTIONS:

- With Phillip Harlon, "Social Studies and Technology," *Instruction,* Vol. 98, No. 1 (Fall, 1987), pp. 9 - 26
- With Phillip Harlon, Mary M. Williams, Harry Kintel, "Teachers and Motivation," *Journal of Instructional Methods,* Vol. 8, No. 6 (December, 1987), pp. 176 - 183
- Executive director, "Computers in the Classroom," four-hour video training program, Virginia State Department of Education and Commission on Higher Education, 1986



circular bullets throughout the resume. Features commonly found in a CV include sections on service performed on professional committees, keynote presentations given, publications written or produced, professional affiliations maintained, and service to the community. Full, dotted, horizontal lines separate the

C O N F I D E N T I A L

**Charles M. Downer** School System Chief Executive Officer ✆ [703] 555-5555

PROFESSIONAL AFFILIATIONS:

- National Association of Supervision and Curriculum Development
- National Association of Secondary School Principals
- National Council of States on In-service Education
- National Education Association
- Virginia Association of School Administrators
- Virginia Association for Supervision and Curriculum Development
- Virginia Education Association
- Virginia Council of School Administration and Supervision
- Phi Delta Kappa (Honorary member of this professional educational fraternity)

SERVICE TO THE COMMUNITY:

- Chairman, Board of Directors, Chamber of Commerce, Alexandria, Virginia
- County Fund Drive Coordinator, Boy Scouts of America
- County Fund Drive Coordinator, American Cancer Society
- Past officer, Rotary Club International
- Past officer, Ruritan National
- Kiwanis Clubs of America
- Jaycees

– 4 –

C O N F I D E N T I A L

positions mentioned in the Professional Experience and Selected Accomplishments section. Achievements are quantified whenever possible. The overall result is a well-designed package of impressive information.

*Curriculum Vitae*

## *Oscar Tirrell*

420 Clarendon Court
Princeton Junction, New Jersey 08550

(609) 275-6508 home
(610) 975-3291 business

### *Profile*

- Known as a self-motivated innovator and risk-taker, with extensive business development and technical experience.
- Developed a new business entity for MetPath, Inc. (parent company). Instrumental in creating and expanding new opportunities within the company.
- Directed the growth of MetTrials from start-up to $6.4 million in three years. Currently maintain operating margins in excess of 40% through the optimization and repurposing of resources.
- Proven leader and business manager who has demonstrated his ability to guide and redirect the business unit through three divisional repositionings.
- Possess strong sales and marketing background with broad experience in Total Quality management. Utilize a high degree of computer literacy.

---

### *Experience*

**Corning Pharmaceutical Services**, Teterboro, NJ — ***1993-Present***

**Current Position:**

***Executive Director, MetTrial, Inc.***, Radnor, PA — ***1993-Present***

Conceptualized and created a new business opportunity for the company; developed a business plan and presented it to the president for approval. Selected a name, logo and color scheme for the new venture and registered same.

Created an organizational structure; designed and implemented a controlled growth plan. Developed services tailored to satisfy client needs and systems integration requirements. Repositioned MetTrials as a partnership of MetPath Laboratories and Corning Pharmaceutical Services to optimize the use of available resources.

Achieved a solid record of business managerial experience, including development of a clinical research business unit.

---

### *Professional Accomplishments*

#### *Business Management*

- Responsible for P&L accountability for MetTrials business unit and other departments.
- Manage multiple departments with staffs having advanced degrees. Oversee staff and operations in multiple locations.
- Created an international partnership providing mutual support for clinical trials in Europe and the United States. Created the "idea factory," a forum designed to encourage innovation and creativity.
- Established cross-functional capabilities for the staff including project management, presentation skills, physician site initiations, client and sales support.
- Developed a staff empowerment structure designed to streamline decision making, optimize staffing, and establish organizational commitment.

22

**Combination.** *Beverly Baskin, Marlboro, New Jersey*

This is another four-page curriculum vitae for an Executive Director. As in the preceding resume, single horizontal lines separate the main sections. A Profile provides initial focusing.

Oscar Tirrell.....Page 2

***Professional Accomplishments*** (continued)

***Research and Development***

- Broad-based experience in laboratory procedures, instrumentation, quality assurance, and operations both human and veterinary.
- Provide consultative support to clinical research clients in developing laboratory test protocols for clinical trials.
- Act as "Pathologist on call" for MetPath. Provide interpretation of data to physicians, correlating clinical information and laboratory results.
- Conduct technical presentations to individual client and at scientific meetings; supervise development and helped evaluate testing kits.

***Sales and Marketing***

- Personally increased sales from start-up to $6.4 million in annual sales within 3 years.
- Commissioned a focus session to assess market positioning for MetTrials.
- Established business development group within MetTrials.
- Managed the creation of two multi-use marketing pieces.
- Directed a national accounts group and oversaw hospital/technical services and laboratories.
- Developed an advertising piece which appeared in several industry journals.
- Created and produced low-cost "leave-behind" piece.
- Established a company-wide MetTrials sales lead compensation structure, for the MetPath sales force, providing a cost-effective method for increasing market penetration.
- Oversaw and participated in MetTrials' presence at a minimum of two trade shows per year. This included the updating of booth graphics on three occasions. Reduced costs by utilizing existing booths.

***Reengineering***

- Reengineered MetTrials as a partnership of MetPath and Corning Pharmaceutical Services within PACT (a division of C.P.S.), blending dedicated resources with the optimized use of available assets. Created a lean and effective operation.
- Repositioned MetTrials as a business unit of SciCor.
- Maximized the outsourcing of services including subcontracting both assembly and shipment of sample kits and automating the transmission of reports. Provided a cost-affective, streamlined service.

***Service Enhancements***

- Created new kit packaging system needed to draw and ship patient samples. Each kit is preassembled, color-coded/visit-specific, and packaged in dispensing containers.
- Developed tailored, flexible, simplified, and streamlined document design and production.
- Commissioned and implemented a data-entry demographic masking system enhancing accuracy and increasing keying speed.
- Conceptualized and oversaw the creation and implementation of a database for MetTrials, featuring a linked bar-coding system which printed patient, visit specific labels as demographic data was applied to the database. This system virtually eliminated the need to complete forms, and supplanted these in cases where the documents were not forwarded to the lab.

A different method of arrangement is that the candidate's experience is presented in three different sections: Experience, Former Positions, and International Experience. The first section, which covers only the individual's work experience as an Executive Director from 1993 to the present, is separated from the other

Oscar Tirrell.....Page 3

---

***Former Positions***

**MetPath Inc.**, Teterboro, NJ 1988-1993
*Director/MetTrials*
*Director of Clinical Research*
*Director of National Accounts*

**Bergen Community College**, Paramus, NJ 1987-1988
*Associate Professor*

**MetPath Inc.**, Teterboro, NJ 1974-1988
*Manager of Research/Industrial/Hospital Services; Medical Professional Technologist*

**New Jersey College of Medicine and Dentistry**, New Brunswick, NJ 1971-1972
*Teaching Assistant*

---

***International Experience***

- Broad international life experiences.
- Completed graduate degrees in France and Italy.
- Traveled throughout the orient.
- Established an international partnership providing mutual support for clinical trials in Europe and the U.S.

---

***Foreign Languages***

Fluent in Italian and French.
Working knowledge of Spanish and German.

---

***Presentations***

- Killer Molecules in the Laboratory: Associates of Clinical Pharmacology conference. May 1992

---

***Total Quality Management***

- Broad experience in Total Quality Management, Quality Assurance processes and regulatory affairs.
- Participated in TQM training programs.
- Member of MetPath Quality Improvement Team (QIT) dedicated to monitoring customer satisfaction.

two sections by a Professional Accomplishments section that runs for almost one and a third pages. In this important section, the candidate's achievements are grouped according to five categories: Business Management, Research and Development, Sales and Marketing, Reengineering, and Service Enhancements.

Oscar Tirrell.....Page 4

---

***Computer Literacy***

- Broad-based experience with Windows software applications including all Microsoft products, WordPerfect, Lotus Suite, Q&A, PerForm Plus, Claris Works.
- Familiarity with multimedia products such as Compel, Media Blitz, and Microsoft Video for Windows.
- Knowledge of systems database products including Oracle 7, Ingress, and Access.
- Training in Visual Basic, C language, multimedia product development and Internet usage is in progress.

---

***Education***

**The Animal Medical Center**, PA, 1984
*(The University of Pennsylvania School of Veterinary Medicine)*
- Post Graduate courses in equine and food animal medicine and surgery.

**The Animal Medical Center**, NY, 1983
- Post Graduate Studies in Clinical Veterinary Medicine.
- Studies in Gastroenterology, Dermatology, Nephrology, Emergency Service, Soft Tissue Surgery, Oncology, and Opthamology.

**University of Bologna**, Italy, 1982
- Doctor of Veterinary Medicine

**University of Grenoble**, France, 1973
- Faculty of Medicine - Graduate Courses in Biology Sciences

**Seton Hall University**, NJ, 1972
- Graduate Courses in Physiology

**Seton Hall University**, NJ, 1971
- BS in Biology/Pre-Med.

---

***Certifications***

Clinical Medical Laboratory Supervisor Certificate and Permit-Department of Health, NY, 1984
Clinical Medical Laboratory Technologist Certificate and Permit-Department of Health, NY, 1973

---

***Professional Affiliations***

Associate of Clinical Pharmacology
American Veterinary Medicine Association
American Association of Clinical Chemists
New York Academy of Sciences
American Management Association
National Accounts Marketing Association

The fourth page details the candidate's computer literacy, education, certifications, and professional affiliations. Small bullets are not put everywhere but call attention to the most important information.

# T. James Wicket

P.O. Box 000 • Clearview, MD 99999 • (410) 000-6666 • (410) 999-4444-(FAX)

Objective

***My job objective is simple and straightforward. I am not just seeking a management position from which I can exercise the talents listed in my resume. I am anxious to return to a work environment where I have interaction with individuals who will work with me to make the business better. I am skilled with people. I want to exercise that skill to its fullest potential.***

Summary of Qualifications

- Assertive, self-motivated and goal directed.
- Excellent organizational skills. Ability to develop realistic and usable plans and programs.
- Ability to resolve difficult situations with diplomacy, tact, and discretion.
- High degree of entrepreneurial and business logic.
- Excellent communications skills.
- Ability to create rapport between associates, customers, and subordinates.
- Proven top performer in sales, management and general management.

Employment Overview

The Wicket Basket Co., Clearview, MD 5/95 to Present

***Owner and Founder*** of successful wholesale mail order business featuring a catalog product line of over 200 styles of imported baskets. Business has experienced a steady growth of 10%-20% per month since its inception in the Spring of 1995.

New Age Baskets, Lincoln, IL 1988 to 10/95

***Owner*** of successful company specializing in the import and wholesale of wicker baskets for the gift and hospitality industries. Increased annual sales from 80M to 500M during term of ownership. Growth and improved performance of company achieved through computerization of inventory, reduced inventory turnaround time, implementing a comprehensive accounts receivable and collections program, improving catalog and advertising initiatives, implementing more cost effective shipping methods, and reducing labor costs and payroll expenses.

Wicket Healthcare, Inc., Cleveland, TN 1974 to 1988

***Vice-President***, (1983 to 1988), directly responsible for the start-up and operation of 80 home care stores in the southwest and northwest region including Texas, Utah, New Mexico, Arizona, Colorado, Oregon, Washington and southern California. Played a major role in all phases of the start-up of each store. Responsible for site location, building acquisition, property improvements, and management recruitment. Managed sales performance in the 80-store district which regularly achieved company's highest sales volumes. District also achieved best performance in profitability and days-sales-outstanding.

***Sales Representative***, (1974 to 1983), for 75 major hospital accounts in the Arizona, New Mexico region. Ranked amoung top five of 350 sales representatives for five consecutive years. First sales representative in company history to earn President's Club status after only five years in sales.

Classic Edition Homes, Inc., Peru, DE 1972 to 1974

***Sales Representative.*** Stimulated growth in new home sales in a slow market area of Peru by implementing innovative, "grass roots" marketing techniques.

United States Air Force, Frazer AFB, ME 1969 to 1972

***Captain, Chief/Combat Training, 26th Air Division, North American Air Defense Command.*** Designated a Master of Air Defense, the highest performance rating in Aerospace Defense Command. Was categorized as a TOP STAR officer. (TOP STAR officers are those believed to have potential for the ultimate rank of a General officer.)

Education

University of Surrey Park, Surrey Park, NJ

***Bachelor of Arts, 1966***

Pre-Law (History and Political Science)

23

**Combination.** *Thomas E. Spann, Easton, Maryland*

The Objective statement may be a candidate's first and only chance to win the attention of the resume's reader. The Objective here in boldface avoids the ordinary and attempts to be heard.

# MARK A. TUCKER

**3117 179th Terrace**
**St. Petersburg, Florida 33703**
**(813) 000-0000**

## ***PROFESSIONAL PROFILE***

Aggressive, results-oriented co-business owner experienced in large volume production operations, business planning, financial management, growing profit margins, gaining market share, customer service, personnel supervision, and staff development. Entrepreneurial minded with proactive, goal-oriented attitude; devised and instituted plan to effectively revamp operations, maximize efficiency, and minimize cost ratios. Track record reflects high-level competency in sales cycle management, facilitating developmental strategies, and producing bottom-line results. Key role in the following areas:

***Operations:*** Structured and implemented company's business plan, arranged daily production activities, monitored inventory and purchasing, and maintained quality control. Conducted equipment evaluation and oversaw proper maintenance. Ensured compliance with all health codes and governmental regulations.

***Financial Management:*** Co-responsible for P&L decisions, capital improvements, developing annual budgets, and preparing yearly financial projections/forecasts. Oversaw accounts receivable and payable, invoicing, collections, and payroll.

***Marketing:*** Directly managed company's sales efforts, solicited new accounts, negotiated contracts, expanded market for product distribution and handled all merchandising promotions. In March 1994, expedited an aggressive sales/marketing plan that successfully grew business from 40 customers (within a 260-mile radius) to 85 customers (in a 400-mile territory) by April 1995. Increase in customer base included one large chain store and 18 independent convenience stores.

***Customer Service:*** Extensively interacted with customers to implement quality service and promote strong vendor/customer relations. Consistently provided follow-up to ensure attention to each customer's requests/needs.

***Administration/ Supervision:*** Charged with personnel functions involving hiring, terminating, training, and scheduling hourly staff. Conducted performance evaluations and instituted applicable disciplinary actions as necessary. Coordinated scheduling of customer delivery routes and developed in-house order sheets and forms for maintaining accurate accounting of inventory. Supervised up to 14 employees including production staff and route drivers.

***Achievements:***

**** Increased size of territory by 35-40% in one year.**
**** Expanded client base by 112% within same time period.**
**** Expedited production by 88.5% while only increasing payroll by 7.8%.**

## ***RELEVANT EXPERIENCE***

**1992 - 1995** MMT FOODS INC. - **Co-Owner** Clearwater, FL

## ***EDUCATION***

ST. PETERSBURG JUNIOR COLLEGE St. Petersburg, FL
**A.A. Degree**

24

**Combination.** *Diane McGoldrick, Tampa, Florida*

This resume was created to accompany documentation for a business loan from a bank after a partnership was dissolved. Six categories help to reveal the applicant's experience and skills.

# Sara Mahan

**123 Hightop Lane • Lincoln, Indiana 55555 • (444) 555-7626**

## Professional Profile

- International banking professional with experience in budget administration, personnel management, auditing, financial reporting, and business development
- Fluently speak German and English and have worked with business professionals worldwide, including Europe, America, Japan, Thailand, Korea, Hong Kong, Singapore, Australia, and New Zealand
- Outstanding communication skills and an ability to create efficient, productive work teams
- Highly developed problem solving skills and a reputation as a decisive, results-oriented manager
- Extremely hard working, dedicated, and efficient; consistently give 110% effort
- Well traveled with a good understanding of European and Asian business conventions and social protocols

## Employment History

❑ Shangri-la Art Gallery, Lincoln, Indiana **1990-1993**
***Owner/Buyer***
- » Imported art work from Southeast Asia and sold through a private gallery
- » Handled all administrative aspects of the business, including buying, customs declarations, personnel management, and accounting

❑ Volans Fine Arts Trading, Singapore and Tokyo **1986-1989**
***Owner/Buyer/Broker***
- » Acquired Asian art in Japan, Singapore, and Thailand for private collectors, building clientele base through Asian business and social contacts

❑ Volunteer Work and Business Entertaining **1983-1989**
As the wife of a banking professional in Singapore, I was not able to receive a work permit; I assisted my partner's career through administrative support, networking, and business entertaining

❑ Bayerische Vereinsbank (Union Bank of Bavaria) **1974-1983**
***Assistant Treasurer/Assistant Controller/Interim Controller***, Chicago, IL (1979-1983)
- » Managed all aspects of the accounting department for the head office of all American branches
- » Coordinated communication between head office in Munich and foreign branches
- » Developed and administered multi-million dollar budgets for all American Branches
- » Managed consolidated management reporting for all American Branches, including P&Ls, security deposits, reserves against deposits, etc.
- » Handled year-end closings and foreign exchange revaluations
- » As bank's liaison officer, worked closely with regulatory auditors

***Accountant/Banker***, Munich, Germany (1977-1979)
- » Compiled P&L information and produced reports for all foreign branches, including London, Tokyo, Luxemburg, Cayman Islands, Chicago, Atlanta, Los Angeles, New York, etc.
- » Coordinated the publishing of monthly, quarterly, semi-annual and annual reports for all foreign branches

***Data Processing Accountant***, Munich, Germany (1976-1977)
- » Accounting representative member of conversion team that computerized all banking systems

***Apprentice Banker***, Munich, Germany (1974-1976)
- » Chosen for bank's specialized job-rotation program and classroom training; top honors student

## Education

- Bank Management Diploma, Chamber of Industry and Commerce for Munich and Upper Bavaria, Germany, 1975
- University of Münster, Germany, majoring in nutrition with course work in economics, 1971-1973
- Course work in Business English, 1976-1977

**25**

**Combination.** *Barbie Dallmann, Charleston, West Virginia*

The rule-breaking use of "I" is an attempt to personalize this resume for someone who had a banking career, married in 1983, developed another career, and now wants to return to banking.

## BEN SCHNEIDER

9215 Pioneer Road ♦ Bartelso, IL 62218
(618) 523-4778

## Creative Marketing / Layout / Design

- Versatile business/project management background, including experience developing comprehensive public relations campaigns. Professional writing skills include radio commercials, press releases, media advisories, newspaper and magazine feature stories, and project reports. Organized promotional events from start to finish.
- Extremely creative; original artwork chosen for an invitational exhibit sponsored by Art St. Louis featuring outstanding college art students.
- Designed invitations, print ads, and event programs. Established project timelines, created press kits, and successfully gained media coverage.
- Proven ability to articulate abstract concepts and turn them into marketable ideas.

## Education

Bachelor of Arts in Art & Marketing, McKendree College, Lebanon, IL (1996)
magna cum laude; GPA 3.9/4.0

- Awarded Most Outstanding Marketing Student in 1996
- Awarded Most Outstanding Art Student in 1996
- Member, Sigma Beta Delta Business Honor Society

## Experience

- 18 years as a successful business owner (1975-1993). Skills included strategic planning, fiscal management, personnel management, business growth, advertising, public relations, customer service, needs analysis, marketing, and diverse clientele management.
- Faber & Partners Public Relations, O'Fallon, IL (Summer Intern, 1995). Notable projects and clients include:

| | Wrote... | Organized... | Designed... | Conducted... |
|---|---|---|---|---|
| **Project/Client** | Press Kits<br>Press Releases<br>Media Advisories<br>Radio Commercials<br>Feature Stories | Special Events<br>Timelines<br>Mailing Lists<br>Ceremonies | Letterhead<br>Invitations<br>Ceremony Programs<br>Mementos<br>Print Ads | Market Research<br>Interviews |
| **Family Fun Fair** | | | X | X |
| **Ganim, Meder, Childers, & Hoering** | | X | | |
| **Lake View Memorial Gardens** | X | | X | |
| **Mid America Bank** | X | | | |
| **St. Mary's Church** | X | | X | |
| **O'Fallon Public Library** | X | X | X | X |

Trained in Adobe Illustrator, Photoshop, and PageMaker

**26**

**Combination.** *John A. Suarez, Troy, Illinois*

The eye-catching table at the bottom of this resume might be read first and shows at a glance the specific tasks the candidate performed for each client. The table supports every point at the top.

# Leonard Nimitz, Esq.

3752 Vista Avenue, New Brunswick, NJ 55555 (201) 555-5555 (201) 555-5555 fax

- **Business Affairs Counsel**
- **Television Pilot Executive Producer**

## Professional Profile

- **Extensive corporate background in business affairs and marketing.**
- **Wide experience in the sports and entertainment industries.**
- **Effectively combine creativity with bottom-line objectives.**
- **A hands-on executive, energized by the pursuit of excellence.**
- **Admitted to New York and New Jersey Bars.**

## Business Affairs Counsel

- **General corporate counsel.** Draft and negotiate licensing, joint venture, employment, restrictive covenant, stockholder, partnership and deferred compensation agreements. Prepare by-laws, equipment and office leases, stock and asset purchase agreements, and promissory notes. Conduct strategic planning for new business formation and development. Prepare memoranda and opinion letters on corporate and commercial issues.
- **Provide extensive legal counsel and business services to independent television and motion picture production companies.** Draft and negotiate production, licensing, distribution and independent contractor agreements. Prepare motion picture private placement memoranda and related subscription/limited partnership agreements. Develop budgets, assist in raising capital, and prepare business and marketing plans.
- **Advised venture capitalist on acquisitions and investments in the sports marketplace.** Evaluated legal and business issues associated with opportunities in merchandising and marketing, minor league baseball and hockey, stadium and arena facilities, Major League Soccer, Major League Baseball, Canadian Football League, and Australian Baseball League.
- **Represented professional sports radio/television broadcaster.** Procured positions in AA minor league baseball and NCAA Division I basketball. Represented client in NFL and NBA radio broadcast negotiations.
- **Structured professional athlete fan clubs.** Designed related merchandising programs including licensed apparel agreements.

## Television Pilot Executive Producer

- **Co-creator and executive producer of *The Body Perfect* — a television pilot for a weekly, thirty minute wellness series hosted by Dan O'Brady and accredited by the American Medical Society.**

27

**Combination.** *Deborah Wile Dib, Medford, New York*

"This resume needed to tie in business expertise and television production experience for a job search focused on the business end of the entertainment industry." The writer "used a bold

# Leonard Nimitz, Esq.

page two

## Television Pilot Executive Producer (continued)

- **Manage show's extensive legal, business and marketing activities.** Negotiate production, distribution, licensing, sponsorship and marketing agreements. Raise capital, develop and oversee budget, and procure corporate affiliations and medical accreditations. Deliver sophisticated sales presentations to top corporate management.
- **Formalized pilot segment concepts and oversaw overall creative development.** Conceptualized segments, assisted in writing, supervised editing, and acted as liaison between production, medical and corporate participants.

## Career Development

- **Owner and Operator** — **1995 to present**
  Nimitz Productions, L.L.C., New Brunswick, NJ
  Law Offices of Loenard Nimitz, Esq., New Brunswick, NJ
- **Associate in Entertainment and Corporate Law** — **1992 to 1995**
  Eichorn, Noble and Julian, Fort Lee, NJ
- **Full-time Law Student** — **1989 to 1992**
  New York University School of Law, New York, NY
- **Marketing Representative, Metropolitan New York Area** — **1983 to 1989**
  Med Pro, Inc., New York, NY
  Levitan Manufacturing Company, Inc., Woodside, NY
  Med Comfort Corporation, New York, NY

## Education

| | | |
|---|---|---|
| ■ J.D. | New York University School of Law, NY | 1992 |
| ■ M.B.A. | Long Island University, Greenvale, NY | 1986 |
| ■ B.A. | State University of New York at New Paltz | 1983 |

## Professional Affiliations

ABA Forum on Entertainment & Sports Law ■ Sports Lawyers Association

NYSBA Entertainment, Arts & Sports Law Section ■ NJSBA Sports Law Committee

approach to capture interest, yet remained as traditional as possible to remain true to the expectations for a legal field resume." Filled, square bullets complement thick horizontal lines. Wide margins, blank lines, and extra space before headings provide adequate white space.

# Blaine See Carter, R.N.

999 Hampton Way
San Diego, California 33333
555.555.5555

## Career Profile

Medical professional with knowledge, experience, and skills to make a valuable contribution to the health care industry. Background includes management, supervision, educational coordinator, instructor, recruiter, trainer, on-going community medical commitments. Thoroughly professional with a high level of interpersonal communication skills.

*Administrative*

- Proven results in the community, implementing new concepts and programs, modifying traditional perceptions to meet diverse needs.
- Proposes basic line budgets and forecasts.
- Experienced in executive level planning, organizing, coordinating and executing, with the ability to perform equally well either as a member of the team or as the leader.

*Management*

- Efficient at scheduling, time management and organization.
- Administrator for several innovative projects and programs.

*Communication*

- Strong oral and written skills in communicating information; documenting complete, concise and reflective data.
- Effective analytical skills compiling and presenting care plans and written reports.

*Medical*

- Excellent knowledge of medical terminology, protocols and responsibilities.
- Ability to identify at-risk patients and assist in non-compliant patients.
- Skilled in Advanced Patient Care.

*Professionalism*

- Establishes priorities in multiple-demanding situations.
- Maintains a positive attitude when interacting with patients, family, physician personnel, peers and subordinates.

*Training*

- Excellent preceptor; developing plans and overseeing progress, offering encouragement when necessary.
- Strong instructing abilities with effective speaking and presentation skills.

*Achievements*

- Successfully developed and executed a Parent Education Program, resulting in utilization by major health care facilities nationwide.
- Implemented and administered pilot program entitled, "Raising Capable People".
- Effectively created scheduling systems, organized, staffed and supervised personnel for new OB/GYN Out-patient clinic.

## Education and Professional Qualifications

*University of California, San Diego* — San Diego, California
**Graduate Credit** - 9 units

*University of California, San Diego* — San Diego, California
**Bachelor of Science Degree / Nursing**

## Of Special Note

*Sea Inn* *An Award Winning Bed and Breakfast* — La Jolla, California
**Owner**, 1990 to 1997

- Created, managed and promoted an award-winning Bed and Breakfast with national recognition, featured on the cover of *California Lifestyles* magazine.
- Responsible for overall operations including business and financial management.

28

**Combination.** *Patricia S. Cash, Prescott, Arizona*

This candidate "wanted to move into an After-Care, Assisted Care Facility Administrator/ Director position. A clean format with bulleted groupings directs the reader to focus on the important

*Page Two* - **Blaine See Carter, R.N.**

## Summary of Experience

*San Marcos Samaritan Village* — San Marcos, California
*An 80 Bed Skilled Nursing Facility* — January 1996 to current

**Nursing Supervisor**, November 1996 to current

- Organize and schedule P.M. nursing staff; supervise quality care to residents.
- Develop, coordinate and implement resident care management.
- Efficiently perform diversified nursing duties including observing complications and symptoms requiring attention or drug modification.
- Maintain professionally accurate and complete documentation (Medicare/caid).
- Interact well with residents; maintain good rapport with physicians and staff.
- Handle medical emergencies and pressures intelligently and competently.

**Staff Nurse**, January to November 1996

- Responsible for daily patient care, including regular administration of medication and related nursing procedures.

*Mira Costa Community College* — Encinitas, California

**Instructor for R.N. Program**, 1990 to 1994

- Created lesson plans, provided instruction and monitored progress of nursing students.

*Nurses' Registry* — San Diego, California

**On Call Temporary Staffing**, 1990

- Provided nursing skills on a temporary basis for majority of the long term care facilities in San Diego.

*California Pioneer Home* — San Diego, California

**Staff Nurse**, 1990

*Scripps Hill Hospital* — San Diego, California

**Perinatal Education Coordinator**, 1978 to 1988

- Developed and instituted a Parent Education Program, with classes on early pregnancy, in hospital post partum support groups, Parents Forum, Big Kids for Babies. Trained and supervised a staff of 60.
- Effectively implemented "Raising Capable People" as adjunct to P.E.P.; training and supervising personnel, managing and administering program concepts.
- Successfully initiated marketing campaign resulting in increased community involvement and hospital census; coordinated and presented educational programs.

*University of California Hospital* — San Diego, California

**Perinatal Education Coordinator**, 1977 to 1978

*San Diego Childbirth Education Association* — San Diego, California

**Instructor, Recruiter and Trainer**, 1975 to 1978

*University of California Hospital* — San Diego, California

**Staff Nurse/Nurse Researcher**, 1975

**Head Nurse, OB/GYN Out-Patient Clinic**, 1971 to 1974

- Recruited to set-up systems, programs, hire and train staff for new clinic.
- Supervised, organized and scheduled a staff of ten professional and non-professionals; created volunteer program, trained personnel in non-essential tasks.

## Affiliations

California Nurses' Association
Sigma Theta Tau

aspects quickly." The "Of Special Note [section] validates her administrative abilities." The use of small caps in headings, subheadings, the names of institutions, and positions unifies the two-page resume visually. The thin-thick lines on both pages also tie the pages together.

**David Johanson** 103 Mill Lane, Greenvale Station, NY ■ (515) 555-5555

**General Manager ■ Business Owner and Operator ■ Entrepreneur**

**Career Profile**

- **Extensive experience in independent and franchised business ownership and business management.** Strong achievements in the areas of marketing, finance, product development, operations, strategic planning, and purchasing.
- **Proven record of success in the building of profitable businesses** by achievement of the highest standards in service, product development, marketing, expense control and asset management. Maintained AAA corporate credit rating and produced profits through multiple recessions.
- **Financial oversight for multi-million dollar operating budgets** with direct and indirect supervision of up to 150 employees. Excel at the enthusiastic motivation of subordinates to achieve corporate objectives.
- **A hands-on administrator and expert troubleshooter energized by the pursuit of excellence.** Keen ability to identify key market trends and profitable opportunities; to plan and direct store openings; and to create effective marketing and merchandising strategies.

**Representative Achievements**

- **Advanced from hairdresser, to beauty shop owner, to founder of *John David Hair Stylists*, a parent corporation of thirty independent and franchised beauty salons with multi-million dollar annual revenue.** Opened new, or purchased existing, under-performing salons; created partnerships or franchises as each salon became profitable. Employed 150 staff members in direct, franchised and partnership situations.
- **Created numerous opportunities for add-on profits.** Developed and marketed full line of cosmetics, beauty supplies, shampoos and hairsprays. Originated concept of salon boutiques; purchased designer clothing for these industry first locations.
- **Conceived and opened first beauty spa on Long Island.** Pioneered concept of "one stop shopping" for beauty services, massage, clothing, and jewelry in an upscale 12,000 square foot building. Spa was featured in a two page color layout in the premier issue of the Sunday Edition of Newsday.
- **Converted spa to cutting-edge *Hideaway* supper club that became prototype for numerous metropolitan area clubs.** Maintained pool and steam rooms and allowed dancing in bathing suits. First to promote male dance reviews to develop mid-week business; concept tripled revenue. Brought in rising talent, including Madonna, K.C. and the Sunshine Band, and other well known artists. Sold club for major profit after fifteen years of operation.
- **Opened and operated area's first "California style" Italian Cafés in Syosset and Smithtown, NY.** Gutted and renovated locations, designed decor and architecture, created innovative restaurants that became popular neighborhood meeting places.

29

**Functional.** *Deborah Wile Dib, Medford, New York*

This "retired business owner/manager wanted to obtain [an] interesting management position." The writer "used a non-dated, functional format with business profiles to demonstrate expertise

**David Johanson** **page two**

## Business Development and Management

**Cocina Italian Café**
**Owner/Operator**
Syosset and Smithtown, NY

***California and city style casual dinning.***

- Conceived, opened, and managed innovative 100 seat, 3,000 square foot café. Opened second location, a 160 seat freestanding restaurant one year later. Gutted and renovated, designed decor and architecture. State-of-the-art restaurants resembled the then new style of California and city cafés. Concept was unique to the local Long Island area.
- Restaurants featured innovative menus, casual dining and contemporary decor with open kitchen concept. Friendly atmosphere and good food promoted repeat business; became neighborhood meeting places.
- Made decision to close in 1996. Skyrocketing expenses, increased competition, and poor local economy were causative factors.

**Hideaway Supper Club**
**Founder and Sole Proprietor**
Lawrence, NY

***Cutting-edge dining, dancing and entertainment venue.***

- Converted previous 12,000 square foot beauty spa location into trend-setting club with capacity for 800 patrons. *Hideaway* became industry prototype for other metropolitan area clubs. Maintained longevity against club industry record of high start-up failures. Operated for fifteen years and sold for major profit.
- Developed cutting-edge concepts: maintained spa pool and steam rooms and promoted dancing in bathing suits. Hired first area male dance review to develop mid-week business. Featured established and rising entertainers; highlighted Madonna early in her career as well as other well known talent. Developed catering operation and private party concept.
- Directed entire renovation and operation of club: managed all personnel, ordered supplies, oversaw bookkeeping and accounting. Hired and fired staff of 25 to 30 for direct or contracted payroll.

**John David Hair Stylists**
**Founder and Owner**
New York City and Long Island, NY

***Chain of thirty independent and franchised beauty salons and spa.***

- Developed corporate operations and negotiated commercial loans for twenty year profitable expansion from single store to multi-million dollar business. Created franchise opportunities and marketing strategies.
- Planned, organized, set up and managed individual store openings and daily operations until store became profitable and was franchised, or put into managed partnership.
- Developed products and packaging for profitable lines of John David cosmetics, hair care and beauty products. Originated concept of salon clothing boutiques. Purchased apparel and accessories for boutiques and supplies and beauty products for chain.
- Spa movement pioneer: opened 12,000 square building featuring full salon and beauty services, massage, and clothing and jewelry boutiques. Converted spa to *Hideaway* after ten years of operation.

and create interest." Reading this resume from beginning to end gives the impression that whatever business this candidate touches will be profitable. Page two displays a unique way to indicate the place of employment and the individual's position: in the left column and with a line.

**RALPH M. JACOBS**

*Licensed Real Estate Broker*

*Certified Residential Specialist* *Certified Buyer Representative*

*Home:*
2 Discovery Lane
Houston, TX 55555
(304) 408-3065

*Business:*
113 Main Street
Houston, TX 55555
(304) 408-7451

**Professional Profile:**

Successful real estate entrepreneur/sales manager with reputation for personal integrity and professional accomplishments. Comprehensive knowledge of housing industry, real estate law, and financing programs. Property management experience as owner of several multi-units. Leadership skills demonstrated through active participation in professional and community organizations at local, state, and national levels.

*Demonstrated ability to:*

- Develop and implement marketing, operational, budgetary, and business plans
- Motivate agents toward improved efficiency, productivity, and service
- Assist clients with all phases of purchasing/selling residential and commercial properties
- Communicate daily with title companies, banks, mortgage brokers, attorneys, etc.
- Present information for home buying seminars and pre-licensure courses

*Achievements/Awards:*

- Grew real estate business from 2-person office to 15-member agency achieving consistent ratings as 1 of the top 3 agencies (in sales) for the Central Houston area; #1 for 1996
- Realtor of the Year, Houston Regional Board of Realtors, 1992
- Consistently meet annual sales objectives in the $2-$3 million-dollar range
- Earned Certified Residential Specialist designation in 1995

**Related Work Experience:**

Owner/Broker, Housing Associates/Jacobs Real Estate, Houston, TX (1989-present)

Sales Agent, General Realty, Houston, TX (1983-1989)

**Professional Affiliations:**

Houston Regional Board of Realtors, Member, 1983-present
Board of Directors (1986-95); President (1991-92); President Elect (1990); Budget & Finance Committee (1988-92); Vice President (1989); Vice Chairman Legislative Committee (1989); Professional Standards Committee (1988); Secretary (1987)

Texas Association of Realtors, Member, 1983-present
Board of Directors (1990-92); Membership Service Committee (1992); Executive Committee (1991)

National Association of Realtors, Charter Member of International Real Estate Division

**30**

**Combination.** *Elizabeth M. Carey, Waterville, Maine*

"This resume was developed for submission to a board that reviewed candidates to a state real estate commission. The client was interviewed and appointed to the board by the governor."

**RALPH M. JACOBS**

*Résumé, Page 2*

**Civic / Community Involvement:**

Texas Chamber and Business Alliance, Board of Directors (1993-present)

Houston Comprehensive Plan Committee, Appointed by Mayor (1996)

Houston Area Chamber of Commerce (Board of Directors, 1992-present; Vice Chairman, 1996)

Best Bank of Texas Advisory Board (Member, 1994-present)

Houston Rotary Club (Member, 1993-present)

**Related Training and Education:**

All State Realtors Institute (1992 Graduate)

Texas Association of Realtors
Leadership Conferences (1988-present); Professional Standards Seminars (1990 & 1992)
State Conventions (1989-present)

Floyd Wickman Real Estate Sales Training Course (1988)

Dale Carnegie Sales and Human Relations Courses (1984-85)

**References:**

Personal and professional references will be furnished upon request.

The Professional Profile highlights the candidate's "knowledge of and achievements in the real estate field, as well as his keen business sense and professional reputation." Distinctive features are the shadowed bullets and the rounded rectangular boxes around the contact information.

# LEWIS P. MONTGOMERY

8000 South Main Street
Longview, Texas 77777

(555) 999-9999 (Office)
(555) 666-8888 (Home)

## AREAS OF EXPERTISE

♦ **Contract Negotiations** ♦ **Public Speaking** ♦ **Sales / Marketing**
♦ **Risk Management** ♦ **Loss Control** ♦ **Policy Interpretation**
♦ **Real Estate Acquisitions / Development / Management**

## HIGHLIGHTS OF QUALIFICATIONS / ACHIEVEMENTS

- **Qualified, efficient professional** with demonstrated versatile experience and expertise.
- Consistently in **Top 10%** in total income/growth. **#1 Fire Producer** (1987, 1988, 1989).
- Successful in negotiations, development, management, and sales of real estate property.
- Cognizant of and adept in all aspects of operations/personnel development/management; risk management; full P&L responsibility; budgeting; payroll; advertising.
- **Licensure:** Group I Insurance; Local Recording Agent; Real Estate Agent.
- Outstanding **public speaking**, **communications,** and **interpersonal** skills; easily establish positive rapport with staff, clients, and business professionals. Conversational Spanish.
- Intensely involved in professional and community organizations/activities/fundraisers.
- Highly self-motivated, profit- and success-oriented, hard-working individual.

## PROFESSIONAL EXPERIENCE

**LEWIS MONTGOMERY INSURANCE AGENCY** — **Longview, Texas**
**Owner / Allstate Insurance Agency** — **1986 – Present**

- Established and developed successful insurance agency from ground up; prospected and acquired account base encompassing 2,500 clients.
- Responsible for complete management of operations and staff of up to five; full P&L responsibility, risk management, payroll, advertising.
- Prepare and manage annual $100,000 operational budget.
- Prospect new business. Handle initial claims.
- Perform insurance inspections for various insurance companies.

**Significant Achievements**

- Consistently in **Top 10% in income and growth**; operate profitable business.
- **# 1 Fire Producer** in 1987, 1988, and 1989 (out of 30+ agents).

**MONTGOMERY INTERESTS** — **Longview, Texas**
**Owner / Manager** — **1980 – Present**

- Acquired in excess of 100 residential, apartment, commercial, and farm properties.
- Manage all aspects of business and staff of up to five. Manage $1 million operational budget.
- Negotiate purchases and sales; arrange for structured financing; taxes; insurance.
- Direct and coordinate contractors engaged in remodeling/refurbishment of property.
- Prepare sales and lease contracts. Lease and manage property.

31

**Combination.** *Ann Klint, Tyler, Texas*

Each page has a border with a thick line at the top and bottom. Each box made by the border is lightly shaded. Diamond bullets call attention to the areas of expertise and the highlights of

**LEWIS P. MONTGOMERY** **Page Two**

**EDUCATION / PROFESSIONAL DEVELOPMENT**

STEPHEN F. AUSTIN STATE UNIVERSITY - Nacogdoches, Texas
Major: **Business**
**Real Estate License; Group I Insurance License**

AMERICAN LEADERSHIP STUDY GROUPS
**International Exchange Student - Europe** (Summer 1979)
Several career-related courses/seminars, including **Risk Management**

**PROFESSIONAL / COMMUNITY AFFILIATIONS / ACTIVITIES / HONORS**

**Council Member**, LONGVIEW CITY COUNCIL (1994-1996)
**Establish and manage $80 million annual budget**

**Board Member**, ALZHEIMER'S ASSOCIATION

**Board Member / Vice President**, LIONS CLUB

**Member**, LONGVIEW CHAMBER OF COMMERCE
**Committee Member**, Longview 2000 Economic Development Steering Committee
**Member**, Vision 2000 Strategic Plan Task Force

**Member**, LONGVIEW INDEPENDENT SCHOOL DISTRICT FOUNDATION
**CPOC Committee Member**, Brown Elementary School

**Board Member**, LONGVIEW/MAIN STREET ADVISORY BOARD (1995)
**Winner of Historical Monument Award for Preservation** (1995)

**Appointed Member / Residential Division Chairman**, MAYOR'S ANTI-CRIME FORCE

**Chairman**, MARCH OF DIMES ***"Stars Behind Bars"***
Raised $17,000 in Pledges

**Past Board Member**, LONGVIEW JAYCEES (1985-1989)
***"Jaycee of the Month"; "Keyman Award"; "President's Award"***

**Past Board Member**, EAST TEXAS COUNCIL OF GOVERNMENT
Instrumental in organization of H.E.A.T. Program

**Past Member**, GOVERNMENT AFFAIRS COMMITTEE (1989-1990)

**Past Board Member / Officer / Membership Chairman**, BOARD OF HISTORIC LONGVIEW

**Volunteer**, UNITED WAY
**Past Board Member and President**, MINI BUS (United Way Activity)

**Annual Volunteer**, HERITAGE ON TOUR

**Member / Insurance Committee Member**, FIRST BAPTIST CHURCH

**32nd Degree Master Mason** - WACO SCOTTISH RITE; **Noble** - SHARON TEMPLE SHRINE

qualifications/achievements. Boldfacing makes certain achievements more visible. In the Professional Experience section the underlined subheading Significant Achievements helps those achievements related to insurance sales to stand out. Community activities occupy more than half of a page.

**SUE SMITH**
(888) 555-9809
69 Old Oaks Trail
Costa, Florida 33333

---

**FOOD & BEVERAGE MANAGEMENT**
**HOSPITALITY EXECUTIVE**

Eighteen-year professional career managing multiple-unit F&B operations … skillful communicator, trainer and mentor able to draw upon expertise in:

Annual Business and Strategic Planning … P&L Management … HR Training & Administration
Field Supervision … Store Design/Setup … Facilities Management & Maintenance
Purchasing & Inventory Management … Food & Labor Cost Controls
Promotions & Special Events … Guest Relations

**CAREER DEVELOPMENT**

AWESOME BAGEL BAKERIES, New City, Utah — 199x to 199x
**Operating Partner**

*Recruited to manage 5 locations within this 17-store, privately-held franchise and direct a management team of 15 with 100+ hourly personnel.*

- Increased net bottom line profit 31% FY96 over FY95.
- Decreased controllable expenses 16.7% FY96 over FY95.
- Executed top-drawer management principles within this 5-store market to deliver 43% of total corporate sales and 50% of gross profits FY96.
- Mentored 5 assistant managers to general management level.
- Introduced cross-merchandising concepts to enhance the shopping experience and build additional profit centers requiring minimal labor.

WALT DISNEY WORLD CO., Lake Buena Vista, Florida — 198x to 199x
**Assistant Food and Beverage Supervisor**

*Managed guest service, product quality, budgeting, cost control, personnel, maintenance, and sanitation functions in 7 locations within 3 theme park operations.*

- Developed management-potential cast members to promotion by meshing pre-Disney experience with traditional company values.
- Selected for EuroDisney opening training team; successfully trained diverse, multi-national staff and management team on schedule.

CHAMPION, INC., Reyes, Florida — 198x to 198x
**Unit Manager**

*Accounted for sales, personnel, cost control, maintenance and security functions.*

- Delivered a net profit percentage increase and raised unit rank to 1st from 18th within 6 months.

32

**Combination.** *Elizabeth J. Axnix, Iowa City, Iowa*

Ample white space is provided by extra blank lines above the section headings and by center-alignment of the opening profile section and the italic descriptive remarks after each position.

**SUE SMITH**

*Page Two*

**CAREER DEVELOPMENT**, *cont.*

CASA BLANCA—GENERAL MILLS RESTAURANT GROUP, Oro, Florida 198x to 198x
**General Manager / Training General Manager**

*Oversaw daily operations of several 300-seat full-service operations and directed a management team of 4 with 140 employees.*

- Coordinated personnel, marketing, operations, finance and information systems functions during 2 new location start ups which resulted in 50% less employee turnover (compared to corporate averages) and a first-year direct cost of sales 10% below industry average.
- Achieved a 10% labor cost reduction and improved management productivity by initiating and co-designing a forecasting system to generate sales projections, labor productivity and labor scheduling.
- Trained subordinate managers to General Manager promotions within 18 months or less.

47 CLUBS OF AMERICA—ELDRED CORPORATION, Pittsburgh, Pennsylvania 197x to 197x
**Unit Manager / Training Manager**

*Managed multi-use entertainment complexes and directed a management team of 5 with 100 employees and generating $2.5MM in annual sales.*

- Coordinated sporting events, special events, and private parties occurring simultaneously with regular operations.
- Conceived and implemented promotional strategies, marketing campaigns, and catering procedures to increase sales and profits.

TGI FRIDAYS, Cleveland, Ohio 197x to 198x
**Manager**

*Maintained bottom-line profitability of a 220-seat facility employing 100+ staff.*

- Planned menus in accordance with quality standards established by corporate to ensure customer satisfaction.

**EDUCATION**

UNIVERSITY OF PITTSBURGH, Pittsburgh, Pennsylvania
**BA—Political Science and Economics** • 197x

**MILITARY SERVICE**

UNITED STATES NAVY • 196x to 197x
*Honorable Discharge*

***COMPLETE REFERENCES AND CREDENTIALS AVAILABLE***

A line 4.5 inches long is perhaps the easiest to read for the size of type in this resume, and the bulleted lines in the Career Development average a little over 4.5 inches. A benefit of such a line length is that the reader can read down a page more rapidly than with margin-to-margin lines.

## Michael J. Armstrong

678 Hidden Cove
Marin City, CA 00000
Phone/Fax (000) 000-0000
Email armstrongmj@westcoast.com/com

**SENIOR MANAGEMENT • INTERNATIONAL BUSINESS DEVELOPMENT**

**CAREER PROFILE**

- Extensive strategic management experience in the United States and abroad, focused on new business and economic development.
- Record of success and innovation in senior management capacities in industry, consulting, and high profile not-for-profit organizations.
- Proven team leadership abilities in over XX countries in Europe, Asia, the Middle East, and Central and South America.
- In-depth experience in coordinating the resources of industry, government agencies, research organizations, and financial institutions.
- Extensive foreign residence, resulting in conversational language ability in French, Italian, and German. Modest ability in Spanish.
- Strong conceptual, analytical, planning, and communication skills.

**ORGANIZATION PROFILE**
*Complete history on page 2*

| | | |
|---|---|---|
| *Industry* | **Major Multi-national Corporation** | **Director, Operations**<br>**Director, Technical Services** |
| | **Major U.S. Corporation** | **Manager, International Operations and Executive Director, Global Development** |
| *Consulting* | **Adams, Baker, Charles & Co.** | **Senior Partner, International Practice** |
| *Non-profit* | **European Business Consortium** | **Chief Executive Officer** |
| | **World Business Consortium** | **Director, Economic Development** |

**EDUCATION**

**Ph.D., Economics**, University of California, 19XX
- Consultant, Industrial Revitalization Corporation, San Francisco, CA
- Research Associate, Department of Applied Economics. Focus on international economic research.

**M.S., Agricultural Economics**, University of Arizona, 19XX
- Consultant, Southwest Development Commission, Phoenix, AZ.
- Research Assistant, Department of Industry Resource Economics

**B.A., Political Science and International Relations**, University of Washington, 19XX

***Selected Training:***

Advanced Executive Development (Major Multi-national Corp.), Managing International Operations (American Management Association), International Joint Ventures (World Trade Center), Managing Foreign Exchange Risk (World Bank), Negotiating Skills (Battelle).

**33**

**Combination.** *Alan D. Ferrell, Lafayette, Indiana*

Besides emphasizing what is important, another tactic in resume writing is withholding what is irrelevant. The topics enclosed within bold horizontal lines and the bulleted statements in the

**M. Armstrong, page 2**

**EXPERIENCE**

**Adams, Baker, Charles & Company**
**Senior Partner, International Practice**, San Francisco, CA, 19XX to present
A strategic consulting firm serving clients in the United States, Europe, Asia, the Middle East, and South America.

- Providing market development, acquisition, strategic planning, and management consulting services to U.S. and foreign corporate, financial, and institutional clients.
- Team leader on assignments involving turnaround management, acquisition analysis, market assessments, strategic planning, and business development.
- Served as CEO of a troubled European company, leading the turnaround team for owners.
- An abstract of consulting assignments is available on request. Clients include a European commercial bank, a European manufacturer, a large Asian company, a chemical industry group, a U.S. trade association, and the World Bank.

**European Business Consortium**
**Chief Executive Officer**, Geneva, 19XX - 19XX
Recruited from industry for an X-year assignment to establish this not-for-profit organization for promoting private sector economic development. Reported to an eminent International Advisory Council.

- Hired/developed staff of XX (XX% local); provided strategic and day-to-day management.
- Achieved self-financing objective by end of second operating year and built $X million capital base. In X years established and built a distribution subsidiary with sales of $XX+ million.
- Established successful initiatives in business investment and finance, distribution, technical training, marketing, trading, publishing, and small enterprise development.

**Major Multi-national Corporation**

**Director, Operations**, Dallas, TX, 19XX - 19XX

- Managed operations of X manufacturing plants in the Southwestern U.S. and X contractors in Mexico. Total annual sales of $XX million.
- Designed and installed new manufacturing equipment; developed new products and marketing programs; developed and implemented quality assurance program; evaluated new ventures.

**Director, Technical Services**, International Division, Houston, TX, 19XX-19XX

- Profit center manager with worldwide responsibility for technical services contracts and trademark and process technology licenses. Also provided technical support to corporate subsidiaries in South America.
- New business development emphasized corporate expansion through joint ventures and acquisitions.

**Major U.S. Corporation**
**Manager, International Operations** and
**Executive Director, Global Development**, Kansas City, MO, 19XX - 19XX

- Profit center manager responsible for development of international business and newly formed Global Development initiative.
- Generated $X million in technical services and training contracts; developed production and marketing joint venture; supervised feasibility studies.
- Conceptualized and guided the establishment of an innovative and highly successful non-profit venture capital institution and development foundation.

**World Business Consortium**
**Director, Economic Development**, Washington, D.C., 19XX - 19XX

- Developed, funded, and managed multi-country projects in Latin America.
- Recruited by Major U.S. Corporation to expand Latin American concepts in other countries.

*Domestic and International References Readily Available*

Career Profile state strongly that the candidate is "highly qualified for senior management in international business development." What is not shown is that much of the candidate's experience is in the fields of food and agriculture. The second profile is a table without lines.

# Susan B. Stephens, M.D.

1255 West Shore Avenue
Lunenburg, MA 01246
Available for Relocation

(508) 582-0000
Facsimile: (508) 583-0000
Email: susan@snell.mit.edu.

## Qualifications

**PHYSICIAN EXECUTIVE** qualified for senior-level management opportunities where strengths in strategic planning, development, and visionary leadership will promote high-growth business ventures. Highlights:

- **Market-Driven Executive** -- Initiated business re-engineering in a 38-physician practice to address the emerging commercialization of medicine; cut operating costs through innovative cost-containment programs; brought consensus among divergent interests during transition to market-focused paradigm.
- **Academic Qualifications** -- MIT Executive MBA program graduate with management and financial skills backed by clinical competence of 15+ years of practice as a board-certified internist and anesthesiologist. Substantial experience in emergency services, aeromedical evacuation, and special operations.
- **International Orientation** -- Advanced the accessibility of health care in third world nations through commitment to international healthcare organizations (eight trips to Honduras, Mexico, and Vietnam as team chief and service as program director for an overseas teaching hospital).
- **White House Fellowship** -- Regional finalist among highly competitive candidate list of 800+; seeking to address global health care issues (special project: research for development of counter-strategies for medical terrorism).

## Professional Experience

**HEALTHCARE MANAGEMENT** -- Partner, Medical Consultants of Fresno, Boston, MA 1/93-Present
Partner, Medical Group, Boston, MA 1/90-12/93

Provide executive leadership as managing partner in a 38-physician group generating $18 million in annual revenue. Lead through hands-on involvement in financial affairs, professional/support staff administration, service planning, patient care, quality improvement, peer review, and credentialing. Well-versed in managed-care operations and negotiation of managed care/capitation contracts. Provide comprehensive anesthesia services and internal medicine consultations for Boston Memorial and other locations. **Accomplishments:**

- Led practice through successful transition to thrive in a managed-care environment utilizing new market-driven, community-oriented patient care model.
- Delivered significant savings through development of operational enhancements and strategic alliances.
- Researched and implemented computerized digital technology for cellular, paging, and voice mail services.
- Consultant for critical start-up of innovative home pain management therapy service.
- Resolved sensitive physician relations issues as member of Medical Staff Quality Council for 300-bed hospital.
- Mentored new physicians, helping to grow practice by 30%.

**OPERATIONS MANAGEMENT** -- Chief, Aerospace Medicine, Virginia Air National Guard 1989-Present

Plan and direct medical services to ensure health and combat readiness of 72 aircrew and over 1,500 ground personnel. Liaison between flying squadron and medical services. Participate regularly in flying missions including active duty deployments and mission qualification in RF4-C, a supersonic fighter aircraft. Directly supervise 25 officers and enlisted personnel. Additionally accountable for public health and safety, bio-environmental engineering, and occupational health issues.

♦ continued ♦

34

**Combination.** *Susan Britton Whitcomb, Fresno, California*

This resume was for a Physician Executive who was pursuing an MBA for a management position with a management care organization or a health-care-related company. The original resume

## Susan B. Stephens, M.D.

**Accomplishments:**

- Selected for fast-track promotion to rank of Major and Lt. Colonel.
- Designed and implemented innovative flying safety and emergency medical training programs.
- Recipient of two Air Force Achievement Medals, Air Force Outstanding Unit Award, Armed Forces Reserve Medal, and National Defense Service Medal.
- Authored 100-pg guide to human factors and physiological stress in flying advanced tactical fighter aircraft, providing flight surgeon support for the zero mishap record during the ANG transition to F-16 aircraft.
- Formerly served as Chief, Clinical Services (1989-1992); Commander, Squadron Medical Element (1984-1989); and General Medical Officer (1982-1984).

**Prior Experience:**

- Clinical Faculty, Department of Internal Medicine, Boston Medical Center 1980-1982
- Attending Physician, Emergency Dept., New Bedford County Medical Center 1979-1980
- Medical Director, Medical Clinic 1978-1979

## Education

**M.B.A., Management** -- Massachusetts Institute of Technology (MIT) 1994-1996
**Residency in Anesthesiology** -- Boston Medical Center, Theilen, MA 1983-1986
**Residency in Internal Medicine** -- Boston Medical Center, Theilen, MA 1979-1981
**M.D.** -- San Francisco State University School of Medicine, San Francisco, CA 1978
**B.S., Biology (cum laude)** -- Arizona State University, Tempe 1973

## Certification, Licensure

**Diplomate** -- National Board of Medical Examiners
**Diplomate** -- American Board of Internal Medicine
**Diplomate** -- American Board of Anesthesiology
**Flight Surgeon** -- USAF School of Aerospace Medicine
**Medical Licensure** -- Massachusetts, Arizona, New York

## Affiliations

American College of Physician Executives
Aerospace Medical Association
American Society of Pathologists
Massachusetts Society of Pathologists
Undersea and Hyperbaric Medical Society
American Medical Association

## Professional Appointments

Utilization Review Committee -- Boston Medical Center
Medical Staff Quality Council -- Boston Medical Center
Chair, Department of Pathology -- Children's Hospital
District Director and Board of Directors -- Massachusetts Society of Pathologists

## Additional Data

Commercial Pilot
Concert Violinist
Conversant in Spanish, French, and Italian

♦ ♦ ♦

was a 9+-page curriculum vitae, which the writer reduced to these two pages. "Emphasis is placed on management achievements rather than clinical experience, publications, etc." The side headings enclosed within horizontal lines are striking, as are this candidate's achievements.

**WINNFRED H. SUCCESS**

0000 East Heather
Anywhere, USA
(000) 000-0000

## EXPERIENCE SUMMARY

**SENIOR EXECUTIVE** with over 20 years experience in agribusiness, demonstrating competency in multiple disciplines:

- **Management:** Experienced in managing full P&L performance for $50 million grower/packer/shipper ... introduced management concepts and executed operating strategies which tripled production and drove net profits to realize an overall 200% increase.
- **Marketing:** Considerable success in identifying market opportunities, expanding channels of distribution, and accessing industry resources to capitalize on new markets which in several cases achieved a 125% or better increase in sales ... managed sales teams in multi-state western region.
- **Consulting:** As agribusiness consultant, specialized in marketing and operational troubleshooting, contract negotiations, opening new markets, and anticipating and positioning companies for changes in industry trends/consumer demands.
- **Development:** Strengths include assembling synergistic business relationships, attracting venture capital, formation of highly profitable business partnerships, and concept development/design of consumer packaging and value-added products.
- **International Orientation:** Directed import/export operations in Mexico and California ... selected for 3-year advanced study/travel group focusing on market opportunities and agricultural practices in the Pacific Rim and China.

## PROFESSIONAL EXPERIENCE

**MANAGING GENERAL PARTNER** -- California Growers, Inc. 1/92-Present
Anywhere, USA

Envisioned concept for commercial cold storage and established start-up venture including formation of corporation, acquisition of financing, budget planning, sales forecasting, site acquisition, and construction management. Manage administrative functions, plant operations, marketing, and operational/expense controls. Additionally involved in farming of deciduous tree fruit operation.

- **Results:** Developed business from zero base to 1.8 million packages annually ... consistently achieved goals for operations and profit margins.

**V.P., FINANCE AND ADMINISTRATION** -- West Coast Fruit Co-op, Inc. 1989-1990
Anywhere, USA

Recruited by venture capitalist to reverse poor performance history. Managed marketing, sales, and daily administration.

- **Results:** Identified and corrected marketing and quality control issues ... launched new in-house label (packaging, marketing, development of domestic/export sales) ... supervised $9 million construction of controlled-atmosphere facility, completing project ahead of schedule ... brought understanding to co-op operations and galvanized growers toward common goals.

35

**Combination.** *Susan Britton Whitcomb, Fresno, California*

This resume has the "look" of a resume for an executive: smaller type; an even right margin (full justification); wide lines in short paragraphs; an Experience Summary first with information

# WINNFRED H. SUCCESS
Page Two

## PROFESSIONAL EXPERIENCE (continued)

AG CONSULTANT/FARM MANAGER -- Farm Management and Consultation — 1990-1991, 1985-1989
Anywhere, USA

Provided agribusiness consulting services and farm management services (six ranches) throughout central California.

- **Results:** Presented proposals to venture capitalist firms for turnkey deciduous tree fruit operations which netted over $1 million in profits ... developed and managed new acreage ... paired growers with packers and marketers for mutually profitable ventures.

**PRESIDENT/CHIEF OPERATING OFFICER** -- California Packing Company — 1983-1985
**PARTNER/PLANT MANAGER** -- California Packing Company — 1973-1983
Anywhere, USA

Directed $50 million deciduous tree fruit and table grape operations for a leading grower/packer/shipper. Experience includes strategic planning, finance/accounting, personnel, operations, marketing, sales, export markets, grower relations, and UFW/ALRB negotiations.

- **Results as President/COO:** Doubled volume of packages three consecutive years (from 1.2 to 4.5 million) ... achieved 200% increase in operating profits during tenure ... procured and directed infusion of outside capital to develop new acreage ... designed and supervised installation of state-of-art packing lines ... designed three facility upgrades over tenure ... negotiated sale to international conglomerate in 1985.

- **Results as Plant Manager:** Achieved operational enhancements in packing plant operations (receiving, packing, storing, shipping) ... directed tree fruit and table grape operations from locations in Mexico, Arizona, and California ... developed software program for tracking of fruit from receipt through shipment (an industry first) ... computerized all elements of operations ... active in numerous industry organizations at the state and federal level.

## EDUCATION

**FELLOW** -- Agricultural Education Foundation

**B.S., AGRIBUSINESS** -- University of California, Davis

## AFFILIATIONS

California Grape and Tree Fruit League
Agricultural Leadership Associates
Agricultural Education Foundation
University of California, Davis Alumni Association, Board of Directors

**References Upon Request**

clustered by category; a Professional Experience section next, arranged chronologically and with achievements (Results) indicated by bullets; some indication of education; and finally a list of professional affiliations. White space through blank lines ensures that the resume is not cluttered.

# Johnson C. Charles

3501 Anystreet Avenue, Southtown, LA 0000 (318) 111-2222

## Objective

A management position with a progressive, established company with opportunity for professional growth.

## Summary of Qualifications

- Highly polished managerial skills with excellent organization skills. Integrate strong leadership skills with a positive, optimistic style that effectively motivates staff.
- Successfully managed and marketed a corporation in both public and private sector.
- Experienced in Human Resource management duties; recruited, trained, and evaluated staff.
- Excellent communication, leadership, negotiations, and troubleshooting skills that interact with clients, staff, and management.
- Creative in formulating special projects and developing program designs.

## Experience

***President/Owner***
C.J.'S TENNIS ASSOCIATION, INC., Southtown, LA (1993 - Present)
Successfully manage an association that contracts tennis pros for club activities in the North Louisiana region.

- Work with board of directors on a regular basis; manage pros' schedules; organize leagues and teaching clinics.
- Schedule events with special pros (including internationally known).
- Set up and manage entire computer system for AP/AR, payroll, taxes and inventory for business.
- Successfully developed and implemented competitive sales and marketing driven management strategies.

***Tennis Manager/Pro***
BAYSIDE COUNTRY CLUB, Bayou, LA (1991 - Present)
Managed Pro Shop, increasing yearly profits by utilizing selective buying and creative merchandising techniques.

- Implemented computerized billing system for Pro Shop for AP/AR and financial statements.
- Successfully organized leagues and increased the percentage of teaching lessons.
- Cut expenses by developing a realistic and workable budget.
- Performed Human Resource management duties, i.e., recruitment, selection, training, and evaluation of staff.

***Tennis Manager/Pro***
CITY OF BAYOU, Bayou, LA (1987 - Present)
Manage two separate facilities of 16 courts as well as one Pro Shop.

- Organized leagues of approximately 420 members.
- Prepared schedules for two full-time pro's. Set up entire computerized billing system for Pro Shop.

***President/Owner***
DOPSON & PETERSON, INC., Anytown, LA (1993)
Co-owner of wholesale convenient store with $56,000 in retail inventory.

- Inventory control; purchasing.
- Hiring, training, and evaluating of all employees.

***Assistant Manager-Tennis Department***
NEVADA BOB'S DISCOUNT GOLF AND TENNIS, Bayou, LA (1985 - 1987)

- Responsible for buying inventory, arranging displays, and sales.

## Education and Training

NORTHTOWN LOUISIANA UNIVERSITY, Anytown, LA
**B.A. (1992)**
Focus: Business and Management

**REFERENCES AVAILABLE UPON REQUEST.**

36

**Combination.** *Melanie Douthit, West Monroe, Louisiana*

A resume for someone who can manage successfully separate facilities simultaneously. Positions in italic are easily spotted. Similarly, establishments in all capital letters can be seen at a glance.

# JACKSON T. STEPHENS

**888 Grand Parkway**
**Atlanta, Georgia 30222**
**(404) 999-9999**

**PROFILE**

Comprehensive experience in **Business Development, Sales,** and **Marketing.** Record of consistent achievement and positive organizational growth through development of new business and successful execution of existing ventures; superior presentation and closing skills. Capable of conceptualizing new opportunities, formulating internationally sponsored enterprises, and conveying the desirability of aspirations to investors and colleagues. Outstanding communication and interpersonal skills.

- Establish and promote excellent rapport and productive environment with executives and decision makers. Proven aptitude for bringing diverse groups together to achieve a common goal; exceptional negotiation and mediation abilities.
- Goal oriented; exhibit a high level of energy and enthusiasm on both self-managed projects or when contributing to team endeavors.
- Monitor factors impacting day-to-day and long-range operations. Recognize trends, analyze potential impact, and initiate appropriate action; remain focused on the "big picture."
- Construct solid community relations and successfully obtain support of key civic, social, and business organizations.

**PROFESSIONAL EXPERIENCE**

THE JACKSON T. STEPHENS COMPANY, Atlanta, Georgia 1992 to Present
***President and Owner***
Created and developed concept for 5-Star luxury hotel; identified site, negotiated options, obtained zoning, directed architectural plans (from schematics through design development), obtained financial commitments and letters of intent from international luxury hotel management companies, and acquired equity resources. Additionally, cultivated and pursued concepts of other multi-family and residential projects in midtown and downtown Atlanta areas.

MANHATTAN MARKETING, New York, New York 1983 to 1992
***Director of Marketing and Sales***
Generated all marketing, public relations, and sales programs for The Zeckendorf Company and World Wide Holdings real estate development companies. Oversaw various aspects of project management including design, construction, pricing, and inventory control. Administered and directed marketing sales programs for several highrise residential condominiums consisting of up to 650 units each with prices up to $2 million per unit. *Met and exceeded all sales goals.*

**AFFILIATIONS**

Georgia Trust for Historic Preservation
Piedmont Park Conservancy
Midtown Alliance
Atlanta Downtown Partnership

**EDUCATION**

UNIVERSITY OF GEORGIA, Athens, Georgia
***Bachelor of Science,*** *Business Administration and Real Estate*

37

**Combination.** *Carol Lawrence, Savannah, Georgia*

An entrepreneur used this resume to network and to test the waters for a possible career change to an officer for a venture capital organization. The Profile shows expertise in development.

# JARAD SMITHERS

140 Maren Court #12 | Vancouver, WA 06902 | Ph: (216) 977-3456

## PROFESSIONAL PROFILE

Aggressive, results-oriented executive with solid track record in strategic marketing, sales administration, product development, business planning, customer relations and project management. Able to effectively utilize resources, maximize sales and achieve P&L goals for start-up companies and established businesses.

- Highly accomplished trainer/motivator with proven ability to build winning sales teams and develop top producers that consistently exceed objectives.
- Experienced in setting up strategic partnerships to optimize marketing opportunities.
- Thoroughly familiar with data and voice networking architectures, PC/LAN technology and database applications.
- Solid network of contacts in the telecommunications industry.

## EXPERIENCE

ADVANCED SOLUTIONS CORP. - Vancouver, WA 1989-Present

**FOUNDER / PRESIDENT**

Built $1.5 million telecommunications business from the ground up. Recruited investors, raised capital and hired/trained sales and support teams. Created strategic business and marketing plans. Managed day-to-day operations and directed sales, telemarketing, customer service and technical support functions. *Sold business in October of 1996; retained by new owner as operations consultant.*

- Set up strategic partnerships with industry giants such as NYNEX, SNET, NEC, MCI and Sprint.
- Trained and developed sales team that produced annual sales volume of $1.2 million.

U.S. WEST - Westbury, NY 1984-1989

**BRANCH MANAGER**

Recruited to salvage non-productive branch of a telecommunications sales operation. Implemented new marketing programs and telemarketing campaigns. Supervised sales manager and directed staff of 19 in sales, customer service, administration and technical support.

- Totally rebuilt and re-trained sales force.
- Successfully developed territory and converted unprofitable operation into #2 ranking branch.

MARTENDALE, LTD. - New York, NY 1977-1984

**MANAGER OF MARKETING**

Developed and implemented plans for strategic marketing, training, telemarketing and sales tracking. Supervised sales team and support staff. Implemented database management system and programs for direct mail, telemarketing and Yellow Page advertising. Originally hired as sales representative; promoted to sales manager after two years.

- Consistently exceeded sales objectives by 50-75%.

## EDUCATION

M.B.A. Portland State University, Portland, OR

38

**Combination.** *Pat Kendall, Aloha, Oregon*

The Professional Profile stands out through double indention. Company names and positions are all uppercase, so boldfacing makes the positions stand out. Centered heads point to the top name.

# JAMES R. LAWSON III

1234 Kingship Avenue
Anytown, Tennessee 00000

Home ■ (000) 000-0000
Office ■ (000) 000-0000

## Professional Qualifications

**BUSINESS DEVELOPMENT**

- Fourteen years of business ownership experience, including product development, new market penetration, and pricing structures.
- Highly skilled in coordinating all aspects of creative process, from concept through delivery of finished product.
- Proven performance record in business development and expansion resulting in increased productivity and sales revenue.

**MANAGEMENT AND LEADERSHIP**

- Effectively utilize human resources to increase productivity and contribute to bottom line profits.
- Cultivate and maintain professional relationships with key personnel.
- Focused on achieving company goals and objectives involving administration of operational procedures, budget adherence, and sales projections.

**MARKETING AND PROMOTIONS**

- Manage promotional activities to increase market recognition and sales.
- Develop creative marketing strategies and promotional materials.
- Strong abilities in special events planning, communication, and organization.

## Career Experience

**OWNER/PRESIDENT** ■ 1982 - 1996
**Lawson Productions, Inc.** ■ Nashville, Tennessee

Developed business from ground floor level. Was actively involved in all business operations with annual sales in excess of $1 million. Sold business in June 1996.

- Full responsibility for contract negotiations, sales projections, and budget preparation.
- Developed and produced trade shows, corporate conferences, and other special events.
- Hands-on involvement in marketing, advertising, public relations, and corporate sponsorships.

**OWNER/PRESIDENT** ■ 1982 - 1996
**American Sports, Inc.** ■ Nashville, TN / Chicago, IL / Portland, OR

With partner, invented and developed concept of "newsport." Generated annual sales of over $2 million. Sold business in June 1996.

- Established retail, wholesale, and commercial field operations.
- Developed procedures for tournament play, referee orientation manual, certification program, safety guidelines, and employee handbooks.
- Supervised and trained 6 general managers and support staff of 18.

**SALES REPRESENTATIVE** ■ 1978 - 1982
**National Cable Company** ■ Nashville, Tennessee

- Supervised 32 door-to-door sales representatives within Davidson County.
- Maintained excellent relations with both existing customers and newly-acquired customer accounts.
- Provided customer service and effectively mediated and resolved customer problems.

## Education

**Bachelor of Business Administration** ■ 1978 ■ Paradise College ■ Honolulu, Hawaii

## Achievements

*Business Leader of the Year* ■ I.N.S.A. ■ 1988, 1995
*Salesman of the Year* ■ National Cable Company
*Eagle Scout* ■ Boy Scouts of America ■ 1969

39

**Combination.** *Carolyn S. Braden, Hendersonville, Tennessee*

After selling two successful businesses, this candidate "wanted a resume that would stress his experience in developing businesses," especially in marketing and promotions. This is the focus.

# STUART RAFKIN

75 Central Park West • New York, NY 10019 • (212) 664-8876

## PROFILE

Successful executive and entrepreneur who has grown an $18 million business in the highly competitive travel industry. Ability to develop effective management and marketing strategies to maintain and increase an expanding customer base. Promote a philosophy of personalized service and relationship building to generate a large repeat and referral business. Strong ability to motivate and supervise employees in creating a productive team environment.

## EXPERIENCE

**INTERNATIONAL TRAVEL SERVICES** **1976 - Present**

**OWNER/PRESIDENT**

Manage all facets of a high profile agency serving the corporate, entertainment, and leisure travel markets. Provide international travel, 24-hour worldwide after-hours service, deluxe executive/VIP services, state-of-the-art airline reservation system, conference and meeting planning, special events, and other travel services.

- Successfully grew high profile travel agency to an annual sales volume of $18 million from a 1983 volume of $1.5 million.
- Carved a marketing niche through creation of a Travel-Entertainment Division encompassing the music, film, television, sports, and fashion industries.
- Enhanced operations to increase efficiency, cost effectiveness, and quality assurance.
  - Expanded state-of-the-art technology and developed a five step manual quality control process to operate a meticulous quality assurance program.
  - Developed a customized reservations system to ensure individual requirements from credit card information, seat and meal preferences to Frequent Flyer Program numbers.
  - Designed a total travel management system to produce detailed tracking reports.
- Developed and directly serviced high profile accounts, including numerous entertainment and corporate clients.
- Coordinated all aspects of worldwide tours and maintained long-term relations with a world renowned rock group (since 1985), a high profile pop singer (since 1985), and a popular actor (since 1983).
- Developed extensive expertise in major domestic and international hotel markets.
- Achieved an uncommon *triple "A"* credit rating with major hotels, airlines, car rental companies, and other vendors.
- Created a highly loyal and effective employee team where the average length of employee service is 10 years, compared to an industry norm of 2 to 3 years.
- Managed travel for the largest single entertainment event in history outside of the United States.
- Coordinated all logistic arrangements for 400 people at a $4 million cable-aired event.

## EDUCATION

Bachelor Degree in Business Administration
State University of New York at Stony Brook, 1974

References Furnished On Request.

**40**

**Combination.** *Etta Barmann, New York, New York*

A resume for a purpose other than a new job. The person, who had built up a successful travel business, wanted to buy a restaurant. The resume shows he could manage the restaurant well.

**Stephen Delling**
**7654 Plains Road**
**Yonkers, NY 10576**
**(914) 554-8876 (H) • (212) 876-9899 (W)**

## Profile

Over 20 years of diversified administrative, accounting, marketing and sales experience with increasing levels of responsibility and promotions.

## Areas of Expertise

- General Administration
- Sales and Marketing
- Training and Supervision
- Promotion and Public Relations
- Accounting and Financial Operations
- Client Relations

## Current Professional Experience (1975-Present)

**President/Sales Executive,** *Delling Associates,* New York, NY

Assumed leadership of major direct specialty advertising and promotional distributorship with sales of $10 million annually.

***Sales/Marketing***
- Develop and maintain accounts with 2500 clients from small entrepreneurial enterprises to Fortune 500 companies.
- Generate an extensive business through telemarketing, personal visits, and referrals in an increasingly competitive environment.

***General Administration***
- Responsible for recruiting, training, and supervising sales and support staff.
- Manage all accounting and financial matters.
- Establish company policies and procedures, and provide leadership for overall strategic direction.
- Interact regularly with importers and domestic factories in sourcing new products and negotiating purchases.
- Function as final authority to resolve client account problems.

***Special Accomplishments***
- Implemented a new computer system with enhanced accounting/reporting functions, as well as restructured financials to improve overall controls.
- Reorganized profit-sharing and health insurance plans to improve cost benefit ratio.
- Improved sales productivity through revamping staff recruitment policies.

## Prior Professional Experience (1971-1975)

**Director of Accounting** (a cabinet-level position), *United Help Organization*, New York, NY
Involved in all areas of accounting for prestigious non-profit organization.

**Controller**, *Collectibles* (a collectable start-up company, within Advertising/Promotion Co.).
Performed variable volume and breakeven budget/cost analysis, control, and f/s reporting.

**Senior Accountant**, *Monetary Corp.*, New York, NY
Worked in mutual funds interfacing with marketing, human resources, and senior management.

## Additional Activities

Board Member and Secretary, General Language Organization

Board Member, International USA Association
Promoted 25th Anniversary Event of organization which promotes international cooperation.

Actively participated in the International Conference of International World Relations Organization.

## Education

**Columbia University**, New York, NY
B.S. in Accounting

*References furnished on request.*

41

**Combination.** *Etta Barmann, New York, New York*

The contact information, Profile, Additional Activities, Education section, references statement, and headings are center-aligned. The client's interest in nonprofit work is evident toward the end.

**MICHAEL STOLFER**
**553 W. 57th St.**
**New York, NY 10039**
**(212) 865-9854**

**OBJECTIVE:** A challenging Administrative or Financial Position which draws upon over 25 years of successful management experience.

***STOLFER ASSOCIATES, INC., New York, NY*** ***1971 to 1996***
**(MANUFACTURER/DISTRIBUTOR OF HEATING EQUIPMENT)**

**PRESIDENT/CO-OWNER (SINCE 1973)**
- Managed all aspects of heating equipment sales and installation for the commercial, institutional, and government markets. The company consisted of the Land Division and the Shipboard Division. Sales volume reached up to $900,000 on an annual basis.

Management/Administration
- Hired and supervised all administrative staff and managers. Oversaw all departments including Sales, Service, and Installation. Also hired outside subcontractors on a project basis.
- Coordinated all operations between departments, administering as many as 25 projects simultaneously.
- Effectively investigated and resolved numerous problems as required.
- In charge of bidding process for federal, state, city, and private contracts.
- Reviewed and evaluated job specs for bids, and ensured compliance with regulations.
- Dealt effectively with union workers.

Purchasing
- Negotiated and purchased equipment, parts, and components from suppliers.

Financial
- Assumed all Controller functions. Possessed check signatory authority. Costed out jobs, reviewed estimates with sales staff for accuracy and project parameters. Maintained all books and ledgers. Administered payroll. In charge of all banking transactions.
- Functioned as Trustee for employee benefits (pension, disability, health).

ACCOMPLISHMENTS:
- Successfully won numerous government and private contracts in a highly competitive environment.
- Ensured the viability of the company, particularly during downturns in the city's economy, by implementing numerous cost cutting and efficiency programs.

***WELL KNOWN CREDIT CORPORATION, New York, NY*** ***1969 to 1971***
**ASSISTANT CREDIT MANAGER**
- Supervised 7 account executives, auditors, and up to 11 receivable clerks for major credit company.
- Regularly interacted with customers regarding the financing of accounts receivables and inventories.

***AUTOMOTIVE FINANCING CORPORATION, New York, NY*** ***1968 to 1969***
**ADMINISTRATIVE AND COLLECTIONS**
- Collected accounts; handled customer service issues and disputes.

**EDUCATION**

B.S., 1966
New York University, New York, NY

**MILITARY**

***UNITED STATES NAVY*** ***1966 to 1968***
**Rank: *Lieutenant***
- Supervised Information and Education Department.
- Managed all personnel records and functions for the base.
- Oversaw operations of Bachelor Officer Quarters, including food service and facility maintenance.
- Supervised stewards and housekeeping staff.
- Managed operations for the Officers Club.

References on request.

42

**Chronological.** *Etta Barmann, New York, New York*

With fewer government contracts, this president disbanded his company and looked for work. His administrative and financial skills are "arranged functionally within a chronological format."

**DAVID CONTENER**

3469 First Avenue • New York, NY 10025 • (212) 456-8765

**PROFILE**

- A highly accomplished executive with over 25 years of successful management and sales experience, including top management of a multi-million dollar reprographics corporation.
- Proven track record of achievement in both established and start-up enterprises.
- Demonstrated history of achieving high levels of performance in situations requiring strong supervisory, communication, organization, and planning expertise.
- Superior marketing, sales, and negotiation capabilities used to maximize productivity.

**SELECTED ACCOMPLISHMENTS**

- Grew company revenues from $540,000 to $6 million annually.
- Purchased two additional businesses and effectively expanded from one location to three.
- Subsequently opened an additional location and operated around-the-clock for the construction industry.
- Planned and purchased innovative, state-of-the-art equipment, which decreased production time and reduced overhead costs.
- Successfully navigated through a one-month long International Brotherhood of Teamsters organizing strike.
- Consistently met all projects on time and under adverse conditions.

**AREAS OF EXPERTISE**

***MANAGEMENT***

As President of Turnkey Associates, Inc.

*General Management*

- Directed all facets of operations for $6 million reprographics firm.
- Administered and implemented organizational policies, procedures, and operations.
- Formulated strategic goals and translated them into operational procedures.
- Negotiated favorable lease structures; negotiated purchase and sale of equipment and companies.
- Developed business plans for launching of new concepts.
- Devised innovative solutions to problems and established preventive measures involved in future expansion.

*Human Resources Management*

- Developed and implemented management and employee training, benefits, and compensations programs.
- Instituted innovative procedures to upgrade professionalism within the organization.
- Negotiated all union contracts.

***SALES/MARKETING***

- Developed and serviced numerous accounts with architects, construction companies, and engineers through bidding, telemarketing, referrals, and repeat business.
- Expanded business through effective sales and marketing strategies.
- Awarded city, state, and federal projects through competitive bidding.

***FINANCE***

- Developed and monitored projects and company budgets.
- Conducted business forecasting to prepare company operating expense budget.
- Identified and cultivated financial resources for expansion.

**PROFESSIONAL HISTORY**

**Sales Executive for a Reprographics Company**, New York, NY
**President, Turnkey Associates, Inc.**, New York, NY

**PROFESSIONAL AFFILIATIONS**

• Society of Reprographic Engineers • Former Secretary - Allied Repro Association, New York
• Former President - US Reprographic Association, New York

**EDUCATION**

**Columbia University**, New York, NY

*References furnished on request.*

43

**Functional.** *Etta Barmann, New York, New York*

This resume calls attention to 25 years of experience; accomplishments; and management, sales/marketing, and financial skills. Because of a time gap, the history section has no dates.

**MICHAEL R. STERNS**

8400 Industrial Parkway
Plain City, Ohio 00000
(000) 000-0000

**CAREER PROFILE**

SENIOR EXECUTIVE with distinguished career in the profitable management of multi-million dollar sales, marketing and manufacturing operations. Consistently successful in increasing revenues and improving bottom-line performance through a series of aggressive reorganization, expansion and management initiatives. Outstanding management and employee relations qualifications. Key skills include:

- General management resources/design management
- Business restructuring/staff development
- Expansion/turnaround strategies
- Return on investment strategies
- New product development
- Manufacturing/Q.A./materials
- Worldwide markets/project development
- New ventures/start-ups

**EXPERIENCE**

HARRISON COMPANY — October 1992 to Present

Headquartered in San Antonia, Texas with operations in North America, Australia, South Africa, India and Japan engaged in the manufacture of capital equipment. As President of the Eaton and Copper Divisions, was responsible for division results including coordinating input/output of all Profit Center teams (e.g., Marketing, Sales, Engineering, Manufacturing, Finance, H.R., Service, etc.) to develop strategic/business plans generating profits/return on investment on a continuing, long-term basis.

**PRESIDENT,** Harrison Company, Eaton, Indiana (October 1994 to Present)
Worldwide supplier of surface mining equipment. Approximate annual revenue of $150 million; 450 employees.

**Achievements:**

- Gained ISO-9001 certification in 15 months.
- Introduced project management concept for high investment, long-term projects.
- Developed project cost control system generating over $4 million savings on first two projects.
- Implemented availability tracking system for field units; raised availability over 5% in two years.
- Evaluated all division products on "stand alone" basis; defined profit contribution by product.
- Introduced shop liaison and procedure control which reduced scrap by 50% during first year.
- Reassigned salaried work force to continue operations, meet customer commitments and profit plan objectives during five-month strike.
- Top producing division for two consecutive years (1995-1996; 40% return on investment).
- Established successful "stand alone" operation in South Africa.

**PRESIDENT**, Copper/Harrison, Lafayette, Indiana (January 1991 to October 1994)
Worldwide supplier of underground mining and material processing equipment. Approximate annual revenue of $100 million; 1,000 employees.

**Achievements:**

- Introduced two new models of continuous miners that contributed over 70% of division's profit.
- Implemented General Manager accountability at each location for cost and lead time control.
- Redesigned chain making (continuous cutting head) facility to reduce cost and lead time by 30%.
- Balanced shop load at North American facilities which increased productivity and profits.
- Upgraded marketing, engineering and manufacturing staff to produce quality products on competitive schedules.
- Introduced quality system to certify and control manufacturing and inspection gauges.
- Identified acquisitions which doubled processing products profits.
- Set-up dedicated service/rebuild center to support customer service.

44

**Combination.** *Susan D. Higgins, Grove City, Ohio*

Sometimes a resume will go back only 10 to 15 years to obscure the age of an older worker. This candidate, however, wanted to be up front about his age and not let it surprise an interviewer.

**MICHAEL R. STERNS**
**Page Two**

**V. P. OPERATIONS,** Copper/Harrison, Eaton, Indiana (January 1987 to January 1991)
Responsible for line functions of Engineering, Manufacturing, Purchasing, Quality, Field Service and Field Construction; coordinated resources to meet customer requirements/company business objectives.

**Achievements:**

- Developed and introduced critical path scheduling for projects/resources.
- Developed effective concurrent team effort of functional departments.
- Brought shop quality up to certified AWS-D1.1 & 14.3 level for welding.
- Identified and installed equipment required to produce AGMA Class 10 gears.
- Reduced WIP and obsolete/slow-moving inventory by $16 million.
- Consolidated/rightsized operation to remain profitable after market downturn in early 80s.
- Set-up joint ventures and/or manufacturing partnerships to supply product on competitive basis worldwide.

**V. P. ENGINEERING,** Copper/Harrison, Eaton, Indiana (October 1982 to January 1987)
Responsible for designing, developing and supporting full-line surface mining equipment to serve worldwide customer base with emphasis on energy sources, iron ore, copper, coal and phosphate mining. Recruited with charter of turning around a stale and unproductive engineering organization.

**Achievements:**

- Reorganized and placed key people in positions of accountability for engineering projects.
- Implemented sophisticated engineering programs (finite element analysis, problem tracking, CADD etc.) to provide proper documentation, standardization and control.
- Designed, developed and put into production: 1) successful "state-of-the-art" hydraulic excavator in less than two years; 2) industry leading dragline; 3) static electric drives for shovels and drills.
- Developed gear design standard to double field service life.

TRACTOR COMPANY, Boise, Idaho — 1979 to 1982
**Director of Engineering** (Managed 100 engineers.)

TRACTOR COMPANY, Grand Rapids, Michigan — 1976 to 1979
**Manager, Advance Features/Concepts** (Recruited to manage new venture products for Tractor Division.)

COUNTERS INC., Homer, Wisconsin — 1965 to 1976
**Design/Chief Engineer,** Crawler Tractor Division

ENGINE REBUILDERS, Fort Wayne, Indiana — 1963 to 1965
**Application Engineer-Power Trains**

**EDUCATION**

**Bachelor of Science, Engineering,** University of Illinois, Urbana, Illinois

ADDITIONAL TRAINING/SEMINARS: A. T. Kearney, *Management Development;* Dale Carnegie Series; Dresser Management Development Series; MAPI, Management Series

**BUSINESS AFFILIATIONS**

Society of Automotive Engineers (SAE)
American Mining Congress (AMC)
Rocky Mountain Coal Mining Institute

**PERSONAL**

Excellent health. Active in sports and fitness training.
Member: Higgins Country Club; Capital Club

The Experience section therefore includes "all his experience as it basically was related to his current occupation." Entries for the current and past three positions include substantial lists of achievements. A concluding Personal section shows that this energetic person was in top health.

♪ GENE SMITH ♪
One Tulip Lane
Sparta, New Jersey 00000
**Tel: (000) 000-0000 • Fax: (000) 000-0000**

## TOP PRODUCING MUSIC EXECUTIVE

***RESULTS ORIENTED*** *professional with a 20-year proven track record in strategic planning, development and business expansion • Ability to foster relationships with recording corporations, labels and artists • Unique talent in discovering new label interests and business ventures • Easily identify up and coming trends with a talent for recognizing cutting-edge styles • Creating and recognizing hit singles • Dynamic, aggressive, persistent and consistent • Extensively versed in studio production • Experienced in both European and U.S. tour management • Confident decision maker and successful risk taker • Knowledge of music spans pop, rock, metal, R&B, alternative, rap, new age and country • Totally versed in state-of-the-art computerized environments • Areas of expertise include:*

- ♪ **ARTIST/LABEL PROJECT MANAGEMENT AND DEVELOPMENT**
- ♪ **NEGOTIATING/SIGNING NEW ARTISTS**
- ♪ **GENERATING, DEVELOPING AND IMPLEMENTING NEW LABEL BUSINESS**
- ♪ **TARGET AND CREATE INNOVATIVE LABEL INVESTMENT OPPORTUNITIES**
- ♪ **PRODUCTION MANAGEMENT AND DISTRIBUTION**

### PROFESSIONAL EXPERIENCE:

CIRCLE PRODUCTIONS — Wayne, New Jersey

***PRESIDENT • 1986 - Present***

Challenged to lead a successful music production company from inception through full operations. Discover and develop extreme talent into cross-over markets. Forecast future trends into mainstream music marketplace.

- Currently managing **Lynn Richardson**, an up and coming female performer.
- Produced MACHINE for **Paul Simon's** production company, *"Night After Night, LTD."*
- Discovered and launched career of **Ann Minogue**, daughter of **Terry Cashman/West through** GRP *"Rap to Rock"* CD compilation of new artists.
- Participant in 20th anniversary **KISS** project and current **KISS** conventions (interviews and personal appearances).
- Maintain high-profile engagement with R&B artist **Elexus Quinn and Ziggy True** and pop/rock artist **Oona Falcon** (major attraction throughout Europe).
- Diverse areas of expertise encompass **Harper-Josef**, a New Age project.
- Contributed to the success of numerous music videos and films.
- Accountable for daily operations, including P&L, budgeting, marketing, strategic planning, staff development and contract negotiations.

(continued...)

45

**Combination.** *Alesia Benedict, Rochelle Park, New Jersey*

A pair of eighth notes enclosing the candidate's name lets the reader know immediately that the candidate's field is music-related and that the resume will display creative touches. A profile

**GENE SMITH** **Tel: (000) 000-0000** **- Page Two -**

**PROFESSIONAL EXPERIENCE continued...**

TOTAL PRODUCTIONS Seaview, New Jersey

***FOUNDER, CO-OWNER • 1982 - 1986***

High-profile position in full service music and video production company. Managed projects for artists and groups. Provided live and video coverage for special events. Launched and produced video-magazine concept in association with The Industry Network System (TINS).

* * * *

Previous employment includes holding Chief Executive Officer position for Naturél Cosmetics, an international/domestic company affiliated with Clairol and Logics International. Details provided upon request.

**PROJECT/ARTIST HIGHLIGHTS:**

- ***Machine*** (Paul Simon's Night After Night productions)
- ***Rod Stewart*** (1988 World Tour)
- ***KISS*** (20th anniversary project)
- ***Oona Falcon*** (European Starlight Express and tour)
- ***Myth*** (Beatles' attorney, Walter Hofer project)
- ***Lynn Richardson*** (up and coming female artist)
- ***Ann Minogue*** (Rap to Rock GRP project)
- ***Elexus Quinn and Ziggy True*** ("Nothing is Meaningless project)
- ***Breakfast Special*** (national tour)
- ***Hunter*** (former members with Billy Squire)
- ***Hawkeye*** ("Great Seal" film documentary, Mill Valley Productions)
- ***Dreams*** in Color (in association with Joe Serling)
- ***Alexia*** (managed by Rolling Stones partner, Pete Rudge)

**PROFESSIONAL ATTRIBUTES:**

- Founding member (drummer) of rock group KISS with Gene Simmons, Paul Stanley and Brooke Ostrander.
- Recipient of numerous awards and tributes in recognition of writing popular songs and lyrics.
- Featured in trade publications including *Modern Drummer*.
- Co-wrote and produced material for successful bands and major production companies.
- Instrumental in production of video projects and film clips.

**EDUCATION:**

Bachelor of Arts degree
University of Miami • Coral Gables, Florida

paragraph of descriptive statements separated by bullets introduces the candidate. Pairs of sixteenth notes serving as bullets point to chief career activities. Boldfacing calls attention to key names in the Professional Experience section and in the Project/Artists Highlights section (page 2).

**JOHN HANCOCK**
12 Augusta Drive
New York, New York 44444
888.555.4051

**PROPERTY AND CASUALTY GENERAL MANAGER**

*offering expertise in organizational restructuring and performance turnaround.*

Effective and innovative leader skilled in strategic planning, change management, consensus building and creating efficient and highly productive insurance organizations within high-growth, emerging, mature and competitive business markets. Career features 16 years' experience in directing day-to-day property and casualty operations, participating in company acquisitions and mergers, and rebuilding problem lines of business.

**CAREER DEVELOPMENT**

UNITED ASSURANCE GROUP, New York, New York **197x to 199x**

198x to 199x—United Casualty Company, Rapids, Ohio

***President and Chief Operating Officer***

Bottom-line accountability for operations of this $200,000,000 insurance organization. Managed daily operations of UCC as well as supervised operations of 2 subsidiary companies. Consistency of performance and the following results contributed to a top property-casualty ranking by Ward Financial Group for 4 consecutive years (000's omitted):

| | 1993 | 1994 | 1995 | 1996* |
|---|---|---|---|---|
| Premium Written | $163,100 | $175,600 | $197,500 | $221,700 |
| Policyholder Surplus | $111,284 | $125,317 | $158,055 | $179,250 |
| Combined Ratio | 102.3% | 99.2% | 97.6% | 99.8% |

*unaudited

***Critical Initiatives***

- Introduced and led corporate-wide planning process; facilitated regular dialogue and collaboration among functional units and between regional offices; provided planning and budgeting guidance; conducted quarterly progress review meetings.
- Co-developed corporate operating structure as a network of autonomous business units, each with own charter, local decision-making authority and accountability, and full P&L responsibility. *Resulted in a more local market driven organization.*
- Consolidated and centralized redundant back office functions *effecting a net reduction of 20 staff positions corporate-wide.*
- Championed design and development of new policy processing system for both commercial and personal lines of business; *achieved project completion on schedule and within budget.*
- Launched a major restructuring which transformed organization into task-focused work teams and streamlined work processes to leverage newly-developed technology. *Key results: Enhanced productivity and net reduction of 67 staff positions.*

*continued ...*

46

**Combination.** *Elizabeth J. Axnix, Iowa City, Iowa*

Two tables are the leading features of this resume for an insurance executive. In spreadsheet format, each table displays four consecutive annual results for three performance indicators:

*Page Two* **JOHN HANCOCK**

**CAREER DEVELOPMENT**, *cont.*

UNITED ASSURANCE GROUP, New York, New York **197x to 199x**

198x to 198x—Another Insurance Company, Orleans, Louisiana

***President and General Manager***

Led the turnaround of this poor performing subsidiary (combined ratios over 110 four consecutive years). Developed and executed revitalization plan which allowed the company to make a significant and consistent contribution to parent company's growth and profitability. Promoted precepts emphasizing teamwork and personal commitment to achieve goals; built team of committed individuals who produced the following results during last four years as general manager (000's omitted):

| | 1985 | 1986 | 1987 | 1988 |
|---|---|---|---|---|
| Premium Written | $8,483 | $10,647 | $13,782 | $12,848 |
| Policyholder Surplus | $7,631 | $8,103 | $9,093 | $10,336 |
| Combined Ratio | 100.9% | 93.2% | 92.2% | 88.4% |

***Critical Initiatives***

- Developed and executed marketing strategy focused on a narrowly-defined niche, utilizing existing resources, staff skills and capabilities. *Key result: Increased market share by 200+%.*
- Managed the dismantling and rebuilding of agency distribution system. *Key result: Reduced agency representation from 361 to 98.*
- Established up-grading of employee skills as top priority: instituted critically needed training, developed in-house training opportunities, personally conducted several training sessions. *Key result: More than 20% of staff earned designations from the Insurance Institute of America.*

197x to 198x—United Casualty Company, New York, New York

***Director of Personnel***

Managed all facets of human resources department including compensation, benefits, training, EEOC compliance and reporting, as well as setting and administrating policy.

I.M. SMITH INSURANCE AGENCY, INC., River Falls, New Hampshire 197x to 197x

***Owner and President***

**EDUCATION**

THE UNIVERSITY OF IOWA, Ohio City, Ohio

**MA—197x**

WILLIAM PENN COLLEGE, Oskaloosa, Ohio

**BA—196x**

premium written, policyholder surplus, and a combined ratio. A single line of italic text focuses the Profile near the top of page one. Key achievements or results are indicated in italic in the two Critical Initiatives sections. Outdenting the dates points to the amount of experience.

# Samantha Day-Smith

4566 N.E. Westridge | Scottsdale, Arizona 97324 | Ph: (503) 345-9076

**PROFESSIONAL PROFILE**

Multi-disciplined executive with broad experience in managing customer service and technical services in the cable television industry. Experienced with strategic planning, budgeting, recruiting, hiring, team building and goal setting.

- Able to effectively assess industry trends and provide leadership in implementing new technology.
- Capable troubleshooter with ability to direct projects through all stages.
- Skilled in managing diverse groups, developing positive relationships across department lines and communicating effectively with employees at all levels.

**EXPERIENCE**

SCOTTSDALE CABLE - Scottsdale, Arizona

**VICE PRESIDENT, CUSTOMER OPERATIONS** (1995-Present)

Oversee activities of 130 employees in five departments: Customer Service, Dispatch, Payment Center, Engineering and Information Technology (MIS). Develop and implement business strategies; oversee five operating budgets and a $4.5 million capital budget.

- Created and installed first scripting program to standardize customer service, repair and diagnosis functions.
- Initiated major changes that integrated field staff, dispatchers and service teams into a centralized Customer Service Department; set up focus groups to address and respond to problems.
- Managed new technology roll-out to field employees using Mobile Data Terminals.

**MANAGER, CORPORATE ACCOUNTING** (1992-1995)

Consolidated multi-million dollar accounting operations. Supervised corporate accounting staff and managed a staff of eight. Prepared ten-year strategic business plan.

- Coordinated start-up of new corporate office; developed operating structure, policies and procedures for the Accounting Department.
- Managed database conversion project for six divisions.

**ASSISTANT CONTROLLER** (1988-1992)

Managed accounting functions for nine cable systems; oversaw consolidation of the U.S. operation. Supervised a staff of eleven.

**EDUCATION**

PORTLAND STATE UNIVERSITY - Portland, Oregon

**B.S. FINANCE** (1988)

CONTINUING EDUCATION

- Management Training/Mapping
- Sales
- Telephony
- Computer Operations

**AFFILIATIONS**

President, Female Executives of Scottsdale

**47**

**Combination.** *Pat Kendall, Aloha, Oregon*

A straightforward, easy-to-grasp resume for a forward-looking vice president. Bold capital letters help you spot her executive roles and finance degree. Bullets point to skills and achievements.

# James Doe

14 Pines Drive • Boston, MA 02364

(617) 555-1638

**Objective**

To obtain a Senior Level position in Store Operations using over 16 years of demonstrated excellence and accomplishment.

**Summary**

- Significant and demonstrated expertise in all areas of retail operations including distribution, transportation, real estate, mail order, new store openings and renovations.
- Excellent use of technology to enhance operations.
- Achieved outstanding results developing and implementing innovative programs
- Demonstrated strong leadership and staff development skills.
- Significant expertise in satisfying customer demands.

**Experience**

1994 to Present — Todd Uniform, Inc. — St. Louis, MO

***Vice President of Operations***

- Responsible for two distribution centers, customer service, product development, production planning, inventory control, catalog sales, and quality control.
- Reduced distribution center payroll by **$600,000** while increasing production output.
- Service level in the distribution center was reduced from 6 days to 2 days.
- Developed and implemented a quality control program reducing errors from 8% to **1.7%.**
- Developed operating procedures and controls which increased distribution inventory accuracy from 82.5% to **98.5%.**
- Reduced customer service payroll by 20% through scheduling improvements and productivity standards.
- Coordinated the implementation of a new automated planning system which reduced backorders by **$900,000.**
- Successfully liquidated $1.7 million of obsolete merchandise and raw materials through tent sales and jobbers sale.

1984 to 1994 — Work 'n Gear Stores (formerly WearGuard) — Hyde Park, MA

***Vice President of Stores (1991 - 1994)***
***Director of Stores (1988 - 1991)***
***Director of Distribution (1984 - 1988)***

- Selected the site and managed the move to a new and larger distribution center of 300,000 sq.ft. Installed state-of-the-art equipment achieving savings of **$500,000.** Recognized as one of the best mail order companies in the country.
- Developed and implemented productivity standards saving **$250,000** in the first year.
- Implemented a quality program reducing errors by 66% which is **80%** below industry standards.
- Developed and implemented a "drop ship" program saving **$500,000** in freight.
- Responsible for 52 stores, 7 district managers and 6 field sales reps. Successfully opened 23 new stores in 11 states. Conducted site evaluation and managed the process of opening each store on time and under budget.
- Developed new store prototype and completed eight remodels and three relocations. All work was completed on time and within budget.
- Created a new concept within the store called the "show room" that is unique in the industry and is geared to attracting more business to business sales. The concept also includes a sales representative on the road. Realized a **12%** increase in revenue.
- Created and successfully installed numerous marketing and selling tools including telemarketing, open house program, outside sales force and training to insure quality.
- Piloted a sophisticated new point-of-sale system to store customer data.

1980 to 1984 — Filene's Department Stores — Boston, MA

***Divisional Director of Production***

- Responsible for processing, shipping/receiving, returns and ticket making in a 320,000 sq.ft. facility.

*Awards*

- Filene's ***Executive of the Quarter*** by reducing costs and maintaining service levels.

**Education**

Bentley College, **B.S.**, Management. — Waltham, MA

**48**

**Combination.** *Steven P. Green, Northboro, Massachusetts*

This resume uses boldfacing to call attention to the important positions held since 1980. Boldfacing enhances also significant achievements expressed in dollars and percentages.

# Frances K. Simon

1847 Plank Street ▸ Neenah, WI 54956 ▸ (414) 752–1874

## Summary of Attributes

- Demonstrated success in training and motivating employees.
- Proven ability to develop an effective rapport with peers, subordinates, customers, management, and community leaders.
- Work ethic characterized by integrity and versatility; work well independently and possess strong management skills.
- Excellent communication, time management, and organizational expertise.

## Experience

City-Wide Dry Cleaners, Appleton, Wisconsin
**Vice President/General Manager** 11/90–Present
Recruited by President to provide management expertise to control overall operations of 18 retail locations and 2 production plants, with a staff of 80.

- interviewing, hiring, evaluating
- marketing, promotion, advertising
- decision making/troubleshooting
- planning, organizing, coordinating
- opening of new locations
- customer service
- payroll, purchasing
- records management
- monthly store meetings
- quality control

*Accomplishments:*

- Increased productivity by 20%.
- Reduced employee turnover by 30%.
- Authored the company's first formal job descriptions.
- Improved quality standards in plant.

ABC Foods, Inc., Milwaukee, Wisconsin 10/86–10/90
**Human Resource Manager** (2/88–10/90)

- Screened, hired, and trained employees in a plant with extremely high turn-over.
- Researched and developed a pre-employment health screening program.

**Assistant Warehouse Manager** (10/86–2/88)

- Supervised 60 employees, including annual performance reviews.

## Education

University of Wisconsin–Milwaukee
B.A. Major: Business/Human Resources 5/88

- Supervisory Leadership Series, 1996
  *Ten-week management training through Chamber of Commerce*
- Group Facilitator Training, 1989

## Professional Organizations

- Human Resource Association of Wisconsin, 1988–Present
- Dry-Cleaners Guild of Wisconsin, 1990–Present
- Management Professionals of the Fox Valley, 11/94–Present

49

**Combination.** *Kathy Keshemberg, Appleton, Wisconsin*

This individual wanted to leave a family-owned business with few chances for further advancement. Emphasis on wide experience qualifies him for more areas in a larger company.

# Stephen A. Williams

1234 Drake Circle
Anytown, State 55555

Residence: (555) 555.5555
Mobile: (555) 555.5555
Pager:(555) 555.5555

**PROFILE**

Senior Sales and Marketing Executive with 15+ years experience in the wood products industry and full P&L responsibility. Implemented organizational initiatives that have consistently improved the financial, market and operational performance of all operations. Designed sales territories, recruited sales personnel, and spearheaded implementation of leading edge strategies to develop strong customer relationships in the marketing of product lines.

- Strategic Planning
- Market/Product Positioning
- Budget/Capital Planning
- Key Account Management
- Productivity Improvement
- Customer Service Management
- Human Resource Affairs
- Contract Negotiation
- Proactive Management

**SELECTED ACHIEVEMENTS**

- Personally responsible for sales of $90 million in wood products.
- Pioneered "Value Added Products" concept with in-house melamine laminate line, cut to size and edge banding, and custom drilling and routing.
- Restructured the sales force resulting in a 17% sales increase over a 12 month period.
- Directed collection operations with credit losses at or below ½ of 1%.
- Demonstrated ability to penetrate new markets by implementing account management initiatives in the Tucson market resulting in sales increase from $50K to $185K in 4 years.

**PROFESSIONAL QUALIFICATIONS**

- Instrumental in building revenues through contributions in marketing strategies, identifying new markets, administration and management.
- Develops rapport and builds relationships with customers and clients through attention to detail in defining needs and providing service and solutions.
- Team-oriented: Recruit, hire, train, motivate and manage productive sales and support teams.
- Proficient in interpersonal relations, load and resource management; strong communication skills with customers, staff and management.

**EXPERIENCE**

*NORTHWEST PACIFIC* 1981 to 1997

**VICE-PRESIDENT/GENERAL AND SALES MANAGER**, 1990 to 1997 Anytown, State

- Full P & L responsibility for a $10 million distribution warehouse and manufacturing company. Scope of responsibility included sales/marketing, plant operations, quality control, product improvement, finance, budgeting, human resources and purchasing.
- Spearheaded company's entry into the State market; successfully opened Anytown facility and led expansion into Another Town and Northern State markets.
- Adept at planning long-term operating, administrative, marketing and financial strategies.

**OUTSIDE SALES**, 1983 to 1990 Anytown, State

- Created direct sales of $1.1million during first year of operations, $4.5 million by the fourth year.
- Developed customer retention program through the introduction of key account management, sales incentives and targeted promotions.

**OUTSIDE SALES**, 1981 to 1983 A Town, Big State

- Increased sales by 140% despite having territory decreased by 50%.

Wood Products expertise in the areas of:

| | | | |
|---|---|---|---|
| Hardwood Plywood | Hi-Pressure Laminate | Thermal fused & rolled Melamine products | Moldings |
| Hardwood Lumber | Particle Board | Fir Plywood | MDF |

**EDUCATION**

University of Big State, Bachelor of Science, Business Administration, 1982 A Town, Big State
Big State University, Major: Business Administration, 1978 to 1981 Hometown, Big State

**SALES** **MANAGEMENT** **MARKETING**

50

**Combination.** *Patricia S. Cash, Prescott, Arizona*

The writer of this resume created a table to "display or 'set apart' areas of expertise or specialization." The table's dark shadow complements the thin-thick lines at the top.

# RUSS REYNOLDS

1214 Fuller Blvd. ✦ Houston, Texas 77008 ✦ (713) 861-3092

**PROFILE:**

**SENIOR BANKING OPERATIONS EXECUTIVE**

Transaction Banking Services • Strategic Planning & Organization Development • Sales Training & Development • Multi-Site Operations Management • Portfolio Development & Management • Loss Prevention Operations • Budgetary Control • Legal Issues & Banking • Regulatory Affairs • Acquisition Analysis • New Branch Start-Up

**PROFESSIONAL EXPERIENCE:**

**SECOND CITY BANK**, Houston, Texas 1977 - Present

*Distinguished management career with one of the highest rated financial institutions in Texas. Expert in creating a dynamic sales culture within multiple branch operations and developing/implementing branch operation strategies, consistently exceeding profitability objectives. Career highlights include:*

**Vice President - Market Area Service Manager**

Promoted from District Sales and Service Manager to direct entire sales and service operations for 74 branches (500 employees). Given complete responsibility for sales and bank operations training, branch auditing, loss prevention, budgetary controls and procedural development and implementation. Chair numerous task force committees. Conduct due diligence on banking acquisitions. Key liaison for legal banking issues. Certified Basic Skills Testing Trainer.

- Assisted in the conversion process of 36-branch acquisition. Consolidated financial and operational systems; retrained new employees on banking systems, culture and protocol; and identified/closed marginally profitable branches.
- Established and directed an internal audit department, resulting in branches exceeding their auditing requirements.
- Developed and launched a cash balancing program which was adopted at all the branches.
- Created and implemented highly successful state-wide Teller Recognition Program.

**Assistant Vice President, District Sales and Service Manager**

Senior Manager with full responsibility for operations, sales, service and budgetary control functions for seven branches in Beaumont, Texas with 100+ employees and a $700 million portfolio. Conducted extensive sales training throughout the branches; served in mentorship capacity for all Branch Managers.

- Chosen as one of 7 Campaign Planners statewide to develop, coordinate and implement sales promotions, special events and community activities throughout the state.
- Transferred to Houston, Texas to spearhead the consolidation of operational functions of 20 branches.

**Assistant Branch Manager**

Directed banking operations and service activities of Nederland, Texas branch (20 employees and $150 million in deposits). Scope of responsibility included recruitment and training, portfolio management and client relationship building.

- Served as Interim Branch Manager; consistently exceeded all sales goals; promoted to Assistant Vice President in Corporate District Office.

**Assistant Vice President of Operations**

Supervised commercial loans, collection and exchange, bookkeeping, teller and lobby operations. Significantly reduced losses by streamlining/tightening security, administrative and operational functions.

**PRIOR:**

Superior Bank & Trust, Garland, Texas 1973 - 1977

Supervisor of Commercial Loans Operations and Collection and Exchange Department.

**EDUCATION:**

Lamar University, Beaumont, Texas

***General Business*** 1975

**CONTINUING PROFESSIONAL DEVELOPMENT:**

Hundreds of hours of Executive Sales and Operational training and development through company and industry-sponsored programs.

51

**Combination.** *Cheryl A. Harland, The Woodlands, Texas*

With the threat of a company takeover, this executive without a college degree wanted a similar position at a larger bank. Smaller print provides much information even with some white space.

# Charlotte Richards

**240 Riverview Boulevard ■ Smallville, KS 77777 ■ (777) 555-8462**

## Qualifications Summary

- Seasoned manager specializing in project development, coordination, and administration
- Master's degree and over 20 years of increasingly responsible assignments
- Strong personnel management background, including staff development and training
- Excellent written communication skills, both clear and precise; extremely detail oriented
- Flexible and innovative with a reputation for tackling challenges with a can-do attitude
- Excellent computer skills in a variety of environments (Mainframe, DOS, Windows, Windows 95); quickly learn new applications; experienced with Internet access

## Management Style

Results-oriented professional with an approachable style. Encourage two-way communication and a team approach to accomplishment. Demanding but flexible. Reputation as a hard-working, reliable leader able to motivate staff to produce consistently high quality.

## Experience

**Kent National Bank, Smallville, Kansas** **1976-Present**

***Vice President of Electronic Banking***

- Forecast and manage $2.5 million budget for statewide electronic banking program
- Manage all aspects of planning, placement, maintenance, and reporting for all ATMs
- Negotiate contracts for ATM placement as well as security services and maintenance
- Plan and develop new markets; continually analyze performance to maximize profits
- Manage and motivate teams of up to 20 staff, from clerical to middle management
- Travel throughout the state conducting marketing training on various bank products

***Highlights:***

- ★ Attained all income, transaction, and market penetration goals for 1995 and 1996 through vigilant operations analysis, creative marketing, and efficient pricing
- ★ Currently coordinating six-month program to add 38 new ATMs to system - personally conducting profitability assessments, securing sites, negotiating rental agreements, ordering equipment, coordinating installation, and establishing fees
- ★ After consolidation, conducted statewide electronic banking assessment, recommending and implementing a program that quickly generated established profit goals

## Education

- Master of Science Degree in Safety Management, Kansas University, 1980
- Bachelor of Arts Degree in Psychology, Kansas University, 1976
- Graduate, Kansas Bankers' Association School of Banking, 1994
- ***Continuing Education:*** 33 post-graduation college hours in banking, including Principles of Banking, Installment Lending, Accounting, Commercial Banking, Business Law, etc.
- ***Seminars & Training:*** Over 1,500 hours of in-house and seminar training in management, planning, administration, supervision, leadership, problem solving, etc.

**52**

**Combination.** *Barbie Dallmann, Charleston, West Virginia*

A strong-looking resume with larger bold type and filled square bullets. Because the candidate wanted to leave banking for a management position, the focus is on her management skills.

(513) 555-2323

## Matthew K. Taylor

8752 Elm Street, Cincinnati, Ohio 45202

**PROFILE**

**Experienced manufacturing manager** with a background that encompasses all aspects of plant operations, labor relations, quality control, and engineering.

- A history of leadership and initiative and a track record of achieving consistent profitability and stability while overseeing considerable growth.
- Demonstrated skill in establishing rapport and building cooperative relationships both within and outside the organization.
- Effective manager able to prioritize resources, instill a teamwork attitude, and motivate staff to excel.
- Thoroughly familiar with manufacturing processes. Equally comfortable on shop floor and in boardroom.

**PROFESSIONAL EXPERIENCE**

CINCINNATI GASKET COMPANY, Cincinnati, Ohio 1971-1996

**Executive Vice President of Manufacturing / Member Board of Directors** (1982-1996)

**Vice President of Manufacturing** (1978-1982)

Directed the manufacturing, engineering, and quality operations of large privately held gasket manufacturer. Managed 6 direct reports (department and plant managers) and 400 full-time union employees. During tenure, company grew from $10MM to $98MM; daily production from 1800 to 6000 gaskets; production employees from 150 to 400. Company continuously profitable.

***Business Management***

- Created company's first engineering department and supervised growth to staff of 4 responsible for overseeing manufacturing systems and methods to ensure efficient production and high quality.
- Spearheaded plant-wide conversion from solvent- to water-based paints to reduce environmental emissions and increase worker safety.
- Managed transportation function for 40 trucks, 70 trailers and 50 warehouses nationwide.
- Began initiative to implement corporate TQM program.

***Human Resources and Labor Relations***

- Negotiated equitable union contracts covering all aspects of compensation and benefits; successful in achieving cost savings including reduction of health care benefits. Maintained outstanding relationships over 25 years with 2 unions.
- Served as trustee on 3 pension plans, working with outside administrators.
- Established company's first human resources department of HR and labor relations professionals to ensure consistency in hiring practices and manage increasingly complex benefits administration.

**Assistant to the President** (1974-1978)

Served as liaison between president and the plant managers and coordinated all work between the company's 2 manufacturing facilities. Maintained costing and inventory system.

- Instrumental in developing company's first computerized costing system.
- Administered all aspects of union contracts, including contract negotiations.

**Quality Control Manager** (1971-1974)

Identified production and quality problems, diagnosed causes, and determined corrective actions. Worked closely with supervisors and production workers to gain their insight into problems and support for changes.

- Successfully handled contract negotiations when union voted in by hourly work force; continued to represent company in all negotiations and communication with 2 unions during tenure with company.

**EDUCATION**

XAVIER UNIVERSITY, Cincinnati, Ohio: **MBA Administration**, 1978

OHIO STATE UNIVERSITY, Columbus, Ohio: **MA Marketing**, 1971; **BS Business**, 1967

53

**Combination.** *Louise Kursmark, Cincinnati, Ohio*

This individual was "retiring after a 25-year career with one company." There is no attempt to mask his age, because at 52 he might still have a 10- to 15-year new career ahead of him.

# CHRISTOPHER A. REYNOLDS

75 Main Street Hartford, CT 06106 (203) 555-5555

**CAREER PROFILE**

Senior Manager with 20 years experience in increasingly responsible positions to the level of Senior Vice President. Consistently increased sales by negotiating contracts to service Fortune 500 and other major companies. Introduced innovative security programs. Managed major corporate reengineering.

**EXPERIENCE**

**Associated Security Contractors (ASC)** 1970 - Present

***Senior Vice President - Central and Northern Connecticut Region*** - Hartford, CT (1986 - Present)

Manage all phases of the largest security company in Connecticut with annual revenues of over $30 million. Negotiate and acquire contracts; monitor sales and marketing activities; oversee labor relations; purchase and budget equipment and supplies; handle customer relations; administer payroll, Workers' Compensation, and liability insurance.

**Accomplishments:**

- Increased sales 25%.
- Managed $21 million payroll for work force of 1500 people.
- Restructured two separate operations into one, reducing operating expenses by 22%.
- Initiated highly innovative security program.

***Regional Manager*** - San Francisco, CA (1978 - 1986)

Managed all phases of the operation of this division: financial performance, contract negotiations, employee supervision, sales operations, and administration.

**Accomplishments:**

- Increased business 600% to over $6 million by winning contracts with American Airlines, General Motors Corporation, and other Fortune 500 companies.
- Expanded number of clients from 15 to 50.
- Improved safety and reduced Workers' Compensation rates by 20%.
- Initiated direct customer billing from regional office, reducing debtor days by 10%.

***Area Sales Manager*** - New York, NY (1970 - 1978)

Monitored activities of 6 sales representatives in the East Side of New York City.

**Accomplishments:**

- Developed Customer Care program.
- Restructured area sales staff.
- Set goals and kept achievement records.

**EDUCATION**

**B.A.** in Business, Queens College, Queens, NY
**A.A.** in Business Management, State University of New York, Stonybrook, NY

**54**

**Combination.** *Wendy Gelberg, Needham, Massachusetts*

This is another resume for a person who has worked for one company during most of his career. Emphasis on significant accomplishments helps to show that he has valuable, competitive skills.

# Calvin Malvin

508 Brittany Woods • Drawbridge, MT 20202 • (555) 555-1166

## Overview

- ❑ Over 20 years' front-line experience within the oil and gas industry; life-long exposure to the business as the only son of an industry professional
- ❑ Over 10 years' management experience including the areas of budgeting, cost control, capital projections, and contract negotiations
- ❑ Possess first-hand, field knowledge of every aspect of oil and gas exploration, development, and production, from prospect evaluation and acquisition through development and ongoing operations and maintenance
- ❑ Over 15 years' supervisory experience with a reputation for thorough knowledge, efficient problem solving, and effective personnel management
- ❑ Extensive network of valuable industry contacts throughout the United States
- ❑ Honest, hardworking, dedicated employee with an exemplary work ethic

## Work History

UNION PROPERTIES DIV. OF OIL RESOURCES, INC., BUCKHANNON, MT 1997-PRESENT

❑ **Vice President and General Manager**

- ✓ Manage the day-to-day company operations, including 12 rotary drilling rigs producing $20 million in annual revenues
- ✓ Supervise directly 6 management employees and indirectly 250 full-time employees
- ✓ Solely responsible for all sales efforts, developing leads, and negotiating contracts

***Accomplishments:***

- ✓ Developed and implemented strategies that increased operating efficiency
- ✓ Restructured organization's key management positions, streamlining operations and drastically improving employee morale
- ✓ Redesigned pricing strategies and improved cost analysis process
- ✓ Renegotiated contracts to mitigate risks

THE HOUSTON OIL COMPANY, HOUSTON, MONTANA 1988-1997
(Merged with Gas Resources Inc., March 1996)

❑ **Operations Manager - Houston, Montana (1/95-2/97)**

- ✓ Coordinated and supervised the day-to-day activities of 25 employees in Montanaa, Arkansas, Oklahoma, and West Virginia
- ✓ Directly supervised maintenance, workovers, and repairs for all FRI-operated production
- ✓ 90% of time spent in the field involved with on-site supervision
- ✓ Coordinated and managed contractors for drilling, well workovers and repairs as well as surface facility and pipeline installations

❑ **General Manager of Montana Operations (5/89-1/95)**

- ✓ Hired, supervised, and managed up to 21 full-time employees
- ✓ Through acquisition and drilling, oversaw the development of 530 wells
- ✓ Developed and administered annual capital and operating budgets in excess of $6 million

***Accomplishments:***

- ✓ Guided region through its most successful period, developing 10 bcf in net reserves
- ✓ Developed projects at a net finding cost of less than 85¢ per mcf
- ✓ Initiated the $6 million acquisition of Seneca Upshur Petroleum Inc. in 1994

❑ **Independent Consultant to FRI (12/88-5/89)**

- ✓ Managed operations startup and established FRI as an operator in Montana
- ✓ Recruited, hired, trained, and supervised office and field employees
- ✓ Directly supervised FRI's first company-operated drilling program

55

**Combination.** *Barbie Dallmann, Charleston, West Virginia*

Because of a company reorganization, this individual and other managers had to look for other work. He had more experience but only a high school education, whereas the other managers

*Calvin Malvin* 2

UNIVERSAL PETROLEUM ASSOCIATES INC., WATERFORD, PENNSYLVANIA 1986-1988

- **President & Manager of Acquisition & Drilling**
  - ✓ Managed all financial aspects of the business
  - ✓ Acquired leasehold acreage and coordinated drilling programs in Pennsylvania
  - ✓ Managed and oversaw the day-to-day activities of six full-time employees
  - ✓ Oversaw operations and maintenance of a 1,000 bpd oil refinery, employing 16 full-time employees
  - ✓ Managed crude oil purchasing and finished product distribution programs
  - ✓ Developed bids, negotiated drilling contracts, and managed leased drilling rig, completion rig, and related support equipment

PROGRESSIVE ENERGY DEVELOPMENT CORPORATION 1985-1988

- **President & Operations Manager**
  - ✓ Operated oil and gas properties in Texas and Montana for foreign investors
  - ✓ Evaluated and selected drilling equipment for the Appalachian Basin
  - ✓ Provided on-site supervision and technical support for the drilling of Triassic test wells in Johnson County, Tennessee, and Chesterfield County, Montana

TRINITY GAS DEVELOPERS, NEW HAVEN, COLORADO 1984-1986

- **Operations Manager**
  - ✓ Supervised the operation and maintenance of producing properties in Montana and Colorado

EASTERN STATES ENERGY CORP., WATERFORD, PENNSYLVANIA 1983-1984

- **Drilling Superintendent**
  - ✓ Supervised multi-well drilling programs in West Virginia and Pennsylvania
  - ✓ Managing partner of contract drilling and services subsidiary company
  - ✓ Assisted in the startup and growth phase of expansion into Pennsylvania
  - ✓ Played a significant role in taking Eastern States from a start-up company to one of the leading independent producers in the northeast

MERRILL NATURAL GAS INC., ROANOKE, VIRGINIA 1980-1983

- **Field Supervisor**
  - ✓ Coordinated and supervised all aspects of single-well drilling programs, including lease acquisitions, well permitting, title curative issues, well site preparation, drilling and completion procedures, well hookups, and ongoing operations
  - ✓ At age 20, oversaw the development and workover of 13 oil wells and the drilling of 3 new wells in New York

## Education & Professional Development

- High school diploma, 1977
- Over 1,000 hours on-the-job, apprenticeship-style training beginning at age 15
  - ✓ By age 18, was promoted to field supervisor and was responsible for three well servicing and workover units operating throughout the Appalachian Basin in West Virginia, Pennsylvania, Ohio, and Kentucky
- Mineral Management Service On-Shore Well Control Certification, 1990-present
- On-Shore Hydrogen Sulfide Training Certification, 1987-present
- Workshops and seminars include:
  - ✓ Department of Environmental Protection workshops
  - ✓ Service company workshops and seminars
- Attendance at and participation in over 20 annual conferences of the Independent Oil and Gas Association of Virginia, West Virginia, and Montana

had master's degrees and doctorates. To help him be more competitive in his job search, the resume focuses on his many experiences, notable accomplishments, and on-the-job training. Shadowed square bullets and boldfacing call attention to the many managerial positions he has held.

## FORD F. SMYTHE

333 Wyoming Lane
New York, New York 14127

716-662-4322
ffsmythe@aol.com

### CONSUMER PRODUCTS MARKETING EXECUTIVE

*Domestic & International*
*Start-Up, Turnaround & High Growth*
*Consolidations / Integrations*

**PROFILE**

Dynamic, results-oriented senior executive with over 20 years of progressive experience in the start-up and management of direct-to-consumer sales, marketing, fulfillment distribution, warehousing, service, merchandising and product packaging.

- Seasoned manager with "common sense" approach to problem solving; highly effective in change management.
- Dedicated teamworker with ability to stimulate staff development, build productive teams and command respect through positive leadership.
- Solid knowledge of information technology, telecommunications call center automation processes and personal computer applications.

*Extensive travel experience and knowledge of international markets and business climates in Europe, Latin America, Japan, Australia and Canada.*

**EXPERIENCE HIGHLIGHTS**

*1994 - 1997* HASBRO - New York, New York

**Vice President** (1995-97)

Built core business operations and led fast-track growth and global market expansion efforts. Coordinated corporate reorganization initiatives. Defined systems and evaluated processes to ensure optimum positioning of new organization in the changing retail marketplace. Managed Consumer Affairs and supervised operations in quality assurance and fulfillment distribution/warehousing.

- Delivered annual savings of $1.1 million by consolidating call center operations; substantially improved service levels and operational efficiencies.
- Integrated Marketing, Sales Support and Service while managing related downsizing efforts.
- Implemented quality tracking system that reduced defective costs, improved brand loyalty and added more than $2 million dollars to the bottom line in the first 18 months.
- Executed multiple direct-to-consumer campaigns that generated over $18 million in additional revenue.

**56**

**Combination.** *Pat Kendall, Aloha, Oregon*

Instead of an Objective, the resume displays—centered—the position title in small caps and headings in italic indicating areas of expertise. The resume is designed so that it is scannable for

## FORD F. SMYTHE / PAGE 2

**EXPERIENCE** HASBRO, INC. - Fort Wayne, Indiana

**Vice President** (1994)

Assumed full P&L responsibility within sales and marketing operations following acquisition. Conducted cost analyses to determine benefit of consolidating the organizations' consumer toll-free call centers.

- Led the transition and subsequent integration of international sales and marketing operations.

*1985 - 1994* KRANSCO GROUP COMPANIES / MATTEL - Fort Wayne, Indiana

**Vice President** / Fun Wheels Division (1989-94)

Administered five departments with direct responsibility for operations of the Corporate Consumer Affairs Call Center and the Field Merchandising Group. Conducted market research and implemented programs to take advantage of marketplace trends.

- Tripled sales in a particular product category (from $48 million to $175 million) and attractively positioned the company for its acquisition by Hasbro.
- Spearheaded the expansion of sales and marketing operations in Europe, Canada, Mexico and Japan.

**Director** / Fun Wheels Division (1985-89)

Recruited to analyze, develop, implement and manage programs to cut quality costs and reduce returns.

- Successfully improved category margins and profit levels by 16%.

*1977 - 1987* LOADSTAR - U.S. Operations

**National Account Manager** / Baltimore, Maryland (1982-87)

Developed and implemented programs for large accounts.

- Served as key member of integration team during acquisition of the General Electric Housewares Division
- Consolidated five regional offices into one central operation.

**Branch Manager** / Birmingham, Alabama (1979-82)

Directed regional operations for the Major Sales and Service branch offices.

**Manager, Service and Sales Center** / Mobile, Alabama (1978-1980)

Opened new regional branch; established and maintained new accounts and consistently met corporate sales quotas.

**College Recruitment Program** / Portland, Oregon (1977-78)

**EDUCATION** UNIVERSITY OF PORTLAND - Portland, Oregon

**Master of Business Administration** (1977)

storage in a database. The body text is Helvetica (11 point), and the opening information (except for the postal address, phone number, and e-mail address) and side headings are in Palatino. Extra word spacing has been added to job titles to separate letters and thus ensure scannability.

# Proven Leadership!

Abrasion-resistant ceramic lined steel fabrications for industry.

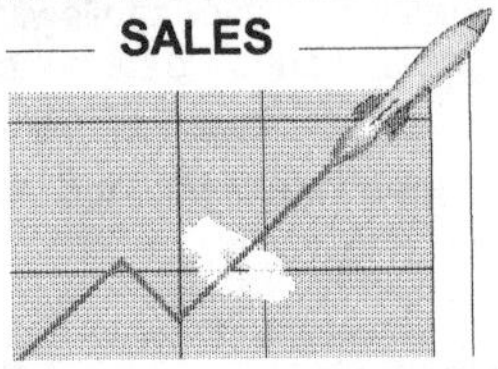


## Carl D. Kelly

10 Longwood Drive
Anderson, IN 46011
**(317) 642-0000**

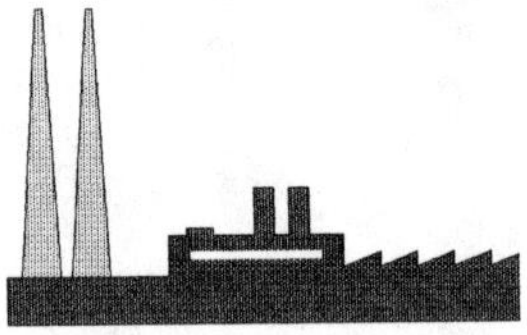

### Summary:

Extensive background and knowledge of steel fabrication, abrasion-resistant ceramic linings and their applications. Solid management & operations skills. Decorated Army Special Forces Sergeant First Class with extensive leadership training & field experience serving in the Mideast and Europe.

### Professional Experience:

Vice President & General Manager, Cerline Ceramic Co., Anderson, IN. In addition to management and operational responsibilities, also retains sole responsibility for engineering and sales. June 1993-Current.

Achievements:
- Company showed modest profit in 1993-94, for the first time in 5 years.
- Reduced general & administrative costs from 27.2% to 19.5%.
- Initiated first successful running inventory and inventory control system.

Sales & Engineering, Cerline Ceramic Co. January 1992-June 1993.

Achievements:
- Conceived and developed sales program for hydrocyclone liners manufactured from A.B. silicone carbide, slipcast alumina oxide ceramic, and Corguard AZS.
- Expanded Cerline Ceramic Co. line of silicones and epoxy products.
- Established effective product quality control program.

*Hands-On Professional Experience with:*

- *Drafting, blueprints, shop drawings*
- *Word processing, spreadsheets*
- *Management, engineering, sales, marketing*
- *Industrial ceramics*

57

**Combination.** *Jon C. Shafer, Anderson, Indiana*

This writer has successfully experimented with color and clip art in resumes. This resume is for an individual who gave up "a promising Army career because, as a family man with kids, it was

Kelly, Page 2

## Professional Experience: (continued)

Achievements:
- Improved design of Cerline patented box elbow.
- Conceived & initiated development of AZS ceramic Pug mill shoes, Pug mill liners, classifier shoes & Log washer paddles traditionally manufactured from Ni-Hard cast iron.

Estimator & Steel Design for ceramic-lined fabrications, Mofab, Inc., Anderson, IN.
Oct.-Dec. 1991

Please note: Prior to military service (below), acquired considerable steel fabrication, sheet metal, sales, shop drawings, and supervisory and shop foreman experience in prior employment with Mofab, Hoosier Fence, Insley Mfg., and Lapel Sheet Metal.

## Military Experience: (and professinal training)

Served in the U.S. Army 1980-1991, Honorable Discharge. Highlights include:

- Army Special Forces, graduated on Commandant's list (limited to top 20% of graduates). Special Forces qualification course, basic and advanced non commissioned officers courses.
- Letter of Commendation, for helicopter assault into U.S. Embassy, Beirut, Lebanon to protect U.S. citizens under fire.
- Army Commendation Medal, Conception & development of advanced operating procedures while instructor at the U.S. Army Special Operations Medical Training Division.
- Soldier of the Month, Soldier of the Quarter, 10th Special Forces Group.
- Several Army Achievement & Commendation Medals, and Foreign Awards.
- Attended more than 15 specialized Army training schools connected with Army Special Forces, including faculty development as an instructor.

**Education:** College courses at Indiana University; Mount Wachusett College, MA; San Antonio College, TX, totaling 83 credit hours, including all core courses. Graduate of Anderson High School, 1974.

*"Sergeant First Class Kelly conceived and developed advanced standard operating procedures which are used throughout the division...demonstrate(s) the highest level of leadership and professionalism...reflects great credit upon himself..."*
— Department of the Army Commendation

time to quit moving around." The writer's task was to call attention to the person's "solid military leadership skills as transferable to leadership in civilian industrial experience." The white-on-color headline at the top of the first page and the closing quotation are effective additions.

# DOUG T. PHILLIPS

**163 Kedron Place**
**Temple Terrace, Florida 33617**
**(813) 000-0000**

***CAREER SUMMARY***

- **Senior-level *Sales Management Professional*** offering demonstrated record of accomplishments reflecting ability to successfully capitalize on emerging growth and profit-related opportunities in competitive markets.
- **Top-Producer** with proven performance in directing management, sales, marketing and financial operations of high-caliber products and/or services within the home building, retail, and manufacturing industries.
- **Highly motivated** with goal-directed/results-oriented work ethic; possess well-defined business acumen and commitment to bottomline results. Consistently exceeded established sales quotas in all sales positions.
- **Proactive leader,** key role in augmenting business management and streamlining efficiency; astute at recognizing areas of improvement, with the vision to develop and implement directives that achieve strong/sustainable results.
- **Articulate communicator,** with excellent presentation, organizational and interpersonal skills; able to effectively delegate authority, motivate staff and interact with all professional levels.

***KEY AREAS OF EXPERTISE***

-- Strategic Business/Sales/Marketing Analysis
-- Motivational Sales Training/Team Building
-- New Product Launch
-- Administrative Operations
-- Formulating Budgets/Forecasts/Projections
-- Corporate Land Acquisitions
-- Contract Negotiations
-- Developing Business Relationships

***PROFESSIONAL EXPERIENCE***

FLORIDA HOMES, INC. - Tampa, FL **1993 - 1996**
**Vice President/Sales Management**

Scope of responsibility was diverse and included managing sales team of up to 20 employees, creating sales training materials, conducting motivational sales training programs, product development/new designs, strategic market planning/multi-media advertising, negotiating land acquisitions/financing terms, reviewing legal documentation, and evaluating demographic studies/surveys. Held full accountability for all financial management and short/long term planning. Cultivated strong alliances with realtors to gain competitive advantage and market position resulting in achieving **#2 Volume Builder ranking in Tampa/ MSA.**

→ Grew volume from $12M to 40M+ in 3 years.
→ Increased number of closings from 104 to 386 in 3 years.
→ Expanded realtor business from 40% to 70% within 3 years.
→ Increased bottomline profits by 3%.
→ Significantly reduced sales staff turnover from 80% to 10%.

AUDIO-VIDEO/APPLIANCES - Springfield, MA **1991 - 1992**
**Sales Manager**

Directly managed sales operations/training; retail/wholesale chain totaling $50M in annual revenues.

→ 1991-1992 - Ranked #1 in sales (exceeded $1.5M); sold 7% extended warranty service.
→ Increased store sales by 100%; grew store sales to $12M in one year.

58

**Combination.** *Diane McGoldrick, Tampa, Florida*

Another resume with the "look" of many resumes for executives. Contributing to this look are such features as small print, wide paragraphs with relatively narrow margins, a substantial

## DOUG T. PHILLIPS

Page Two

***PROFESSIONAL EXPERIENCE** (continued)*

S V M INC. **1985 - 1991**
**Store Manager** - Orange, CT (1989-1991)

Exhibited high-level sales management ability that led to the successful turnaround and profitability of three-store chain totaling $50M in annual sales. During tenure spearheaded management of all three locations achieving increased volume and profits at each store. Charged with facilitating administrative and operational activities of new store opening from concept through turnkey stages.

- Store volume and profit margin exceeded first-year projections by 10%.
- Warranty sales were 20% above projections.
- Structured six-step selling phases program/trained 30 sales associates.

**Store Manager** - Springfield, MA (1987-1989)

- Increased profit margin by 5% in one year.
- Grew sales from $8M to 10M in one year.

**Store Manager** - Framingham, MA (1985-1987)

- Directly responsible for $1.5M in annual sales.
- Increased profits 15% via increased warranty sales and effective sales training.
- Increased volume from $6M to $10M in two years.

J&B PLASTICS - Leominster, MA **1983 - 1985**
**Sales Manager**

Oversaw activities of 12 national sales representatives for plastics manufacturer. Position required managing and coordinating 12 national trade shows annually, combined with servicing major accounts such as Bradlees, K-Mart, Zayre, Spags, and Stop & Go.

- Annual sales exceeded $3M.

PAUL SCHOFIELD INC. - San Diego, CA **1979 - 1982**
**General Manager**

Accountable for sales endeavors of commercial painting contractor including vendor contacts, supervision of 20 employees, scheduling and monitoring work assignments. Handled $1M in gross annual sales.

***EDUCATION***

SAN DIEGO STATE
**Bachelor of Arts - Business Management** (1982)

***PROFESSIONAL TRAINING***

Completed numerous management and sales training seminars/programs with national trainers such as:
- Bob Schultz - *New Home Sales Management*
- David Stone - *Top Gun Training*
- Zig Ziegler - *Sales/Motivational Training*

profile or qualifications summary near the top of the first page, lists of bulleted achievements, and some kind of Professional section near the end (Professional Affiliations, Professional Training , or some other). In short, much material needs to be stated briefly and tastefully.

**ADAM ADMINISTRATOR**
119 Old Stable Road
Lynchburg, Virginia 24503
(804) 384-4600

## CORPORATE FINANCE, MIS & ADMINISTRATION EXECUTIVE

***Expertise in Start-Up, Turnaround & Fast-Track Growth Operations***

Professional qualifications in strategic planning, corporate finance, accounting, budgeting, banking, lending, contract negotiations and leading edge MIS technologies. Combine strong forecasting, analytical and negotiations expertise with consistent achievement in personnel management, team building and productivity/quality improvement Contributed millions of dollars through efforts in operations reengineering, cost reduction and revenue growth.

**Professional Certifications**

Certified Public Accountant, State of Virginia, 1992
NASD Series 7 Registered Representative, 1988

**Computer Skills**

Lotus, Word, MCBA, BPI, Peachtree, Media Plus, Norton Utilities, DOS, Windows, Procomm, Word Perfect

## PROFESSIONAL EXPERIENCE

**BUSINESS DAILY**, Lynchburg, Virginia 1987 to 1994

*National business and financial newspaper with annual revenues rapidly approaching $100 million and an average annual sales increase of 35% throughout the past two years. Recognized as one of the fastest growing newspapers in the U.S. with circulation growth of 61% in two years. Major competitor of The Wall Street Journal.*

**Vice President** (1992 to 1994)

High-profile executive management position leading the financial, accounting, MIS, legal, contract, marketing, production, distribution and customer service for multi-site operations (main facility and eight remote printing sites). Led the introduction of a multi-tiered program of financial and operating analyses to reduce operating costs and position for long-term financial growth. Performed cost/benefit analyses on virtually all operations throughout the corporation. Directed a team of 100 employees and 1500 independent contractors.

***Financial & MIS Achievements:***

- Reduced average marketing cost per order by 50% through redesign of subscription marketing programs.
- Renegotiated existing contracts with third-party printing companies for a net annual cost reduction of $1.2 million.
- Saved $1.8+ million annually and accelerated market growth via restructure of national distribution network.
- Identified and capitalized upon opportunity to increase revenue stream through negotiation of on-line service agreements with Reuters, Prodigy and other international networks. Structured financial transactions and negotiated contracts that currently generate an additional $600,000 in revenues to the corporation.
- Managed high-profile and complex negotiations with airports throughout the U.S. for product placement. Prepared detailed cost/benefit analyses to determine pricing for maximum return on service delivery.
- Analyzed production requirements for regions throughout the U.S. to determine need for expanded facilities. Prepared detailed cost/benefit analyses, identified sites, negotiated printing contracts, acquired capital equipment, and coordinated the entire start-up of each new production center.

59

**Combination.** *Wendy S. Enelow, Lynchburg, Virginia*

Many of the executive resume features mentioned in the remarks about the preceding resume are evident also in this resume. Some horizontal, thin-thick lines are interrupted by centered

**ADAM ADMINISTRATOR** - *Page Two*

***Operational Achievements:***

- Orchestrated a massive reengineering of the entire production process to resolve issues impeding productivity, quality and efficiency of the operation. Implemented a series of strategic management initiatives that successfully realigned production and supported growth.
- Designed a new commission structure for telemarketing personnel which increased productivity by 20% with no additional expense to the corporation.
- Restructured customer service operations from a complaint/data entry function into a sales and retention business unit with a resulting 50% revenue increase.
- Instrumental in the consolidation and relocation of the corporation and all affiliates ($7 million project).

**Controller** (1987 to 1992)

Promoted from Accounting Manager to Controller within four months. Given full responsibility for establishing a formal accounting and finance department to accommodate the corporation's rapid growth/expansion. Hired and directed a staff of 11 responsible for accounts payable, accounts receivable, general ledger, monthly financial statements, budgets and variance analyses. Personally managed all corporate financing, leasing and banking activities.

Conducted detailed analyses of all critical functions to provide CEO with information essential to managing growth and improving profitability. Designed analytical methods and reporting systems for financial, marketing and production departments. Prepared cost analyses to identify cost overrides and resolve issues impacting revenue/profit growth. Played a key role in the preparation of five-year business plans for investors and lending institutions.

***Achievements:***

- Reduced expenditures by $4.2 million annually during first 18 months following reorganization of nationwide distribution network.
- Initiated and developed the first departmental fiscal budgeting system with monthly variance reports.
- Implemented credit and collection policies for advertising sales that reduced uncollected receivables by 80%.
- Negotiated a $2 million secured lease/finance arrangement for the purchase of new production equipment at 2% below prime. In addition, negotiated a $1 million revolving line of credit for the corporation.

**A SIGN CO.**, Austin, Texas 1985 to 1987

**Controller**

Managed accounts payable/receivable, general ledger and financial reporting for a $1 million sign manufacturing and advertising company. Worked in cooperation with CPA to prepare monthly sales and annual income tax filings.

## EDUCATION

**Bachelor of Administration in Accounting**, University of Virginia, Lynchburg, Virginia, 1985

## PROFESSIONAL AFFILIATIONS

American Institute of Certified Public Accountants
Society of Certified Public Accountants
American Management Association

headings and are visually appealing. The italic paragraph near the top of the Professional Experience section conveys a powerful message. Side subheadings indicate where achievements are listed. The bulleted achievement statements are impressive because of their number and their amounts.

**EMMELINE WHITCOMB, P.A., J.D.**
1234 North Washoe
Denver, Colorado 80283
(303) 222-0000

**QUALIFICATIONS SUMMARY**

**SENIOR MANAGEMENT TEAM MEMBER** combining 12+ years in the medical and legal professions, with career highlights including:

- As VP Medical Affairs, impressive record of addressing risk management/quality assurance, contracting, legal, physician relations, and managed care issues, positively impacting administration and medical affairs in anticipation of industry trends.
- As Risk Management Specialist for Children's Hospital, Denver, reviewed and managed contracts and implemented safety and risk management programs which considerably reduced legal fees, insurance premiums, and medical malpractice claims.
- Successful litigation experience as Associate Attorney with plaintiff medical malpractice litigation firm.
- Prior background as Board-Certified Physician Assistant in acute care hospital.
- Assistant Professor of Medicine with University of Virginia College of Medicine.
- Credentials include Juris Doctor, B.H.S. in Public Health, and Board Certification as Physician Assistant.

**PROFESSIONAL EXPERIENCE**

**VICE PRESIDENT, MEDICAL AFFAIRS** 1991-Present
Children's Hospital, Denver, Colorado

**Medical Affairs:** Manage administrative, financial, and technical activities of the Medical Affairs Division for 346-bed regional children's hospital, reporting to CEO and COO. Manage medical staff relations with 625 physicians and 275 active medical staff. Represent administration at all Medical Staff Committee meetings. Coordinate physician recruitment. Executive Council member, representing Medical Affairs at Board of Trustees meetings.

**Management/Administration:** Establish new medical programs with subspecialists and coordinate operations with hospital administration through matrix management techniques. Manage Infection Control, Quality Assurance/Risk Management, Medical Staff Office, Residency Program, Medical Library, Continuing Education, and Medical Affairs Administration with staff of 20. Manage budgeting and financial reporting functions.

**Legal Affairs:** Serve as liaison for all legal issues. Prepare, review, and maintain over 100 physician and medical service contracts and leases.

- Instrumental in design and development of Independent Physician Association and Physician Hospital Organization for managed care.
- Facilitated creation of Pediatric Research Division.
- Directed Medical Affairs Department in receiving JCAHO accreditation with commendation.
- Provided in-house legal services which reduced legal fees approximately 50%.
- Implemented risk management programs to reduce insurance premiums and malpractice legal fees.
- Directed successful recruiting strategies to meet physician recruitment goals.
- Controlled $8+ million operating budget, consistently finishing three consecutive years under budget.
- Promoted from Assistant Vice President, Medical Affairs in less than one year (one of two non-physicians to hold VP, Medical Affairs position among 50 children's hospitals nationwide).

**60**

**Combination.** *Susan Britton Whitcomb, Fresno, California*

A resume for an individual who had been a physician assistant and as an attorney directed legal affairs for a children's hospital. The original resume was three pages. Much of the information

**EMMELINE WHITCOMB, P.A., J.D.** **Page Two**

## PROFESSIONAL EXPERIENCE (continued)

**MEDICAL LEGAL CONSULTANT** 1990-1991
Charleston, West Virginia

Consultant services included review of medical records to assess liability and damages in personal injury, workers' compensation, and medical malpractice for plaintiff and defense law firms. Additionally,

- Drafted West Virginia Academy of Physician Assistants' proposed legislation for PA section of Medical Practice Act (approximately three-quarters of legislative language was adopted).
- Lobbied state and federal legislators regarding Physician Assistant prescriptive practices and Medicare reimbursement.

**PRIOR EXPERIENCE**

- Litigation Associate -- Dietrich & Noble, Attorneys at Law, Charleston, West Virginia 1988-1990
- Physician Assistant -- University Hospital of Jacksonville, Florida 1985-1988

## PUBLICATIONS, EDITORIAL ACTIVITIES

Editorial Board, *Journal of the American Academy of Physician Assistants* (1993-Present)
"Negotiating an Employment Contract," *Clinician's Reference Guide*, 1995.
"The Physician Assistant's Scope of Practice," *Journal of the American Academy of Physician Assistants*, 1994.
Peer reviewed chapter on Litigation for the "Liability Handbook" for health care providers.
Peer reviewed "The Physician Assistant as an Expert Witness," a position paper for the American Academy of Physician Assistants, 1992.

## PUBLIC SPEAKING

Speaker for pharmaceutical company Johnson & Johnson on medical malpractice prevention:

- "The Legal Workshop or How You Too Can Think Like an Attorney"
- "Legal Relationships, in Sickness and in Health, For Richer, For Poorer"
- "Documenting for the Lawyer Looking Over Your Shoulder"

Numerous presentations to the business and medical communities on health-related topics.

## EDUCATION

**Juris Doctorate** -- University of Colorado, School of Law (1987)
- Honors in appellate advocacy; member of Honor Court prosecutorial staff

**Physician Assistant Program** -- San Francisco State University, San Francisco, California (1982)
- Dean's List (6 semesters); Who's Who in American Colleges; Student Exec. Council, Medical Center

**Bachelor of Health Sciences in Public Health** -- University of Texas, Austin (1979)
- Graduated with Distinction; Founder, Committee on Ethics and Responsibilities

## AFFILIATIONS (partial list)

Colorado Society for Health Care Attorneys; Medical Group Management Association; American Academy of Physician Assistants (active involvement, including service on Judicial Affairs committee 3 years); West Virginia Academy of Physician Assistants (active involvement, including service on Board of Directors)

**References Upon Request**

was for the first entry in the Professional Experience section. Instead of putting all that information into one "overly-thick paragraph," the writer clustered information under three subheadings. The Qualifications Summary ties together the person's medical and legal work.

# CHRISTOPHER S. JADEN

369 Harborside Drive
Lakeland, Florida 33810
(941) 555-5555

**SENIOR SALES AND MARKETING EXECUTIVE**

***Expert in Strategy Development and Corporate Sales Expansion for Multi-Locational Residential Communities***

Dynamic sales and marketing leader with expertise in creating profit-driven marketing strategies designed to stimulate sales and increase presence within the industry. Recognized for innovation in strategic planning, operations management, and building leading edge marketing programs that have achieved strong and sustainable results.

## PROFESSIONAL EXPERIENCE

**1991 to Present** **Vice President of Sales and Marketing** **ANSEL PROPERTIES, Lakeland, Florida**
*(Company specializing in the development, marketing and management of all-adult manufactured housing communities)*

Recruited to re-engineer and turn around the sales and marketing functions for this nationally ranked premier developer. Initially restructured the sales and marketing department, analyzed existing sales methods, and developed new programs and strategies to re-direct sales focus. Work closely with President and other senior operating executives to position the corporation for continued growth and market expansion.

- Administer and direct all aspects of the firm's marketing activities; engage in long and short range business planning; devise and implement effective marketing strategies and sales campaigns.
- Produce radio and television commercials; coordinate with advertising agencies to produce print ads for publication in newspapers and nationwide publications including *Modern Maturity, AARP Bulletin, Golf Magazine,* and *Golf Digest.*
- Prepare and conduct quarterly training presentations for junior sales executives.

**1989 to Present** **General Manager - Sunshine Village** **ANSEL PROPERTIES, Lakeland, Florida**
*(Company produced record sales for the state of Florida in this adult lifestyle golfing community with 1564 units)*

Responsible for the management and marketing with operations in facilities management, recreational sporting activities, and food.

- Direct all activities related to the daily operation of the community; work with other senior executives to ensure that the lifestyle of the community is preserved and that residents' needs and concerns are resolved efficiently.
- Develop and implement sales and marketing strategies to further promote the community's growth and increase community presence.
- Manage a staff of 60 employed in the areas of sales/marketing, property maintenance, golf course maintenance, groundskeeping, resident relations, and the clubhouse/snack bar operation.

**61**

**Combination.** *E. René Hart, Lakeland, Florida*

Compound (thin-thick-thin) horizontal lines are a distinctive feature of this resume. (Depending on light conditions, the clarity of your vision, and your distance from the resume, such lines can

**CHRISTOPHER S. JADEN** *Page Two*

## PROFESSIONAL EXPERIENCE (continued)

**1985 to 1989** **Vice President** **FLORIDA MARKETING COMPANY, Winter Haven, Florida**
*(Company specializing in all aspects of sales and marketing for adult resorts and retirement communities)*

Held full responsibility and decision making authority for sales and marketing, staff sales training, and strategic planning and corporate development.

- Designed and presented sales seminars for the Florida Living Expo, a trade show for adult resorts and communities.
- Trained junior sales representatives in new and established sales strategies.
- Directed the company's telemarketing and direct mail programs.
- Procured and followed up on new leads.

**1983 to 1985** **Project Manager** **KEEGAN ENTERPRISES, Thonotosassa, Florida**
*(Company specializing in manufactured housing development and management )*

Direct sales/marketing and all aspects of operations and facilities management for this manufactured housing development company.

- Managed all phases of the company's daily operation, including construction, sales, and service.
- Developed a fly-and-buy program.
- Produced and edited television commercials and videos; developed and refined direct mail and telemarketing programs.
- Played a significant role developing FHA Title II financing for the project, which was the first manufactured housing community in Florida to achieve this.

| | | |
|---|---|---|
| **1977 to 1983** | **Vice President/General Manager** | **SOUTHEAST FINANCIAL** |
| **1974 to 1977** | **Vice President** | **DEALER SERVICE CONSULTANTS, INC.** |
| **1970 to 1974** | **Sales Manager** | **SCHWARTZ MOBILE HOME SALES** |
| **1968 to 1970** | **Field Service Manager** | **WARNER & SWASEY CO.** |

## EDUCATION

**Bachelor of Arts - Business Administration** (1968)
Florida Southern College • Lakeland, Florida

make the white space between them look gray. ) After each company name, the parenthetical remark in italic helps to acquaint the reader with each company. Note how the companies served from 1968 to 1983 are mentioned without elaboration in a list that resembles a work history.

# *Jordan J. Phillips*

199 West Street
Bangor, Maine 04401
(207)555-5555

***Objective:*** **Nurse Manager / Nursing Supervisor**

## *Career Highlights:*

- Over six years of experience at Bayview Hospital as Assistant Director of Nursing Services and was selected as Acting Vice President of Nursing.
- Twenty-one years of experience at Coastal Osteopathic Hospital as Staff Nurse, OR and 3-11 Supervisor, Director of Nursing of Acute Care and Geriatric Units, and Acting Administrator for Hospital (during bankruptcy)
- Proven record of success as a leader in nursing administration. Excellent communication and organizational skills.

## *Certifications:*

- State of Maine - Registered Nurse License
- American Nursing Association - Certification in Nursing Administration

## *Areas of Expertise:*

- Management and Administration
- Interpersonal Relations
- Teaching and Training
- Staffing
- Staff Development
- Problem Resolution
- Clinical Knowledge
- Personnel Selection

## *Professional Experience:*

**Bayview Hospital, Bangor, Maine** **1990 - 1996**
*Acting Vice President of Nursing (1996)*
*Assistant Vice President of Nursing (1990 - 1996)*
*Evening Supervisor (1990)*

- Assisted in the development and implementation of philosophy and goals of the Nursing Department. Assisted with the preparation and monitoring of the Nursing Department operating and capital expense budgets.
- Determined staffing patterns for individual units for maximum efficiency and effectiveness. Served as GRASP Coordinator for Nursing Department.
- Provided direct supervision, management, and evaluation of Nurse Managers. Made goal rounds on all nursing units in order to assess the quality of nursing care provided. Recommended alternatives in plan of care to address identified needs.
- Collaborated with Vice President of Patient Care to solve people, system, procedural, or policy problems as they arose.
- Prepared quarterly and annual reports for nursing units in collaboration with Nurse Managers. Participated in management development programs.
- Monitored and implemented required changes in or additions to achieve Nursing Department's accreditation requirements.

62

**Combination.** *Joan M. Roberts, Bangor, Maine*

This candidate, a nursing administrator, was laid off after 25 years in the medical field. Her career path showed "progressive growth in nursing and nurse management," so the writer decided

***Jordan J. Phillips***

*Page Two*

- Promoted patient relations and participated in public relations activities to increase community awareness of hospital and nursing services.
- Maintained clinical and managerial proficiency through continuing education programs and participation in professional organizations.

**Coastal Osteopathic Hospital, Bangor, Maine** **1969 - 1989**
***Acting Hospital Administrator (1989)***
***Director of Nursing / Assistant Administrator - Pavilion & Hospital (1970 - 1989)***

- Directed nursing services in both acute care and geriatric settings. Supervised nursing staff.
- Performed administrative duties and oversaw Pharmacy, Lab, X-ray, Respiratory Therapy, and PromptCare Departments. Acted as Hospital Administrator during bankruptcy proceedings.

*From 1963 - 1969 held positions as Director of Health Services, Staff Nurse M/S, OR Supervisor, and Float Charge Nurse in Chicago and Bangor.*

## *Education & Professional Development:*

**University of Maine, Orono, Maine** **1989 - Present**
*Completing courses in the Nursing Program*

**Eastern Maine General Hospital School of Nursing, Bangor, Maine** **1963**
*Diploma*

Recent Professional Development:

- Executive Nurse Management Program - Hospital Corporation of America (1986)
- Explanation of The New L/T Care Survey Process (1986) - ME Health Care Association
- Nursing Executive Management Program (1986) - The Center for Health Studies, TN
- Legal Aspects of Nursing Practice in Long-Term Patient Care Management (1986)
- Director Nursing Seminar (1985) - MCA Northeast Regional Conference (1985)
- Certification in Nursing Administration (1985 - 1989) - American Nurses' Association
- Husson College - Accounting (1985)

## *Professional Affiliations:*

Nursing Advisory Committee - Eastern Maine Technical College (1994 - 1995)
Organization of Maine Nurse Executives (1974 - 1989)

## *Community Involvement:*

United Way - Received Distinguished Volunteer Service Award
Greater Bangor Chamber of Commerce Building Bridges Program
Hospitality Assurance - Values Integration Process Mentor - St. Joseph Hospital
Penobscot Job Corps - Vocational Curriculum Advisory Committee

***References Available Upon Request***

"to use the Career Highlights section to grab the attention of the reader." In Maine, competition for management positions in health care was tremendous, so the person needed "the most powerful resume possible." She now works for the largest home health agency in the area.

# Dorothy A. Belmont

760 Lincoln Street
Rock Valley, IA 55555

000/000-0000

## Profile

***Accounts receivable factoring executive** offering an extensive industry background, which enables valuable insights into new operating procedures, techniques and competitors' developments. Proficient in identifying problem situations and providing sound solutions, supportive of company's goals. Astute managerial and communication skills, demonstrated in effective staff training, interdepartmental relationships, and client negotiations.*

## Career History

1989–1996

FIDELITY COMMERCIAL CORPORATION, SIOUX FALLS, SD

**Vice President of Operations**

- Managed $800 million accounts receivable factoring operations for department and specialty store clients all across the country. Working with a complement of 3 supervisors and 14 employees, oversaw functions consisting of sales coding, cash application, and adjustments.
- Restructured the accounts receivable department and trained personnel in proper methods of cash application, cash-on-account entries and daily recycle reconciliations.
- Cross trained adjusters to support cash application personnel during peak periods, resulting in reduced overtime, increased productivity, and improved quality control.
- Worked closely with supervisors and staff to ensure consistency of quality performance on an ongoing basis. Encouraged them to contribute their ideas to increase efficiency and productivity.
- Established comprehensive record keeping systems for controlling customer remittances/refunds while also facilitating research of cash-on-account entries.
- Developed new coding procedures, which have effectively reduced the duplication of customer accounts as well as coding errors.
- Streamlined process for controlling accounting documents and reports, which has eliminated the tedious job of filing daily, weekly and monthly paperwork by adjustor without compromising established policies.
- Set up programs on in-house PC that strengthened integrity of documentation related to customers' write-offs, recoveries, monthly income accounts, unused credits and cash entries.
- Assisted in the implementation of the Fidelity Order Entry/Credit Approval System to better manage a high volume of customer activity.
- Implemented the posting of store numbers for all large department store accounts. This has served as an aid to the collectors, facilitated in the application of large payments, and reduced cash-on-account entries for the same customers.
- Visited customer/clients to resolve unusual problems related to adjustments and chargebacks.

»»»

63

**Combination.** *Melanie A. Noonan, West Paterson, New Jersey*

The subject of this resume was over 60 but did not want to retire. Her career displayed impressive growth from clerical positions to vice president of operations. After a merger she lost

## Dorothy A. Belmont

Page 2

1975-1989

NATIONSBANK FACTORING GROUP, SIOUX FALLS, SD

**Assistant Vice President / Head of Accounts Receivable, Adjustment and Collection Departments** (1983-89)

- Reported directly to Senior Vice President and had responsibility for overall accounts receivable operations consisting of 300,000 credit card customer accounts, which generated yearly volume of $2 billion.
- Prepared yearly budget and salary administration for staff of 115.
- Planned and controlled day-to-day operations, which included employee training, evaluation and counseling.
- Wrote department procedures and designed required forms.
- Initiated cross training programs to enhance productivity, quality of service and job performance.
- Assisted in coordinating the merger of two major accounts receivable operations.
- Instituted auditing controls and procedures for collection of past due accounts.

**Assistant Treasurer / Head of Adjustment and Collection Department** (1975-83)

- Assigned the responsibility of reorganizing and coordinating workflow of the general accounting department.
- Reconciled accounts and established internal auditing procedures.

Prior to 1975

**Assistant Manager, Accounts Receivable Department**

**Accounts Receivable Supervisor**

**Senior Accounts Receivable Clerk**

**Accounts Receivable Ledger Clerk**

### Education

UNIVERSITY OF CHICAGO — B.S. Accounting with concentration in Finance

Numerous accounting and management development courses throughout employment with NationsBank and Fidelity Commercial Corporation.

### Membership

National Factor Controllers Association

her job. To make her appealing to new banks entering the area, the writer played up the individual's daily administrative activities and played down her age by omitting dates of titles before 1975 and not indicating the date of her degree. Note the unusual bullets and how they are used.

**LARRY LAWYER**
123 ABC Street
Anywhere, YZ 45678
Home (987) 123-4567

**EXECUTIVE PROFILE**

Top-flight executive career combining experience in Business Management and Corporate Law.

- As **CEO and Vice President** of two affiliated corporations, provided strategic, operational, financial, human resource and technology leadership for substantial revenue and profit gains.
- As **Associate General Counsel**, directed high-profile and successful business law, litigation and legislative affairs.
- MBA and JD Degrees. Published Journal and Book Author.

**PROFESSIONAL EXPERIENCE**

**Second Vice President / Associate General Counsel** 1975 to Present
**THE INSURANCE COMPANY (TIC)**, Anywhere, YZ

Member of the Senior Executive Management Team of this diversified insurance company with more than 1200 employees and a total portfolio valued in excess of $2 billion. Provide expert legal counsel to President and other top executives to protect the corporation, its business interests and assets.

Personally direct the efforts of over 40 law firms managing 200+ litigation cases arising from the firm's $13 billion life, accident and health insurance portfolio. Formulate legal strategy to positively position TIC for proactive defense of each case and consult with outside counsel regarding legal theory and case law. Direct ERISA, EEOC, employment, securities, corporate, life/health insurance, intellectual property, antitrust, commercial and unfair trade litigation, and international law.

***Management Achievements:***

- Launched the introduction of computerized case management and billing technology. Managed project from initial cost justification through hardware/software selection to final installation and training.
- Created a standardized reporting, disclosure and billing policy for outside law firms that reduced internal legal costs by 10% while improving level and quality of service.
- Established and administered the corporation's pension plan for 13 consecutive years. Built plan from start-up to over $1 billion.
- Designed and led in-house professional training seminars on topics including Claims Law and Procedures, Employee Benefits Law, Employment Law and Commercial Law. In addition, led annual seminar on Franchise Selection for accountants, attorneys and investors.

***Legal Achievements:***

- Assumed personal control of an employee benefits case where TIC was facing a $7 million judgement and a $1 million settlement. Identified applicable case law and legal theory which supported a total reversal of initial judgement. Followed through with a malpractice suit against original law firm and won $750,000 settlement.
- Provided legal documentation and justification that allowed TIC to pursue action resulting in an injunction for return of technology from former subsidiary owner/president.
- Supplied legal theory and case law for landmark decision involving suit for $6 million in pension assets by several of the company's former employees. Won favorable decision following extensive litigation. Case has subsequently been quoted on numerous occasions by other courts throughout the U.S.
- Developed ERISA legal memorandum package for outside law firms that has established clear standards for compliance and significantly reduced potential litigation losses to TIC.

**64**

**Combination.** *Wendy S. Enelow, Lynchburg, Virginia*

Partial thin-thick-thin lines direct the eye to the main side headings and to the candidate's name at the top of page two. Small bullets point to key information in the Executive Profile and to

## LARRY LAWYER

**President / CEO / Corporate Counsel** 1991 to 1993
**TIC CREDIT UNION**, Anywhere, YZ

Full P&L and operating management responsibility for affiliated credit union. Spearheaded an aggressive turnaround of the entire business organization, resolved internal operating problems, implemented policies and procedures to recover outstanding debt, and revitalized income and asset growth. Retained full-time responsibilities as Second Vice President and Associate General Counsel with parent corporation during this special two-year assignment.

- Increased assets from $1.8 million to $2.25 million with concurrent profit improvement of 100+%.
- Launched a high-profile marketing program targeted to niche consumer markets. Increased loan activity by 150% within one month and achieved the lowest default rate in the organization's history.
- Improved rating from the National Credit Union Administration to the highest possible category.
- Pioneered the introduction of a series of employee empowerment, participative management and team building initiatives that resolved long-standing issues impacting quality, productivity and service.

**Adjunct Instructor - Business Law** 1980 to 1990
**THE UNIVERSITY**, Anywhere, YZ

Taught undergraduate and graduate courses in Business Law, Employment, Contracts, Uniform Commercial Code, Corporations, Securities, Antitrust and Intellectual Property. (Concurrent with full-time executive positions at TIC.)

**Financial Trial Attorney** 1971 to 1975
**U.S. SECURITIES & EXCHANGE COMMISSION**, Washington, D.C.

Reviewed/analyzed offering circular for more than 50 stock issues. In addition, planned and directed litigation of securities fraud cases. Won high-profile securities fraud cases against oil and gas operators, financial service corporations, and a famous television evangelist.

## EDUCATION

**Master of Business Administration**, The University, Anywhere, YZ 1979
**Masters in Corporation Law**, The University School of Law, Anywhere, YZ 1971
**Juris Doctor**, The University School of Law, Anywhere, YZ 1969
**Bachelor of Arts in Psychology**, The University, Anywhere, YZ 1963

**Licensed** to practice law in Louisiana and District of Columbia
**NASD Series #7 (Registered Representative) and #24 (Registered Principal)**

## PROFESSIONAL AFFILIATIONS

**Past President & Current Director**, Local Chapter of American Corporate Council Association
**Member**, American Business Law Association
**Member**, American Bar Association
**Member**, District of Columbia Bar Association
**Member**, State Bar Association

achievements in the Professional Experience section. The candidate is both an executive with an MBA and an attorney with a JD degree. These dual roles are indicated in the Profile, and achievements for each role are presented under separate side headings in the Experience section.

## Paul Salem

**483 Dowling Street • Medford, NY 11763 • (555)-555-5555**

---

**Commercial Lending • Risk Management • Government Loan Programs**

---

**Career Profile**

**Commercial lending professional with extensive experience in structuring innovative and traditional business loans using in-depth knowledge of risk reduction, risk sharing and government guarantee loan programs.**

**Employ analysis and creativity to form shrewd and inventive partnerships with banks and businesses. Believe that profitability, customer service and portfolio quality are primary factors of success in this competitive industry.**

---

**Representative Achievements in Financing**

**Management Buyout**
- Proposed $1.4MM conventional mortgage loan participation to member bank as part of a $2.8MM financing project for an aerospace manufacturing concern. Solution reduced bank's total exposure and increased future financing flexibility.

**Reorganization**
- Conceived innovative strategy to payoff a $1.8MM FDIC debt with $900M. Combined a $450M conventional first mortgage with a $500M SBA 7(a) second mortgage. Financing prevented bankruptcy filing.

**New York City Benefit Program**
- Pioneered the first loan under the NYCIDA Straight Lease program. Deal opened the door to a steady flow of NYCIDA business and saved company over $250M in real estate tax payments over twenty years.

**Start-up**
- Provided $500M in start-up funding to a 50 year old prepared foods company venturing into the restaurant business. Created a "no lose" situation by structuring a bank participation loan that reduced risk and retained a valued customer.

**Joint Real Estate Purchase**
- Closed the first SBA 504 second mortgage loan in which two unrelated companies jointly purchased property that both occupied as tenants. Utilized little known revised eligibility guidelines to complete this ground-breaking deal.

**Refinancing**
- Structured non-SBA conventional term loan with bank participant to refinance a short term debt severely hampering cash flow. Extended loan maturity significantly reduced debt service requirements and enhanced bank/customer relationship.

**Portfolio Review**
- Analyzed bank mortgage loan portfolio to determine suitability for major loan purchase. Completed complex transaction in two weeks. Deal represented a total purchase of $5MM and assisted member bank in the realignment of portfolio.

**65**

**Combination.** *Deborah Wile Dib, Medford, New York*

A resume spread over three full pages. The number of line spaces on the third page could have been reduced, but a full page looks better than a partial one. Extra blank lines have been added

## Paul Salem

**page two**

---

**Commercial Lending Experience**

**VICE-PRESIDENT** **1991 to present**

**New York Commercial Development Corp. (NYCDC)**
**Empire State Commercial Development Corp. (ESCDC)**
**New York, NY**

*NYCDC and ESCDC represent a consortium of New York State banks to provide access to capital for the promotion of commercial business growth and expansion. As Vice-president, partner with member banks to structure loan proposals for small to mid-size business concerns. Use extensive knowledge of risk sharing, and state and federal government loan programs to develop creative and fiscally sound financing that manages risk and creates profit opportunities.*

**Special Programs**
- Small Business Administration (SBA): Preferred Lenders Program, 7(a), 504 second mortgage loans, Low Doc, and Fastrack.
- Job Development Authority (JDA) and enhanced JDA/504 second mortgage loans.
- New York City Industrial Development Agency (NYCIDA) Straight Lease Program.
- Empire State Development Corporation (ESDC) Linked Deposit Program.

**Closings**
- Produced $15MM in loan closings ranging from $100M to $1MM; averaged $4MM in closings and generated $85M in fee income over past two years.
- Doubled size of NYBDC Long Island loan portfolio and enhanced customer relationships for member banks.
- Interacted with legal counsel and formulated closing agendas.

**Origination**
- Cultivate, develop and maintain loan source referral network of banks, CPAs, attorneys, and economic developers.
- Organize loan program seminars for commercial lenders.

**Analysis**
- Conduct in-depth financial analysis and evaluate credit risk.
- Prepare loan presentations: written, for NYBDC regional loan committees, and verbal, for NYBDC Board of Directors.
- Negotiate loan terms and conditions; institute loan covenants; analyze adequacy of collateral.
- Coordinate and obtain government guarantees; plot and meet rigorous committee deadlines.

**Servicing**
- Maintained loan losses to an all-time low in fiscal year 1996.
- Evaluate loan portfolio quality through frequent financial reviews, appraisals of collateral sufficiency, and site visits.

so that the information on the third page reaches the bottom margin. Because most of the blank lines have been added with horizontal lines, which have extra white space on the first two pages, the additional blank lines on page three look natural. Boldfacing effectively makes evident the contact information, career-field

## Paul Salem

**page three**

---

**Lending Experience (continued)**

**COMMERCIAL LOAN OFFICER** **1988 to 1991**

**Commercial Loan Brokerage**
**New York, NY**

*Northeast regional non-bank SBA lender specializing in SBA 7(a) loans.*

- Developed $6.25MM in loans representing 25% of this non-bank's $25MM SBA loan portfolio.
- Gained knowledge of secondary market loan sales as institutional investments.
- Maintained an extensive network of accountant and broker referral sources.
- Strengthened relationships with local SBA offices.

**Related Credit Experience**

**OPERATIONS MANAGER AND CREDIT ANALYST** **1980 to 1988**

**TRW**
**New York, NY**

*TRW is one of the largest providers of consumer and business credit information.*

- Assigned commercial credit ratings to Long Island businesses.
- Obtained and analyzed financial statements.
- Supervised team of six credit analysts.

---

**Computer Skills**

Word for Windows • Lotus 123 • Stan5 Financial Spreadsheets

**Education**

**Bachelor of Science in Business Economics**
State University of New York at New Paltz

**Continuing Education**
- TRW credit and financial analysis courses
- Kent Stickler motivational training seminar

---

**Professional Affiliations**

- National Association of Development Companies (NADCO)
- National Association of Government Guarantee Lenders (NAGGL)
- Long Island Association (LIA)
- Long Island Business Development Council (LIBDC)
- Guest panelist for National Association of Women Business Owners (NAWBO)

headline, Career Profile text, headings, subheadings, positions, company names, and dates. If the eye sweeps through the resume, the mind can comprehend the resume's organization at a glance, which is a valued characteristic of a best resume.

**Michael Lefkowitz**

32 Bob White Road
Tarrytown, NY 55555
(555) 555-5555

**Senior Level Consultative Sales and Marketing Specialist**

## Professional Profile

- **Seventeen years progressive advancement in sales, marketing, management and product development for TRW, one of the world's largest provider of consumer and business information. Surpassed sales goals and achieved corporate recognition in each position held.**
- **Create unique, industry specific business information programs and products. Develop profitable, information sharing partnerships. Trusted by accounts to maintain integrity of confidential data. Tackle complex projects; devise inventive and cost-effective solutions.**
- **Direct and motivate sales teams to produce optimum creativity and bottom-line performance. Initiate, research and develop innovative and profitable sales opportunities. Compose sophisticated proposals and marketing materials.**
- **Self-directed, focused and goal oriented; invest whatever time and effort necessary to get job done. Fair and approachable, with strong people skills; work effectively with all levels of sales and management to achieve objectives.**

## Career Development

**TRW BUSINESS INFORMATION SERVICES** — **1980 to present**

**Assistant Vice-President** — (1995 to present)

**Sales and Marketing Specialist serving the business information needs of the utility and energy industries. Major accounts include Con Edison, Duke Power, Florida Power & Light and others.** Assign and achieve revenue growth targets. Create and implement strategic marketing initiatives, sales channel strategies and third party alliances. Develop new products, services and sales collateral material. Compose and deliver sophisticated account presentations to all levels of management.

- **Generated 56.3% total revenue growth and $2.5M in new database marketing revenue** in 1996. Numbers represent the highest growth of all vertical market segments.
- **Increased revenue dramatically by identification of unique business information needs of utilities industry**. Created and trained seven "regional champions" to focus on regional utilities and demonstrate growth potential to regional sales associates. Identified all major nationwide utilities—top 100 with $500M+ in annual sales—and developed customized strategic sales marketing presentation that illustrated link between TRW products and the utilities' business information needs.
- **Created $300K in new sales and increased average sale by 15% prior to product release** by development of the first industry specific desktop database—*Street Smart*, for the utility/energy industry. Devised solution to satisfy need for industry specific information not represented in existing TRW solutions. Corporation is now planning to develop for additional industries.

**66**

**Combination.** *Deborah Wile Dib, Medford, New York*

Another three-page resume by the same writer. It was for a senior-level executive and resulted in his acquiring a high six-figure position. When a resume is more than one page, the writer must

## Michael Lefkowitz page two

### Career Development (continued)

**TRW Business Information Services (continued)**

**Assistant-Vice President (continued)**

- **Conceived and developed an innovative business alliance with the WEFA Group** (a macro economic information agency) to provide utility customers with valuable industry specific usage and growth information essential to the creation of a strategic and tactical database indispensable to utilities in transition. Alliance is evolving into a mutually beneficial and profitable information sharing relationship with projected 1997 revenue in excess of $4M.
- **Established an alliance with The International Revenue Protection Association (I.U.R.P.A.) that will produce projected 1997 revenue in excess of $1M.** Partnered to create an initiative to acquire utility customer data to develop an energy consumption model. Current objective is to expand initiative to utility marketing applications, By utilizing this information, *Street Smart* will be the most industry specific vertical market database available.
- **Partnered with Baraket & Chamberlin** (a consulting firm providing strategic market assessment and analysis). New alliance has produced $400K in incremental revenue, with outstanding potential for additional revenue.
- **Additional accomplishments include** (1) the production of several new sales by development of an internal customized utility customer file match process that enhanced match rates, improving results up to 20%; (2) the development of industry specific marketing materials; (3) the production of direct mail piece that generated $522K in new business; (4) the recent completion of work on comprehensive utilities industry sales brochure

**Director of Personalized Sales and Solutions** (1992 to 1995)

**Managed team of highly consultative sales professionals. Produced customized solutions for business information needs of Fortune 1000 accounts.** Results of several proposals incorporated as standard corporate products. Performed operation reviews to determine needs and identify solutions. Created proposals, developed systems, provided field training. Assisted in closing sales of custom models. Exceeded annual objectives and received four quarterly Overachievement Recognition awards. Chosen as integral member of three successful internal breakthrough teams.

- **Conceived and developed new Financial Focus CD ROM product that sold $400K in first year** while competing with Lotus One Source for market share. Received corporate recognition for new product development.
- **Worked closely with a major utility customer to develop a customized process** to analyze and monitor major customers and identify commercial customers most likely to go bankrupt. System returned $500K investment of $60K and is still in use today.
- **Developed Lotus Notes bankruptcy notification service** providing a major telecommunications company with daily bankruptcy information for seven states. Service provides a quick, cost efficient and effective process to minimize losses with significant ROI.
- **Formulated batch scoring process for major leasing company** that enhanced efficiency of mail campaigns. Built model predicting risk of severe delinquency that scored prospects and issued pre-approved credit limits.

ensure that the resume looks the same across the two or more pages. Visual similarity, or unity, is achieved in this resume by a header on pages two and three that resembles the contact information on the first page. The thick horizontal lines on each of the three pages thus help to tie the three pages together visually.

**Michael Lefkowitz** **page three**

## Career Development (continued)

**TRW Business Information Services (continued)**

**District Sales Manager** (1988 to 1992)

**Directed Long Island branch office with annual revenue of $8M.** Supervised fifteen sales associates and five support staff members. Controlled operations and budget, hired/fired/promoted personnel. Instituted successful new bonus and incentive programs.

- **Recognized for best hiring, retention and team development record in region.** Ten sales representatives achieved Senior Sales, National Sales and Sales Management positions.
- **Office first in region and third in country for new product sales.** Achieved Regional District Manager of the Year award in 1989 and 1990.

**Divisional Sales Manager** (1984 to 1988)

**Managed seven sales professionals in Long Island office.** Marketed new and existing products, acquired new relationships and trained customers and associates. Consistently exceeded new business and new product sales targets.

- **Placed second in National Sales Contest** in 1985 and 1986; third in 1987.

**Account Representative** (1980 to 1984)

Established new accounts, increased current account sales, exceeded yearly sales targets.

- **Awarded prestigious Presidential Citation in 1984** for achievement of 178% of sales gain objective. Won New Business award in 1980.

## Computer Skills

- IBM and compatibles; Windows 95 applications; Fluent in Microsoft Word, Excel and PowerPoint

## Education

- **B.S. in Business Administration, Princeton University, Princeton, NJ** **1978**

## Professional Development

| | | |
|---|---|---|
| ■ **System Analyst Program** | 4 hour course | New York University, New York, NY |
| ■ **Negotiation for Senior Executives** | 2 day seminar | Harvard University, Cambridge, MA |
| ■ **Consultative Sales Techniques** | certification course | Forum Corporation, Boston, MA |
| ■ **Targeted Selection Process** | workshop | TRW, corporate training |
| ■ **Performance Management** | workshop | TRW, corporate training |

## Personal Interests

- 8 handicap golfer and soccer coach. Participate in community fundraising and Make-a-Wish Foundation

The filled square bullets perform the same task. By appearing in all the sections of the resume to call attention to key statements, achievements, skills, education, professional training, and personal interests, the bullets unify all the pages.

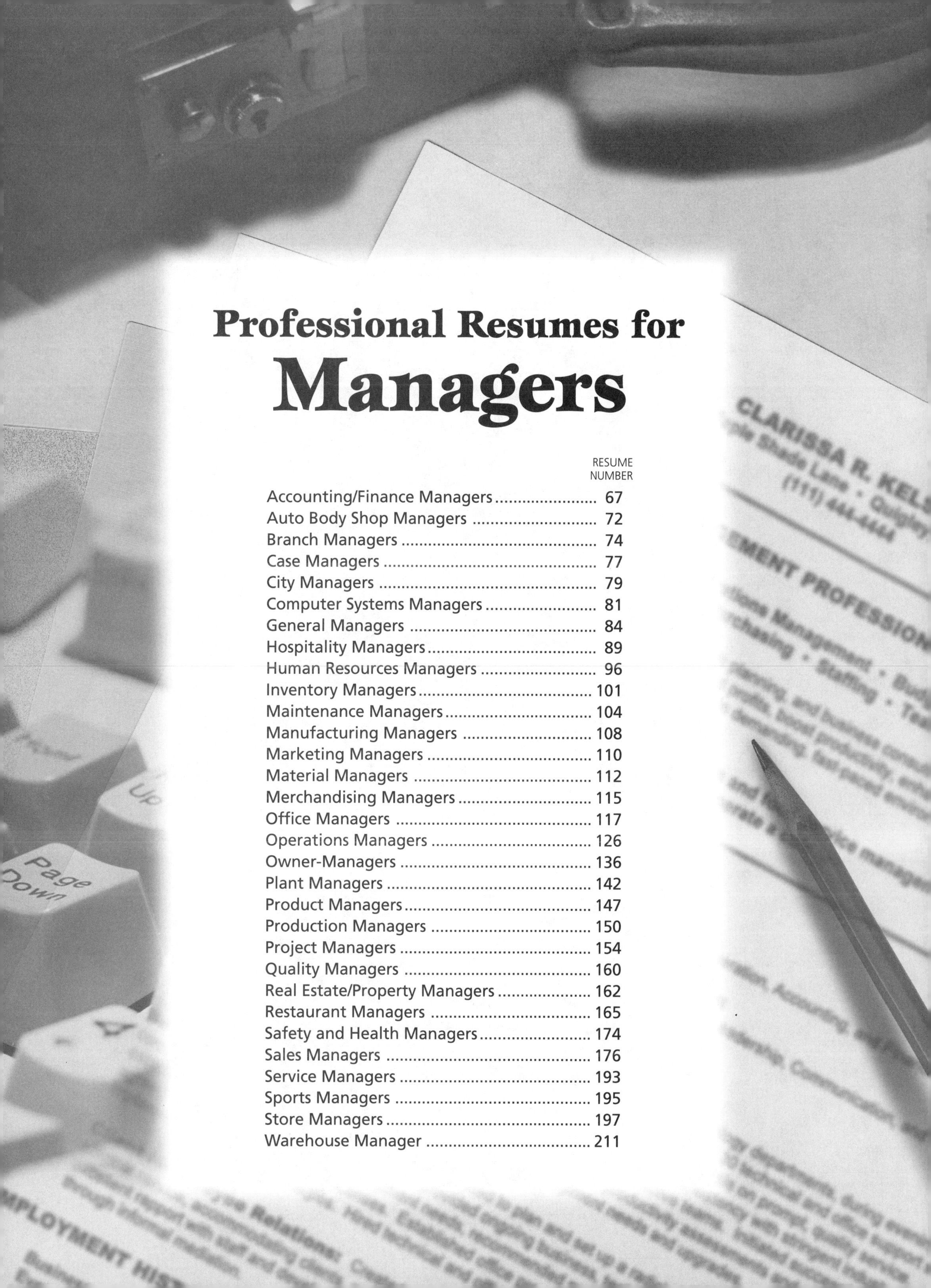

# Professional Resumes for Managers

# Robert R. Taxman

861 South Court Street
Fremont, Ohio 55555

(555) 555-5555 residence
(555) 555-5555 work

**PROFESSIONAL SUMMARY**

***Attorney*** and ***CPA*** with 22 years of diverse tax experience. Involves 17 years with global Fortune 500 manufacturing corporation. Background experience includes federal, state, and local income, property, ERISA, foreign, payroll, sales and use, reorganizations, employee benefits, expatriate, VAT, and intercompany pricing. Strong track record structuring transactions which are tax efficient and accomplishing desired business results.

**EMPLOYMENT HISTORY**

**Foodstuffs Company, Fremont, Ohio**

*A $1.25 billion multi-national manufacturer of food products and services*

***Director of Tax Research and Planning*** 1990 - present

- Sole tax attorney devoted to tax research and project planning

***Tax Manager*** 1978 - 1990

- Management of a staff of four providing state and local compliance
- Provided guidance to members of corporate accounting departments on preparation and review federal compliance
- Full responsibility for all federal and state tax audits including protests and settlements
- Worked closely with legal, international, accounting, planning, and treasury departments in tax planning strategies

Andersen & Andrews, Tax Department, Chicago, Illinois 1973 - 1978

**EDUCATION**

**B.A. Accounting**
University of Illinois, 1970

**J.D.**
University of Kansas, 1973

**PROFESSIONAL AFFILIATIONS**

Illinois Bar Association, 1974
Ohio Bar Association
Illinois CPA, 1980
American Bar Association
Tax Executive Institute
Tax Advisory Committee for Ohio Manufacturers Association

67

**Combination.** *Patricia L. Nieboer, Fremont, Michigan*

A thick-thin horizontal line separates an unusually large name from the rest of the contact information. The person's preceding role as tax manager is discussed more than his current role.

**MARGE RINGER**

**2000 Maple Avenue • Hoboken, New Jersey 07000 • (201) 000-0000**

**PROFILE:**
- Experienced in operations management and task force leadership.
- Proven ability to develop/implement new computerized systems.
- Substantial knowledge of medical billing and insurance regulations.
- Strong interpersonal and training skills.

**EXPERIENCE:** MAJOR LABORATORY SERVICES, Fair Lawn, NJ — 1988-Date

***Manager/Special Projects***

*Billing Systems*

* Instrumental part of management team to restructure Billing Department in order to accommodate increased growth.
* Streamlined paper flow. Established parameters for new billing system. Wrote procedures and data entry manuals.
* Collaborated with MIS staff, software vendors and consultants. Customized system to handle the complexities of Medicare/caid regulations as well as billing internal/external lab services.
* Implemented system which successfully handled a patient base that tripled in 5 years and billed out $120 million annually. Trained staff in operations.

*Contracts*

* Set up a network of reference labs nationwide to control staggering costs in conjunction with Technical Resource Manager.
* Negotiated fees and generated contracts with both national and local labs. Reduced yearly cost by $2 million while servicing twice the number of patients.

*A/P Systems*

* Headed up the decentralization of the A/P function in division. Set up administrative procedures and trained staff to process multimillion dollar payables per month.
* Effectively utilized company's "home grown" computer system while researching and evaluating new programs.

DOCUMENT CLEARING HOUSE, Newark, NJ — 1983-1988

***Customer Service Supervisor***

*Customer Service*

* Interfaced extensively with clients. Supervised processing of all customer requested revisions and documentation. Troubleshot problems and handled difficult situations.
* Participated in formal and informal public relations meetings.

*Training*

* Trained and motivated staff of with full time telephone transcribers. Trained temp staff of 30 during rush seasonal work loads.
* Rewrote department training procedures and protocol manuals.

**EDUCATION:** County Community College, Monticello, NY - Business Administration
*Phi Sigma Omicron National Honor Society*

Trenton State College, Wayne, NJ - B.A. Degree

Professional Seminars in Customer Service, Communication, Management

NASD #7 License Program, Certified

**68**

**Combination.** *Vivian Belen, Fair Lawn, New Jersey*

The Profile calls attention to the individual's skills; the Experience section indicates the person's achievements. A series of italic subheadings in the left column focus on special accomplishments.

## HELEN M. DAVIS

465 Williams Court, Norwood, OH 00000

(555) 555-5555

### OBJECTIVE

Administrative management position involving accounting support, staff supervision and customer service.

### EXPERIENCE

**CARLETON DISTRIBUTING, INC.**, Cincinnati, OH 1985 to Present

*One of the nation's largest paperback book wholesalers to the retail marketplace, serving accounts that include Wal-Mart and Pennywise stores.*

*Held positions of: **Manager, Accounts Payable Department** (since 1991); promoted from **Distribution/ Customer Service Supervisor** (1986-91) and **Order Taker** (1985-86).*

### SKILLS AND ACCOMPLISHMENTS

**Direct interface with President and CEO.**

★ Entrusted and empowered to make daily decisions of a consequential nature for the company's benefit.

**Ability to create order from chaos.**

★ Took a badly run and neglected department and after only three months, organized filing system, brought accounts up to date, and kept the operation running smoothly thereafter.

**Multi-talented and adaptable to changing work environments.**

★ Built accounts payable department during company's expansion from having sole responsibility to taking charge over a staff of three. Performed diversified duties simultaneously while maintaining focus under the pressures of an increased workload.

**Encourage a participative management style and team approach to problem solving.**

★ With hands-on involvement and understanding of all processes, hired a loyal and dedicated staff who work well together. Defined each job in the department, delegated duties and set priorities. As a result, improved productivity and quality of output as well as enhanced employee morale.

**Strong aptitude for detail intensive numerical work, particularly involving opportunities to recover lost profits.**

★ Handled 40-50 vendor accounts monthly, some with a hundred or more individual line items. Checked for appropriate deductions, returns, chargebacks or discounts for special incentives. Prepared net monthly payments totalling $6-7 million. Brought many accounts current for the first time in the history of the company. Identified and claimed over $90,000 in unapplied credits that were over five years old.

**Represent company with courtesy and professionalism under difficult circumstances.**

★ Responded to suppliers' requests for payment, frequently having to convey negative information without resorting to dishonesty. This has resulted in retention of good business relationships and credibility with all accounts. Also provided account status and problem solving support for a national sales force of 75.

**Proactive change agent with foresight to identify operational weaknesses and prevent their recurrence.**

★ In an area never before addressed, created and implemented warehouse procedures for receipt of returned merchandise. This established control over receiving paperwork to prove delivery in disputes of significant monetary value.

**Computer literate in both PC and on-line systems.**

★ Utilized Excel and Word for Windows as well as Access database for the entry and maintenance of financial data and correspondence. Worked with controller and systems analyst to modify applications for automated vendor tracking system on AS/400 computer using Alliance software customized for the publishing industry.

### EDUCATION

Completed 85 credits toward B.S. in Business Administration, Foxcroft College, Cleveland, OH.

69

**Combination.** *Melanie A. Noonan, West Paterson, New Jersey*

Statements with boldfacing draw the reader's attention to the individual's skills. Star bullets point to significant achievements. A tasteful thin-thick line divides the contact information at the top.

# MATT S. PETERS

**196 Swed Circle**
**Yorktown Heights, NY 10598**
**(914) 962-1997**

**OBJECTIVE**

A Financial Management position in the consumer goods industry which will utilize my manufacturing background, expertise in accounting and financial analysis and benefit from my successful, results-oriented track record.

**SUMMARY**

- More than six years experience in ***Operations Finance*** and ***Accounting*** with increasing responsibilities relating to: **General Ledger** and **Consolidations Accounting**, **Financial Planning** and **Reporting**, **Overhead Budgeting**, **Cost Analysis**, and **Capital Budgeting.**
- **Demonstrated expertise** in ***annual*** and ***strategic planning***; proven ability to ***manage key business opportunities*** and risks while consistently meeting deadlines.
- Substantial **hands-on experience** in the **implementation** and **management** of **state-of-the-art information systems,** ***supporting major business initiatives.***
- Organized, take-charge finance professional with exceptional follow-through abilities and excellent ***time management*** and ***cost containment skills.***
- ***High caliber*** interpersonal ***communication*** and ***presentation skills***; proven ability to **work well with** both **individuals** and **teams**, employing ***TQM*** principles.
- Computer Literate; significant hands-on expertise using the following Information Systems: Lotus 1-2-3, Harvard Graphics, Micro Control (LAN), M&D F/A System, System W, Masterpiece G/L System, Microsoft: Word, Excel, Powerpoint & Access, WordPerfect, Commander Prism, DBase, and Paradox.

**PERFORMANCE PROFILE**

- Significant experience in **Accounting**, **Operations Finance**, and **Financial Systems.**
- Demonstrated proficiency in preparing capital and material requirements plans.
- ***Successfully*** **manage project timetables** while **monitoring key performance indicators.**
- Expertise in **Asset Management**, and **Demand Planning**.

**EXPERIENCE**
April 1991 - Present

**KRAFT GENERAL FOODS USA, OPERATIONS AND TECHNOLOGY DIVISION,** White Plains, NY
**Fast-track promotions through a series of increasingly responsible Analytical and Financial Management positions.**

**Assistant Manager:** Capital & Productivity Group August 1993-Present

- **Manage $76M Capital Expenditure** budget for four divisions. Develop, prioritize, and evaluate capital programs which support ***profit increasing***, and ***strategic marketing initiatives.***
- ***Control $15M*** of P&L impacts of capital (start-up costs, expense portion of capital, disposals, and first year depreciation).
- Act as financial liaison between division HQ and eleven manufacturing sites: apprise management of plan performance; provide input in capital planning forums, and identify opportunities/risks and funding resources.
- ***Orchestrated procedural re-design*** of capital authorization process ***slashing process from six weeks to two.***
- ***Instrumental*** in the ***TQM development*** of a greatly improved capital\productivity tracking system.
- Supervise/oversee daily activities of a financial analyst; direct activities of accounting/analytical staff at multiple manufacturing sites.
- ***Credited*** with pulling together the 1995 ***OB Capital plan***; ***$200M.***

**70**

**Combination.** *Mark D. Berkowitz, Yorktown Heights, New York*

The writer of this resume likes to use boldface, bold italic, underlining, and bold underlining to direct the reader's eye to key words and phrases. Such a technique is helpful to readers who are

**MATT S. PETERS** ***page 2***

**EXPERIENCE**

*Continued*

**Financial Associate:** Manufacturing Cost Group September 1992-August 1993

- **Conducted major analyses** for management, i.e. facility shutdown study, lease vs. buy and historical cost profiles.
- ***Spearheaded*** a **$20M repair/maintenance cost breakdown analysis** resulting in a ***20% cost reduction*** and a **first year savings** of ***$1.6M***
- **Performed needs analyses** related to information requests. Evaluate needs/costs prior to making recommendations regarding product sourcing.
- ***Served*** as ***Plant Analyst for two manufacturing facilities***, developing O.B.'s, and revised forecasts concerning variable, fixed, raw and packaging material estimates.

**Senior Financial Analyst:** Planning & Reporting February 1992-September 1992

- **Developed time tables** and standardized reporting requirements for O & T headquarter units and plants.
- Prepared internal monthly management reports and various FP&A reports.

**Financial Analyst:** Overhead Budgeting Analysis April 1991-February 1992

- ***Developed*** annual ***operating budgets*** totaling **$150M** for Operations headquarter units.
- ***Monitored*** and reported variances of ***headquarter budgets***: ***productivity*** performance and ***headcount*** variances.

May 1988 - April 1991

**KRAFT GENERAL FOODS INTERNATIONAL, CORPORATE ACCOUNTING,** Rye Brook, NY

**Promoted through a series of accounting and analytical positions.**

**Senior Accounting Analyst:** World Trade/Latin American Group September 1989-April 1991

- **Developed and implemented** all cost center budgets for Latin American units.
- ***Credited with recovering*** in ***excess of $1M*** in ***outstanding receivables*** from international clients.

**Accounting Analyst:** Consolidations May 1988-September 1989

- Consolidated P&L and balance sheet data of international units and performed ***cash flow*** analyses.

**EDUCATION**

**PACE UNIVERSITY - LUBIN SCHOOL,** White Plains, NY
**Masters of Business Administration** 1992
**Major:** ***Finance***

**IONA COLLEGE**, New Rochelle, NY
**Bachelor of Business Administration** 1988
**Major:** ***Finance***

in a hurry and might be inclined to skip over whole passages. If you skim over the resume and read just the enhanced text, you gain a strong impression of the candidate without reading every word. The interruption of the border by the name is distinctive. Work is continuous from May 1988.

**JUDITH B. GINSBERG**

36 Bond Street
Bridgewater, NJ 08807
(201) 581-3758 (w)
(908) 231-0185 (h)

**SUMMARY OF QUALIFICATIONS**

Motivated, energetic, professional advocate for the deaf community. Continuously educates the public and corporations on the hearing impaired through role model behavior and public appearances. Contributes significantly to the community and associations for the hearing impaired.

**PROFESSIONAL ACCOMPLISHMENTS**

- Demonstrated AT&T equipment at the National Special Needs Center at the Telecommunications Deaf Incorporated (TDI) Convention.
- Delivered public speaking appearances for the hearing ear dog.
- Counseled hearing impaired children and their parents on how to compensate for hearing impairment.
- Translated senior management speech into American Sign Language.
- Trained Phone Center Store representatives on special needs equipment for convention exhibit.
- Participated in Job Accommodations Specialist Training seminar.
- Delivered workshops on Consumer Products that are compatible with hearing aids.
- Created Hearing Aid Compatible display for Phone Center Stores.

**AFFILIATIONS AND OFFICES HELD**

- Treasurer: Garden State Chapter, Association for Late Deafened Adults (ALDA)
  Member: National Chapter
- Business Manager: Employee Technical Advisory Panel (ETAP)
- Northwest Jersey Association of the Deaf (NWJAD)
- Self Help for the Hard of Hearing (SHHH) Member: National, NYC and Westchester chapters

**PROFESSIONAL EXPERIENCE**

**AT&T** **1983 - present**

***Promoted to positions with increasing responsibilities and ongoing professional development.***

**Assistant Staff Manager - Lease Asset Specialist** **1995 - present**

Consumer Products

- Serves as subject matter expert for various departments to develop products for the hearing impaired.
- Represented Consumer Products and demonstrated products at IDEAL (Individuals With Disabilities: Enabling Advocacy Link) Convention.
- Served as member of *Take Our Daughters to Work Committee* and delivered workshop for students on being hearing impaired in a hearing world.
- Conducts Inventory Management of leased telephones and ancillary products.
- Obtains and analyzes reports from Lease Products Availability, Inventory Purchases, new products, and repairs to initiate Forecasting and Production planning.

**71**

**Combination.** *Fran Kelley, Waldwick, New Jersey*

An easy-to-read resume with centered headings, unifying bullets, and adequate white space. The left-aligned contact information provides ample white space at the beginning of the resume, and

**JUDITH B. GINSBERG** page 2

---

**Assistant Staff Manager - Consumer Lease Services** **1991 - 1995**
Consumer Products

- Reduced costs $300,000.00 per year through initiation of a ram-bundling procedure for billing inserts.
- Developed and delivered an innovative sensitivity package and audiotape to over 300 Phone Center Stores to promote better understanding of the hearing impaired customer. (Tape allows a hearing person to hear what a hearing impaired person hears.)
- Designed store signage and recommended equipment for testing by hearing impaired customers.
- Developed a system for reporting defective vendor inserts that resulted in cost rebates for the client.
- Developed monthly program usage inventory reports.
- Managed monthly marketing programs using the equipment bill envelope for all lease and direct marketing clients.
- Implemented monthly programs to provide instruction on cycle, pocket, priority and quantities for monthly usage.
- Monitored the preparation and data generation of cycle reports (percentage forecasting of bar-codes to actual usage.)
- Prepared monthly delivery schedule for tracking due dates and accuracy of insert shipments to the Bill Print Center for 22,000,00 inserts per month.
- Resolved sudden and unexpected program changes by quickly developing and supplying new procedural instructions.

**Associate Manager - Financial Planning & Analysis** **1989 - 1991**
Communication Services

- Promoted to compile financial data for use by senior management.
- Converted data from one system to another.

**Reports Clerk** **1985 - 1989**
End User Organization

- Promoted to provide financial analysis reports for budget analysts for monthly book close.
- Collected financial information for use in special projects.

**Word Processor** **1983 - 1985**
Support Services

- Provided office support for intercompany client groups.
- Edited and proofread Tariff documents.

---

**EDUCATION**
AA , Accounting, Collegiate Business Institute

**LANGUAGES**
Total Communication - fluent; American Sign Language - some knowledge

**COMPUTER SKILLS**
LOTUS, Freelance, Focus, Word 6.0, Excel

the centered information about Education, Languages, and Computer Skills supplies extra white space at the end. Under each position in the Professional Experience section is a subheading (Consumer Products, Communication Services, etc.) that indicates the key area of activity.

# JEREMY R. JAMISON

**16 Westervelt Lane**
**Barrister, NJ 88888**
**(999) 555-5555**

## SUMMARY

**EXPERIENCED AUTO BODY SHOP MANAGER** with a 20-year background in the auto body industry. Strong combination of business management and technical skills. Expertise in business start-up and development, operations management, customer service, staff supervision and training, employee relations, and cash management. Committed to quality workmanship and ethical conduct.

## TECHNICAL PROFICIENCY / CERTIFICATION

- Skilled in general body work, unibody repair, and welding.
- Strong paint preparation / painting background and experience with Glasuriut, Diamont, and Sikkens paint systems.
- Knowledge of full range of body shop equipment and equipment operation.
- I-CAR Airbag and ABS Certification, 1994
- I-CAR Certification, 1993

## MANAGEMENT EXPERIENCE

**BODY SHOP MANAGER, Cranmoor Collision, New York, NY** 1992 - Present
Manage all aspects of this quality, high-volume production shop with annual revenues of $1.3 million. Oversee general auto body and major collision repairs on late model vehicles, from economy cars to $100,000+ luxury sedans. Concurrently function as body shop manager, paint department foreman, and quality control manager; supervise a staff of eight technicians. Scope of responsibility includes staffing, client relations, scheduling, estimating, parts ordering, troubleshooting, and cash management.

- Played a major role in business start-up and expansion; collaborated with owner in converting a parking garage into a highly profitable, well-organized, and fully equipped shop, handling over 85 car repairs each month and generating over $110,000 in monthly revenues.
- Developed a large repeat and referral business with numerous high-profile clients.
- Recruited and retained an expert multicultural staff in an industry known for high turnover; retained entire technical staff for over 3-1/2 years.
- Set up an automated estimating and parts management system (Autoquote / Mitchell Data).
- Established solid business relationships with over 30 vendors.

**BODY SHOP FOREMAN, Classic Auto Body, Dumont, NJ** 1991
Supervised five body shop technicians in this high-volume, 18-employee business generating over $2.8 million in annual revenues. Scheduled and oversaw repairs on 100+ cars / month, with a major focus on quality control. Related with insurance companies on projects.

## RELATED EXPERIENCE

**HEAVY COLLISION TECHNICIAN, Jon Craig Auto Body, South Sands, NJ** 1992
Restored cars to pre-accident condition for this busy auto body shop. Performed body work, unibody repair, welding, paint preparation, and painting; gained experience with various paint systems.

**SALES REPRESENTATIVE, Auto Liner Co., NJ / PA / MD / New England** 1983 - 1990
Promoted state-of-the-art unibody frame repair equipment throughout the Northeast. Conducted demonstrations for owners, managers, and technicians. Managed entire sales process from cold-calling to closing sales and providing regular follow-up. Trained technicians at client sites in use of equipment. Generated over $750,000 in annual sales.

**HEAVY COLLISION SUBCONTRACTOR, Steve's Auto Body, Clark, NJ** 1979 - 1983
Achieved recognition as one of the best heavy collision experts in the area, within three years. Gained extensive experience in body work, unibody repair, and welding. Emphasized to owner the importance of delivering quality service, leading to a 30 percent increase in client base. Advanced rapidly from entry-level helper to high caliber technician.

## PROFESSIONAL DEVELOPMENT / EDUCATION

Completed workshops in Shop Productivity, Estimating, Wheel Alignment, and Communication.
Attended Davis and Elkins College, Elkins, WV.

72

**Combination.** *Rhoda Kopy, Toms River, New Jersey*

The individual's name in bold caps, followed by a partial horizontal line, establishes the style for the headings. Positions are in all-uppercase letters as well. The result is a strong resume.

# JACK L. SMITHERS

5342 S.W. 162nd | Aloha, Oregon 97007 | (503) 649-2709

**BACKGROUND SUMMARY**

Service-oriented body shop manager with 15+ years of experience. Committed to high standards of excellence in workmanship and customer service.

- Up-to-date knowledge of auto industry trends, high-tech equipment and environmental regulations.
- Thoroughly familiar with staff certification and training requirements.
- Experienced in using computers for parts tracking, estimating, billing and body shop operations.
- Profit-conscious manager with successful experience in marketing, new business development and customer relations.

CERTIFICATIONS - ASE Certified Auto Painting & Body Repair . . . Certified Collision Damage Repair and Refinishing . . . PPG Certified Deltron Advanced Refinishing and Color Adjustment . . . CCC Advanced Collision Computer Estimating Certified . . . General Motors Corporation: STG Certified; HVLP; Base Coat/Clear Coat & Color Tinting and Adjustment . . . Allstate Pro Shop Certificate in Customer Satisfaction.

**EXPERIENCE**

HILLSBORO CHEVROLET INC. - Hillsboro, Oregon

**Auto Body Shop Manager** (5/90-Present)

Manage body shop operations for this Allstate direct repair shop; also complete warranty work and body/paint projects for commercial trucks and RVs. Oversee office staff and supervise eight technicians; organize work flow to maximize productivity.

*Accomplishments:* Developed marketing campaigns (targeted toward insurance companies) that increased gross sales from $57,000 to $78,000 and resulted in substantial improvements in customer service. Trimmed material expenses by over 30%.

GLADSTONE FORD - Gladstone, Oregon

**Auto Painter** (3/92-5/90)

Hired, trained and supervised two assistant painters. Delegated assignments, ordered materials and maintained supply inventory.

J&J AUTO SALES - Prineville, Oregon

**Shop Manager** (4/90-2/92)

Managed shop operations and ensured high quality of all painting/body work projects. Supervised three technicians and one shop assistant; coordinated work flow and purchased materials. Reduced costs by continually monitoring expenses.

PORTLAND AUTO BODY - Portland, Oregon

**Owner / Manager** (3/80-4/90)

Built business into a profitable enterprise with a staff of eight. Managed shop operations, hired/trained technicians and maintained positive relations with customers.

**EDUCATION**

PORTLAND COMMUNITY COLLEGE - Portland, Oregon

**Auto Collision Estimating** (1995)

CASPER COLLEGE - McMinnville, Oregon

**Business Administration / Marketing** (50 credit hours, 1990-93)

73

**Combination.** *Pat Kendall, Aloha, Oregon*

A resume for a blue-collar manager. Ellipses (. . .) in Certifications paragraph save space. Experience section stresses management skills; accomplishments are in a separate paragraph.

# Marketing Consumer Lending
## Mortgage Loan Processing
## Client/Customer Relations

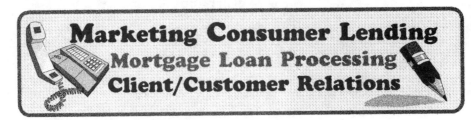

**Melissa Merrill**
1400 W. 700 S.
Pendleton, IN 46000
**(317) 778-0000**

**Major Achievement:**

Handled marketing for a new credit union branch opening, including TV commercial coordination, opening and reception. First year generated $3 million per month in CU business in gaining new client base.

**Professional Experience:**

<u>Assistant Branch Manager</u> Sep 1995-Mar 1996

*Star Financial Bank, Pendleton.* Processed mortgage loans, consumer loans, scheduled tellers, conducting training, and supervised branch in the absence of the branch manager.

<u>Mortgage Officer</u> Feb 1993-Mar 1995

*AGE Federal Credit Union, Albany, GA.* Approved all mortgage loans & construction loans, approved consumer loans, credit cards, etc. Interviewed clients. Managed processors, handled public relations with Realtors and builders.

<u>Mortgage Administrative Assistant</u> 1989-1993

*AGE Federal Credit Union.* Processed all first and second mortgages. Handled client interviews and processed all applications. Arranged for appraisals, title searches and issued loans. Handled security deeds.

Previously served as Loan Processing Supervisor and Student Loan Supervisor with management of employees and consumer lending. *Term of employment with AGE totals approximately 10 years, starting in 1985.*

Note: Previously served, also, as a mortgage service representative with Georgia Federal, Albany, GA 1981-85.

---

**Education:**

Continuing education at St. Louis University, consumer lending; CUNA Training School, mortgage loans; STAR Member Services, consumer lending.

- **"Outstanding performance...have worked diligently and shown (the) desire.."**
  —Outstanding Employee Award
- **Numerous letters of commendation.**
- **American Cancer Society; Eastern Star; Clean-Up America Committee; Pendleton Lion's Club.**

74

**Chronological.** *Jon C. Shafer, Anderson, Indiana*

Another resume with experimental clip art. Rounded, shaded rectangular boxes show areas of expertise and contact information. The bulleted items make a strong ending. A balanced design.

## ROBERT W. PALMER

**(616) 555-5678**

**413 Woodfield Circle, #2**
**Kalamazoo, Michigan 49079**

**QUALIFICATIONS**

| | | |
|---|---|---|
| **Personnel Management** | **Employee Relations & Issues** | **Compensation Administration** |
| **Organizational Behavior** | **Production & Quality Control** | **Small Business Management** |
| **Team / Consensus Building** | **Scheduling / Work Delegation** | **Group Presentation Skills** |
| **IBM & Macintosh Computers** | **Strategic / Logistics Planning** | **Business Law & Accounting** |

**EDUCATION**

**Bachelor of Business Administration,** 1992, WESTERN MICHIGAN UNIVERSITY, KALAMAZOO, MICHIGAN
Major: Management with Human Resource Concentration – Minors: Economics and General Business
Major GPA: **3.75 / 4.00** – Overall GPA: **3.61 / 4.00** – Graduated *cum laude*
Financed **100%** of my educational and living expenses

**Additional Training & Certifications**

Notary Public Certification ... Primary Leadership Development ... Total Quality Leadership ... Attrition Analysis & Management ... Principles of Banking & Branch Management ... Mutual Funds ... Analyzing Financial Statements ... Bank Investments & Funds Management ... Enrolled in Haworth Business College to pursue MBA in Finance (part-time basis).

**EXPERIENCE**

***Assistant Branch Manager I, Lending,*** *August 1994 to present*
*FIRST FEDERAL BANK OF SOUTHWEST MICHIGAN, KALAMAZOO, MICHIGAN*

- Manage office of eight tellers and one customer service representative to include training, scheduling, motivation, performance evaluations, and payroll.
- Interview and qualify loan applicants, preparing all supporting loan documentation.
- Prepare managerial reports in accordance with "Management Control" program.
- Establish staff sales goals and monitor progress of annual sales plan.
- Assist in the administration of established regulations, policies, and procedures.

***Management Trainee,*** *March 1992 to August 1994*
*GOLD BANK OF MICHIGAN, MATTAWAN, MICHIGAN*

- Provided recommendations regarding consumer loan requests, including setup of lending portfolios.
- Compiled statistical data and prepared branch productivity reports on a regular basis.
- Supervised project staff members in evaluating quality service delivery for management training program.
- Coordinated efforts between the Branch Network and Marketing Department during successful transition of "Number One" card to Visa debit card system.

***Armor Platoon Leader, Second Lieutenant,*** *July 1994 to present*
*MICHIGAN ARMY NATIONAL GUARD, CADILLAC, MICHIGAN*

- Train and supervise 15-member teams to ensure 100% mission readiness.
- Provide mentoring to junior leaders to enhance individual professional development.
- Prepare and coordinate short- and long-range training schedules to include logistical support.
- Accountable for millions of dollars in equipment to include quality control assurance standards.

***Career Counselor,*** *May 1991 to July 1994*
*MICHIGAN ARMY NATIONAL GUARD, JACKSON, MICHIGAN*

- Given personal responsibility for 150 individuals and overall growth responsibility for 600 soldiers.
- Provided career planning and attrition management training to personnel supervisors.

Previous employment: **Package Load Supervisor,** UPS (1992–1994); **Senior Customer Service Associate,** Montgomery Ward (1990–1992); and **Stinger Missile Section Sergeant,** U.S. Army (1985–1990). Additional details upon request.

**HONORS / AWARDS / MEMBERSHIPS**

Distinguished Honor Graduate, Officers Candidate School ... Honor Graduate, Army Leadership Development Course ... Non-Commissioned Officer of the Year ... Army Team Chief of the Year ... Phi Theta Kappa International Honor Society Member ... Phi Kappa Phi Scholastic Honor Society Member ... Beta Gamma Sigma Business Honor Society Member.

**75**

**Combination.** *Mary Roberts, Tarpon Springs, Florida*

The Qualifications section is flexible. It can be changed for different target industries or jobs, and it can include course work, skills, or experiences. The target field here is Human Resources.

**Peter J. Hopson**
3624 Grandview Blvd.
Flint, Michigan 48555
(810) 555-8548

## PROFILE

Seasoned administrator with thorough knowledge of the transportation industry.

## EMPLOYMENT HISTORY

Superior Automotive Operations, Inc. • Detroit, Michigan
(Doing business as Superior Auto Transit Inc./Quality Carriers Inc.)
**Branch Manager** - Detroit and Windsor Facilities (1985-1994)

- Maintained and directed fleet of 175-200 tractor trailer units and Teamster-affiliated drivers.
- Participated in labor negotiations.
- Monitored branch profitability.
- Supervised vehicle rail-loading and release operations.
- Calculated freight rates.
- Assured on-time delivery of vehicles.
- Oversaw safety management program.

Beckman Transport • Salerno, Ontario
(Division of Great Dane Truck Lines, Co., Ltd.)
**Operations Manager/Systems Coordinator** (1963-1984)

- Managed operations of six high volume freight terminals.
- Supervised 250-unit fleet, union-affiliated drivers and office staff.
- Developed familiarity with U.S. and Canadian customs procedures.
- Directed operational functions including dispatching, billing, and vehicle maintenance.
- Managed rate negotiations and claim dispositions with shippers.
- Monitored budget.

Thomas Transport Co. Ltd. • Toronto, Ontario
**Operations Manager** (1961-1963)

- Managed office and fleet operations.
- Maintained inventory control.
- Promoted from clerk position.

*Additional Background:* Immigrated to Canada in 1957 after completion of electrician apprenticeship and employment as journeyman in Germany.

## PROFESSIONAL AFFILIATIONS

Current or past member of:

- Wayne Co. Traffic Club, Board of Directors
- Traffic Club of Ontario
- Motor Vehicle's Safety Association of Toronto

## PROFESSIONAL DEVELOPMENT

Extensive training in:

- S.P.C. programs
- Human resource development
- Quality improvement process
- Labor negotiations
- Budgetary responsibility

## PERSONAL

- Married, no children
- Excellent health, no physical limitations
- Willing to relocate

76

**Combination.** *Janet L. Beckstrom, Flint, Michigan*

A resume for a retired worker with no formal education past high school. After the contact information, a pair of dual lines enclose the rest of the resume. Positions in boldface stand out.

# Heather L. Gifford

322 North Elm Street · White Cloud, Michigan 49349 · 616-689-5555

## CAREER OBJECTIVE

Professional Social Worker seeking to contribute comprehensive education, training, and experience to a challenging and rewarding position working with youths and their families in casework capacity.

## PROFESSIONAL QUALIFICATIONS

Caring and sympathetic to client needs. Dependable and reliable. Personable. Excellent rapport with county agencies, school officials, children and parents. Exceptional counseling skills. Self motivated and enthusiastic.

## EDUCATION

**Bachelor of Arts, Criminal Justice**, May 1994
Michigan State University, East Lansing, Michigan
Dean's List 4 Semesters

## PROFESSIONAL EXPERIENCE

**Case Manager**
*Bethany Christian Services*, Fremont, Michigan, May 1994 - present

- Provide individual and family crisis intervention and guidance for juveniles 10 - 20 years. Work with runaway and homeless teens offering counseling services and providing resources and information. Serve as advocate for clients in court and with community agencies. Document and update confidential records and participate in on-call rotation. Act as mentor.

**Juvenile Court Officer/Student Intern**
*Ingham County Probate Court*, Lansing, Michigan, Spring 1994

- Worked with severely neglected and abused youths and their families in the *Intensive Neglect Services Department*. Assisted in identifying the issues that each family needed to address. Assisted in developing and managing case service plans. Conducted case contacts to clients homes on a daily basis. Transport clients to and from various programs and appointments.
- Conducted case contacts to clients schools on a weekly basis for the *Delinquent Probation Department*. Assisted in writing investigative reports, reviewed summaries, and various court orders and petitions.

**Student Coordinator, Volunteer Probation Officer Program**
*Service Learning Center, MSU*, East Lansing, Michigan, 1992 - 1994

- Recruited, interviewed, trained, and supervised approximately 35 MSU student volunteers. Created and designed the first VPOP monthly newsletter. Planned and lead two reflection meetings. Worked in a professional relationship with the Ingham County Probate Court.
- As Student Volunteer, served as a positive role model in two one-on-one relationships. Obtained professional experience with confidentiality, responsibility and commitment to both the children and the court.

77

**Combination.** *Patricia L. Nieboer, Fremont, Michigan*

The contact information, section headings, and Education data are centered in this resume. A thick-thin line divides the contact information. Work sites are indented from positions held.

**KAREN CROSBY, R.N., B.S.N., C.C.M.**
**16 Brooksweld Road**
**Canton Massachusetts 02021**
**(617) 828-3587**

**PROFESSIONAL SUMMARY:**

**Certified Case Manager** with 20 years professional experience as Clinic Administrator, Quality/Patient Care Coordinator and Nurse Liaison specializing in clinical assessment of catastrophic cases for rehabilitation, subacute, and skilled nursing facilities. Coordinates the delivery of services to patients and families, manages the financial resources of the patient assuring cost effectiveness of treatment, facilitates and monitors the discharge planning process, and serves as patient and family advocate to coordinate and direct effective communication regarding patient's care. Demonstrates creativity, initiative and sound problem-solving skills to meet challenges of changing health care environment.

**PROFESSIONAL HIGHLIGHTS:**

- Established 15 bed skilled nursing center and coordinated admission process with 40 bed rehabilitation center. Developed and implemented policies and procedures, quality assurance and utilization review programs. Hired and educated staff; developed criteria through interdisciplinary team approach.
- Developed and implemented an HMO/PPO health network. Conducted concurrent review of inpatient hospitalization and discharge planning. Established and monitored Medical Staff Credentialling Committee.
- Evaluated and assessed all inpatient admissions at St. John's Episcopal Hospital for Quality Assurance and Utilization Review. Served on Newborn and Premature Service/Prenatal Committee and Newborn and Premature Record Screening Committee.
- Instrumental in preparing Healthsource Rehabilitation Hospital for successful JCAHO Certification. Chosen as facility's first nurse/liaison to assess patients and coordinate all aspects of admission.
- Developed and implemented an orientation program for nursing; conducted monthly in-services programs; chaired Peer Review Committee.

**PROFESSIONAL EXPERIENCE:**

**HEALTHSOURCE REHABILITATION CENTER**, Stoughton, MA 1993 - Present
Rehabilitation Case Manager/Nurse Liaison
Developed and implemented admissions process; assessed rehabilitation, skilled nursing, subacute patients for admission, focusing on Integrated Program Model approach.

**MEMORIAL HOSPITAL**, Cambridge, MA 1991 - 1992
Special Procedures/Recovery Room Nurse
Admitted and monitored patients in preoperative holding area. Assessed discharges and admissions to hospital.

**ST. JOSEPH HOSPITAL**, Providence, RI 1989 - 1991
Internal Case Manager/Nurse Liaison
Performed case management and marketing of rehabilitation and skilled nursing units. Evaluated and assessed rehabilitation potential through concurrent review and physical examination.

**78**

**Combination.** *Cheryl A. Harland, The Woodlands, Texas*

A double horizontal line is a header line on both pages. An additional line on page one is interrupted by the phone number to call attention to it. Section headings stacked in the left

**KAREN CROSBY, R.N., C.C.M.** **PAGE TWO**

---

**PROFESSIONAL EXPERIENCE:** (Cont'd.)

**HEALTHSOURCE REHABILITATION CENTER**, Stoughton, MA 1988 - 1989
Nurse Educator/Nurse Liaison
Evaluated and assessed patients to determine rehabilitation potential. Conducted hospital-wide orientation programs and in-service nursing education programs.

**TRAVELERS HEALTH NETWORK**, Providence, RI 1987 - 1988
Internal Case Manager/Patient Care Coordinator
Performed concurrent review of inpatient hospitalization and discharge planning. Oriented physicians and hospital staff to policies and procedures of HMO/PPO.

**ST. JOHN'S EPISCOPAL HOSPITAL**, Newport, RI 1986
Quality Assurance Coordinator
Screened 100% of inpatient admissions for Quality Assurance and Utilization Review.

**KELSEY-SEYBOLD CLINIC**, Providence, RI 1984 - 1986
Clinic Administrator
Provided leadership and guidance to staff on daily clinical operations.

**NORTHEAST MEDICAL CENTER**, Newport, RI 1980 - 1984
Intensive Care Nurse
Assisted in 10 bed surgical intensive care unit - Multiple Trauma, Emergency Room, and Medical Intensive Care Rotation.

**EDUCATION:**

University of Massachusetts
Boston, Massachusetts
**B.S.**, Nursing 1975

**CERTIFICATIONS:**

Certified Case Manager 1994
Registered Nurse in Rhode Island and Massachusetts

**TEACHING AFFILIATION:**

Massachusetts Community College
Nurse/Health Aide course approved by the Massachusetts Education Agency

**PROFESSIONAL AFFILIATIONS:**

Case Managers Society of America
American Association of Rehabilitation Nurses
- National and Northeast Chapters

President, New England Medical Center Neurological Nurses Society
Massachusetts Head Injury Association - Board Member
Continuity of Care - Northeast Chapter
Northeast Insurance Association

---

column make this resume one that could be made as a 3-column, 1-row table without lines, where the section headings are in the first column, the narrow second column is left empty, and the main information is in the third column. Word wrapping and pressing Enter push the single row down the page.

**JOSEPH L. GUSKA**
99 Oak Drive
Melbourne, FL 32934
(407) 555-5275

**OBJECTIVE**

To examine further opportunities in Professional Management within a compatible forward-looking organization.

**SUMMARY OF QUALIFICATIONS**

- Experienced in executive level City Administration (Assistant City Management)
- Experienced in upper level County Government Management (DPW Director)
- Creative abilities in operational procedures
- Substantial General Management Experience -- Service and Heavy Industry
- Successful in grant applications
- Skilled in budgeting, forecasting, business planning, and revenue maximization
- Experienced in Plant Maintenance Supervision; ability to effectively determine labor, parts, and equipment needs; ability to train, motivate, and direct employees
- Background in Labor Relations and Supervision of hourly and salaried professional personnel
- Marketing experience, including Administrative Work Flow Analysis
- Self-Motivated; Adaptable; Operations Oriented; Excellent Leadership and Management

**MEMBERSHIP**

- American Public Works Association
- International City Management Association
- Florida City & County Management Association
- Brevard County City Managers Association

**PROFESSIONAL PROFILE**

CITY OF COCOA, Cocoa, Florida — 10/94 to Present
**Assistant City Manager** - (10/94 to Present)
Responsible for management of Information Systems, Facilities Maintenance, Fleet Maintenance, Public Information Office, Engineering and Public Works departments. Manage $14.2 Million combined budget. Also handle special projects for the City Manager and act as the City Manager during his absence.

**Public Works Director** - (09/91 to 10/94)
Directed the City's Engineering, Traffic, Transportation, Recycling, CIP and road and drainage maintenance efforts. Responsible for approximately $6.6 Million budget and approximately 95 employees.

ORANGE COUNTY GOVERNMENT, Orange County, FL — 06/87 to 09/91
**Manager -- Department of Public Works**
Responsible for the management functions within the Public Works Department of planning, organizing, controlling, and leading. Manage the County-wide Transportation Management Program consisting of: pavement management, capital improvement planning, maintenance operations, related budgets (currently $6.6 million). Responsible for development and operation of the Public Works Department in relation to organizing and implementing a Work Management System. Responsible to citizens and other user Departments in a positive team environment.

continued

79

**Combination.** *Laura A. DeCarlo, Melbourne, Florida*

A resume for a person whose professional work history spanned 20+ years. The writer removed all irrelevant and old job positions and eliminated information in order to focus the resume.

**JOSEPH L. GUSKA** **Resume Page 2**

**PROFESSIONAL PROFILE continued**

**Assistant Manager -- Department of Public Works**
Manage the Road & Bridge Division and Community Relations as they pertain to Road & Bridge Operations. Responsible for day-to-day work planning, act as liaison to Fleet Maintenance. Perform ongoing analysis of administrative and operational work methods with regard to streamlining the work flow. Developed a Work Management Program to organize and utilize labor and materials more efficiently.

- Developed Five-Year Equipment Replacement Plan.
- Revised Departmental Cost Accounting Methods.
- Streamlined Payroll Internal Reporting.
- Selected and Implemented a Fleet Maintenance Analysis System.

GENERAL MOTORS CORPORATION, Central Foundry Division, Pontiac, MI 1979 to 1987
**General Supervisor -- Planning and Control Department** - (1984 to 05/87)
Directed the activities of eight salaried and three clerical personnel involved in the planning function for this large manufacturing complex. Held full profit and loss responsibility. Performed budget forecasting for materials and labor annual budget of $16 million and audited budget compliance. Involved in financial planning, cost estimating, and project cost control. Resolved scheduling conflicts between production departments and plant maintenance, and coordinated materials and job scope for major repairs or equipment maintenance. Devised long and short-range business plans and recommended enhancements to upper management. Served as liaison between U.A.W. and plant Labor Relations to investigate and resolve disputes.

**General Supervisor -- Plant Maintenance** - (1979 to 1984)
Managed service and repair of equipment for full product lines, including determining necessary parts, labor, and equipment for daily and major repairs. Directed efforts of eleven salaried supervisors and one hundred skilled trades people. Educated new supervisors in safety, product quality, cost control, and labor relations.

ROADWAY EXPRESS COMPANY, Toledo, OH 1977 to 1979
**Maintenance Supervisor**
Managed and organized the maintenance of highway tractors and trailers, in accordance with Department of Transportation standards and delivery and time constraints.

**EDUCATION**

**M.A. Degree, Business Management** - 1984
CENTRAL MICHIGAN UNIVERSITY, Mt. Pleasant, MI

**B.S. Degree, Finance/Economics** - 1975
DEFIANCE COLLEGE, Defiance, OH

Hanging indentation, in which all the information is tabbed past the section headings, makes them visible. The result is a resume whose overall arrangement can be seen at a glance. The writer used bullets in this resume to break up its length. Boldfacing helps positions stand out.

# Alan A. Aladin

0000 N. West Avenue
Anywhere, USA

Residence (000) 000-0000
Cellular (000) 000-0000

## Career Summary

Over twenty years of leadership experience in **GOVERNMENT ADMINISTRATION** and **MUNICIPAL OPERATIONS**, most recently as Director of Public Services and Interim City Manager for the City of Bilton with prior experience in Public Works with the County of Attowa. Additional business management experience in the private sector. Strengths include:

- Management/Administration
- Budgeting & Fiscal Management
- Project/Program/Department Management
- Marketing & Economic Development
- Public/Private Sector Alliances
- Staff Development/Empowerment

Effective communicator and team builder with ability to lead and inspire, reach consensus, and identify and attain goals. Held leadership roles in industry-related associations at the local, state, and national levels.

## Qualifications

**MANAGEMENT:** Proactive executive experienced in strategic planning, development, and management of diverse municipal departments. Made significant contributions impacting operational, budgetary, staffing, resource, and management needs. Prepared and controlled annual operating budgets of up to $22 million. Directly supervised up to 41 employees. *Contributions:*

- Envisioned and brought to fruition a business sense to government which, during my tenure, enabled general fund to increase from $3.2 to $32.6 million and the reserve fund from $870,000 to $11.5 million.
- Recruited, hired, and developed personnel into a strong, proactive, problem-solving management team.
- Introduced management concepts and strategies which created win/win partnerships with the community.

**ADMINISTRATION:** Served as Interim City Manager on several occasions for a city of 10,000. As Director of Public Services, directly supervise Directors of Public Works, Utilities, Planning, and Economic Development. Administered numerous projects, grants and joint ventures. *Contributions:*

- Held vital role in City development and expansion during a period of explosive growth and revitalization.
- Directed the City's recovery from a devastating earthquake ($51 million in damages); coordinated full-scale disaster response (demolition, new construction, public services, redevelopment).
- Initiated legislation to bring entire city under redevelopment status (without sharing tax increment with other agencies); lobbied for special bill to acquire an additional $5.1 million in state disaster assistance.

**ECONOMIC DEVELOPMENT:** Supported a strong public/private partnership toward diversified growth and prosperity in difficult economic times. Sourced and conducted negotiations with new industries. Created assessment districts and other financing vehicles for public improvements. *Contributions:*

- Planned and achieved economic diversification from a sole-source to a multi-faceted economy, generating $255+ million in new development and stimulating a population growth from 4,800 to 10,000.
- Attracted new industry, in one instance alone creating 1,100 new jobs in the $50,000 salary range.
- Encouraged economic development which supported $57 million in new construction (1,271 SF/MF units).
- Structured two new apartment complex projects which will generate $1.3 million in tax increment over 20 years, with no cost basis to the City.

♦ ♦ ♦

80

**Functional.** *Susan Britton Whitcomb, Fresno, California*

No dates are given in this resume. Instead, a Career Summary calls attention to the individual's strengths and skills. The Qualifications section shows his achievements under three categories.

# Charles W. Broadway

2000 Victoria Boulevard
Sandhurst, Alabama 36100
[555] 555-5555

*Transformed my people from computer phobics to PC wizards!*
*– Pharmacy Manager*

*Best trouble shooter I've ever seen.*
*– Network Administrator*

*A valuable addition to our computer teaching staff.*
*– Director of Adult Education*

*Got our data base talking to our word processor after two others had tried and failed.*
*– Office Manager*

**Objective:** As computer systems administrator, to provide comprehensive, high-quality support to meet the needs of a growing firm.

**Profile:** ◆ Solves complex problems ◆ Translates needs into systems that deliver results fast ◆ Cares enough to be sure they work right the first time ◆ Enjoys helping people be more productive ◆ Excellent trouble shooter ◆ Can assemble systems from parts

**Record of Achievement:**

**TURNING URGENT NEEDS INTO CAPABLE SYSTEMS:** Planned and set up all computer support for new pharmacy outlet. Chosen to resolve conflicting communications, civil engineering and data automation priorities.

***Results:*** Face-to-face meetings with all contractors turned friction into teamwork. Revised plan allows for growth without extra cost. New facility helps handle 3,300 prescriptions a day and meets critical accuracy standards.

**PROVIDING SYSTEMS THAT WORK RIGHT THE FIRST TIME:** Found bottlenecks that crippled our ability to serve customers quickly and accurately. My recommendations to upgrade hardware, software and procedures accepted by senior manager without change.

***Results:*** Printing time cut by 30 percent. Clerks saving 20,000 keystrokes a week. Waiting time dropped from seven minutes to a few seconds for each transaction. Downtime cut from hours a month to 30 minutes in three years. Total cost for upgrade: $600.

**SERVING THE USER:** Designed, validated and installed automated voice system a major hospital uses to track 15,000 prescriptions a week. Customers now call 24 hours a day to order medicine and know exactly when their prescriptions will be ready.

***Results:*** Hundreds of man hours saved. Customers love it. Employee morale jumped.

**Work History**

- Pharmacy Computer Systems Manager: Connelly Air Force Base, Iowa (Mar 91 - Present)
- Pharmacy Technician: Connelly Air Force Base, Iowa (Feb 90 - Present)
- Computer Sales Associate: Techno Masters, Miami, Florida (Jul 89 - Dec 89)

**Education:** B.S., Central University (**Business** minor), Spring 94

81

**Combination.** *Donald P. Orlando, Montgomery, Alabama*

A resume for a person leaving the Air Force. The Profile indicates his skills for civilian work. He has had no experience in his target field, but the testimonials show that he is a "gifted amateur."

**LAWRENCE STEIN**
5516 Tree Lane • Kent, New Jersey 00000
**Tel: 555-555-5555 • Email: xxxxxxxxx@aol.com**

**TECHNOLOGY MANAGEMENT**

*Delivering Technology Solutions to Improve Organizational Productivity and Efficiency:*

**Applications Development & Management**
**Client / Server Architecture**
**Remote Access Systems**
**Business Process Re-engineering**
**LAN / WAN Technologies**
**Customer Support & Training**

**PROFILE SUMMARY**

Accomplished, results-oriented technology professional with expertise in leading the design, development and implementation of leading-edge systems • Adept in evaluating critical business needs and developing creative solutions to improve performance • A strong team player with outstanding communication skills and the ability to build consensus • An effective manager in developing, training and leading technical staffs to achieve peak productivity • Solid record for commitment to superior customer service and support.

**PROFESSIONAL EXPERIENCE**

**ABC INSURANCE COMPANY (1969-1996)**

**MANAGER, APPLIED TECHNOLOGY GROUP** - Broadway, New Jersey (1994-1996)
Promoted to head group that designed, developed and implemented Network and Client/Server solutions in support of corporate compliance initiatives. Developed and directed team of 25 programmers, systems and business analysts. Served on software selection committee.

- ***Implemented national WAN with remote access capabilities for 400 users.***
- ***Aided company in rectifying and preventing future multi-million dollar compliance penalties.***
- ***Initiated customer support programs including hotline, help desk and user training.***
- ***Partnered with users to design, develop and implement numerous Client/Server applications.***
- ***Led introduction of Windows NT within company.***
- ***Assumed key role in formalizing telecommuting program for Broadway office.***
- ***Served on committee to develop plans for corporate-wide consumer complex data base.***

**SENIOR PROJECT MANAGER** - New York, New York and Bridgewater, New Jersey (1987-1994)
Managed 15 programmers, systems and business analysts in development and implementation of system modifications for Commission Payroll operations.

- ***Saved over $2 million annually through staff reductions while maintaining productivity.***
- ***Modernized payroll system, reducing staff and lead time required for system modifications.***
- ***Led task force in developing one of first laser check printing applications.***
- ***Led development efforts for one of first EFT arrangements for a commission payroll in the nation.***
- ***Pioneered introduction of PC technology, Windows applications and training courses for users, improving efficiency and morale.***
- ***Created communication tools to inform sales staff of important changes and their impact, dramatically improving customer satisfaction.***

82

**Combination.** *Alesia Benedict, Rochelle Park, New Jersey*

A double-line page border and centered contact information, headings, and Technical Skills and Education sections are evident design and layout features. The Technology Management section

**LAWRENCE STEIN**
**Tel: 555-555-5555 • Email: xxxxxxxxx@aol.com**
**Page Two**

**ABC INSURANCE COMPANY experience continued...**

**PROJECT MANAGER, CENTURY 21 INSURANCE** - New York, New York (1985-1987)
Spearheaded corporate initiative to provide administrative support for new insurance distribution system. Provided supervision to staff of 10 business and systems analysts.

- ***Ensured successful, on-time opening of new administrative support office.***
- ***Coordinated implementation of system and procedural changes to accommodate unique requirements of new office.***

**PROJECT MANAGER, COMMISSION COMPLEX** - New York, New York (1982-1985)
Directed up to 25 programmers and business analysts in designing and implementing new commission reporting and calculation systems to support corporate marketing strategies.

**PROJECT ASSISTANT** - New York, New York (1979-1982)
Supervised a team of 10 programmers in the development and implementation of one of the first CICS applications company-wide.

**PRIOR EXPERIENCE** includes increasingly responsible positions in Auditing and Systems support.

**TECHNICAL SKILLS**

SQL Server
Visual Basic
Powerbuilder
Windows NT, 95 and 3.1
IRMA Workstation for Windows
Microsoft Office, Access and RAS
Microfocus Workbench (COBOL and CICS)

**EDUCATION**

***B.A. in Economics / Concentrations in Accounting and Sociology***
Waynesburg College, Waynesburg, Pennsylvania

***Additional Seminars and Courses:***
Management • Programming • Systems Development • Negotiating Skills • Insurance

presents first a slogan-like statement in italic and then the person's fields of expertise. The Profile Summary indicates his skills. A tactic for the Professional Experience section is to explain responsibilities in a brief paragraph and then use diamond bullets to point to achievements.

# PATRICIA L. HALLOWELL

**4445 Lake Drive ◆ Tampa, Florida 33624 ◆ ( 813) 000-0000**

***CAREER SUMMARY***

Self-directed individual with diverse experience in ***customer relations, sales, diverse managerial functions (including project management), and computer programming/software applications.*** Articulate communicator, exhibiting strong analytical, presentation and organizational skills. Offer a conscientious work ethic and a demonstrated record of efficiency, reliability and commitment to job performance. Conversant with writing COBOL programs. Computer knowledge includes DOS, Windows, Microsoft, Electronic Data Interface, WordPerfect and Excel. Held interim positions during periods of home management.

***EDUCATION***

**M.S. Degree - Management** - Rensselaer Polytechnic Institute (1982)
**B.S. Degree - Mathematics** - Memphis State University *(Graduated Cum Laude)* (1968)
**Basic and Intermediate Accounting courses** - Middle Tennessee State University (1994)

***EMPLOYMENT HISTORY***

**MJT, INC.** - Brentwood, TN **1990 - 1996**
**Document Specialist**
- Tenure included 6-year contract assignment at ***General Electric Information Systems.*** Prepared and tested latest software releases of ANSI and Edifact standards affiliated with Electronic Data Interface (EDI). Utilized PC DOS/Windows applications for testing.

**NATIONAL BANK** - Nashville, TN **1989**
**Trust Department Accountant** (Part-time position)
- Coordinated preparation of Federal and State Tax Returns for 400 trust accounts. Reviewed and verified data from in-house and outside vendor computer reports.

**DISCOVERY TOYS** - Lexington, KY and Franklin, TN **1984 - 1987**
**Educational Sales Consultant**

**SOUTHERN NEW ENGLAND TELEPHONE COMPANY** - New Haven, CT **1976 - 1984**
***Self-motivation, initiative and high-level performance led to progressive promotions.***

**Account Executive** (1982-1984)
- Managed portfolio of 1,000 accounts equalling $7MM in revenue. Client base included small businesses, professionals and non-profit organizations.
- Performed cold calling and sales of Dimension and Horizon upgraded telephone systems; concurrently maintained customer relations.

**Project Manager** (1979-1982)
- Served as liaison to internal departments in conjunction with directing implementation of complex AT&T computer system (Camis) used to develop and administer $240M capital budget. Completed project on time and within budget.
- Designed and wrote computer graphics applications for DEC time share system utilized for capital budget analysis.
- Continued to provide system support; initiated cost-effective plans to reduce annual expenses by $100,000.
- Coordinated activities of twelve people in four departments; directly supervised two staff members.

**Data Systems Personnel Coordinator** (1976-1979)
- Spearheaded directives for personnel expansion during period of growth from 500 to 1,000 programmers.

**AETNA INSURANCE COMPANY** - Philadelphia, PA **1975 - 1976**
**Computer Programmer/Analyst**

**UNION CARBIDE** - Memphis, TN **1972 - 1975**
**Computer Programmer/Analyst** - IBM Mainframe

**GENESCO** - Nashville, TN **1969 - 1972**
**Computer Programmer** - Accounting Programs

## 83

**Combination.** *Diane McGoldrick, Tampa, Florida*

This resume is for a "'trailing spouse' who had held several positions and worked part-time during periods of 'home management.'" The resume looks in every way like an executive resume.

## MARC R. CASTINGS

25 Seaside Avenue | Wells, Maine 05505 | (207) 555-5055

### OBJECTIVE

A versatile manufacturing professional with broad experience including supervision and staff development, in-depth knowledge of production systems/castings, and problem solving abilities seeks a management position in manufacturing that offers challenge and growth potential. Ability to develop staff will contribute to the productivity and profitability of a Company.

### SUMMARY OF QUALIFICATIONS

**Areas of expertise: Production Supervisor. . . Casting. . . Quality Control**

- Over 20 years experience in hands-on manufacturing environments, with extensive knowledge of a full range of castings, i.e., sand, permanent, investment and ceramic block.
- Detail and profit oriented, with proven ability to identify, repair, analyze and solve problems.
- Conceived and implemented conversion of Precision Castings from an Iron Foundry to a Specialty Alloy Foundry, increasing sales from $300,000/yr. (1982) to $1.5 million/yr. (1986).
- Instrumental in developing method to cast high alloys in permanent metal molds (High Molds™).
- Successful ability to supervise, motivate, train and increase productivity.
- Thorough familiarity with all operating procedures and shop equipment, combined with in-depth knowledge of materials, metallurgic components and quality control factors regulating the machining, finishing and inspection of a wide variety of work pieces.
- Experienced in providing independent consulting services instructing management on melting practices, tooling design, production parameters, temperature controls & safety procedures.
- Administration/profit & loss experience managing Foundries with sales of $5+ Million/yr.
- Extensive experience in PT, RT, UT, Dimensional and Visual methods of inspections.
- Utilized excellent communication skills performing marketing & sales responsibilities.

### EDUCATION

**Industrial Engineering Technician Training** • 1965-1969
Portsmouth Naval Shipyard - Kittery, Maine
Completed 2 1/2 years of a 3 year program before cutbacks eliminated program training.

**Molder (Castings) - Journeyman's Certificate** • 1960-1964
Portsmouth Naval Shipyard - Kittery, Maine
Apprenticeship - Foundry Technology

**Diploma** • 1960
Thornton Academy - Saco, Maine

**Specialized Training:**
- Machine Shop Training
- Non-Destructive Testing - PT & RT (Level II)
- Credit and Career Advancement courses - New Hampshire Vocational Technical Institute

### WORK HISTORY

**General Manager** • 1995
Pine State Castings, Inc. - Buxton, Maine

**General Manager/Consultant** • 1993 to 1995
Bayside Co., Inc. (Stainless Steel Foundry start-up) - Boston, Massachusetts

**Production Coordinator/Planner** • 1989 to 1992
Branyen Brothers, Inc. - Dover, New Hampshire

**Self Employed (mechanical contracting)** • 1987 to 1988

**President** • 1982 to 1987
Precision Castings, Inc. - North Conway, New Hampshire

**Vice-President** • 1978 to 1982
White Mountain Foundries, U.S. Metallurgical Products, Inc. - Portsmouth, New Hampshire

**Marketing Development Manager** • 1976 to 1978
R.M. Foundry - Portland, Maine

**Production / Quality Control Supervisor** • 1972 to 1976
Gorham Metallurgical Products - Gorham, Maine

### REFERENCES

Available upon request

84

**Combination.** *Patricia Martel, Saco, Maine*

The writer has reduced the point size and line spacing so that the presented information can fit on one page. The writer has also shaded lightly the contact information within horizontal lines.

# EMMA COHEN

15 Avenue I • Brooklyn, New York • 12121
(718) 222-3333

## SUMMARY

**Experienced Retail Manager** with proven strength in Customer Service, Sales, and Negotiations. Skilled at marketing, advertising, strategic planning, and promoting products. Highly analytical and logical with excellent research and writing skills. Successful in developing strategies to attract new customers and maintain their loyalty.

## EXPERIENCE

NORTHERN HOME STORES, Brooklyn, NY

**General Manager,** 1993 to present

Oversee fifteen 5,000 square foot stores/warehouses throughout the U.S. Supervise twenty employees. Foster an atmosphere of teamwork and empower staff to make decisions. Design store layouts to maximize attractiveness and sales. Represent company and promote products to retail operations.

- Increased sales by 15% in 1996 and helped company achieve its highest sales level in 15 years.
- Coordinate monthly store exhibits that draw 10,000 customers.
- Overhauled pricing structure that increased profits by 10%.
- Implemented employee retention plan that reduced staff turnover rate by 50%.

**Assistant Manager,** 1991 to 1993

Assisted with staff supervision and product marketing. Designed layout and wrote copy for quarterly product catalogues. Promoted to General Manager.

AMERICAN STORES, Forest Hills, NY

**National Inventory Director,** 1988 to 1991

Inspected operations throughout the U.S. and solved inventory problems.

- Developed comprehensive system for handling damaged furniture.
- Decreased defective furniture by 75% in California and 85% in New York.
- Successfully negotiated with factories to receive credits for furniture.
- Improved appearance of warehouses and stores.

APEX INVESTMENT CORPORATION, New York, NY

**Account Executive,** 1985 to 1988

Researched and visited companies to determine growth potential. Advised investors on strategies and helped them make informed decisions.

- Managed up to 75 accounts worth a total of $300,000.
- Earned Series 7 and Series 63 Licenses.

## COMPUTERS

- Proficient in Microsoft Office (Word, Excel, Access, PowerPoint)
- Knowledge of WordPerfect, Lotus 1-2-3, Quotron, and PageMaker

## EDUCATION

**B.A. in Economics,** 1985
**St. John's University,** Jamaica, NY
Financed education 100%

**85**

**Combination.** *Kim Isaacs, Jackson Heights, New York*

An easy-to-read resume. The shaded, shadowed box attracts attention to the person's strengths and skills. For each position in boldface, the writer states duties and then bullets achievements.

# ARTHUR ROSSITER

2434 West Bellevue
Denver, CO 80508
(303) 233-3332
arossiter@aol.com


## PROFESSIONAL GOAL

MANAGER: TECHNOLOGY SERVICE CENTER / TECHNICAL OPERATIONS / COMPUTER SUPPORT

## QUALIFICATIONS SUMMARY

QUALIFIED for opportunities with an organization that will benefit from cross-functional talents in the areas of management, sales, service, and technology. Experienced in start-up, turnaround, expansion, and management of multi-unit technical/service operations. Characterized by colleagues and customers as having:

- Effective, hands-on management style and strong team-building skills.
- Excellent analytical, problem-solving, technical, and communication skills.
- An unsurpassed commitment to customer service, directly impacting customer referrals and repeat business.

## PROFESSIONAL EXPERIENCE

PEAK COMPUTER SERVICES, Denver, Colorado — 1986-1997
*(Authorized Service Center -- Novell Gold, Compaq, IBM, Epson, Okidata)*

General Manager -- Directed successful start-up, growth, and operation of computer business servicing the Denver metro area. Provided full range of hardware and software support, specializing in Novel and Windows NT network management support. Hired and supervised technical and support team of 18. Developed and managed marketing, accounting, and operations systems which supported a tenfold increase in sales. Secured and renewed annual service contracts totaling approximately $2.5 million.

- Led company to achieve consistent growth of approximately 30% annually.
- Restructured company in early 1990's to meet changing market conditions, achieving a 150+% increase in net profit.
- Maintained a call-back rate of less than 4%.
- Increased average volume per technician to 4.78 service calls per day.
- Maintained a 73% average billable rate for technicians.
- Recruited and retained technical talent, providing staff development and mentoring which enabled several to obtain certification as Microsoft Certified Technician and Novell Certified Network Engineer.
- Earned outstanding customer survey marks from outside audit (98% satisfaction rate). Comments from customer response cards: "Your folks are very patient with those of us who test their patience!" ... "excellent representation" ... "I have told others of your excellent service."

DIGITIZER SYSTEMS GROUP, INC., Los Angeles, California — 1984-1986

Northern California Service Manager -- Developed new territory, opening and managing branches in San Jose and Oakland. Secured minicomputer maintenance contracts valued in excess of $300,000 with companies such as National Semi-Conductor, Stanford Research, and GenRad.

◆◆◆

86

**Combination.** *Susan Britton Whitcomb, Fresno, California*

After selling his company, this person used the title General Manager to avoid overwhelming a potential employer. An Education section is omitted since the person had no formal education.

## JOHN W. SMITH

**1111 Any Street, Hometown, FL 22333 ▪ (000) 000-000**

**Qualifications For**

**SENIOR LEVEL OPERATIONS / MARKETING MANAGER**

### PROFESSIONAL SUMMARY

- Results-driven executive with strong background in general management, sales, marketing and distribution.
- Ability to listen to customers, understand their needs, and create customized solutions.
- Entrepreneurial spirit, team motivator, customer-oriented with keen sense of urgency.
- Highly capable strategic thinker and team player with strong tactical implementation capability.

### AREAS OF EXPERTISE

- Operations Management
- Strategic Development
- Cost & Safety Control
- Business Expansion
- Team Builder
- Multi-Facility Management
- Quality Control
- Hiring
- Business/Finance Management
- Fleet Management
- Sales Diversification
- Crisis Management

### PROFESSIONAL HISTORY

**A Wonderful Company, Inc., Anytown, FL** 10/92 - Present
***General Manager***
This is a $6.8 million industrial process and equipment firm with branch locations servicing over six states. The company leases and sells industrial floor care equipment and chemicals and provides 24 hour a day support to its customers.

- Manage day-to-day operations for a multi-state, multimillion dollar company.
- Responsible for all company operations including marketing, sales, customer service, employee supervision, and product development.
- Identify, develop and implement new business opportunities in order to diversify the company's interests while preserving the core business.
- Developed and refined new programs to improve floor maintenance process, and bring the company into a more "environmentally friendly" position by decreasing use of chemicals.
- Increased sales volume by over 300% in less than four years.
- Developed, negotiated and manage contract for national company with sites throughout the Southeast.

87

**Combination.** *Jean West, Indian Rocks Beach, Florida*

Double horizontal lines serve as part of a header for each page. Single horizontal lines separate main sections. The headings, Qualifications section, and Academic Credentials are centered.

**JOHN W. SMITH** **Page Two**

**A Wonderful Company, Inc.** - continued:

- Created new industry process and successfully negotiated contract to test for a 408-store national company for contract worth $16.5 million.
- Increased volume from $3.2 million in 1992 to $6.8 million in 1996.
- Negotiated financing for a $750,000 line of credit with Republic Bank.
- Located site, negotiated purchase, planned and supervised remodeling of 35,000 square foot corporate headquarters and warehouse.
- Negotiated and set-up operations for Big Time Grocery Stores, Inc. in Someplace, Florida with annual sales of $1.4 million at 113 locations.
- Set up sales with an import/export operation in Miami, Florida for annual sales of $312,000.
- Spearheaded operations in Florida, Georgia, and Alabama for 51 new store locations in the Panhandle/Big Bend area with annual sales of $663,000.
- Manage fleet of 24 service trucks and technicians. Implemented strategies to decrease service calls and improve customer service.
- Successful at building and leading a professional discipline within the organization resulting in improved quality control in all divisions for complete customer satisfaction.

**ABC Plumbing, Hometown, FL** 10/89 - 4/92
***President (10/90 - 4/92)***

- Responsible for overall operations and employee supervision of a $3.6 million commercial contract including five residential service vehicles.
- Directed company growth from $1.2 million in 1989 to $3.6 million in sales in 1992.
- Negotiated financing of $1.3 million of working capital from private sources.
- Developed business relationships with general contractors to secure profitable projects.
- Planned, negotiated and secured extensive commercial contracts, including Big Time Resort, Grand Convention Center, and ABC Hospital.
- Additional projects included new school contracts in My, Yours, Ours, and Their counties.
- Supervised retail operations selling plumbing products and services to the general public and contractors.

***Project Manager (10/89 - 10/90)***

- Supervised entire field operations.

**ABC Construction, Hometown, FL** Summers 1985 - 1987
***Assistant Field Superintendent***

**ACADEMIC CREDENTIALS**

Florida State University, Gainesville, FL (1982 - 1989)
*Construction Management with emphasis in*
*Landscape Architecture & Engineering Technology.*

**REFERENCES AVAILABLE UPON REQUEST**

The paragraph under the first company in the Professional History section describes the company. Bullets point to responsibilities and achievements. Whenever possible, the achievements are quantified—mostly in dollar amounts. Bold italic helps the four different positions stand out.

# Wayne Marshall

P.O. Box 2343 • Houghton, Michigan 49458
(616) 639-1258

## SUMMARY OF QUALIFICATIONS

- ✓ Strong Managerial Background
- ✓ Business Planning
- ✓ Cost Estimating
- ✓ Budgetary Controls
- ✓ Scheduling
- ✓ Manpower Forecasting
- ✓ Cost Reduction
- ✓ Labor Relations
- ✓ OSHA
- ✓ Hiring and Training of Personnel
- ✓ Supervision of Personnel
- ✓ Achieve Manufacturing and Profit Goals

## PROFESSIONAL EXPERIENCE

***General Manager Contract Machining/Consultant*** ***September 1986 to September 1992***
**Smith Associates, Adrian, Michigan**

Made recommendations to reduce costs, provided cost estimating, worked with suppliers to improve company image and allow for credit and improved cash flow. Reversed 3-1 ratio from payable to receivables. Performed all general management functions. Instrumental in obtaining GP 3 rating by General Motors and Grade 2 Rating with Rockwell International. Developed and implemented personnel and production control systems. Hired and trained personnel. Responsible for industrial engineering functions and sales as well as extensive troubleshooting, and consulting.

***Successfully turned the company from near bankruptcy to profitability in two years.***

***President Assembly and Machining*** ***October 1986 to September 1990***
**Financial Managers, Inc., Tecumseh, Michigan**

Responsible for all day-to-day operations of the company.

***Process Technician*** ***September 1976 to October 1984***
**General Mills, Grand Rapids, Michigan**

Responsible for maintaining the operating process. Knowledgeable in mechanical and electrical operations for the purpose of updating equipment process. Quality assurance on raw materials and finished product. Conducted classroom training for operators, mechanics and new process technicians. Was instrumental in the change from conventional to the technician mode of operating.

***Auditor of Daily Business - Hotel Restaurant and Lounge*** ***February 1976 to September 1976***
**Clarion Inn, Houghton, Michigan**

Responsible for verification of accuracy and compiling of day's business and monies. Redesigned manager's process of reconciliation and lowered the possibility of human error.

88

**Combination.** *Christina M. Popa, Adrian, Michigan*

A two-page resume with an uncluttered look because of the centered titles, the amount of line spacing, and left-aligned information that does not fill whole lines. Large small caps are used for

Resume of Wayne Marshall
Page 2

## PROFESSIONAL EXPERIENCE (Continued)

***General Foreman*** *July 1974 to July 1975*
**B & D Corporation, Louisville, Kentucky**

Auto parts machining, auto jacks, and hoist machining and assembly. All duties related to automotive chuck lathes, engine lathes, in-line boring, radical arm drills, multi-spindle drill and tap, shearing, welding, press operation, and assembly. Forecasted budget and production. Interfaced with engineering and union.

***General Foreman*** *October 1973 to June 1974*
**General Products, Inc., Kansas City, Kansas**

Manufactured heavy equipment. Shift Superintendent functions over total plant for fabricating, machining, welding, assembly, and painting.

## OTHER WORK EXPERIENCE

***General Foreman Machining***
**Kentucky Stamping Corporation**

***Foreman Machining and Assembly***
**General Motors Corporation**

***Foreman Press Room***
**Quaker Printing Press**

## EDUCATION

**SPC Training** — Smith Associates

**Basic and Advanced Production Supervisor Training** — General Motors Corporation

**Labor Relations Courses** — General Motors Corporation

**Process Technician Classroom and On-The-Job Training** — General Mills

**Quality Assurance** — General Motors Corporation and General Mills

**Personnel Management School** — United States Army

**Lotus 1-2-3, Accounts Receivable Collections** — Jackson Community College, Jackson, Michigan

**Digital Electronics** — Jackson Community College, Jackson, Michigan

**Graduate** — Adrian High School, Adrian, Michigan

***References available upon request.***

the person's name in the contact information. The check marks direct attention to the items in the Summary of Qualifications. In the Professional Experience section, the use of bold italic for each of the positions held makes it easy for the eye to pick them out in a sweep through the resume.

# MATTHEW LANDREW

123 Hotel Circle
Convention City, Arizona 55555

Voice: 555.555.5555
Data: 555.555.5555

## PROFILE

Proven record in executive, operations, and program management, staff supervision, customer service, marketing and sales. Extensive hands-on experience in virtually every area from maintenance to human resources to front desk. Progressed through the ranks to management positions and principal in entrepreneurial endeavor.

## HOSPITALITY

- Twelve years industry experience.
- Responsible for daily audit, balancing of all revenue outlets, track expenditures within budgeted guidelines.
- Provides daily and monthly profit reports.
- Maintains accurate postings of guests' room charges, taxes and incidental charges.

## MANAGEMENT AND ADMINISTRATION

- Effectively plans projects, assesses tasks involved, makes manpower assignments, and provides scheduling, training and assistance.
- Strong interpersonal skills are evident in the ability to interface with customers, colleagues and vendors.
- Supervised up to 60 hospitality personnel in all aspects of motel operations.
- Manages accounts payable, receivables, collections and payroll.
- Tracks expenditures within budgeted guidelines. Provides daily and monthly reports to owners.

## MAINTENANCE AND TROUBLESHOOTING

- Ability to evaluate and troubleshoot utilizing problem solving capabilities.
- Knowledge of operating procedures and equipment to accomplish repairs quickly and efficiently.
- Performs quality assurance inspections of rooms, common areas and grounds. Ensures all facilities were safe, clean and well maintained.

## CUSTOMER SERVICE AND SALES

- Develops rapport and builds relationships with customers through attention to detail in defining needs and providing service and solutions.
- Coordinates corporate and group reservations, accommodations and conference rooms.

## CAREER EXPERIENCE

| | | |
|---|---|---|
| **MANAGER**, 77 rooms | Mountain View, Convention City, AZ | 1996 to current |
| **PRINCIPAL** (1/3 interest), 43 rooms | Shilo Inn, Anywhere, AZ | 1994 to 1996 |
| **MANAGER**, 103 rooms | Double Tree, Somewhere, AZ | 1993 to 1994 |
| **MANAGER**, 77 rooms | Comfort Inn, Desert, AZ | 1991 to 1993 |
| **PRINCIPAL** (1/3 interest), 78 rooms | Econolodge, Durango, CO | 1990 to 1991 |
| **MANAGER**, 24 rooms | Rodeway Inn, Somewhere, AZ | 1989 to 1990 |
| **MANAGER**, 24 rooms | Sleep Inn, Desert, AZ | 1987 to 1989 |
| **MANAGER**, 24 rooms | Twiggs Motel, Somewhere, AZ | 1985 to 1987 |

## AFFILIATIONS

Convention City Chamber of Commerce
Asian-American Hotel-Motel Association

## PROFESSIONAL DEVELOPMENT

Seminars and Training Sessions in Hotel, Motel Management, Business Practices and Customer Service sponsored by Econolodge and Comfort Inns, among others.

*MANAGEMENT* *HOSPITALITY* *OPERATIONS*

**89**

**Combination.** *Patricia S. Cash, Prescott, Arizona*

This person needed a "Presentation of Qualifications" for a bank loan to buy his own motel. The resume serves this purpose and validates "his risk worthiness" through continuous employment.

## TOM VALVE

9876 Abercrombie Road ◆ Cincinnati, Ohio ◆ 45000
(123) 456-7890

### OBJECTIVE:

Progressive management position with a growth-oriented country club in which I can immediately apply my knowledge and experience of all aspects of country-club development, together with my marketing, interpersonal and leadership skills, while continuing to develop them to their maximum potential.

### KEY SKILLS PROFILE:

- An accomplished professional in all aspects of the development and growth of premier country club environments: marketing; staff hiring and training; labor management; cost control; menu design; all clubhouse operations, including bar and restaurant, valet, housekeeping, locker-rooms, and maintenance.
- Leading-edge skills in inventory control and management, and in the conceptualization and implementation of comprehensive, accessible record-keeping systems.
- Top-rank communicator with ability to inject creative ideas and generate action across all levels of an organization.
- Function effectively both as an independent, self-motivated individual and as an active, contributing team member.
- Able to bring together diverse individuals to form a unified team, and motivate them to identify personally with key objectives. Exceptional ability to identify potential interpersonal barriers and communication problems and take the steps necessary to circumvent them. Solid record of team leadership, with the capacity to train, mentor and develop both new and long-standing team members.
- Customer-oriented, with demonstrated ability to develop an instant rapport and build lasting relationships with prospective and existing members, through maximum attention to detail in determining their real needs and preferences, then providing service and quality beyond expectation.
- Strong advocate of the need to develop & continuously enhance knowledge of products, processes, and market trends.

### EXPERIENCE PROFILE:

**BUCKINGHAM COUNTRY CLUB**, Gano, Ohio — **October 1993 - Present**

***Clubhouse Manager*** — ***May 1994 - Present***

- Responsible for all aspects of the development, marketing and operation of this premier (developer-owned) country club: food & beverage operations; valet service; housekeeping; maintenance; locker-room; golf-course food & beverage service.
- Acted as Interim Club Manager during candidate search for General Manager, with particular focus on the design and development of new clubhouse.
- Developed, wrote and edited an employee handbook.
- Selected and oversaw outside contractors for pool maintenance.

***Dining Room Manager*** — ***October 1993 - May 1994***

- Oversaw up to 15 full-time staff in the operation of an upscale dining facility attached to the Swim & Tennis Club.
- Responsible for bar operations, including purchasing, inventory, hiring staff, training, scheduling, and quality control. Maintained Cost of Goods at 25%.
- Coordinated all golf outings and banquet events.

**SHERATON HOTELS**, Cincinnati, Ohio — **July 1990 - October 1993**

***Room Service Supervisor***

- Supervised a staff of 10 in the Room Service Department.
- Selected to coordinate and organize a special banquet event involving nine bars and 18 bartenders, with total sales exceeding $200,000.

### EDUCATION & TRAINING:

- Henry's Harbor High School, Henry's Harbor, Illinois. College prep. Graduated 1983.
- Lake Erie College, Henry's Harbor, Illinois. Completed two years' study of *Business Administration* and *Marketing*. 1983 - 1985.
- Completed a multi-session course in *Total Quality Management* sponsored by Sheraton Hotels, 1992.
- *Business Management Institute I*, Kentucky State University, sponsored by CMAA, October 1994.
- *Business Management Institute II*, Cal-Poly State, Celeste, California, sponsored by CMAA, September 1995.

**90**

**Combination.** *Barry Hunt, Cincinnati, Ohio*

Small print and narrow margins allow the writer to put much information on one page. Bullets, italic, and different vertical alignments through careful tabbing make the resume easy to read.

# TANYA SMITHERS

13244 Long Beach Blvd. #H-2
Manhattan Beach, California 90234
310/786-9055

**OBJECTIVE**

Position as CONCIERGE.

**PROFESSIONAL PROFILE**

Highly motivated professional with strong service orientation and ability to successfully handle a high level of responsibility.

- Friendly, outgoing personality; able to communicate effectively with the public and project a positive image.
- Experienced with front desk and general office operations (i.e., 10-key, typing, data entry, faxing, cashiering and paperwork management).
- Computer literate.

*As a professional nanny, gained extensive hands-on experience with household management and administration of day-to-day operations. Acquired the ability to deal effectively with people of all ages, work well under pressure and independently resolve problems.*

**EDUCATION**

PORTLAND STATE UNIVERSITY - Portland, Oregon

**A.A. Hotel Management** (1991)

Comprehensive hotel management training program encompassing:

- Accounting
- Travel / Tourism
- Hotel Law
- Front Office Management
- Food and Beverage Management
- Marketing Principles

**RELATED EMPLOYMENT**

FRONT DESK CLERK - The Executive Club, Arlington, Virginia (9/89-7/90)
Independently managed front desk operations on weekends for this all-suite hotel. Checked-in guests, processed financial transactions, performed data entry and provided prompt customer service.

**OTHER EXPERIENCE**

HOUSEHOLD MANAGER / NANNY - Washington, D.C. (7/86-9/97)
Managed day-to-day household activities for family of four. Handled purchasing duties, cooked meals and functioned as chauffeur.

MARKETING ASSISTANT - Ensco Corporation, Portland, Oregon (5/84-6/86)
Coordinated office operations, provided clerical support and prepared business documents for sales manager and staff of 13.

**REFERENCES**

Professional references and letters of recommendation provided upon request.

## 91

**Combination.** *Pat Kendall, Aloha, Oregon*

This resume's carefully designed format helped the person overcome some negatives, such as a six-year-old, hospitality-related education, and to land a job as a concierge at a Marriott Hotel.

# FARE OF
# CAROLINE CURRIER

1234 North 16th Avenue
Somewhere, Florida 33006
(305) 954-1256

92

**Combination.** *Shelley M. Nachum, Fort Lauderdale, Florida*

This individual wanted a "'creative' resume in the form of a menu for a restaurant manager position." The candidate "had a graphic designer design paper so that it folded like a menu."

## STARTER...

A position in Restaurant Management which will capitalize on my past experience and offer responsibility and opportunity for growth.

## SPECIALTIES...

- Detail-oriented
- Organized
- Communication skills
- People-oriented
- Motivator
- Customer relations

## MAIN COURSES...

**BACHELOR OF SCIENCE IN HOSPITALITY MANAGEMENT..........1983**
*Florida International University, Miami, Florida*

**ASSOCIATE IN APPLIED SCIENCE IN HOTEL, RESTAURANT, & INSTITUTION MANAGEMENT..........1981**
**ASSOCIATE IN APPLIED SCIENCE IN GENERAL BUSINESS..........1991**
*Community College, New Jersey*

Selections included:

- *Business Communications*
- *Employee Motivation and Productivity*
- *Business Organization & Management*
- *Small Business Management*
- *Sanitation in Food Service*
- *Restaurant Management*
- *Purchasing & Menu Planning*
- *Catering Management*

**CERTIFICATE IN BARTENDING/MIXOLOGY..........1984**
*International Bartending Institute, Pompano, Florida*

## AND MORE...

Dean's Honor List - Spring 1989 and Spring 1990
Vice President of Hotel, Restaurant, & Institutional Club
Club Managers Association of America

## A LA CARTE...

"Food Service Managers" Certification from the State of New Jersey
"Serving Alcohol With Care" Certification
"National Sanitation Foundation" Certification

The writer "created the categories and filled in the information accordingly." She also selected a display type that "adds to the effectiveness." The result was an unusual resume that "received a lot of compliments and comments." After each centered head with a creative name, you can spot the important sections: an

## ENTREES...

**STEAKHOUSE & CANTINA........................................................1994 - 1995**
*Miami, Florida*
Assistant General Manager; Bartending/Marketing
Oversaw 250-seat restaurant and supervised staff of 40. Interviewed, hired, and trained employees; collected all revenue, reconciled sales slips and compiled daily sales report for home office; performed direct customer relations; responsible for nightly shut down of entire restaurant.

Started with restaurant tending to guests and servicing of restaurant. Conducted inventory on all bar products on weekly basis. Bartended at two privately catered parties. Promoted to Assistant General Manager.

**PREZERRIOS..........................................................................1993-1994**
*Miami, Florida*
Service
Prepared restaurant for guest service, attended and maintained guests' needs. Held thorough knowledge of all menu items, including contents and preparation techniques.

## ON THE SIDE...

**THE GRAND...............................................................Fall Semester, 1992**
*Boca, Florida* (Internship)
Garde Manager
Performed preparation work for station and other areas of kitchen. Worked on cold line preparing a la carte salads and desserts.

**ITALIAN RESTAURANT........................................................1990 - 1991**
*Trenton, New Jersey* (Part-time)
Maitre d'
Acted as hostess, as well as oversaw restaurant while manager attended to other duties. Collected monies and handled customers.

**HYATT REGENCY HOTEL......................................................1987 - 1989**
*Edison, New Jersey* (Part-time)
Food and Beverage Cashier
Handled monies and settled guest checks at Crystal Garden Restaurant. Took and ensured complete delivery of in-room dining orders. Made regular nightly deposits to hotel for both outlets.

**REFERENCES AVAILABLE UPON REQUEST**

objective; a summary of skills; education, honors, and certification sections; an experience section, and an additional experience section. Ellipses after the headings, leader dots before dates, and filled circular bullets tie together the second and third pages.

**Robert L. Norwood**

3220 Mountain Ridge Road Montgomery, Alabama 36100 ☎ [334] 555 -1575 Residence

*"In club management, he has no peers."*
*- Two star general and club board chairman*

*"Bob Norwood is the finest club manager I have known in over 27 years."*
*- Executive and board member*

*"Brilliant organizer."*
*- Senior decision maker*

OBJECTIVE: To give members of The Four Hills Country Club unsurpassed service and outstanding value.

PROFILE: ❖ Seasoned manager in all aspects of club operations ❖ Expert in delivering great service and great value ❖ Master at building and leading teams of employees to *want* to be the best.

SELECTED EXAMPLES OF SUCCESS:

**SEASONED MANAGER WHO GETS RESULTS**: Selected to manage a club that might not have met its next payroll. Literally lived in the club for the first week. Turned fragmented staff into well-trained team. Put reputation on the line with members.

> ***Payoffs:*** **Cut $19,000 a month** in personnel costs without reducing staff. Designed and executed programs that attracted *and kept* membership. One indicator of success: **food revenue up** nearly **50% in four months**.

**DELIVERING GREAT SERVICE AND GREAT VALUE:** Not satisfied with the high membership he inherited when hired as new manager. "Sparkplug" behind an all new program of benefits for families: gave them more services at great savings. Children's serving line – built to their height – a big success.

> ***Payoffs:*** **Membership up 18%** in eighteen months. Cash flow considerably improved.

**LEADING EMPLOYEES TO BE THEIR BEST:** Transformed the cleaning staff from "time-clock punchers" to pros. Gave them new uniforms, new lockers – and total responsibility for making our club shine.

> ***Payoffs:*** **Sick leave dropped by 60%** across the board. **Turnover went** from nearly 100% a year **to zero**. All our staff couldn't wait to get to work. Members prouder than ever to show visitors their club.

93

**Combination.** *Donald P. Orlando, Montgomery, Alabama*

"Even after my client had been hired by a civilian country club, I had to overcome strong stereotypes against retiring senior military people. Those who manage country clubs focus

**Robert L. Norwood**, General Manager [334] 555-1575 Residence

WORK HISTORY:

- *General Manager,* Awahnee Country Club, Clartin, Alabama
  1996 - Present

  Hired to guide $2 million restoration and expansion for this full-service, 600-member club. Facilities include dining room, grill, snack bar, swimming pool, tennis courts, 18-hole golf course, and driving range.

More than 25 years of increasing responsibility in club management with the United States Air Force, including these most recent positions:

- *Club Manager,* Sharpton Officers' Club, Sharpton Air Force Base, Texas, January 1994 - 1996

  Chosen over 33 other experienced applicants, including others with years more experience, to manage this 3,000-member club. Facility entertained very senior decision makers from Federal and state governments, business and community leaders, and high ranking representatives of some 32 foreign governments. Supervised staff of 83.

- *Club Manager* later promoted to *General Manager,* Club Complex, Royal Air Force Compton, Compton, England, June 1991 - January 1994

  Selected from 25 well-qualified applicants to run this complex of three clubs. Served nearly 2,200 members and their families. Provided nearly 20% return on sales despite currency fluctuations that eroded buying power. Responsible for 200 full and part time employees.

- *Director,* International Club Complex, Brunssum, The Netherlands, June 1983 - December 1989

  Reported directly to boards and committees representing 16 foreign nations. Turned around restaurant losses of $50,000 a year to generate profits of $200,000 annually. Oversaw $100,000 in improvements in a single year: all completed on time, all paid for before renovations completed. Led staff of 200.

CERTIFICATIONS:

- In top two percent of managers who held credentials as a Certified Military Club Executive, International Military Club Executive Association, 1978.
- Formerly Air Force's chief instructor preparing club managers to handle food and beverage operations, manage finances, conduct marketing and accommodate special functions.

MEMBERSHIP:

- Club Managers Association of America

EDUCATION:

- Associate of Arts, **Restaurant Management,** Community College of the Air Force, Maxwell Air Force Base, Alabama, June 1978

Page two

on customer service, cost control, and profits—things they feel military people know little about. I used expert testimony and quantified examples to overcome these obstacles." The testimonials and "payoffs" in boldface on the first page *do* get you to come to attention and take notice.

Presentation of Qualifications

for

**JOHN Q. JONES**
000 Street
Anaheim, CA 00000
Telephone: (714) 000-0000

---

**SUMMARY OF QUALIFICATIONS**

- Experience and corresponding expertise in the field of **HOTEL MANAGEMENT** has been acquired through specialized training and extensive practical application with fine, full-service hotels ranging in size from 250 to 2,000 rooms.
- Overall personnel management skills include training, supervising and motivating staff to surpass company standards in every aspect of their duties.
- Excel in the development of an efficient business operation and team-oriented working atmosphere.
- Manage a wide range of functions; skilled in the coordination of complex and multi-departmental activities.
- Interface well with all levels of administration and management, various personnel and clientele.
- Able to quickly establish a strong rapport with individuals from diverse backgrounds and disciplines, communicating in both **Spanish** and **English.**
- Implement effective problem resolutions with tact and ease.
- Expertise in an environment that requires heightened levels of leadership, resourcefulness and responsibility.

**Key Strengths Include:**

- Proven record of outstanding **Sales** and **Marketing** achievements. Develop wide-scale and strategic planning for new market openings. Devise and implement innovative promotionals. Maintain strong client relations with an exceptional level of sales conversion.
- Instill professional standards of **Customer Service** with staff, making recommendations for continuous improvement in quality of service.
- Experienced as an **Asset Manager** with profit and loss responsibility for all divisions. Evaluate profit centers and prepare cost summaries.
- Command excellent communication skills, both verbally and in writing. Proven ability to explain complex procedures and issues to others.
- Selected as "Citizen of the Year" in 1992 and participated in numerous community activities and volunteer service.

**94**

**Combination.** *Christine Edick, Orange, California*

This resume "had to be 'keyword' specific and follow certain guidelines dictated by the hotel industry in this area (next page). Keywords were highlighted and placed on page one together

**JOHN Q. JONES** **Page Two**

## PROFESSIONAL BACKGROUND

**GENERAL MANAGER - Hyatt Regency Alicante** - Anaheim, CA

- Direct and administer total operational responsibility for this upscale hotel which caters to conventions, corporations and leisure clientele.
- Manage $15,000,000 annual revenues and a staff for this 400 room hotel.
- Instrumentally involved in sales effort of a 10 member Sales team.
- Coordinate marketing strategies to increase exposure through customer presentations, promotional and creative advertising.
- Enhanced customer service satisfaction utilizing intensive service training and motivation.

**Accomplishments:** Doubled amount of meeting space on property from 20,000 sq. ft. to 40,000 sq. ft. to efficiently accommodate increasing number of clientele. Total increase realized is in excess of 31%. Consistently outperformed competition as measured by Smith Travel Reporter. Yield of penetration index has averaged over 115% for the past two years. Increased revenues and profits for every year in an economically depressed area. Maintain the highest level of customer satisfaction, averaging above 99% in our positive response survey. (1990 to Present)

**GENERAL MANAGER - Hyatt Edgewater** - Long Beach, CA

- Managed all aspects of operations for this 250 room hotel with full-service property catering primarily to groups and corporate clientele.
- Implemented measures to improve skills and stability of Sales force, in addition to asset and operation control.
- Emphasized attention to excellence in service and client requests.
- Established business relations with key customers, resulting in continued business and customer referrals.
- Instituted and coordinated a marketing committee to raise the hotel's profile through promotionals, civic involvement and advertising.

**Accomplishments: Successfully increased sales in both room rentals and food/beverage service.** Established a prominent role in the community and contacts with service organizations such as the **Rotary** and the **Chamber of Commerce**. Sponsored and organized receptions and Chef's Tables hosting local civic and community leaders. **Placed on the Board of Directors and Executive Committee of the Long Beach Convention and Visitors Council**.

**EXECUTIVE ASSISTANT MANAGER, ROOMS**

Hyatt Regency - Dallas, TX (1989)
Hyatt Regency - Dearborn, MI (1987-1988)
Hyatt Regency - Oakland, CA (1985-1987)
Hyatt - Burlingame (1984-1985)

**ASSISTANT ROOMS DIVISION MANAGER - Hyatt Regency Grand** - Cypress, CA

Opened a 900 room luxury resort property. In addition to supervising related areas for Rooms Division, managed the Health Club and Recreation facilities. Assisted in initial staffing of entire division. (1983 to 1984)

## PROFESSIONAL AND CIVIC AFFILIATIONS

Executive Board, Chamber of Commerce
Anaheim Convention and Visitor Bureau
Anaheim Area Hotel/Motel Association

## EDUCATIONAL BACKGROUND

Glassboro College - Glassboro, NJ

with 'strengths' to catch the reader's eye." Boldfacing in the second Accomplishments section on page two perpetuates the boldfacing that was used on the first page. The Professional Background section shows continuous work for (and therefore loyalty to) Hyatt/Hyatt Regency Hotels since 1983.

# ADAM Q. MIDAH

10010 DILLWIDDEN NORTH
SOUTHVILLE, ILLINOIS 60060
000 444.0004

## PROFESSIONAL SYNOPSIS

Twelve-year commitment to the same company, in management positions, with increasingly demanding responsibilities.

Accustomed to fast-paced, high-volume, and quick decisions in an environment that is changeable, and is dependant on critical timing.

Highly reliable, capable, and dependable. Manages with authority and integrity.

## QUALIFICATIONS SUMMARY

*MANAGEMENT*

- Responsible for over 200 employees including: management, administration, drivers, and kitchen workers.

*OPERATIONS*

- Directly responsible for developing and implementing company quality standards.
- Interpret P&L statements to adjust staffing, plan budgets, and relate business issues.

*HUMAN RESOURCES*

- Monitor within the company structure to continually improve employee relations and concerns; develop team concepts – in union/non-union environments.

*TRAINING*

- Taught classes on sanitation and other topics complying with NRA criteria.

## CAREER HIGHLIGHTS

- Restructured procedures, executed innovative strategies ... resulting in ten-percent increased company profits over a two-year period.
- Developed a strategic plan for reduction of personnel by one-third; implemented phase-in process, compiled feed-back, assimilated customer buy-in ... resulting in six-percent wage decrease company wide.
- One of five in 24,000 to be selected on CORE transportation committee ... resolving critical customer service issues.
- Successfully managed the largest flight kitchen, within the largest transportation department, in the United States.
- Directed food service operations for thirteen Kaiser Permante hospitals in the San Francisco Bay area.

**95**

**Combination.** *Lorie Lebert, Novi, Michigan*

The eye-catching element in this resume is the thickening of a full horizontal line just over the centered contact information and each centered heading. The thickening is actually a thick, short

*Page 2 of Résumé for:*

**ADAM Q. MIDAH**

**EMPLOYMENT HISTORY**

*CORPORATION INTERNATIONAL,* 1984 to 1996
*$32 million operation, servicing airlines with in-flight meal requirements; previously owned by Services In Flight*

**SUPPORT SERVICES MANAGER** of Transportation, 1994 to 1996 . . . . . . . . . . . . . . . . City, State
- $32 million sales, 12 direct reporting managers, 200 hourly employees, 400 flights daily, and 106,000 meals weekly.

**ACTING GENERAL MANAGER,** 1993 to 1994 . . . . . . . . . . . . . . . . . . . . . . . . . . . . . . City, State
- $12 million sales, 7 direct reporting managers, 200 hourly employees, 13 hospitals, 60 flights daily, 35,000 meals weekly.

**OPERATIONS MANAGER** [Services In-flight], 1990 to 1993 . . . . . . . . . . . . . . . . . . . . City, State
- Same as *"Acting General Manager."*

**ASSISTANT MANAGER,** 1984 to 1990 . . . . . . . . . . . . . . . . . . . . . . . . . . . . . . . . . . . City, State
- $14 million sales, 2 supervisors, 40 hourly employees, 80 flights daily, 40,000 meals weekly.

**EDUCATION AND TRAINING**

*OREGON STATE UNIVERSITY* . . . . . . . . . . . . . . . . . . . . . . . . . . . . . . . . . . . . . . . . . . . . . . City, State
**BACHELOR OF SCIENCE DEGREE,** 1985
- *Double Major:* Hotel and Restaurant
- *Minor:* Finance

Dale Carnegie – *Sales and Management* Course

*"Dimensions in Leadership"*

TCT *"Total-Cycle-Time"* Process Mapping

Re-engineering Processing

Commitment to Excellence

Services *"Back to Basics"* Courses

Numerous in-house sessions dealing with a wide range of topics

line overlay that is centered over a thin, full line. Another distinctive feature is the use of four categories as side headings in the Qualifications Summary. Right-pointing arrow tips serve as bullets, which help to tie together the two pages and point to the achievements in the History.

# PATRICIA SMITH

111 Mountain Avenue • Glenns Falls, NY 00000 • (914) 999-9999

## HUMAN RESOURCES / ADMINISTRATION

Offering a solid background in corporate Human Resources with strengths in administration and systems development.... Considered a problem solver who improves operational efficiency through implementation of sound Human Resources practices.... *Areas of expertise include:*

Policy & Procedures / Benefits / Employment Law / Employee Relations
Recruitment / Staffing / Training / HRIS / Payroll

***Selected Accomplishments***

- Established Human Resources function at rapidly growing company assisting development of three additional locations.
- Initiated automated payroll and HRIS systems substantially upgrading personnel reporting.
- Created innovative employee relations programs which improved morale and reduced turnover.

**CAREER EXPERIENCE:**

DENTAL ASSOCIATES, Harrison, NY — 1995-Present

**Human Resources Manager**

Responsible for full scope of Human Resources activities as well as payroll/HRIS administration for this multi-site provider of managed care dental services. Part of management team which spearheaded expansion plans to four locations with staff of 125.

- Develop and monitor personnel policy/procedures ensuring compliance with all government regulations. Revised handbook and implemented policies for ADA and Family Leave Act.
- Set up many "first-of-their-kind" employee relations programs including benefits orientation, attendance awards, *Pat on the Back* recognition and post-hire evaluations.
- Wrote industry standard job descriptions to support extensive recruitment effort. Effectively utilized community resources to reduce advertising costs.
- Coached supervisory staff to implement disciplinary policy and resolve personnel issues. Conducted training sessions emphasizing documentation. Minimized unemployment liability.
- Improved Worker's Compensation exposure through affiliation with an occupational health service. Realized a reduction of medical costs and fraudulent claims.
- Continually brainstormed with employee teams to troubleshoot operations and improve efficiency. Resulted in reorganization of insurance claim verification process.

MAJOR BRANDS OUTLET, INC., High Lawn, NY — 1992-1995

**Human Resources Administrator**

Corporate Human Resources administration for major retailer with 28 locations and staff of 1,000.

- Implemented Abra HRIS system to produce EEO reports and analyze employee turnover.
- Administered collective bargaining agreement including salary schedule for unionized employees.
- Coordinated outplacement process for over 500 employees during Chapter XI downsizing. Collaborated with State Emergency Response Team and consulting firms to effect transition.

**EDUCATION/PROFESSIONAL:**

International University, White Plains, NY -- CERTIFICATE IN HUMAN RESOURCES MANAGEMENT, 1995
- Member, Society for Human Resources Management (SHRM)
William Holland College, Wayne, NY -- BA Degree (in progress)
Colby Junior College, New London, Connecticut -- AA Degree

**TECHNICAL:** ADP Payroll — MS-Office — Lotus 1-2-3 — WordPerfect — Email

**96**

**Combination.** *Vivian Belen, Fair Lawn, New Jersey*

To play up the candidate's management experience, the writer created a centered keyword list (see "areas of expertise"), made a Selected Accomplishments section, and boldfaced the positions.

**James J. Jones**
**2222 Jones Beach Blvd.**
**Elmira, NY 00000**
**000-000-0000 (Home)**

To play a key management role within a dynamic and challenging Human Resources environment.

FODD SERVICES COMPANY, INC., Elmira, NY

1994 to Present **HUMAN RESOURCE MANAGER**

Directs the administration and implementation of plant human resource systems, such as, employee relations, wage and benefit compensation, government regulatory compliance, employee training and development, quality work teams, recruitment-EEO/AAP, workers' compensation administration and plant safety to ensure plant, regional and corporate human resources objectives are met. The plant employs approximately 250 employees. The climate is highly people, production and results oriented. The plant is non union in all areas. Consequently, positive employee relations emphasis is a constant requirement.

GRAND CENTRAL MANUFACTURING COMPANY
TURBO PRODUCTIONS DIVISION, Washington Heights, NY

1991 to 1993 **HUMAN RESOURCES SPECIALIST**

Managed the selection, orientation, and placement for all Division exempt staff levels. Handled all salary negotiations, benefits, relocations, and other generalist duties. Performed all other human resources duties as assigned. Responsible for training in areas such as Drug Awareness, Total Quality Management, Workforce Diversity, ADA, and Sexual Harassment. Conducted interviewing skills workshops, managed college and university relations program, wrote AAP Plan for Division, managed Associate Engineering Program, served as EEO Representative. Responsible for the implementation of ISO-9001 certification for Human Resources Department. Trained and participated in self directed work teams.

JACKS TECHNICAL AUTOMATION, Corey Heights, OH

1986 to 1990 **HUMAN RESOURCES CONSULTANT/GENERALIST**

Responsible for the professional recruitment and placement of technical exempt and non-exempt positions and college recruitment program. Participated in training within the company and development of field managers. Handled all salary negotiations, benefits, relocations, and other generalist issues. Also, responsible for EEO/AAP issues and other employee relations duties as assigned.

GENERAL MILLS COMPANY, Philadelphia, PA

1983 to 1986 **LABOR RELATIONS SUPERVISOR**

Managed all labor relation activities of plant's 600 employees (485 hourly-union).

LOUISIANA GENERAL OIL COMPANY, Gordon, LA

1980 to 1983 **HUMAN RESOURCES REPRESENTATIVE**

Responsible and performed all HR generalist duties.

**EDUCATION**

ST. MICHAEL'S COLLEGE, Valley Beach, NY (1978 to 1980)
**Master's Degree in Industrial Relations** GPA: 3.5/4.0
Major: Labor Relations & Personnel Administration

ELMIRA CITY COLLEGE, Elmira, NY (1974 to 1978)
**Bachelor of Science in Sociology** GPA: 3.5/4.0
Emphasis: Business

97

**Chronological.** *Betty Geller, Elmira, New York*

Sixteen years of work experience have been put on just one page with enough white space for easy reading. Job positions are all uppercase and in boldface for emphasis. Degrees are bold also.

## NATHAN D. AGELY

*100 Full Circle*
*Milton, WA 00000*

*Home 000-000-0000*
*Office 000-000-0000*

**Human Resources Management, drawing on nearly 15 years of HR generalist experience with two major corporations. Strong record of contribution in corporate headquarters, division headquarters, manufacturing, distribution, and sales / marketing environments.**

### *PRIMARY AREAS OF EMPHASIS*

- Team Building / Self-Directed Work Teams
- Management Development / Succession Planning
- Total Quality and Employee Involvement Efforts
- Professional Employment and College Recruiting
- Employee Relations
- Organization Development
- Employee Training and Orientation
- EEO / AA / Diversity Training

### *EXPERIENCE*

**BOEING, INC.**, Seattle, WA
The world's largest manufacturer of commercial aircraft.

**Manager, Recruiting Automation**, 9/93 - present
- Member of implementation team consolidating recruiting services for all operating areas.
- Specific responsibility for automation projects required by the team to maximize efficiencies.
- Performed external bench marking and internal customer surveys; used inputs to reengineer the recruiting function to best meet customer needs in a new organizational structure.
- Installed an automated employment management system; developed support processes and trained users from all operating areas.
- Handling a variety of professional recruiting assignments.
- Supervise staff of six.

**BOEING PRIVATE INDUSTRIES**, Tacoma, WA
A $2 billion Boeing subsidiary manufacturing private aircraft.

**Manager, Employee Relations and Organization Development**, 8/92 - 9/93
- Provided broad HR support to client groups including Field Sales, Marketing, Distribution, and Manufacturing.
- Special emphasis on succession planning; training and training needs analysis; and quality practices to stimulate organizational effectiveness.
- Ensured resources available to implement Employee Involvement and move toward self-directed work teams.
- Provided guidance on consolidation and downsizing efforts.

**Manager, Recruiting and Employment**, 9/90 - 8/92
- Direct all recruiting activity, managing a staff of 7. Filled an average of 250 jobs annually, from support staff to Director level.
- Set Affirmative Action strategies/goals with the Management Board; prepared AA plans.
- Developed and installed a state-of-the-art Employment Management and Applicant Tracking System.

**98**

**Combination.** *Alan D. Ferrell, Lafayette, Indiana*

The individual's name at the top and the centered italic headings are in small caps with boldfacing. The company names in the Experience section are all uppercase and bold. The

***Agely, page 2***

**INTEL PLASTICS CORPORATION**, Portland, OR
The $1.8 billion plastics subsidiary of Intel, the world's most successful marketer of semiconductors.

**Manager, Employee Relations - Corporate Office**, 1/89 - 8/90
- Recruited during a period of rapid growth to develop and implement an employee relations function covering 450 employees. Reported to Director of HR.
- Broad HR generalist responsibilities, including policy formulation. Established training and orientation programs for corporate office and remote facility use.
- Member of task force consolidating Total Quality and Employee Involvement efforts.

**BOEING SECRET SERVICES**, Tacoma, WA
A wholly-owned Boeing subsidiary manufacturing high-security government and military aircraft.

**Manager, Human Resources - Tacoma Plant**, 12/87 - 1/89
- Selected to manage the closing and transfer of this manufacturing operation to another Boeing facility.
- Developed and implemented plant closing strategies and coordinated the transfer of technology to the new facility while managing day-to-day employee relations activities.
- Worked with the multi-discipline business venture team, consulting in all HR areas.

**Manager, Employment and Employee Relations - Division HQ**, 8/86 - 12/87
- Provided employment, college recruiting, and EEO / AA coordination for headquarters and field sales employees.
- Handled day-to-day employee relations issues; facilitated management development training programs; and conducted interventions, third party consultation and team building sessions.

**Senior Human Resources Administrator - Division HQ**, 10/84 - 8/86

**Benefits Administrator - Division HQ**, 3/83 - 10/84

**Supervisor, Distribution - Tacoma Plant**, 4/82 - 3/83

**UNIVERSITY OF WASHINGTON**, Seattle
**Student Personnel Administrator**, 8/80 - 4/82

## *EDUCATION*

**Master of Science, Counseling**, emphasis in Personnel, Oregon College, Salem, OR, 1980

**Bachelor of Science**, Oregon College, 1978

## *LEADERSHIP AND AWARDS*

Leadership Development Program (CCL)
Boeing Achievement Award (2)
Chair, National User Conference, 1994

NTL Interaction Lab, Team Building, Basic OD
Certified Instructor - Frontline Leadership, MPG
Advanced Employee Relations Law Certificate
Behavioral Interviewing (DDI)

## *PROFESSIONAL AFFILIATIONS*

Society for Human Resource Management
Human Resource Systems Professionals

Employment Management Association

positions and the degrees have bold upper- and lowercase letters. The profile in the shadowed, full-width box near the top sets the tone for the rest of the resume. To offset the candidate's big-company orientation, the writer includes employee involvement in each position description.

**Irene Stephens**

1111 North Hill Street • Radcliff, Kentucky 40100 • (502) 351-1111

## Objective

**Training Manager / Human Resources Manager**

## Qualifications

- Held positions of increasing responsibility in management, operations, and training.
- Work well with people, both individually and as part of a team.
- Positive attitude reflected in personal determination, discipline, and dedication.
- Highly adaptable. Thrive on change and respond in a positive manner to new responsibilities and tasks.
- Excellent written and verbal skills.

## Management & Organization

- As department manager of a newly formed organization, assisted the director in developing and implementing company policies. Participated in the initial company goal-analysis, and assisted in the development of a goal task list.
- Managed, planned, and conducted worldwide movement of employees and chemical equipment for training purposes. Inspected equipment, ensured that associates were properly certified, and that all administrative paperwork was in place.
- Within 30 days, structured and established a new company, trained 62 new employees, coordinated all travel arrangements, and physically relocated the company.
- Established and monitored strict inventory control measures to ensure property accountability.
- Managed a heavy equipment company, and supervised the administration, operations, maintenance, transportation, and communications departments within the company, as well as the 30 employees.
- Organized social functions for employees and their families to improve company morale and teamwork.

## Personnel Management and Development

- Selected for position as the manager of a new and unique regional training organization. Assisted with establishment and set up of the organization. Trained teams of personnel to evaluate and conduct training in other companies across an eight-state area. Supervised and instilled a sense of teamwork among the 371 subordinates.
- Set and maintained high standards. Provided daily motivation and training to ensure employees realized that their work was meaningful. Influenced and encouraged personnel to participate in self-improvement processes.
- Managed and supervised as many as 80 personnel. Wrote employee appraisals and conducted counseling with subordinate supervisors on career development and progression, unsatisfactory job performance, and selection for attendance at special training courses.
- Coached and mentored junior and mid-level supervisors. Utilizing drive, determination, and discipline, built the most cohesive and effective leadership team in the organization.
- Ensured that promotions and awards were fair and equal. Acted as president of the company's internal-promotion panel and served as member on the organization's awards selection panel for subordinate supervisors.

*(Continued on page 2)*

**99**

**Combination.** *Connie S. Stevens, Radcliff, Kentucky*

This resume displays strength because of the extra-bold centered name in the contact information, the bold thin-thick lines making a header on each page, the extra-bold centered

**Irene Stephens** **Page 2**

- ➤ Ensured work-loads were evenly distributed. Demanded and maintained quality and safety in all areas.
- ➤ Established a work-site education program for employees to start or complete bachelor or associate degrees. Coordinated all phases of the program with local colleges, professors, and other qualified instructors. Arranged meeting times and places for classes before work, during lunch, and after work.
- ➤ Ensured that training was fairly and equally distributed. Assisted with the selection of employees for special training and courses. Evaluated the effectiveness of all training programs.
- ➤ Assisted in developing the requirements, standards, and validation methodology for Trainer Certification.

## Communication

- ➤ Frequently acted as spokesperson for the organization. Prepared and conducted briefings with top level management officials.
- ➤ Acted as principal advisor to the company's director on all matters dealing with junior and mid-level supervisors.

## Education

**Master's Degree** in **Business Management** • Dec 90
University of Kentucky • Lexington, KY

**Bachelor of Science** in **Business Administration** • May 83
**Bachelor of Science** in **Psychology** • May 83
University of Kentucky • Lexington, KY

## Career Path

| | |
|---|---|
| Feb 91 - Present | Any Large Heavy Equipment Manufacturing Plant • Louisville, KY<br>**Human Resources Manager** |
| Jan 88 - Feb 91 | Any Training Organization • Louisville, KY<br>**Training Manager** |
| Jun 83 - Jan 88 | Any Chemical Plant • Louisville, KY<br>**Assistant Training Manager** |

headings, the square bullets in the Qualifications section, and the arrow-tip bullets in the three main sections following the Qualifications. The arrow-tip bulleted items are grammatically parallel in having verbs in the past tense. The career path has been continuous since June 1983.

## Marie Smith

123 Major Street • Santa Clara, CA 95456 • (408) 664-8765

### Objective

A challenging Human Resources position, contributing to corporate success while continuing to grow in my profession.

### Professional Capabilities

- Recruiting and Hiring
- Payroll Processing
- Compensation Planning
- Training and Development
- Manpower Planning
- Policy Development
- Employee Relations
- Benefits Administration
- 401k, Pension
- AAP, EEO
- UI, SDI, WC
- Safety, OSHA

### Human Resources Experience

*Human Resources Manager* 1987 - 1992
**AKG Acoustics, Inc. (formerly Orban Associates)** San Francisco, CA

Primary responsibilities included hiring, employee relations, benefit and salary administration, policy development and implementation. Supervised a Recruiter, HRIS Assistant and Personnel Administrator while working in two locations.

- Improved efficiency of employment functions.
- Developed policies consistent with labor laws and good employee relations while counseling managers about administrative consistency.
- Corrected implementation of 401k and pension plans.
- Purchased better health insurance at a 12% cost reduction.
- Made benefits understandable and accessible to multicultural workforce.
- Upgraded managers' employee relations, counseling and disciplinary skills.

*Personnel Manager* 1982 - 1987
**Hillestad Corporation** San Jose, CA

Recruited and hired employees. Developed managers' counseling and performance appraisal skills. Supervised employee relations and disciplinary actions including terminations.

- Instituted accurate payroll processing and better salary administration planning.
- Developed policies, health insurance and 401k plan benefits understandable to employees.
- Saved money by improving unemployment insurance and workers' compensation administration.
- Reduced UI rate annually.

*Regional Personnel Coordinator* Position: 1973 - 1978 Company: 1970 - 1982
**Deluxe Check Printers** San Jose and Los Angeles, CA

Worked through 8 Plant Managers to initiate and monitor personnel policies and practices. Initiated Affirmative Action Plans for all plants, revamped orientation program and co-developed 4 in-house management training programs.

- Trained Interviewers and Training Coordinators, wrote manuals, and conducted seminars at various levels.
- Wrote job descriptions and evaluations.
- Audited each plant's hiring, AAP progress, manpower planning, wage administration and disciplinary actions. Conducted attitude surveys.

**100**

**Combination.** *Gary Watkins, San Jose, California*

A single, full, horizontal line serves as part of a header on each page. The three bulleted columns in the Professional Capabilities section have items that could be altered to adapt the resume to a

**Marie Smith** page 2

## Other Work Experience

*Administrative Support* 1994 - Present
**Sony Electronics Research Labs** San Jose, CA

Audit and track invoices, purchases requisitions, expense reports and accounting documents going to San Diego for payment. Make corrections, obtain approval signatures and verify that policy is being followed.

Improved the turn around time for San Jose payments routed through the San Diego operation by improving procedures and accuracy. Learned Microsoft Word and Excel for Macintosh.

*Assistant Manager* 1994
**Stride Rite Corporation** San Jose, CA

Ordered and displayed stock, trained new hires, directed staff, documented sales and inventory transactions, handled banking, balanced cash and assisted customers.

*Sales Associate* 1992 - 1993
**Macy's West** Santa Clara, CA

Developed clientele, assisted customers, planned displays and record keeping for the children's shoe department.

*Consulting and Temporary Assignments* 1992

## Education

*Bachelor of Arts, Natural Science Major, Math Minor*
**California State University, San Jose**

*Continuing Education*
**Professional Seminars**

Interviewing, Affirmative Action, California and US Labor Law, ADA, Wage Administration (Hay and Market Based), Maintaining Non-Union Status, Workers Compensation for California, Hazcom, OSHA Manufacturing Regulations, Management Problem Solving Skills, Termination Practices, COBRA Updated Unemployment Insurance Rate Management.

different objective or position. Bulleted items in the Human Resources Experience and Other Work Experience sections show both duties and achievements. Positions in italic and company names in boldface are easily seen. Professional seminars attended make a strong ending.

**ANDREW EVANS**
**900 Philodendron Ln. #555 • Santa Clara, CA 95000**
**(555) 555-5555**

---

**OBJECTIVE:** Position as a Purchasing/Traffic Manager. Willing to travel as required.

**QUALIFICATIONS:**
- Over 15 years of experience involving purchasing/traffic responsibilities.
- Proven management, leadership, and organizational skills.
- Effective performance in a multi-task environment; experienced decision-maker.
- Strong communication skills; ability to develop productive work relationships with others.
- Computer skills: Real World (purchasing software); CC Mail on network.

**EXPERIENCE:**

**Worldwide Corporation.**, Mountain View, CA 1993-Present
**PURCHASING/LOGISTICS MANAGER**
*Responsible for procurement of materials and equipment for factories in Singapore, Germany, and the United Kingdom. Also responsible for import/export to and from these countries.*
- Supervise, train, and evaluate four employees in purchasing, shipping/receiving, and traffic.
- Compare air/freight rates of providers, perform cost analysis, and set guidelines for cost-effective shipment to various international locations. Negotiate rates and delivery terms with freight forwarders, Federal Express, and UPS.
- Interface extensively with other departments to coordinate shipping/traffic activities.
- Respond to customer inquiries received by customer service department, regarding billing questions or freight invoice issues.
- Implement corporate purchasing policies and strategy.

**Accomplishments include:**
- Conducted survey to determine shipping needs; used data to establish shipping department cut-off times and communicated schedule to everyone involved.
- Improved ship-alert system and associated procedures between the U.S. and Singapore.
- Designed shipment routing program which has reduced freight costs by up to $25,000 per year.
- Established quality improvement team to resolve shipping/traffic deficiencies and improve inter-department cooperation.

**Advanced Electronics**, Cupertino, CA 1984-1993
**PURCHASING/TRAFFIC SUPERVISOR**
- Managed all activities related to direct, indirect, and capital equipment purchases.
- Sourced and qualified both domestic and international/off-shore vendors, with an emphasis on quality and cost-effectiveness.

**Robbins-Atkins Manufacturing**, Palo Alto, CA 1981-1983
**INVENTORY CONTROL SUPERVISOR**
- Supervised purchasing, shipping/receiving and stockroom activities.
- Implemented quality circle program to improve inter-plant communications.

**PROFESSIONAL AFFILIATIONS:** Member, Professional Association of Exporters and Importers

**EDUCATION/TRAINING:**
- Associate of Arts degree in Business Administration, Mission College, Santa Clara, CA, 1980
- Workshops in Purchasing Negotiation and Sales Tax

**101**

**Combination.** *Georgia Adamson, Campbell, California*

The writer used distinctive bullets "to add visual impact." In the Experience section, the writer also created an Accomplishments subsection for the current position to stress recent work.

## PABLO RODRIGUEZ

1203 Park Drive
Pineville, North Carolina 28134
(704) 555-1774

### SUMMARY OF QUALIFICATIONS

- 10 years of broad-based retail management experience, with an emphasis on buying, inventory control, sales, promotions, and merchandising for men's sportswear, designer clothes, furnishings, and suits.
- Keen analytical skills. Proven ability to identify current and emerging fashion trends that satisfy both the customer's need for value and the company's need for profit.
- Accustomed to working with sales representatives, vendors, managers and other buyers in fast-paced and highly competitive environments.
- Effective at implementing successful purchasing and merchandising strategies that maximize available resources, sales and budgetary limitations.

### VENDOR RELATIONS/BUYING EXPERIENCE

| | | | | |
|---|---|---|---|---|
| Haggar | Levi-Strauss | Tommy Hilfiger | Anne Klein | Bugle Boy |
| Wembley | Polo/Chaps | Alexander Julian | Warren Sewell | Izod |
| Generra | Jordache | Calvin Klein | Men's Claiborne | Gant |

### MANAGEMENT EXPERIENCE

**Inventory Control Manager** Richmar Fashions, Fort Mill, SC 1993-Present
*Annual Sales Volume: $3 million*
Coordinate the timely computer input of customer and vendor purchase orders, shipping and receiving data, and credit information. Evaluate inventory and advise buyers of optimum stock levels. Communicate with vendors on reorders and return requests. Manage accounts receivable and customer service functions. Prepare sales activity reports to plan merchandising and distribution strategies.

**Assistant Store Manager** Stein Mart, Winston Salem, NC 1992-1993
*Annual Sales Volume: $6 million*
Helped manage all daily store activities. Trained department managers and newly hired sales associates on customer service, sales, and merchandising techniques. Orchestrated a successful accessories promotion that ranked second in the region and one of the best in the country.

**Divisional Manager, Menswear** Belk Hudson, Brunswick, GA 1991-1992
*Annual Sales Volume: $4.3 million*
Oversaw all advertising and buying activities for three stores. Trained sales personnel on merchandising, customer service, inventory control, and reordering procedures. Introduced a new product line and coordinated a successful Levi's promotion.

**Sales Manager** Rich's, Atlanta, GA 1986-1991
*Annual Sales Volume: $2.3 million*
Supervised a 12-member staff and managed promotions, advertising, displays, and inventory. Evaluated sales performance and implemented successful incentive programs. Coordinated with buyers on inventory levels and sales trends.

### EDUCATION

**Bachelor of Science Degree** Business Administration/Marketing University of Akron, OH

References Available Upon Request

102

**Combination.** *John A. Suarez, Troy, Illinois*

This person wanted to return to buying. The writer plays up buying in the Summary, creates a Buying Experience section, and emphasizes titles more than dates in Management Experience.

# Katherine Marie Nickerson

3212 Uncle Sam's Parkway • Wilmington, NC 28412 • (000) 111-2222

**Profile**

***Purchasing . . . Inventory Management . . . Logistics***

Dynamic career professional with demonstrated proficiency in all areas including:

- Purchasing
- Contract Negotiation & Administration
- Vendor Sourcing
- Transportation / Logistics
- JIT & Inventory Management
- ISO & Quality Adherence

Career track record of improvements to each area of responsibility particularly in generating cost savings for the company.

Strong interpersonal skills with a proven ability to interact with individuals on all levels of an organization.

**Experience**

***Big Time Corporation***, Wilmington, NC 1973 - Present

Full responsibility for purchasing, delivery, and all related activities required to secure raw materials to support world-class manufacturing facilities. Received several company commendations for performance.

***Purchasing***

- Purchase essential ingredients and finishes for three sites.
- Coordinate purchase of refined and spent glycol for six plant sites and methanolysis feedstock for one plant.
- Adhere to strict quality standards in selection of materials while achieving cost goals. Well-versed in ISO.
- Locate materials for emergency and shut-down situations to minimize downtime and costs.

***Contract Administration***

- Authorize releases against contracts.
- Manage all on-site service contracts with responsibility for sourcing, bidding, negotiation, and selection of vendors.
- Interact with contractors and plant personnel evaluating fulfillment of contract.

***Inventory Management***

- Reconcile accounts and maintain inventory records for raw materials and supplies at several plants.
- Instrumental participant in establishing production rates based on inventory availability.
- Interact with personnel on the floor of refinery fine-tuning manufacturing process to increase quality of raw materials.

***Logistics***

- Maintain and coordinate rail car fleet for transportation of glycol. Achieved significant cost reductions for transportation expenses and improved utilization of fleet.
- Extensive experience in logistics researching and negotiating contracts for truck and rail transportation to meet product needs.

**References**

Provided upon request

**103**

**Combination.** *Sandy Adcox Saburn, Wilmington, North Carolina*

This individual, who had worked more than 20 years for one company, feared that she couldn't do anything else. Her experience is divided into four main skill areas to show its breadth.

# JOHN GOULSBY ▪ 4921 117th Street ▪ Fennville MI 49408 ▪ 222-444-0044

▪ ELECTRICAL TROUBLESHOOTING//COMPUTERIZED CONTROLS ▪ MECHANICAL TROUBLESHOOTING//MACHINE DESIGN ▪

## Career Objective

**Position as Facilities Maintenance Supervisor/Coordinator in a progressive organization where I can utilize knowledge and expertise to implement profit-oriented results.**

## Summary of Qualifications

- **15+ years experience in hands-on mechanical and industrial maintenance field including 10+ years in operations management as supervisor/engineer and third shift lead mechanic.**
- **Knowledge of computerized maintenance management systems and processes; solid experience in preventive maintenance and repair of:**
  - manual and computer operated motor controllers, power control centers, new runs for lighting systems and outlets, motor operated equipment, power systems for computer equipment.
- **Comprehensive background in areas of:**
  - safety (HAZMAT), quality assurance and continuous improvement concepts, materials handling and distribution--JIT; preventive maintenance programs; and numerous manufacturing processes.

## Leadership Abilities

- Detail-oriented and results-driven, with proven ability to identify, analyze, and repair problems.
- Ability to perform effectively despite sudden setbacks and changing priorities.
- Strong planning, organizational, and estimating skills; with long-term focus on the bottom line.
- Ability to determine the cause and justify the resulting cost overruns of completed projects.
- Excellent communication and interpersonal skills; ability to supervise, motivate, train, and increase productivity.

## Technical Skills

- **Utilize troubleshooting publications to solve problems; interpret blueprints, schematics, manuals, and specification requirements for:**
  - PLC's, water treatment plant equipment: tank farms, cooling towers, chillers; AC/DC drives; check weighers; prototypes; welders; conveyor components; hydraulic, pneumatic, and digital equipment, and a variety of electrical and electronic meters, calipers, and scales.

## Computer Knowledge

- **Excellent working knowledge of computer systems and programs to include**: Windows 95: Lotus 123, Microsoft Word, Oracle, and numerous troubleshooting equipment and software.

## Education

1978. **A.A/S: Electronics**, Lyons Technical Institute, Upper Darby, PA.

## Work History

| | |
|---|---|
| 1995-Pres. | **Manager**, B&G Services/Electrical, A/C, Refrigeration, Heavy Equipment Repair, Fennville, MI. |
| 1990-1995. | **Maintenance Mechanic A, Third Shift Lead Mechanic**, Clorox Company, Chicago, IL. |
| 1985-1990. | **Plant Engineer, Production Supervisor**, Servie Ice, (formerly Sparkle Ice & Tucson Ice) Tucson, AZ. |
| 1984-1985. | **Operations Manager, Production Supervisor**, Mountain Ice, Tucson, AZ. |
| 1982-1984. | **Maintenance Mechanic, Electrician, Setup Assistant**, Sundance Press, Tucson, AZ. |
| 1981. | **Apprentice Refrigeration Technician/Electrician**, Don Reed's Refrigeration, Plainwell, MI. |
| 1979-1980. | **Welder, Rollform Operator, Production Assistant**, Pullman Industries, Inc., Pullman, MI. |
| 1977-1978. | **Apprentice**: Radio/Television Communications Equipment, National Allied Signal, Philadelphia, PA. |

## Certifications/Licensures

1988-1990. • State of Arizona General Contractor Mechanical License.

**104**

**Combination.** *Randall S. Clair, Parchment, Michigan*

A resume that uses small type and wide lines to pack a lot of information on one page. Full horizontal lines separate the many sections visually and therefore make the resume easy to read.

# F. Patrick Hassey

1009 Vallejo Way • Sacramento, California 95818 • (916) 446-6151

***OBJECTIVE*** A position as General Manager.

***PROFILE***

- More than 15 years progressive experience in water and wastewater management.
- Strong leader, program developer, capable decision maker, and adept problem solver.
- Employ participative management style endorsing team building environment.
- Excellent communication, organizational, and time-management abilities.

***EDUCATION***

B.A., Management, Saint Mary's College, Moraga, CA
A.S., Mechanical Electrical Technology, Sacramento City College, Sacramento, CA

***RELEVANT EXPERIENCE AND ACCOMPLISHMENTS***

**MANAGEMENT**

- Administered $5 million annual operating budget in directing operation, maintenance and repair of 3,200-mile sanitary sewer collection system.
- Directed staff of 50 full-time personnel through one assistant and 5 supervisors.
- Supervised operation of 35 MGD, Grade V, secondary wastewater treatment plant; 7 sanitary lift stations; 19 water wells; and 150-mile water distribution system.
- Conducted personnel evaluations; training; hiring, dismissals, transfers, and disciplinary actions; and coordinated in-house educational programs.
- Chaired committees and facilitated various meetings and work groups.

**WATER/WASTEWATER**

- Systematized laboratory testing, submitted regulatory reports, and prepared annual budget.
- Improved effluent quality from 85 percent BOD, and suspended solids removal within 6 months to 97 percent and 98 percent removal, respectively.

**PROGRAM/PROJECT DEVELOPMENT**

- Created and implemented emergency procedure manuals, developed equipment and contract specifications.
- Established cost effective operations parameters assuring management's objectives.
- Authored 5-year personnel plan for wastewater collections system and water meter shop.
  - Provided rationale and justification for both personnel and equipment.
- Developed employment examinations from entrance level through 2 ranks of supervisors.
- Conducted analysis of 24-hour shift schedules, and developed alternative schedules identifying $100,000 annual cost savings.
- Scripted and produced video, coordinated on-site inspection and interviews that won Sacramento CSD No. 1 the 1995 CWEA Collection System of the Year award.

**105**

**Combination.** *Nancy Karvonen, Willits, California*

A resume for a Maintenance Manager. Headings are all uppercase and in italic. This enables the three roman subheadings in the Relevant Experience and Accomplishments section to stand out.

# F. Patrick Hassey

*Page Two*

*EMPLOYMENT HISTORY*

1990-present **Underground Construction/ Maintenance Manager •** County of Sacramento
Plan, budget, and direct work of water distribution and wastewater collections system repair, maintenance, and construction crews.

1988-1990 **Water/Wastewater Supervisor •** City of Lodi, Lodi
Supervised operation, maintenance and repair of sanitary sewer collection and water distribution systems. Coordinated development of underground utilities mapping system to accommodate future growth.

1986-1988 Underwent complete recovery and retraining from medical condition.

1983-1986 **Plant Shift Supervisor •** Vallejo Sanitation and Control District, Vallejo
Supervised and participated in operation of 15 MGD physical-chemical wastewater treatment plant.

1982-1983 **Consultant •** Barnes and Associates, Oakland
Analyzed workers compensation claims for 11-city risk management group. Developed cost base for all departments in each city.

1980-1982 **Safety/Training Officer •** Central Contra Costa Sanitary District, Martinez
Facilitated and directed implementation and maintenance of comprehensive district-wide safety, health, and training program. Acted as liaison for California Administrative Law, Occupational Safety and Health, Engineering Technology, and Water/Wastewater Systems.

*LICENSES*

- **Grade V Wastewater Operator**
- Grade IV Collection System Maintenance
- Grade II Water Treatment Operator

*AWARDS/ HONORS*

- WECF Member Association Safety Award
- Gerson Chanin Award
  *Outstanding Published Contributions to Bulletin of the California Water Environment Association*
- CWEA Collection Systems Committee, *Ambassador*

*PROFESSIONAL AFFILIATIONS*

- California Water Environment Association (CWEA)
  - Collection System Committee, *Chairman*
- Water Environment Federation (WEF)
- American Public Works Association (APWA)
- Greater Central Valley Collection System Committee (GCVCSC)

*PUBLICATIONS*

- CWEA Bulletin
  *Published 6 articles on training, and innovative technology.*
- Sacramento County Water Quality Division
  *Reactive and Proactive Maintenance Labor Requirement Study*
- Sacramento County Water Quality Division
  *Performance Evaluation of New Sika Robotics In-Line Sewer Repair System*
- Barnes and Associates
  *Contra Costa County Risk Management Authority Analysis and Evaluation of Workers Compensation Claims*

Employment History dates show steady work since 1980, and the positions indicate the different roles of this person. In referring to his technical articles, the Awards/Honors and Publications sections break any stereotypes readers might have about maintenance managers.

**HOWARD COLBERG**
**445 E. 35th Street**
**New York, NY 10016**
**(212) 124-7743**

**SUMMARY OF QUALIFICATIONS**

Dedicated Maintenance Manager with 10 years of progressive experience in all aspects of building operations for a large community building in New York City. Excellent technical, organizational, and interpersonal skills. Ability to supervise and motivate employees for improved productivity. Highly motivated and cooperative individual who can interact well with visitors, employees, and management.

SKILLS INCLUDE THE FOLLOWING AREAS:

| | | |
|---|---|---|
| Electrical | Plumbing | Carpentry |
| HVAC (some) | Glazing | Painting |
| Pool/Gym Maintenance | General repair/maintenance | Grounds Maintenance |
| Supervising outside contractors | Drywall | Plexiglass and countertop installation |

**MANAGEMENT EXPERIENCE**

**NYC COMMUNITY CENTER** — New York, NY
***Maintenance Manager*** — 1988 to 1996

- Supervise and perform all facets of building maintenance and repair for 7-story, 46,000 sq. ft. community center built in 1945, which includes community recreation and meeting rooms, restaurant, pool and gymnasium and garden/greenhouse areas. Capacity is approximately 700 individuals for the senior and youth centers.
- Promoted rapidly from initial position as a maintenance worker.
- Maintain all building standards and codes to comply with NYC regulations.
- Oversee operation of HVAC equipment as required; perform light plumbing, painting, and carpentry. Maintain and repair all interior and external areas. Supervise substantial electrical work as required.
- Supervise subcontractors during various renovation projects such as new door and window installations.
- Oversee building operations for numerous social and fundraising events, which consist of transporting chairs and tables, supervising guest safety and security, and other logistics of the events.

**ADDITIONAL EXPERIENCE**

**CONRAD RAILROAD** — New York, NY
***High Tension Lineman in Local #3 Union*** — 1983 to 1988

**UNITED STATES ARMY** — Germany & Texas
***Fire Control Missile Mechanic*** — 1976 to 1983
Rank: E-5; Honorable Discharge

Commendations: Good Conduct Medal, Army Service Ribbon, Overseas Service Medal

**EDUCATION/TRAINING/CERTIFICATES**

United States Army - High School Graduate
Sprinkler City, T-1 License, 1/94
Supervise low BSI/Oil Burner #6, 2/94
Department of Health, Swimming Pool Operation, Technology Certificate, 9/90
Driver's License: Class 6G

**REFERENCES**

Furnished upon request.

**106**

**Combination.** *Etta Barmann, New York, New York*

The 4-row, 3-column table indicates the person's skills in electricity, plumbing, and carpentry. Five years of union work as a High Tension Lineman show that he knows how to handle wiring.

PROFESSIONAL
PROFILE

TONYA LIZA SALSIDO

**Facilities Maintenance Manager**

107

**Combination.** *Fran Holsinger, Tempe, Arizona*

This is the front cover of a folded 11" x 17" sheet of paper that was originally colored. When you open the cover, you see the rest of the resume spread over two pages. The back cover is left blank.

# TONYA LIZA SALSIDO

124 S. International St. | Mesa, AZ 55555 | [555] 000-0000

## EDUCATION:

FULLERTON COMMUNITY COLLEGE - Fullerton, CA
Major: Pre-Law 1992 -1993

## SUMMARY OF QUALIFICATIONS:

- Over 10 years supervisory/facility management experience....
- Supervised 30 county/150-200 participants in county work program....
- Maintained 25+ buildings in Hughes Aircraft complex....
- Interviewed/hired/trained/scheduled/evaluated/disciplined employees....
- Trained/supervised employees without constraint of language barrier....
- Outsourced special services....requested bids from vendors to supply services....
- Prepared payroll information....
- Generated significant savings through providing on-site equipment repairs....
- Purchased equipment/supplies....
- Utilized Team Concept to set pace/direction of department....improved morale in all areas....
- Oversaw set-up of city convention center for conventions/ceremonies/functions....worked with sound systems/lighting....
- Devised/monitored inventory control system....
- Cognizant of O.S.H.A. guidelines/requirements for employee safety ....
- Instituted bi-weekly employees meetings to resolve issues/concerns...
- Articulate....good sense of humor....dependable....organized....detail oriented....team player....adaptable....able to establish rapport with peers/upper management....efficient....excellent follow-through.... timely....

This is another Maintenance Manager resume that breaks any stereotype someone might have about maintenance managers. The candidate here is a woman who, for four years, maintained more than twenty-five buildings in the Hughes Aircraft complex. The Summary of Qualifications lists this and other impressive

professional profile

PROFESSIONAL HIGHLIGHTS:

**FACILITIES/MAINTENANCE MANAGEMENT**

- Scheduled/supervised employees....
- Inspected work performances to assure compliance to required standards...
- Developed/coordinated training sessions....
- Monitored performances of county work program participants....
- Responded to/solved complaints from customers....
- Maintained appropriate levels of safety performance....
- Negotiated with vendors....
- Provided input into budget preparations....
- Met budget guidelines....
- Instituted "Open Door" policy with employees....
- Improved operations of large city maintenance department....
- Handled operations of 4 sq block convention center....
- Supervised security personnel....
- Created round table discussions with other departments to resolve job security issues....
- Reduced outside vendor contracts/costs through utilizing internal personnel to provide services....
- Authorized requisitioning of supplies/equipment....
- Devised program to increase cost efficiency....

EMPLOYERS:

**VARSITY CONTRACTOR** - Glendale, AZ
*Area Manager:* 1994 - 1995

**HUGHES AIRCRAFT CORP** - Fullerton, CA
*Manager:* 1988 - 1992

**CALIFORNIA INSTITUTE OF TECHNOLOGY** - Pasadena, CA
*Supervisor:* 1987 - 1988

**CITY OF CINCINNATI** - Cincinnati, OH
*Maintenance Manager:* 1972 - 1987

managerial experiences this person has had. Listed at the end of the Summary are personal traits, which are transferable skills this person could take with her to any kind of new job or career. The Highlights section contains a mix of duties and achievements.

# JOHN A. THOMAS

1234 South Bloom Street
Kalamazoo, MI 49007

Home: (616) 555-1212
Office: (616) 555-2121

## PROFILE

Skilled hands-on manager of personnel and contracted projects involving the **design, development, and manufacture of tooling**. Currently targeting related management positions to further challenge and share my expertise and successful experience in the areas of:

- ▲ Employee Training, Motivation, Development, Supervision, and Productivity
- ▲ Manufacturing Troubleshooting and Problem Solving
- ▲ Prototype Development and Design
- ▲ Customer Relations
- ▲ Process Engineering

*Computer skills include Windows, Microsoft Office (Word, Excel, Powerpoint), WordPerfect, and DOS. Currently learning Unigraphics computer-aided-design (CAD) system; knowledge of MasterCam.*

## EMPLOYMENT

PEG MIDWEST TECHNICAL CENTER, BATTLE CREEK, MICHIGAN

**Tooling Manager** sharing responsibility for 54 employees producing new tooling for $6.5 million division (annual sales), including new plastic injection and die cast molds, as well as all repairs for PEC Michigan's 32-press custom molding facility. (1993–present)

METAL PROCESSING., KALAMAZOO, MICHIGAN

**Manufacturing Manager** directly accountable to company owner for all trim die design and building, custom wire and conventional EDM, duplication, copy die milling, and CNC milling personnel and procedures for 45-employee company generating $5+ million in sales. (1991–1993)

BO-KAL, INC., TEMPERANCE, MICHIGAN

**Tool and Die / Mold Journeyman** responsible for the repair of plastic molds and building of specialized machinery for $2 million company. (Interim position, 1990–1991)

MODERN TOOLS / LIBBEY-OWENS-FORD DIVISION, TOLEDO, OHIO

**Tool and Die Supervisor** in charge of personnel (26 direct / 50 indirect) and contracted projects involving the design, development, and manufacture of tooling for the automotive and aerospace industries for division having over $6 million in annual sales. (1983–1990)

Previous positions included Machine and Maintenance Foreman, Tool and Die / Mold Leader, Tool and Die /Mold Journeyman, and Tool and Die Apprentice. (1970–1983)

## PROFESSIONAL DEVELOPMENT

- How to Build & Improve Customer Service
- Front Line Leadership I, II, & III
- Employee Involvement (Facilitator)
- Performance Review Training
- Employee Assistance
- Dale Carnegie Personal Development
- Maintaining Customer Satisfaction
- QS 9000 Workshops
- Bloodborne Pathogens Compliance
- Accident Investigation Training
- Advanced Time & Self Management
- Producing Results with Others
- Supervising the Workforce
- Worker's Right to Know

## EDUCATION

KALAMAZOO VALLEY COMMUNITY COLLEGE, KALAMAZOO, MICHIGAN
Completed coursework toward Associate Degree in Business.

108

**Combination.** *Mary Roberts, Tarpon Springs, Florida*

The resume opens in an ordinary way with a Profile that indicates the individual's different areas of experience and expertise in tooling. Computer skills are listed in italic. At this point, rules

**JOHN A. THOMAS**
**Page 2 of 2**

**Home: (616) 555-1212**
**Office: (616) 555-2121**

**SELECTED CAREER HIGHLIGHTS**

**Leadership / Employee Relations**

- Supervised and scheduled [up to] 76 Die Welding, EDM, WEDM, Gundrill, CNC, Conventional Duplicator, and Boring Mill workers in both union and non-union environments.
- Interviewed, hired, and trained employees to establish new night shift and increase efficiency of machinery and hours; conducted regular performance evaluations and determined merit raises.
- Developed and implemented several new leader systems to improve manufacturing quality and quantity.
- Conducted weekly production meetings to coordinate quality control, engineering, sales, accounting, and / or manufacturing personnel, resulting in better flow of information between departments, improved procedural effectiveness, and adherence to job safety practices.
- Originated use of Lake Michigan College pre-apprenticeship program to upgrade new apprentice qualifications and speed return on employee training investment.
- Participated in the start-up and continuation of an Employee Involvement program which resulted in overall improvement of employee morale.
- Chaired committee that developed and implemented an innovative system to re-quote work and computerize data which improved work scheduling and accuracy of build hours charged.

**Technical / Operational Achievements**

- Established new evaluation system to separate merit raises from performance evaluations which resulted in a more productive environment to discuss individual improvement.
- Replaced three-tier tracking system--time, job, and work cards--with one-card system which eliminated duplication of clerical efforts and allowed precision job cost tracking.
- Created new computerized priority report program which facilitated tracking of work in progress and backlogs.
- Realigned large machine burden to more closely match profit centers and establish a more accurate shop rate.
- Instrumental in the purchase of new CNC equipment and the upgrade of existing CNC equipment to include 75% rebuild of mold shop following $5.5 million dollar fire loss.
- Developed and implemented new job priority tracking system, measuring against quoted hours and delivery dates, to maintain better control of work in progress.
- Traveled to customer locations to provide on-site supervision of new die tryouts which required extensive troubleshooting, problem solving, and customer relations skills.
- Provided quotes for new mold builds, engineering changes, and mold repair work (for all employers).
- Created and coordinated new system to increase "on time" deliveries to 98%.

**Salary & Benefits Negotiable ... Willing to Relocate ... References Upon Request**

become broken on purpose. The writer presents the Employment section next and reaches further back in time than three jobs or ten years to show knowledge about industry standards. The writer also puts career highlights and achievements on the second page for an impressive last page.

# William Robert Jennings

6183 East Drive • Adrian, Michigan 49286
(517) 442-6517 Residence • (517) 442-2285 ext. 294 Work

## QUALIFICATIONS SUMMARY

▸ Strong management and organizational skills ◂
▸ 28 years experience in the automotive industry ◂
▸ Progressive experiences in personnel, sales, and production management ◂
▸ Identified track record in problem solving, training, and motivational tactics ◂
▸ Able to set goals, prioritize tasks, structure operations, and handle multiple projects simultaneously ◂
▸ Excellent oral and written communication, proficient evaluation, and analytical and deductive abilities ◂

## SUMMARY OF EXPERIENCE

### Production Management

- Manage stamping and weld assembly production, equipment and facilities maintenance, and labor.
- Review and analyze production and maintenance reports. Troubleshoot operating problems and improve product quality.
- Revise production schedules and priorities for on-time delivery as a result of equipment failures or operating problems.
- Develop and design programs to meet long- and short-range objectives and goals.
- Utilize team building concepts in the planning process.
- Handle EEO and OSHA problems and ensure guidelines are met.
- Act as labor and management liaison.
- Successfully reduced manufacturing costs and increased company profitability.
- Managed Kaizen Department, educating workers through example on how to identify and eliminate wastes.
- Assisted Production Engineering by developing various production equipment constructed from concepts and built in-house.

### Personnel Management

- Supervised labor contract and benefits coordination.
- Administrated safety and security policies.
- Developed corporate safety policies and education.
- Assisted in start-up hiring and education of 350 employees while coordinating work schedules.
- Responsible for handling and resolution of personnel problems.
- Chair grievance procedure second step meetings for protested labor and contract disputes, disciplinary problems, and policy modifications.
- Increased labor efficiency by motivating problem resolution resulting in improved harmony and decreased absenteeism.
- Developed and maintained very successful suggestion systems.

### Sales

- Managed sales contracts, product diversification, and new business coordination.
- Increased sales by $15 million per year within a 2 year assignment.
- Developed continuing internal quoting procedures and responsibilities.
- Developed continuing sales budgets and procedures.

**109**

**Combination.** *Christina M. Popa, Adrian, Michigan*

An unusual feature in this resume is the use of a pair of bullets to enclose each line in the Qualifications Summary. Because each bullet in a pair points to the text, the eye is led to read

Resume of William Robert Jennings
Page 2

## WORK HISTORY

WASHTENAW STAMPING CORPORATION, ADRIAN, MICHIGAN

| | |
|---|---|
| **Manufacturing Area Manager** | August 1992-Present |
| **Assistant Manager Sales** | August 1991-August 1992 |
| **Assistant Manager Kaizen** | November 1989-August 1991 |
| **Safety and Health Specialist** | August 1988-November 1989 |

JEEP OF AMERICA, INC., SOUTH HAVEN STAMPING PLANT,
SOUTH HAVEN, VIRGINIA

| | |
|---|---|
| **Administrator of Safety and Security** | October 1986-August 1988 |
| **Supervisor of Hourly Personnel/Industrial Relations** | December 1979-October 1986 |

GENERAL MOTORS AUTOMOTIVE DIVISION, BOWLING GREEN, OHIO

| | |
|---|---|
| **UAW Bargaining Unit Representative** | March 1967-December 1979 |

## SEMINARS

- *QS-9000*—Sponsored by Technologies, Inc., January-December 1995

| | |
|---|---|
| Education | Development of Implementation Plan |
| Gap Analysis | Assignment of Project Teams |
| 23 Element Training | Development of Schedules |
| Internal Auditor Training | Projected Certification December 1995 |

- *Effective Time Management Skills*—Sponsored by Educational Marketing Services, Inc., March 1995
- *UAW/Management Labor Conference, "Participative Worksite Process"*—Sponsored by The Labor-Management Council for Economic Renewal, October 1994
- *Team Problem Solving*—Sponsored by LTEC, April 1994
- *Kaizen and the JIT/Toyota Production System*—Sponsored by University of Dayton School of Engineering, May 1990 and June 1994
- *Using Microsoft Works*—Sponsored by LTEC, February 1994
- *MRP II Overview*—Sponsored by NIST/Midwest Manufacturing Technology Center, November 1993
- *Excell*—Sponsored by LTEC, October 1993
- *The Basics of Plant and Production Management*—Sponsored by Keye Productivity Center, September 1993
- *Windows*—Sponsored by LTEC, June 1993
- *Introduction to Computers and Information Processing*—Sponsored by LTEC, February 1993

## EDUCATION

SOUTH HAVEN STATE COLLEGE, INSTITUTE, NORFOLK, VIRGINIA
**Major:** Business Administration

BOWLING GREEN STATE UNIVERSITY, BOWLING GREEN, OHIO
**Major:** Chemical Engineering—Math

FINLEY STATE UNIVERSITY, FINLEY, OHIO
**Major:** Industrial Arts Secondary Education

each line of text and rethink it before moving to the next line. A strong tactic is the clustering of information under three side headings in the Summary of Experience. Groups of related points are easier to read than one long list. Work-related seminars appear before formal education.

**OVERVIEW**

***Self-motivated professional with a strong background in the transportation industry. Progressively increased responsibilities. Proven results ... increasing company revenue, developing cost savings programs, market development, and product awareness. Excellent upper management expertise.***

**SELECTED CAREER HIGHLIGHTS**

- Responsible for establishing a successful Smith/Major office in (major city) for sales and service, resulting in increased market penetration.
- Developed and implemented a "Major First Assist" 24-hour roadside assistance program to support Class 8 vehicles.
- Established an "LPG Bridging Strategy" to maintain the customer base and position to reenter the market, generating 600+ unit sales and enhanced customers' satisfaction.
- Structured and achieved a Hendrickson suspension program that increased dealer/customer acceptance and awareness and notable increase in unit sales.
- Championed a fleet credit card program (launched 2Q/96).
- Designed SVS buy/lease program, featuring a one price with custom option packages which resulted in reduction of product complexity and increased long-term customer loyalty.
- Formed a car hauler task force project for AB88.
- Team member on QFD "Voice of the Customer" which involved customers in research, evaluation, and recommendations toward development of Ford's new AB88 product line.
- Member of cost-cutting team to identify cost-reduction opportunities with vendors, engineering, and product content.
- Developed an innovative national "Walk Around" sales consultant contest ... resulting in increased product knowledge and customer presentation skills.
- Championed warranty consolidation team.

**SUMMARY OF QUALIFICATIONS**

- Excellent program/project and general business manager.
- Creative in problem-solving and cost-cutting issues.
- Demonstrates skill in managing several tasks simultaneously.
- Works cooperatively on teams as well as independently toward excellence and quality in corporate objectives and goals.

**110**

**Combination.** *Lorie Lebert, Novi, Michigan*

The name and other contact information are on the outside cover not included here. The opening section is called an Overview (rather than a Profile) because it focuses not just on the

| | | |
|---|---|---|
| **PROFESSIONAL EXPERIENCE** | *MAJOR MOTOR COMPANY* | |
| | **MARKETING PROGRAMS MANAGER**, 1994- Current | City, State |
| | ▸ Commercial Truck Division | |
| | **NATIONAL ACCOUNTS MANAGER** , 1989-94 | City, State |
| | ▸ Fleet and Leasing Department | |
| | **REGIONAL OPERATIONS MANAGER**, 1986-89 | |
| | ▸ Southeast Region | |
| | **NATIONAL ACCOUNTS MANAGER**, 1983-86 | |
| | ▸ Smith Account Manager | |
| | **SALES ENGINEER**, 1983 | |
| | ▸ Heavy Truck Fleet and Leasing Department | |
| | **HEAVY TRUCK MERCHANDISING MANAGER**, 1980-83 | City, State |
| | ▸ Sales/Marketing – City District | |
| | **TRUCK SALES SPECIALIST**, 1979 -80 | |
| | ▸ City District | |
| | *TRANSPORT AMERICA, INC.* | City, State |
| | **FLEET OPERATIONS MANAGER**, 1975-79 | |
| | *WELL-KNOWN TRUCK RENTAL* | |
| | **BRANCH MANAGER**, 1974-75 | City, State |
| | ▸ Full-service truck leasing and daily rental | |
| | **ACCOUNT MANAGER**, 1974 | City, State |
| | ▸ Full-service truck leasing | |
| | *INTERNATIONAL CORPORATION* | City, State |
| | **ZONE MANAGER**, 1972-74 | City, State |
| | **TRUCK RETAIL SALES REPRESENTATIVE**, 1972 | City, State |
| | **Training Program-Sales & Service**, 1971-72 | |
| **EDUCATION AND TRAINING** | *CORNELL UNIVERSITY* | Ithaca, New York |
| | **BACHELOR OF SCIENCE DEGREE**, 1970 | |
| | ▸ Major: *Industrial/Labor Relations* | |
| | ▸ Numerous training programs, seminars, workshops, skills training | |
| **OTHER INFORMATION** | Member: Commercial Trucking University Associates | |
| | QFD Marketing Committee | |
| | Vendor Task Force | |
| | HN80 Launch Team | |
| | Trade Show Team Member | |
| | Cost-Reduction Team Member | |

person but also on the results of his work. The use of the heading "Selected Career Highlights" suggests that more could have been included with those listed here. The Experience section shows steady work since a year after this person's graduation from college. This resume was his "first-ever" resume!

# IAN FOLKNER

22 SideWay Court
Janesville, Wisconsin 53545
(608) 555-5555

## SENIOR OPERATIONS & MANAGEMENT EXECUTIVE

*Marketing...Procurement...Distribution...P&L Performance*

Key management resource for industrial supply and electronics companies, with a solid track record of initiating and reengineering process improvements, developing strategic marketing plans, and integrating technology with long-range sales and profitability plans. Proven ability to shorten production and processing cycles, generate new revenue streams, and improve individual and team performance levels.

**Key strengths include:**

Strategic Planning
Direct Marketing
Demand Forecasting
Distribution Resource Planning
Procurement
EDI/Supplier Partnerships
Inventory Management
Product Management

Expertise in developing direct marketing strategies to identify, penetrate, and expand key customer segments. Consistently achieved high standards relating to inventory service levels, inventory turns, obsolete inventory, cost of goods sold, and gross profit margins.

## CURRENT EMPLOYMENT

LAB SAFETY SUPPLY, INC., Janesville, Wisconsin, 1990-Present
*(direct marketer of personal and industrial safety products; a division of W.W. Grainger)*

**Business Unit Manager** (1994-Present): Develop and implement company-wide marketing strategies for three customer segments currently totaling 250,000 and increasing by more than 40,000 locations per year. Coordinated merchandising and circulation plans to maximize revenue and contribution stream.

- Implemented new planning processes that reduced catalog production time by 50%.
- Improved product margins and cut marketing expenditures 25% while maintaining sales levels.
- Expanded product lines and grew new product sales at twice the company growth rate. Currently positioning department for 15% increase in new product sales, up from 9% in 1994.
- Played a key role in reengineering the company from an acquisition-based organization to a customer-focused retention and development-based organization. Implemented cross-functional teams, focus groups, and visitation programs to better understand customer needs.

**Procurement Manager** (1990-1994): Led a 30-member department responsible for purchasing more than $100M per year. Oversaw quotations, risk assessment, and pricing.

- Implemented automated demand forecasting and distribution resource planning capabilities that improved buyer productivity 25%.
- Improved inventory turns from 5.5 to 7.6 while increasing line service level from 93% to 97%.
- Reduced overstocked inventory from 3% to 1%.
- Negotiated cost reduction programs with suppliers equal to 2% of cost of goods sold.
- Implemented supplier business guidelines to improve receiving and accounts payable productivity.
- Developed pricing strategies that ensured competitive price positioning and developed quantity break structure that increased average order size by 3%.

**111**

**Combination.** *John A. Suarez, Troy, Illinois*

According to the writer, the opening summary "brings out" what the candidate can do, "and the rest shows what he had done." The summary, which was nonexistent in the original version

**IAN FOLKNER** **2**

## PREVIOUS EXPERIENCE

NEWARK ELECTRONICS, Chicago, Illinois, 1984-1990
*(business to business direct marketer of electronic components; division of Premier Industrial Corporation)*

**Director of Purchasing** (1986-1990): Managed buying operations for a 40-person department purchasing more than $150M annually. Identified need and implemented American Software inventory management system to support multiple distribution centers.

- Oversaw the production and distribution of more than one million catalogs annually.
- Implemented EDI system for purchase orders.

**Purchasing Manager** (1984-1996): Managed the purchasing of all connector and relay product lines. Implemented gross profit improvement systems, e-mail capabilities, and vendor management programs.

- Improved line service level from 85% to 95%.
- Negotiated cost savings equal to 7% of cost of goods sold.

MCMASTER CARR INDUSTRIAL SUPPLY COMPANY, Chicago, Illinois, 1979-1984
*(business to business direct marketer of industrial maintenance products)*

**Physical Distribution Manager** (1982-1984): Managed all operational aspects of a 24-person receiving department.

- Raised productivity 9.5% in the first six months with excellent quality standards.
- Developed an automated stock-out fill system to complement an on-line receiving system.
- Developed a training manual concerning the handling of receiving problems and their impact on accounts payable.

**Supply Side Operations Coordinator** (1982): Identified, implemented, and evaluated inventory projects.

- Developed strategies for purchase programs and solved supplier problems on a corporate rather than a branch basis.
- Coordinated a project designed to study procurement costs and annual carrying costs for warehouse space.

**Accounts Payable Supervisor** (1979-1981): Coordinated all daily operational aspects in an 18-person department.

- Implemented an on-line accounts payable system that improved productivity 30%.
- Developed and implemented a cash forecasting system along with cash variance reporting.
- Coordinated the payment of all invoices for stocking and opening of a new distribution center.

## EDUCATION/PROFESSIONAL ORGANIZATIONS

M.B.A. in General Business, Loyola University of Chicago
B.B. in Accounting, Western Illinois University, Macomb, Illinois
National Association of Purchasing Managers
American Production and Inventory Control Society

References Available Upon Request

of the resume, shows the extent of the individual's strengths and abilities. The Current Employment section covers the person's last two positions with his current employer. The Previous Experience section on the second page is less developed. See the helpful italic explanation of each company.

**BARBARA H. CATYALA**
5356 River Road • Hackensack, New Jersey 00000
**Tel: (000) 000-0000 • Email: 00000.000.000**

## CAREER OBJECTIVE:

EXPERIENCED manufacturing professional seeks a position with advancement opportunities that will utilize acquired skills and knowledge to contribute to organizational success. Areas of expertise include:

MATERIAL MANAGEMENT • INVENTORY MANAGEMENT • MIS MANAGEMENT

## PROFILE SUMMARY:

A dedicated and results-oriented manager with over 12 years experience within a manufacturing environment. Possesses outstanding organizational, analytical and interpersonal skills. Proven ability to define critical problem areas/weaknesses and institute improved processes for maximum efficiency. Excels in driving productivity and profits while streamlining procedures. Builds staff to peak levels of performance, instituting a team-approach. Computer proficiency includes DEC, VAX, VMS, Fortran, Datatrieve, Basic, DCL, PC's, Windows 95 and Microsoft Suite.

## DEMONSTRATED STRENGTHS:

| | | |
|---|---|---|
| *Material Flow Management* | *MRP Systems* | *Inventory Control* |
| *Process Re-Engineering* | *New Process Development* | *Materials Management* |
| *Information Processing* | | *Data Management* |

## SELECTED ACHIEVEMENTS:

- **Consistent record of leading and developing departments from initial start-up phase to successful operations. Requested by senior management to establish and guide the Customer Service, Inventory Control and MIS departments from initial start-up phase to successful operation.**
- **Spearheaded the implementation of ABC Codes for stock items and instituted daily cycle counting: increased productivity while reducing staffing expenses and improved accuracy from 62% to 96%.**
- **Slashed pick-per line time from 7 minutes per line to 3 minutes per line.**
- **Streamlined the time needed in recording physical inventory from 5 days to 3 days, substantially improving productivity and profitability.**
- **Implemented a forecast policy which analyzed sales history and predicted future sales trends, and also pioneered an MRP policy: combined policies were instrumental in slashing product delivered lead times from 120 days to 5 days and in driving annual sales from $12 million to $52 million.**
- **Replaced telephone system from a 32 line in-house MYTEL PBX system to a 250 line, full feature NYNEX Centrex Intellipath system with ISDN and voicemail.**
- **Converted computing from a DEC VAX mainframe and VT terminals to a PC/MC network on the VAX.**

112

**Combination.** *Alesia Benedict, Rochelle Park, New Jersey*

The purpose of the strong achievements on the first page is to overcome the lack of a college degree. On page two, promotions within the same company "show strong performance." Note

**BARBARA H. CATYALA** **(000) 000-0000** **- Page Two -**

## PROFESSIONAL EXPERIENCE:

**INTERNATIONAL DYNAMICS, INC.** - New York, New York **1982 - Present**

***MIS MANAGER (1991-Present)***
High profile position reporting directly to the Vice President of Finance and Chief Operating Officer. Accountable for the development and maintenance of operational procedures for information processing. Recruit, motivate and lead a staff of programmers, network administrators and network technicians. Assess needs to develop new information processing systems and improve program design. Successfully interface with corporate MIS Department in co-aligning strategies and achieving goals. Develop and submit bids. Negotiate and secure contracts.Liaison between users and programmers to determine systems and programming requirements. Implement and manage complex telecommunication systems.

***MATERIAL CONTROL MANAGER (1988-1991)***
Reporting to the Director of Operations, managed daily operations including shipping, receiving, warehouse and inventory control. Led and managed a staff of 22 employees. Identified and resolved critical problem areas to ensure efficiency and timely project completion. Increased department competency of all material handling personnel through strategic staff re-engineering. Served as a liaison with department heads to ensure efficiency, timely completion and increased productivity.

***INVENTORY ADMINISTRATOR (1988)***
Developed, controlled and managed Inventory Control Department, including cycle counting, physical inventories and all inventory transaction processing. Accountable for inventory accuracy and material movement process. Provided leadership to departmental staff. Reduced recording of physical inventory from quarterly to bi-yearly basis. Instituted daily cycle counting and increased accuracy levels. Reported to the Director of Operations.

***CUSTOMER SERVICE SUPERVISOR (1982-1988)***
Developed department from inception through full operation. Communicated extensively with customers to provide delivery dates, product configuration and expediting. Managed staff to peak levels of performance.

**HOTEL MAYER** - New York, New York **1978 - 1982**

***ACCOUNTING TECHNICIAN***
Processed daily receipts through computer system; reconciled receipts and balanced subsidiary ledger. Accountable for $10,000 petty cash. Coordinated payroll. Trained and developed night auditors.

## EDUCATIONAL BACKGROUND:

S.U.N.Y. • Plattsburg, New York • Psychology Major

**Regularly attend in-house training seminars in:**
Inventory Management
Fortran, Datatrieve, BASIC, DCL
VAX Clustering • VAX Operations

the varieties of alignment and indentation. Contact information and headings are centered. The Profile Summary displays double indention. Strengths and the header (page 2) show left-, center-, and right-alignment. Achievements and Experience have hanging indents with full justification.

## Lee Stephens

123 Whiteoaks Drive ◆ Radcliff, Kentucky 40100 ◆ (502) 555-1111

### OBJECTIVE

A responsible position that will utilize my expertise in
**Material Management / Distribution / Human Resources**

### SUMMARY

- More than 20 years of management and leadership experience in logistics, human resources, and training.
- Excellent verbal and written communication skills. Able to work independently or with a team.
- Skilled in directing, coordinating, and motivating staff to successfully complete objectives. Adept at planning and carrying out administrative responsibilities. Reliable and goal-oriented.
- Proficient in the provision of support service, resolving problems, handling sourcing of suppliers, purchasing, account management, and inventory control.

### HIGHLIGHTS OF PROFESSIONAL EXPERIENCE

#### Supply / Inventory Management

- ➡ Managed stock control, accounting, procurement and inventory control of supplies, clothing, and equipment. Supervised storage, receiving, issue, materiel handling, supply locator systems, and supply security operations. Coordinated logistical activities. Analyzed statistical data to improve supply methods and procedures. Performed assistance visits and provided solutions to supply problems.
- ➡ Ensured facility maintenance was accomplished. When funds were not immediately available, ensured that maintenance and repairs were placed on the "new work" list and were given a high priority. Developed suspense system for tracking work orders.
- ➡ Planned and coordinated activities for the organization. Requisitioned or purchased equipment and ensured that it was available when needed. Established contact and invited outside agencies to attend the activities. Wrote itineraries and provided participants with transportation, food, and lodging.

#### Special Operations

- ➡ Supported special operations for an organization of 3,000 personnel.
- ➡ Managed and maintained a large inventory warehouse containing supplies and diverse types of equipment key to this special operations organization, such as cargo nets, tie-down sling nets, pallets, rappeling equipment, ropes, parachutes, scuba diving equipment, etc. Ensured that all necessary equipment was available for special teams to conduct exercises on a worldwide basis.
- ➡ Directed all logistical reports for lost or damaged items.
- ➡ Administered innovative project to replace conventional clothing and equipment with much stronger materials that would withstand the extremely rugged use received in special forces training. Researched requirements and possibilities. Coordinated and observed testing procedures which were implemented at Smith Laboratories. After project met quality standards, oversaw fielding and implementation throughout six companies.
- ➡ Coordinated the project and arranged for Smith Laboratories to develop new food supplies which contained more vitamins and other supplements necessary for added endurance.
- ➡ Prepared packages, equipment, and vehicles which were delivered via aircraft for night flight equipment drops from personnel/equipment transports. Loaded the aircraft. Properly strapped/tied-down/rigged/sling-loaded equipment and vehicles so that the cargo would not break lose while in flight and would be fully balanced when released from the aircraft. Taught Air Transportability and Refresher Sling Load Classes.

**113**

**Functional.** *Connie S. Stevens, Radcliff, Kentucky*

The one and only job—a military position with dates but without comment—does not make this a combination resume. The individual retired as a Sergeant Major in material management, but

**Lee Stephens** Page 2

**Human Resources**

- ➡ Supervised mid-level managers and employees. Wrote performance evaluations and conducted counseling. Determined job-related, equal opportunity, affirmative action training needs and ensured they were accomplished.
- ➡ Devised and implemented a career development program for junior managers. Determined needs and arranged for courses, materials, and funding. Provided guidelines for the managers to instruct and train their subordinates. The program encompassed 780 managers and employees. Result was better trained managers and employees, increased efficiency, and higher morale.
- ➡ Served as President of the boards for selection of "Employee of the Month" and "Employee of the Quarter." Headed the incentive awards program for managers and employees.

**Management**

- ➡ Provided advice and counsel to the director of a district maintenance headquarters. Established plans and procedures for each department. Coordinated administration and support services. Administered, monitored, and reviewed all reports submitted by department managers for the director's approval and signature. Reports were primarily logistical and administrative in nature.
- ➡ Presided over weekly meetings with subordinate mid-level managers. Informed them of goals, new objectives, and problems within the organization.
- ➡ Traveled from Asia to "sister" companies in Hawaii. Presented briefings in preparation for training activities. Performed inspections of sister companies. Wrote reports to provide solutions to any problems encountered during inspection or assistance visits. Coordinated possible solutions with upper echelon, then implemented the plans and provided feedback on the progress.
  - ➡ Assessed the losses and damages that occurred from an oil spill. Determined the equipment, supplies, manpower, and dollars it would take to correct the situation and bring the land and equipment back up to high-quality standard. Implemented the plan and rectified the problem in less than three months.
- ➡ Managed the budget for supply/material management center of a large organization. Responsible for property accountability. Evaluated needs and divided annual monies for supplies among the various offices. Ensured that all offices stayed within their allotted budget. Acted as approval authority on most expenditures.
- ➡ Managed and supervised maintenance of mechanical equipment. Planned layout of maintenance shops and facilities. Supervised production and quality control.

**PROFESSIONAL WORK EXPERIENCE**

- ➡ U.S. ARMY • 1975 - 1995 • Retired with Rank of **Sergeant Major**

**EDUCATION**

- ➡ WEBSTER UNIVERSITY • Webster, KY
  **A.S.** in **Business Management** • Degree Conferred 1985

**CAREER TRAINING COURSES**

Microsoft Computer Software, 80 Hours
Advanced Leadership/Human Resource Development, 6 Months
Advanced Logistics Training, 2 Months
Mid-Level Management and Leadership, 2 Months
Leadership and Personnel Training, 2 Months
Leadership Training, 2 Months
Stock Control and Accounting, 2 Months

most of his career was in special forces (Green Beret, Delta Force). His experience did not translate well into civilian life. "Not very many employers are looking for people who specialize in counterterrorism." The writer "'civilianized' his military job experience as much as possible."

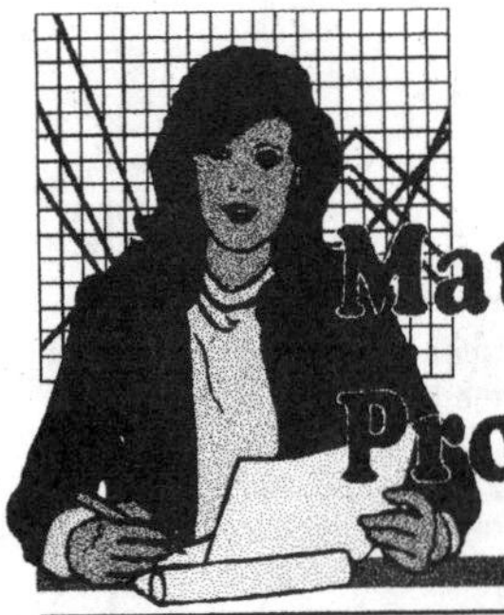

# Purchasing
# Materials Expediting
# Property & Casualty

**Robin Darrelson**
700 West State Street
Pendleton, IN 46064
**(317) 778-8888**

- **Solid background in purchasing, inventory control.**
- **Strong leadership and customer service skills.**
- **Sales & servicing of property & casualty, life & health insurance, and money market products.**
- **Managed half-million budget for operations of up to three hospital dormitory facilities.**

**Professional Experience:**

Material Manager Expediter
Rapid Design Services, Anderson, IN. 1994-95. RDS is a division of Delphi Automotive Systems. Managed all aspects of material management and inventory control. Purchasing of raw materials and components, plastic parts, wiring and batteries. Vendor sourcing and negotiations. Pricing, expediting shipments.

Registered Agent
The Prudential Company, Anderson, IN. 1993-94. Sales and servicing of property & casualty, and life & health insurance packages. Also money market products.

Courier
Federal Express, Muncie, IN. 1990-92. Tracking and locating packages, inventory control, record keeping, ensuring quality customer relations and service.

Staff Sergeant, U.S. Air Force (reserve)
Wright-Patterson AFB, Dayton, OH. 1986-94. In reserve status, responsible for managing all aspects of military dormitory operations; budget, inventory control, supervising work details, maintenance, supplies and equipment.

Dormitory Manager, U.S. Air Force
USAF Regional Hospital, Elmendorf, Alaska. 1983-86. Active duty, managed $.5 million annual budget and operational aspects of up to three hospital dormitories. Purchasing, equipment & services, negotiating with civilian vendors, reviewing & monitoring contracts, quality control.

**Education & Training**

National Assn. of Securities Deailers, Carmel, IN. Series 6 & Series 63 security licenses.

Pathfinders, Indianapolis. All requirements for life & health, property & casualty license.

U.S. Air Force. Supply management, personnel management.

Anchorage Community College.

- **Implemented inventory control system, effectively raising inventory accuracy and ability to meet production deadlines.**
- **Planned, implemented, supervised rehabilitation project that earned "best dormitories ever seen" by USAF inspectors.**
- **Contributed to Fed-Ex Muncie branch being recognized by earning Malcolm Baldridge Award.**
- **Some14 years "hands-on" expertise with materials mgt.**
- **Solid leadership skills, results-oriented.**
- **Excellent trouble-shooting skills, creative problem solver.**
- **Stong work ethic, proven ability under deadlines & budgets.**
- **Highly principled, proven ability in project management.**

**114**

**Combination.** *Jon C. Shafer, Anderson, Indiana*

Yet another example of the experimental use of clip art. Except for a year in insurance and securities, this candidate's career has been material-related. Note balance in the resume's design.

# Aaron Mark Geller

323 Grove Street
Elmira, New York 00000
**(000) 000-0000**

**Objective:** Position as **Visual Merchandising Manager**, multiple or single store, or other management-level position involving merchandise presentation and/or store design.

**Experience:**

DEPARTMENT STORE — 1989 - Present

**Visual Merchandising Manager** - *Crystal Mall, Crystal, New York*
Responsible for implementation of corporate presentation policies. Handle all aspects of shop set up, fashion presentation, and in-store signage. Coordinate fashion shows and special events. (1992 - Present)

**Visual Merchandising Manager** - *Crystal City Region, New York*
Developed and implemented merchandise presentation for 3-store department store group (Ithaca, Elmira, Big Flats). Communicated policies to store management, coordinated fixture set-up, seasonal shops, and trim. Supervised visual personnel. Oversaw fashion shows and all special events. (1989 - 1992)

DEPARTMENT STORE — 1985 - 1989

**Display Director** - *Elmira, New York*
Developed presentation strategy for family owned 3-store department store group. Responsible for purchase of all pertinent material (mannequins, props, trim, etc.). Supervised visual staff and sign shop. Developed and presented budgets. Oversaw design and construction of floats for annual Christmas Parade.

AARON & AARON DEPARTMENT STORES — 1982 - 1985

**Display Stylist** - *Buffalo, New York*
Produced in-store and window presentations for 9-store department store chain under direction of display manager. Handled in-store production of props and trim.

**Education:**

UNIVERSITY OF BINGHAMTON - *Binghamton, New York*
**Master of Fine Arts** (1979)
Sculpture and 3-Dimensional Design (on graduate assistantship)

ELMIRA CITY COLLEGE - *Elmira, New York*
**Bachelor of Fine Arts** (1976)
Sculpture (minor in Art History)

**Activities:**

- Assistant Scoutmaster, Boy Scouts of America
- Enjoy running, reading, artwork, and family activities

**References Available Upon Request**

**115**

**Chronological.** *Betty Geller, Elmira, New York*

The objective is targeted. "Skills, achievements, and duties are listed under the specific jobs." The "two-column format is easy to read" and can be made as a table with all but two lines removed.

# DAVID MIDDLETON

111 Henry Boulevard • Fair Woods, NY 00000 • (914) 777-5555

**Highly qualified Retail Management professional** with extensive experience in merchandising a product line, purchasing and controlling inventory. Skilled in negotiating and making profitable buying decisions. *Areas of expertise include:*

Merchandising/Buying / Forecasting / Inventory Control
Advertising / Customer Service / Sales Training/Supervision

**SELECTED ACCOMPLISHMENTS:**

- Successful record of advancement from trainee to management.
- Motivated and trained a staff of Sales Associates to achieve highest sales revenues nationwide.
- Exceeded corporate standard for unsampled inventory reduction by 3.5%.
- Developed new merchandising strategies which effectively used display space to maximize sales.

**CAREER EXPERIENCE:**

MAJOR FURNITURE, Garden Place New York — 1988-Present

**Merchandise Manager/Assistant Branch Manager**

Control $2.5 million home furniture and decor inventory budget for largest furniture retailer in U.S. Direct supervision of sales associates, decorators and clerical staff at flagship store.

- Develop new merchandising strategies which included promoting high-end product line. Doubled monthly sales and substantially increased gross margin percentages.
- Continually research sales history and shop the competition to meet customers' needs and tastes. Contributed to store's overall profitability by expanding contemporary line.
- Plan product displays for a 90,000 square foot showroom. Increased bedding business from 5% to 9% of total sales through display emphasis and more attractive decorating.
- Monitor inventory closely using IBM AS/4000 system. Prepare purchase orders to ensure availability of stock.
- Aggressively negotiate with manufacturers to resolve defective merchandise claims. Reduced branch exceptions from 5% to 1.5% of total inventory - bringing store from bottom to top 20%.
- Collaborate with regional merchandise managers to select styles and develop price points for promotions. Created copy for print advertising.
- Manage and train a staff of 28 Sales Associates. Conduct daily motivational meetings continuing to maintain sales leadership nationwide.
- Serve as Branch Manager supervising both cashier and customer service operations.

**Buyer - Paterson & Newark, NJ Branches**

Purchased case goods and upholstery negotiating directly with Manufacturer's Reps for best prices.

- Developed price structure and authorized markdowns/clearance merchandise. Reduced "old age" inventory consistently meeting goal of zero standard.
- Part of Northeast District buying team which selected new merchandise and styles for all stores.

**EDUCATION:**

St. Thomas College, Spring Lake, New York - B.S. Degree/Business Administration, 1988

References available upon request.

**116**

**Combination.** *Vivian Belen, Fair Lawn, New Jersey*

The writer combined a profile statement, a centered keyword list, and an accomplishments section "to maximize this candidate's management experience with just one employer."

**Office**

**Retail**

**Customer Relations**

**Kay Wellington**

**2 Downing Street**
**Middletown, IN 47356**

**(317) 354-0000**

**Objective:**

I am a working mother returning to the job market. Seeking an office position where I can put my word processing and shorthand skills to best use, or a retail environment where I have management experience with customer relations skills. Seeking growth opportunities in either.

**Skills:**

- **WordPerfect**
- **Lotus 1-2-3**
- **Data Base III**
- **Word Star**
- **Shorthand, 70 wpm**
- **Typing, 55 wpm**
- **Dictaphone/Transcrptn**
- **Bus. Communications**

**Work Experience:**

- Head office manager, Eavey's Market, Middletown. Scheduling, bookkeeping, stock, inventory, trained employees, cash balance and deposits. Started as cashier; promoted to office manager in two weeks.
- Customer service, communications and computer operator for Rex TV/Appliances, Anderson. Did data entries on layaways, cash sales and daily information.
- Management, bookkeeping, inventory, personnel and customer relations for Subway Sandwiches & Salads. Trained in temporary management. Worked at two stores, Nora (Indianapolis) and Kohl's Plaza, Anderson.

**Education:**

International Business College, Indianapolis, Secretarial Science, 1989.

**117**

**Combination.** *Jon C. Shafer, Anderson, Indiana*

A resume for a "working mom." The clip art image, the Objective box, and the Education box are shaded, tying together visually the resume's top and bottom. The Skills box links the other boxes.

**CAROLYN L. VERBECK-BRINDLE**
24 Kirchner Avenue
Hyde Park, New York 12538
(914) 555-5555

---

**Office Administrator** A established record of increasingly responsible decision making experience in all phases of office and personnel management. Skilled in the development and implementation of operational strategies that promote sound business practice.

***AREAS of EXPERTISE***

- Office Management
- Budget Administration
- Customer Service
- Staff Recruitment
- Training & Development
- Bookkeeping/Billing

***QUALIFICATION HIGHLIGHTS***

- Outstanding ability to work with community, governmental and professional groups
- Effective in budgeting and long-range planning; able to prioritize, delegate and motivate
- Extensive experience in developing programs from concept to ongoing operation
- Exceptional skill in personnel supervision and training program coordination

***RELEVANT EXPERIENCE & SKILLS***

***Management & Administration***

- Supervised the daily operation of 23-person agency program including office administration, staffing, training, general accounting, and client contacts
- Designed and implemented dBASE program to assist in tracking clients of home delivered meals
- Prepared and administered $500,000 annual operating budget
- Analyzed statistical data and compiled weekly, monthly, and annual projection reports
- Performed bookkeeping functions: Accounts Payable/Receivable, Bank Reconciliations, Sales Tax Payments, Customer Billing/Invoicing

***Organizing & Coordinating***

- Initiated itemized bidding specification process; evaluated bids and presented recommendations
- Conducted feasibility study to centralize operations; projected savings of $20,000 annually
- Coordinated and developed in-service staff training programs

***Marketing & Public Relations***

- Conducted high-energy cold calling campaign, opening new sales territory for a start-up business
- Developed ideas for creating new business, prioritized work projects, and implemented follow-up procedures, resulting in more efficient and profitable work flow

***EMPLOYMENT HISTORY***

| | | |
|---|---|---|
| Office Manager/Sales Representative | Leslie Graphics, Inc., Hopewell Jct., NY | 1994-Present |
| Project Director | Dutchess County Office for Aging, Poughkeepsie, NY | 1981-1994 |
| Manager & Public Relations Coordinator | McDonald's Restaurant, Hyde Park, NY | 1977-1981 |

***EDUCATION/CAREER DEVELOPMENT***

Bachelor of Science, Business Administration, University of Tulsa, OK
Various Management and Supervisory Training Seminars

***COMMUNITY ACTIVITIES***

| | |
|---|---|
| Member, Past President, New York State Association of Nutrition and Aging Service Programs | 1981-1994 |
| Member, Past President and Vice-President, Hyde Park Board of Education | 1972-1984 |

**118**

**Combination.** *Marian K. Kozlowski, Poughkeepsie, New York*

All the sections commonly found in a resume for executives and managers are on one page for this older person. The grouping of experience and skills by three subheads makes reading easier.

**JO-ANN GERARDO**
22-3 B Loudon Drive
Fishkill, New York 12524
(914) 555-5555

**Executive/Administrative Assistant** Extensive background in administrative and secretarial positions with small and large companies. Particularly strong, organizational, problem solving and customer service skills. A highly motivated, committed, people-oriented team player.

***HIGHLIGHTS OF QUALIFICATIONS***

- More than 14 years of professional experience in administrative/executive assistance
- Ability to execute a number of projects simultaneously
- Able to assess organizational needs and implement administrative procedures
- Exceptional communication and interpersonal skills
- Development of procedures to increase collection of delinquent accounts
- Ability to supervise employees and work well with all levels of management in a professional, diplomatic and tactful manner

**PROFESSIONAL EXPERIENCE**

Orthopedic Physical Therapy, Mamaroneck, NY (1994-Present)

**OFFICE MANAGER**

- Coordinate and direct all supportive services of physical therapy staff
  - Handle incoming calls and mail; greet clients
  - Verify and arrange patient appointments
- Administer EZCLAIM electronic billing for Medicare, Blue Cross/Blue Shield
- Manage "PTOS" billing system (Physical Therapy Office System)
  - Track insurance claims and payments
  - Reconcile accounts receivable
  - Increase cash flow through implementation of electronic billing system
- Coordinate purchase of all office equipment and medical supplies

IBM Corporation, Poughkeepsie and White Plains, NY (1981-1993)

**ADMINISTRATIVE SPECIALIST**

- Developed and delivered personnel data management system presentation to 2600 managers
- Set up and directed "Help Desk" function
- Led education task force to develop on-line user guide for personnel application (PDMS)

**EXECUTIVE ASSISTANT**

- Provided administrative support to vice-president of General Products Division
- Trained and supervised secretarial staff; coordinated work flow; encouraged team atmosphere

**EXECUTIVE SECRETARY**

- Scheduled and maintained appointment calendars; prepared correspondence
- Coordinated travel arrangements; prepared detailed itineraries

**SECRETARY**

- Maintained confidential personnel/payroll records of benefits administration department
- Provided support to 14 managers of financial planning department

**EDUCATION/TRAINING**

Effective Communications / Time Management / Personal Development / Market Driven Quality Training
Microsoft Word for Windows / WordPerfect / Displaywrite

**119**

**Combination.** *Marian K. Kozlowski, Poughkeepsie, New York*

This person worked twelve years for one company before getting her current job. She had never taken college courses. Her training occurred only in employer-conducted, in-house workshops.

## SUSAN IMPANI

3846 W. 235th Street • Riverdale, NY 10463 • (718) 543-8756

### PROFILE

- ✓ Three years in medical office administration for a high profile practice utilizing proven management and supervisory skills.
- ✓ Able to communicate effectively with medical personnel, support staff, and patients.
- ✓ Significantly enhanced office organization and developed improved staff utilization.
- ✓ Increased cash flow and reduced costs through effective administrative procedures.

### EDUCATION

*Candidate, Bachelor of Science in Health Management and Hospital Administration, Mt. Cedars*

### ---MEDICAL OFFICE ADMINISTRATION EXPERIENCE---

*Office Manager* — *1993 to Present*
**Physical Therapy Associates** — New York, NY

- Manage administrative functions for NYC office of high volume physical medicine practice.
- Contribute to the smooth running of the office and client satisfaction through efficient operation and productive relationships with staff and patients.
- Interview, supervise, and evaluate administrative support staff; assign all job tasks.
- Responsible for patient scheduling and all front desk activities.
- Oversee operations of Billing Department, including full charge of collection procedures.
- Manage patient litigation cases. Institute liens, plan patient-attorney conferences, negotiate OSB on settlements, collect fees and schedule court appearances.
- Direct timely purchase of supplies, as well as maintenance of equipment and facilities.
- Fully versed in CPT codes, rules, and regulations.
- Experienced with Medical Management Program.

**Achievements**

- Created new systemized forms and office procedures contributing to overall office efficiency.
- Reduced high employee turnover through creation of more favorable office environment.
- Actively contributed to increased profitability from $1 million to $2.5 million over a four year period.
- Developed a team approach for effective employee evaluation.
- Gained significant control over billing practice. Reduced outstanding liens. Implemented new systemized payment policies. Instituted new criteria to accept more profitable cases; reduced overhead by decreasing clerical staff.

### ---ADDITIONAL EXPERIENCE---

*Administrative Assistant/Sales Manager* — *1990 to 1993*
**Manchester Funding Corporation** — New York, NY

- Prepared, maintained, and expedited a variety of reports for Sales Department, including Contracts of Sale Reports, Sponsor-Purchase Finance Reports, Vacancy Buyout, and Goals Reports.
- Coordinated activities between Sales, Legal, and Budgeting Departments.
- Trained and motivated sales staff.

*Sales Manager* — *1988 to 1990*
**New York Realty Corporation** — New York, NY

- Directed 8 on-site sales offices.
- Managed conversion of 12 buildings from inception through closing.
- Designed and oversaw all phases of renovation.
- Coordinated vacancies with management and prepared interim leases.

*References furnished on request.*

**120**

**Combination.** *Etta Barmann, New York, New York*

The location of the Education section near the top seems unusual because the person has no degree. The degree in progress, however, is a sign of her new commitment to a medical field.

# Office & Business Manager, Solid at Research, Organized, Excellent Customer Service Skills

**Joan Collins**
100 Tacket Way
Daleville, IN 47000
**(317) 378-0000**

**Qualifications:**

- **Very strong organizational skills.**
- **Particularly adept in customer relations.**
- **Innovative thinker with great initiative.**
- **Research oriented & thorough.**
- **Training/teaching experience, solid ability in employee relations.**

**Professional Experience:**

Office Manager/Examiner, Rowland Title Co., Anderson, IN. May 1991-current.

Supervision of various administrative and procedural functions, including the tasks performed by 15 employees. Primary functions of this office revolve around real estate title research and title insurance examinations of court and in-house records for the purpose of ongoing real estate transactions & closing.

Peripheral, yet essential functions include regular customer service as it relates to record research, answering customer questions, review and preparation of commitments & policies, assurances of proper title closings, monitoring all procedures and making changes as needed, accounts receivable/payable, and related real estate title & title insurance matters.

Tax Processing Supervisor, H & R Block. 1982-92.

Involved in the development and implementation of H & R Blocks "Rapid Refund" program. Supervised 15-20 employees and responsible for quality control service to franchise offices and 14 satellite offices. Taught basic income tax classes and yearly refresher course for employees. In charge of records, business volume reports and budgets. Seasonal, Nov-April.

Bookkeeping Dept., American National Bank. 1988-89.

Customer service for account information, balanced cashier checks and PMOs, processed & mailed statements, closed accounts, maintained files for cancelled checks, checked for signatures on checks, and related duties. Seasonal: May-Oct.

Note: went to Rowland Title full time from American National, continued with H & R Block through 1992.

---

Strong organizational & managerial skills...efficient...friendly.

Created a complete employee policy handbook.

Great motivator...a "people-person" with tact...diplomacy.

**121**

**Combination.** *Jon C. Shafer, Anderson, Indiana*

The profile in headline style (initial caps in major words) in the top box reads like a headline. The contact information in inverse (white-on-black, light-on-dark) format captures attention.

**Melissa A. Evans**

2914 Ford Parkway • Flint, MI 48555 • (810) 555-9039

**PROFILE**

Professional with knowledge and significant experience in all aspects of medical and office assisting, including surgery involving local anesthesia. Excellent interpersonal skills; able to develop rapport with patients and medical staff. Detail-oriented and thorough. Computer literate; outstanding keyboarding skills.

**HIGHLIGHTS OF EXPERIENCE**

*Administrative/Office Management*

- Managed office staff including, hiring, training, supervising and dismissing.
- Interacted with patients on a consultation basis; arranged referral appointments and facility scheduling.
- Processed medical records and billing: transcription, ICD & CPT coding, MHSC billing, insurance company and private pay billing, collections.
- Managed financial recordkeeping: general accounting, payroll, banking; ordered O.R. and office supplies.
- Provided administrative support for up to 14 physicians; maintained professional working environment.

*Medical/Plastic Surgery Assisting*

- Proficient in utilizing various lasers.
- Trained in operation of computer imaging program: taking and printing pre- and post-operative photos; manipulating photos to enable patients to visualize possible results.
- Performed patient counseling; acted as liaison between physician and patients.
- Assisted with all outpatient surgical procedures including liposuction, liposculpture, and permanent makeup application; performed dressing changes and removal of suture/staples/steri-strips.
- Processed laboratory samples and recorded results.
- Maintained sterility of instruments and autoclaving; operated cautery and plume evacuators.

**PROFESSIONAL EXPERIENCE**

Plastic Surgery Specialists • Flint, MI [formerly Windsor, Ontario] (1990-1995)
**Office Manager/Assistant**

London Medical Center • London, ON - Canada (1987-1990)
**Assistant to Administrative Secretary**

**EDUCATION and TRAINING**

*Medical Secretary Transcriptionist Program* - Helmsford Institute/Career College • Vancouver, BC (1986-1987)
*General Coursework* toward Bachelor of Arts degree - London University • London, ON (1985-1986)

"Laser Nurse Specialist Training Course" - U.S. Medical Education Foundation • Cincinnati, OH (1995)
"Physician's Choice" - The Institute for Advanced Medical Aesthetics (APSA) • Phoenix, AZ (1995)
"Vital Signs of a Health Practice" - McLaren Regional Medical Center • Flint, MI (1995)
"Risk Management Strategies" - Genesys Regional Medical Center • Flint, MI (1994)
"MIOSHA Continuing Medical Education" - Hurley Hospital • Flint, MI (1994)
"Coding 1 Seminar" - Association of Plastic Surgery Assistants • Chicago, IL (1994)
"Annual Educational Seminar" - Association of Plastic Surgery Assistants • New Orleans, LA (1993)
"Beyond Secretary" - Careertrack's Continuing Education Seminar • Winnipeg, MB (1992)

**CERTIFICATIONS**

- Community CPR and Community First Aid & Safety (American Red Cross)
- Laser Safety Officer ($CO_2$ and Candela lasers)
- Chemical Peel Anesthetist (administer chemical peels, skin care and camouflage treatment methods)

**AFFILIATIONS**

- Association of Plastic Surgery Assistants (since 1993)
- The Society of Plastic Surgical Skin Care Specialists
- Lipoplasty Society

*References available on request.*

**122**

**Combination.** *Janet L. Beckstrom, Flint, Michigan*

When a one-page resume has much information, horizontal lines that separate the sections will make them visible at a glance. Reduced line spacing helps to fit everything on one page.

## *Susan J. Smith*

***RR 2 Box 1234***
***Bayside, Maine 00000***
***(207) 555-5555***

***Objective:*** ***Bakery / Deli Management***

### *Areas of Expertise:*

- Restaurant Management
- Scheduling
- Customer Relations
- Staff Training and Development
- Employee Supervision
- Negotiation with Sales Representatives
- Problem Resolution
- Baking and Recipe Creation

### *Professional Experience:*

**The Deli Shop Plus, Deli & Bakery, Bayside, Maine** **1982 - Present**
***Manager***
Overall responsibility for the management and supervision of a kosher restaurant serving direct customers, commercial, and wholesale accounts. Supervise 5 - 10 employees. Negotiate with sales representatives in person and on the telephone to secure the best quality, quantity, and price of product. Estimate quantity of product to order based on upcoming projects. Manage wholesale business, which reflects 20 - 25% of revenue. Responsible for training and supervising the daily routines of keeping a kosher kitchen. Gained and retained extensive knowledge of Jewish religion and culture.

**Key Accomplishments**:

- No employee turnover in four years. Current staff is dependable, efficient, and content.
- Played major role in designing new display area resulting in increased business.
- Created 100% of bread recipes used and some soup and pastry recipes.
- Achieve high ratings on food and sanitation inspections.
- Attended buying trips, including the Fancy Food Show and the Kosher Food Show at the Javitz Center in New York City, to identify new products.

**Country Catering, East Bayside, Maine** **1990 - 1993**
***Owner / Caterer***
Established cake decorating and catering business. Prepared and decorated cakes for all occasions. Managed all financial and marketing aspects of business.

### *Education:*

**Eastern Maine Technical College, Bangor, Maine** **1982**
***Diploma - Food Technology Program***

**Subject Areas**:
- *Sanitation in Food Service*
- *Restaurant Management*
- *Psychology*
- *Customer Service & Selling*
- *Merchandising*
- *Food Preparation*

***References Available Upon Request***

**123**

**Combination.** *Joan M. Roberts, Bangor, Maine*

This person enjoyed her work in sales, customer service, and bookkeeping but wanted to change employers. The writer created the Profile and Skill Areas sections to show the person's interests.

**CHARLENE A. TRAVIS**
1212 Rosewood Drive
Hinsbrook, IL 00000
(555) 000-0000

**PROFILE**

**Office Manager** with nine years experience who enjoys the challenge of a fast-paced office with diverse responsibilities. Computer literate; Microsoft Office professional. Detail oriented and accurate; type 70+ wpm.

**EXPERIENCE**

**Office Manager** 1986 to Date
HOME RESOURCE, Hinsbrook, IL
(retail flooring and window treatments)

- Direct full range of activities in this busy office; supervise two part-time clerks. Manage office independently during the owner's frequent absences. Work in cooperation with sales staff, and coordinate schedules with estimators and installers.
- Possess strong customer service skills: handle heavy volume of telephone calls, resolving customer problems with speed and diplomacy.
- Manage bookkeeping function, including the following:
  - accounts receivable
  - accounts payable
  - payroll and payroll taxes
  - job costing
  - cash receipts and disbursements
  - bank reconciliations
  - inventory tracking
  - invoicing / billing
- Streamlined office operations by setting priorities and eliminating redundant routines.

**Secretary** 1984 to 1986
BEST-TEMP EMPLOYMENT AGENCY, Hinsbrook, IL

- Conducted orientations for applicants, administered tests, and assisted with placements. Developed competency on an IBM PC.

**EDUCATION**

**A.A.S. Degree, Office Administration** 1984
SEYMOUR COMMUNITY COLLEGE, Seymour, IL

- Maintained perfect attendance record and high grades while working 20 hours per week.

124

**Combination.** *Jennie Dowden, Flossmoor, Illinois*

Putting the contact information between lines directs attention to the information. Careful line spacing produces adequate white space. Diamond bullets lead the eye to important statements.

# Britain J. Walker

*294 E. Walnut • Phoenix, Arizona 85555 • (520) 555-7777*

**PROFESSIONAL PROFILE**

» Over 25 years of administrative experience in academic medicine
» Acted as program coordinator for internal medicine residency program
» Trained, supervised, coordinated, motivated, and evaluated staff of eight
» Prepared budgets, monitored receipts and disbursements, and oversaw accounting functions; provided budgetary and purchasing recommendations
» Dependable, honest, hard working, and highly confidential; good mediator with outstanding communication skills; work well under pressure

**SKILLS**

» Administrative Office Management
» Personnel Supervision and Motivation
» Budgeting, Purchasing, and Inventory
» Coordination of Residency Rotations
» Preparation for AMA Inspections/Audits
» Written and Oral Communications
» Word Processing (Word Perfect 5.1) and Medical Transcription

**EMPLOYMENT HISTORY**

UNIVERSITY OF ARIZONA MEDICAL CENTER **1966-1996**
Phoenix, Arizona

- ***Office Manager - Department of Medicine*** - 1985-1996
  » Oversaw day-to-day operations of Department of Medicine
  » Administered residency program, including rotations and record keeping
  » Coordinated secretarial support for 76 full- and part-time faculty
  » Acted as confidential secretary to chairman, Dr. Shawn Chillag
- ***Secretary to the Chairman - Department of Medicine*** - 1974-1985
  » Dr. John Poindexter, 1977-1988
  » Dr. Barbara Dallmann, 1974-1976
- ***Secretary - Institutional Research, President's Office*** - 1969-1974
  » Statistical analysis and reporting
  » Confidentiality and precise typing skills required
- ***Secretary - Dean of Women*** - 1966-1968
  » Handled highly confidential student records

**EDUCATION**

» ***Associate Degree in Business Administration***, Waysworth Business College
» ***History Major***, two years, University or Arizona

**MANAGEMENT TRAINING**

"The Legal Aspects of Hiring and Firing," Padgett Thompson
"Business Writing Skills," Keye Production Center
"How to Supervise People," National Seminars
"The Organized Manager," Padgett Thompson
"Basic Supervision Seminar," Padgett Thompson

**PROFESSIONAL AFFILIATIONS**

Member, Office Manager's Association, Phoenix, Arizona
Member, National Association of Female Executives

125

**Combination.** *Barbie Dallmann, Charleston, West Virginia*

A thick-thin line stretches across the contact information, drawing attention to the person's name. Chevrons (») are used as bullets in most of the resume and with filled bullets in the History.

## Lawrence D. Rasmone

8250 Spring Mill Road
Indianapolis, Indiana 46250

Telephone and Message:
(317) 251-7340

**OPERATIONS MANAGEMENT / CONSULTANT**

***Program Management / Marketing / Customer Development / Strategic & Operational Planning Manufacturing / Proposals / Negotiations / Contract Structuring / Total Quality Management***

**PROFILE**

Creative and results-driven executive effective in understanding the overall industry position, links in relationships and appropriate competitive strategies in market development, contracts and procurement, general operations management.

Energetic and decisive leadership with successes guiding projects from concept through negotiations. Specialized expertise in the planning and management of manufacturing while organizing and supporting quality control requirements and cost reduction methods for ongoing manufacturing of a reliable and cost effective product.

Solid technical training, team building, management development and customer service skills. Chief negotiator for facility: developing proposals, structuring contracts, optimizing technical compliance and internal operational activities. Security Clearance: DoD Secret level.

Can provide an interchangeable mix of capabilities that can be shifted on demand to promote, expedite, and maximize performance of corporate short and long range objectives.

**PROFESSIONAL EXPERIENCE**

**Smith & Eimeldingen**, Indianapolis, Indiana 1964 - Jun 1997
*Clients include: Raytheon, Hughes, McDonnell-Douglas, Texas Instruments, Thiokol, and U.S. government.*

**Manager, Contracts & Procurement - ERI Operations** (1991-Jun 1997)
**Program Manager- ERI Division** (1990-1991)
**Manager, Contracts, Sales and Marketing- ERI Division** (1987-1990)
**Program Manager, Nuclear Equipment Division** (1981-1985)
***-prior responsibilities**: program management, contract and proposal administration* (1964-1981)

Manager responsible for connecting interrelationships between strategy and implementation to support general operations and business development. Beginning in 1964 supported a strong operational focus working with high-dollar, long duration contracts for nuclear equipment, and in 1987 placed in multiple strategic positions for sales/marketing; program planning and management; since 1991, prepared and negotiated proposals for contracts with an annual value of $15-20 million. Report to General Manager. ***Contributions include:***

**Contracts & Procurement**
- Held responsibility as the chief negotiator for all proposals with average annual value of $15 million-plus.
- Directed Purchasing Department with a $15 million -plus volume. Developed solid infrastructure that produced a cost reduction of 5% a year.
- Managed all contracts from the initial negotiations throughout the manufacturing operations. Acted as intermediary between customer and company with both the private customer and Department of Defense.

**Program Management**
- Following negotiations, continued with projects as Program Manager, and in the last 10 years directed company's small to medium range programs that brought yearly revenues from $750,000 - $6 million as well as led 4-key military programs through to successful conclusions.
- Conceived strategies and coordinated logistics that brought planning into action connecting the infrastructure to result in successful execution, cost control, customer interface and scheduler performance.
- Managed large networks of internal personnel that extended over multiple disciplines.

**Sales & Marketing - Business Customer Development**
- Identified critical growth paths that optimized market and product leadership positions. Contacted industries, prepared proposals - selling and opening communications to new customer bases.
- Brought together customer requirements, technical compliance and internal operational activities.

**EDUCATION**

**Master of Business Administration**, Indiana University, Bloomington, Indiana 1982
**Bachelor of Science**, Mechanical Technology, The Ohio University, Columbus, Ohio 1964

126

**Combination.** *Mary Ann Finch Vandivier, Zionsville, Indiana*

A resume for someone who worked for the same company for thirty-three years—ever since graduation. Only the last four positions are listed. Contributions are grouped under subheadings.

# STACY GARCIA

1414 Elm Lane • Staten Island, New York • 10314
(718) 222-2255

## LETTERS OF CREDIT / COLLECTIONS SUPERVISOR

**OVERVIEW**

- Highly experienced administrator in Letters of Credit and Bank Collections.
- Track record of setting-up new departments and improving operating efficiency.
- Spearhead departmental growth by millions of dollars annually.
- Outstanding skills in presentations, project management, and strategic planning.
- Excellent interpersonal relations with customers, businesses, and employees.
- Effective communicator; Bilingual English-Spanish, written and verbal.

**EXPERIENCE**

**1990 to present** AMERICAN BANK, New York, NY
**Operations Officer/Manager of Documentary Services Department**

- Supervise the processing of all letters of credit, including:
  - issuances
  - amendments
  - negotiations acceptances
  - discounts
  - reimbursements
  - assignment of proceeds
  - advices
  - transfers
  - finance
- Plan and implement operations for Documentary Services Department.
- Establish departmental policies and procedures to maximize efficiency.
- Train and supervise 35 employees in letters of credit and collection methods.
- Establish a rapport with business contacts to enhance customer relations.
- Negotiate and process issuance of Commercial and Stand-By Letters of Credit.
- Handle issuance of steamship guaranties and airway bill releases.
- Complete process of import and export clean and documentary collections.
- Calculate pre- and post-export finance and issue Trust Receipts.
- Enforce Bank operating procedures and controls to maintain auditory compliance.
- Monitor workflow to ensure that all work is completed within deadlines.
- Prepare reports related to the production of the department.

**1985 to 1990** NATIONAL WESTMINSTER BANK, New York, NY
**Letters of Credit/Collection Specialist**

- Received and processed letters of credit and collection items for 50 accounts daily.
- Logged and checked documents and reviewed for accuracy.
- Traced unpaid items and handled transfer of funds.

**1982 to 1985** WINTHROP TRUST COMPANY, New York, NY
**Collection Specialist/Supervisor**

- Performed collections and supervised four Collection Clerks.

**COMPUTERS** Advanced user of Microsoft Word, Excel, PowerPoint, Access, WordPerfect, Lotus 1-2-3, and dBASE.

**EDUCATION** **Bachelor of Business Administration - Finance,** 1990
WAGNER COLLEGE, Staten Island, NY
Financed education 100%

**127**

**Combination.** *Kim Isaacs, Jackson Heights, New York*

An easy-to-read resume because of all caps for company names, boldfacing for job titles, horizontal lines enclosing the occupation, headings and dates in the left column, and white space.

# Claudette Ford-Worthy

3388 Oakwood Road • Columbus, Illinois 60606 • (555) 555-4447

## Qualifications Summary

- Six years small business management experience, with specialization in personnel management, staff development, and team building
- Highly articulate with a natural instinct for creative marketing strategies
- Adept at designing new systems and procedures to maximize workplace efficiency
- Respected, affable team leader with a record of inspiring high morale and productivity
- Well versed in many computer programs, including DOS and Windows applications
- Highly energetic professional; a life-long learner with a reputation for welcoming challenge and overcoming adversity

## Professional Experience

PROTECTED RESOURCES COMPANY, Columbus, Illinois 1990-Present

**Operations Manager**

*Areas of Responsibility:*

- Managed team of 17, coordinating service schedules and interacting with clients to arrange for over 100 technical calls per day
- Purchased all company supplies, equipment, fleet vehicles, and resale merchandise
- Served as safety director, evaluating work environment and coordinating training
- Edited *The Safety Voice*, the monthly newsletter of the Illinois Safety Council
- Managed credit and collections functions, keeping annual write-offs to less than 1%

*Major Accomplishments:*

- Directed the relocation and merger of two companies, including the consolidation of inventories, personnel, administrative procedures, and accounting functions
- While safety director, company received the Governor's Safety Award for its outstanding safety record
- Researched and wrote company's OSHA hazardous material communication plan; implemented the program and conducted the training company wide
- Achieved company's highest inside sales for 1995

## Education

- **Business Administration,** Westerville College, Westerville, Colorado, 1988-1990
- **Associate of Applied Sciences in Business,** National Education Center, Westerville, Colorado, 1988, GPA 4.0
- **Continuing Education,** 1990-1995, topics included:
  - Hazardous Communications
  - Americans with Disabilities Act
  - Managing Multiple Projects
  - Confined Space Training
  - Skill Path Career Development
  - Team Building

## Affiliations

- Illinois Safety Council
- National Association of Female Executives
- Columbus YWCA, active with community volunteer programs
- Shaolin martial arts

128

**Combination.** *Barbie Dallmann, Charleston, West Virginia*

An attractive font for the person's name and the side headings, decorative bullets, and white space make this a friendly resume. The focus is on her past responsibilities and achievements.

# Orin K. Francis

1234 East Saratoga
Johnston, MO 65483

(455) 224-5582
ofrancis@msn.com

## INFORMATION SYSTEMS / TELECOMMUNICATION SYSTEMS

**Focus on mid- to large-scale business or healthcare organizations**

**Management:** Skilled in planning and implementing business-driven technology initiatives to improve efficiency and boost profit. Planned and/or negotiated programs that delivered a hard dollar savings of more than $237,500 for the past fiscal year. Solid customer service (internal and external), problem-solving, and change agent skills.

**User Training:** Equipped users (from executives and physicians to clerical support) with technical skills and confidence to make the most of advanced technology. Wrote and/or assisted with editing of more than 400 pages of user-friendly technical manuals.

**Technical:** Provided system management (DEC Vax 4000 minicomputers and PC's) for regional hospital and 6 satellite units. Experienced in installation, troubleshooting, repair, administration, and upgrades. Software: Excel, Word, Power Point, as well as dial-up networking, database, alpha-numeric paging, and OLE applications.

## Professional Experience

INTEGRATED HEALTHCARE SYSTEM, Johnston, Missouri 1987-1997

Advanced through positions as:

**Manager of Operations, Hospital Information Systems (HIS) Department (1992-1997)**
**Lead Computer Operator (1989-1992); Computer Operator (1987-1989)**

Accountable for information systems, telecommunications systems, and wireless technology supporting 1,800+ users. Hired, trained, and supervised Computer Operations team (DEC platform supported 1,000+ PC's, printers, terminals, modems, faxes, and other peripheral devices). Monitored data management (document input, processing, generation, backup). Managed wireless, paging, and voice technology. Negotiated and monitored fees and service contracts.

**Profit Enhancement:**

- Delivered a savings of approximately $192,000 in annual telephone fees through use analysis and line consolidation.
- Cut more than $55,000 in annual paging and cellular fees through renegotiation of vendor contracts.
- Analyzed proposals and selected long distance carrier for projected savings of $50,000 over ensuing 2-year term.
- Re-tooled position and cross-trained support staff to accommodate greater work volume without increasing technical staff (users increased from 1,200 to 1,800 with an addition of 3 mini computers).

**Productivity Enhancement:**

- Trained users in software and basic trouble-shooting, enabling technical staff to devote more time to complex issues.
- Wrote technical manuals for departments hospital-wide, standardizing 100+ computer procedures.
- Introduced dial-up networking capabilities to improve off-site physicians' and administrators' access to data.
- Initiated alpha-numeric paging technology, improving cost savings and response time for emergency care.
- Assisted with error-free installation of new $2 million telephone system linking headquarters with satellite locations.

## Education

**Bachelor of Science Program in Business Administration / Management** ~ Missouri State College

**References Upon Request**

**129**

**Combination.** *Susan Britton Whitcomb, Fresno, California*

The bold lines help you see the main sections at a glance. Note the side headings in the opening, summary section to help you to see the person's key areas and a summary of achievements.

# James Dervisian

123 Truvale Avenue
Avila, California 94321
(805) 432-4312

**SENIOR MANAGER -- FOOD PROCESSING / MANUFACTURING**

*Unwavering commitment to quality, productivity, and profitability.*

## Professional Experience

MAJOR BAKING COMPANY, Santa Cruz, California 1984-Present

Manage production operations for national distributor of snack foods and regional distribution of specialty breads. Report directly to CEO. Promoted through increasingly responsible positions including 3 years as Bakery Manager and 2 years as Supervisor of Cracker lines.

**Selected to turnaround bakery operations, re-establishing company's reputation as leading manufacturer of specialty breads.**

- Rebuilt bakery department -- from zero staff, hired and trained an ethnically-diverse crew (many with limited English skills); encouraged and rewarded team members for ideas that improved productivity and quality.
- Improved quality to recapture critical sales, virtually tripling production volume -- reversed department's reputation as a "loss leader" to become a financially viable profit center.
- Maximized profits through elimination of overtime, intensive cross-training, and procedural enhancements.
- Achieved approx. 15% reduction in staffing with concurrent increase in production and quality.
- Controlled shrinkage and losses in retail store, reducing write-offs from $1,000 per month to as low as $12.
- Formulated 3 new doughs for a key account -- corporate reps asserted the formulations were best-tasting in company's history (accomplished this with no formal food science training).

**Planned, directed, and controlled 6,000-pound-per-shift operation for cracker products.**

- Increased pound-per-person production by 12%.
- Reduced scrap to record low (5-10 pounds per shift) through emphasis on cross-training.
- Eliminated downtime through improvements in materials planning and scheduling.
- Standardized procedures and wrote company's first manuals for sanitation, production, and retail operations.

**Well-rounded knowledge:**

- Production: materials handling; oven and packaging operations (TL Green oven, Hayssen form & fill, shrink wrap, Adco, Do-boy); packaging; sanitation (advanced training from American Institute of Baking); quality control (color/moisture/weight requirements, conditioners, packaging, standardized procedures).
- General Management: production tracking/analysis, cost accounting, inventory management, purchasing, supervision of retail bakery operations and route sales, computer operations (MAS 90 program for accounting and inventory management; Unix-based system).
- Comments from performance evaluations: "quality-conscious . . . go get `em attitude . . . never needs supervising . . . always strives to exceed her quotas . . . thinks ahead . . . always busy . . . when you need a job done well, you give that job to James."

## Education

**San Jose State University** -- ongoing part-time studies toward Degree in Business (senior status with 3.8 GPA)

**References Upon Request**

130

**Chronological.** *Susan Britton Whitcomb, Fresno, California*

Achievements and skills of a functional resume are given here in a one-company, chronological resume. The italic line is a profile. The bold lines are for grouping data. See the final comments.

# DANIEL DAVIES

111 Montgomery Place • New Maywood, New York 00000 • (914) 999-6666

***DATABASE MANAGEMENT / DIRECT MARKETING***

**Senior level manager** offers extensive background in developing/maintaining targeted databases.... Proven ability to run a profitable direct mail and catalog publication operation with accomplishments in customer retention and cost control.... Effective leader who excels in planning and bringing jobs in under cost.

**Areas of Expertise**

Database Maintenance / Direct Mail / Mass Mailings / Mail Merge / Merge/Purge
Lead Generation Fulfillment / Postal Presort Requirements
List Selection / Database Strategies / Customer Sales

**CAREER EXPERIENCE:**

TECHNICAL SERVICES, INC., West Center, NY (1983-Date)

**Operations Manager**

Part of senior management team for this direct marketing/publishing company with sales of $5 million. Assume P&L responsibility for direct mail operation overseeing production, office administration, accounting and customer relations.

- Manage a highly focused database of over 250,000 records targeted to Electronic/Computer Design Engineers and Managers. Supervise maintenance process achieving an extremely low undeliverable rate (under 1%) for industry.
- Plan and supervise approximately 50 mass mailings per month in a lettershop environment. Credited for maintaining top efficiency contributing to high customer retention rate.
- Responsible for complete production of catalog publications which generate approximately 41% of sales revenue. Coordinate digital pre-press, printing and distribution with vendors for a bimonthly catalog of 36 pages with circulation of 85,000.
- Oversee lead generation fulfillment operation. Introduced electronic transmission to advertisers by modem decreasing turnaround time.
- Work closely with sales staff and customers on estimating jobs. Consistently bring in jobs under cost based on production planning methods and cost controls.
- Serve as key contact with clients advising on best approach to projects and building strong working relationships.
- Advanced to senior management staff from initial position of Customer Service Rep.

**EDUCATION:**

University of Maine, Augusta -- Business Administration

**TECHNICAL:**

| | |
|---|---|
| Tandem VLX | IBM PC/Windows Environment |
| MS-Office 4.3 | Lotus 1-2-3 |
| ACCPAC BPI Accounting | |

References available upon request.

131

**Combination.** *Vivian Belen, Fair Lawn, New Jersey*

By the time you read about the one and only company, you know the candidate's management areas, his senior level, and areas of expertise that are expressed in keywords separated by slashes.

## LENNY HORRIGAN

75 Highway Drive
Swansea, Illinois 62221
(618) 555-9736
Email: horrigan@transcom.safb.af.mil

### SUMMARY OF QUALIFICATIONS

**TRANSPORTATION MANAGER** with 20 years of senior-level experience in operations, training, security and communications. Proven ability to coordinate multimodal air, motor, rail and water transportation activities requiring complex networks of key human and material resources. Oversee strategic planning functions with budgets in excess of $2.5 million. Successful track record of improving cost and quality controls, customer service, productivity and overall performance levels.

### PROFESSIONAL EXPERIENCE

United States Army, 1976-Present
Current rank: Lieutenant Colonel, U.S. Transportation Command
**GLOBAL TRANSPORTATION AND OPERATIONS MANAGER**

Selected Accomplishments:

- Served as Executive and Operations Officer of the only Army line-haul transportation battalion in Korea consisting of headquarters, two medium truck companies, four trailer transfer points and a trailer maintenance center. The 450 vehicles and trailers accumulated more than three million miles annually hauling government cargo along a 350-mile line of communication.
- Directed the movement of more than 1,000 commercial containers during a Korean trucker's strike while simultaneously downsizing the organization.
- Managed all air and surface transportation assets for an 11-country, 3,500-member peacekeeping force in the Middle East. Planned and coordinated the effective utilization of all aircraft and wheel cargo vehicles.
- Supervised an administrative-use vehicle fleet, motor pool operations and maintenance shops consisting of more than 200 personnel and 550 vehicles.
- Managed a 196-man transportation unit responsible for the maintenance and operation of 111 vehicles including tractor-trailer combinations with both bulk fuel and dry cargo capability and 5-ton cargo trucks.
- Developed and improved internal procedures for the movement of cargo and passengers across international boundaries.
- Referred to by superiors as "a recognized master at developing and conducting challenging, realistic and productive training" for a transportation assistance unit. Evaluated the logistics of simulated military operations; provided corrective input via after-action reports.

### EDUCATION/SPECIALIZED TRAINING

- M.S. Degree, Logistics Management, Florida Institute of Technology, Melbourne, Florida
- B.A. Degree, History, Midwestern State University, Wichita Falls, Texas
- Logistics Executive Development Course

### AFFILIATIONS

National Defense Transportation Organization

REFERENCES AVAILABLE UPON REQUEST

**132**

**Combination.** *John A. Suarez, Troy, Illinois*

The left-aligned headings underscored by a full horizontal line are spotted easily. The subheading "Selected Accomplishments" implies there are more. Dates are omitted in the Education section.

SCANNABLE RÉSUMÉ

**LENNY HORRIGAN**

75 Highway Drive
Swansea, Illinois 62221
(618) 555-9736
Email: horrigan@transcom.safb.af.mil

**KEY WORDS**

Senior Transportation Manager. 20 years experience. Global and domestic operations. Multimodal air, motor, rail and water transportation activities. Strategic human and material resource planning. Budgets in excess of $2.5 million. Cost reductions. ITV management. Quality controls. Customer service. Training. Security. Communications. Productivity. Line-haul transportation. Asset utilization. Capacity planning. Fuel and dry cargo capability. Wheel cargo vehicles. Maintenance. Tractor trailers. Masters Degree in Logistics Management.

**PROFESSIONAL EXPERIENCE**

United States Army, 1976-Present
Current rank: Lieutenant Colonel, U.S. Transportation Command
**JOINT MOBILITY OPERATIONS MANAGER**

**Selected Accomplishments:**

- Served as Executive and Operations Officer of the only Army line-haul transportation battalion in Korea consisting of headquarters, two medium truck companies, four trailer transfer points and a trailer maintenance center. The 450 vehicles and trailers accumulated more than three million miles annually hauling government cargo along a 350-mile line of communication.
- Directed the movement of more than 1,000 commercial containers during a Korean trucker's strike while simultaneously downsizing the organization.
- Managed all air and surface transportation assets for an 11-country, 3,500-member peacekeeping force in the Middle East. Planned and coordinated the effective utilization of all aircraft and wheel cargo vehicles.
- Supervised an administrative-use vehicle fleet, motor pool operations and maintenance shops consisting of more than 200 personnel and 550 vehicles.
- Managed a 196-man transportation unit responsible for the maintenance and operation of 111 vehicles including tractor-trailer combinations with both bulk fuel and dry cargo capability and 5-ton cargo trucks.
- Developed and improved internal procedures for the movement of cargo and passengers across international boundaries.
- Referred to by superiors as "a recognized master at developing and conducting challenging, realistic and productive training" for a transportation assistance unit. Evaluated the logistics of simulated military operations; provided corrective input via after-action reports.

**EDUCATION AND SPECIALIZED TRAINING**

- M.S. Degree, Logistics Management, Florida Institute of Technology, Melbourne, FL
- B.A. Degree, History, Midwestern State University, Wichita Falls, TX
- Logistics Executive Development Course

**AFFILIATIONS**

National Defense Transportation Organization

REFERENCES AVAILABLE UPON REQUEST

133

**Combination.** *John A. Suarez, Troy, Illinois*

A scannable version of the preceding resume. Note the sans serif font, the absence of lines, the "KEY WORDS" section, and the replacement of the slash with "AND" in the Education heading.

# JESSALYN S. MORGAN

***369 Harborside Drive***
***Lakeland, Florida 33810***
***(941) 555-5555***


## SENIOR OPERATIONS MANAGER

***Expert in Personnel, Facilities and Operations Management***

***Strategic Corporate Planning / Quality Control / Contract Administration***
***Human Resources / Labor Relations / Customer Service / Production Planning and Management***

Senior management professional with over twenty years' experience managing fast-paced telecommunications operations for one of the nation's largest telecommunications providers. Broad-based knowledge and experience encompassing operations and technical management, human resources, and telecommunications administration.

## PROFESSIONAL EXPERIENCE

### FLORIDA SOUTH COMMUNICATIONS, Miami, Florida

*A major telecommunications service provider, Florida South provides residence, business, data, cellular, video, and carrier services to 16 million customers with an annual revenue of over $620 million.*

**1995-1996 Area Manager - Field Operations Support**

- Provided administrative and technical support to an Installation/Maintenance and Network Services district comprised of over 800 employees; managed an annual budget of over $55 million.
- Served as the District's primary liaison with the senior executive staff; served as back-up for the Director of Operations.
- Coordinated large projects within the District, including a new program enabling employees to obtain a college degree while on the job.
- Implemented Florida South's procedural changes and trained staff accordingly; supervised Union interactions.
- Oversaw the District's results-tracking and analysis; prepared correspondence and reports.

**1994-1995 Area Operations Manager/Switching Administration**

- Directed surveillance, analysis, maintenance, and provisioning of all service installations in central offices and the overall network operations.
- Supervised seven management and 22 craft employees requiring a thorough knowledge of various electronic and digital switching technologies and network facilities.

**1991-1994 Area Operations Manager/Circuit Provisioning Center**

- Provisioned all special service circuits, message trunks, and carrier orders throughout the Southeast with more than 960,000 access lines.
- Supervised 17 management and six craft employees who engineered the detailed electronic design of circuit and cable equipment for over 22,000 square miles of territory.
- Managed the processing of over 30,000 orders annually, ensuring that all quality and production objectives were consistently exceeded.
- Provided developmental cross-training for engineering and administrative support personnel, successfully eliminating the need for addition to the existing work force.
- Supervised the center's closedown and transition of work to another area; successfully reassigned or secured retirement benefits for all employees in the group.

**1989-1991 Manager - Network Services Results**

- Supervised monthly compilation and calculation of performance measurements for 144 central office entities.
- Effectively integrated technical telecommunications practices into network switching results indices.

134

**Combination.** *E. René Hart, Lakeland, Florida*

A thin-thick line and a thick-thin line enclose the opening section, which functions as a profile and a summary of qualifications. Another thin-thick line is part of a header on page two.

***JESSALYN S. MORGAN*** ***Page Two***

## PROFESSIONAL EXPERIENCE (continued)

**FLORIDA SOUTH COMMUNICATIONS, Miami, Florida**

| | |
|---|---|
| 1989 | Acting Area Operations Manager - Central Area Switching Control Center |
| 1985-1989 | Foreman - Dispatch Administration |
| 1984-1985 | Network Administration Engineer |
| 1980-1984 | Foreman - Dispatch Administration |
| 1976-1980 | Central Office Foreman |

## EDUCATION

**Bachelor of Science - Business Management** (1995)
South Florida State College, Hollywood, Florida

## TECHNICAL SKILLS SUMMARY

| | |
|---|---|
| Lotus 1-2-3 | Excel |
| Lotus Notes | Professional Write |
| First Choice | WORD for Windows |
| Harvard Graphics | Microsoft Works 4.0 |

## COMMUNITY ACTIVITIES

- Served as volunteer tutor in an elementary school for a business/education project.
- Served as Professional Development Program Director for the Florida South Central Area Association of Management Women.
- Served on the Board of Directors for the Florida Tel-Com Federal Credit Union.
- Represented Florida South on Career Night at all South Miami junior high schools and on Career Day at Belle Glade Heights Senior High School.
- Designed and coordinated two Work Shadow Programs for Lauderdale and North Miami Junior High Schools for Florida South. Worked on the committee for Take Your Daughters to Work Day.
- Served as a member of the South Florida Business and Professional Women's Association.

The Professional Experience section shows work for the same company since 1976. In italic after the company name is a comment about the size of the company. As Area Manager, the candidate coordinated a college-degree-on-the-job program. She herself benefited from it (see Education).

# Hunter A. Lawrence

121 Hardscrabble Road ■ Chappaqua, New York 10514 ■ (914) 555-0000

Administrative and Customer Service ■ Human Resources ■ Travel Services Management

## Professional Profile

Diversified and solid management career with particular expertise in multi-site operations management. Focus on planning of major conventions. Significant experience as outside travel agent and coordinator of corporate travel plans. Highly visible manager with superior communication skills critical in providing quality customer service. Innovative style used in support-staff recruitment, hiring and training. Personal travel throughout the United States, Europe, South America and Russia.

## Management Accomplishments

**OUTSOURCE COMPANY, INC.** 1992–present

*Long-term assignments for management services firm supporting corporations in the major markets.*

**TOP-TIER COMPANY** 1993–present
**Manager of Administrative Operations** at three locations: Montvale, New Jersey, Westbury, New York and New York City. Oversaw customer-service centers in Montvale and Westbury.

- Currently manage nine full-time contract employees, directing mailroom shipping and receiving functions, reproduction and copy services.
- Manage budget, payroll and personnel requirements. Allocate resources and meet with regulatory compliance, including safety standards.
- Employ persuasive and thorough communication and research skills to recruit and interview new hires. Interpret specifications of positions, define culture of each site and evaluate employees' skills and abilities to fit company's needs.
- Created concept for, and implemented, customer-satisfaction surveys in response to company commission to study economic feasibility of copy centers. Client evaluation of services resulted in a 90% approval rating, surpassing the mark of previous service supplier by more than 25%.
- Adept at purchasing and inventory management, evaluated bids on copier leases to achieve cost savings of $150,000 over previous year's contracts.
- Facilitated workflow through development of site-specific procedural manuals. Translated technical language into clear, readily usable terms.

**ABC CORPORATION, INTERNATIONAL HEADQUARTERS,** White Plains, New York 1992–1993
**Site Manager** in charge of American Express contract for travel services. Directed Customer Centers supporting client education, video conferencing, audio-visual services and graphic arts control. Maintained telecommunications system, internal assets and capital equipment.

- Collaborated with department managers in reviewing travel reports, resulting in a reduced travel budget and a company-wide $275,000 increase in surplus operating revenue.
- Instituted a program rewarding video conference usage that contributed to further reductions in travel costs.
- Selected as Team Leader for Travel Quality Council, representing staff from Outsource, ABC and American Express. Council monitored services, customer satisfaction and cost control for travel provided to ABC.

135

**Combination.** *Phyllis B. Shabad, Ossining, New York*

The writer emphasized this candidate's "long and substantial management career because he never went to college." When the candidate was downsized from "ABC," he continued his

**Hunter A. Lawrence** page two

**ABC CORPORATION, VARIOUS U.S. AND INTERNATIONAL DIVISIONS** 1979–1992

*Held increasingly responsible positions in **Management, Personnel, Recruiting, Accounting** and **Customer Service.** Broad experience in facilities management, including food and travel services, secretarial support, education enrollments and internal asset security.*

- Detail-oriented travel manager who ensured swift resolution of problems arising from corporate travel policy. Reconciled discrepancies and implemented cost controls. Thorough knowledge of reservation transactions, including booking and ticketing. Interfaced with brokers and assembled packages. Finalized plans with on-line reservation systems.
- Successfully managed logistical planning of arrivals, departures and dining accommodations for over 1,200 attendees at each of four Latin American Sales Recognition Conventions held in Nashville, Orlando, New Orleans and Miami.
- Directed $500,000 site renovation of cafeteria, accompanied by a facilities upgrade of food preparation and refrigeration equipment.
- Spearheaded team effort to initiate customer promotion program, bringing food service operations to a break-even point and eliminating need for corporate subsidy.
- Streamlined expenses of sales unit and held down costs through attrition and consolidation.
- Progressive human resource manager in entry-level recruiting, interviewing and hiring. Maximized staff performance and boosted morale through career development, focusing on coaching, training and skills assessment.
- Recognized for accuracy, organization and thoroughness in financial records management, accounting and international billing processing. Coordinated monthly salary compensations for American ABC employees on assignment in Europe. Monitored accounts receivable collection operations for 8 ABC branches.

## Related Activities and Achievements

**Awards**

In recognition of exceptional performance for contributions to quality service, received ABC Customer Service Award. Also earned Regional Managers and District Managers Awards.

**Professional Development**

Certified by NYU Travel Management Program. Coursework included managing business and personal travel.

Attended Pitney-Bowes workshops on mailroom operations.

Regularly attend series of National Postal Forum seminars on new products, services and government regulations.

Participated in numerous ABC management training programs.

**Computer Literacy**

Utilize Lotus 1-2-3 and AmiPro, as well as internal corporate systems, for accounting solutions.

career by subcontracting to an outsourcing firm and never had a gap in his employment record. Bulleted items include achievements as duties. The side headings for the Related Activities and Achievements section end the resume on a strong note and help to offset no Education section.

## JAMES M. LEESON

**555 Remson Street · Schenectady, New York 55555 · (555) 555-5555**

**OBJECTIVE:** A position in the construction trades - focus on my carpentry skills.

**PROFILE:**

- Hands-on knowledge of all phases of construction.
- Dependable, self-motivated; assume responsibility to get the job done.
- Possess strong organization, communication and customer service skills.
- Take pride in quality workmanship and complete customer satisfaction.
- Resourceful in solving problems and maximizing resources.
- Ability to learn new skills quickly; perform under pressure to meet deadlines.

**RELEVANT EXPERIENCE:**

**SOUTHERN ADIRONDACK CONSTRUCTION CO.,** Schenectady, NY
Owner/Manager - 1995 - 1996

- Direct involvement in all phases of the construction process from start to finish including designing the job, print reading, footings to finish work.
- Complete projects on time while meeting strict budget requirements.
- Locate qualified vendors; negotiate with subcontractors.
- Estimate and bid jobs; acquire zoning variance and building permits.
- Purchase and expedite materials/equipment; maintain quality control.
- Assess customers' needs and advise on layout and materials required; explain cost and benefits of products in relation to their needs.

**PHIL MARTELL,** Scotia, NY
Carpenter - 1991 - 1995

- Performed all phases of carpentry and general construction work including layout of job, footings, concrete work, framing, and trim work.
- Estimated and bid jobs; ensured that work is completed on schedule and to the customer's satisfaction.

**FUNSTON OF SCOTIA, GLULAM SYSTEMS, INC.,** Scotia, NY
Yard Foreman - 1984 - 1991

- Supervised and delegated work to a staff of 11 employees.
- Responsible for ordering materials, all receiving functions; ran inventories.
- Resolved a wide range of customer problems; assisted with layout of job and arranged for timely delivery of materials.

**EDUCATION:**

Canton Agriculture & Technical College, Canton, NY - 1980 - 1983
**Associates Degree in Agriculture & Wood Products Engineering**
**Associates Degree in Animal Husbandry**

**VOLUNTEER/COMMUNITY INVOLVEMENT:**

Volunteer Fireman, West Charlton Fire Dept. - 7 years

**REFERENCES:**

Available on request.

**136**

**Combination.** *Barbara Beaulieu, Scotia, New York*

The resume of an individual who, as a carpenter and owner of a construction company, is the manager of it. Bulleted items call attention to his managerial skills. His titles are underlined.

**MARGARET ANDERSON**

9247 Colgate Lane • Davison, Michigan 48555 • (810) 555-7394

**HIGHLIGHTS OF QUALIFICATIONS**

- Strong people skills: easily establish rapport with customers, peers and management; extremely customer service focused.
- Thorough understanding of financial concepts and procedures based on significant experience in banking and credit unions as well as small business operations.
- Able to listen to and interpret customer needs, develop plans to meet those needs, and implement programs with mutually beneficial results.
- Proven problem-solving and decision-making skills.
- Adept at prioritizing, handling and completing multiple tasks simultaneously.
- Employee training and supervisory experience.

**EMPLOYMENT HISTORY**

**Owner-Manager** • Country Designs Unlimited • Grand Blanc, MI (1990-1995)
- Owned and managed retail store with custom framing service.
- Increased sales over 30% from previous owner.
- Developed store's reputation by emphasizing customer satisfaction and quality service.

**Customer Service Representative** • Martin Inc. • Flint, MI (1989-1990)
- Collaborated with customer institutions to set up and adapt data processing service.
- Determined features of accounts, procedures and computer interface.

**Visa Coordinator/Loan Officer** • Benton Municipal Credit Union • Benton, MI (1986-1989)
- Established and organized Visa card program from ground up.
- Acted as loan officer to review and approve/disapprove loan applications within specified guidelines.

**Supervisor** • U.S. Army Credit Union • Alexandria, VA (1984-1986)
- Oversaw daily operations of institution with six employees.
- Processed mortgage loan applications.

**Customer Service Specialist** • Community Bank of Flint • Flint, MI (1978-1984)
- Designated by manager to assist customers whose accounts totaled over $100,000.
- Promoted from teller position.

**EDUCATION**

**Seminars** on relevant topics:
- Financial Planning
- Security in Financial Institutions
- Dealing with Difficult Employees
- Business Taxes
- Beginning Your Own Business
- Custom Framing

**Business Management** coursework • Cole Community College • Cole, MI 1975-1976
- Participated in Business Co-op program.

**AFFILIATION**

American Business Women's Association (former member)

*References available upon request.*

137

**Combination.** *Janet L. Beckstrom, Flint, Michigan*

A resume for a small business owner who is returning to the job market. Bold diamond bullets catch attention better than small circular bullets. Boldfacing helps the positions stand out.

## ARTHUR QUINLAN

115 Second Avenue • Orangeburg, NY 55555 • (000) 000-0000

### PROFILE

Entrepreneurial manager with over 30 years experience in all aspects of interior planning and furnishing. Skilled in all business matters requiring negotiating, decision making and strong customer service orientation. Ability to strategize, organize and manage projects start to finish, and to achieve client satisfaction within time and budgetary framework. Scope of effectiveness extends to:

***Site selection*** of office or retail space consistent with client requirements, local zoning ordinances and financial resources.

***Evaluation of suitability for occupancy*** dependent on business purpose, with consideration to factors such as floor space allocation, lighting, air circulation, and accommodations for employees' and/or patrons' comfort and safety.

***Layout assistance*** with regard to placement of doorways, electrical or telephone outlets, furnishings, fixtures, signs, equipment and sales inventory for maximum efficiency and visual impact.

***Vast resource network*** of factory direct furniture, carpeting, fabric and interior accessories suppliers.

***Cooperative working relationships*** with building trades contractors and property managers.

***Advice in matters of interior design or merchandising*** to create appropriate ambience and enhance professional image of clients.

***Troubleshooting of client problems*** in areas of merchandise delivery, warehousing, selling, advertising and financing from a business owner's standpoint.

### EXPERIENCE

1986–1995 CLASSIC CHARM BOUTIQUE, Warwick, NY and Tuxedo, NY

- Owner/manager of a very successful home furnishings and accessories business, started from scratch with 4000 square feet and doubled in volume every year thereafter.
- In partnership with wife, employed a staff of six full- and part-time sales associates in two locations.
- Designed, arranged and stocked stores with a diversified line of merchandise appealing to client preferences.
- Established numerous industry contacts, enabling most favorable buying conditions to maximize profitability.
- Provided attentive service and decorating advice which increased business growth through referrals. Had very little need to advertise.

1970–1986 HOUSE OF OAK AND MAPLE, Brunswick, NJ

- Owner of 22,000 square foot store carrying a full line of traditional furnishings and accessories for residential and business environments. Employed staff of 14.
- Took over unprofitable business from former owner experiencing financing difficulties. Reversed negative trend after one year through hands-on management in all areas.
- Increased business growth by 30-40% in following years by reestablishing credit, building reputation with suppliers, improving merchandising, and revising financial system and advertising methods.
- Sold business at outset of major shift in the case goods industry to concentrate on smaller, more profitable specialty retail operation.

1963–1970 PARK MANOR FURNITURE CO., Edison, NJ

- Managed family's 15,000 square foot general furniture store. Acquired a comprehensive knowledge of the business including furniture craftsmanship and buying.

***Business and personal references will be provided upon request.***

**138**

**Combination.** *Melanie A. Noonan, West Paterson, New Jersey*

A resume for a manager over age 50. The lines make the contact information stand out. The Profile indicates both skills and areas of effectiveness. Some of the bullets show achievements.

# *Matthew C. Hatson*

653 River Road, Grosse Ile, MI 48138
H: (313) 555-7654 ◆ W: (313) 333-1324

## Career Highlights

Manager with extensive background in Engineering, Logistics, and Human Resources. Skilled troubleshooter, leader, negotiator, and communicator with a proven ability to increase profitability, productivity, efficiency, and morale.

***Engineering*** Directed UPS staff in job planning, workload/workforce balancing, and documentation control. Developed and maintained long-range plans for operations, training, and inspections. Developed a "Master Operating Plan" (M.O.P.)–a standardized procedure for processing Canadian shipments through Customs–for Detroit Area. The plan streamlined procedures and resulted in improved productivity and a decrease in errors. The M.O.P. was used as a nationwide model, and I was sent to Seattle, Buffalo, Minneapolis and Montreal to implement the program. Served as mediator with Customs. Increased pieces per hour by 300%, reduced fines, and improved morale.

***Logistics*** Set up UPS facilities to handle package flow. Successfully managed Midwest shipping and distribution of the Diet Pepsi "Gotta Have It" promotion. Midwest operation was the most efficient in the U.S. Brought consistency to Time-in-Transit nationwide.

***Management*** Trained in operations, logistics, personnel management, customer service, production management, inventory control and shipping. Successfully set up Customer Service Export Hold Center as a troubleshooting center for problem packages. Currently manage a restaurant, and a $35,000/per month budget. Experienced with negotiating union contracts; work well with Teamsters.

***Human Resources*** Excellent leadership skills with the ability to motivate and direct staff. Have supervised staff of up to 150–both hourly employees and salaried supervisors. Developed training video for pre-work communication meeting. As Hub Training Supervisor, hired and trained 69 people in two months, with no turnover during the Christmas rush. Opened Madison Heights UPS facility and trained Management on hiring and keeping employees.

## Professional History

**ST. MARTIN'S,** La Salle, MI — 1994 - Present
Owner/Manager

**UNITED PARCEL SERVICE** — 1985 - 1994
Volume Reconciliation Supervisor, Livonia Hub Supervisor, Night Sort Supervisor

## Education

**UNIVERSITY OF MICHIGAN**
Computer Science/Marketing — 1983 - 1988

**GROSSE ILE HIGH SCHOOL,** Grosse Ile, Michigan — Graduated in 1978

**139**

**Combination.** *Deborah L. Schuster, Newport, Michigan*

This proven logistics manager for a major shipping company had purchased and managed a restaurant but wanted to return to logistics. The four expertise areas play up logistics experience.

**STEVEN T. SCHOR**
**5407 Allendale Drive ◆ Lutz, Florida 33549**
**(813) 000-0000**

**SENIOR LEVEL OPERATIONS MANAGER**

Record of progressive leadership and ability to deliver strong, sustainable results in productivity and efficiency improvement, project management, financial management, needs assessment, program development and augmenting human resource activities for large-scale operations.

**EXECUTIVE SUMMARY**

***Senior Operations Professional*** with an accomplished military career encompassing over 25 years of diverse, high-profile experience. Exercised conceptual and innovative strategies to effectively promote program efficacy. Entrepreneurial minded with experience in P&L, preparing financial projections/forecasts, regulating policies/procedures, personnel management and facilities operations. Articulate communicator with excellent training, keen analytical ability, prudent decision-making skills and meticulous organizational expertise.

**DEMONSTRATED SKILLS**

-- Regional Planning
-- Turn-around Operations
-- Procurement/Distribution
-- Time Management
-- Public Relations Liaison
-- Proposal Development
-- Investigative Research
-- Automated Systems
-- Contract Negotiations
-- Operational Logistics

**COMPUTER SKILLS**

Windows and DOS-based programs, WordPerfect, Microsoft, Excel
Familiar with programming

**EDUCATION**

STATE UNIVERSITY OF NEW YORK AT BUFFALO
**Bachelor of Arts Degree in English** *(Magna Cum Laude; Phi Beta Kappa)*

**Graduate,** Commander and General Staff College

**Graduate,** Health Care Administration

**EXPERIENCE**

UNI-TEL - Albany, NY **1994 - 1997**
**Owner/Manager**
Pioneered start-up of coin-operated telephone business. Oversaw all aspects of management and operations inclusive of site selection, traffic flow analysis, contracting and installation/maintenance services. Performed accounting, record keeping and subcontracting functions.

309TH FIELD HOSPITAL - Boston, MA **1992 - 1993**
**Chief Plans and Medical Operations Officer / Major**
-- Spearheaded administrative and financial management responsibilities involving budget maintenance, human resource functions, senior-level planning, procurement activities and facilities management for all medically-related operations.
-- Directed reserve staff of medical service professionals and administrative personnel; oversaw operations of 14 unit medical training managers for 450 reserve personnel.
-- Designed, developed and implemented a myriad of innovative, adjunct programs to streamline operational infrastructure and re-engineering existing training programs.
-- Formulated long range projections and financial plans; oversaw preparation of procedural manuals, authored comprehensive technical proposals and interpreted regulations and policies.

**140**

**Combination.** *Diane McGoldrick, Tampa, Florida*

The current Owner/Manager title differs considerably from the candidate's previous titles. A task of the resume is to display in the opening section skills and qualifications that will be needed in

**STEVEN T. SCHOR** **Page Two**

HEADQUARTERS FIRST U.S. ARMY - Fort George A. Meade, MD **1989 - 1992**
**Personnel Officer / Captain**
-- Charged with providing administrative support to 850 physicians (coordinated their mobilization during Desert Store); processing personnel actions, enforcing regulatory changes and maintaining security of classified information.
-- Key role in human resource functions; designed, developed and implemented policies/procedures and staffing programs resulting in **90% retention of qualified personnel.**

UNITED STATES DEPARTMENT OF AGRICULTURE - Buffalo, NY **1986 - 1989**
**Federal Grain Inspector**
-- Duty involved biological testing of flours and grains, verification of radiological contamination specimens, analyzing purity of grain products and interpreting weight compliance codes with federal regulations.
-- Initiated recommendations for safety procedures and modifications to OSHA guidelines.

338TH GENERAL HOSPITAL - Niagara Falls, NY **1985 - 1986**
**Chief Health Care Administrator / Captain**
-- Orchestrated planning and coordination of a managed health care delivery system for 600 military employees.
-- Presided over procurement services and supplies; budget administration; vendor selection; contract negotiations; facilities management; automation and communications.
-- Established logistical management programs, assembled project teams, prioritized assignments, tracked milestones to ensure timely completion of assignments and conducted all supervisory/human resource functions for administrative professionals and related technical/clerical support staff.

SURGEON GENERAL'S OFFICE - Phoenix, AZ **1985**
**Medical Personnel Administrator / Captain**
-- Directed recruitment activities of medical personnel and counseled applicants regarding career opportunities, benefits, programs and responsibilities.
-- Designed and conducted market analysis, identified specialty shortages, composed comprehensive recruiting strategies to obtain qualified medical personnel for hard-to-fill occupations and delineated parameters for recruiting actions. **Attained 90% strength level in a difficult market.**
-- Instrumental in establishing a medical affiliation with the University of Arizona Medical School.

EVACUATION HOSPITAL - Niagara Falls, NY **1979 - 1984**
**Administrative Specialist / First Lieutenant**
-- Supported senior-level administrative staff members, logistics operations and management of human resources functions.
-- Performed operational audits, developed labor utilization plans to maximize staffing operations, evaluated programs, maintained controls for total quality management and oversaw hospital budget.
-- **Generated 30% savings** in food costs via ingenious sourcing, conducting cost analyses and astute inventory management.

U.S. ARMY **1976 - 1979**
**Recruiting Specialist** - Niagara Falls, NY
-- Coordinated recruiting campaigns, facilitated improvements in training programs and provided budgeting/forecasting assistance.

**CAREER ACHIEVEMENTS**

*During military tenure have earned numerous meritorious honors and commendations such as:*

Meritorious Service Medal
Army Achievement Medal (3)

**MILITARY STATUS**

Major, U.S. Army (Inactive)

any new operation. The two-column list of skills in the "Demonstrated Skills" section is flexible and can be tailored to a specific job target. Note the use of boldfacing—particularly, in the position titles, in the dates, and toward the end of the bulleted lists in the Experience section.

# Donna J. Watson

4444 Blue Lake Drive, Tullahoma, Tennessee 37388 Tel: (615) 555-4117

***Over ten years experience in management and sales with a broad knowledge of all levels of a retail environment. Excellent track record in public relations and customer service through experience in retail sales and the housing and rental markets. Established ability in dealing with financial issues, marketing, and employee relations.***

## BUSINESS EXPERIENCE

Retail Management • Customer Service • Sales • Employee Supervision/Relations
Budgeting • Public Relations • Advertising & Marketing • Inventory Control
Cash Flow Planning • Cost Analysis • Accounts Payable/Receivable • Payroll
Housing Management • Tenant Issues • Inspections • Shipping/Receiving

## TECHNICAL SKILLS

- Windows 95
- PC operations
- Lotus 1-2-3
- Microsoft Office
- Peachtree
- Inventory Software

## EMPLOYMENT HISTORY

***Owner/Manager***

***Watson's Televisions, Tullahoma, Tennessee. 1/85 to present.***
Own and manage retail store with direct sales of televisions, satellite systems, home entertainment systems, and electronic equipment. Plan marketing and advertising campaigns; provide customer service; negotiate with vendors and suppliers; manage payroll and employee issues. Budget expenditures and manage cash flow; track profit and loss; supervise bookkeeping and accounts.

***Inventory Manager***

***George Dickel Distillery, Tullahoma, Tennessee. 1/84-1/85.***
Supervised shipping/receiving in the bottling department for large whiskey distillery. Tracked flow of packaging using computer inventory system. Performed general office duties.

***Administrative Assistant***

***Tullahoma Housing Authority, Tullahoma, Tennessee. 6/79-12/83.***
Provided administrative support to the Executive Director. Received and reviewed applications for housing; interviewed prospective tenants to establish eligibility and determine rental rates. Prepared lease contracts and informed tenants of rules and regulations. Collected rents and prepared reports. Inspected units and compiled reports of needed maintenance or renovations. Attended Board meetings and maintained minutes and records. Assisted in accounting and reporting of all monies collected.

## EDUCATION

*1978-1979* — ***Shelbyville Technical School****, Shelbyville, Tennessee. Business Systems.*

*1975-1978* — ***Middle Tennessee State University****, Murfreesboro, Tennessee. Completed approximately 70 semester hours toward a Bachelor of Business Administration degree.*

**141**

**Combination.** *Tracy A. Bumpus, Manchester, Tennessee*

The writer calls this a "shotgun" resume for a candidate who wasn't sure of what she was looking for. Italic is used for the profile, side headings, company names, and the Education section.

# BRUCE HAGGER

238 Stockford Place • Riverside, Missouri 69771
(218) 666-7800

## WORK EXPERIENCE

**ABC, INC. -** One of the leading manufacturers of business forms in the United States, with fifteen manufacturing facilities and coast-to-coast distribution and sales coverage.

**Plant Manager, Riverside, Missouri** 1993 to Present
Responsible for the operation of production facility and distribution center. Manage 105 employees, including nine supervisors. Over $73 million production in 1993.

**Manager Print and Distribution Centers, Albion, Michigan** 1991 to 1993
Responsible for six print centers plus nationwide distribution system that included 11 ABC, Inc. facilities and 35+ outside warehouses. Managed 165 employees including, 13 supervisors.

**Plant Manager, Berkley, Mississippi** 1986 to 1991
Responsible for start-up and operation of production facility and warehouse. Managed 41 employees, including four supervisors. Plant produced over $23 million in 1990.

**Assistant Plant Manager, Riverside, Missouri** 1982 to 1986
Responsible for operation of production facility and warehouse control center directing 14 additional warehouses. Also responsible for supervision of 176 employees, including 15 supervisors and 161 non-exempt personnel. This plant produced in excess of $83 million in 1985 and surpassed $95 million in 1986.

**Production Manager, Riverside, Missouri** 1980 to 1982
Responsible for start-up of new plant, including hiring of personnel, training of new employees, operational organization, and production.

**General Supervisor, San Antonio, Texas** 1975 to 1980
Responsible for operation of preparatory and shipping departments and warehouse facilities. Supervised staff of 29, including two supervisors. Output of preparatory department was doubled while cost of operation was reduced by more than 50%.

**General Supervisor, San Antonio, Texas** 1974 to 1975
Responsible for quality control department. Supervised staff of two, including one supervisor.

**General Supervisor, San Antonio, Texas** 1970 to 1974
Responsible for production control and outside supply departments. Supervised staff of 22, including three supervisors.

**Customer Service Supervisor, San Antonio, Texas** 1968 to 1970
Responsible for supervision of customer service, expediting of production, and shipping departments. Supervised staff of six.

**Plant Expeditor, San Antonio, Texas** 1958 to 1968
Responsible for movement of all orders throughout plant. Also worked in other capacities of plant, including operation of collator and printing press.

## EDUCATION

Sexton High School, San Antonio, Texas

## HONORS

Valedictorian of graduating class

## ACTIVITIES & INTERESTS

Member of Rotary Clubs International

CONFIDENTIAL – PRESENTLY EMPLOYED

**142**

**Chronological.** *Christina M. Popa, Adrian, Michigan*

The writer of this resume liked it because it clearly shows the individual's "continual promotions within one company." The fact that he had only "a high school education is hardly noticeable."

## DON LEYRITZ

30 Money Lane
Freeburg, Illinois 62243
(618) 555-8873

### PROFESSIONAL PROFILE

Extensive background managing all plant operations for a $7M commercial printing company, with successful track record for maximizing resources, sales, production, quality and overall profitability. Hands-on knowledge of 4-color and aqueous coating processes. Areas of expertise include:

| | | |
|---|---|---|
| Warehousing | Manufacturing | Inventory Management |
| Vendor Relations | Sales Targeting | Industry Standards |
| Quality Control | Estimating | Customer Service |

### CURRENT POSITION

Adsell Printing, St. Louis, MO 1985-Present

**Printing Plant Manager:** Oversee operations in five departments: Prep, Pressroom, Bindery, Shipping & Receiving, and Warehousing. Supervise 85 employees. Coordinate paper buyouts, prep and press inventory, layout for printing jobs, and all printing and binding production.

**KEY ACCOMPLISHMENTS**

- Redesigned prep department to allow business to handle modernized mailing requirements. ***Result:*** Doubled press capacity while cutting binding costs in half.
- Restructured relationship with major paper supplier, allowing stock to be purchased on an "as needed" from a designated off-site supply. ***Result:*** Company required 30% less inventory space in-house and earned a 20% discount on all merchandise in return for exclusive business.
- Started a new estimating program on large print orders. ***Result:*** Saved $500-$1000 per week previously lost in negotiating paper prices that were inconsistent with original estimates.
- Implemented and managed an in-house consignment plan that replaced the costly and time-consuming process of purchasing key printing and proofing supplies as needed. ***Result:*** Company maintained and replenished a $15,000-20,000 inventory, significantly decreasing press downtime.
- Learned a previously unused computer function to track supply inventory levels. ***Result:*** Negotiated better pricing through extensive knowledge of actual usage and sales trends.
- Negotiated an exclusive two-year deal with a major manufacturer. ***Result:*** Company was given more than $45,000 worth of processing and proofing equipment to replace its manual systems. In addition, vendor supplied engineers to oversee a relocation and create an efficient business layout.

### PREVIOUS EXPERIENCE

**Plant Manager/Assistant General Manager**, Register, Inc., St. Louis, MO 1978-1985
**General Manager**, Fritz Litho (sister company of Register, Inc.), St. Louis, MO 1976-1977
**Printing Salesman**, Register, Inc., St. Louis, MO 1974-1976

REFERENCES AVAILABLE UPON REQUEST

**143**

**Combination.** *John A. Suarez, Troy, Illinois*

Evident are several strong resume features: headings seen readily by full lines, expertise areas in flexible columns, a duties paragraph, and bulleted key accomplishments. See the use of "Result."

**WILLIAM G. CARSON**

**Extensive management and technical expertise in power plant operations.**

**GOAL - Director, Plant Operations, Union Hospital**

**EXPERIENCE:**

**A BIG MUTUAL INSURANCE COMPANY,** Indianapolis, Indiana 1979-9/94

**FACILITIES MANAGER/DIRECTOR:** Managed 160,000-square-foot facility and grounds: mechanical systems, Liebert computer room equipment, landscaping, housekeeping, and security. Supervised three managers and 19 technical and office support staff.

- Developed and managed mechanical maintenance program with 0% downtime on major HVAC components.
- Re-engineered dual duct and chilled water HVAC system; gained annual savings of $120,000; directed system planning and installation.
- Initiated $460,000 savings during company downsizing.
- Organized Facilities Management Division.
- Conceived and organized unique concept in housekeeping.
- Established award-winning landscaping program, recognized by Mayor Hudnut.
- Specified and implemented new concept in modular space saving furniture.
- Developed budget control procedure generating variance reports and expediting results.
- Negotiated transactions of real estate and leasing agreements for facilities in six states.
- Managed corporate automobile fleet program consisting of up to 160 units, including set up of computerized tracking system.

**TOOLEY F. FREEZE, INC.,** Indianapolis, Indiana 1960-1979

**SERVICE MANAGER** for large commercial and industrial mechanical contractor, including installation and preventive maintenance. Supervised crew of 20 technicians.

- Organized inventory control system.
- Managed total company purchasing operation.

**EDUCATION:**

- Business Administration, Indiana Central University, Indianapolis, Indiana.
- Personnel Management, Motivation, and Interpersonal Skills; Mechanical Contractors Association, Indianapolis, Indiana.
- Factory Design and Engineering, commercial refrigeration equipment, Frick Company, Waynesboro, Pennsylvania.

**ACTIVITIES:**

- The Masonic Lodge, Anytown, Indiana (Past Master, 1975).
- St. Anthony's Lutheran Church, Anytown, Indiana (Past Council President).
- American Legion Post #791, Cissna Park, Illinois.

***5037 Norman Drive • Indianapolis, Indiana 46228 • (317) 578-5656***

**144**

**Chronological.** *Carole E. Pefley, Indianapolis, Indiana*

A different feature is that the contact information is split between the resume's top (the individual's name) and bottom (the address and phone number). A specific goal is centered.

# CHRISTOPHER S. JADEN

*369 Harborside Drive*
*Lakeland, Florida 33810*
*Home: (941) 555-5555*

## CAREER PROFILE

Plant/Operations Manager with over ten years experience managing fast-paced production and distribution operations. Implemented organizational change initiatives that have consistently improved financial, market, and operational performance. Analytical thinker and planner able to develop and implement effective operations and management strategies aimed at promoting company growth and increasing productivity. Exceptional leader with a team-oriented management style.

- Strategic Planning
- Market/Product Positioning
- ISO9000, HAACP, SPC Processes
- Customer Service Management
- Budget/Capital Planning
- Productivity Improvement
- PC and MIS Technology
- Materials Management
- Production/Planning Management
- Distribution/Warehousing Management
- Human Resources Administration
- Contract Negotiation/Implementation

## PROFESSIONAL EXPERIENCE

**MAMA'S FAVORITES (*a division of Family Foods Company*) - Tampa, Florida** ***1994 to Present***
**Plant Manager**

- ➢ Senior management executive with full responsibility for operations, quality control, engineering, production, distribution, purchasing, human resources, accounting, and maintenance activities.
- ➢ Oversee product distribution averaging $91 million in annual sales value to distributors throughout the southeastern United States.
- ➢ Work cooperatively with seven similar plant facilities to forecast product requirements, plan distribution for marketing promotions, and observe operations to enhance overall company performance and productivity.
- ➢ Direct a staff of nine department managers; control a $51 million operating budget.
- ➢ Strong familiarity with BPCS (business operations integration and planning) and ELKE (preventive maintenance) software.

***ACCOMPLISHMENTS***

- ➢ Instrumental in the development and start-up of two state-of-the-art baking facilities in Tampa, Florida and Atlanta, Georgia.
- ➢ Through systems automation and staff reorganization:
  - reduced plant downtime by 50%.
  - improved processing yields by $300,000 annually.
  - improved labor efficiency by $350,000 annually.
- ➢ Implemented a productivity improvement program for fiscal year 1996, realizing over $800,000 in savings annually.
- ➢ Improved conversion cost/lb by 6% in 1996, with a 16% increase in May and June alone.
- ➢ Maintained controllable expenses of $600,000, keeping within the constraints of the original budget.
- ➢ Reduced ingredient and container inventories by 9.2%, with production up 9.4%.
- ➢ Played a significant role in the company's achievement of the ISO9000 certification.
- ➢ Led the successful turnaround of the customer service organization and reduced consumer complaints by 32%.
- ➢ Implemented HACCP, resulting in a 41% decrease in foreign object complaints.
- ➢ Through an increased awareness and focus on plant safety, successfully reduced recordable injuries by 13% with no lost time accidents.
- ➢ Reduced employee discipline counselings by 58%; reduced chargeable absentee rate by 38%.

**145**

**Combination.** *E. René Hart, Lakeland, Florida*

Larger-than-average side headings complement the larger-than-average name in the contact information. The rest of the contact information, the parenthetical explanations of company

**CHRISTOPHER S. JADEN** -2-

## PROFESSIONAL EXPERIENCE (continued)

**HEARTS-A-FLUTTER CHOCOLATE (*a division of Family Foods Company*) - Atlanta, Georgia** ***1993-1994***
**Plant Manager**

➢ Completely re-engineered the production process through:
  - addition of a third shift and production line during peak production periods.
  - maximization of existing staff and increased use of temporary employees.
  - reduction of the finished product inventory by 900,000 lbs annually.

➢ Reduced outside storage costs by $120,000 each year; closed one outside storage facility altogether.

**MAMA'S FAVORITES - Boise, Idaho** ***1990-1993***
**Operations Manager-Bakery Production**

**MAMA'S FAVORITES - Tampa, Florida** ***1987-1990***
**Operations Manager-Bakery/Biscuit Production**

**MAMA'S FAVORITES - Buffalo, New York** ***1986-1987***
**Operations Manager**

## EDUCATION

Bachelor of Science - Political Science (*1974*)
George Mason University - Washington, D.C.

Currently pursuing a Master of Business Administration
University of South Florida - Tampa, Florida

## CONTINUING EDUCATION AND TRAINING

Boise Food Executive Program - Ithaca, New York (*1992*)
Executive Techniques Workshop - Tampa, Florida (*1989*)
University of Toledo Confection School - Toledo, Ohio (*1993*)

## CIVIC ACTIVITIES

Board of Directors - West Area Economic Development Council
Coach - Carrollwood Baseball League
Hillsborough County School Board Improvement Committee
United Way Allocation Committee

names, and the dates are in italic. Two kinds of bullets are used for different levels of bulleted statements. At the end of the Career Profile are three columns of bulleted areas of expertise. You will recall that such columns are flexible: they can be changed to target a specific position.

HARRY ALBRIGHTON
9926 California Court
Wilmington, North Carolina 28412
(000) 111-2222

***Manufacturing Manager / Operations Manager / Plant Manager / Production Supervisor***

Results-driven, hands-on operations manager with 20+ years experience leading manufacturing plants. Strong general management qualifications in:

| | |
|---|---|
| Manufacturing | Production Scheduling and Control |
| Budgeting & Financial Controls | Inventory/Materials Management |
| Regulatory & Safety Compliance | Personnel Administration |

Successfully turned around Rose Hill, NC site which had shown annual losses to profitable status in less than 6 months. Since that time site has continued to be profitable, most often ranked as the most profitable of Beautiful Pants Division Plants.

Significant improvements made to quality and efficiency through implementation of quality and production control measures.

## EXPERIENCE

BEAUTIFUL INDUSTRIES

**Plant Manager** - Rose Hill, NC 1990 - Present

Full accountability for operations and profitability of a 110 employee cut and sew plant making mens sportswear and pants. Manage all daily operations including production, quality control, regulatory compliance, human resource, and financial functions.

- Direct all safety, environment, and health functions; developed policies and guidelines to ensure OSHA and other regulatory compliance.
- Reorganized plant's policies and procedures which resulted in increased production and improved efficiency.
- Solicited outside contracts to fill in production schedule as needed to best utilize manpower and facilities.
- Designed and implemented an in-line quality system which significantly reduced waste and rejects from QC inspections.

**Plant Manager** - Atlanta, GA 1978 - 1990

Directed operations for a manufacturing facility, producer of mens pants and sportswear, with 150 employees making significant accomplishments and consistently meeting or exceeding corporate goals.

- Introduced new strategies and policies that led to improved profitability.
- Successfully led site through expansions in production, facilities, and manpower.
- Maintained close interaction with supervisors and operators fostering a team environment.

146

**Combination.** *Sandy Adcox Saburn, Wilmington, North Carolina*

The opening section includes descriptive labels for previous positions, strong qualification areas, and main achievements for this person planning to step down to stay in his geographical area.

## Harry Albrighton - Page Two

### Experience (continued)

TINSLETOWN COMPANY - Outerwear Division
**Production Manager** - Denver, CO 1974 - 1978
Full responsibility for safe and efficient production of plant producing nylon and quilted jackets with a work force of 210. Made recommendations and modifications to production process that led to increased efficiency.

**Industrial Engineer** - Palm Beach, FL 1973 - 1974
Oversaw production in contract plants producing jackets. Ensured quality of work completed and compliance with corporate standards.

**Junior Engineer** - Birmingham, AL 1972 - 1973
Trained as Industrial Engineer in time studies, methods costing, and other various engineering duties.

### Education

**Bachelor of Science Degree** - University of Southern Mississippi, 1972

### Additional Training

**Machining Technology Courses** - Universal Community College
Gaining knowledge of manual lathes, milling techniques, CNC machines, and various measuring and testing equipment. Anticipated graduation: Fall 1997

### Professional Membership

Member - North Carolina Rotary

### References

Provided upon request

"The resume focuses on a broad range of skills in manufacturing management but is not industry specific. His education in machining was left in, even though it was not managerial, to show added skills but placed at the end so as not to distract from the other skills."

**PAUL PETERSON**
5555 Sandy Hill Drive
Anytown, U.S.A. 55555
(000) 000-0000

**SUMMARY OF QUALIFICATIONS**

Versatile, highly motivated professional with extensive experience in business administration and operations management within a manufacturing environment. Particularly skilled in project planning with an emphasis on the ability to understand the entire scope of a project and develop processes and procedures that effectively comply with established objectives. Hands-on experience in control and compliance as required by Good Manufacturing Practices.

**SIGNIFICANT ACHIEVEMENTS**

- **Reduced complaint closing processing time by 50%** through the introduction of a statistical method for determining appropriate failure investigation and corrective action.
- Created, implemented and directly controlled the development and marketing efforts for a new product release. **Product has contributed a net profit of $200,000 each year since introduction.**
- **Increased productivity by 25%** by streamlining data entry procedures and implementing a telephone order entry system which allowed for paperless processing.

**PERSONAL SUMMARY**

Excellent analytical and interpersonal skills . . . Ability to quickly learn, master and apply new procedures and techniques . . . Flexible . . . Skilled in verbal and written communication . . . Ability to assess problems and develop and implement solutions . . .

**COMPUTER SKILLS**

Proficient in WordPerfect, Microsoft Word, Word for Windows, Lotus 1-2-3, Excel, PowerPoint, Harvard Graphics, Visio, Flow 3, SuperProject, Time Line, MS Project, and Paradox (DOS and Windows version) . . .

**EDUCATION**

Bachelor of Arts, Management
Any University, U.S.A.
*(cum laude)*

147

**Combination.** *Sheryl Wilde, San Diego, California*

Contact information, uppercase and underlined section headings, uppercase positions, and company names are all centered for easy reading down a page. The current job title and

**PROFESSIONAL EXPERIENCE**
***Paul Peterson, Page Two***

***PRODUCT MONITORING MANAGER***
***ABC Corporation, Anytown, U.S.A.***

- Created and directed the development of a new department for reporting and investigating product malfunctions in compliance with Good Manufacturing Practices and the Medical Device Reporting Act.
- Developed and administered 1.5M departmental budget. **Implemented controls which resulted in department coming in significantly under budget.**
- Successfully directed a cross-functional team of 40 to review over 65,000 product malfunction issues to determine compliance to FDA medical device reporting requirements.
- Developed policy and procedure manuals, and flowcharted the entire process which contributed to overall division quality systems procedures.

**PRODUCT SUPPORT MANAGER - HOSPITAL ACCESSORIES**
***XYZ Corporation, Anytown, U.S.A.***

- Directly responsible for planning, organizing, implementing, and controlling four separate projects. Projects included the development and marketing of two products, the implementation of an Electronic Data Interchange order entry system, and the production of a company-wide product catalog. **All projects were completed on time and within budget.**
- Recruited cross-functional team members; performed product benefit analysis; directed product definition, design, pilot, production and sales introduction phases.

**REGION ADMINISTRATION MANAGER**
***ABC Corporation, Anytown, U.S.A.***

- Managed day-to-day activities of ten administrative employees responsible for order entry, service contract sales, credit management, inventory control, warehouse and shipping, and facility maintenance.
- Developed job classifications and corresponding pay scales; developed policy and procedure manual for all administrative employee activities. **Was the first Region Administration Manager to be awarded stock options due to the successful implementation of these policies.**
- Administered employee benefits and compensation for all region staff.

**NATIONAL FIELD SERVICE ADMINISTRATION MANAGER**
***Any Company, Anytown, U.S.A.***

- Directed activities of 150+ employees at 17 office sites in the U.S.
- Worked with in-house consultant to develop strategy to improve field operations. **Potential annual savings upon implementation of recommendations was 1.4M. Plan was implemented one year after leaving the company.**
- Coordinated recruiting efforts and training of staff.
- Documented methods and procedures relating to service policy.
- Wrote specifications for enhancement to on-line systems efficiency and performance.

company locations are in bold italic. Other items in boldface are achievements on page one and at least one achievement for each position on page two. Sections often put at the end of a resume (Personal Summary, Education, etc.) are on page one so that all job experience is on the whole of page two.

**DARREN McCLOUD**
1987 Cherry Road
Wood Dale, Illinois 55555
(555) 555-5555

*Seeking an executive management position with a dynamic company that will effectively utilize my successful marketing, sales management, and procurement experience.*

**PROFESSIONAL PROFILE**

- Profit-driven professional offering over 20 years of successful experience in sales and marketing management.
- Experienced in coordinating sales, marketing, broker, and distribution networks in major markets; manages all strategic planning and competitive analyses.
- Expert in developing successful private label programs, from comprehensive costing structures through graphic design/packaging, which have been sold nationally to major grocery retailers, food service distributors, mass merchandisers, and drug chains.
- Proven ability to convert profit losing operations to profit gainers through development and implementation of strategic marketing plans.
- Hire, train, supervise, and motivate sales teams and operations management at virtually all levels.
- Executive-level talents in product development and introduction, innovative marketing and business administration, including full responsibility for P&L and new ventures.
- Accomplished sales professional demonstrated by consistent record of achieving and exceeding sales goals. Accustomed to high-profile networking and managing major key accounts.

**CAREER HIGHLIGHTS**

***GUNLOCH PURCHASING, INC.***; Northlake, Illinois — July 1994 - Present
A cooperative private label buying group.

**Product Manager, Perishables - Retail and Foodservice**
Responsible for over $300 million in procurement for 45 wholesalers servicing 20,000 plus supermarkets internationally.
- Created a Central Billed Egg program which will bring 15,000,000 dozen eggs in-house, resulting in over $500,000 of new, net income.
- Created and sourced a 100 SKU "Thaw and Sell" premium in-store bakery program for supermarkets without in-store bakeries.
- Accountable for the procurement of over 3,000,000 cases of ice cream and ice cream novelties.
- Totally responsible for all foodservice perishables for food service members that exceed $8 billion in revenue.

***LEMITZ MANUFACTURING***; Franklin Park, Illinois — August 1990 - July 1994

**Vice-President of Sales and Marketing**
Managed all sales and marketing functions for this manufacturer. Reported directly to President. Total P&L responsibility for sales and marketing departments.
- Restructured, expanded, and managed national network of food brokers covering grocery/frozen food, deli/bakery, convenience stores, membership wholesale clubs, and food service.
- Established company as a premier private label manufacturer in this category for both major retail and food service accounts.
- Developed and implemented marketing strategies thereby increasing sales from $3 million to $7 million within 15 months, to $11.8 million in 24 months; and to $20 million plus when the company was sold to a multi billion dollar Canadian food conglomerate.

**148**

**Combination.** *Georgia Veith, Elmhurst, Illinois*

This is another resume that has the look of a resume for executives, managers, and other administrators. What contributes to this appearance is the smaller type, narrower margins,

***CHAMPION FOODS***; Chicago, Illinois — November 1988 - August 1990

**Executive Vice President, Sales & Marketing**
Accountable for all sales and marketing functions for this manufacturer of super premium frozen pizzas. Reported directly to President.
- Targeted alternative sources and expanded market for company's products to major market categories, including grocery retail, convenience stores/vending, private label/co-packing arrangements, membership wholesale clubs, and institutional/food service.
- Increased sales from $3 million to $7.2 million with extremely limited financial resources.

***GHS INTERNATIONAL,*** A division of *Staley Continental, Inc.* — February 1977 - November 1988
A then publicly traded multi-billion food conglomerate.

**Vice President, National Accounts** (6/87 - 11/88)
Developed and maintained multi-unit accounts nationally for the Distribution Division of *Staley Continental, Inc.* Reported directly to President.
- Increased accounts from $17 million to $102 million within 21 months.

**Vice President, Corporate Sales** (2/87 - 6/87)
High profile networking with multi-unit accounts nationwide. Represented all food service divisions (distribution, manufacturing, customized distribution) for *Staley Continental.*

**General Sales Manager** (8/85 - 2/87)
Managed 50 person sales force covering northern Illinois, southern Wisconsin, and western Indiana for *Continental Chicago*, the largest branch of the largest region.
- Expanded product market through effective market analyses and training/motivation of sales team.
- Achieved record sales and profit results for this division and record growth of sales versus prior year.
- Awarded Master Circle for performing within top 2% of nationwide sales force.

**Central Region Multi-Unit Account Manager** (6/84 - 8/85)
Managed all multi-unit accounts which were served by two or more divisions within the Central Region of *C.F.S. Continental* (the largest region). Reported directly to Group Vice President.
- Maintained continuity for multi-unit accounts that crossed branch boundaries.
- Total responsibility approximately 40% of total region's sales, i.e., $350 million.

**Director of Marketing, National Sales Manager** (7/81 - 8/84)
Managed 15 person nationwide sales force and a brokerage network of over 30 independent brokerage firms for *Houston Foods*, a manufacturing division of *CFS Continental.* Promoted out of this division into *Continental Food Service Co.*

**Regional Sales Manager** (5/80 - 7/81) / **Sales Representative** (2/77 - 5/80)

## EDUCATIONAL BACKGROUND

**Bachelor of Arts, Graduated in 1971**; *Northern Illinois University,* DeKalb, Illinois
American Management Association (AMA) courses in Sales, Marketing, and Fundamentals of Finance and Accounting for Non-Financial Executives
Hamilton Strategic Management Group - successfully completed college accredited, comprehensive strategic planning seminars sponsored by AMA
*Illinois Benedictine* Post-graduate coursework in Marketing and Advertising.

## PROFESSIONAL AFFILIATIONS

PLMA (Private Label Manufacturers Association)
IFDA (International Food Distribution Association)
IFMA (International Food Manufacturing Association)

extended Profile, extensive record of employment with managerial duties and achievements at one or more companies, and list of professional affiliations. The Work Experience section is called "Career Highlights" possibly because of the unexplained hiatus between 11/88 and 8/90.

# NEIL SCHOENFELD

363 Morningstar Court
Philadelphia, Pennsylvania 34423
(215) 334-1212

**PROFILE**

- Results-driven professional with twelve years of successful management experience.
- Proven ability to implement strategic plans and spearhead company growth.
- Respected leader, motivator, negotiator, and resourceful problem-solver.
- Consistent track record of exceeding sales targets and leading sales teams.
- Readily develop a rapport with customers and generate repeat business.
- Computer literate; Able to work in Windows, MS-DOS, and Macintosh systems.

**EXPERIENCE**

**PHILADELPHIA EDUCATIONAL SYSTEMS, INC.,** Philadelphia, PA

**Product Development Manager,** 1992 to 1997

Devised marketing strategies and delivered presentations to educational institutions in Pennsylvania, Connecticut, and New York. Sold educational materials and trained new users of system. Trained, supervised, and evaluated Sales Representatives. Negotiated with educational administrators such as Superintendents, Principals, Deans, and PTA leaders.

Accomplishments:

- Helped company grow from obscurity to a market leader.
- Achieved steady sales volume increase from $120,000 (1992) to $750,000 (1997).
- Signed the company's first collegiate contract and 2 district contracts.
- Ranked #1 in Northeast for Sales in 1997.
- Received awards for outstanding sales in 1994, 1995, and 1996.

**VANGUARD OFFICE PRODUCTS, INC.,** Scranton, PA

**District Manager,** 1988 to 1992

Trained and supervised new Sales Representatives for international office supplies company. Initiated national contracts and revived dormant accounts.

Accomplishments:

- Assisted company achieve sales growth from $800,000 (1988) to $2.5 million (1992).
- Slashed excess inventory which saved company $250,000.
- Landed multimillion dollar contracts with major U.S. companies.

**Sales Representative,** 1986 to 1988

Listened to customer needs and recommended products. Implemented volume-based sales discounts for key dealerships. Leadership, loyalty, and initiative earned promotion to District Manager.

**Customer Service Representative,** 1982 to 1986

Handled customer inquiries regarding orders and provided timely solutions. Achieved team award for best performing territory.

**EDUCATION**

**PENNSYLVANIA STATE UNIVERSITY,** University Park, PA

**B.A. in Business Administration,** Major in Marketing, 1982

149

**Combination.** *Kim Isaacs, Jackson Heights, New York*

Double lines draw the reader's attention to the enclosed Profile information. "Separate job listings for each company showcase promotions. Impressive titles are in bold to make them stand out."

**DAVID K. GREENE**
1234 Tanglewood Cove
Nice Place, Arizona 55555
555.555.5555

**OVERVIEW**

Offers a broad spectrum of diverse experience in management, production, training, customer service and program development. Dependable, self-motivated; assumes responsibility necessary to get job done.

**SUMMARY OF ACHIEVEMENTS**

- Benchmarked drill press operation by ***reducing*** two person production to one, with no loss of manufacturing time.
- Initiated and implemented program that significantly ***decreased*** employee overtime while increasing supervision, at ***no additional cost.***
- ***Co-created*** program to raise young abandoned wild animals, resulting in a better balanced, less stressful and more manageable animal in captivity. Implemented in regional zoo.

**KEY SKILLS**

- Hands on TQM management style and leadership skills have resulted in four promotions with increasing responsibilities.
- Demonstrated ability to supervise, motivate, train and increase productivity.
- Proficient in interpersonal relations, load and resource management.
- Strong written and oral communication skills with individuals at all levels of an organization.
- Performs effectively both as an autonomous, self-motivated individual and as an active, contributing team member.
- Adept at evaluation and troubleshooting, utilizing problem solving capabilities.
- Monitors operations to ensure safe and effective performance of personnel; maintain high level of production and quality of product.

**EXPERIENCE**

*SILVERSTONE & COMPANY, INC.*, Central, Arizona — 1991 to current

*ALPHA DIVISION*, 1992 to present

**SET UP - FLOOR MANAGER**

- Supervise, monitor, train and motivate up to 20 production line personnel.
- Responsibilities include: set-up machinery, expedite and inspect product, troubleshoot production line, schedule work and load resource.
- Prepare written and oral reports for Inspection and Assembly Departments.
- Implements preventive maintenance program to assure optimum manufacturing efficiency and maximum product output.
- Verifies employee time cards, prepares performance evaluations.
- Ensures that work meets specified standards and safety codes (OSHA, state, etc.).

*BETA DIVISION*, 1991 to 1992

- Transferred to Alpha Division
- Involved in the steel straightening aspect of Golf Club production.

*MOUNTAIN SMALL ANIMAL HOSPITAL*, Central, Arizona — 1990 to 1991

**ANIMAL TECHNICIAN**

*LOCAL PARK ZOO*, Prescott, Arizona — 1989 to 1990

**ATTENDANT**

- Conducted guest tours; attended animals, observed for illness or injuries and uncharacteristic behavior patterns.

***ADDITIONAL EXPERIENCE*** — 1979 to 1989

**Restaurant Support Services** - Progressed from food prep assistant to shift supervisor.

- Responsible for food preparation and presentation and training of new employees.

**EDUCATION**

*CENTRAL COMMUNITY COLLEGE* — 1994 to 1997 — Central, Arizona

**BACHELOR OF SCIENCE DEGREE** - in process - Maintains 3.92 GPA while working full time.
Major: Ecology and Evolutionary Biology

*INDIAN HILLS COMMUNITY COLLEGE* — 1983 to 1985 — Another State

**AAS DEGREE** - Food Service

**150**

**Combination.** *Patricia S. Cash, Prescott, Arizona*

The contact information has a distinctive "drop cap" in a shadowed box. The bullets in the Experience section match this box. Small caps are used in names, headings, titles, and degrees.

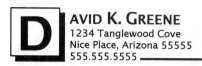

**_Joel Brask_**
*0000 Elvira Place, Apt. C*
*Elmira, New York 00000*
*(000) 000-0000*

**Objective:** *Production Management with profit and loss responsibility, providing hands-on leadership, direction and focus with positive results and outcomes.*

**Professional Experience:**

***Grandview Packaging*** *- Elvira, New York* *April 1996 to Present*
(Pharmaceutical Packaging)

**Printing Manager** *- 35 employees within 4 departments including: sheeting, in house ink department, offset press operation, and off-line U.V. coating with special adhesive applications. Responsibilities include introduction of a First Time Quality Program, streamline ink operation, track and trend performance numbers. Create analytical teams for problem-solving and performance evaluation.*

- *Developed performance expectations for the ink and pressroom departments, setting guidelines for measurable objective results.*
- *Evaluated and implemented one ink and coating supplier, resulting in a $40,000 annual savings by combining supplies and consumables.*
- *Introduced First Time Quality Program with attribute checklists for individual departments along with defined default specifications.*
- *Revised film and proofing specifications to ensure accurate pressroom reproduction.*

***Harley Davidson Container Corporation*** *- Johnstown, Delaware* *December 1994 to March 1996*
(Consumer Packaging)

**Production Manager** *- 100 employees with sole responsibility for efficient plant performance. Interpreted, trended, and compared data history and recommended corrective actions and led implementation of positive change efforts. Responsible for development of a safe, quality driven, customer focused, cost effective production organization.*

- *Implemented 24 hour Daily Production Status Board enabling organization to capture all relevant performance numbers, safety incidents, quality complaints and financial information.*
- *Charted weekly Uptime, Maintenance, Delay, and Makeready percentage in conjunction with scheduled hours.*
- *Established "Production Targets" for Estimating System to allow for a more competitive advantage.*
- *Project Manager for the relocation of 7 pieces of finishing equipment. Increased throughput and pull through by 20% within 2 month time frame. Created new case pack stands enabling machines to increase speeds.*
- *Assisted in writing and assembling procedures for Quality Assurance System to ensure first time quality. Objectivity and measurable results allowed for establishing customer default specs and adhered to industry standards.*

***Valley Stream Media Services*** *- Belleville, Maryland* *April 1994 to December 1994*
(Software Packaging)

**Assembly Operations Manager** *- 175 employees, 2 shift operation. Scheduled 5 assembly lines with automated shrink lines and heat tunnels. Re-engineered and configured lines for continuous process improvement. Directed labor applications to meet fluctuations in labor force to variances in production scheduling.*

- *Created and implemented new production reporting system to track detail related to productivity.*
- *Initiated a computerized schedule report for all operations, reducing paperwork and the need for extensive meetings.*
- *Researched and justified purchase of carousel 43 bin collator, to enable a dedicated work cell for JIT service for specific customers.*
- *Continuously trained and updated employees on the Management System philosophy in a certified 9002 environment.*

**151**

**Chronological.** *Betty Geller, Elmira, New York*

A standard chronological resume in format only. Everything is in italic, except section headings, parenthetical explanations of company names, and job titles—making these items quickly visible.

***JOEL BRASK*** ***Page 2***

***Harley Davidson Container Corporation*** - *Brentwood, California* *1990 to 1994*
(Consumer Packaging)

**Litho/Flexo Manager** - *62 employees within the Prepress, Litho, Flexo, Bobst Cutting Departments with generated sales in excess of $16 million. Fully responsible for throughput, purchasing, quality control, inventory supplies, budgets, and capital expenditures.*

- *Reduced marketing waste by 40%, with the creation of continuous improvement project teams, with full empowerment and accountability to the employees.*
- *Introduced tracking system to identify and quantify delay time on production equipment.*
- *Exposed and trained employees on the use of Statistical Process Control Methods, including: Brainstorming, Pareto Charting, Fish Bone Diagrams and Nominal Group Technique.*
- *Justified and purchased Blanket bar adapters for the operation, which created a savings of $20,000 per year.*
- *Implemented the use of an alcohol substitute in the pressroom one year before Maryland law mandated reduction. The direct result of the elimination of alcohol was a $23,000 cost reduction per year in addition reduced VOC's.*
- *Negotiated the purchase of a 50" Woodward Aerator, and a Retrofit Dahlgren Blanket Coater.*

***The Printing Shop*** - *Brookhaven, California* *1979 to 1990*
(Commercial Printing)

**Production Manager** - *Duties included planning and scheduling. Supervised work flow from order entry to delivered product.*

- *Streamlined operation for efficient production flow through team spirit concepts and employee empowerment.*
- *Evaluated the need for capital expansion by machine and labor capacities as well as JIT of customers.*

## Education:

- *Western Vocational High School, Diploma (1979) - Printing Related*

## Professional Training:

- *Productivity Incorporated: Quick Changeover (S.M.E.D.)*
- *Barry Quality Incorporated: The Right Way to Manage Facilitator Workshop*
- *Max Division Corporation: Doctor Blade Seminar*
- *Printers Service: Fountain Solutions & Alcohol Substitutes*
- *Valley Stream Ink Company: Pigments, Vehicles & Resins*

After each job title is (1) a paragraph that indicates duties and responsibilities for that position and (2) a bulleted list of accomplishments. Dates are right-aligned. The Education section, which shows only a high school diploma, is put near the end. The Training section strengthens the end.

# Marc Aigner

14 Sundale Place ★ Scarsdale, NY 10583 ★ (914) 555-0000

**Feature Films ★ Theatre ★ Television ★ Shorts ★ Video ★ Documentaries**

**Creative Profile**

Highly creative **production manager** and **independent filmmaker** with more than 15 years of diversified industry experience. Well-regarded, warm and energetic **teacher** who readily shares technical expertise and passion for filmmaking. Outstanding management, communication and collaborative skills that help get the job done. Effective troubleshooter whose strengths include ***producing, directing, writing*** and ***editing***. Expertise in ***camerawork*** and ***direction of photography***.

**Career Highlights**

" ... particular strengths are commitment, energy, knowledge of cameras and concern for students."
—Tom Gunning, Author, "D.W. Griffith and the Origins of American Narrative Film."

" Mr. Aigner has many of the same admirable personal values that former Film Chair Avakian possessed" ... "he is patient and willing to help in problem-solving, and takes a personal interest in student projects."
—Richard Dawson, NYU colleague.

★ **Management**

***Manage university Film Production Office and Facilities, including sound stage, film, video, computer-editing, mixing and transfer rooms and equipment.***

- Spearheaded and managed a turnaround operation for university film department. Improved viability and quality of production/post-production film equipment by determining complex repair needs and establishing controls.
- Served as catalyst for increased productivity among faculty and students for on-time project completion of independent films.
- Creatively used budget allocations for staffing needs and facilities upgrades.

★ **Independent Filmmaking**

***Collaborated in the making of numerous feature, television, short and documentary films.***

- Director of Photography/Producer: "European and Poetic," 90 min. Stefano Mario Baratti, Director.
- Writer/Producer/Director: "Gypsy Cab," 16mm, 30 min., in color. Original project filmed on location in The Bronx, depicting an immigrant man's struggle to adapt to a new life. Screened at area film festival.
- Cameraman: "Vinal," 16mm, 30 min., in color. Director, Marissa Benedetto.
- Assistant Director: "The Suitors," 35mm, 90 min. Director, G. Ebrahimian.
- Cameraman: "Bone White," 16mm, 60 min., in color.
- Director of Photography: "Vanitas," 16mm, 60 min., in black and white. Stefano Mario Baratti, Director.
- Production/Camera Assistant: Ebra Films. Several documentary projects for BBC, French and Italian Television.

★ **Instruction**

***Hire and supervise work/study students, offering group and one-on-one instruction. Support film faculty in organizing film festivals and outside screenings.***

- Designed and taught course *Production Workshop* focusing on proper operation of cameras, lighting, sound, editing, mixing and transfer equipment.
- Simplified instructional methodology and improved student morale by completely rewiring sound-mixing studio, creating universal access to sophisticated controls.

**152**

**Combination.** *Phyllis B. Shabad, Ossining, New York*

A resume for a creative manager. The top graphic captures the eye immediately, and the triple line then draws attention to the name in the contact information. The reader sees also the line of

**Marc Aigner**
Page Two

**Employment History**

1990-present — **Film Production Manager** and **Instructional Support**, Film Department, New York University, New York, NY.

1988-1989 — **Cameraman.** WVVA-TV (NBC affiliate), Bluefield, West Virginia.

1982-1988 — **Independent Filmmaker.** Ebra Films, New York, NY.

**Education**

New York University, New York, NY:
**Bachelor of Fine Arts in Film Production**, 1985.
Additional coursework in engineering.

**Special Talents**

**Languages:**
Trilingual—Fluency in written and spoken English/French; spoken Italian.

**Technical:**
- Adept in using all 16mm and 35mm film equipment, and applying latest technology such as DVD.
- Use specialized software such as *Movie Magic* and *Final Draft.*

**Related Professional Activities**

Participated in several film productions that appeared at the:
**Sundance Film Festival**, 1997 (Winner—First Prize).
**Empire State Exhibition Film Festival**, 1995.
**Cannes Film Festival**, 1988.

fields and star bullets, whose density (blackness) is the same as the name. From there, the second graphic pulls the eye to the left column where the reader spots the two testimonials. To control the placement of the graphics, the writer used both word processing and desktop publishing.

## MARK L. TRIPSO

3987 Rinhand Court Oakbrook Terrace, Illinois 60181
Telephone: 708.397.2940

### SUMMARY

Experienced **Creative** professional seeking position in **Corporate Communications** or **Marketing** capacity.

Possesses a unique sense of innovation and resourcefulness with proven expertise in devising original solutions to complex problems. Excellent research and analytical skills; investigates alternatives thoroughly, focusing on all relevant details. Strong sales, marketing, and customer service orientation. Works effectively with employees at all levels. Excellent retention of information. Hardworking and dependable with a strong work ethic.

### PROFESSIONAL EXPERIENCE

**HEREK STUDIO; Chicago, Illinois** **September 1990 — January 1993**
World's largest production studio in terms of equipment and employees.
***Group Production Manager***

- Significantly contributed to account base through aggressive sales and marketing techniques and contacts developed through prior ownership of production art studio. Exceeded commission expectations by 33%.
- Prepared cost and time estimates.
- Interacted with clients in concept development and throughout various production phases.
- Oversaw project operations from start to finish and ensured adherence to deadlines.
- Worked with production and design staff in an extremely fast-paced environment to produce comps, layouts, and camera-ready art.

**VISIONS; Chicago, Illinois** **June 1989 — June 1990**
***Production Manager*** - Responsibilities same as above.

**TRIPSO GRAPHICS, LTD; Chicago, Illinois** **November 1978 — June 1989**
***Owner and President***

- Initiated the start-up of an art production studio for advertising. Developed it into a business clearing an average of $200,000 annually through strong abilities in sales and client service.
- Start-up efforts included locating a facility and negotiating lease space, researching and purchasing equipment, and hiring and training support staff (between one and five personnel over the eleven years).
- Interacted with clients to devise optimal design and production solutions. Ensured jobs were executed on budget and on schedule.
- 95% of business was from Leo Burnett, who knew they were paying a premium price, but believed that *Tripso Graphics* was the best and the price was well worth it. Other clients included *Ogilvie Mather, J. Walter Thompson, BBDO* and *Foote, Cone and Belding*. Accounts included Kellogg's, Philip Morris, Pillsbury, United Airlines, Proctor and Gamble, Parker Pen, Schwinn, and Navistar.

**JACOBS & LIVINI STUDIO; Chicago, Illinois** **October 1974 — August 1978**
***Sales Representative***
Started with this advertising production studio as a keyliner, then promoted to Sales Representative in 1975. Solicited work from clients / prospective clients and saw projects through from start to finish.

### EDUCATION

Completed two years of fine arts education at *Concord College* (Concord, Connecticut) and *Randall State University* (Jabot, Texas).

153

**Combination.** *Georgia Veith, Elmhurst, Illinois*

The Summary, which includes an objective statement and a profile including skills, nudges this resume into the Combination column. The design is visible at a glance, and so are the job titles.

**William S. Buckmaster ▪ 5596 Cimmarron ▪ Ada MI 49301 ▪ 333-000-2255**

**PROJECT MANAGEMENT ▪ CUSTOMER RELATIONS ▪ PRODUCT DESIGN ▪ QUALITY ASSESSMENT**

*Automated Buffing & Polishing Systems • Ergonomic Workstations • Tool Balancers • End-Of-Arm Tooling • Gas-Powered Burden Carriers • Surgical Equipment*

**Current Focus**

Position as Project Manager/Coordinator utilizing diverse engineering experience and strengths in customer and vendor relations.

**Background**

History of advancement into positions of increased responsibility for area manufacturing organizations; broad base of design, engineering and manufacturing knowledge; experience in researching all aspects of material and design data; demonstrated success in planning and implementation of complex projects; technical expertise in the application of manufacturing processes/materials.

**Personal Qualities**

- Accomplished facilitator; skilled at problem mediation and resolution while successfully upholding company objectives.
- Excellent planning and organization skills; ability to prioritize and handle a multitude of details at once; highly adaptable to rapidly changing requirements and situations; strong sense of responsibility as a professional team worker.
- Task-oriented and precise, with high performance standards; committed to a goal-directed work environment; interact effectively with a wide range of personalities; effective in presentation of products and services.

**Professional History**

| | | |
|---|---|---|
| 1994-PRES. | PROJECT MANAGER. | Hanson Machinery Co., Kalamazoo, MI. |
| 1990-1994. | PRODUCT DEVELOPMENT ENGINEER. | Aero-Dynamics, Kalamazoo, MI. |
| 1987-1990. | PROJECT ENGINEER. | Prab Robots, Kalamazoo, MI. |
| 1979-1987. | APPLICATION ENGINEER. | Kalamazoo Manufacturing Company, Plainwell, MI. |
| 1967-1979. | SENIOR LAYOUT DRAFTSMAN. | Stryker Corporation, Kalamazoo, MI. |

**Highlights of Accomplishments**

**Hanson Machinery Co.** - As project manager for our buffing and polishing systems, I am heavily involved with the customer from project start-up through product delivery. In this key role as liaison, I facilitate the transfer of information, provide technical support, and contribute leadership to our many departments and outside vendors. Throughout the project cycle of ensuring the highest degree of quality and top-notch customer service, other major responsibilities include equipment evaluation, process development and improvement, resource optimization, general problem solving, supporting and participating in team activities as well as in-house meetings involving the customer, and training.

**Aero-Dynamics** - My work in the design and development of ergonomic workstations brought me in direct contact with our customers. I worked closely with our sales representatives to provide accurate, technical information and to ensure smooth installation. Every workstation sales order was reviewed by me to ensure proper product application. In an earlier role as Project Engineer, I completely redesigned three tool balancers replacing metal fabrications with plastic injection molded and aluminum die cast parts.

**Prab Robots** - I was heavily involved in end-of-arm tooling and peripheral equipment design and engineering. All customer contact was performed by me and I worked closely with our purchasing, accounting, and manufacturing departments to ensure the end-result was of the highest degree. My beginning title at Prab was Mechanical Engineer and I worked closely with shop personnel; an ability to work effectively with all levels resulted in my advancement and subsequent interaction with our customers.

**Kalamazoo Manufacturing** - I was responsible for the design and development of burden carrier vehicles from concept to production. Throughout the development stage, I worked closely with our vendors and, later on in the process, with our sales team. I accompanied our sales representatives to customer locations and provided technical support and assisted in selecting vehicles and options based on their needs. The government purchased a line of our carriers which entailed building to military specifications. Beneath my umbrella of responsibility fell Experimental, Blueprint, Drafting, and Engineering departments.

**Stryker Corporation** - My springboard to where I am today, Stryker gave me in-depth technical exposure. From Detail Draftsman to Layout Draftsman to Senior Layout Draftsman, my work at Stryker provided the pathway for my role as Engineer.

**Education**

| | |
|---|---|
| 1978. | BACHELOR OF SCIENCE: Mechanical Engineering, Western Michigan University, Kalamazoo, MI |
| 1978. | ASSOCIATE OF APPLIED SCIENCE: Drafting & Design, Kellogg Community College, Battle Creek, MI. |

***Excellent Professional References Available Upon Request***

**154**

**Combination.** *Randall S. Clair, Parchment, Michigan*

A resume with a printed look. This innovative writer pushes the limit in reducing font size. The writer has the candidate show friendliness by daring to tell achievements in the first person.

MARTIN P. ABERNATHY
3100 North Plaza Drive ▪ St. Clair MI 48079 ▪ 555-222-5522

***Expertise in all phases of the Commercial and Residential Construction Industry...***

▪ ***PROJECT DEVELOPMENT*** ▪ ***PUBLIC RELATIONS*** ▪ ***SITE MANAGEMENT*** ▪

• ***Condominiums*** • ***Health Care Facilities*** • ***Apartment Complexes*** • ***Retirement Centers*** • ***Office Buildings*** • ***Warehouses***

## Objective

▸ **Position as Manager for a well-established construction development firm utilizing a diversity of commercial project experience.**

## Qualifications Summary

▸ **Experienced Construction Project Manager with 25+ years experience in commercial construction.**
- Technical expertise in all phases of project coordination to include contract negotiation, engineering, estimating, preparation of construction documents, materials, site punchout and completion through certificate of occupancy.

## Strengths

▸ **Excellent presentation and communication skills; actively promote a positive, proactive manner with contractors, management, and clients.**
- Skilled in maintaining a balanced, objective viewpoint during contract negotiations and in addressing problems and issues; highly effective leadership skills with an established track record of achievements.
- Maintain near-100% success rate for completing construction projects within budget and on time.
- Enjoy the challenge of new projects and handling several priorities at once.

## Professional Experience

***as Independent Builder***

| | | | | |
|---|---|---|---|---|
| Scope of Projects: | Residential units and small apartment complexes: | | unit value: $50K - $500K. | |

***as Construction Manager***

| | | | | |
|---|---|---|---|---|
| Scope of Projects: | Seagull Estates Condominiums: | $15 million. | Canterbury Place Condominiums: | $6.5 million. |
| | Conroy Estates Condominiums: | $5.3 million. | Eagle Valley Retirement Center: | $4.5 million. |
| | Village Green Apartments: | $3.6 million. | Kissimmee Memorial Hospital: | $.25 million. |

***as Builder-Developer***

| | | | | |
|---|---|---|---|---|
| Scope of Projects: | Ambassador Park Condominiums: | $7.5 million. | Country Center Shopping Mall: | $6.3 million. |
| | Park Elmwood Office, (*Phase) II: | $2.3 million. | | |

***as Managing Partner***

| | | | | |
|---|---|---|---|---|
| Scope of Projects: | Park Elmwood Office, *I: | $1.5 million. | Taco Bell Restaurant: | $.25 million. |
| | Fleenor Auto Store: | $.20 million. | | |

***as Operations Manager***

| | | | | |
|---|---|---|---|---|
| Scope of Projects: | Tomahawk Village, *I, II: | $12 million. | Tippecanoe Village Apartments: | $6.1 million. |
| | Flanner & Buchanan Mortuary, *I: | $.75 million. | Flanner & Buchanan Mortuary, *II: | $.50 million. |
| | Lodestar Office Building: | $.50 million. | | |

***as Field Supervisor***

| | | | | |
|---|---|---|---|---|
| Scope of Projects: | Fox Harbour Apartments: | $10.1 million. | Turtle Creek Apartments, *I: | $7.9 million. |
| | Turtle Creek Convalescent Center, *II: | $4.5 million. | Turtle Creek Apartments, *II: | $4.4 million. |
| | Turtle Creek Convalescent Center, *I: | $2.5 million. | Colonial Mortgage Company: | $2 million. |
| | Turtle Creek Apartments, *III: | $1.1 million. | | |

***as Project Superintendent***

| | | | | |
|---|---|---|---|---|
| Scope of Projects: | Laurel Lake Apartments, *II: | $3.6 million. | Old Towne Village Apartments: | $3.1 million. |
| | Wheel Estates Mobile Home Park, I, II: | $5.6 million. | | |

## Work History

- 1993-Pres. **Builder.** Martin P. Abernathy, Georgia and Florida.
- 1987-1993. **Construction Manager.** Five Star Industries, Phoenix, AZ.
- 1983-1987. **Builder-Developer.** Martin P. Abernathy, Indianapolis, IN.
- 1979-1983. **Project Manager.** Abernathy/Johnson Development Company, Detroit, MI.
- 1974-1979. **Operations Manager.** Thunderhawk Construction Company, San Diego, CA.
- 1971-1974. **Field Supervisor.** Houk's Realty and Builders, Inc., Atlanta, GA.
- 1967-1971. **Project Superintendent.** Houk's Realty and Builders, Inc., Atlanta, GA.

## Education

1964-1967. Indiana University School of Business, Business Administration, Bloomington, IN.
1962-1964. Purdue University, School of Architectural Engineering Technology, Indianapolis, IN.

*Excellent professional and business-related references enclosed.*

**155**

**Combination.** *Randall S. Clair, Parchment, Michigan*

A distinctive table in the Professional Experience section. The order of the rows matches the positions in the Work History. Projects read from left to right, line by line, in descending order.

# Hobson H. Pepperdyne

**75 Parkwood Plaza • Omaha, Nebraska 68666 • (402) 555-2225**

## Professional Overview

- Over 15 years project management experience, specializing in technical telecommunications
- Over 10 years computer experience with emphasis on engineering and technical applications
- Managed over 25 projects, including budgetary accountability for up to $7 million per project
- All projects completed within budget guidelines; every deadline was met
- Meticulously compared contract specifications to vendor performance; was 100% successful in obtaining refunds in excess of $100,000 per project where specifications were not met
- Received highest performance bonus three years in a row within a field of 40 engineers
- Within one year led 35-person section from last to first place in statewide performance rating
- Reliable, highly focused, and exceedingly detail oriented with a reputation for excellence
- Good team management and communication skills across all levels

## Education

- Bachelor's Degree, Nebraska Institute of Technology, Montgomery, Nebraska
- Post-graduate study in business administration, Nebraska Graduate College, Institute, WV
- Two years specialized engineering training, Bell Labs, New Jersey and BellCore, Chicago
- Over 1,800 hours performance-oriented in-house management training

## Experience

**NORTHWESTERN BELL, OMAHA, NEBRASKA • 1962-1991**

- Project Engineer/Project Manager • 1979-1991
- Manager • 1977-1979
- Assistant Manager • 1972-1977
- Office Manager/Operator/Customer Service Representative • 1962-1972

**Project Management Highlights**

- Planned, sized, ordered, and coordinated installation of statewide toll service equipment, the largest, most expensive project in the company's history - $7 million
- Budgeted, purchased, and supervised installation of equipment that doubled capacity and centralized statewide directory assistance service to Omaha - $2 million
- Coordinated project to install in Omaha the most complex telephone switching equipment in the United States (based on features and size) - $4 million
- Managed project to retrofit 16 switching offices from mechanical to electronic operation utilizing the same equipment space - $48 million

**Management Highlights**

- Managed Network Services budget, workforce, and message data forecasting for two years with an annual budget exceeding $18 million
- Took over a section of 35 directory assistance operators with consistently poor ratings and led them from last to first place in statewide performance within one year
- Supervised on-duty forces of up to 60 operators

**156**

**Combination.** *Barbie Dallmann, Charleston, West Virginia*

This individual worked his way up from long-distance operator to project manager. Because he held so many positions over the years, the focus is on his accomplishments rather than his duties.

# RUDOLPF AUGUSTINE

84 RED ROSE ROAD
CENTER ISLAND, NY 55555
(555) 555-5555

SPECIALTY FOODS CONSULTANT ♦ FRESH PRODUCE AUTHORITY ♦ ORGANICS SPECIALIST

## CAREER PROFILE

- Extensive experience in the specialty and natural foods industries serving as consultant, manager, store designer, buyer, and lecturer.
- Expert in wholesale and retail sale of conventional and organic produce with total annual volume as high as $5 million. Achieve produce profit margins of up to 42%.
- Working background in all United States regional markets—understand variances in food products, growing seasons, local economies and consumer buying patterns.
- Active proponent of sustainable farming methods and profitable organic market development. Keen interest in historical and political perspectives on food and food production. Believe that eating is a political act.
- Recognized by Florence Fabricant in The New York Times for establishing the best organic produce selection in New York City.

## REPRESENTATIVE CUSTOMERS AND CLIENTS

- Balducci's
- Gourmet Buys
- Postrio
- Berkeley Bowl
- Hudson River Club
- Monterey Market
- Union Square Café
- Red Horse Market
- TKO Farms
- Wild By Nature
- Andronico's
- Souen

## ACHIEVEMENTS AND QUALIFICATIONS

- Expert in forecasting, planning, trend spotting, and creating new opportunities. Specialist in cost and inventory control. Have increased product movement and reduced spoilage at every retail or wholesale client/employer.
- Increase typical produce department percentage of store sales from 15% to 25%-35%. Run a profit margin usually 6 to 8 points over regional average. Total annual volume in produce has been $250,000 to $5 million.
- Experienced buyer with wide knowledge of farmers and wholesalers in key growing areas of the United States. Understand regional and cultural negotiating and buying patterns. Expert in foraging for the freshest and most unusual produce.
- Adept in the innovative and profitable presentation of produce and all types of specialty foods. Create effective and prize-winning displays using unusual props—mix texture and color, identify and react to food and visual trends.
- Directed design, construction and opening management of $2 million annual sales, 4,000 square foot, full-line specialty foods store. Determined floor layout, product placement, lighting, fixturing, signage, and back-room production arrangements/equipment. Scouted for antiques and unusual fixtures to enhance store concept.
- Facility for selling to the specialty and organics customer and to the customer with a highly developed palate and a sense of aesthetic character—food stylists, personal and professional chefs, world travelers, society figures and international clients. Develop and maintain an excellent rapport with customers accustomed to the best in quality and service.
- Interact with customers on a personal and instructional level that creates a redirected purchasing pattern based on a seasonal sensibility for produce and an understanding of ingredients. Direct total purchase for a loyal following of customers who shop with an "open list" and ask "what's good today?"

157

**Combination.** *Deborah Wile Dib, Medford, New York*

The exceptional graphic with the contact information is the first indication that this is an exceptional resume for a creative "food-industry professional with numerous management and

# RUDOLPF AUGUSTINE

PAGE TWO

**EXPERIENCE AS CONSULTANT, MANAGER AND BUYER**

1997 **Gourmet Buys**
Glen Head, NY
**Store Designer**
**Construction Project Manager**
**Store Opening Manager**

1996 **Amagansett Farmers Market**
Amagansett, NY
**Produce Consultant**

1995 **Wild By Nature (a Division of King Kullen Supermarkets)**
East Setauket, NY
**Produce Manager**

1995 **North Country Market**
Setauket, NY
**Produce Consultant**
**Manager**

1994 **Need Lettuce**
Madison, WI
**Produce Consultant**

1994 **Magic Mill**
Madison, WI
**Produce Consultant**

1993 **Red Horse Market**
East Hampton, NY
**Produce Consultant**
**Manager/Buyer**

1992 **Balducci's**
New York, NY
**Produce Manager**
**Assistant Produce Manager**

1991 **TKO Farms**
Salinas, CA
**Stall Manager/**
**San Francisco Produce Terminal**
**Sales Manager/Bay Area**

1990 **Native Farms Organics**
New York, NY
**Owner/Operator/Buyer**

1989 **Del Tomaso**
Oakland, CA
**Buyer**

1988 **Living Foods**
Berkeley, CA
**Front End Supervisor**
**Produce Clerk**

**REPRESENTATIVE SPECIALTY AND ORGANIC FOODS PRESENTATIONS**

- **"Locally Grown Foods—Opening the Market to Local Businesses".**
  Presented to local farmers and retailers.
  Cornell Cooperative Extension, Riverhead, New York, coordinated by NOFA (Northeast Organic Farmer's Alliance) (1996)
- **"Historical and Practical Perspectives on Food and Food Choices".**
  Presented to professional chefs.
  The Women's Culinary Alliance, New York City (1994)
- **Developed and presented numerous in-store demonstrations.**
  Balducci's, Red Horse Market, Del Tomaso and Native Farms
- **Created and led educational farm tours for the trade and for the public.**
  Discussed growing methods and farm history.
  Lectured on preparing and eating farm fresh produce.
  TKO farms, Salinas, CA and Fairview Gardens, Goleta, CA (1991-1992)
- **Spoke on effective methods of produce air shipping.**
  Participant in panel formed to discuss future of organic foods industry.
  California Certified Organic Farmers, Santa Cruz, CA (1991)
- **Created and produced regional, international and specialty produce tasting program and display.**
  Summer Tasting Fair at Festival of the Lakes, Oakland, CA (1991)
- **Produced multi-media "Stewards of the Earth" program for Earth Day.**
  Speakers included Frances Moore Lappe and Michael Ableman.
  Zellerbach Hall, University of California Berkley Campus (1990)

consulting positions." The font for the contact information, the headline, and the section headings are distinctive, and the original resume was printed on an earthy-toned, granite-flecked paper. The two-column "Experience as Consultant, Manager and Buyer" section is unique.

# PAUL M. SEITZ

75 Main Street
New York, New York 10019
(212) 555-6284

***Project Manager*** Extensive technical and project management experience in information systems hardware, combined with degree in finance/business management. Skilled in managing the day-to-day operations of a nation-wide Large Systems Support Center. Adept at leading teams of diverse groups of people to accomplish common goal. Highly motivated, committed team player with strong organizational and analytical skills.

***QUALIFICATION HIGHLIGHTS:***

- Over 17 years progressive technical services and project management experience
- Exceptional leadership skills; able to motivate and assess staff, delegate responsibility
- Proven ability to problem solve and meet deadlines within demanding environments
- Consistently recognized by management for superior performance, management skills, and problem solving ability

***SUMMARY of EXPERIENCE:***

- Spearhead joint venture in development of duplex processor element
  - Effectively reduce code load time by 93%
  - Uncover/resolve 220 design problems in hardware, software, and documentation
- Provide technical support to customers; ensure implementation of correct product service strategy
- Design training programs on advanced AIX 9076 power parallel processor and RS/6000 platform
  - Interface with IBM Europe to assess needs/requirements for participants from 16 countries
  - Coordinate curriculum; schedule instructors, materials and equipment
  - Manage and administer $70,000 project budget
- Develop and implement two-phase system specialist training program; oversee 24-person team
- Coordinate with Product Engineering to diagnose Large System hardware problems/design issues
- Knowledge of LAN architecture and client servers
- Experienced in building business cases to support capital funding projects
- Skilled in operation of MVS/VM systems and open system architecture (UNIX and AIX)

***EMPLOYMENT HISTORY:***

*IBM Corporation,* White Plains and Buffalo, NY — *1979-Present*
**INFORMATION SYSTEMS PROJECT MANAGER**
**OPERATIONS SUPPORT SPECIALIST**
**SYSTEM SUPPORT SPECIALIST**
**FIELD TECHNICIAN/CUSTOMER ENGINEER**

***EDUCATION/TRAINING:***

**Bachelor of Science,** Business Management, Concentration: Finance G.P.A.: 3.6 — *Fall, 1996*
Pace University, Pleasantville, NY

**Associate in Applied Science,** Electrical Engineering — *1978*
Jamestown Community College, Jamestown, NY

***AWARDS/HONORS:***

Branch Manager's Award / Outstanding Achievement Awards / IBM Peer Recognition Award
National Honor Society for Scholastic Achievement / Dean's List

**158**

**Combination.** *Marian K. Kozlowski, Poughkeepsie, New York*

The candidate was completing a business degree and wanted to advance from technical to managerial services. The challenge was choosing the right technical information to include.

# Professional Profile

HARLEN SIMPSOON

159

**Combination.** *Fran Holsinger, Tempe, Arizona*

Another of the writer's two-page resumes with a front cover. The Summary of Qualifications includes statements about experience, duties, and skills. Included are personal skills, which, as

# HARLEN SIMPSOON

110 Rose Way Dr. Tempe, AZ 55555 [555] 000-0000

## SUMMARY OF QUALIFICATIONS:

- Over 10 years experience as Project Manager/Engineer/ Superintendent.... extensive experience in concrete structures/forms...
- Established/monitored project budgets/forecasts....oversaw projects of up to $18 million dollars....
- Coordinated daily activities of 24 subcontractors/24 suppliers....
- Wrote/negotiated contracts with subs/suppliers....
- Liaison with Owner during duration of project....
- Familiar with government funded projects/requirements....
- Scheduled/supervised up to 30+ employees....
- Worked closely with Operation/Construction Managers....
- Prepared complete estimates for securing projects....
- Recorded 800+ days without a loss time accident in district....
- Delegated responsibilities appropriately for various aspects of project....
- Composed/tracked all project records/inventory control....
- Estimated/prepared/mediated contract changes....
- Endeavored to bring projects on or under time/budget....
- Computer literate: Lotus 1-2-3/Windows Release 4/Primavera/Best-PCL's estimating systems/Excel 5.0/Word/WordPerfect 6.0/J.D. Edwards system forecasting....
- Excellent communication skills....strive for perfection....responsible.... team player....organized....detail oriented....adaptable....good listener....objective.....open minded....

## EDUCATION:

UNIVERSITY OF NORTHERN IOWA - Cedar Falls, IA
Bachelors of Technology: Construction Management

transferable skills, are useful in most any new career or field. The Professional Highlights section is a bulleted list of duties, responsibilities, and other activities. The Major Projects section is subdivided by three different positions held. The bulleted items listed for each position appear as accomplishments. The display font used

**professional profile**

## PROFESSIONAL HIGHLIGHTS:

PCL CIVIL CONSTRUCTORS, INC. - Tempe, AZ

***Project Manager/Project Engineer:*** 1987 to present

- Accounted for time/cost quality/general overall project performance....
- Controlled project to meet schedules/contractual obligations....
- Interpreted specifications/ensured construction met specs/on-time/ within budget....
- Designed/analyzed construction techniques/equipment applications/ temporary structures/services....
- Coordinated/controlled all engineering functions for project....
- Tracked progress claims/project records/productivity analysis/diaries...
- Administered subcontracts/major purchase orders....
- Procured materials....
- Documented all changed conditions/recorded impact on costs/ schedules....
- Controlled As-built drawings/submittals/Operating & Maintenance manuals....

## MAJOR PROJECTS:

***Project Manager/Project Engineer***

- Santa Ana Watershed Project Authority: Regional Rapid Infiltration/ Extraction (RIX) Site Facilities - $18 million
- San Pasqual Aquatic Treatment Facility Contract #2 - $6 million
- Williams AFB: Apron Slab Replacement - $4 million
- City of Mesa: 72nd St. Improvement Project - $4 million
- Salt River Project: Interconnection Facility - $4.5 million
- U.S. Bureau of Reclamation: Joint Distribution System Phase II - $6 million

***Carpenter Foreman:***

- U.S. Bureau of Reclamation: Central Distribution System Units I & IV -$ 9 million
- Arizona Department of Transportation: Phoenix-Cordes Junction Highway - $ 9 million

***Assistant Superintendent:*** (*Flatiron Structures Co. - Longmont, CO*)

- Colorado Department of Transportation: Mile-High Dog Track Overpass - $2.5 million
- Colorado Department of Transportation: Santa Fe & Evans Interchange - $2 million
- Colorado Department of Transportation: Glenwood Canyon I-70 Widening - $10 million

for the individual's name on the front cover is used also for the section headings. A different style of bullet is used in each section, preventing a kind of monotony that arises when the same bullet style is used throughout a multipage resume.

**ROBERT L. THORNTON**
**10099 County Road 18**
**Tyler, Texas 75700**
**(903) 555-0099**

## PROFESSIONAL QUALIFICATIONS

- **Highly innovative, proactive quality / manufacturing professional** with eight years of experience and expertise in **Quality Inspection / Control / Management ♦ Engineering / R&D Technology Failure Mode and Effects Analysis ♦ Time / Motion Production Processes Studies ♦ Product Identification / Traceability ♦ Quality Audits ♦ SPC**. Limited **Plant Management** experience.
- **Strategic Planning / Development** aptitude; structured / created quality department, quality program, training program, and production maintenance schedules and manuals for all processes; **significantly slashed internal and external scrap rates, production time, and required man-hours**.
- Proficiency in **troubleshooting, malfunction identification, technical maintenance / repair, calibration and gage R&R procedures**, and **corrective / preventative action**.
- Exceptionally **computer literate**: MS-Office, Works for Windows, WordPerfect; spreadsheets, flow-charts, SPC program.
- Outstanding **leadership, conflict / dispute resolution, communication**, and **interpersonal** skills; interface effectively with engineers and people of diverse socioeconomic backgrounds and cultures; quickly resolve problems / conflicts in diplomatic, professional manner. **Team-** and **results-oriented.**

## EDUCATION

THE UNIVERSITY OF TEXAS AT DALLAS – Dallas, Texas
**Bachelor of Business Administration Degree** (1989)

## PROFESSIONAL EXPERIENCE

BEST INSULATION, INC. – Tyler, Texas 1995 – Present

**Quality Manager**

- Recruited to establish and implement Quality Program for ISO-9000-equivalent system for manufacturer of insulation products for HVAC industry and blow mold plastics for The Trane Company; **highly successful in progressing to Level III compliance** required for United Technologies-Carrier Vendor Certification.
- Serve in capacity of Plant Manager during manager's absence. Indirectly supervise production staff of 50.
- **Structured entire department**; **established Quality Program** and **created policy and procedure manual**.
- **Inaugurated Training Program**; conducted training classes.
- **Designed/implemented control plans**; perform capability analysis.
- **Developed periodic maintenance schedules**; **created manual** to comply with manufacturer's specifications and recommendations for maintenance.
- Review contracts; perform document and data control; administer quality records.
- Solely responsible for inspection of all products from receipt of materials through shipment of final product; control measuring and test equipment and nonconforming products.
- Execute internal quality audits; take corrective and preventative action, as necessary.
- Designed/created/published quarterly newsletter.
- Created/documented work instructions.
- Conducted time / motion studies on production processes and implemented strategies based on findings which **drastically slashed internal and external scrap rates**, **production time**, and **required man-hours** and **accelerated production, sales, and profitability**.
- **Significantly reduced defective PPMs**. Goal: 375 PPM; Actual: 26 PPM/YTD; Parts Produced: 978,514.

**160**

**Combination.** *Ann Klint, Tyler, Texas*

A resume for an effective candidate whose career has been progressively developing from engineering technology to technological management. The writer uses boldfacing to call

**ROBERT L. THORNTON** **Page Two**

**SOUND INDUSTRIES, INC.** - Fort Worth, Texas 1989 - 1995

**Customer Service / Technical Representative** (1994–1995)

- Supervised contract labor force; extensively interacted with technicians via phone to troubleshoot problems and provide technical support for OEM industrial water heaters and boilers.
- Responsible for warranty service performed on defective equipment.
- Solicited and negotiated estimates for jobs; ensured work was completed promptly and accurately.
- Specified parts; placed orders; shipped parts, as needed.

**Quality Control Inspector** (1993–1994)

- Performed final inspection for finished goods.
- Ensured manufacturing personnel complied with regulations (U.L. Laboratories, ULC, A.S.M.E.).
- Promoted to Customer Service / Technical Representative.

**Engineering Technician** (1990–1993)

- Designed and determined instrument specifications; performed bill of material maintenance.
- Coordinated and ensured compliance with various regulatory agencies.
- **Team Leader** in implementation of new computer system.
- Served as liaison between Engineering and Manufacturing.
- Performed drafting and limited AutoCAD.
- Promoted to Quality Control Inspector.

**Research and Development Technician** (1989–1990)

- Conducted R&D for new product lines.
- Promoted to Engineering Technician.

♦ ♦ **Professional References Furnished On Request** ♦ ♦

attention to the individual's effectiveness and management skills. The highest concentration of boldfacing is the first bulleted item in the Professional Qualifications section. If a reader reads anything in the resume, it will be that first bulleted item. The other boldfacing pulls the eye down the page.

# C. Mitchell Harrington

456 West Garrison Street • Stillwater, MD 00000 • (410) 877-7777

## Objective

Management level position in quality assurance.

## Highlights of Qualifications

• Certified quality engineer (ASQC).
• Five years experience in Statistical Process Control.
• Extensive experience in industrial production supervision, purchasing and inventory.
• Experience in leadership training, technical training and staff development.
• Excellent communications and problem-solving skills.
• Works well with people on all levels.
• Supervisory/Management background
• Strong computer skills---word processing/spreadsheet/some data base applications.

## Experience

### Benson and Benson, Inc., Westview, MD

***Training and Development Manager*** **(10/92 to present)**

Responsible for developing and implementing all technical and leadership training for 1,200 associates. Developed and coordinated training on q.a.d. computer software. Served as administrator of TQP Phase II, Westview.

***Value Improvement Analyst*** **(1/91 to 10/920)**

Served as senior manufacturing planner for Quality Improvement Team. Responsible for tracking unit cost data on consumer power tools. Coordinated and tracked value improvement projects. Handled administrative details of implementing TQP training.

***Process Improvement Analyst*** **(10/88 to 1/91)**

Responsible for data analysis on scrap and waste. Worked directly with department manager on cost reduction projects. Developed Manufacturing Problem Solving training module which was used in TQP Phase I program.

***Quality Control Engineer*** **(10/87 to 10/88)**

Senior quality engineer for Household and Outdoor products manufactured in Westview. Served as quality engineer on new product development team. Served on team that developed automated SPC system. Developed course materials and taught SPC classes.

***Production Line Supervisor*** **(8/84 to 10/87**

Supervised 80 associates. Served as a leader in the JIT pilot lot project. Published in a national magazine for pioneer work in cross training. Developed and implemented a visible inventory program.

***Manager Tool Crib (MRO Buyer)*** **(1/80 to 8/84)**

Managed department budget, inventory control and financial accounting systems. Responsible for the purchase of all plant operational supplies, non-capital machinery, tooling and service contracts. Led team responsible for identifying and implementing $290,000 in cost reductions through engineering and process changes. Designed automated record keeping functions of the tool crib.

***Purchasing Agent OEM*** **(8/78 to 1/80)**

Managed annual purchases of $25 million in metals, fasteners, and labels commodities. Served on Value Analysis teams in this department.

### Self Employed **(7/74 to 8/78)**

***Owner and operator of a machine shop.***

### Give and Take Clothing Co., Preston, CA **(9/72 to 7/74)**

***Sales and Business Consultant***

Responsible for opening 40 plus new retail stores and for providing assistance to 60 independent franchises in the United States.

### Allied Drug Co., Spartan, OK **(10/69 to 8/72)**

***Ethical Drug Sales Representative***

### United States Army **(10/67 to 10/69)**

***Attained rank of Captain. USAR***

161

**Combination.** *Thomas E. Spann, Easton, Maryland*

The contact information, bold section titles, objective statement, qualification highlights, and contact information on the second page are centered. The rest of the information is left-aligned.

# C. Mitchell Harrington

456 West Garrison Street • Stillwater, MD 00000 • (410) 877-7777

## Education

Bloomberg College, Bloomberg, DE
***Masters in Business Education---1988***

Whitehaven University, Plainsview,MT
***Bachelor of Science Degree, Business Administration---1967***

Eastville College, Bakersfield, CA
***Certified Instructor***

East RiverUniversity, Greenville, NH
***Adjunct Professor--Industrial Technology Department***

## Community Service

Stillwater Town Council, Stillwater, MD
***Councilman, 4th Ward (Currently serving in third term)***

WestEnd Regional Technology Council, Rocky Bluff, MD
***Member, Advisory Committee***

Stillwater Business Management Council, Stillwater, MD
***Member, Board of Directors***

Christmas is Giving Festival Inc., Stillwater, MD
***Event Chairman***

A distinctive feature uniting the two pages visually is the use of shaded boxes for the section headings. Another feature is the use of small caps for the contact information and company names (including the designation "Self-Employed"). Bold italic makes the job titles stand out.

**ELLEN MONROE SMITH**

***123 West Main Street • Anytown, Tennessee 00000*** ***(000) 000-0000***

## OBJECTIVE

Seeking a career opportunity in **PROPERTY MANAGEMENT** requiring skill and experience in negotiations, management, leasing, and accounting activities.

## PROFESSIONAL EXPERIENCE

**PROPERTY MANAGEMENT**

- Seven years of property management experience; management portfolio included 96 single units, 8 four-plexes, 6 duplexes, and 4 single family residences
- Coordinate tenant improvements, lease negotiations, and contracted services
- Provide cost-efficient monitoring of all property accounting, monthly reports, tenant relations, & maintenance

**COMMUNICATION**

- Excellent communication, public relations, and motivation skills that effectively interact with tenants, vendors, staff, and executive management
- Liaison for landlord in the areas of collections, introducing new policies, and policy enforcement
- Strong abilities in fundraising and working with community, civic, and charitable organizations

**ADMINISTRATION**

- Experienced in all aspects of personnel development, including interviewing, hiring, training, and supervising support staff of up to 15 employees
- Extensive background in retail management, materials management, bookkeeping, payroll, cash management, inventory, shipping and receiving
- Prioritize and complete numerous concurrent assignments while meeting time and organizational goals

## EDUCATION

**CONTINUAL LEARNING INSTITUTE** • 1993 • Capital City, Tennessee
Real Estate Property Management • Emphasis on Leases, Contracts, Rental Property, Tenant-Owner Relations, Repairs, Maintenance, Inspection, Marketing

**OLD WEST COLLEGE** • 1990 - 1991 • Anywhere, Montana
Focus on Introduction to Law, Business Law, Family Law, and Business Contracts

**ADULT EDUCATION CENTER** • 1987 & 1980 • Anywhere, Montana
Numerous courses in Accounting, Legal and Business Forms, Introduction to Computers, DOS, Quicken

## EMPLOYMENT HISTORY

**STORE MANAGER/REGIONAL MANAGER IN TRAINING** • 1993 - Present
***Ladies Petite Dress Shop*** • Peachtree Mall • Anytown, Tennessee

**MANAGER/SUPERVISOR** • 1991 - 1993
***ABC Corporation/Lingerie Division*** • Capital City, Tennessee

**PROPERTY MANAGER** • 1983 - 1990
***Rocky Mountain Properties*** • Anywhere, Montana

**CO-OWNER/OFFICE MANAGER** • 1980 - 1983
***XYZ Flooring Systems*** • Anywhere, Montana

---

***Additional Information Available Upon Request***

**162**

**Combination.** *Carolyn S. Braden, Hendersonville, Tennessee*

The writer uses three categories as side headings in the Professional Experience section to group kinds of experience, to break up a long section, and to draw attention to important strengths.

**ALANA J. ALLENSON**
123 River Walk Way
St. Louis, MO 00000
**(314) 555-1212**

**OBJECTIVE**

A career growth opportunity in the **real estate development/management** industry where I can draw on diverse experiences in accounting, legal, and administrative management.

**Assisting the owners of a St. Louis commercial and residential real estate company** pending graduation and completion of my job search in the real estate industry.

**STRENGTHS**

- **Nearly ten years of experience in a challenging variety of work settings, including a legal practice emphasizing real estate and a real estate agency.** Responsibilities focused on accounting, bookkeeping, office and legal administration.
- Strong computer skills with experience in Lotus 1-2-3, PerfectCalc, C and Basic programming languages, WordPerfect 5.1, Wang Word Processing, and MS Word.
- Work ethic characterized by versatility, an inquisitive nature, the ability to work independently, and very strong organization skills.

**EDUCATION**

**Bachelor of Arts, Economics,** May, 1996
**Washington University,** John M. Olin School of Business, St. Louis, MO

- Earned a 3.1 GPA in Economics and a 3.2 in Psychology while working 20 to 30 hours weekly to earn 100% of college/living expenses.

Associates Degrees in Accounting and Business Administration, 1993
Anderson Community College, Bloomfield Hills, Michigan

**EXPERIENCE**

**Business Administration**
Birdsong & Best, P.C., Dearborn, MI, 5/91 to 5/94

- Recruited from prior employer to manage all aspects of administration for this **Real Estate**, General Civil, Corporate, and Probate practice.
- **Provided operating and financial management for real estate partnerships.**
- Substantially improved profit and cash flow by implementing a computerized time and billing program and other operating procedures, including an in-house computerized tax preparation program.
- Duties included preparation of billings, accounts payable/receivable ledgers, cash receipts ledgers, pleadings, and other court documents.
- Managed multiple bank accounts, client estates, purchasing, and equipment service and support contracts.

**Office Manager**
ABC Partners, Ltd., Dearborn, MI, 5/88 to 5/91

- Managed the billing, taxes, and payroll accounts.
- Handled all administrative duties for up to six unrelated practitioners.

**Assistant Manager**
Michigan China Company, Birmingham, MI, 8/86 to 12/88

- Sales, marketing, inventory, and personnel responsibilities for this growing retail china and crystal store. Assisted with bookkeeping and expansion to second store.

**Administrative Assistant**
Sandra J. Fleischman, P.C., Dearborn, MI, 8/87 to 5/88

- Office administration for a General Practice attorney. Part-time while at Michigan China.

**163**

**Combination.** *Alan D. Ferrell, Lafayette, Indiana*

The target of this resume is the real estate industry. The person, however, "does not have a strong real estate background." The writer boldfaces whatever information is relevant to real estate.

**Meredith Lee**

98 Seaview Avenue, Revere, MA 02151 • (617) 555-9821

**PROFESSIONAL PROFILE**

Experienced **property manager** with a solid record of industry accomplishments.

- Proactive business manager who combines close attention to detail with planning and goal-setting to achieve long-range objectives.
- Creative problem solver and effective negotiator.
- Highly motivated and enthusiastic; able to manage multiple projects simultaneously.
- Strong leadership skills and the ability to manage and motivate staff.

**EDUCATION**

MBA BOSTON UNIVERSITY, 1986 • Concentration in Finance
BA PACE UNIVERSITY, 1983 • Majors in Economics and Finance

**EXPERIENCE**

1990-Present

**Property Manager** • HUB PROPERTIES, Boston, Massachusetts

Provide total property management for 52 buildings comprising 260 residential and retail units. Responsible for building management and maintenance, marketing, leasing, tenant relations and retention, financial reporting, budgeting, collections, negotiating contracts with tenants and vendors. Supervise staff of 6.

- Maintain occupancy rate in mid-90% range through combination of pro-active measures (effective marketing; thorough screening of prospective tenants; cultivating referrals through a bonus system) and a strong customer service focus that results in excellent tenant retention and low turnover.
- Consistently achieve a satisfactory return on the owner's investment.
- Instrumental in the purchase of 11 pieces of real estate, providing analysis of building, neighborhood, and leasing prospects as well as detailed cost estimates for remodeling/repairs.
- Achieved successful turnaround of newly purchased vacant or poorly run buildings, applying an intensive effort to make them marketable and income-producing within a short time frame.
- Analyzed company's computer needs and installed updated system that includes word processing, spreadsheet, and property management and construction software.

1986-1990

**Project Manager** • BODY STOPS, INC., New York, New York

Managed the development and maintenance of all Body Stops retail stores in Northeast Division (15–25 new stores per year) from Letter of Understanding through opening.

- Ensured construction met quality standards and stores were completed within established time frames and budgets.
- Managed $12MM construction budget and additional maintenance budget.
- Directed all remodeling of existing and acquired stores.
- Established and maintained positive working relationships with general contractors, architects, vendors, property owners and company officials.
- Developed a computerized revitalization program for existing stores to produce long-term financial forecasts, monitor budgets and expenses, and ensure completion of annual maintenance programs.

1983-1986

**Project Cost Accountant** • WASTE MATERIALS CO., Hauppage, New York

Coordinated field accounting on EPA-contracted hazardous-waste cleanup projects. Tracked financial data and generated financial and close-out reports on approximately 25 ongoing projects representing yearly contracts of $12 million.

**164**

**Combination.** *Louise Kursmark, Cincinnati, Ohio*

A vertical line and several horizontal lines (one full and three partial) break a page into small areas. For the first two positions, a paragraph tells of duties, and bullets show accomplishments.

## Joel I. Nicklaus

**400000 Dreamboat Drive • ELmira, New York 00000 • (000) 000-0000**

**PROFILE:**

Seeking a challenging **Management** position in the Hotel/Restaurant field. Highlights include:

- Proven administrative, management, supervisory and training abilities.
- Experience in restaurant operations: scheduling, purchasing and inventory control.
- Knowledge of computers: WordPerfect, dBase III, Lotus 1-2-3, Window Works 2.0.
- Strong organizational, problem-solving, interpersonal and communication skills.
- Language skills: Spanish, Italian and French.

**EDUCATION:**

ELMIRA CITY COMMUNITY COLLEGE, Elmira, New York
**A.A.S., Hotel/Restaurant Management** - 1995
*Honors:* GPA: 3.9/4.0; Phi Theta Kappa (1994-95); Dean's List (Fall 1993-Spring 1995)
*Relevant Courses:* Food Service & Preparation I&II, Food Service Purchasing, Food Service Industrial & Governmental Relations, Food & Labor Cost Control, Hospitality Marketing, Nutrition.

ST. JOHN'S UNIVERSITY, St. Johns, New York
**English Literature Major** (90 credits) - 1968/71

*New York State Sanitation Certification*

**EXPERIENCE:**

FRIENDLY'S RESTAURANT, Bartlett, New York
**Management Internship,** January 1994 to May 1994
- Enhanced skills in all phases of restaurant management.

THE BAR, Valley Hope, Pennsylvania
**Bartender,** January 1987 to October 1992
- Ordered liquor and beer, handled receiving and inventory control procedures.
- Worked with suppliers and vendors, inspectors and maintenance personnel.

THE VALLEY MISTIC RESTAURANT, New York, New York
**Manager,** July 1986 to January 1987
- Oversaw all daily operations for restaurant specializing in Italian and American cuisine.
- Supervised kitchen/wait staff and bartender. Responsible for scheduling and training.
- Duties included staff development, ordering, inventory control and documentation.

PICTURE PRETTY INC., New York, New York
**Owner/Manager,** March 1978 to July 1986
- Created, designed and manufactured photographs and posters for the retail and wholesale trade.
- Supervised 11 employees at two locations; handled scheduling and performance evaluations.
- Wrote, designed, and handled layouts and paste-up for annual multi-page catalogs and bi-monthly mailings. Worked with printers.
- Developed and promoted publicity and multiple articles in the *New York Times, New York Daily News, New York Magazine, Los Angeles Times, Good Housekeeping,* etc.

**ACTIVITIES/INTERESTS:**

- Hotel/Restaurant Association Club, Elmira City Community College
- Publications Office/Patient Volunteer, Valley Home Regional Medical Center

**- References Available Upon Request -**

**165**

**Combination.** *Betty Geller, Elmira, New York*

A resume for an older worker who returned to school for a Hotel/Restaurant Management degree. Relevant education is therefore put early. The Profile has both an objective and a skills summary.

**Suzanne Weeks**
35-83 35th Street
Brooklyn, NY 11215
(718) 225-8787

**OBJECTIVE** CORPORATE MEETING MANAGER/PLANNER

**PROFILE**

- Significant experience in convention and meeting planning for major organizations and corporations.
- Expertise in all areas of food and beverage operations, room and travel packages, meeting set-ups, and recreational packages.
- Ability to understand and work within corporate budgets and constraints as well as negotiate the optimal packages to meet organizational requirements.
- Excellent skills in sales, marketing, customer service, and negotiation.
- Strong understanding of corporate planning needs and budgets.

**RELATED EXPERIENCE**

4/93 to Present

THE RITZ-JEFFREY HOTEL—4-star property New York, NY
**Food and Beverage Manager** (Promoted from Assistant F & B Manager)
- ♣ Oversee and coordinate receptions, banquets and meetings for high level corporate and prestige events at luxury suite hotel. Select menus and wine lists, coordinate with sales department for room reservations, arrange for audio-visual equipment with outside vendors, and negotiate required contracts.
- ♣ Client companies include Entertainment Communications, Trans-Land Corporation, TCG Companies, and other major organizations.
- ♣ Regularly solicit corporate meeting planners to develop new accounts as well as to solidify current accounts.
- ♣ Organize hotel seminars for top travel agents, meeting planners, and editors in conjunction with sales department.
- ♣ Direct all food and beverage operations for all outlets.
- ♣ Manage an annual budget of $8 million with a staff of nineteen.

**ADDITIONAL EXPERIENCE**

5/92 - 4/93

THE SHELTON-LOCK HOTEL-4-star property New York, NY
**Shift Bar Manager**
- ♣ Arranged special food and beverage functions such as FAM trips, VIP dinners, cocktail parties, and sales events.

11/91 - 5/92

HOTEL NEW YORK-4-star property New York, NY
**Assistant Room Service/Minibar Manager**
- ♣ Co-managed daily operations for room service and minibar departments of a 725 room hotel.
- ♣ Coordinated special hospitality parties for groups.

1990

HOTEL GENEVA HILTON-5-star property Geneva, Switzerland
**Member of Banqueting Department**
- ♣ Worked as part of a banqueting brigade serving up to 2,000 clients in French, English, and Gueridon styles of service.

**EDUCATION**

NEW YORK UNIVERSITY New York, NY
**Bachelor of Science**, May 1991
**Major: Hotel Restaurant Management**

INSTITUTE SWISS Geneva, Switzerland
**Certificate of Hotel Management**

**REFERENCES** Available upon request.

**166**

**Combination.** *Etta Barmann, New York, New York*

This individual wanted to become a meeting manager/planner. The Profile lists her relevant skills, and shamrock bullets indicate her related experience. Her name is put in a personable font.

# Ronald W. Eastwood

**Objective:** A management position in the Food or Food Service Industry.

**Profile:**

- 13 years of experience in the Food Service Industry; 4 years in Restaurant Management.
- Strong record of cutting costs, increasing sales, and reducing waste.
- Excellent employee management skills. Improve morale and motivate staff through incentives, employee training, and improving the work atmosphere.

**Experience:**

**Wallabey's**, Detroit, Michigan — January 1991-Present
*Dining Room Manager (6/94-Present)*
*Beverage Manager (7/92-6/94)*
*Bartender (1/91-7/92)*

Manage dining room for one of the top grossing restaurants in Michigan. Supervise an average of 50 employees per shift. Handle hiring, training, scheduling, and labor tracking. Control inventory and order front-of-the-house supplies. Oversee guest service and handle any customer complaints. Accountable for all monies, including cash drawer and bank deposits.

- **Cost Controls:** Reduced inventory by tracking a year's worth of sales and planning accordingly. Reduce payroll by careful employee scheduling. Reduced liquor costs through improved security, bartender retraining, and inventory control.
- **Sales:** Increased sales by training waitstaff in suggestive selling and by educating them about the products. Also introduced waitstaff sales incentives.
- **Awards:** Won "House of Seagrams" cocktail award, and was featured in an article by the Michigan Beverage Journal.

**East Side Charley's**, Harper Woods, Michigan — March 1986-December 1991
*Bartender (12/86-1/91)*
*Server (3/86-12/86)*

- Trained for and earned in-house certification to train new employees.

**L-Bow Room**, Mt. Clemens, Michigan — July 1983-March 1986
*Room Service, Bussed Tables*

**Education:**

*Graduate (1985)*
**Clintondale High School,** Mt. Clemens, Michigan

**Additional Training:** Attended numerous in-house seminars on management, sales, and employee training.

**23 Elm Street, Monroe, MI 48161**
**(313) 555-3344**

167

**Combination.** *Deborah L. Schuster, Newport, Michigan*

A slightly rounded font (Soutane) is used for this manager of a laid-back restaurant. Lines frame the page, and contact information is put last—"You don't need it until you read it" (the resume).

**VINCENT B. CLEMENZA**

4455 West Whiteside #1C
Park Ridge, IL 60068
708/555-9531

**EXPERIENCE:**

- Proven abilities in business operations and personalized customer service, including full responsibility for troubleshooting and system streamlining.
- Plan and conduct sales presentations in a professional manner; handle research, status reporting and account updating.
- Skilled in general accounting and bookkeeping with a strong aptitude for figures; organize stocking, inventory control and cost-effective purchasing.

**EMPLOYMENT:**

Perry's, Des Plaines, IL — 1991-3/94
**Manager**
Responsible for direct customer service, sales and special event planning at this full-service restaurant.
Coordinated budgets and the purchase of food, beverages and supplies; provided data for monthly reconciliations.
Trained and supervised all personnel in food preparation, front/back house operations and problem solving for peak customer satisfaction.
Organized catered events including banquets, parties and weddings.

* Worked directly with the owner in the startup of this second location.
* Promoted to this position from driver.

Ryan Temporary Service, Chicago, IL — Full and Part-Time, 1989
**Personnel Representative**
Worked directly with client companies for the placement of temporary staff in clerical, sales and customer service positions.

JJ's Bedding & Furniture, Niles, IL — 1981-1988
**Sales / Business Operations**
Communicated daily with customers to determine and meet their needs for high-quality furniture.
Routed and expedited trucks; supervised delivery staff on a daily basis.
Resolved customer complaints with tact and professionalism; developed a strong referral business.

**EDUCATION:**

Oakton Community College, Des Plaines, IL
**Associates Degree** — Graduated 1988

Completed a total of 40 credit hours; GPA: 3/87/4.0 at OCC and:

Northeastern Illinois University
Courses included intensive study in English and Communications.

168

**Combination.** *Steven Provenzano, Schaumburg, Illinois*

A clean-cut resume whose design is easily grasped at a glance. A line separates the contact information from the rest of the resume. Boldfacing makes the job titles and degree stand out.

# Susan J. Smith

*RR 2 Box 1234*
*Bayside, Maine 00000*
*(207) 555-5555*

**Objective:** ***Bakery / Deli Management***

## Areas of Expertise:

- Restaurant Management
- Scheduling
- Customer Relations
- Staff Training and Development
- Employee Supervision
- Negotiation with Sales Representatives
- Problem Resolution
- Baking and Recipe Creation

## Professional Experience:

**The Deli Shop Plus, Deli & Bakery, Bayside, Maine** **1982 - Present**
***Manager***
Overall responsibility for the management and supervision of a kosher restaurant serving direct customers, commercial, and wholesale accounts. Supervise 5 - 10 employees. Negotiate with sales representatives in person and on the telephone to secure the best quality, quantity, and price of product. Estimate quantity of product to order based on upcoming projects. Manage wholesale business, which reflects 20 - 25% of revenue. Responsible for training and supervising the daily routines of keeping a kosher kitchen. Gained and retained extensive knowledge of Jewish religion and culture.

**Key Accomplishments**:

- No employee turnover in four years. Current staff is dependable, efficient, and content.
- Played major role in designing new display area resulting in increased business.
- Created 100% of bread recipes used and some soup and pastry recipes.
- Achieve high ratings on food and sanitation inspections.
- Attended buying trips, including the Fancy Food Show and the Kosher Food Show at the Javitz Center in New York City, to identify new products.

**Country Catering, East Bayside, Maine** **1990 - 1993**
***Owner / Caterer***
Established cake decorating and catering business. Prepared and decorated cakes for all occasions. Managed all financial and marketing aspects of business.

## Education:

**Eastern Maine Technical College, Bangor, Maine** 1982
***Diploma - Food Technology Program***

**Subject Areas**:
- *Sanitation in Food Service*
- *Restaurant Management*
- *Psychology*
- *Customer Service & Selling*
- *Merchandising*
- *Food Preparation*

***References Available Upon Request***

**169**

**Combination.** *Joan M. Roberts, Bangor, Maine*

This busy manager of a deli and bagel shop wanted the greater challenges of restaurant management. The writer focused on areas of expertise that would entice a new employer.

# Jeff R. Sherrie

*3175 Shell Lane, LaBelle, FL 33935* *Telephone: 941-675-7977*

## Objective and Summary

**A management position in the food and beverage industry**
that builds upon expertise in strategic and daily operations planning and upon a reputation for a motivational hands-on management style.
Specific experience includes:

- Profit and loss responsibility
- Purchasing
- New-start facility design and planning
- Hospitality industry software
- Employee development

## Food Industry Experience

*Manager of Food and Beverage Department*, 1993-present
SEMINOLE INDIAN CASINO, Immokalee, FL
Total responsibility for all food and beverage operations for 46,000 square foot facility with over $3.5 million in sales. Includes a full service restaurant, gaming palace with full service bar, poker room with cocktail sales, bingo hall with concession stands and mobile cart sales. Hire, train and direct the development of over 80 employees. Hire all entertainment.

- Acclaimed by food critics with three out of four stars for food quality and service.
- Managed the customization and installation of Pinnacle Posi-Touch software, an automated PC/networking system to generate accounting reports, and fully integrate sales and cost analysis, product inventory and material requirements planning.
- Special commendation from state health inspectors for exceptional kitchen sanitation and maintenance.
- Selected to serve on corporate committee to implement and design company-wide new hire orientation training program.
- PC proficiency in Lotus 123, WordPerfect 6.0, Deluxe Print Shop.

*Manger of Club House Operations*, 1990-93
THE CLUB PELICAN BAY, Naples, FL
Responsible for ensuring an impeccable dining experience for over 1000 members in this exclusive club facility which includes two dining rooms, two banquet rooms and two bars with total seating capacity of over 400. Arranged special functions requiring attention to protocol, strict compliance to club regulations and ability to elicit cooperation and team work among the wait/kitchen/bar staff of 50.

**170**

**Combination.** *Deborah C. Sherrie, Charlotte, North Carolina*

The graphic and extra large font for the name in the contact information make this resume stand out at once. A full line under each section heading enables the reader to size up the resume's

**Jeff R. Sherrie**, page 2

*Owner/Manager*, 1985-90
YESTERDAY'S AT OLCOTT BEACH, Olcott Beach, NY
Created the nostalgic theme, decor and menu for restaurant facility. Renovated the existing 125 year old structure and constructed a building extension in keeping with the original architecture. Designed the floor plan and kitchen layout. Purchased kitchen equipment.

- ➢ Successfully built a profitable new business which resulted in a notably gainful sale.

## Other Experience

*Salesperson/Office Manager*, 1984-89
J.R. SHERRIE REALTY, Lockport, NY
Listed and sold commercial, residential and farm properties. Managed bookkeeping for local rental properties. Wrote all advertisements. Organized open houses.

*Manager/Technician*, 1982-84
MARK TWAIN'S RESTAURANT, Ft. Lauderdale, FL
Repaired and maintained computerized animated show consisting of 8 characters, and a game room of over 150 video games. Assistant Manager of Restaurant Operations.

## Education and Training

*A.S., Computer Technology,* specialty in fiber optics and robotics
Alfred State University of New York, Agriculture & Technical College, Alfred, NY, 1982

*Center for Food Service Education*, Houston, TX, 1995. 16 CEC hours
Topics included: Financial statement analysis. Labor, food and beverage cost control.
Point of sales. Hospitality industry software and hardware.
Menu pricing and layout.

*The Responsible Vendor Training Program*, current
Provided by Beverage Law Institute of Tallahassee, FL

CPR Certified

## Other Activities

Designed and constructed present home.

parts at a glance. Boldfacing brings the objective into view. A distinctive bullet ties together the two pages visually. Uppercase letters make the restaurant or company names readily apparent. Italic helps you spot job titles and kinds of education. The large sans serif font is easy to read.

# KENNETH M. STILWELL

8976 Bender Square
Worthington, Ohio 00000
[614] 555-5555

**OBJECTIVE** **Administrative position in business, government, or education.**

**QUALIFICATIONS SUMMARY**

- Over fifteen years of management success supervising persons of all educational, technical, and skill levels.
- Proven ability to recruit, train, and motivate productive team members.
- Significant experience developing computerized solutions for management problems.
- Demonstrated planning, leadership, and communication skills.

**EXPERIENCE**

**JONES MANAGEMENT, INC.**, Columbus, Ohio (1992 to present)

- Took over as ***Senior Restaurant Manager*** of million-dollar-a-year fast-food restaurant in May, 1994. Brought annual sales to $1.2 million. Develop and implement monthly budget. Analyze potential impact of promotions and seasonal events, and project expenses required to meet expected sales. Plan and budget for special projects.
- Supervise forty-one employees including eight managers and six full-time workers. Write annual performance evaluations and weekly updates for management staff. Advise District Manager on hiring and firing of managers.
- Train new employees. Through giving regular individualized attention maintain staff turnover at much lower rate than industry average.
- Oversee second restaurant. Respond to emergency needs and consult regularly with its manager.
- Served for a year as ***Restaurant Manager*** at busiest of company's twelve stores (1993 to 1994).
- Worked as ***Assistant Manager*** at two restaurants during training period (1992 to 1993).

**U.S. ARMY** (1978 to 1992)

- Served as ***Operations Officer***, Fort McKavett, Texas (1991 to 1992). Held rank of Major. Managed daily operation of 750-person, 150-vehicle field artillery battalion. Directly supervised thirty people in four offices. Developed and implemented training plans. Planned, managed, and did projections for $2 million training budget. Created comprehensive training evaluation program eventually adopted for other Fort McKavett units. Exceeded training standards by maintaining over 90% qualification status.

**171**

**Combination.** *John D. King, Bloomington, Indiana*

A resume for an individual who has successfully made the transition from military to civilian life and now wants to move from successful restaurant management to administrative work in

**KENNETH M. STILWELL** (page two)

- As ***Fire Support Coordinator***, Fort McKavett, Texas (1990 to 1991), wrote plans and orders for 21,000-person organization during overseas deployment. Supervised target analysis and production team during combat operations. Became Project Officer overseeing construction and staffing of desert facility for washing 7,500 vehicles to meet United States Department of Agriculture and Customs Department standards prior to return. Completed project under budget and ahead of schedule.
- Assigned as ***Assistant Professor of Military Science*** at The Ohio State University, Columbus, Ohio (1987 to 1990). Taught undergraduate Military Science courses at all levels. Counseled students concerning academic performance, scholarships and financial assistance, and career opportunities.
- Wrote department's computing plan. Analyzed and projected equipment and software needs over five year period. Converted all student files to a computerized data base.
- Developed and implemented program's marketing plan including budget development, campaign planning advertising, and public affairs promotion. Supervised and trained eight other officers for marketing effort. Assigned territories and market segments, and continually assessed results. Personally recruited at thirty-five Ohio high schools. Program doubled overall enrollment and number of scholarship students, and tripled freshman participation. Later maintained equivalent market coverage despite 15% budget reduction.
- As ***Executive Officer***, Schwaebisch Gmeund, Germany (1986 to 1987), supervised inventory control, supply accountability, maintenance management, and procurement. Instituted management program which led to winning award as best unit out of twelve.
- Earlier served as ***Commissioned Officer***, Fort Sill, Oklahoma (1978 to 1986), holding a succession of progressively more demanding positions.

**EDUCATION AND TRAINING**

**Bachelor of Arts in Criminal Justice** (1978)
University of Wisconsin, Madison, Wisconsin

**Graduate Study**
The Ohio State University, Columbus, Ohio

- Completed eighteen credit hours toward Master of Science in Education degree in College Student Personnel Administration. Maintained 3.7+ grade point average (on 4.0 scale).

**Diploma** (1992)
Command and General Staff College, Fort Leavenworth, Kansas

**Computer Competence**

- Experienced in use of WordPerfect 5.1, Harvard Graphics, Lotus 1-2-3, DBase III Plus, Reflex, Norton Utilities, and several communications programs.

business, government, or education. With flush-left section headings and hanging indentation throughout, the overall layout of the resume is easy to spot. The use of boldface for job titles helps them to stand out in text. Boldface is effective in the Education and Training section too.

# Jeffrey P. Walker

◆ 9803 McClain Drive ◆ Bayview, Michigan 48555 ◆ 810-555-8733 ◆

## PROFILE

- Productive, efficient manager who excels in challenging, fast-paced environment; calm under pressure.
- Personable leader whose ability to maintain rapport with employees is based on mutual respect.
- Effective written and verbal communicator including one-on-one and group settings.
- Innovative thinker who is not afraid to design and implement new solutions.
- Adept at problem identification and problem resolution.

## SUMMARY OF EXPERIENCE

*Management*
- Oversee operations of employee/patient/public cafeteria and grill, serving approximately 2,000 daily.
- Circulate throughout public areas to monitor customer service and respond to patron concerns.
- Share responsibilities including supervision with other managers and chef for additional operations (patient service, catering, food preparation).
- Develop and successfully implement staff and product cost cutting measures as required.
- Interact with corporate officials, outside event coordinators and other staff to plan special events.

*Supervision*
- Motivate, supervise and evaluate employees on three shifts.
- Conduct regular meetings with subordinates to discuss procedural and other topics.
- Resolve employee disputes and respond to union grievances as necessary.
- Oversee training for new employees.

*Operations*
- Program, trouble-shoot and reconcile computerized cash registers. Investigate register shortages.
- Anticipate and resolve problems created by staff or food shortages.
- Conduct Quality Assurance Audits; identify problems and initiate appropriate corrective action.
- Prepare for and interact with officials during routine and surprise health inspections.

*Food Service*
- Collaborate with dietitian and chef to develop and adapt cyclical menus; coordinate customized menus with staff in two affiliate hospitals.
- Monitor portion size, supply and general appearance of hot food; sanitation and appearance of serving and dining areas; and salad, soup and dessert bars.
- Project food orders based on experience, review of past menu performance, and product availability.

## EMPLOYMENT HISTORY

HOPE METHODIST GENERAL HOSPITAL • Bayview, MI — 1977-Present
**Cafeteria Manager**

## EDUCATION

WESTERN MICHIGAN UNIVERSITY • Kalamazoo, MI
**Bachelor of Science - Food Systems Economics and Management** — 1977

Professional development through employer (complete list available on request) — Ongoing

## COMMUNITY INVOLVEMENT

**Member** - Muscular Dystrophy Association • Bayview, MI — 1985-Present
**Volunteer Treasurer** – Discovery Day Care Center • Bayview, MI — 1992-1994
Prepared weekly payroll for twelve employees.

*References available on request.*

172

**Combination.** *Janet L. Beckstrom, Flint, Michigan*

A preparation-for-the-ax resume. For twenty years since graduation, this person has been a good manager. His employer, though, is "restructuring," so this loyal, effective manager may be fired.

**PRESENTING**

**DAVID M. SMITH**

**IN**

**"A RESTAURATEUR FOR ALL SEASONS"**
***A NEW YORK PRODUCTION***

**STYLE:**

Providing service with panache, David offers a unique style of food presentation and customer service that has ingratiated him to clients throughout the United States and Paradise Island.

**CREDITS:**

A 20 year Hospitality Professional with extensive Restaurant, Banquet, Meetings Management, Resort, Front and Back of House experience.

**REVIEWS:**

An accomplished chef, he prepares a veritable cornucopia of culinary styles to titilate your senses.

David M. Smith • 455 FDR Drive • New York, N.Y. 10002 • (212) 677 - 1111

173

**Combination.** *Martin Weitzman, New York, New York*

An innovative resume designed as a program for a stage production. The graphic on this front cover is an immediate indication that this is not "another resume." The title of the production is

A profit driven and service oriented professional, David is adept at controlling food and beverage costs while maintaining the highest levels of customer service. His ability to develop customer loyalty can be traced directly to his eagerness to go the extra mile. Whether directing kitchen activities, planning and managing banquets or his flair for providing a true dining experience with unique tableside meal preparation, he is a true Hospitality original.

His hands-on managerial and culinary experience encompasses:

- Restaurant, Banquet and Meetings Management and Planning.
- P & L responsibility.
- Recruiting and staffing of new and existing restaurants.
- Planning eclectic menus based on locale, season, pricing, facility and profitability structures.
- Determining costing, portioning and selection of specials.
- Developing and implementing time and cost effective kitchen procedures and techniques.
- Overseeing wait staff to ensure guest and customer satisfaction.
- Training, developing, scheduling and motivating Front and Back of House staffs.
- Union and non-union labor relations.
- Selecting vendors and negotiating most favorable pricing to ensure maximum profitability.
- Maintaining strong inventory control procedures for food, beverage and non-food items to minimize waste and spoilage.
- Implementing automated billing and scheduling systems.
- Tracking employee time and preparing payroll sheets.

**REVIEWS:**

*"Thank you for making the American Bar Association 1993 annual meeting a success"*
*"Chef David Smith has worked his culinary wonders in Shandaken, New York City, the Bahamas, Colorado, Florida, the Virgin Islands and Canada "*
*"Outstanding, quite possibly the best I ever had"*
*"A fabulous Executive Chef "*
*"Chef David Smith, who helped create distinctive tropical cuisine for Club Meds in Paradise Island and Denver, Colorado "*
*"A culinary genius "*
*"David was always there to make sure all was well. He is very efficient and a pleasure to work with "*
*"David Smith did a wonderful job and I congratulate you "*
*"Thank you for going beyond the call of duty "*
*"It was a great feeling knowing everything was in your capable hands"*
*"Special thanks to David Smith for his tireless attention and professional bearing "*

David Smith • 455 FDR Drive • New York, NY 10002• (212) 677 - 1111

cleverly a profile statement that "says it all." The headings Style, Credits, and Reviews function as categories of a Summary of Qualifications. At the top of page two is a summary of skills, followed by a bulleted list of duties and responsibilities. The creative Reviews section is a series of testimonials that function as a string

**CREDITS:**

Loews New York Hotel, New York, NY — 1989 - Present
**Sr. Assistant Restaurant Manager - Lexington Avenue Grill**
**Maitre D' Hotel**
**Assistant Banquet Manager**

Sugar Maples Resort, Maplecrest, NY — 1981 - 1989
**Chef**

Elka Park, Hunter Mountain, NY
**Club Manager and Chef**

One Fifth, New York, NY
**Chef De Cuisine**

Garvins Restaurant, New York, NY
**Night Line Chef**

Park Ten, New York, NY
**Sous Chef**

The Tropics International, South Miami Beach, FL
**Executive Chef**

Aldo's Black Pearl, Sarasota, FL
**Restaurant Chef**

Club Med, Colorado, and Paradise Island
**Specialty Chef/Cuisine Team**

**EDUCATION:**

Star Service Competence Program — 1994

Train The Trainer Seminar , New York, NY — 1991
**Certificate**

Management Assessment, New York, NY — 1991
**Certificate**

New York Food and Restaurant School, New York, NY — 1989
**Certificate in Restaurant Management**
**Merit Award in Professionalism**

Auberge des 4 Sasion, Shandaken, NY — 1974 - 1979
**Apprenticeship in Classical French Cuisine**

David Smith • 455 FDR Drive • New York, NY 10002 • (212) 677 - 1111

of achievements. The Credits section presents a work history but with dates for only the last two, long-term positions. The Education section shows that the person continues to advance his expertise. Boldface makes positions and certificates easily seen.

**SUZANNE RIFFE, CSP, CHMM**

5814 Linhurst Ave.
Troy, Michigan 00000
(555) 555-5555

---

**OBJECTIVE**

Position as **Safety and Health / Environmental Manager** for an industrial manufacturer.

**HIGHLIGHTS OF QUALIFICATIONS**

- Four years multi-plant experience directing the Safety, Health and Environmental functions in a heavy manufacturing environment. Report to the Director of Human Resources.
- In-depth knowledge of OSHA and EPA regulations, with a successful record of compliance audits.
- Effective leadership skills: Adept at organizing, directing, training and motivating employees to achieve a common goal.
- Strong interpersonal skills: Develop rapport and work well with staff of all levels in organization.
- Experienced PC user. Maintain and update records on Excel 5.0. Utilize computer to maintain OSHA log, track accident statistics and schedule training.

**PROFESSIONAL EXPERIENCE**

***Safety and Health***

- Conduct health and safety audits to ensure compliance with OSHA standards for Wolf's three production plants of 900 employees. Reduced recordable incident rate by 35 percent and lost time incident rate by 50 percent over a two-year period by implementing a program to correct potential hazards.
- Identified major ergonomic problems during a job safety analysis; conducted employee training that resulted in a 42 percent reduction in repetitive trauma injuries.
- Revised and implemented Lockout/Tagout training program. Updated health and safety training manual for employees.

***Environmental***

- Administer the hazardous waste disposal and waste minimization programs. As a result of waste monitoring and recycling, hazardous waste has been reduced by 46 percent.
- Led team that developed and implemented the storm water pollution plan.

***Management / Leadership***

- Established departmental safety committees, working with production employees to improve safety and ensure that employees' point of view was considered.
- Designed well-received incentive and award system to promote safety in the workplace.
- Responsible for supervising and training Safety and Health Intern and two clerical staff.

**EMPLOYMENT HISTORY**

| | | |
|---|---|---|
| **Safety & Health Specialist** | WOLF Manufacturing, Inc., Holley, MI | 1990 to Date |
| **Safety & Health Intern** | WOLF Manufacturing, Inc., Pontiac, MI | 1988 to 1990 |

**EDUCATION / CERTIFICATIONS**

**B. S., Occupational Safety and Health,** Ferris State University, Big Rapids, MI, 1988

Certified Safety Professional and Certified Hazardous Materials Manager

**174**

**Combination.** *Jennie Dowden, Flossmoor, Illinois*

Boldface guides the eye down the page from the uppercase name at the top to the degree at the bottom. The Experience section groups duties and achievements according to three categories.

**DAVID I. TRASHBURN**
1881 Elk Creek Run
Westbrook, Maine 21212
**555.555.1234**(*call for fax*)
*e-mail: trashburn@aol.com*

**ENVIRONMENTAL MANAGEMENT SPECIALIST**

*Experience in the areas of:*

- Waste Management
- ISO 14000 Environmental Standards
- Environmental Management
- Topography / Geology / Hydrogeology
- Life-Cycle Assessment
- Environmental Monitoring
- Waste Analysis
- Universal Treatment Standards
- Regulatory Compliance
- EMS Audits

## SUMMARY OF QUALIFICATIONS

- Experience in environment disciplines: air, water, waste disposal, emergency planning, and chemistry.
- Certified Storm Water Operator – State of Maine
- Licensed and Registered Sanitarian – State of Maine
- Knowledge of OSHA, MIOSHA, EPA/RCRA, UST, SARA Title III, DOT, and local, state, and federal compliance regulations.
- Trained in EMS – Environmental Management System.

## SELECTED ACCOMPLISHMENTS

- Formulated ground water monitoring/tracing system for the State of Maine – Department of Environmental Quality.
- Developed environmental audit package documentation for companies.
- Formulated policies in response to compliance issues.
- Worked with the Department of Transportation to establish all training requirements and on-going professional development.

## EXPERIENCE

*ENVIRONMENTAL SERVICES, INC.* — Franklin, Maine
*Licensed training and test sanitation facility*
**ENVIRONMENTAL MANAGER**, 1986-current
**LABORATORY MANAGER**, 1984-86 — **ENVIRONMENTAL CHEMIST**, 1984

- Ensure company compliance to regulations for corporate environmental goals.
- Primary contact for auditing officials; developed audit package documentation.
- Maintain on-going association with contractors, consultants, and governmental regulatory agencies.
- Collaborate with members on Process Committee and Safety Committee.
- Manage a professional staff of 7 (chemists and office personnel), including recruiting, hiring, training, mentoring, and evaluating.
- Supervise ground water monitoring program.
- Work within government: local, state, and federal guidelines.

*WASHINGTON COUNTY HEALTH DEPARTMENT* — Augusta, Maine
**ENVIRONMENTAL SANITARIAN SUPERVISOR**, 1980-84 — **ENVIRONMENTAL SANITARIAN**, 1972-80

- Identified, alleviated, and solved environmental issues.
- Performed preventive and corrective measures to prevent pollution and develop corrective solutions.

## EDUCATION AND PROFESSIONAL DEVELOPMENT

*UNIVERSITY OF MAINE* — Augusta, Maine
**MS CANDIDATE** —Discipline: *Water Resource Management* — *in process*
*MINOR STATE UNIVERSITY* — Bar Harbor, Maine
**BACHELOR OF SCIENCE DEGREE** — 1972
Major: *Environmental Health Management*

Attend annual seminars, workshops, and courses to remain current with technology.

**175**

**Combination.** *Lorie Lebert, Novi, Michigan*

Lines enclosing the name make it the first item seen. Note that the lines get progressively thinner. In the Experience section, three positions are grouped to avoid repeating similar duties.

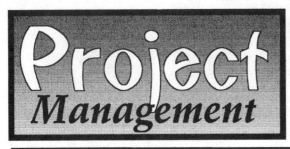

# Project Management

- Organizational skills, research and information gathering.
- Solid at analysis of data and evaluating alternate solutions.
- Identifying optimal approaches.
- Negotiating toward decisions, implementation, carry-through to plan completion.

**Bruce Westfeld**
4000 Meadowlark Lane
Anderson, IN 46000

**(317) 643-3000**

**Professional Experience:**

Sales Manager — Wesco, Inc., Noblesville, IN

Wesco is a producer of novelty and promotional items, and meat snacks. Novelty items include stuffed animals and similar products, e.g., novelty animals and cartoon characters featured in fast-food restaurant chain special meal promotions, etc. Meat products include such items as smoked beef snacks found in convenience stores, restaurants & bars. Supervise six sales executives assigned to 6 exclusive Indiana sales regions servicing businesses and corporate accounts. In charge of business retention and development of new business growth, training seminars, sales development and strategies. June 1995-current.

Director of Operations — Everybody's Oil Corporation, Anderson, IN

Everybody's Oil Corp. is a 14-store convenience Food Store chain. Was with the company for 20 years, spanning from 1975-1995. In charge of merchandising, purchasing, promotions, implementation of company policies/procedures, gross profit requirements, recruitment & retention and supervision of managers. Previously served as Director of Loss Prevention & Security involving monitoring inventory and cash shortages, trend sheets development, "mystery" shopper programs, cash audits, planning/organizing company seminars on shrink & loss control. Also, as an administrator, developed OSHA manual, identified discrimination laws, considerable regulatory experience, unemployment comp. hearings, and related responsibilities.

**Education:**

B. S. Degree, Ball State University, Muncie, IN. Major: History. Minor: Political Science

*Looking for an opportunity to contribute to a project management environment. It is stimulating to be able to pull together various elements into an integrated, coordinated and effective teamwork role from start to finish.*

**Well-Organized Excellent Communiations Hands-On Experience Effective**

**176**

**Combination.** *Jon C. Shafer, Anderson, Indiana*

The resume opens and closes with phrases about skills. Experience paragraphs tell about the company and the person's duties and achievements. The goal is stated next to the lower graphic.

# Michelle Lindsey

5842 Apple Creek Lane • Appleton, Wisconsin 54914 • (414) 784-4781

***Highly motivated professional with excellent training, staff development, and presentation abilities. Creatively develop course concepts and curriculum. Comfortable teaching both small and large groups. Strong communication, interpersonal relations, leadership, and management skills.***

## Career Highlights

### *Training and Staff Development*

- Designed and implemented an innovative classroom training program for new employees. Program included overview of corporate strategies, visual presentation of objectives and processes, and hands-on training of actual systems.
- Selected by management and peers to present training strategy to top executives. Emphasized the importance of training and employee development in relation to the success of the company. Recognized by Division President for the effectiveness of this presentation.
- Realized significant office productivity increases through implementation of new training procedures and elimination of redundancy.

### *Management*

- Led customer service team through work delegation utilizing AS400 system, staff motivation, and statistical analysis.
- Orchestrated human resource functions including hiring, reviews, compensation issues, and promotions.
- Sole responsibility for planning and scheduling manufacturing production for Fortune 500 company.

### *Sales and Marketing*

- Researched and recommended cost savings solutions for customers within sales territory based on a needs and benefits analysis.
- Effectively utilized presentation, communication, and organizational skills.
- Developed and executed marketing strategies on a continual basis. Strong emphasis on time and territory management.

## Education

University of Wisconsin
Milwaukee, Wisconsin

- Currently working toward **Bachelor of Science** in **Business Administration**
  *(matriculation expected May 1997)*

## Employment History

XYZ Corporation
Appleton, Wisconsin

- Area Sales Manager
  1995 – Present
- Customer Service Supervisor
  1990 – 1995

ABC Chemical Company
Neenah, Wisconsin

- Office Manager
  1989 – 1990

Weber Foods
Milwaukee, Wisconsin

- Distribution Coordinator
  1988 – 1989

Ellis General Finance
Milwaukee, Wisconsin

- Assistant Manager
  1986 – 1988

177

**Combination.** *Kathy Keshemberg, Appleton, Wisconsin*

Because of downsizing, this person was moved from training to sales. She wants a new training position. Combination format lets her list her work history and play up her training experience.

**LANCE F. WORTHINGTON**
**784 Conte Lane ■ Morris Heights, NJ 88888**
**(555) 555-5555**

**SALES AND MARKETING MANAGEMENT**
***- Fine Wine Industry -***

Top-Performing Sales and Marketing Professional with 15 years of experience in the fine wine industry, representing wines from every major wine region worldwide. Outstanding success in promoting products, including small niche brands, to on-premise and off-premise accounts, even in areas known for marginal fine wine sales. Expertise in:

- ■ Key Account Relationship Management
- ■ Client Training and Support
- ■ Strategic Planning
- ■ Marketing Presentations
- ■ Product Introduction
- ■ Incentive Planning

***Track record of consistent revenue growth in a highly competitive and challenging market.***

## PROFESSIONAL EXPERIENCE

■ **SALES REPRESENTATIVE / BRAND MANAGER, Select Choices, Dalsing, NJ** 1994 - Present

Promote numerous specialty brands of fine wine to central New Jersey on-premise establishments, fine wine shops, and large retail chains, for this fine wine wholesaler and niche brand marketer. Represent wines from every major wine region in the world. Scope of responsibility includes management of entire sales process, marketing, account management, client training, and promotional package development.

- Played a key role in the start-up and rapid growth of the business; assisted in defining the direction of the company, developing marketing strategies, and establishing human resource requirements.
- Generated over $750,000 in niche brand sales revenues annually; consistently achieved 30% increase in monthly revenues, compared with prior years' figures for the same months.
- Significantly increased sales of fine burgundy wine in central New Jersey, a product known to be a "hard-sell" in this area; personally sold over 400 cases in 1996.
- Cultivated a client base of over 120 active accounts; established relationships based on trust and quality service.
- Demonstrated creativity and resourcefulness in developing and marketing promotional packages that increased revenues and freed up warehouse space.
- Provided expert guidance to restaurants regarding interpretation of and compliance with ABC regulations.
- Planned and conducted customized client training seminars on wines and wine sales..

■ **SALES AND MARKETING CONSULTANT, Tallington Industries, North Aimes, NJ** 1987 - 1994

Specialized in the sale of fine wines and national brand liquors to on-premise businesses (hotels / restaurants) in New Jersey for this wholesaler / distributor.

- Top-performing sales representative; achieved revenue growth annually.
- Drove up territory sales from $480,000 to $1.6 million, with 80% of revenue from wine sales.
- Demonstrated expertise in building brands on premise; effectively billboarded niche brands in restaurants.
- Initiated and implemented wine education seminars at client sites to boost wait staffs' knowledge and increase sales.

■ **SALES AND MARKETING CONSULTANT, International Beverages, Hanley, NJ** 1982 - 1987

Represented small / niche wine and beer brands throughout New Jersey as a sales representative with a small family-owned beer and wine distribution company; specialized in sales to on-premise establishments.

- Consistently achieved status as top sales representative out of ten.
- Opened 180 accounts, including four large casinos, and serviced 300 accounts.
- Guided retail and wholesale accounts in devising new marketing and pricing strategies, leading to increased sales.
- Collaborated in the design of a warehouse ramp system and an improved restaurant delivery system.

## PROFESSIONAL DEVELOPMENT / EDUCATION

Windows of the World Wine Course ■ Korbrand Wine Training Seminar ■ New Jersey Sommelier Wine Course
Associate's Degree in Business Administration, 1979 ■ Somerset County College, Branchburg, NJ

## INTERESTS

Aerobatic Flying ■ Piloting ■ Backcountry Hiking and Skiing

**178**

**Combination.** *Rhoda Kopy, Toms River, New Jersey*

A pair of thick-thin lines enclose the profile section, which includes areas of expertise. In the Experience section, paragraphs show duties, and bullets mark achievements.

# KAROL J. GRAVES

111 South Division Street • Morenci, Michigan 49286
(517) 587-4512

## PROFILE

Eleven years of experience in the financial industry with expertise in client sales and service, personnel management and community development. Diplomatic negotiator with excellent verbal and written communication skills. Uphold and maintain the highest standards of ethics and integrity in all business and personal dealings.

## EXPERIENCE

Social Bank, Ann Arbor, Michigan
**Sales Manager** December 1994-Present

- Develop and manage tactical sales plan to enhance the sales and service activities of ten direct reports.
- Establish, cultivate and grow portfolio of profitable client relationships.
- Promote commercial loan, deposit and investment products through an aggressive sales calling initiative.

**Client Sales Specialist** March 1994-November 1994

- Served as primary point of contact for providing financial products and services to existing portfolio of clients.
- Prospected and developed new consumer client relationships.
- Identified additional client needs and coordinated with appropriate products, services and bank personnel.

**Mortgage Sales Administration** 1992-1994

- Served as sales liaison between Social Mortgage Company and Social Bank personnel and customer base.
- Oversaw closings of approved real estate loans through final disbursement of funds.
- Fully trained mortgage originator.

Second Federal Savings Bank, Arbor Springs, Michigan
**Senior Mortgage Loan Sale Representative** 1991-1992

- Implemented efficient formation of securities for sale into the secondary market.
- Coordinated verification, tracking and efficient delivery of trades performed by the department.
- Negotiated sale of mortgage-backed securities with government bond traders.

Trust Savings Bank, Britton, Michigan
**Training Manager/Personnel Assistant** 1990-1991

- Designed, developed and implemented in-house training and development program; facilitated regularly scheduled instructional sessions for bank personnel.
- Created and administered specialized teller training program.
- Supported personnel function by executing payroll and cafeteria plan functions, as well as benefit billings and employee orientations.

## EDUCATION

Southern Michigan University, Coldwater, Michigan
**Bachelor of Science, Special Education and Business Education** December 1989
***Magna Cum Laude***

## MEMBERSHIP ORGANIZATIONS

- Leadership Ypsilanti
- Ypsilanti Chamber of Commerce
- SMU Alumni Association
- Golden Key
- Alexander Graham Bell Association
- United Methodist Church

***Excellent personal and professional references available upon request.***

**179**

**Combination.** *Christina M. Popa, Adrian, Michigan*

A resume for an individual who has worked for three banks since graduation and has worked her way up to Sales Manager for her current employer. Round bullets show duties and achievements.

# ROSA A. WATERS

156 Main Court
Virginia Beach, Virginia 23466
804 • 604 • 3058

**OBJECTIVE**

To secure a responsible and challenging position in managed health care, national accounts management or institutional sales combined with research study placements where my extensive experience will benefit the employer and offer an opportunity for personal and continued professional growth.

**SUMMARY of QUALIFICATIONS**

- Over twelve years experience in the pharmaceutical sales field effectively analyzing individual departmental and institutional sales needs; rapidly promoted through the pharmaceutical sales field.
- Effectively communicate and interact with medical and paramedical personnel; able to translate technical complicated information into readily understood data and concepts.
- Plan and organize data, programs, and resources to meet situational objectives while demonstrating a high degree of self-motivation, creativity and initiative to attain results within an independent environment.
- Solid interpersonal skills; effectively establish myself as a credible, reliable resource for peers, supervisors, and customers.
- Positively motivated and influenced the thinking and behavior of others.

**PROFESSIONAL EXPERIENCE**

**XYZ Corporation**, Pleasant Grove, Connecticut 1994-**Present**
Digital Communications Recording Systems Division
Area Sales Manager, Virginia Beach Branch

**Rich Laboratories**, Nowhere, New Jersey 1979-1993
Pharmaceutical Representative, Central Division
Senior Territory Manager, Boston, Eastern Division

**Interim Employment**: Pharmacy Technician - First Aid Pharmacy Corporation, Plainview, Virginia
Retail Sales - East of Eden, Virginia Beach, Virginia, Bow & Arrow Ltd, Freeport, Maine

**ACHIEVEMENTS**

- Recognized by Corporate Sales Manager for initiatives in sales department feedback and suggestions based on my evaluation of the needs of the health-care professional, the pharmaceutical representative, and the pharmaceutical company.
- Performance ranking of #1 or #2 representative for the last twelve years. Considered by managers as a *role model* for divisions and region.
- Achieved exceptionally fast market share penetration for products such as Rocephin and Versed.
- Recipient of multiple President's Achievement Awards (1985, 1986, 1987). Also received the President's Achievement Award Ring.

**Other interests and experiences include** Basic Life Support and First Aid Instructor for the American Heart Association and American Red Cross through a vocational institute.

**EDUCATION**

**Bachelor of Science**, University of Smithson, Wisconsin, 1979.
Additional educational requirements met with increasing challenges and responsibilities.

**REFERENCES AVAILABLE UPON REQUEST**

**180**

**Combination.** *Anne G. Kramer, Virginia Beach, Virginia*

With a dynamic personality and an excellent background, this person was thought overqualified. The pharmaceutical industry was targeted, and this resume was sent to state drug companies.

**ALAN FREEBERG**

**765 E. 39th Street • New York, NY 10016 • (212) 889-7645**

**PROFILE**

- Dedicated Sales Manager with over 8 years of successful sales and sales management experience with rapid promotions and responsibilities.
- Consistently exceeded quota and won numerous company awards.
- Generated and expanded business through establishing an excellent reputation.
- Excellent Sales Manager who can train and motivate a powerful sales team for enhanced productivity and profitability.

**EXPERIENCE**

**DESMOND CORPORATION,** New York, NY 1987-Present
105 branch offices throughout the U.S. and $425 million in annual sales volume.

Rapidly advanced through the company from Sales Rep to Field Sales Manager and District Sales Manager for high volume Manhattan territory.

Major Sales Accomplishments include

- Qualified twice for Circle of Excellence (top revenue group in company).
- Qualified for top 5 sales reps in company (out of 480 reps); 4th in revenue, 5th in sales.
- Selected as Most Valuable Player in sales district.
- Led the Manhattan office with the most sales and revenue in its history.
- Ranked #1 in the company for the month of January.
- Qualified 6 times for the company conference.

**DISTRICT SALES MANAGER—MANHATTAN TERRITORY** (6/94-PRESENT)
**FIELD SALES MANAGER—MANHATTAN TERRITORY** (6/93-6/94)

- Supervise, train and evaluate a team of 9 sales reps, generating a total sales volume of $2.5 million annually.
- Consistently exceeding quotas for territory Exceeded 130% of sales quota in second year as Field Sales Manager.
- Recruit and hire sales staff; conduct all field and classroom training and motivational seminars.
- Develop and implement business/activity plans and oversee prospect management for territory.
- Assumed additional responsibilities for Manhattan District Office upon promotion to District Sales Manager. Oversee all administrative and operational matters, with final authority and P & L accountability, including funds allocation, budgeting, and vendor relations.

**SALES REPRESENTATIVE— MANHATTAN TERRITORY** (11/88-6/93)

- Developed/serviced corporate accounts throughout Manhattan territory.
- Generated leads through cold calling and canvassing; solicited referrals from accountants, bankers, and client base.
- Prepared detailed proposals, conducted sales presentations, and negotiated client contracts.
- Gained detailed product knowledge and comprehensive understanding of sales techniques through completion of twelve week intensive training program at company headquarters.
- Followed through on vital aspects of account sales and service; functioned as key contact for client service issues and problems.

**EDUCATION** **State University of New York at Stony Brook**
B.A. in Business Administration, 1988

**REFERENCES** Furnished on request.

**181**

**Combination.** *Etta Barmann, New York, New York*

Accomplishments are stressed over duties for this District Sales Manager, who "grew with the company." To avoid repetition, the writer grouped together the duties of the manager positions.

# Timothy P. Joyce

777 North Main Street
Cincinnati, Ohio 45222
(513) 555-7777

**OBJECTIVE**

Vice President of Sales or equivalent.

**PROFILE**

Highly motivated **sales management professional** with a strong track record of successful sales and account development. Proven ability to select, train, and motivate sales staff to achieve ambitious goals.

Strategic planner skilled at both short- and long-range goal setting. Strong ability to accomplish objectives by focusing on essential activities.

Effective communicator with excellent relationship-building skills.

**PROFESSIONAL EXPERIENCE**

**Sales Manager** • NATIONAL OFFICE SUPPLY, Cincinnati, Ohio — 1993-Present

Direct a 12-member sales force in the Northern Kentucky/Southwestern Ohio area in the sale of office products and supplies to commercial accounts of all sizes.

*Sales Management*

- Instrumental in invigorating an organization with flat sales for the previous five years. Increased sales 300% in two years ($2.4 million to $8 million).
- Office recognized for largest sales increase in the past two years among 80 branch offices and 33 distribution centers nationwide.
- Pioneered innovative recruiting program on college campuses.
- Expanded sales to existing client base and established new accounts, including 4 very large accounts with annual sales in excess of $1 million each.

*Staff Development*

- Selected, hired, trained, coached and managed highly motivated individuals and gave them the tools and training necessary to succeed.
- Direct sales staff in forecasting and setting sales goals. Focus on the individual skills and needs of each account executive, executing an individual strategy for each.
- Encourage sales through creative incentives while relying primarily upon the professionalism and self-motivation of sales staff.

*Customer Relations*

- Promote positive ongoing customer relationships and serve as a problem-solver and resource to customers.
- Communicate to sales staff a focus on customer service and communication.

**Account Executive** • EXPRESS COMPUTER SUPPLY, INC., Cincinnati, Ohio — 1983-93

- Ranked #5 among 60 account executives in sales to commercial accounts.
- Consistently achieved annual sales increases in the 15-20% range.
- Developed territory from ground up and expanded sales from zero to $2 million.
- Developed accounts through a unique presentation to each prospect and a commitment to service, follow-up, and meeting customer needs.
- Successfully regained several large accounts that had been lost to competitors due to pricing issues.

**EDUCATION**

Bachelor of Business Administration, 1983 • UNIVERSITY OF NOTRE DAME, South Bend, Indiana
Studies toward MBA degree; completed all but 2 courses • XAVIER UNIVERSITY, Cincinnati, Ohio

Learning International training — PSS (Professional Selling Skills); PSS Coaching; ADS (Account Development Strategies); Building Interpersonal Relationships; Leadership Skills

Team Building for Managers — National Office Supply corporate headquarters, Atlanta, Georgia

Willing to relocate. References provided upon request.

**182**

**Combination.** *Louise Kursmark, Cincinnati, Ohio*

The Objective states "Vice President" because the successful person wants to advance, not seek a lower position. To avoid a lengthy list, the achievements are grouped under three subheadings.

## ANDREA BETH CONNOLLY

115 West 81st Street
New York, New York 11228
Phone: (212) 222-1211 • Beeper: (917) 123-5566

**OBJECTIVE**

Northeast Regional Sales Director position

**PROFILE**

- Senior sales executive with expertise in marketing, developing new accounts, and leading successful sales teams.
- Specialized knowledge of automated window and door mechanisms.
- Talent for negotiating, preparing custom proposals, and securing new contracts.
- Bilingual English-Spanish with experience conducting international business.
- Computer literate with proficiency in Microsoft Word, Excel, and PowerPoint.

**EXPERIENCE**

**ADVANCED MECHANISMS,** Cranbury, NJ
*Distributor for Apex Technology products*

**International Sales Manager,** 1993 to 1997

- Handled $2 million accounts for export to South America and the Caribbean. Prepared proposals and estimates. Delivered presentations on automated products. Trained new sales representatives.
  - Increased company's international market share by 55%.
  - Secured more than 200 new corporate contracts.
  - Opened 5 lucrative international territories.
  - Led 10-member team to devise strategic marketing plan.
  - Delivered keynote address at International Technologies Convention.

**Local Sales Manager,** 1991 to 1993

- Designed and presented proposals for local companies.
- Earned promotion based on sales ability, dedication, and product knowledge.

**Installation Helper,** 1990 to 1991

- Assisted with automated installations and learned technical aspects of business.
- Received commendation letters for efficiency in responding to service calls.

**WALKER GIFT SHOP,** Woodbridge, NJ
*Mall-based retail store selling gifts and novelties*

**Manager,** 1988 to 1990

- Recruited to manage 2000-square foot store and improve declining sales. Led a team of 10 sales staff.
  - Increased sales by 5% in 1991, 7% in 1992, 15% in 1993, and 12% in 1994.
  - Eliminated unpopular products and set-up inventory tracking system for $300,000 in merchandise.
  - Reorganized displays and store layout to maximize appeal.

**EDUCATION**

**NEW YORK UNIVERSITY,** New York, NY
**Bachelor of Science in Marketing,** 1988

*Professional Courses:*

- Winning Proposals
- Making Presentations
- Motivational Techniques
- Sales Tactics
- Ethics in Sales
- Marketing Techniques

**183**

**Combination.** *Kim Isaacs, Jackson Heights, New York*

This person was applying for a job at Apex Technology, mentioned in the Experience section. The Profile shows her main qualifications for the position. Smaller bullets show her achievements.

## WILLIAM T. GREGORY

1 Scenic Highway | Lawrenceville, Georgia 30246 | (404) 978-8888

**SUMMARY OF QUALIFICATIONS**

Twenty years experience in **Sales and Management** with focus on MRO (Maintenance, Repair, and Operating) products and equipment. Excellent interpersonal, analytical, and leadership skills. Ability to administer multiple responsibilities, set priorities, and communicate ideas to others. Enthusiastic, creative, and committed.

- Design and implement sales strategies to develop accounts, ensure services consistently meet or exceed standards and specifications, and enhance profitability.

  ✓ ***Increased sales from $70,000 to $1,900,000 between 1977 and 1990.***
  ✓ ***Ranked in top 10% of sales force for six consecutive years, 1985 to 1990.***

- Define sales, operations, and management objectives; outline constraints; and implement appropriate actions to meet specifications and deadlines. Perform routine analysis and comparisons to document status of operations and programs.
- Monitor factors impacting day-to-day and long-range operations. Recognize and mitigate concerns associated with revisions in operations and program management.
- Prepare forecasts; employ long-range planning strategies.
- Function as liaison between sales force and suppliers; establish positive rapport with individuals of diverse backgrounds and professional levels.
- Generate high levels of productivity, customer satisfaction, and compliance with industry standards through emphasis on team building and ownership.
- Negotiate customer contracts; respond to questions and problems; detail and result oriented.
- Manage sales operations as a working supervisor; directed, motivated, and evaluated staff of thirteen. Trained and directed the growth of two Market Development Specialists.

**EXPERIENCE**

SAFETY FIRST, INC., New York, New York — 1977 to Present
*Subsidiary of Well-Known-Leader-In-Field*
***District Sales Manager,*** *Atlanta, Georgia 1993 to Present*
***Manager, Sales Development,*** *Richmond, Virginia 1991 to 1993*
***National Accounts Manager,*** *Richmond, Virginia 1991*
***Territory Manager,*** *Philadelphia, Pennsylvania 1977 to 1990*

**AFFILIATIONS**

American Society of Safety Engineers
American Industrial Hygiene Association

**EDUCATION**

EMBRY-RIDDLE AERONAUTICAL UNIVERSITY, Daytona Beach, Florida
***Bachelor of Science Degree in Aviation Maintenance Management***

184

**Combination.** *Carol Lawrence, Savannah, Georgia*

Check marks in the Summary draw attention to exceptional sales achievements. Instead of telling about the duties of each position at the same company, this Summary avoids needless repetition.

## CHRIS A. SMITH

400 Anywhere Street • Anywhere, USA 00000
(555) 555-5555

**OBJECTIVE**

Dynamic, energetic professional seeks Sales/Marketing position with a company that will benefit from my proven ability to generate new business, and service and develop existing accounts.

**SUMMARY OF QUALIFICATIONS**

- Sixteen years experience in public relations, sales, and marketing
- Excellent organizational and analytic skills; exceptional attention to detail; quick grasp of technical product and service
- Ability to create and present an excellent image of the company and its services
- Coordinate and communicate well with clientele and management at all levels
- Strong interpersonal and communication skills to establish and maintain client relationship

**PROFESSIONAL EXPERIENCE**

ANYBODY CO., Anytown, USA — October 0000 - July 0000
*Territorial Sales Manager*
- Serviced all existing and new customers in a seven-county region in Northeast Anywhere
- Made cold calls and field visits to new customers, significantly increasing accounts
- Directly responsible for completion of sales transaction from inception to final payment, including shipment, customer service, and quality assurance

ANYCOMPANY INTERNATIONAL, Anytown, USA — April 0000 - October 0000
*Sales Representative/Inspector*
**Achievements**
- **Received Top 10 Sales Recognition Award (several times)**
- **Received Top Regional Sales (November 0000)**

BEST COMPANY, INC., Anytown, USA — January 0000 - April 0000
*Sales/Customer Service*
- Daily contact with medical professionals and staff, setting appointments and demonstrating medical equipment
- Attended ophthalmological trade shows throughout the United States promoting the Company's full line of medical instrumentation
- Directly responsible for customer service, marketing, quality control and maintaining good customer relations

TOWNSHIP OF ANYWHERE, Anywhere, USA — April 0000 - January 0000
*Administrative Officer of the Planning Board/Board of Adjustment*
*Zoning Officer*
- Organized and administered all Planning Board and Zoning Board matters
- Maintained, inspected, and enforced all zoning regulations of the County Municipal Code
- Liaison between town officials and citizens to resolve matters in a quick and effective manner
- Attended all Planning Board and Board of Adjustment meetings every month

**Achievement**
- **Received Outstanding Service Award for the Township of Anywhere - January 0000**

**EDUCATION**

Bachelor of Science, Management — 0000
University of Anywhere, Anywhere, USA

**ACTIVITIES**

Management Club - President, Vice-President, Member

*References available upon request*

185

**Combination.** *M. Carol Heider, Tampa, Florida*

A wide double line separates the contact information from the rest of the resume. Company names are uppercase, and job titles are in italic. Boldfacing makes the achievements stand out.

confidential

# N. Jonathan Coster

1715 Normand Drive
Memphis, Tennessee 37100

[615] 555-5555
njcoster@msn.com

WHAT I BRING TO EDUTECH AS A **DIRECTOR OF SALES AND TRAINING:**

- **Skill** that penetrates and holds tough new markets.
- **Experience** that guides people to higher goals.
- **Knowledge** that keeps production costs low.

RECENT WORK HISTORY WITH EXAMPLES OF SUCCESS:

- June 96 – Present: **National Sales Manager**, Education Technology, Plano, Texas
  *Education Technology is the national leader in bringing the newest technologies into the educational market. Annual sales projection: $2M.*
  - Report directly to CEO. Supervise 20 sales professionals.
  - Hired away by president to build national sales force from scratch. Single-handedly created our marketing plan, budgets, territories, quotas, cost of sales, pricing, sales manual, and presentations. ***Payoffs:*** Twenty sales professionals **covering 33 states in just 90 days**.
  - Penetrated market dominated by single competitor who enjoyed 18-month lead. We were unknowns. Our products cost four times his. ***Payoffs:* Beating sales projections by 20%**. Now at 70% of quota despite late start in very short buying season.
  - Expanded our market vertically through strong presentations to senior executives and administrators. ***Payoffs:* Customers'** central decision makers now **"pre-selling"** our products and services.

- November 89 – June 96: **District Manager,** Reference Division *promoted to* **Midwest Sales Manager,** Electronic Learning Division *promoted to* **Southeastern Regional Manager,** Instructional Materials Division, Encyclopaedia Britannica Educational Corporation, Chicago, Illinois
  *Britannica is the former global industry leader in reference materials for libraries and media centers. Annual sales: $35M.*
  - Sold new curriculum products at 10 times the unit cost of "tried and true" traditional materials offered by competitors. Proved cost-per-student attractive. Positioned our lines as key to the Federal and state funding on which our customers lived. Increased student achievement and boosted teacher efficiency. ***Payoffs:* Beat** as many as **15 competitors to win large sales** in three of four state adoption presentations.
  - Turned around sales in economically depressed territory after seven other professionals failed to make their goals for five years. Targeted the right market segments. ***Payoffs:*** Topped six other publishers. Made sales targets and **sold entire catalog** product line. My first job in educational sales.

- February 86 – November 89: **Director of Admissions**, Southeastern Paralegal Institute, Nashville, Tennessee
  *Southeastern Paralegal is the only school in the Southeast sanctioned by the American Bar Association.*
  - Built admissions department from the ground up. Coordinated placement of our students as interns with prospective employers. ***Payoffs:* Increased enrollment 333%**.

confidential

186

**Combination.** *Donald P. Orlando, Montgomery, Alabama*

This candidate "sought to build upon his solid track record selling educationally related material." Because of "his background and energy he lined up interviews for positions at senior

confidential

N. Jonathan Coster | Director of Sales and Training | [615] 555-5555

ADDITIONAL WORK EXPERIENCE:

- January 84 – February 86: **Director of Admissions, Corporate Programs Administrator** and Faculty Member, Davidson Educational Center, Nashville Tennessee
- May 83 – Feb 84: **Field Representative**, United States Chamber of Commerce, Washington, D.C.
- May 81 – May 83: **Institutional Sales Manager** and **Operations Manager,** Page and Taylor's Sporting Goods, Clarksville, Tennessee
- Aug 76 – May 81: **Academic Department Head** and Assistant Athletic Director, Houston County School System, Erin, Tennessee

AWARDS:

- Seven consecutive memberships in President's Club (120% of sales goals) or Honors Club (110% of goals), Encyclopaedia Britannica Educational Corporation.
- "Rookie of the Year" for highest grossing new salesperson, Encyclopaedia Britannica Educational Corporation.
- Five time winner as "Instructor of the Quarter," Davidson Educational Center.

PROFESSIONAL DEVELOPMENT AND EDUCATION:

- Management Internship, Encyclopaedia Britannica, 91 – 92 *Chosen by VP for Corporate Planning as one of five from 300 eligibles to be groomed for more managerial responsibility.*
- **Practica for College Recruiting Professionals**, College Administrators' Institute, Harvard University, Boston, Massachusetts, 86 – 87 *Passed competitive examination and interviews to attend this program fully paid by my employer.*
- Pursued M.S., **Educational Administration**, Appalachian State University, Boone, North Carolina, **GPA 3.8**, 78 – 79
- Pursued M.S., **Educational Administration**, Austin Peay State University, Clarksville, Tennessee, 76 – 78
- B.S., **History** and **English** (double major), Middle Tennessee State University, Murfreesboro, Tennessee, **cum laude**, 76

COMPUTER LITERACY:

- Expert: Internet search techniques, Decide Right (decision analysis software), MAC OS, Write Now, Inspiration, Publish It Now, MultiMedia Level III
- Proficient: HTML, Java, Winsock, Excel, Windows 3.x, Windows 95, ACT!, Word for Windows, WordPerfect 6.1, Quicken, MS Money, PowerPoint

SPECIAL SKILLS

- Strong background in technical writing and the drafting of educational proposals and grant applications

confidential *Page two*

levels quickly." What he must have taken to his interviews was this sophisticated resume. Note the phone symbol in the contact information; the special bullets; the use of boldface, italic, and bold italic; the small caps; the header on page two; and correct capitalization of software names.

# JONATHAN F. GOLDBERG

3-A Tiffany Court ❐ ❐ ❐ Lansdale, PA 00000 ❐ ❐ ❐ [000] 000-0000

## CAREER SUMMARY

- Dynamic telecommunications executive with over nine years industry experience, six of those years in the burgeoning cellular telecommunications marketplace.
- Strong entrepreneurial spirit to manage start-up operations, develop major accounts, initiate cost effective procedures and expand on customer services to maximize competitive edge.
- Extensive knowledge in the areas of:
  - Switching equipment and hardware for regular and cellular telephony from a wide range of manufacturers.
  - T1 and proprietary network hookups.
  - Capability and limitation of all long distance carrier products.
  - Security technology to avert air piracy of user PINs.

## PROFESSIONAL EXPERIENCE

EXCELL MOBILE COMMMUNICATIONS, Philadelphia, PA 1992-Present

***Regional Sales Manager** for the most profitable of Excell's markets, extending from Philadelphia to New York City, producing annual revenues of $30-50 million per year. Control a $16 million budget and oversee 34 direct reports responsible for direct sales, telemarketing and service functions. Personally service large volume accounts.*

- Increased sales over 300% within one year of assuming position in one of the country's most difficult to manage markets due to geographically convoluted boundaries.
- Overcame higher than average overlapping competition from AT&T Wireless Services (formerly Bell Atlantic and Nynex), McCaw, Metrophone and other national resellers to capture 50% of area's cellular users (population area of two million).
- Restructured ineffective sales force into a highly productive and motivated team of three major account executives and 15 sales representatives, operating at 110% of quota to date.
- Negotiated and secured purchasing agreements for user equipment from manufacturers such as Motorola, NEC, Ericsson, Uniden, Mitsubishi and others.
- Conducted all training seminars for supervisors and sales representatives.
- Created more efficient administrative systems which ensured tight control over costs, provided for equitable sales compensation, and positive gains in customer, employee and sales distributor satisfaction.
- Introduced mobile servicing of accounts that eventually developed into the area's first installation and service center.
- Acted as area liaison for the AT&T Wireless Services national accounts program, which sets up cellular service with Fortune 100 companies throughout the country.

More ❐❐❐

187

**Combination.** *Melanie A. Noonan, West Paterson, New Jersey*

The person's mid-sized wireless telecommunications company was "about to be acquired by a giant in the field." Under new ownership, he wanted to continue in high-level sales. To grab and

# JONATHAN F. GOLDBERG

❐ Continued ❐

STRATOS CELLULAR, Richmond, VA 1990-1992

***General Manager*** *in an entrepreneurial venture with three partners.*

- ❐ Built a cellular system from the ground up. This included arrangement of financing, set-up of towers, and purchase of switch and retail units, reaching an operational status in less than a year.
- ❐ Selected appropriate product mix based on analysis of market, and established and coordinated ordering procedures.
- ❐ Established, managed and trained a distribution network of 19, covering an area from Washington, DC to the Carolinas, and opened two free standing retail outlets in Virginia. Oversaw functions of cellular dealers, direct sales force, office support staff and customer service representatives.
- ❐ Designed customer rate plans, phone pricing schedules, distributor territorial borders, advertising/promotional campaigns, and all administrative procedures necessary for profitable operations.
- ❐ Positioned business to induce attractive offer from the Cellular One organization, netting a profit of $2 million.

SPRINT CORPORATION, New York, NY 1988-1990

***Account Representative*** *for a major long distance carrier.*

- ❐ Acquired various new, large volume corporate accounts through in depth analysis of their communication needs.
- ❐ Expanded the product mix, introducing upgrades to increase effectiveness and efficiency for existing accounts.

ISOTEC COMMUNICATIONS, New York, NY 1985-1987

***Sales Representative*** *for medium sized distributor of PBX systems that have a capacity of up to 400 lines.*

- ❐ Designed, coordinated and implemented hardware and software solutions to address specific telecommunication problem areas.
- ❐ Cultivated over 65 larger corporate accounts, achieving 140% of quota.
- ❐ Attained membership in President's Club for gaining additional percentage of market share in the industry.

## EDUCATION

**New York University**, New York, NY
Bachelor of Science in Business Administration 1986
*Major: Marketing* *Minor: Finance*

hold the reader's attention, the writer used a 3-D border echoed by similar 3-D bullets and subbullets. Furthermore, a 3-D font (with a different shadow direction) was used for the name in the contact information and for the section headings. Bold italic makes the job titles stand out.

# PETER A. PORTHKERRIS

0000 N. West • Anywhere, USA • Office (000) 000-0000

## EXPERTISE

**SALES / SALES MANAGEMENT** -- Thrive in fast-paced, competitive environments as evidenced by stellar sales performance in regional management and key account management with a leading Fortune 500 consumer products manufacturer. Strengths include recruiting, developing and motivating market dominant sales teams, as well as maximizing sales through effective merchandising, advertising, and account management skills.

**Highlights** as District Manager include increasing volume in excess of 44% in a multi-million dollar territory ... as Key Account Manager, boosted sales 163% and showed a 10-1 ROI for marketing funds.

## PROFESSIONAL EXPERIENCE

**FORTUNE 500 COMPANY** 12/91 to Present

**DISTRICT MANAGER** for six-state Western Area (1/94 to Present)

Promoted to manage high-volume district with sales in excess of $7.8 million. Plan and execute sales and marketing plans for accounts in California, Arizona, New Mexico, Nevada, Utah, and western Texas.

Implement district sales volume plans for sales budgets, profit, spending, and category goals (space, location, inventory, merchandising, distribution, pricing, promotion). Foster relationships with buyers and key retail personnel. Manage financial resources pertaining to salary budget, product development, and expense reports. Hire, train, and motivate six Territory Managers to achieve individual and management goals.

**Achievements:**

- Led sales team to attain district-wide increase from $4.9 million to $7.8 million in sales.
- Exceeded 1994 goal of 7% increase with a 21% increase and 1995 goal of 16% with a 42% increase.
- Reduced returns to net sales from 22% in 1993 to 7% in 1995 (below company standard of 14%).
- Personally developed and presented Category/Brand Analysis to national account, resulting in space increase to a consistent 4-ft. set in 114 stores, netting an incremental order of $220,000.
- Hired, developed, and promoted high profile Territory Manager to District Manager in just eight months.

**KEY ACCOUNT MANAGER / REGIONAL TRAINING MANAGER** (12/91 to 1/94)

Managed territory retail accounts to maximize existing sales opportunities and establish new product distribution in Division. Additionally accountable as Regional Training Manager for initial training of new Territory Managers in Washington, Oregon, and California.

**Achievements:**

- As Territory Manager, achieved 1992 net sales increase of 142% and 1993 net sales increase of 112%.
- Promoted in 1993 to manage large grocery (67 doors) key account; achieved first year net sales increase of 174%; designed all creative marketing and advertising programs for leading drug store account.
- Managed marketing funds of $80,000 per annum, showing a return on investment of as much as 10-1.

**188**

**Combination.** *Susan Britton Whitcomb, Fresno, California*

The bold horizontal line separates the contact information on the first page and serves as a header on the second page. The other horizontal lines point to the section headings and make

## Peter A. Porthkerris

Page Two

### Professional Experience

**Achievements (continued):**

- Established leadership role within district as presenter at district sales meetings; designed a Marketing Development program subsequently adopted for national use.
- Received top honors from Divisional Vice President for three consecutive years (an award reserved for 5-10 individuals nationwide).
- Presented and closed blanket purchase order programs with WalMart, resulting in over $139,000 in incremental business for the district.
- Representative list of accounts managed throughout tenure with company includes all major drug, grocery, wholesale, and mass merchandisers.

**THE CENTRAL COMPANY** 8/82 to 7/87

ACCOUNT SYSTEMS ANALYST

Managed, installed, and maintained systems for 85 commercial accounts.

- Increased customer retention through monitoring account activities and 24-hour availability.
- Developed system which reduced system installation by two full hours.
- Decreased time required for monthly inventory by three hours through use of database.

### Education

**Minnesota State University, Minneapolis** 1985 to 1989

- **B.S., Business Administration** (5/89)
- Concentration in **Marketing**

**United States Air Force** 3/84 to 6/90 reserves; 6/82 to 3/84 active

- Electrical Power Production Specialist Course
- 3700 Technical Training wing, Lamont AFB, Massachusetts (Honors Graduate)

**Fortune 500 Company Schools**

- Initial Training; Effective Public Speaking; Conceptual Selling Skills

### Computer Skills

WordPerfect 6.1, Quattro, Lotus 1-2-3, WordPerfect Presentations

### Interests

Continued educational advancement, travel, reading, painting, scuba diving, softball, golf, and snow skiing.

**References Provided Upon Request**

them easy to spot. Both the company names and the job positions are all uppercase, but underlining makes the positions stand out. "Achievements" side headings introduce impressive accomplishments of this individual. Small, right-pointing bullets help to unify the two pages.

## Peter R. Whitney

*640 West Bayside*
*Whitneyville, Maine 00000*
*(207) 555-5555*

### *Profile:*

Banking and financial management executive with over twenty years of progressive experience in Maine. Proven record of success with mergers and acquisitions, business development, and commercial lending. Broadly based exposure to consumer and commercial financial environments. Creative and effective problem solver with excellent written and oral communication skills. Demonstrated ability for meeting objectives. Team player with strong leadership abilities. Community leader.

### *Honors & Recognition:*

- *First recipient of the Volunteer Banker of the Year Award in 1990 from the Coastal Bankers Association.*
- *Malcolm Baldridge Project Leader for Coastal Bank of Maine's 1995 Assessment Application.*

### *Professional Experience:*

**COASTAL BANK OF MAINE, Machias, Maine** **1989 - Present**

***Sales Manager, Small Business Lending for Maine (1995 - Present)***

- Responsible for development of $250 million small business loan portfolio. Manage the sales process, marketing, and business development throughout the state of Maine. Oversee and direct the activities of 15 relationship managers from Kittery to Fort Kent.

***Senior Vice President / Area Sales Manager - Eastern District (1989 - Present)***
*(Eastern District is Coastal Bank of Maine's largest, most profitable and fastest growing district.)*

- Responsible for overall retail management of 16 office regional branch network. Maintain and service major commercial loan relationships and provide business development focus throughout region.
- Served as Project Leader of merger of existing banks to form one entity. Spearheaded the design and opening of new branches including Coastal Plaza. Project Leader in acquiring divested branches.
- Recognized by executive management for success in business development. Conduct presentations at state sales meetings. Maintain presence in the community through leadership on various boards and as a keynote speaker for community organizations.

**COASTAL BANK OF EASTERN MAINE, Machias, Maine** **1986 - 1989**

***Executive Vice President / Chief Operating Officer***

- Responsible for the day-to-day administrative management of the bank including the supervision of all branch managers and department heads. Oversaw the development of the branch system, including the functions related to establishing new banking offices within the market.
- Project leader role in the major acquisition of ten branch offices ($100 million in assets) purchased from Summit and Telstar Bank. Continued involvement in commercial lending function. Approximately $200 million asset size at time of consolidation.

**189**

**Combination.** *Joan M. Roberts, Bangor, Maine*

This candidate, "a bank executive, was being recruited by another financial institution," and he "needed his first resume in over twenty years." The prospective employer knew of him but

***Peter R. Whitney***

***Page Two***

**CITIZENS BANK OF EASTERN MAINE, Machias, Maine** **1978 - 1986**

***Senior Vice President / Branch Administrator (1982 - 1986)***

- Responsible for the supervision of branch office managers and insuring maximum operating efficiency and profitability of the branch system including the Financial Control Department of the Bank.
- Actively involved in the business development function, lending to and servicing private client accounts. Responsible for the bank investment portfolio. Instrumental in the development, management, and implementation of all automated systems.

***Vice President / Director of Personnel (1978 - 1981)***

- Assumed project leader position of Bank Merger Coordinator, organizing and directing the financial operations and personnel phases of the merger between Liberty National Bank in Ellsworth and Depositors Trust Company of Eastern Maine.
- Major responsibilities included personnel administration, municipal and commercial lending, and bank investment portfolio.

**CITIZENS BANK OF MACHIAS, Machias, Maine** **1976 - 1978**

***Vice President***

- Major responsibilities included personnel and operations administration, bank investment portfolio, and municipal and commercial lending. Second to President in all areas except loan administration. Assumed a major role in successfully reversing the negative earning trends in this bank.

**FREEDOM BANK IN ELLSWORTH, Ellsworth, Maine** **1969 - 1976**

***Vice President / Cashier (Treasurer) / Operation Officer / Management Trainee***

- Broad responsibilities included personnel and branch administration in addition to Cashier's duties. Considered a senior level management position with specific functional responsibilities including accounting, financial and regulatory reporting, internal audit, bank investments, budgeting, purchasing, and bank real estate. Responsible for all bank operations.

## *Education & Professional Development:*

**Harvard University, Boston, Massachusetts**
***Roberts' Graduate School of Banking***

**University of Coastal Maine, Machias, Maine**
***B.S. Business Administration; Major: Finance***

## *Community Involvement:*

*Bayside Healthcare - Strategic Planning Committee and Audit Committee*
*Coastal Hospital - Trustee / Executive Committee*
*Business Committee of 50 - Treasurer / Director*
*The Youth Foundation - Trustee / Investment Committee*
*Freedom Place, Inc. - Past President, Treasurer, and Director*
*Machias Halfway House - Past President, Treasurer and Director*
*Bayside YMCA - Past President and Director, currently Investment Committee Member*

wanted to know the specifics of his background. He wanted his resume to "capture the progression of his career and his accomplishments." The individual "is now president of the bank that recruited him." Note the record of employment from 1969 and where italic is used in this resume.

**EDWARD G. LONG**
**1000 Willbanks Drive**
**Dallas, Texas 75200**
**(214) 555-3333**

**HIGHLIGHTS OF QUALIFICATIONS / ACCOMPLISHMENTS**

- **Highly efficient, profit-conscious professional** with 14 years of rapid progression in the **hospitality / food service industry**.
- **Top Performer**. Proven track record of increasing sales, market share, and profit margins while controlling costs in highly competitive market.
- Excellent **organizational**, **time management**, **problem-solving**, and **team building** abilities.
- Full P&L, cost-control, and personnel development/management responsibilities.
- Exceptional **customer service**, **communication**, and **interpersonal** skills; establish and maintain positive rapport with staff, customers/clients, and business professionals.
- **Regional Task Force member**; implemented new "Customer-Driven Menu Cycle."
- **Selected as Regional Representative for Imperial's Menu Task Force.**
- **Instrumental in installation and implementation of Imperial's FoodCo Program.**
- Served as **District Safety Coordinator** for Fiscal Year 1991; no LTIFs.
- **Negotiated/finalized multiple-year contracts with clients.**
- **Successfully implemented labor productivity, capital coverage, and growth initiative to Southern Region.**
- **Achieved score of over 95% on Associate Satisfaction Survey.**

**PROFESSIONAL EXPERIENCE**

**IMPERIAL EDUCATION SERVICES** **1988 – Present**

**District Manager In Residence, Dallas, Texas** (11/94–Present)

- Efficiently manage six accounts in North Texas and Oklahoma; independently opened three accounts.
- Manage annual sales budget of $11 million and annual profit budget of $275,000.
- Direct six food service directors and nine food service managers.

**Food Service Director–Dallas Junior College, Dallas, Texas** (12/93–11/94)

- Relocated to Dallas to open new account.
- Responsible for resident dining, retail, catering, and concessions and a staff of 60-65.
- Generated $1.3 million sales revenue annually.

**Resident Dining Director–North Texas University, Denton, Texas** (08/92–12/93)

- Relocated to Denton as member of Imperial's opening management team.
- Trained and directed staff of 80 engaged in serving multi-meal plan formats to 1,000 residents.
- Assisted in establishment of budget for account.
- Instrumental in upgrading facility.
- Provided services to faculty in dining hall.

**190**

**Combination.** *Ann Klint, Tyler, Texas*

Each page has a double-line border, shading within the border, and a thin-thick line that separates the contact information from the rest of the resume and serves as part of a header at

**EDWARD G. LONG** **Page Two**

**IMPERIAL EDUCATION SERVICES** (Continued)

**Food Service Director–Renton Community College, Renton, Washington** (12/90–08/92)

- Directed full-time and part-time staff of 40.
- Oversaw retail operation, resident dining program, catering, and vending.
- Served as District Safety Coordinator; performed account audits; made presentations at safety meetings; served as resource to district; created/distributed monthly safety brochures; promoted safety on campus.

**Unit Manager–University of California, Santa Cruz, California** (1989–1990)

- Supervised production manager and full-time/part-time staff of 60.
- Responsible for unit feeding of 525 residents.

**Production Manager–University of California, Santa Cruz, California** (1988–1989)

- Supervised full-time and part-time staff of 60; oversaw daily food production.

**HAMILTON, INC., Little Rock, Arkansas** **08/87 - 08/88**

**District Manager**

- Trained and directed restaurant managers of five restaurants; generated approximately $7 million in sales annually.
- Controlled costs which significantly increased profit margin.

**PROFESSIONAL DEVELOPMENT**

IMPERIAL MANAGEMENT TRAINING PROGRAM

**American Correspondence – Hotel & Restaurant Management Training**

**ADA Training**

**Ethics Training**

**Analytical Tools**

**Management Seminar**

**Principles of Management**

**Introduction to Management**

~ ~ ***References Furnished Upon Request*** ~ ~

the top of page two. Large diamond bullets point to qualifications and accomplishments in boldface in the Highlights section. Small diamond bullets call attention to responsibilities and achievements in the Professional Experience section. Boldface makes the job titles stand out.

1215 W. Hudson Avenue
Tampa, Florida 33614

# JAMES L. CONNOR

(813) 000-0000

## SALES MANAGEMENT / MERCHANDISING

**Sales/Marketing ◆ Wholesale/Retail Operations ◆ Personnel Management**

### CAREER PROFILE

Fast-track promotions through a series of increasingly responsible positions. Advanced rapidly via exhibiting high-level performance resulting in consistent improvements in sales, earnings and customer satisfaction. Instituted conceptual and creative approaches to marketing and merchandising. Goal-directed and detail-oriented with well-developed business savvy; successfully implemented effective short and long-term strategic plans resulting in strong, sustainable bottomline results. Able to motivate others and maximize productivity.

### AREAS OF EXPERTISE

- Operations Management
- Financial Management
- Customer Relations
- Retail Buying
- Store Design / Set-up
- Personnel Supervision
- Staff / Management Training
- Inventory Control
- Advertising / Media Buying
- Promotions
- Forecasting
- Merchandising

### CAREER HIGHLIGHTS

**Retail Sales Management**

Proactive ***Store Manager*** with demonstrated ability to consistently maintain or exceed profitability status through strategic planning; executed cost-saving incentives; structured purchasing and inventory controls; created and implemented promotions; and exercised prudent decision-making skills. Strong communication and interpersonal skills contributed to establishing long-term vendor relations and effectively supervising up to 40 employees.; performed all human resource functions and strengthened employee relations. Record of successfully growing business and commitment to quality customer service led to promotion as ***Area Supervisor*** involving a broader scope of managerial responsibilities, in conjunction with overseeing retail operations of 12 store locations. Applied experience gained as Store Manager to identify and assess needs, problem-solve, troubleshoot, increase productivity and profitability, and facilitate smooth-running operations.

**Wholesale/Distribution Operations**

***Area Sales Manager*** with full accountability for overseeing 15 truck routes in a sizable territory consisting of the Sarasota, Lakeland and Tampa Bay areas. Attention to detail and well-developed organizational skills contributed to efficiently prioritizing and coordinating service requirements for retail grocery chains, convenience stores, and independent food markets. Managed 20 employees including two supervisors.

**191**

**Combination.** *Diane McGoldrick, Tampa, Florida*

A resume for a victim of downsizing. A thin-thick line and a thick-thin line below it enclose the headline and make it stand out. A second thick-thin line is part of a header on page two. The

## JAMES L. CONNOR

Page Two

**Marketing / Merchandising**

Extremely pivotal role as ***Merchandiser / Director of Marketing / Buyer*** for 400+ convenience stores. Spearheaded all aspects of advertising, visual merchandising, promotions, buying, pricing, and P&L activities. Provided visionary leadership in organizing new store grand openings, promoting optimum product mix sales strategies, and orchestrating point-of sale merchandising to launch monthly promotions. Visible position requiring interaction with media to coordinate television/radio commercials. Recognized for contributions to reengineering store design that became prototype for future locations. Chaired Buying Committee.

**Personnel Management / Training**

An efficient manager of people with proven ability to successfully motivate others. Learned by doing and effectively integrated hands-on experience with formal and on-the-job training programs to generate progressive team development.

**EMPLOYMENT HISTORY**

HENRY'S FOODS - Tampa, Florida **1988 - 1996**
**Area Sales Manager** (1993 - 1996)
**Branch Manager** (1988 - 1993)

CIRCLE K CORPORATION - Tampa, Florida Division **1972 - 1988**
*(formerly Shop & Go)*
**Merchandiser/Director of Marketing/Buyer** (1982 - 1988)
**Area Supervisor** (1975 - 1982)
**Store Manager** (1974 - 1975)
**Assistant Store Manager** (1973 - 1974)
**Clerk** (1972 - 1973)

**Achievements**

➔ **Recipient of Award for Outstanding Achievement in Loss Prevention**

**EDUCATION**

***Food Merchandising Certificate*** CORNELL UNIVERSITY
***Business Administration*** SUMTER COMMUNITY COLLEGE

**SUPPLEMENTAL TRAINING**

Completed numerous hours of comprehensive training in the following:

Practical Supervision for Managing Modern Food Stores
Convenience Store Merchandising I & II

bulleted areas of expertise in three columns can be easily altered to target a specific career, field, or job position. Information in the Career Highlights section is organized under four bold and underlined side headings. Bold italic helps job titles stand out in the text under these headings.

Dept. XYZ/797 Job Code 00/00

JAMES N. OVERTON
14403 Lake Ellen Cove
Tampa, Florida 33618
(813) 000-0000

MARKETING AND SALES MANAGEMENT / TELECOMMUNICATIONS INDUSTRY

Expertise in sales/marketing of complex products and technologies within high-growth, emerging, mature and competitive business markets.

CAREER PROFILE

- Senior Sales/Marketing Account Executive with an accomplished career span reflecting top-producing, sales leadership in progressively responsible positions; aggressively capitalize on opportunities to expand/gain market share and increase revenues.

- Spearhead management of multi-state territories/large account base; key role in cultivating high-profit, long-term relationships; contract negotiations; product/service/price presentations and "closing the sale."

- Execute customer-driven initiatives focused on developing product knowledge, structuring education/training programs and planning/ implementing the re-engineering of high-tech systems.

AREAS OF DEMONSTRATED SKILL

- Key Account Relationship Management
- Sales Cycle Management
- Sales Training and Development
- Strategic Sales and Market Planning
- Budgeting and Forecasting
- Competitive New Product Launch
- Pricing and Service Management

PERSONAL STRENGTHS

- Results-oriented, innovative idea generator with keen analytical ability, adept in tracking industry trends; astute at recognizing areas in need of improvement, with the vision to develop and institute applicable solutions.

- Proactive leader with competent decision-making skills; able to take charge and facilitate directives that achieve strong/sustainable results. Work well under pressure and against deadlines.

- Articulate communicator, excellent organizational and interpersonal skills, proficiency in training/motivating sales

192

**Combination.** *Diane McGoldrick, Tampa, Florida*

This four-page resume, which looks typewritten, might come as a shock and seems out of place with all of the laser-printed resumes that have been displayed. This resume, however, is

force, building team concepts and effectively interacting with decision-makers of all technical/professional levels.

EDUCATION

UNIVERSITY OF TAMPA - Tampa, FL
B.S. Degree - Business Administration

PROFESSIONAL EXPERIENCE

DIGITAL TELECOMMUNICATIONS INC. - Tampa, FL 1997
District Sales Manager

Charged with penetrating and developing a nine-state marketing area within the BellSouth Region.

- Initiated innovative strategic plans focused on posturing company for future growth with multiple accounts
- Within in five months rendered multiple orders to MCI corporate headquaraters
- Analyzed, prepared and submitted Business Case Proposals to BellSouth
- Positioned GTE-Florida for first large order entry

ABC COMMUNICATIONS CORPORATION - Dallas, TX 1992 - 1997
Account Director (Tampa, FL)

Pioneered establishment of first Sales Office in Florida. Challenged to build competitive, complete product line presence emphasizing transmission/access products to GTE (Florida/East Coast Region). Accountable for all ABC contracts in designated Region including new applications for product development. Consistently have met/exceeded quotas throughout tenure.

- Successfully positioned ABC as a quality rated vendor with GTE
- Took Region from $1.5M to $4.0M within 18 months
- Cultivated strong customer relationships with SouthTel that generated productivity and profit
- 1994 - President's Club

FUJITSU AMERICA, INC. - Atlanta, GA 1984 - 1992
Regional Sales Manager

Conducted technical sales, coordination of all account activities, systems engineering and customer service support areas. Initially responsible for IXC sales in Southeast; succeeded by business

presented as a scannable resume. The fact that the resume spills onto a fourth page is no matter because "length is not a consideration" when you scan a resume into a database. Furthermore, nouns, or keywords, are more important than verbs in a scannable resume, so words like *managed, directed,* and *supervised* are

development of BellSouth Services. Directed nine-state market penetration and management of multi-million dollar sales program for BellSouth. Formulated forecasts for production planning, product presentations and account plans. Position required extensive knowledge of transmission/network type products and personal contacts with all levels of engineering.

- Fourth salesperson hired in USA by Fujitsu
- Achieved high-level IOP/OSP sales experience
- Directed opening of Atlanta Sales Office

SOUTHTEL COMPANY 1966 - 1984

Network Sales/Market Manager - Durham, NC (1981-1984)

Managed network segment of sales market and oversaw staff support functions in special services, data, coin and toll markets. Served as inter-departmental liaison and coordinator accountable for sales training, structuring objectives, strategic planning and implementation of new business programs, system development of complex sales (multi-company) opportunities, management of special facilities ordering, and publication of market results. Supervised 15 employees.

- Initiated first fiber project at Research Triangle Park (RTP)
- Championed new SouthTel market entry

General Sales Manager - Durham, NC (1976-1980)

Monitored business product and network/business sales throughout eight sales units in Southeastern U.S. Conducted market segmentation studies, analyzed applicable sales responses, prioritized work flow and maintained budget. Actively participated in staff development, training and customer education programs. Managed 90 employees.

- Instrumental role in establishing administration of data base software for PABX Systems
- Key role in cultivating and developing expertise of sales staff

Area Sales Manager - Tampa, FL (1971-1976)

Oversaw management of four business units and 30 employees; together with training/developing personnel, structuring/implementing policies and procedures, calculating budgets and preparing revenue operating plans.

- Accountable for successful penetration of Tampa market
- Led competitive sales campaigns to capture CPE market share

less preferred than their noun forms: *manager, director,* and *supervisor.* The "Areas of Demonstrated Skill" section is a place where it is advantageous to insert keywords and relevant nouns that might be search criteria in a database search. The more keywords are found in a resume in a search, the more competitive

Product Seminar Leader - Tampa, FL (1970-1971)

Highly visible position requiring extensive interaction with customers and intra-company personnel. Created and presented telecommunications programs to select customer audience.

Sales Manager - St. Petersburg, FL (1968-1970)

Directed implementation of unit sales programs, policies and practices. Supervised 5 employees.

Communication Consultant - St. Petersburg, FL (1966-1968)

Analyzed and determined telecommunications products to enhance business of customers, developed definitive proposals and closed the sale.

MILITARY

U.S. NAVY - Retired Active Reserves, Rank: Captain (O-6)

that resume is, and the more likely the subject of that resume will be contacted by an employer for further inquiry. In this scannable resume, notice the simple serif font and the absence of horizontal lines.

# TIMOTHY P. WILSON

10 W. 5th Street ▪ Troy, MI 48000
(313) 555-1234

## *Objective*

A Logistical/Maintenance Management Position.

## *Summary of Qualifications*

Seventeen years training, education, and practical experience in **maintenance and transportation operations management**–in both military and civilian environments–with a detailed working knowledge in:

- Managing transportation, logistics and maintenance of military vehicles and weapons systems.
- Overseeing transportation operations.
- Overseeing repair and maintenance of heavy semi-tractor/trailer vehicles; and managing the parts department to support that maintenance.
- Project management and organizational development.
- Recruiting, staffing, training, supervising, and managing personnel.
- Creating a synergistic work environment–maximizing productivity of personnel and equipment.
- Administering safety and security programs and risk assessment.
- Managing budgets and records, including computer-generated tracking systems.

## *Experience*

**PK TRUCKING**, Ann Arbor, Michigan — February, 1993 - Present
(One of the nation's leading transport companies)

**Parts Manager** (Promotion) (8/94 - Present)

- Manage Parts Department with $100,000 base parts inventory, supporting maintenance for 7,600 trucks and 12,500 trailers.
- Oversee five employees, including day-to-day supervision, hiring, training, scheduling, and promotions.
- Manage inventory, including cost analysis of vendor-supplied items.
- Order, receive, and inspect parts; and return obsolete or defective items.
- Instituted vigorous housecleaning program to reorganize storage rooms for greater efficiency. Purged and reorganized filing system.
- Developed comprehensive training and retraining program for both new and old employees, which increased productivity.

**Shop Foreman** (Promotion) (9/93 - 8/94)

- Oversaw all aspects of maintenance, preventive maintenance, and repair of heavy over-the-road semi-tractors.
  **Region Covered:** Upper Midwest and parts of Canada. **Volume:** 75-200 Vehicles per day.
- Scheduled, assigned, and monitored repair activities; directly supervised twelve mechanics.

193

**Combination.** *Deborah L. Schuster, Newport, Michigan*

Two pages were needed for the resume of this individual, who had extensive, relevant military experience and "a strong background in Maintenance Management and Logistics." The challenge

Timothy P. Wilson Resume/2

**PK TRUCKING** (Continued)

**Driver Supervisor/Yard Control** (2/93 - 9/93)

- Scheduled and supervised incoming and outgoing freight.
- Coordinated assignment of equipment, preplanning and dispatching.
- Handled high volume paperwork, including customs requirements.

---

## *Military Experience (1977 - 1992)*

**US ARMY** 1977 - 1992

**Warrant Officer** (86 - 92)

- Directed battalion-sized transportation, logistics, and maintenance operations, including: Driver/Operator training and testing; Automated parts supply and maintenance management systems; Motor vehicle dispatch and utilization; Scheduling; All mechanical repair, maintenance, and quality control for a wide variety of machinery, equipment, vehicles, and weapons systems; and Records Management–both manual and computer, including (TAMMS).
- Formulated policies and procedures for transportation, logistics, and maintenance, including timetables, assignment of drivers/cargo, and procedures for monitoring movement.
- Conducted assessment studies of facilities configuration, maintenance operations, actuaries, equipment/personnel utilization. Initiated improvements based on the analysis. *Result: Improved efficiency of operations.*
- Trained, directed, and supervised mechanics and technicians.

**1977-1986**: Received consistent promotions from Private to Staff Sergeant, and ultimately to Warrant Officer.

**Military Awards:**
Excellent personal and professional evaluations with numerous awards, honors, and recognition for outstanding technical skills, exemplary performance, outstanding achievement, meritorious service, individual initiative, professionalism, and proficiency.

---

## *Education*

**A.A. Degree - Technical Education:**
Piece Community College, Tacoma, Washington 1990

**U.S. Army Warrant Officer Training School**
Aberdeen Proving Grounds, Maryland 1986

**Basic, Advanced, and Senior Leadership/Management Training, and NCO/Enlisted Technical Training**
U.S. Army Institute for Professional Development 1977 - 1986

---

for the writer was summarizing this person's military and civilian backgrounds "with equal emphasis." Horizontal lines were used to break up the resume into sections, and bullets made the information more readable. Both backgrounds were merged in the Summary, a skills "snapshot."

Professional Profile

BRADLEY BOSSLE

194

**Combination.** *Fran Holsinger, Tempe, Arizona*

This page is the outside, front cover of an 11" x 17" folded sheet. The two pages that follow appear on the inside spread, or pages 2 and 3. The front cover's title is eye-catching because it

# BRADLEY BOSSLE

1100 W. Lancaster Way #1-105 Tempe, AZ 55555 [555] 000-0000

## SUMMARY OF QUALIFICATIONS:

- Extensive experience in Management/Sales/Training....
- Increased/maintained one-third of company customer base of $80,000/week in sales....expanded sales volume by $3,000/week....
- Controlled material costs/developed budget projections....
- Consistently exceeded sales quotas....reduced loss of accounts to less than 4%....
- Interviewed/hired/trained/evaluated drivers....supervised 8 service routes/drivers....utilized TQM system....
- Built insurance customer base from 0 - 700+ in 2 years....
- Maintained control of $80 million U.S Air Force weapons stockpile....
- Supervised 32 member crew....
- Implemented innovative management/leadership initiatives which improved unit morale/production....
- Established Service Advisory Council to ensure patron's satisfaction with outstanding results....
- Received certification as Emergency Actions Officer (EAO) in record time while performing Support Officer's duties....
- Excellent communication skills....decisive....accurate/timely with decisions....efficient....astute....dependable....detail oriented....seek challenges....work well under stress/crisis situations....

## EDUCATION:

UNIVERSITY OF MONTANA - Missoula, MT
*Masters Degree: Business Administration*
ST. MICHAEL'S COLLEGE - Winooski, VT
*Bachelor of Arts: Business Administration - Finance*

## ADDITIONAL EDUCATION/TRAINING:

AIR UNIVERSITY - Squadron Officers School - Maxwell AFB, AL - Upper Level Management Course
Meticulous Hiring - TQM - Continuous Process Improvement
Requirements Base Selling - Service Leadership

has been rotated 90 degrees. On page two, a pair of triple lines enclose most of the contact information, and a third triple line is part of a header on page three. The Summary includes experience, duties, achievements, and skills. The ellipses separating the skills make it possible to alter the listing to target the Qualifications to a

**professional profile**

PROFESSIONAL HIGHLIGHTS:

**SALES**

- Oversaw complete operations for uniform rental service....
- Established new Insurance Agency....built clientele base....
- Prepared P & L's for service area....
- Controlled material costs....
- Created route driver training evaluation system which improved efficiency....
- Negotiated contracts with major accounts....
- Marketed Life/Health/Property/Casualty insurances....
- Maintained extremely low delinquency rate....
- Gave presentations to commercial/business prospects....

**MANAGEMENT/TRAINING**

- Managed stockpile/release of $80 million in weapons for U.S. Air Force in Germany....
- Supervised 32 staff members....
- Provided complete services support for American Community....
- Assured adequate recreation center programs for personnel....
- Implemented innovative management/leadership initiatives which improved unit moral/production....
- Wrote monthly certification tests....briefed other controllers on detailed procedures....
- Directed interior renovation of base's Consolidated Open Mess....
- Increased MWR profits....revised dining facility services....
- Trained Missile Launch Crews to perform Emergency War Orders (EWO) mission of wing....
- Trained over 180 crew members....instrumental in Malmstrom AFB being recognized as "Best Missile Wing in SAC"....
- Continually performed above peers....

EMPLOYERS:

CINTAS CORPORATION - Tampa, FL
***Service Manager:*** 1995 - 1996
AMERICAN FAMILY INSURANCE CO. - Apache Junction, AZ
***Agency Owner:*** 1993 - 1995
U.S. AIR FORCE - Memmingen, Germany
***Captain:*** 1986 - 1992

specific job opening. Positions on page three are bold, italic, and underlined. A different bullet style is used for the Sales and Management/Training sections. Both of these sections indicate achievements as well as duties and responsibilities.

# CRAIG LAWRENCE

Phone: (714) 787-2222
E-mail: CLawrence@aol.com

714 Plank Boulevard
Orange, California 92929

---

## JOB TARGET

A position as a Soccer Tournament Manager

## SUMMARY OF QUALIFICATIONS

- 20 years of experience as a soccer league and tournament manager, director, player, referee, and coach.
- Expertise in athletic events planning, public relations, marketing, and advertising.
- Currently manage 75 soccer teams, advise 300 teams, and organize 4 to 5 major tournaments annually.
- Secured more than 25 regular sponsors for soccer tournaments and events.
- Excellent communication skills; Bilingual English-Spanish with international contacts.

## SOCCER LEAGUES ESTABLISHED

| | | |
|---|---|---|
| 1997 | California South Soccer League | Executive Director/Founder |
| 1995 | Metro Soccer League | Executive Director/Founder |
| 1993 | Indoor Soccer International Team | Executive Director/Founder |
| 1993 | Hispanic Soccer Coaching School | Executive Director/Founder |
| 1987 | Orange County League Referee Association | Executive Director/Founder |
| 1985 | Young Adult Soccer School | Executive Director/Founder |

## SOCCER COMMITTEE EXPERIENCE

| | | |
|---|---|---|
| 1988 to 1998 | California Soccer Association | Public Relations Director |
| 1994 to 1998 | West Coast Soccer Association | Press Director |
| 1996 to 1998 | Clearbrook Soccer Association | Assistant Program Director |
| 1996 to 1998 | National Soccer League | Special Events Coordinator |
| 1996 to 1998 | Oakland Soccer League | Special Events Assistant |
| 1997 to 1998 | Riverside Soccer Club | Assistant Events Coordinator |
| 1995 to 1997 | Western Indoor Soccer League | Public Relations Director |

## SELECTED SOCCER TOURNAMENTS

| | |
|---|---|
| 1998 | The First Indoor Interstate Championship for Young Adults |
| 1997 | California Soccer Association State Cup Championship |
| 1996 | Western Indoor Soccer League Tournament of Champions |
| 1995 | Indoor Soccer International Tournament |
| 1995 | West Coast Division Playoff Game |
| 1994 | West Coast Soccer Association Tournament |
| 1993 | Metro Soccer League Championship Game |

References and Professional Portfolio Furnished Upon Request

**195**

**Combination.** *Kim Isaacs, Jackson Heights, New York*

The soccer ball graphic creates "visual appeal." Impressive qualifications, leagues established, committee experience, and tournaments show this person's extensive soccer experience.

# CHUCK MORRIS

**125 West 72nd Street, Apt. 11C • New York, NY 10035**
**(212) 776-0087**

**OBJECTIVE**

TO APPLY BUSINESS MANAGEMENT EXPERIENCE TO THE SPORTS INDUSTRY

**PROFILE**

- Highly motivated New Business Development Manager with MBA combines a strong interest and background in the sports industry with 8 years of successful business experience in the corporate world.
- Expertise in finance, sales, marketing, and management.
- Strong persuasive, negotiation, public relations, and creative problem-solving skills.
- Proven track record of making sound business decisions and planning strategically.
- Able to work under pressure and meet deadlines.

**BUSINESS EXPERIENCE**

**NYC Bank**, New York, NY — 1988 - Present

*New Business Development Manager* (1995 - Present)
- Heavily involved in new business development of corporate accounts.
- Developed a portfolio of business loans through new lead prospecting, as well as fulfilling the needs of existing corporate customers.

*Sales Manager* (1992- 1995)
- Consistently achieved sales goals by managing sales efforts/sales team within the branch.
- Effectively trained and developed branch personnel.
- Established sales and marketing initiatives to increase market share through business development and effective cross-selling to customer base.

*Select Banker* (1990 - 1992)
- Managed portfolios for priority customers.
- Assisted in start-up of new branch office and built strong customer base.

*Sales Representative* (1988 - 1989)
- Prospected for clients and conducted large group presentations to market bank products.

**SPORTS EXPERIENCE**

**Sports Radio Network**, New York, NY — 1993 - Present

*Reporter*
- Covered NY Giants and Jets home games and interviewed players for comments.
- Interviews were aired on affiliated radio stations across the country.
- Employed as a producer for worldwide NHL radio coverage of 1994 and 1995 Chaps Cup Finals.
- Covered 1994 NHL Finals in Atlanta, Georgia for syndicated radio reports.

**Phil Panahoe Productions**, New York, NY — 1992 - 1993

*Producer*
- Created and produced weekly Sports Preview Show on QED 950 AM in New York.
- Program received good press from the media, including the Daily News and New York Post. Columnist for the New York Post described the program as a "Concise analysis and coverage."
- Planned format and booked guests, creating a comprehensive look at NHL games.
- Contacted potential advertisers and sold advertising time.

**Cable Sports Network**, Atlanta, GA — 1984 - 1987

*Sports Intern*
- Gained experience in editing and producing sports programming.
- Compiled and edited videotapes of sporting events and selected highlights for viewing.
- Brainstormed for new story ideas and features.

**EDUCATION**

**NYC University**, New York, NY
**Graduate School of Business Administration**
*MBA in Finance*, 1993

**Derploin University**, Gainsville, FL
**School of Business Administration**
*BBA in Finance*, 1987

*References Furnished On Request.*

**196**

**Combination.** *David Feurst, New York, New York*

The individual had considerable management and marketing experience and wanted to combine it with his "great love for sports." Both areas are featured so that readers can see the connection.

## PETER S. MANAGER

1122 Waterford Court • Somewhere, NJ 11223
(555) 555-5555

***MANAGEMENT / SALES REP / MANUFACTURING REP***
Expertise in...Servicing Existing Accounts...New Account Development...Team Building

**SUMMARY OF QUALIFICATIONS**

- Strong presentation, negotiation, and sales closing skills. Utilize verbal communication and listening abilities to identify client needs and/or problems; superior grasp of product knowledge.
- Solid work ethic; ability to set short- and long-term goals; computer literate.
- Extremely focused on identifying potential problem areas, minimizing issues, formulating and executing competent solutions.
- Assimilation of company goals/objectives involving the analysis and administration of operational procedures, annual budgets, and future projections.

**PROFESSIONAL EXPERIENCE**

BEST DEPARTMENT STORE, Anywhere, NJ, FL — 1995 - Present
***Department Manager***
Responsible for inventory control of hard lines including ordering merchandise, stocking shelves, and setting displays.

- *Largest turnover of merchandise in store.*
- *Instituted methods to increase productivity and reduced work force.*

ANASCH'S INC, Anywhere, NJ — 1994 - 1995
***Regional Sales Manager***
Wholesale dry cleaning establishment headquartered in Small Town, NJ. Territory encompassed the state of New Jersey, from Anywhere to Somewhere.

- *Established route; started with 10 accounts and generated approximately 40 new accounts per month.*

WHOLESALE CLEANERS, INC., Anywhere, NJ — 1986 - 1994
***President***
Mid-sized cleaning established with on-premises cleaning facilities generating approximately $700,00 in annual revenues. Hired, trained, supervised, and evaluated 13+ employees. Complete P&L and budget responsibility.

- *Founder and majority stockholder; turned profit in first year.*
- *First wholesale dry cleaner to cater exclusively to the hotel industry.*
- *Major clients included Best Known hotel, Better Known hotel, and Grand hotels.*
- *Successfully negotiated profitable sale.*

Early relevant career experience includes: ***General Manager*** of large local cleaner with $1 million+ in revenues. Directly responsible for P&L, budget, hiring, training, supervising of 48+ employees. Redesigned physical facilities thus improving productivity. Increased sales; initiated computerized sales system; initiated development of new outlets in downtown locations. ***Office Manager*** of large wholesale printing supply company. Clients included printers throughout the state of New Jersey. Responsible for inventory, sales, and customer service.

**EDUCATION**

University of New Jersey, Anywhere, NJ — 1983
***Major: Management***
Community College, Anywhere, NJ
***Associate of Science, Business Management*** — 1982

**MILITARY/AFFILIATIONS**

United States Navy Reserve

- Honorable Discharge — 1982
- Citation, The Commander Submarine Force, U.S. Atlantic Fleet

Rotary Club — 1985 - 1987

**197**

**Combination.** *M. Carol Heider, Tampa, Florida*

After being in business successfully for himself, this older person sold his business and was "now looking for a permanent managerial job" with growth potential. Bold and italic are used effectively.

**SUZANNA P. YORK**
4392 Maiden Lane
Bay City, Michigan 48555 810-555-3841

**PROFESSIONAL HIGHLIGHTS**

- Experienced in managing outlets of higher level retail chains.
- Manage district's designated training store in which training programs and orientations were conducted.
- Administered budgets mandated by company while exceeding previous years' sales.
- Developed and implemented district's training sessions for all new hires.
- Completed paperwork for all new employees as required by federal regulations.
- Directed all general accounting, payroll and accounts payable functions, including collections.
- Certified skills and developed promotions of assistant managers to store manager level.
- Monitored and audited store managers' training of employees to meet company deadlines.
- Assisted District Manager in developing programs to promote positive work experience which ensures longer employee retention for company.
- Assisted District Manager in interviewing and hiring management candidates for area stores.
- Monitored store inventory and suggested purchases; processed monthly inventory.
- Defined and closely monitored short- and long-term goals and objectives.
- Selected to receive additional training in preparation for promotion to District Manager position while continuing to manage store full-time.
- Exhibit proficiency in customer relations to ensure growing level of customer retention.
- Implemented and maintained internal & external security procedures to maximize company's profits.

**PERSONAL ATTRIBUTES**

- Highly organized—able to prioritize, delegate and follow through to completion.
- Strong ability to effectively communicate with all levels of management.
- Proven interpersonal and group management skills.
- Focused on task-related activities.
- Excel at taking initiative to gain knowledge and expand job performance; possess strong drive to succeed.

**EMPLOYMENT HISTORY**

Office Products & More • Bay City, Michigan
**District Trainer** 1995-Present
**Store Manager** 1991-Present
**Senior Assistant Manager** 1990-1991

TJ Maxx • Saginaw, Michigan
**Assistant Manager** 1986-1987 & 1988-1990

The Limited Express • Bay City, Michigan
**Lingerie Supervisor** 1988

**EDUCATION**

Delta College • University Center, Michigan
**Associate Degree in Arts** 1988-1992

Great Lakes College • Saginaw, Michigan
**Business Management** 1984-1986

**REFERENCES** Available upon request.

198

**Combination.** *Janet L. Beckstrom, Flint, Michigan*

A full horizontal line before each section makes the page design readily visible. The writer learned that this person had recently been promoted to District Manager in her new job.

**_Barbara L. Daniels_ ▪ _2987 Hillcrest Street_ ▪ _Grand Rapids MI 49053_ ▪ _222-444-4422_**

***Current Objective***

**Challenging opportunity in sales/management/merchandising utilizing proven track record of success to contribute to corporate expansion and profitability.**

***Summary***

**Seasoned Manager with an impressive background with national retailers; comprehensive experience in coordinating efforts for new store openings "*". Currently provide visionary leadership and management for operation with 150+ employees.**
- demonstrated aptitude for sound planning and decision-making to effectively resolve problems and enhance sales and productivity.
- reputation as an efficient manager of people and resources with a record of integrity, dependability, and exceptional customer service.

***Profile***

**14 years successful experience in retail business management; resourceful, well-organized, and flexible;**
- excellent communication and interpersonal relations skills; proven results building and motivating winning teams that exceed objectives and meet the ever-changing needs of the customer.

***Work History***

| | | | |
|---|---|---|---|
| 1988-Pres. | **KOHL'S** | | |
| | Store Manager. * | Grand Rapids, MI. | 1994-Present. |
| | Store Manager. | Farmington, MI. | 1993-1994. |
| | Assistant Store Manager. | Macomb, MI. | 1991-1993. |
| | Assistant Store Manager. * | Farmington, MI. | 1990-1991. |
| | Assistant Store Manager. | Troy, MI. | 1988-1990. |
| 1984-1988. | **HUDSON'S** | | |
| | Selling Manager. | Ann Arbor, MI. | 1987-1988. |
| | Merchandise Manager. | Battle Creek, MI. | 1987. |
| | Area Merchandise Manager. | Dearborn, MI. | 1984-1987. |
| 1984. | **MACY'S** | | |
| | Junior Manager. * | Houston, TX. | 1984. |
| 1982-1984. | **FOLEY'S** | | |
| | Group Sales Manager. | Houston, TX. | 1982-1984. |
| | (Started as Management Trainee) | | |

***Education***

| | | | |
|---|---|---|---|
| | **MICHIGAN STATE UNIVERSITY** | East Lansing, MI. | 1982. |
| | B/S., Retail Management. | | |

***Professional Accomplishments***

**1988-Pres; Kohl's: Presently direct and monitor management team of 4 Assistant Managers, 27 Supervisors in training, presentation, marketing, advertising, merchandising, and housekeeping functions:**
- unit has realized an increase in annual sales of 16% from 1994; gross profit margins increased by 7% from 1994.
- since 1994: have maintained a unit ranking of #1 in the organization for United Way contributions and #1 in the district for customer service scores; currently rank 35 in the nation (out of 128 units) for customer service scores.
- since 1988: employ a positive, comprehensive style for recruiting and training department supervisors and overseeing a broad-base of activities including sales technique, customer service, goal-setting, inventory control, and employee performance.

**1984-1988; Hudson's, Macy's: Recruited, trained and supervised merchandise managers and sales associates in merchandising techniques, shop creation and setup, and customer service:**
- interacted with corporate buying office for product selection and inventory; produced vendor seminars and in-store fashion shows; trained and directed supervisors and sales associates in sales and merchandising techniques; provided guidance in reaching sales goals.
- hands-on experience in opening new store: developed floor plan, fixtures, and product line for first Houston-based Macy's; trained new sales associates in corporate policies and procedures; involved in full-circle *ramp-up*.

***References:*** **Excellent professional references available upon request.**

199

**Combination.** *Randall S. Clair, Parchment, Michigan*

Another of this writer's resumes that have fine print, narrow margins, and a table to fit much information on one page with yet some white space. Work and Education appear in the table.

# Leon B. Preston

43 Waterfowl Road • Henderson, MD 99999 • (000) 000-0000

**Objective**

***Candidate for B.S. degree in Accounting, seeking field-related employment for summer of 1996. Desire an intern position offering maximum potential for practical application of accounting skills and training.***

**Highlights of Qualifications**

- Successfully completed Accounting Program Admission Test (12/95), a prerequisite for senior studies in accounting at Salisbury State University.
- First-hand field experience in individual income tax preparation through participation in the Volunteer Income Tax Assistance program administered by Clinton State University. (Participation continues through 1996 tax season)
- Knowledge of Turbo Tax and journal entry accounting systems, as well as DOS, Windows, Excel, and MS Word.
- Associates of Arts Degree in Business Administration. (Completed studies with G.P.A. of 3.5)
- Six years supervisory/management experience in retail sales.
- Active member of the Institute of Management Accountants.

**Education**

**Clinton State University, Clinton, MD**
*Candidate for Bachelor of Science, Accounting (5/97).*
Studies have included Intermediate Accounting I and II, Financial Management, Management and Organizational Behavior, Personal and Corporate Income Tax Preparation and Marketing.

**Preston College, Forestville, MD**
*Associate of Arts Degree, 1995.*
Coursework in Accounting I and II, Macroeconomics, Microeconomics, Microcomputer Applications, Introduction to DOS, and Introduction to Spreadsheet and Data Base operations.

**Experience**

**The Athlete's Space Inc., Brady, MD** 8/94 to 9/95
*Manager*
Supervised staff of five employees and oversaw all aspects of day-to-day store operations including counter sales, inventory management, maintaining daily sales records and reports, banking transactions, customer relations and store opening and closing.

**Movietime Inc., Easton, MD** 11/88 to 8/94
*Assistant Manager*
Responsible for all aspects of day-to-day store operations including counter sales, inventory control, marketing, daily cash transactions and daily computer entry.

**Pace Markets Inc., Easton, MD** 6/88 to 11/88
*Clerk*
In addition to handling grocery/video sales, also responsible for stocking inventory and assisting customers as needed. (First job obtained while in high school)

**Strengths**

- Excellent team management skills.
- Well organized. Goal directed.
- Gets along easily with people.
- Hard working. Dependable.

**200**

**Combination.** *Thomas E. Spann, Easton, Maryland*

A resume for a college student who, as a past manager, is looking for a summer intern position. Smaller section headings in the left column help the business and institution names stand out.

# Innovative, Results-Oriented Business Manager

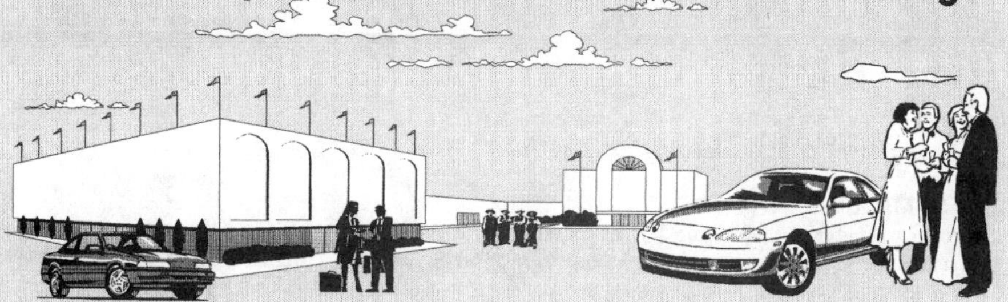

**Exceptional sales and profit figures...are the results of hard work, dedication and commitment to be successful...to advance based on quality, performance.**

## Ben Cartwright

700 Pondorosa Drive
Chesterfield, IN 46017

- Excellent Leadership Skills
- $8 Million in Sales
- Committed to Success

(317) 378-0000

Professional Experience:

- **Assistant Manager**, Wal-Mart, Noblesville, IN, May 1993-present. Responsible for $8 million in sales, $2 million in inventory, supervise 65-70 associates. Have produced excellent sales and profit figures.

- **Department Manager**, Wal-Mart, Indianapolis, Feb. 1991-May 1993.

- **Manager**, F.W. Woolworth, Calumet City, IL. Sales volume $2.1 million annually. Previously manager of Woolworth store in Dowagiac, MI; and asst. mgr. of store in Anderson, IN. With Woolworth from 1986 to 1991, during which period Woolworth began phasing out stores in the Midwest.

Special Skills/Abilities:

- Extensive Management Training
- Sales & Merchandising
- Customer Service
- Gross Profits/Loss Prevention
- Accounting/Cost Controls
- Freight Receiving/Inventory Control
- Personnel & Hiring

Education:

Ball State University, Muncie, IN.
Business and Math Major. 1983-85.

Lebanon High School, IN 1983.

2-year Management Training Program, Woolworth/other training programs.

**"Dedicated, concerned for store and organization."**

**"Hardworking...ability to generate sales."**

—District Manager, Woolworth

201

**Combination.** *Jon C. Shafer, Anderson, Indiana*

The person was in the retail shopping center business, so the writer provided shopping center clip art. In the bottom box are "strong 'anchor' supporting statements from a previous employer."

# DEBRA ALLEVA

128 Homeline Drive
Elmira, New York 00000

Telephone:
(607) 000-0000

**OBJECTIVE:**
A management position utilizing retailing skills.

**CAREER SUMMARY:**
Strong managerial background with experience in retailing, purchasing, human resources, sales, customer service and support. Expertise in organizing and prioritizing work related tasks. Skilled supervisor and trainer. Accustomed to working in a team-oriented environment. Excellent interpersonal skills.

**PROFESSIONAL EXPERIENCE:**

ELMIRA RETAIL STORE, Elmira, New York — 3/93 to Present
**Assistant Manager**
Duties include management of daily operations for 80,000 sq. ft. store, office and personnel administration and supervision of the Home Department. Interviewed, hired, trained and scheduled support personnel. Provided evaluation based on productivity, customer response, attendance and work habits. Adhered to payroll and expense budgets and ensured the security of cash, fixed assets and inventory.

ROCHESTER RETAIL STORE, Rochester, New York — 11/89 to 3/93
**Manager**
Managed a 56,000 sq. ft. department store with $3 million in annual sales and 30 Floor Associates. Coordinated tasks with a management team of three department supervisor. Developed merchandise plans, tracked sales, interviewed and hired staff. Maintained budgets and ensured complete customer satisfaction.

J. HANLEY & COMPANY, Elmira, New York — 1/89 - 11/89
**Manager**
Performed the same duties as aforementioned position.

WARD BROTHERS, Lewiston, Maine — 11/73 to 11/88
**Administrative Assistant**
Also functioned as Sportswear Buyer, Assistant Dress Buyer and Department Manager.

**EDUCATION/TRAINING:**
HUSSON COLLEGE, Bangor, Maine
**Associate's Degree in Business Administration** - May 1973

**Ward Bros.:** Workshops on Purchasing and Merchandising; attended Regional Trade Shows.

**Elmira Retail Store:** Several Management, Supervisory and Customer Service Seminars, as well as in-house training programs.

**COMMUNITY ACTIVITIES:**
- Vice President, Downtown Elmira Inc. (1992)
- Secretary, Downtown Elmira Inc. (1990)
- President/Member, Elmira Central School District HSO (1989-Present)
- Volunteer for Cinderella Softball Team (1989-Present)
- Fund raising for various non-profit organizations

**REFERENCES AVAILABLE UPON REQUEST**

**202**

**Combination.** *Betty Geller, Elmira, New York*

Without the Career Summary, the format would be a standard chronological design. A set of thin-thick lines encloses the body of the resume. Job titles are bold and underlined to stand out.

# DONALD DIAMOND

5624 Main Street ♦ Queens, NY 11423 ♦ (718) 555-5345 (H)

**PROFILE**

Five years of progressive management experience in service industries.

Strong supervisory and operational background with demonstrated ability to increase efficiency of operations and improve profitability. Excellent customer service orientation. Function effectively under pressure with strong time management skills.

**RELEVANT EXPERIENCE**

1990 to Present — **LUXURY DEPARTMENT STORE,** New York, NY

**Manager, Special Services (1992-Present)**
**Manager, Client Services (1992-1994)**
**Customer Service Manager (1990-1992)**

AS MANAGER OF SPECIAL SERVICES:

- ♦ Manage all facets of Special Services Department generating a volume of $18 million annually. Supervise, schedule and train 14 shoppers and administrative staff. Oversee sales, customer service, operations, and merchandising.
- ♦ Devise and implement strategies to maximize profitability.
- ♦ Instrumental in the successful management of $5 million Greeter Program.
- ♦ Oversee operations and staffing for Direct Sales Division. In the process of growing the men's business.
- ♦ Coordinate store-wide fashion shows and special events, covering all aspects from models to wardrobe selection.
- ♦ Function in a public relations capacity by conducting store-wide tours for corporate and non-profit groups.

**Achievements:**

- ♦ Increased business 42.8% in 1995 over prior year through improved staff training and recruiting new personnel in order to meet sales goals. Enhanced organizational efficiency and departmental harmony.
- ♦ Elevated customer satisfaction and reduced complaints to minimal levels.
- ♦ Recognized 3x in store's newsletter for *Outstanding Customer Service.*

AS MANAGER OF CLIENT SERVICES:

- ♦ Established and managed department, implementing an 800 customer service number to track the flow of shipments. This area has grown and is a highly successful operation.

AS CUSTOMER SERVICE MANAGER:

- ♦ Decreased customer returns by 9% through emphasizing other areas of redress.

1988 to 1990 — **SPEEDY COURIER SERVICE,** Queens, NY

**Customer Service Manager**

- ♦ Oversaw a staff of eight (8) customer service representatives for courier service.
- ♦ Successfully retained 42% of Rapid Courier's prior clients after its purchase by Speedy Courtier Service.

1987 to 1988 — **RAPID COURIER,** Nassau County, NY

**Customer Service Representative**

- ♦ Managed all aspects of customer service for international courier service.

**EDUCATION**

**Queens High School,** Queens, NY
Diploma, 1986

**REFERENCES**

Available on request.

203

**Combination.** *Etta Barmann, New York, New York*

Although "Diamond" may be a fictitious name, bullets matching the name can be an effective complement. Only the most recent position for an employer is detailed along with achievements.

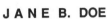

**J A N E B. DOE**
555 Main Street
Anytown, USA 00000
(000) 000-0000

***Objective:*** To obtain a challenging, growth-oriented position within the Coffee Industry where I can contribute my knowledge, experience, and love of the business.

***Qualifications:***

- Energetic and creative self-starter; exceptional passion for the coffee industry.
- Avid, independent researcher of coffee backgrounds and characteristics.
- Demonstrate working knowledge of blending, roasting, and flavoring processes.
- Strong sales, management, and customer service background.

***Relevant Experience:***

**GIFT BASKETS GALORE,** Anytown, USA *6/92 - Present*
*Retail store, specializing in gourmet foods, liquor, and coffee.*
**Store Manager**

- Responsible for all operations of this store; *invited to remain on staff after business was acquired by new owner in February 1993.*
- Generate sales through creative merchandising, i.e., designing attractive point of purchase and window displays.
- Assist owner in planning advertising, brochures and marketing programs.
- Supervise and train employees; assist owner in hiring and interviewing process.
- Attend gift shows and research various catalogs to discover new and unusual merchandise.
- **Increased corporate accounts from one to 15 through effective networking and merchandising efforts.**
- **Designed special gift baskets, regularly featured in Country Business, which continually generate a high volume of sales.**
- **Serve as in-store consultant for specialty coffees.**

**COFFEE UNLIMITED,** Anytown, USA *1/88-1/89*
*Specialty coffee roasting and retail establishment.*
**Shift Supervisor**

- Managed total store operations; supervised and trained employees.
- Gained experience in blending and flavoring coffee beans.
- Assisted with the roasting process.
- Researched all coffee background and characteristics.
- Acted as informational resource on coffee for customers.
- Assisted owner with initiating design and implementation of new store location.

***Other Experience:***

**IN-HOME CHILD CARE,** Anytown, USA *1/91-6/93*

**INSURANCE-ALL,** Anytown, USA *10/88-12/90*
**Postal Operator**

- Expedited incoming and outgoing postal services, both internally and for regional offices.

***Education:***

**Bachelor of Arts - English (May 1993),** Any State University, Anytown, USA
**General Curriculum,** Any State University, Anytown, USA
*Independently financed 100% of entire college education*

***Computer Skills:*** Basic IBM/compatibles PC functions; word processing; data entry.

**204**

**Combination.** *Joellyn Wittenstein, Buffalo Grove, Illinois*

The coffee cup clip art is fitting for this manager seeking a career in the coffee industry. The section headings are right-aligned within the left column (without lines). Note use of boldface.

# Extensive knowledge of building materials industry & applications

Ken Donaldson
200 Jones Ave., Anderson, IN 46012
(317) 643-0000

**Objective:** Seeking primarily inside sales with potential management responsibilities in lumber and building supplies industry.

**Professional Experience:**

Store Manager, Interstate Lumber, Indianapolis. In charge of store operations, personnel, hiring, training, cost control, inventory control, contractor sales.

Inside Sales, Shannon Door, Carmel, IN. Primary responsibilities: inside sales, inventory control, purchasing. 1992-95.

Inside Contractor Sales, Lowes Lumber, Indianapolis. Primary responsibilities: Process orders, schedule deliveries, quote prices and process special order items and materials. 1989-92.

15 Years with Wickes Lumber, in 4 Indiana cities: Indianapolis, Anderson, Bloomfield and Kokomo; also stores in Illinois, Iowa, and Kentucky.

**Achievements:**

- Earned top state sales and profit award.
- 4 times qualified in the top 10 in sales/profits nationally.
- Korean War Veteran.

**Special Skills & Abilities:**

Extensive knowledge of lumber/building materials.

Excellent skills in customer relations.

Strong managerial abilities.

Solid sales skills and profit-driven.

**Exceptional skills in inside sales & solid customer relations.**

**Top sales & profit performance "top 10" nationally 4 times.**

205

**Combination.** *Jon C. Shafer, Anderson, Indiana*

This manager was a middle-aged man with only a high school education but with much knowledge in his single field: building materials. The task, then, is to play up this knowledge.

# WILLIAM KOLLER

55 W. 57th Street, Apt. 4K
New York, NY 10019
(212) 545-9876 (H)


## SUMMARY OF QUALIFICATIONS

15 years of successful retail management experience focusing on the health and nutrition industry. Marathon runner and sports enthusiast who embodies the Sports Apparel TKG philosophy. Dedicated and enthusiastic manager who can build a powerful team. Proven track record of bringing fresh ideas and creativity to sales/marketing, merchandising, and staffing.

## RETAIL EXPERIENCE

**Management/Sales, Apparel For U**, New York, NY (1991-Present)
Oversee sales and customer service for athletic apparel store with an extensive Sports Apparel TKG merchandise selection. Supervise and motivate two sales associates. Develop new ideas to increase store profitability including strategic purchases, effective floor & window displays, and local health club promotions.

**Owner/Manager, The Health Store**, Riverdale, NY (1984-1991)
Established and managed a health and nutrition store catering to an upscale customer base with annual sales of $700,000. Hired, supervised, trained and evaluated a staff of 6. Developed a strong community presence and profitability through extensive marketing and promotional efforts.

- Realized 10-year sales goal after only 5 years.
- Turned around store after purchase from previous owner. Rebuilt operation from ground up including complete store redesign.
- Built an entire athletic department with supplements to improve endurance and performance.
- Developed a reputation as a fitness and nutrition expert. Spoke at local schools about related topics. Trained for marathons through community runs. Displayed personal marathon photos in the store. Featured on radio talk shows. Created newsletters and other marketing materials.

**Manager, Nature Health and Foods**, New York, NY (1981-1984)
Directed all aspects of health and nutrition store which sported the third largest volume of its type in New York City with annual sales in the millions. Trained and supervised a staff of 15. Improved staff rapport, team effort and morale. Evaluated inventory and established a more effective merchandise mix over previous manager. Effectively directed operations in high pressure environment.

**Manager, Health Etc.**, New York, NY (1979-1981)
Tripled volume in less than a year from $18,000 to $36,000 week. Managed every aspect of the operation from buying and merchandising to visual display and staffing.

## SPORTS EXPERIENCE

**Associate Producer, WNBC Sports for Everyone**, New York, NY (1978-1979)
Assisted in coverage of professional sporting events, including NY Yankee baseball and Volvo Grand Prix tennis matches at Madison Square Garden. Freelance producer for major college football games.

**Marathon Runner** since 1983. Have run in 8 marathons, including the New York City marathon, San Francisco marathon, and Marine Corps marathon.

## EDUCATION

B.A. Sociology, Lehman College, 1977

**206**

**Combination.** *Etta Barmann, New York, New York*

This resume is "highly targeted" to the company referred to in the Profile. The person wanted to work for this company, so the resume shows his retail and sports experience—and his motivation.

# DAVID T. DOSTIE

P.O. Box 777, West Woods, ME 00000
(207) 000-0000

## EXPERIENCE

**K-mart Corporation**, Troy, Michigan

***Positions Held:*** Manager, Sporting Goods & Automotive Departments
River City, Maine . . . . . . . . . . . . . . . . . . . . . . . (1984-Present)
Dover, Delaware . . . . . . . . . . . . . . . . . . . . . . . (1981-84)
W. Lebanon, New Hampshire . . . . . . . . . . . . . . . (1979-81)
Assistant Manager, Sporting Goods Department
Northern City, Maine . . . . . . . . . . . . . . . . . . . . (1978-79)

***Summary of Responsibilities:***

- One of seven core management personnel at one of the company's largest stores in the state; participate in key decisions affecting store operations.
- Oversee all aspects of managing sporting goods and automotive departments (with combined annual sales of over $1 million) including supervision of personnel, advertising, promotions, pricing, merchandising, unit integrity, and customer service.
- Order, receive, check, and control inventory, maintaining appropriate mix according to company guidelines.
- Experienced in hiring, firing, scheduling, and training employees, including training personnel from other locations to become department managers.
- Maintain strong communications with management and employees to ensure a team effort toward meeting company goals.

***Selected Achievements:***

- Consistently achieved scores of "above company expectations" on performance evaluations throughout 18-year association with K-mart.
- Repeatedly exceeds corporate sales and profitability goals, largely attributable to low annual percentage of invisible waste. Met 120% of corporate goals for profitability in 1995.
- Appointed as second lead person within the district to make decisions on promotional buys for stores in Maine and New Hampshire.
- One of three-member team sent to stores within the district to evaluate, make recommendations for and oversee reset/layout of stores.

## EDUCATION

A.S. Business Management, Regional Technical College, Northern City, Maine (1978)

Continuing Professional Development: Ongoing attendance at seminars and inservice programs on topics such as Retail Management, Safety, Sales, Communications, and Product Knowledge

207

**Combination.** *Becky J. Davis, Waterville, Maine*

For a person with 18 years at one company, this is a "no-frills" resume that quickly starts showing his experience and achievements. He sent 5 resumes, had 5 interviews, and got 4 job offers!

# DAVID M. MERCHANDISER

12587 New York Avenue, Winterpark, NC 69317 (555) 898-9898

**MANAGEMENT • BUYER**

Experienced professional with a proven track record in merchandising and closing sales. Solid management, communication, situation assessment, problem solving, and organizational skills. Expertise in:

- Floor Management
- Product Ordering/Distribution
- Quality Control/Improvement
- Merchandising/Inventory Control
- Personnel Training/Supervision
- Retail Sales Management/Customer Service

**PROFESSIONAL EXPERIENCE**

***Buyer/Sales Manager*** 1987 - Present
GOOD FURNITURE, Ft. Myers/Jacksonville, FL

Primary responsibility for the coordination of merchandise inventory for four high volume furniture stores. Maintain $3M inventory; plan and prepare budget. Work independently with little or no supervision. Familiar with custom software maintenance programs. Take charge in manager's absence. Key responsibilities include:

- Train, schedule, supervise, and evaluate the work performance of a staff of 10+.
- Maintain/update inventory, documents, and control procedures.
- Recommend procedural changes to expedite product movement, control, and accountability.
- Set advertising and coordinate product movement through four Metro stores.
- Meet with manufacturer's reps to resolve problems regarding defective products.
- Instrumental in closing of floor sales.
- Voted "Employee of the Month."

***Audio/Video Manager*** 1984 - 1987
BEST APPLIANCE, Anywhere, OH

Supervised entire audio/visual department. Scope of responsibilities included merchandising/displaying of established and new product offerings. In charge of inventory control functions.

***Appliance Sales/Cashier Supervision*** 1982 - 1984
DISCOUNT LAND, Anywhere, OH

Responsibilities included audio/visual sales, inventory control, and customer service.

***Assistant Manager*** 1980 - 1982
DISCOUNT WORLD, Anywhere, OH

Supervision of 30+ personnel. Reported directly to President. Diverse responsibilities included personnel training, employee scheduling, sales, merchandising, product management, pricing, advertising, customer service, and opening and closing store.

***Manager*** 1979 - 1980
HIP FASHIONS, Anywhere, OH

Responsibilities included supervision and scheduling of 5+ personnel, merchandising, displays, and overseeing store operations.

## 208

**Combination.** *M. Carol Heider, Tampa, Florida*

Horizontal lines enclosing the centered headings make them, together with the individual's large name in italic small caps, the first items seen. For some reason, there's no Education section.

## Raymond H. Wilson

832 Newport Rd., Newport, MI 48166
(313) 555-3130

### Summary

**Retail Manager**

- 16 years experience in retail, 12 in retail management for a major chain.
- Experienced in operations, budgeting, merchandising, customer service, purchasing, and inventory control.
- Strong customer service orientation; work well with the public.
- Excellent leadership skills–can communicate effectively with employees and motivate them to perform at their best. Can set direction for the team. Hands-on approach to training.
- Can effectively manage budget and save costs.
- Flexible–proven ability to adapt to corporate changes in operations or personnel.
- 16-year record of dependability and loyalty to the company.

### Experience

**WAL-MART**, Monroe, Michigan 1980-Present

Replenishment Manager, 1994-Present
Operations Assistant Manager, 1992-1994 (Promotion)
Customer Service Manager, 1990-1992
Merchandising Assistant-Hardlines, 1987-1990 (Promotion)
Store Assistant Manager, 1984-1987 (Promotion)
Floor Supervisor, 1981-1984 (Promotion)
Stock Person-Patio, 1980-1981

- Assist in overseeing day-to day operations of entire store.
- Have managed up to 40 employees, including scheduling, training, supervising daily assignments, and evaluating performance.
- Monitor expenditures of all store supplies, ensuring that they are within budget.
- Increase profits through effective displays and merchandising.
- Numerous customer service awards.

### Education

**EASTERN MICHIGAN UNIVERSITY**, Ypsilanti, Michigan
Three Years of Credits towards BA in Mathematics

**MONROE HIGH SCHOOL**, Monroe, Michigan
Graduate

**209**

**Combination.** *Deborah L. Schuster, Newport, Michigan*

A resume with good white space. Thick partial lines call attention to the name or headings under them. Because of reorganization, highlights are given for all the positions rather than for each.

## *Quincy P. Evans*

***9872 Town Court North***
***Lawrenceville, New Jersey 08648***
***Residence: (609) 799-2998***
***Business: (609) 799-5409***

### *Summary Of Qualifications*

Broad-based experience in the following areas :

- Operations
- Supervisory Management
- Recruiting/Human Relations
- Inventory Control
- Financial Reporting
- District Management
- Marketing
- Customer Relations

### *Professional Accomplishments*

#### *District Operations*

- **Responsible for a group of stores in the Southern New Jersey area**, in addition to operating my own $2.5 million unit.
- Aid stores in daily operations from sales reporting, inventory control, and visual set-up.
- Assist District Manager with weekly and monthly projects as well as weekly and monthly sales reporting.
- Conduct presentations at semi-annual Manager and Assistant Manager meetings.
- Responsible for the development of merchandise programs, ranging from the creation of new programs to the expansion of merchandise needs for area stores.
- Perform market research for the purpose of investigating new store locations. Target customer demographics and review perspective locations from a "grass roots" marketing standpoint.

#### *Financial Reporting*

- **Responsible for preparing District Wage Budgets** based on store running rates and store volume.
- Assisted in establishing volume goals based on Corporate Budgets.
- Set up expense budget reduction plans based on corporate restraints and guidelines.
- Coordinated a communication compliance program to ensure follow-up in all aspects of store operations.
- Conduct presentation as to the importance of reducing controllable expenses at the store level.

#### *Supervisory Management*

- **Responsible for the development of personnel** through a management training program.
- Involved in the re-development of the Corporate Management Training Program with the Vice-President of Personnel.
- Assist area stores with personnel needs from recruiting activities to training methods.
- Supervise a staff ranging from 12-18 employees at the store level. Responsible for managers' personal growth and development.
- Interact daily with District, Regional, and General Managers regarding sales programs, merchandise needs, daily inquiries, and customer service requests.
- Participate in continuing education and Human Resource Development programs to enhance managerial skills.

**210**

**Combination.** *Beverly Baskin, Marlboro, New Jersey*

The individual's name, section headings, and subheadings are in italic. Accomplishments are listed according to three subheadings: District Operations, Financial Reporting, and Supervisory

**Quincy P. Evans**

Page 2

## Experience

**FOOT LOCKER**, Lawrenceville, NJ
***Manager Trainer - Southern New Jersey Area*** 1985-Present

Tenure with this organization has resulted in promotions as follows:

| | |
|---|---|
| *Manager Trainer, Lawrenceville, NJ* | *Nov. 1994* |
| *Manager Trainer, New York, NY* | *Aug. 1993* |
| *Manager Trainer, Eatontown, NJ* | *Oct. 1992* |
| *Manager, Marketplace Mall, Henrietta, NY* | *May 1989* |
| *Manager, Midtown Mall, Rochester, NY* | *Dec. 1987* |
| *Manager, Camellias Mall, Syracuse, NY* | *Feb. 1987* |

## Recognition and Awards

- Named and promoted to Manager Trainer in 1991.
- Recruiter of the Year awarded 1989 and 1993.
- 100,000+ Gain Awards in 1987, 1989, 1993.
- Coach's Award 1993.
- Inventory Control and Loss Prevention Awards 1987, 1988, 1989, 1990, 1991, 1993, 1994.
- Assisted Personnel Vice President in 1994 with the Re-development of the Management Training Program.
- Developed and trained 20 employees to manage their own stores.
- Awarded "Best Profit Percent in West New York" in 1989.
- Managed six stores with volumes ranging from $600,000 to $2.5 million.
- Managed the corporate flagship store for 1993 and 1994 in New York City.

## Education

BS in Accounting, 1985
University of Scranton, Scranton, PA

## Personal

- Married; excellent health; one child.
- Mobile and willing to relocate.
- Activities include golf, softball, swimming.
- Involved in community activities and child's school activities.

Management. Boldface is used for the chief responsibility under each category. On this page is a list of promotions and their dates. The Recognition and Awards section amounts to an additional list of achievements. A Personal section seems appropriate for a personnel trainer.

**JAMES R. JOHNSON** ***Warehouse Management***

5099 S.W. Main Street, Beaverton, Oregon 97007 Ph: (503) 644-9088

**QUALIFIED BY**

- Over 11 years' experience managing warehouse operations and multi-million dollar inventories.
- Solid skills in shipping/receiving, staff management, record keeping and paperwork processing.
- Comprehensive knowledge of hardlines buying, vendor negotiations and salvage management systems.
- Experience with Excel, Word, Windows and computerized inventory management systems.

**EXPERIENCE**

FRED MEYER INC. - Portland, Oregon

**Manager, Hardlines Salvage Warehouse** (3/86-10/97)

Managed salvage warehouse that processed $25 million in goods annually. Hired, trained, supervised and evaluated 43 employees; coordinated operations in warehousing, shipping/receiving and office support. Developed and published manuals (for 52 stores and buyers) that detailed policies and procedures for the processing defective merchandise.

*Developed programs and systems that saved more than $3 million dollars annually:*

- Set up in-house facility to repair defective merchandise.
- Developed innovative parts ordering system.
- Implemented product testing program to determine quality of goods.

**Shipping & Receiving Clerk** (4/82-3/86)

Handled routine shipping/receiving duties and prepared vendor returns for common carrier or UPS shipment.

**Assistant Manager, Catalog Sales** (1/77-4/82)

Assisted with the set up and design of Fred Meyer's first retail catalog sales showroom. Supervised daily operations and coordinated shipping, receiving and stockroom activities.

**EDUCATION**

PORTLAND STATE UNIVERSITY - Portland, Oregon

**B.S. Business Administration** (1977)

ADDITIONAL TRAINING:

- Advanced Computer Operations
- Dealing with Difficult People
- Computerized Inventory Management
- Quality Control

**REFERENCES** Provided upon request.

**211**

**Combination.** *Pat Kendall, Aloha, Oregon*

Placing the objective (Warehouse Management) in the upper-right corner "adds interest and balance" to the page. One-page format focuses on career highlights rather than job descriptions.

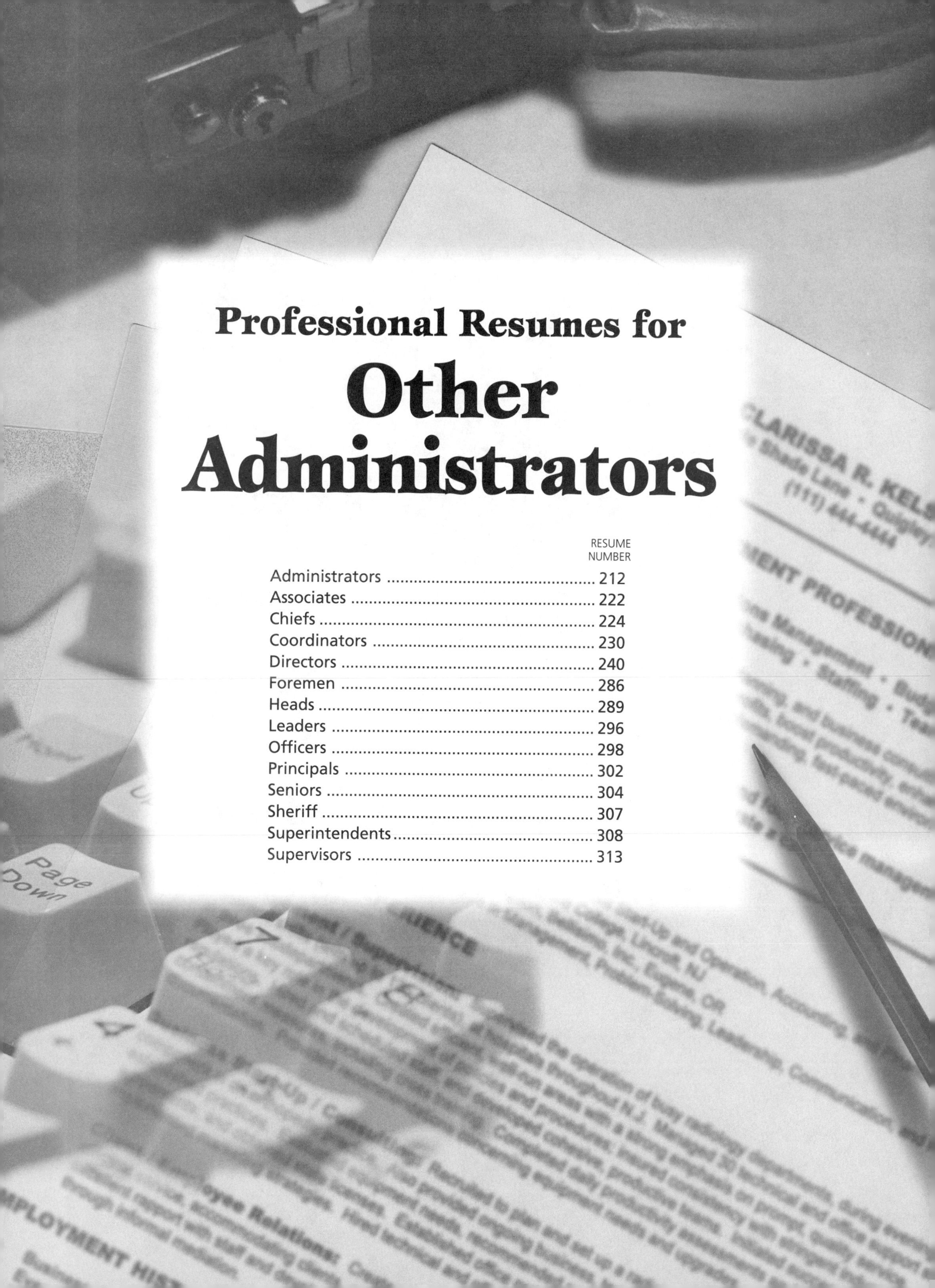

## Professional Resumes for

# Other Administrators

# Marlena Johnson

6788 Woodview Place • Woodburn, Oregon 97007 • 503 / 655-7834

**Objective**

Management position in a teamwork-oriented medical environment where programmatic and therapeutic skills can be effectively utilized.

**Summary**

Highly qualified in planning, developing and coordinating programs and support services for the medically fragile, physically and developmentally disabled population.

- Expert in providing crisis intervention, group and individual counseling, intake assessment and discharge planning.
- Solid knowledge of Total Quality Management and related issues.
- Accustomed to working as an interdisciplinary team member; able to work cooperatively with staff at all levels.

**Education**

M.S.W. - Portland State University, Portland, Oregon

B.S. Elementary Education - Marylhurst College, Marylhurst, Oregon

A.C.S.W. (Academy Certified)

**Experience**

ST. VINCENT CENTERS FOR CHILDREN - Portland, Oregon

**Program Administrator** (1993-Present)

Manage four residential homes for medically fragile, multiple-handicapped adolescents and young adults. Design and monitor proactive programs and behavior management systems to meet residents' needs. Act as support group facilitator and provide individual counseling as needed. Oversee daily operations and ensure compliance with state and federal requirements.

*Activities & Accomplishments:*

- Set up organization's first two group homes for physically disabled adolescents.
- Recognized for "excellent contributions" in 1994.
- Board member, Washington County Association for Retarded Citizens.
- Chairperson, Human Rights Committee.

CENTER FOR HANDICAPPED CHILDREN - Portland, Oregon

**Director of Social Services** (1986-1993)

Coordinated the development of individual habilitation plans for physically and mentally handicapped children in a 38-bed facility. Provided counseling for children and their families; directed small therapy groups with 6-18 participants.

*Activities & Accomplishments:*

- Set up and administered the ADVENT volunteer program.
- Chairperson, Human Rights Task Force.

**References**

References and letters of recommendation provided upon request.

**212**

**Combination.** *Pat Kendall, Aloha, Oregon*

The horizontal lines make the sections readily visible. Because of the master's degree and certification, the Education section is put earlier than the end. Bold job titles stand out.

## CAROLYN HAPWORTH

410 Kentucky Lane, Norridgewock, ME 04957
Phone/Fax: (207) 639-7307

**OVERVIEW**

Six years' experience as SYSTEMS ADMINISTRATOR for multi-location company with Retail and Maintenance Divisions. Program/application proficiencies include Windows, MS-DOS, WordPerfect, MS Word, Write, Lotus 1-2-3, and Excel. Technical, organizational, and interpersonal skills demonstrated in the following areas of responsibility:

- √ **AS400 System Technical Support**
- √ **Troubleshooting / Problem Solving**
- √ **Local Area Network Administration**
- √ **System Installation / Configuration**
- √ **PC Training / Telephone Support**
- √ **Hardware / Software Purchasing**

**WORK EXPERIENCE**

TRUCKS "R" US RENTAL, Skowhegan, ME — 1987 to present

**Systems Administrator**, 1990-present

- Provide technical support to 10 locations on following equipment: PCS, laptops, Memorex telex, printers, and handhelds for the AS400 system.
- Install, configure, and test all hardware and software; perform limited on-site training.
- Guide employees—primarily by phone—in troubleshooting and correcting system problems and answering variety of computer-related questions.
- Communicate with headquarters to research pricing and order software/hardware.
- Serve as LAN administrator for the district office requiring some installation of components and technical assistance with computer upgrades.
- Organized all logistical and technical aspects of setting up several offices. Scheduled wiring crews, set up and linked computers, communicated with office representatives, and tested all equipment for proper functioning.

**Human Resources Assistant**, 1987-present

- Answer benefit questions, program multi-line telephone system, make deposits, reconcile petty cash fund, order forms for all locations, and write vendor checks.

MAINE RENTERS ASSOCIATION, Clinton, ME — 1984 to 1986

**Supervisor**

- Accountable for 5 employees, the building's security system, membership mailings, and office support functions.

**EDUCATION and TRAINING**

Novell LAN Networking, VALCOM (1995)

Candidate, A.S. in Computer Science Degree, Husson College, Bangor, ME (1994-present)
Achievement Award, Dean's List every module, GPA: 3.8

Carrabec High School, Carrabec, ME (1984 Graduate)

**213**

**Combination.** *Elizabeth M. Carey, Waterville, Maine*

This administrator had no completed degree, so the Education and Training section is put at the end. Check bullets point to her skill areas in the Overview. Dash bullets show mostly duties.

# Katherine T. Lennard

410 West Market Square
Cambridge, MA 00000

Home: (617) 000-0000
Work: (617) 000-0000

**Professional Profile**

***Certified Nursing Home Administrator*** with ten-year record of successful fiscal, human resource, medical, and ethical management of nursing care facilities. Significant areas of responsibility and achievement have included:

- Supervision of up to 85 administrative, medical, and ancillary personnel.
- Implementation of policies and procedures to comply with state and federal mandates.
- Formulation of sound budgets and fiscal controls to maintain profitability; turned nonprofitable facility around to show a profit in 18 months.
- Initiated and developed resident case mix and census development strategies with nontraditional populations to maximize profitability.
- Established programs addressing quality assurance and community involvement.
- Served as co-chairperson of corporate mock survey team for 3 years.
- Co-wrote application to become one of only three long term care facilities in the country selected for Multidisciplinary HIV/AIDS Traineeship.
- Appointed by State Commissioner of Mental Health to serve on Quality Improvement Council
- Current facility has received numerous recognitions for outstanding resident care, community involvement, team building, and staff to resident/family interaction.

**Experience**

**Northeast Associates** (1986 to Present)
Parent corporation with multiple nursing care facilities in Maine, New Hampshire, and Massachusetts

*Administrator* – Manfield Living Center (67-bed SNF/ICF), Harrington, MA (1989-Present)
*Administrator* – Southfield Manor (54-bed ICF), Southfield, MA (1987-89)
*Administrator-in-Training* – Newburgh Estates (85-bed ICF), Newburgh, MA (1986-87)

**Waltham-Weston Hospital**, Waltham, Massachusetts (1984-86)

*Day Supervisor, Domestic Services* – Supervised domestic service activities and assisted in direction of staff of 18.

**Licensure / Education**

Certified Nursing Home Administrator – The American College of Health Care Administrators (1995)
Commonwealth of Massachusetts, Nursing Home Administrator's License
Bachelor of Arts, Health Care Administration – University of New Hampshire (1985)
Continuing Education: Approximately 30 CEUs per year in Health Care and Medical Management; Dale Carnegie Course

**Affiliations**

Massachusetts Chapter, American College of Health Care Administrators – Current Chapter President
American Heart Association – Board of Directors
Gamma Corporation of Alpha Omicron Pi – Past President, Past Treasurer

214

**Combination.** *Becky J. Davis, Waterville, Maine*

Ornate bullets call attention to significant responsibilities and achievements of this individual. By putting them here in the Profile instead of under each position, the writer has avoided repetition.

MAUREEN M. HORTON
159 River Road
Highland, New York 12528
(914) 555-3776

---

Office Administrator Diversified background encompassing office administration, information management systems, personnel, and copyright publication. Particularly strong organizational and problem solving skills. Highly motivated, committed, people-oriented team player.

***HIGHLIGHTS of QUALIFICATIONS***

* Thirteen years administrative and information management systems experience
* Able to work effectively within a variety of organizational structures
* Exceptional communication and interpersonal skills
* Ability to execute a number of projects simultaneously

**PROFESSIONAL EXPERIENCE**

IBM Corporation, Yorktown Heights, NY (1982-1995)

**INFORMATION MANAGEMENT SYSTEMS ANALYST**

- Spearhead project to distribute research reports via Internet, resulting in 75% time savings
- Calculate and review statistical data prior to submission for copyright and publication
- Maintain on-line archival bibliographic records of scientific and technical releases

**PUBLICATION PROCEDURES ADMINISTRATOR**

- Provide departmental notification of any changes in copyright application procedures
- Produce and distribute monthly publication statistics
- Arrange non-confidential technical visits of foreign competitors and dignitaries
- Act as liaison between Research department and outside vendors

**PERSONNEL ADMINISTRATIVE ANALYST**

- Train and supervise Personnel Information Center staff
- Administrator of Corporate Employee Resource Information System (CERIS)
- Track employee transfers; develop and disseminate demographic reports to senior management
- Coordinate summer intern hiring program; conduct group orientation for new employees

**PROGRAMMING SYSTEMS SUPPORT ADMINISTRATOR**

- Oversee computer user helpdesk, provide support, establish new user ID's

**SECRETARY**

- Provide administrative assistance to senior management
  - Typing, filing, telephones
  - Maintain appointment calendar
  - Prepare presentations

**GENERAL CLERK**

- Support recruiting and personnel management staff
- Code and data input new applicant records; circulate candidate files to management
  - Schedule interviews
  - Administer employment tests
  - Generate offer letters

**EDUCATION**

**Bachelor of Science,** Business Administration, Mercy College, Dobbs Ferry, NY (1990)

**COMPUTER SKILLS**

VM/CMS / SCRIPT/VS / Windows / OS/2 / LOTUS 1-2-3 / Lotus Notes / WordPerfect / Internet

## 215

**Combination.** *Marian K. Kozlowski, Poughkeepsie, New York*

The person's name, the side headings, and the job titles are all uppercase and bold. In addition, the headings and the company name are underlined. Skills are in the Highlights and at the end.

*Linda Berber* **(616) 555-9282**

**2937 Lakeshore Drive**
**Kalamazoo, MI 49009**

PROFILE

Detail-oriented and conscientious individual with the ability to efficiently prioritize and / or manage multiple tasks. Outgoing personality; can quickly establish rapport with persons from diverse backgrounds and at all professional levels. Can work equally well on an independent basis, with little direct supervision, or in a leadership capacity, motivating and supervising others. Computer literate (IBM-compatible PCs).

QUALIFICATIONS

- ✔ General Office Management
- ✔ Interpersonal Communications
- ✔ Operation of Office Equipment
- ✔ Accounting / Recordkeeping
- ✔ Preparation of Management Reports
- ✔ Use of Multi-Line Phone Systems
- ✔ Windows / Word Perfect
- ✔ dBase / Lotus / Excel
- ✔ Newsletter Preparation

EXPERIENCE

***James Dean and Bros, Kalamazoo, Michigan, 1980–present***

*– Walnut Trail Apartments / Newport Village Apartments (2,856 units), 1992–present*
*– Concord Place / Mount Royal / Seville Apartments (1,234 units), 1985–1992*
*– Wingate Apartments (1,017 units), 1980–1985*

**OFFICE ADMINISTRATOR**
Currently in charge of all day-to-day activities and administration of 2 offices with 13 staff members. General responsibilities include interviewing, hiring, and training office support personnel; reviewing potential resident applications; verification of background information; credit reporting; and preparation of weekly and monthly management reports. Assist with budgets, market analysis, newsletter preparation, and organization of activities for community residents. Locate vacated debtors and pursue for collection which requires current knowledge of small claims court and wage garnishment procedures. Recent highlights:

- Decreased rental unit vacancies from **14%** in 1992 to **4%** in 1995.
- Increased closings from **37%** in 1991 to **49%** in 1994.
- Personally collected the following amounts from vacated debtors (1992–1995):
  – **$14,500 / 1992** – **$19,000 / 1993** – **$19,300 / 1994** – **$22,400 / 1995**
- Assisted in revision of company management manual, which included presentation of new policies and procedures to personnel in other communities.
- Coordinated and conducted "open house" days to aggressively promote rental units to the public.
- Designed more efficient lease forms which were easier to use.
- Prepared appropriate paperwork and represented company in Small Claims Court procedures.
- Coordinated all activities related to company-owned and operated cable television system.
- Trained office personnel and assistant managers.
- Participated in numerous seminars pertaining to leasing, vacated debtor collections, management, sales, time management, communication, and telephone techniques / skills.

***Custom Lock and Safe, Inc., Grand Rapids, Michigan, 1977–1980***
**SECRETARY**

EDUCATION

Kalamazoo Valley Community College, Kalamazoo, Michigan
Completed coursework toward Associate Degree, 1983.

REFERENCES PROVIDED UPON REQUEST

**216**

**Combination.** *Mary Roberts, Tarpon Springs, Florida*

Qualifications listed in columns are easily altered to target a resume to a specific job. By showing duties and achievements of the position rather than by apartments, the writer avoided repetition.

**ERNEST A. KILMER**
60 Willow Cross Road
Hyde Park, New York 12538
(914) 471-6224

---

***AREAS OF EXPERTISE***

**Purchasing & Procurement / Inventory Control / Facilities Management / Contract Negotiations**

---

***QUALIFICATION HIGHLIGHTS***

- Extensive purchasing and product procurement experience
    - Performed purchasing of all commodities, raw materials, and supplies
    - Negotiated cost effective subcontract agreements
    - Integrated "Just-in-Time" principles with suppliers resulting in significant inventory reduction
    - Developed world class supplier relationships, reducing order lead time and pricing
    - Achieved substantial reductions in purchasing budgets through effective negotiating and cost control

- Effective in personnel and facilities management
    - Supervised, trained, and motivated purchasing staff
    - Managed operations and facilities for international manufacturer
    - Outlined and justified capital equipment expenditures

- Excellent communication skills
    - Dynamic, bright, high energy level professional team player
    - Superior customer service skills
    - Proficient in PC operation with knowledge of word processing and spreadsheet applications

---

***EXPERIENCE***

**Procurement Administrator**
Stewart Stamping Corporation, Yonkers, NY

**Procurement Contracts Administrator**
IBM Corp., Poughkeepsie, NY

---

***AWARDS/HONORS***

Participating Recipient of Malcolm Baldridge Quality Award
Recipient of Outstanding Negotiation Award
Member of IBM Million Dollar Cost Savings Club

---

***EDUCATION/TRAINING***

Dutchess Community College
Management Training Program

Presentation Skills
Effective Negotiating Skills

**217**

**Functional.** *Marian K. Kozlowski, Poughkeepsie, New York*

No dates appear in this resume for a successful Administrator. Areas of Expertise appear in a headline. Key duties and achievements are grouped according to three experience or skill areas.

## David T. Forbes

108 Elmwood Drive ■ Anytown, MI 48000 ■ 313-555-0000

**Objective:**

To obtain a position in Health Care Administration.

**Education:**

**University of Michigan** — **Ann Arbor, Michigan**
*Bachelor of Science - Institutional Health Care Administration* — 1994

**Eastern Michigan University** — **Ypsilanti, Michigan**
*Bachelor of Business Administration - Finance* — 1983

**Abilities:**

- Planning, implementing, and managing a health care program or department; and supervising day-to-day operations.
- Implementing revenue enhancement and cost reduction programs.
- Determining staffing needs of facility.
- Supervising accounts receivable to ensure high collection rate.
- Knowledge of government, insurance, and accrediting regulations as they apply to the hospital industry.
- Extensive background in financial management. Effective financial planning skills.
- Excellent management, supervisory, and leadership skills, with the ability to train and motivate staff.

**Achievements:**

**Hospital Planning**

- Prepared a draft business plan for Emergency Room renovations at Harper Hospital. Assessed patient flow to determine staffing and physical requirements. Presented the final plan to the Vice President and Legal Counsel. The draft was used in implementing the final plan, which resulted in more efficient patient flow.

**Management and Financial**

- As branch manager for a financial corporation, directed all operations, managed $40M in assets, supervised all personnel, sales, customer service, accounting, and provided administrative support. Brought Toledo branch back in compliance with corporation policies and standards. Developed checklists that increased accuracy and decreased risk to the firm.

**Experience:**

**Harper Hospital** — **Detroit, Michigan**
*Administrative Resident* — January, 1994 to March, 1994

**American Financial Corporation** — **Toledo, Ohio**
*Branch Manager* — 1986 to 1993

**World Commodities, Inc.** — **Southfield, Michigan**
*Commodities Broker* — 1985 to 1986

**First Bank of Michigan** — **Southfield, Michigan**
*Collection Agent* — 1984 to 1985

**218**

**Combination.** *Deborah L. Schuster, Newport, Michigan*

With another bachelor's degree, this person wants to change careers from Financial Manager to Health Care Administrator. The focus is on his abilities through education, not from experience.

**CHRISTINE R. THOMPSON**
**5033 Mahanna Springs**
**Dallas, Texas 75200**
**(214) 888-0000**

## HIGHLIGHTS OF QUALIFICATIONS

- **Highly self-motivated Juris Doctor** with five years of experience in the legal field and expertise in **Trial Preparation / Prosecution • Courtroom Presentation / Management • Case Strategy Legal Research**; First and Second Chair trial experience in felony and misdemeanor cases.
- Solid understanding and interpretation of local and state statutes / laws.
- Impressive **organizational** and **time management** abilities; remain poised, confident, and professional during stressful situations and under stringent deadlines.
- **Marketing / Advertising strengths; creative / innovative.**
- Exceptional **writing**, **presentation**, **communication**, and **interpersonal** skills; establish positive rapport with clients and team members.

## EDUCATION

ST. MARY'S UNIVERSITY SCHOOL OF LAW – San Antonio, Texas
**Doctor of Jurisprudence Degree**

SOUTHERN METHODIST UNIVERSITY – Dallas, Texas
**Bachelor of Fine Arts Degree**
Major: **Advertising**
Achieved "**Honorable Mention: Advertising Excellence,**" Campaign for a Drug-Free America

## PROFESSIONAL EXPERIENCE

DALLAS COUNTY CRIMINAL DISTRICT ATTORNEY'S OFFICE — Dallas, Texas
**Assistant District Attorney** — 1995 – Present

- Serve as **Administrative Chief of the Court** and **Lead Prosecutor** of the 100th Judicial District Court.
- Prepare for trial and prosecute all felony cases assigned to specified Court, with concentration on victims of violent crimes. **Achieved 94% conviction rate** in **40 felony jury trials.**
- Coach/prepare expert witnesses for trial.
- **Successfully procured four life sentences for aggravated sexual assault of a child defendant.**
- **Prosecuted two gang members** for murder; **successfully attained 99- and 75-year sentences.**

HARRIS COUNTY / DISTRICT COUNTY'S OFFICE — Austin, Texas
**Assistant District Attorney** — 1993 – 1995

- Prosecuted all juvenile misdemeanor and felony offenders and adult misdemeanor offenses.
- Participated in 20 misdemeanor jury trials; **achieved 85% conviction rate.**
- Acquired appellate practice in the 20th Court of Appeals.
- Represented County in all civil proceedings. Served as member of Juvenile Crime Task Force.
- **Successfully received longest sentence of juvenile tried by determinate sentencing.**

219

**Combination.** *Ann Klint, Tyler, Texas*

This Assistant District Attorney served as Administrative Chief of the Court, but she wanted a position as an attorney with a law firm. The Highlights of Qualifications show that she "has

**CHRISTINE R. THOMPSON** **Page Two**

MAYES, RAWLINS, & MOORE San Antonio, Texas
**Law Clerk** 1992 - 1993

- Assisted in case strategy, witness and trial preparation, preparation of pleadings, analysis and response to pre-trial discovery. Participated in criminal and civil cases.
- Performed extensive legal research and writing pertaining to products liability and medical malpractice cases.
- Acquired extensive education in medical malpractice and employment Title VII law.

BEST, LONG, STEVENS & BLACK San Antonio, Texas
**Law Clerk** 1991 - 1992

- Performed legal research and participated in trials pertaining to insurance defense and workers' compensation for large insurance defense firm.
- Drafted petitions, motions, and various other legal documents.

## PROFESSIONAL SPEAKING ENGAGEMENTS / ACTIVITIES

**Presenter**, TEXAS ATTORNEYS ASSOCIATION
(Conducted mock trials; educated claims adjuster on liability and risk management issues)

**Speaker**, ISSUES IN EDUCATION SYMPOSIUM
(Interpreted legislation for education lawyers and school district leaders)
**Rated as "Outstanding Speaker"**

**World Legal Problems** - International Seminar, Innsbruck, Austria

**Student Teacher**, TEXAS YOUNG LAWYERS ASSOCIATION
(Taught Bill of Rights to 6th grade students)

**Participant**, CLIENT COUNSELING COMPETITION

## PROFESSIONAL AFFILIATIONS

AMERICAN BAR ASSOCIATION
STATE BAR OF TEXAS
DALLAS COUNTY BAR ASSOCIATION
TEXAS DISTRICT AND COUNTY ATTORNEYS ASSOCIATION
DALLAS COUNTY YOUNG LAWYERS ASSOCIATION
TEXAS COLLEGE OF THE BAR (Past Member)

◆ ◆ **Professional References and Writing Samples Furnished On Request** ◆ ◆

additional strengths in marketing and advertising." Note the unusual thick-thin border at the left and top of each page. The significant Education section is put early. Bulleted Experience items show duties and achievements. The Activities and Affiliations sections make the end impressive.

## Norma L. Kennedy, PHR

120 Windmill Dr., Southfield, MI 48000
(810) 555-3321


### Career Summary

- Human resources manager with six years generalist experience.
- Results-oriented, with highly developed problem-solving, decision-making, and leadership abilities.
- Trained in effective communication and conflict resolution.

### Accomplishments

**Personnel Management**

- Managed human resources and payroll for 250 employees at four Data Trust locations.
- Recruited, interviewed, hired, counselled, and separated employees.
- Managed $4.5 million annual payroll budget and $160,000 employee relations budget.
- Supervised major update of job descriptions.
- Developed, implemented and administered Personnel Policies and Procedures Manual. Results were a significant reduction in absenteeism, and more equitable disciplinary procedures.
- Reduced turnover from 22% to 10% over a two-year period.

**Training**

- Minimized EEO complaints by training supervisors and managers to effectively handle employee relations.
- Organized Human Resources team to develop a presentation of managed health care plan to 1,650 employees.
- Make recommendations about employee training and cross training.
- Train and supervise support staff.

**Administration**

- Manage corporate benefits programs for major financial institution. Administer health and welfare benefits for 4,500 employees, including health, dental, life, disability, Worker's Compensation, and pensions.
- Supervised the consolidation of more than 12,000 employee records during merger of the bank's two largest regions.
- Successfully met four-week project deadline - which had been reduced from 12 weeks - during conversion to an automated pension database.

220

**Combination.** *Deborah L. Schuster, Newport, Michigan*

Spreading this resume over two pages enables the important Accomplishments section to dominate the first page. With that, the Education section, which shows the person's lack of a

Norma L. Kennedy, PHR — Page 2

## Employment

**Michigan National Bank** — Canton, Michigan
*Benefits Administrator* — 1993 to Present

**Data Trust Corporation** — Livonia, Michigan
*Personnel Manager (1986-1993), Personnel Representative (1981-1986)* — 1981 to 1993

**State Farm Insurance Company** — Dearborn, Michigan
*Office Manager* — 1976 to 1980

## Education

**Oakland Community College** — Auburn Hills, Michigan
*Pursuing Degree in Human Resources*

**Society for Human Resource Management** — Dearborn Chapter
*Certified - Human Resource Professional (PHR)*

**Plymouth High School** — Plymouth, Michigan
*Diploma* — 1975

## Professional Organizations

Human Resources Association of Greater Detroit
Society for Human Resource Management
American Business Women's Association
National Association for Female Executives

degree, can be downplayed near the end of page two. In effect, the first page is functional, and the second page is chronological. Using the functional format on page one, the writer is able to emphasize the person's "Personnel Management and Generalist experience/accomplishments."

**DONALD D. VINCE**
332 First Avenue • D4 • North Tempe, Nevada 00000
**Tel: (000) 000-0000 • Email: 0000.000.000**

## HEALTHCARE ADMINISTRATOR

**RESULTS ORIENTED** professional with comprehensive experience in all business areas, utilizing extensive experience to guide companies to maximum levels of profitability and productivity • Aggressive, persistent and consistent • Demonstrated leadership, time management and problem solving skills with the ability to set priorities to ensure favorable outcomes • Confident decision maker • Bilingual: English/Spanish.

## PROFESSIONAL AFFILIATIONS:

**SAINT PETER'S MEDICAL CENTER** North Tempe, Nevada
*Administrator, Diagnostic Pathology and Laboratory Medicine* *1992 - Present*

- High profile management position accountable for corporate operations of multi-campus department; oversees strategic planning of department while ensuring mission/goals of medical center come to fruition.
- Controls multi-million dollar operating and capital expense budgets.
- Manages, motivates and develops a direct staff of 15 managerial level reports; accountable for 450 indirect staff employees.
- Leadership role in laboratory information systems projects including design of clinical information system for medical center.
- Develops and designs laboratory services for new ambulatory care facility.
- Successfully negotiates, secures and institutes managed care contracts for laboratory services.
- Interfaces with vendors and secures capital equipment contracts.

*Achievements/Highlights:*

- ♦ *Developed aggressive outreach program for laboratory services, including Client Services, generating a 6% increase in tests with a $350,000 decrease in expenses.*
- ♦ *Currently chairs departmental Labor Management Committee, including facilitating training for associate departments.*
- ♦ *Active member in Patient Care Innovation Team.*
- ♦ *Lead role in re-engineering efforts for the department and entire Medical Center; reduced departmental operating expenses by over $1.6 million.*
- ♦ *Achieved a series of fast track promotions to attain current position.*

**BROOKLYN HEIGHTS MEDICAL CENTER** Brooklyn, New York
*Assistant Director, Infection Control* *1990 - 1992*

- Oversaw critical operations pertaining to infection control for entire facility, comprised of 2 campuses.
- Provided in-service education for all staff members; interfaced extensively with various hospital departments to ensure organizational goals were attained.
- Accountable for budget administration, staffing needs and special projects.

*Achievements/Highlights:*

- ♦ *Instituted and managed a major vaccination program for the NYC Department of Health.*
- ♦ *Developed, implemented and managed a comprehensive, internal vaccine program for staff.*
- ♦ *Served as a liaison to the community and developed a successful outreach program, promoting education and increasing awareness.*

221

**Combination.** *Alesia Benedict, Rochelle Park, New Jersey*

A double border on each page, boldface for the contact numbers and centered headings, underlining for the employers, and italic for the positions are all signs of planning for a strong

**DONALD D. VINCE**
**(201) 768-9677**
**- Page Two -**

## PROFESSIONAL AFFILIATIONS continued...

**MOUNT VERNON HOSPITAL** — Mount Vernon, New York
*Supervisor, Microbiology Department* — *1989 - 1990*

- Managed daily activities including staff development, purchasing and budget control.
- Interfaced with physicians, nurses and various medical staff.

*Achievements/Highlights:*

- ♦ *Created and developed Quality Assurance Program.*
- ♦ *Converted laboratory operations to a computerized environment.*
- ♦ *Generated departmental policies and procedures manual.*
- ♦ *Active member of the Infection Control Committee.*

**MEMORIAL SLOAN-KETTERING CANCER CENTER** — New York, New York
*Technologist II* — *1984 - 1989*

- Assigned to special projects and held leadership role in Lab Computer System projects..
- Liaison for troubleshooting system between lab and MIS group.

**WOODHULL MEDICAL CENTER** — Brooklyn, New York
*Phlebotomist* — *1984 - 1986*

**WYCKOFF HEIGHTS HOSPITAL** — Brooklyn, New York
*Laboratory Technologist Trainee* — *1983 - 1984*

## ACADEMIC CREDENTIALS:

New School for Social Research • New York, New York
M.S. in Health Care Administration • GPA 3.9/4.0

York College • Jamaica, New York
B.S. in Medical Technology • GPA 3.6/4.0

## PROFESSIONAL AFFILIATIONS:

Clinical Laboratory Management Association (CLMA)
American Association of Clinical Chemistry (AACC)
American Society of Microbiology (ASM)
College of American Pathologist (CAP)

## COMPUTER SKILLS:

Windows • DOS • WordPerfect • Paradox • Lotus 1-2-3 • various laboratory software applications

design. With short terms of employment at a couple of the employers, and to avoid the appearance of "job hopping," the writer built the Achievements/Highlights sections, strengthened them with diamond bullets, and right-aligned the dates to "minimize attention" to them.

G. ALBERT WILSON
*Attorney-at-Law*
30 Franklin Rose Road • Englewood, New Jersey 00000
(555) 555-5555

## AREAS of EXPERTISE

| | | |
|---|---|---|
| COMMERCIAL LITIGATION | BANKRUPTCY / FORECLOSURE | QUIET TITLE |
| LENDER LIABILITY | SPORTS LAW | ENVIRONMENTAL LAW |
| REAL ESTATE | PUBLIC UTILITIES | WORK OUTS |

## PROFESSIONAL EXPERIENCE

**KAUFFMAN & BURN** — Fort May, New Jersey
A firm specializing in commercial litigation and diverse real estate matters.

***Senior Associate*** — ***1988 - Present***
- Accountable for firm litigation team including overseeing complex matters in state and federal courts.
- Interface with clients which include insurance companies, financial institutions, title insurance companies, real estate developers, professional athletes and marketing companies.
- Conduct discovery, draft briefs and pleadings and successfully try cases.
- Review associates' files, deliberate strategies, review briefs/pleadings and assist associate attorneys in trial preparations.

***Selected Achievements:***
- ♦ ***Successfully tried a novel foreclosure matter where mortgage was outside the chain of title.***
- ♦ ***Increased billable hours 30% defending security guard companies.***
- ♦ ***Oversaw diversification/expansion of litigation due to real estate market decline.***
- ♦ ***Expanded practice regarding sports marketing and generated $130,000 in additional revenues.***
- ♦ ***Profitably promoted, developed and sold three multifamily buildings.***

**NEW JERSEY ATTORNEY GENERAL'S OFFICE** — Newark, New Jersey

***Deputy Attorney General*** — ***1987 - 1988***
- Represented Public Utility Commission and agency staff in state and appellate courts.
- Tried major utility rate cases and enforcement actions for gas, electric and solid waste companies.
- Counseled utility commissioners, developed policy and interfaced with division directors.
- Provided legal expertise for the Department of Environmental Protection.

***Selected Achievements:***
- ♦ ***Assigned to special task force regarding investigation and prosecution of organized crime into solid waste industry.***
- ♦ ***Counseled commissioners during hearing to debar a solid waste hauler.***
- ♦ ***Obtained favorable published opinion pertaining to the allocation of sewerage capacity and antitrust issues.***

(continued...)

**222**

**Combination.** *Alesia Benedict, Rochelle Park, New Jersey*

By the same writer, another resume showing some of the same tactics but also some different ones. Diamond-bulleted achievements and right-aligned dates divert attention from short stays

**G. ALBERT WISLON** **(555) 555-5555** **-Page Two-**

**PROFESSIONAL EXPERIENCE continued . . . . . . . . . . . . . . . . . . . . . . . . . . . . . . .**

**STERN, STEIGER, CROLAND & CONWAY** Morristown, New Jersey
A 26 member firm concentrating in commercial litigation and matrimonial law.

***Associate*** ***1985 - 1987***

- Managed 50+ cases for an insurance company involving surety bonds, real estate syndication, RICO, fraud in addition to an active caseload of complex commercial and non-commercial matters.
- Tried cases in state and federal courts.
- Extensively interfaced with clients and prepared complaints, interrogatories, motions and briefs.
- Conducted depositions and researched commercial litigation matters.

***Selected Achievements:***

- ***Successfully managed all aspects of insurance cases which generated over $100,000 in annual revenue.***
- ***Assisted in a commercial nuisance case that resulted in trial verdict of $383,000 compensatory damages and $100,000 punitive damages.***

**EDUCATIONAL BACKGROUND . . . . . . . . . . . . . . . . . . . . . . . . . . . . . . . . . . .**

**RUTGERS SCHOOL of LAW** - Camden, New Jersey
Juris Doctor (1985)

- Moot Court Best Oral Argument (Commercial Law, Real Estate, Taxation, Environmental Law)
- Teaching Assistant for Legal Research and Writing Class (Performance rated A+)
- Coordinated tutorial program for affirmative action students
- Dean's List

**YALE UNIVERSITY** - New Haven, Connecticut
Bachelor of Arts in Economics and Political Science (1981)

- John M. Brodie Memorial Scholar Athlete Award
- Captain of Wrestling Team
- Officer/Charter Member of Black Athletes at Yale Organization

**CONTINUING EDUCATION . . . . . . . . . . . . . . . . . . . . . . . . . . . . . . . . . . . . .**

Institute of Continuing Legal Education / Practicing Law Institute

- Representing Professional Athletes and Teams
- Revised Business Corporations Act
- Trial Preparation
- Mastering the Art of Direct and Cross Examination
- Entertainment Law
- Mock Trial of a Bankruptcy Case
- Power of the Bankruptcy Court Under Section 105

**BAR ADMISSIONS . . . . . . . . . . . . . . . . . . . . . . . . . . . . . . . . . . . . . . . . . . .**

State of New Jersey
Federal District Courts of New Jersey and Southern District of New York
State of Connecticut

**PROFESSIONAL MEMBERSHIPS . . . . . . . . . . . . . . . . . . . . . . . . . . . . . . . . .**

New Jersey Bar Association
Bergen County Bar Association
Bergen County Bar Arbitration Panel
Garden State Bar Association

at a couple of work sites. Notable differences are period leaders after the side headings, areas of expertise in three columns (left-aligned, centered, and right-aligned), bold italic for the achievements, and a series of strong sections at the end that are important to the field of law.

# CRAIG CALANDRA

(000) 000-0000 • 0000 N. West • Anywhere, USA

## EXPERIENCE SUMMARY

**Over 10 years' commission sales experience in highly competitive industries and markets. Strengths include:**

- Relationship selling
- New business development
- Quality account service
- Sales lead generation
- Presentations and negotiations
- Structuring financing
- Long-term account loyalty
- Productivity and profitability

## PROFESSIONAL EXPERIENCE

**SALES ASSOCIATE** -- The Property Professionals (formerly FTR, Inc.) 1990-1994
Fullerton, Thiesen, Roberts, Inc. (FTR) 1983-1988

- Managed sales and leasing of commercial medical and office properties ... specialized in medical office leasing and dominated market in city's northeast sector (despite soft economy and market volatility).
- From "no" client list, built a diverse list of clients representing a wide range of medical, distribution, manufacturing, and general service businesses.
- Serviced clients in analyzing office sites, evaluating leasing terms and conditions, and coordinating construction of improvements.
- Secured exclusive contracts for leasing of professional office complexes ranging in size from 18,000 to 48,600 sq.ft., with combined market value of approximately $6.5 million.
- Negotiated lease terms, rental rates, and interior improvement allowances.

**LEASING MANAGER** -- Management Investment Professionals 1988-1990

- Managed central valley income property portfolio consisting of retail shopping centers, office buildings, and mini-storage facilities; negotiated leases for national, regional, and local tenants; managed budgets, occupancy levels, and facilities maintenance; and supervised on-site managers.
- Assisted in sale negotiations for multi-million dollar properties; prepared income and expense pro formas; analyzed financial data; and conducted market analyses.
- Focused on increasing occupancy and decreasing operating expenses to improve profitability and marketability for future sale.

**SALES AGENT** -- Advertising Executives 1981-1983

- Experienced in sales of intangibles, developing new business through cold calling, referrals, telemarketing, and direct sales.

## EDUCATION

**B.A. DEGREE**, History/Sociology -- University of Nevada, Las Vegas 1971

■ ■ ■

**223**

**Combination.** *Susan Britton Whitcomb, Fresno, California*

Font enhancements are not accidental; they are planned and used consistently to increase readability. The three bullets at the end are the writer's indication that this resume ends here.

# ROBERT SMITH

333 Oak Street • Bayonne, New Jersey 07333 • (201) 999-9999

*—— A position utilizing a background in CHEMISTRY & CHEMICAL OPERATIONS. ——*

*Offering strengths in Technical Knowledge / Workflow Planning / Leadership.*

**CHEMICAL INDUSTRY EXPERIENCE:**

WORLD CHEMICALS, Fair Lawn, New Jersey 1989-1992

**Chief Chemical Operator**

Responsible for maintaining standard operating procedures for this manufacturer of salicylic acid with a 24 hour operation. Monitored temperature, vacuum & pressure and specific gravity.

- Treated raw batches with chemicals to bring pH and specific gravity into set ranges. Performed all routine maintenance on shift.
- Handled complete start-up and shut down of facility. Inspected equipment on daily basis to ensure proper mechanical operations.
- Promoted within six months from Chemical Operator based on merit.

**ADMINISTRATIVE/CUSTOMER SERVICE EXPERIENCE:**

SAFE RECORDS, Englewood , New Jersey 1993-Present

**Records Center Specialist/ Lead Person**

Service client accounts for this archival storage operation of magnetic computer tapes and disks.

- Update inventory database of 250,000 tapes/disks using a networked system on daily basis. Troubleshoot problems requiring extensive research into past transactions.
- Interface with clients regarding requests to ship materials. Consistently achieve two hour turnaround time for emergency requests.
- Visit client sites to ensure that proper media is available to restore system.
- Prepare inventory reports for clients from database. Create custom formats to meet client's specifications.

**COMMUNITY SERVICE:**

MIDDLETOWN FIRE DEPARTMENT, Middle, New Jersey 1987-1990

**Volunteer Firefighter**

- Participated in all community service activities. Completed hazardous materials training sequence.

**EDUCATION/TECHNICAL:**

State College, Newark, New Jersey - Chemistry Major

- Computer literate: America OnLine user - Windows 95 - Database - WordPerfect

*References available upon request.*

**224**

**Combination.** *Vivian Belen, Fair Lawn, New Jersey*

The format looks chronological, but note the order of employment. The most recent job is placed second. The person wants to return to the chemical field, so the most relevant work is first.

# JAMES BRADFORD, M.D.

Business:
1255 W. 24th, Clovis, NM 75432
Conf. Voice Mail: (201) 555-5555

Residence:
34 N. 9th, Clovis, NM 75432
Home/Fax: (201) 444-4423

## QUALIFICATIONS

**EXPERIENCED MANAGEMENT PROFESSIONAL** with administrative competence reflected by positive impacts in the areas of operations, program planning/service development, and profit performance. Strengths include:

- Critical Start-up, Turnaround
- Regional Strategic Planning, Implementation
- Capital & Operations Budgeting
- Recruitment of Key Personnel
- Teambuilding, Training & Development
- Operations/Service Planning & Management

## PROFESSIONAL EXPERIENCE

### MANAGEMENT:

**Directly accountable for P&L performance** of a high-volume outpatient medical facility staffed with 22 physicians and support team of 57. Manage through hands-on involvement in operations, financial affairs, professional/support staff administration, service planning, patient care, and quality improvement.

- Successful in leading department though critical reorganization and turnaround.
- Improved customer perceived satisfaction by 9% through retraining of medical staff.
- Managed a culturally diverse staff using a consensus building model.
- Designed staffing plan which accommodates tremendous seasonal fluctuations in demand for services; system improved accessibility to care despite annual decreases in operating budget.

**Member of executive management team** challenged with critical start-up and management of new 120-bed hospital. Participated in strategic planning, policy development, minimum training requirements, etc. to obtain state accreditation. Ongoing management responsibilities as Chief of Pediatric Medical Staff includes daily operations, quality improvement process, patient care, peer review, physician discipline, and credentialing.

- Team member directly involved in budget planning, capital acquisitions, space planning, staffing mix, scope of services, physician/management recruitment, and infrastructure development.
- Instituted medical staff policies and established physician credentialing process.
- Obtained JCAHO accreditation with no significant deficiencies on first attempt.
- Realigned services to assure quality of care and staff expertise.

**Serve at corporate level as member of Regional Chiefs** for the Medicus Medical Group, collaborating on issues relating to regional strategic priorities impacting 26 facilities throughout a four-state area.

- Co-developed systems relating to physician relations, customer service, quality of care, accessibility to care, patient satisfaction, salary recommendations, and education.
- Provided leadership in consolidation of services to support the "Centers of Excellence" model.

### FISCAL ACCOUNTABILITY:

Participate in allocation process for $43 million in operating funds. Directly administer $3 million departmental budget. Determined capital appropriations for advanced medical and information technologies. Manage and approve over $200,000 in professional fees to outside providers.

- Member of management team which met budget expectations for facility while adhering to corporate directive of no involuntary reduction of FTE's.
- Participated in negotiation of fee agreements and service parameters with outside providers.
- Managed transition from FTE-based budget to dollar-based budget.
- Intricate knowledge of fiscal issues associated with managed care.

**225**

**Combination.** *Susan Britton Whitcomb, Fresno, California*

The Employment Summary at the end keeps this format from being altogether functional. The occasion for the resume was a doctor who got "fed up with managed care restrictions

# JAMES BRADFORD, M.D.

Page Two

## PROFESSIONAL EXPERIENCE (Continued)

**HUMAN RESOURCE MANAGEMENT:**

Directly supervise management team consisting of 2 nurse managers and 14 physicians supported by technical and clerical staff of 20+ FTE's. Consult on hiring, discipline, dismissals, and evaluations. Manage physician recruitment, discipline, and evaluations.

- Catalyst for internal reengineering of management structure -- brought staffing in line with regional norms (from 30+ FTE's to 20 without sacrificing service quality), achieved performance improvement through cross-training and teambuilding, and turned-around department to record levels for morale, cooperation, and commitment.
- Launched a physician/staff retraining series to meet the challenge of healthcare initiatives in a fast-paced, customer-driven environment.
- Balanced resources to support new "open access" policy which enabled customers same-day access to services.
- Resolved complex service issues and customer concerns.

## EDUCATION

UNIVERSITY OF COLORADO

- **M.D.** (1969)
- **B.S., Business Administration** (1966)

PROFESSIONAL DEVELOPMENT SEMINARS (partial list)

- **Leadership Development Process** -- Program includes training in TQM, CQI, DISC Personality Profiling, Teambuilding, and Managing Transition and Change.

- **Physician's Management Course** -- Program includes training in Leadership Styles, Legal Issues, Problem-Solving & Decision-Making, Cultural Diversity, Communication Styles, Recruitment, Hiring, Evaluations, and Managing Employee Performance.

- **Managing in a Union Environment** -- Program includes training in EEO, Cultural Diversity, Sexual Harassment Issues, Progressive Discipline, Seniority, and Grievance Processes.

## EMPLOYMENT SUMMARY

| | |
|---|---|
| Chief of Pediatrics, Medicus Foundation Hospital, Albuquerque, New Mexico | 1994-Present |
| Chief of Pediatrics, Medicus Foundation Hospital, Albuquerque, New Mexico | 1992-Present |
| Pediatrician, Medicus Hospital, Albuquerque, New Mexico | 1988-Present |
| Private Practice, Albuquerque, New Mexico | 1979-1988 |
| Emergency Department Physician, Christian Hospitals, Denver, Colorado | 1975-1978 |
| Staff Pediatrician, US Army Hospital, Ft. Carson, Colorado | 1972-1975 |
| Intern and Resident, Walter Reed Army Medical Center | 1969-1972 |

**References Upon Request**

and decided he would rather manage/administer than practice medicine." The writer drew from the person's "Chief of Pediatrics experience, special assignments, and leadership training." M.D. was used after the name at the top to get attention, not to find a clinical job.

**PETER J. TURNER**
55432 Marvin Drive #4
Melbourne, FL 32901
(407) 255-9292

---

**OBJECTIVE**

To secure a position utilizing experience in Studio Engineering/Broadcasting, Post Production, Distance Learning and Fiber Optics Technology.

**PROFESSIONAL PROFILE**

UNITED STATES AIR FORCE

**Chief Studio Engineer** (11/94 to Present) • **Lead Technician** (9/93 to 11/94)

**Accomplishments**

- Spearheaded interactive Distance Learning System via satellite uplink and $T_1$ line with two-way audio and video for DoD's Defense Equal Opportunity Management Institute (DEOMI)
  - Reduced costs by over 50% and improved quality of product by setting up new policy on recycle tapes
  - Reduced down time, establishing a 99% error-free environment by implementing a Preventive Maintenance Inspection schedule for control booth
  - Reduced man power and setup time 25% by designing and implementing an accessible procedure for conducting remote shoots
  - Implemented new tracking systems for tapes pre and post production
- Commended for obtaining Student Leader status....instrumental in modifying the training program resulting in a positive approach to a highly disciplined system
- Received numerous letters of appreciation for outstanding acheivement in performing remote shoots, designing and installing camera systems, and all other aspects of production for various U.S.A.F. and DoD events

**Projects and Experience**

- Designed and installed Civil Engineering Supply Warehouse 7 camera security system
- Developed and installed 14 camera security system for Child Development Center
- Engineered, designed, and installed two studios and broadcast control room for DEOMI
- Chief Engineer for daily satellite downlinks
- Supervised Guest Lecture Production and daily video documentation of all classes and lectures
- Coordinated and set up equipment for various U.S.A.F. ceremonies, video projection, switching and editing for live broadcasts
- Performed live on-air broadcast with multiple camera shoots in each studio via LAN line
- Computer literate in Microsoft Word, Power Point, Excel, Amiga, and other Dos programs
- Assisted in remote production shoots for video documentation of the Space Shuttle and unmanned launches at Cape Canaveral and Kennedy Space Center as well as other shoots
- Performed troubleshooting and maintenance to the component level on all consumer and broadcast quality audio visual equipment with minimal down time

continued

226

**Functional.** *Laura A. DeCarlo, Melbourne, Florida*

The one-line date statement under the centered heading, United States Air Force, is not enough to give this functional resume a combination format. Leaving studio engineering in the Air Force,

**TURNER** **RESUME PAGE 2**

## EQUIPMENT

| | |
|---|---|
| VTR's: | Sony Betacam SP, Sony Hi8 Sony 3/4 U-matic, Panasonic Universal VHS, Numerous 1/2, Panasonic SVHS AG-7800 |
| TBC's: | Nova Sync 3, Sigma, Drive Image |
| Projectors: | Sony RGB and LCD, Sharp LCD, Barco RGB, Ampro RGB, NEC RGB |
| Switchers: | Panasonic WJ-MX50, Sony DVS-2000C/DFS-500, Amiga Video Toaster 4000, Grass Valley 250 |
| Satellite Transmission: | C&KU Band Up & Downlink |
| Cameras: | Panasonic 300CLE, Sony BVW-D600 Betacam SP ENG, Sony BVP-370 Studio Camera, Sony EVW-300L Hi8, Panasonic AG-DP800 |
| Editing Systems: | BUE-2000 Sony, Panasonic AG-7800 |
| RF Modulators: | Blonder Tongue, Jerrold |
| Fiber Optics: | ALS |
| Audio: | IRP Audio System, Telex Wireless Mics, Yamaha Audio Mixer |
| Routing Switches: | Sigma 16x16, Grass Valley 32x32 |
| Computer: | Amiga 4000 Toaster, IBM PC Presentation System |
| Presentation Stands: | Canon, Elmo & 35mm Slide to Video |
| Character Generator: | Grass Valley Presto 200Plus |
| Teleprompter: | QTV FDP-9 |
| Remote Systems: | AMX Full Remote Prodigy System, TSM Pan & Tilt Cameras |

## EDUCATION

**Pursuing Bachelor of Science in Electrical Engineering**
FLORIDA INSTITUTE OF TECHNOLOGY, Melbourne, Florida

**Fiber Optics Simplified** - Advanced Technology and Management Program
ACOM TECHNOLOGY UNIVERSITY
- Fiber Optics Communication History
- How to Construct Fibers & Fiber Cables & Evaluate Fiber Options
- Discussion of the Components: LED's & Laser Diodes, Connectors & Splices
- Discussion of Couplers & Multiplexers, & Optical Amplifiers
- System Design & the Fiber Future

**Apprentice TV Equipment Specialist Course,** 1120 hours
UNITED STATES AIR FORCE

**Basic Electronics Principles**
UNITED STATES AIR FORCE

this person wanted a scannable resume with keywords that would help him get a civilian job in studio engineering. The purpose of the Equipment section was to show that he was "up to speed." In a couple of months, he was employed in studio engineering.

**Janet Grady, RN, MSN**
1215 Norwood Lane ♦ Montgomery , Alabama 36100 ♦ ☎ [334] 555-5555

VALUE TO GLIDE MEMORIAL: As your **Director of Practice Management**, direct nursing care that gives peace of mind to patients, families, and your board of directors.

CAPABILITIES YOU CAN USE AT ONCE:

- **Vision** to see how people can focus themselves toward excellence,
- **Leadership** to build, guide and maintain very high quality nursing services,
- **Energy** to overcome challenges quickly and correctly, and
- **Poise** in helping everyone - from senior decision makers to nurses' aides - achieve goals they are proud of.

WORK HISTORY WITH EXAMPLES OF SUCCESS:

More than 20 years of increasingly responsibility with the Department of Veterans' Affairs including these most recent assignments:

- *Promoted to* Chief, Nursing Service, VA Medical Center, Norman, Oklahoma, 89 - 98
  - Led sluggish medical center to their **highest accreditation score ever.**
  - **Cut critical shortage of 52 RNs** to 15 in two years.
  - **Arranged $100,000 in** VA-sponsored **tuition** reimbursement **awards** for students seeking nursing degrees. Recruited 72 students. During the first year, 12 LPNs completed an accredited RN program.
- Associate Chief, Nursing Service, VA Medical Center, Groton, Connecticut 86 - 89
  - Guided groups to **solve problems in every area**. Sample: Cut admission time in half.
  - **Increased patient satisfaction** in psychiatry wards from 55 to 98%.
  - Placed ward secretaries on each nursing team. **Saved cost of 6 positions**. Order entry **error rate dropped from 31% to 8%.**
- Assistant Chief, Nursing Service, VA Administration Central Office, Austin, Texas, 86
  - Produced first major study of patient falls in VA medical centers during this preceptorship. **My recommendations and findings adopted for further study at all 172 centers.**

At the VA Medical Center, Logansport, Ohio:

- *Promoted to* Associate Chief for Clinical Practice, Surgery Ambulatory Care and Patient Escort Service, 85 - 86
  - Built system to get patients to the right appointment on time: **nearly doubled rate at which patients could be seen.**
  - Introduced nurse practitioners to **free physicians for other tasks** and allow patients to be seen by same care giver consistently.
- *Promoted to* Acting Assistant Chief, Nursing Service, 84 - 85

**227**

**Combination.** *Donald P. Orlando, Montgomery, Alabama*

"This package was very hard to write because the client was so self-effacing. However, as I gathered information about her, she saw her true worth for the first time. And so, this resume

Janet Grady, RN, MSN | **Director of Practice Management** | [334] 555-5555

EDUCATION:

- M. S. N., Carlisle College of Nursing, Carlisle, Pennsylvania, 78
- B. S. N., Michaels College of Nursing at Central University, Laneton, Vermont, 70

ADJUNCT FACULTY APPOINTMENTS:

- School of Nursing, Central State University, Central, Alabama
- Selton University School of Nursing and Allied Health, Selton, Alabama

PUBLICATIONS IN THE FIELD OF NURSING:

- "An Educational Partnership/Tuition Reimbursement Project," Journal of Nursing Education, October, 94
- "Patient Fall Prevention Study at One VA Medical Center," VA Preceptorship Training Archives, November, 92
- With Camilla Bowles, "The COPD Patient's General Knowledge of His Health Problems and His Re-admission to a Pulmonary Disease Service," Unpublished thesis, 78

COMPUTER LITERACY: Fully proficient in proprietary scheduling, budgeting, resource control and education software.

AWARDS AND HONORS:

- Leadership VA: One of 30 selected from 5,000 eligibles to attend four workshops on national-level issues, 89
- Director's Commendation: The highest award the VA gives, 89
- Distinguished Black Woman in Health Care, Marlin State University School of Social Work, Marlin, Louisiana, 86
- Nurse of the Year: Chosen by 150 colleagues, Marlin Chapter, National Black Nurses' Association, 83
- "Who's Who in America," 77 - 78
- Achievement Award, Chamber of Commerce, Marlin, Louisiana, 77

MEMBERSHIPS:

- First President and co-founder of The Association of Chiefs of Nursing Services, an organization consisting of all 172 chief nurses from VA medical centers nationwide.
- Chair, Professional Organization for Health Care Issues, Shelton County Woman's Commission, 86 - 89.
- President, Marlin Chapter of the National Black Nurses Association, 83 - 86.
- Life member, American Lung Association.
- Member, Sigma Theta Tau nursing society. Increased membership from 75 to 300 in one year.

SERVICE TO MY COMMUNITY:

- Created community-based hypertension screening for 200 - 275 elderly citizens.
- Organized two, annual on-the-spot screening for breast cancer, AIDS, blood pressure Screened 5,000 women the first year; nearly 10,000 the second year.

Page two

did more than get her interviews. It was a self-development tool. It also helped her negotiate for salary and benefits from a strong position." Many professional resume writers can tell such a story. Pulling and organizing information from a client is a process of self-discovery for the client.

**ROBERT S. DAVIDSON**

3971 Chelsea Circle • Burton, Michigan 48519
(810) 555-3912

**PROFILE**

Seasoned administrator with law enforcement and public administration background. Skilled in **public** and **employee relations, negotiation, financial management** and **research analysis.**

**HIGHLIGHTS OF QUALIFICATIONS**

- Administrative experience at Chief and Mayoral levels.
- Highly effective in motivating and supervising people.
- Outstanding record in labor relations.
- Strong leader by example.
- Respected by peers and subordinates.
- Well developed investigative skills.

**PROFESSIONAL EXPERIENCE**

MARYVILLE [MICHIGAN] POLICE DEPARTMENT 1990-1995
**Chief of Police**
- Administered 30-member department.
- Realized significant drug case forfeiture returns.
- Implemented specialized training for officers resulting in certification.

LAKEVILLE [MICHIGAN] POLICE DEPARTMENT 1986-1990
**Chief of Police**
- Improved vehicle equipment.
- Promoted subordinate education.

BAY CITY [MICHIGAN] POLICE DEPARTMENT 1965-1986
**Positions of Increasing Responsibility**

*Planning, Research and Training (1983)*
- Served as grant coordinator for Alcohol Enforcement Task Force of Genesee County encompassing fifteen police agencies.
- Assisted in preparation of grant proposals; monitored funded programs.
- Coordinated various studies and research projects, both in-house and in cooperation with other agencies and associations.

*Neighborhood Foot Patrol (1981)*
- Acted as Administrative Assistant to Deputy Chief in charge of Foot Patrol Bureau.
- Performed budget, research and statistical analysis.
- Developed and implemented new programs.

*Special Operations (1974)*
- Investigated cases involving vice and narcotics.
- Organized raids when appropriate.

*Patrol and Traffic Bureaus (1965-1972)*

GRAND RAPIDS [MICHIGAN] POLICE DEPARTMENT 1962-1965
**Patrol Officer**

**228**

**Combination.** *Janet L. Beckstrom, Flint, Michigan*

This resume opens and closes with center-justified sections: the contact information and Profile at the beginning, and the Professional Affiliations section at the end. The Highlights of

**ROBERT S. DAVIDSON** (810) 555-3912

## EDUCATION

UNIVERSITY OF MICHIGAN 1987
**Bachelor of Arts in Public Administration**
*Major:* Psychology
*Minor:* Criminal Justice

**Law Enforcement Development** Ongoing
Attended numerous seminars and classes addressing administrative practices, investigative techniques and human relations.

## PREVIOUS COMMUNITY INVOLVEMENT

City of Mason City, Michigan — Mayor; City Council Member; Planning Commission Member

Jackson County Small Cities Association — Chairman; Vice Chairman

Parks and Recreation Advisory Board — Chairman; Vice Chairman

Jackson County Water and Waste Board — Member

Lions Club International — Current Member

## PROFESSIONAL AFFILIATIONS

Michigan Association of Chiefs of Police

Fraternal Order of Police

Jackson County Police Chiefs' Association
(Served as Vice President and Secretary-Treasurer)

Grant County Association of Chiefs of Police

*Excellent professional and personal references available on request.*

Qualifications section is centered but not center-justified. In the Professional Experience section, which shows continual work for 33 years, the job titles are bold for easy spotting. Also in boldface are the Positions of Increasing Responsibility in the Bay City Police Department.

**ROBERT CARPENTER**
4877 McDonald Avenue • Metropolis, Michigan 48555
(810) 555-9865

## PROFILE

Seasoned law enforcement administrator. Skilled in community and labor relations. Counseling and classroom teaching experience.

## HIGHLIGHTS OF ACCOMPLISHMENTS

- Secured over $5 million in federal grant funding to enhance police services.
- Enhanced minority representation on Metropolis Police Department.
- Implemented Drug Enforcement Task Force with federal agencies.
- Expanded Metropolis Police Community Policing program.
- Developed and established Leon Banks full service police precinct and three police mini-stations.
- Established Community Officers Patrolling Streets program.
- Developed and implemented Metropolis Police Mounted Horse program.
- Expanded Community-School Liaison program.
- Organized and implemented juvenile curfew violations program.
- Renovated key areas in police department headquarters.
- Reorganized and revitalized the Police Activities League (PAL) program.
- Expanded Drug Awareness Resistance Education (DARE) program.

## PROFESSIONAL HISTORY

CITY OF FLINT POLICE DEPARTMENT • Metropolis, MI 1970-1996
**Chief of Police** (1991-1996)
**Deputy Chief of Police** (1987-1991)
**Police Captain** (1986-1987)
**Police Lieutenant** (1983-1986)
**Community Service Supervisor** (1982-1983)
**Patrol Sergeant** (1980-1982)
**Detective Sergeant** (1976-1980)
**Accident Investigator** (1973-1977)
**Patrolman** (1970-1973)

## RELATED EXPERIENCE

DELTA COLLEGE • Saginaw, MI 1983-Present
**Instructor** - Criminal Justice

BASIC SKILL CENTER • Lennon, MI 1976-1977
**Instructor** - Law Enforcement

METROPOLIS ADULT HIGH SCHOOL • Metropolis, MI 1974-1976
**Instructor**

LINCOLN COUNTY TRAFFIC SAFETY COMMISSION • Metropolis, MI 1972-1974
**Instructor** - Defensive driving techniques

FIVE STAR ACADEMY • Metropolis, MI 1972-1975
**Instructor** and **Counselor**

**229**

**Combination.** *Janet L. Beckstrom, Flint, Michigan*

This career police officer retired in his early fifties and wanted another job, possibly using his postgraduate degree in counseling. The Highlights of Accomplishments lists those achievements

**Robert Carpenter** (810) 555-9865

## *EDUCATION*

CENTRAL MICHIGAN UNIVERSITY • Mt. Pleasant, MI

**Master of Arts** in Educational Leadership 1983

*Specialization:* Community Administration

**Master of Arts** in Guidance and Counseling 1974

JAMESTOWN STATE UNIVERSITY • Jamestown, AL

**Bachelor of Science** in Education/Social Science Studies 1968

*Program Minor:* Political Science

## *PROFESSIONAL TRAINING AND CERTIFICATIONS*

| | |
|---|---|
| State of Michigan Secondary Administration Certificate | 1996 |
| State of Michigan Teaching Certificate | 1995 |
| Total Quality Service Training | 1993 |
| Rotary International Group Study Exchange - South Africa | 1982 |
| Human Relations Seminar (International Chiefs of Police) | 1977 |
| Supervisory Training (City of Metropolis) | 1976 |
| Michigan Law Enforcement Training Council - Certified Instructor | 1975 |
| Michigan Law Enforcement Training Council - Certified Officer | 1970 |
| State of Michigan Traffic Accident Investigation | 1974 |

*References available on request.*

that are most relevant to his new career goal. Because getting another police position is not a concern, the Professional History section lists the positions held without elaboration. The Related Experience section is important because it indicates his roles as instructor—a related objective.

# PAULA B. TEACH

P.O. Box 550 • Biddeford, ME • 05505
(207) 555-5505

**PROFILE**

Offering over twenty years of demonstrated teaching/case management and community outreach expertise. Area of expertise in special education and high risk students. Adept at all aspects of cooperative facilitation. Excellent written and verbal communication skills with proven effectiveness in public relations.

**SUMMARY OF QUALIFICATIONS**

- Over 20 years experience providing educational instruction and psychological and emotional support to students to foster improved self-knowledge and self-esteem, and promoting empowerment and community integration.
- Exhibit a high degree of enthusiasm for establishing a creative, stimulating and positive environment for students through which they can develop and grow to their full potential.
- Excellent interpersonal communication skills; sensitive and responsive to students needs, and able to build instant rapport with students and parents, and maintain rapport through effective communication and listening abilities.
- Demonstrated conflict resolution techniques by utilizing compromise, negotiation and mediation.
- Accomplished facilitator; able to work with diverse individuals from all economic backgrounds.

**EDUCATION**

**M.L.S.W. in Social Work**
University of Southern Maine - Orono, Maine
**Degree Date: 1990**

**B.S. (+30) in Secondary Education**
Boston University - Boston, Massachusetts
**Degree Date: 1969**

**Continuing Education** · 1969 to present
Area of study: Masters in education
Attended various courses at the University of Southern Maine / UNE / University of New Hampshire.

**PROFESSIONAL EXPERIENCE**

**Transitional Coordinator for Special Education** · 1991 to Present
Thorton Academy - Saco, Maine
- Team Leader / Cooperative Facilitator for special education and high risk students.
- Responsible for identifying students needs and managing all aspects of case management.
- Extensive experience coordinating all aspect of community integration; proficient in developing case plans addressing students needs and goals; active participant in PET meetings making appropriate recommendations to achieve student's goals; providing one-on-one training and instruction, issuing job assignments, traveling to job locations to monitor and oversee job performance, and completing all necessary evaluations and progress records.
- Developed and maintained rapport with all services to ensure that a team effort is achieved.
- Utilized excellent interpersonal communication skills promoting public support and awareness.

**Teacher** · 1972 to 1989
Massabesic Junior High - Alfred, Maine
- Awarded *Teacher of the Year* in 1985.
- Taught a Basic Life Skill course to entire student body.
- Provided pre-vocational training to special education students on a one-to-one basis.

**PROFESSIONAL ASSOCIATIONS**

- The Association of Cooperative Education Educators · 1993 - present
- The National Association of Social Workers · 1992 - present
- The York County Council on Transition · 1991 - present
- The National Education Association · 1974 - present
- The Maine Teacher's Association · 1974 - present

**VOLUNTEER ASSOCIATIONS**

Massabesic P.T.O. · 1985 - present.
- Vice President for 3 years; Chairperson for 2 years; Treasurer for 3 years.

**230**

**Combination.** *Patricia Martel, Saco, Maine*

Distinctive features of this resume include (1) reduced line spacing to fit much information on one page and still have considerable white space and (2) special, bent-ribbon bullets at the end.

# Delilah Bran

0000 North West Circle
Anywhere, USA
(000) 000-0000

## Strengths

**Sales** -- business development, account retention, presentations, merchandising

**Management** -- store operations, customer service, bookkeeping

**Planning** -- new store openings, promotions, special events, publicity

## Experience

**The Consignment Counter,** Anywhere, USA 1988-1993
Co-owner and consignment coordinator for consignment showroom featuring fine furniture, china, crystal, and estate items. Developed new business through referral network with retail furniture stores, relationships with over 700 consignors, and presentations to community groups and military families.

**Results**

- Managed business start-up functions: lease negotiations, 4,000-sq.ft. showroom layout/design, operating systems, marketing, advertising, etc.
- Achieved consistent and strong growth, with annual sales increases of over 45% for six consecutive years.
- Secured free publicity through local newspaper feature, radio coverage with leading talkshow host, and Chamber of Commerce functions.

**Delilah Bran Catering,** Anywhere, USA 1981-1990
Specialized in California contemporary cuisine for private dinner parties and special events.

**Results**

- Established reputation for unique menus, fresh ingredients, and artistic presentation.
- Client comments: "your hors d'oeuvres were beautifully displayed and so delectable...not the same old catering trays which tend to taste the same."

**Exquisite Dining,** Anywhere, USA 1986-1988
Waitperson for award-winning restaurant featured in *Bon Appétit.*

**Results**

- Selected to open for dinner shift; took all food orders from memory, averaging $1,000 in sales per evening.
- Owner/Chef's remarks: "by far the best waitperson in my restaurant."

**The Eatery,** Anywhere, USA 1985-1986

**Results**

- Averaged highest ticket sales per night among wait staff of 25.
- Promoted to trainer in just four months.

**The Cooking Center/Billing's Appliance,** Anywhere, USA 1980-1983

**Results**

- #1 in commission sales in both stores for three consecutive years.
- Developed and presented biweekly 3-hour demonstrative cooking classes.

## Education

**Business & Home Economics,** CSU Fresno and Fresno City College

## Pastimes

Fine Dining / International Foods, Cooking / Entertaining, Travel, Reading

231

**Combination.** *Susan Britton Whitcomb, Fresno, California*

The crossed horizontal and vertical lines establish the zones for the information. Distinctive in the lower-left zone are the Results subheadings that call extra attention to the achievements.

# whatever you're doing..

**..is the most important thing in the world !**

---

That's why you may need me..

## Tammy Walker

..on your team !

---

**Creative thinking that was meant to be in a creative environment.**

My career objectives are:

- **Contribute significantly in a creative environment with an ad agency, PR firm, marketing organization or related endeavor.**
- **Working with ideas, conceptual development.**
- **Putting together a persuasive campaign to achieve public acceptance of an idea, or consumer confidence in a product or service.**
- **Selling the desirability of objectives, and meeting those objectives and achieving the desired results.**

232

**Functional.** *Jon C. Shafer, Anderson, Indiana*

This writer experiments with clip art only when a client wants to give it a try. This was his first full-color resume. It got the individual an ad agency interview but no job offer. "The resume then

## Experience:

- Currently working as a Personnel Coordinator for Indiana Temporaries, Anderson, IN. In charge of coordinating placement of clerical job applicants. (**Note:** this is a good organization for whom I enjoy working, but it is not in my chosen career field, which is why I am seeking entry into a creative environment with advertising, marketing, PR.)

- Most recently was an account representative for The Add Sheet, which is a national advertising weekly publication published by Gannet. There I worked on design and layout for ads for more than 400 clients, acquired through cold calls and referrals. Was **top salesperson** for 1 1/2 years, received **national recognition** for a bridal shop ad I designed. This ad was used in The Add Sheet's national ad training booklet.

- Customer service/retail sales associate, Elder Beerman/Meis Department Stores, Anderson and Muncie, IN. Manager of girls junior department; in charge of retail displays, layout and design of department.

## Education/related experience:

- B.S. Degree, Ball State University, Muncie, IN. Major: Journalism-Advertising. Minor: marketing.

- Advertising practicum for the Muncie Civic Theater. Wrote development and promotional fund-raising letters.

- Served as tour guide for Student Orientation Committee at Ball State.

Where you can reach me...

**(317) 640-0000**

**Tammy Walker**

1000 Pricewood Pkwy
Anderson, IN 46013

led to the local newspaper creating a position for her in its advertising department." The resume was circulated among the "top brass" of the newspaper chain and praised for the resume's originality and use of color. One of the interested newspaper executives called it "the 'perfect' resume."

# Susan K. Schumm, R.N., M.S.A.

805 South County Line Road
Hebron, Indiana 46341 (219) 996-6110

## Objective

Professional Healthcare Management/Administration leading to executive responsibility utilizing my managerial, organizational, and hands-on skills to strengthen a facility's operations.

## Profile

- Over 23 years of multifaceted nursing and management skills; Develop protocol to improve patient care; Cross-train staff to enhance flexibility/control budget; Monitor outcomes of cost-effective management/reimbursement; and Accountability of quality/utilization measures.
- Self-motivated and positive attitude to meet/exceed goals unsupervised as well as in team member/team leader role.
- Effective interpersonal skills; Organized, detailed-minded problem-solver; and Interested in career opportunity with a progressive organization that values and rewards results.
- Have professional and personal relationships with many of the key influential physicians and decision-makers in the medical and business community in Northwest Indiana region.

## Professional Experience

### Coordinator Quality Utilization & Case Management — 1999-Present

*ABC Center,* Hobart, Indiana

**Responsibilities:**

Assess and monitor all admissions for medical necessity, severity of illness, and appropriateness of care; Negotiate with insurance carriers for allowable care and length of stay; Interview patients to expedite discharge planning; **Quality Liaison/Assistant to the Chairman** of Cardiac Quality Review Committee, Critical Care Committee, Department of Medicine Committee, and Medicine Quality Committee; Supervise, organize, and direct all Physician Peer Review, collect data, conduct statistical analysis, and present current educational issues; Coordinate and implement 1995 Healthcare Quality Improvement Project for Medicare; Previously established, coordinated, and monitored Cardiac Rehab patients' exercise and educational activities; Supervised patient billing; Scheduled and inserviced employees; and Managed department's quality program.

**Accomplishments:**

- Promoted from Cardiac Rehab to Quality Utilization and Case Management Coordinator due to highly professional manner of implementing, coordinating, and executing administrative and healthcare tasks.
- Certified Professional in Healthcare Quality (CPHQ), Certification.
- Total Quality Management Leadership Training (TQM), 1999, Certification.

### Guest Lecturer — 1999-Present

*ABC University North Central,* Department of General Business, Westville, Indiana

**Responsibilities:**

Lecture, discuss, and instruct the **Medical Terminology** education program, Spring and Fall semesters, to adult students to stay competitive in their profession.

**233**

**Combination.** *Susan K. Schumm, Hebron, Indiana*

A resume that makes an impressive two-page spread. The first double line makes the end of the contact information readily visible, and the second double line is part of the header on page two.

# Susan K. Schumm, R.N., M.S.A.

Page 2

**Assistant Administrator** 1999-1999

*ABC Healthcare Center,* Merrillville, Indiana

**Responsibilities:**

Managed and marketed aspects of a long-term care facility; Arranged and monitored with hospitals' patients discharge planning; Identified and implemented complete, long-term careplan of patients; Attained administrative training in all state rules and regulations; and Performed all other administrative tasks.

**Accomplishments:**

- Comprehensive Health Facility Administrator, Indiana, Certification.

**Shift Director** 1999-1999

*ABC Medical Center, Inc.,* Crown Point, Indiana

**Responsibilities:**

Directed, verified, and evaluated staff to deliver quality care to a 350-bed hospital; Structured problem-solving skills to promote quality service and staff satisfaction; and Quality Liaison for all admissions, emergencies and medical/surgical procedures.

**Assistant Nurse Manager/Charge Nurse/Staff Nurse** 1999-1999

*XYZ Medical Center,* Hobart, Indiana

**Responsibilities:**

Managed and developed a clinically cohesive and efficient Intensive Care Unit; Trained staff to operate equipment; Updated staff on current educational issues; Evaluated staff; Computed time cards; and Initiated and set up budget guidelines.

**Accomplishments:**

- Advanced Cardiac Life Support (ACLS), Certification.

**Charge Nurse/Staff Nurse** 1999-1999

*ABC Clinic,* Merrillville, Indiana

**Responsibilities:**

Clinically managed the acute care patients for the Emergency Room and Outpatient Surgery.

## Education

**Master of Science Healthcare Administration** 1999

*University of Notre Dame,* South Bend, Indiana

**Bachelor of Arts Sociology/Psychology** 1999

*Indiana University Northwest Campus,* Gary, Indiana

**Associate of Arts Nursing** 1999

*Indiana University Northwest Campus,* Gary, Indiana

### Certification

- Registered Nurse, Indiana and Illinois License, 1999

## References

Furnished upon request.

Diamond bullets are used for Profile statements, Accomplishments in the Professional Experience section, and Registered Nurse certification. Her job titles are in boldface, and the names of her employers are in italic. Hanging indentation makes the section headings stand out.

**MELODIE KIMBER**

## HUMAN SERVICE POSITION

Directly involved in human service work since 1991 in positions of increasing responsibility and authority ... experience in grant writing and government contracts ... diligent, compassionate and thorough professional who is committed to excellence ... effective communicator and motivator ... work well under pressure ... thrive in atmosphere of challenge, creativity and variety ... flexible work style—can adapt quickly to changing work and client needs ... assertive, hands-on leader with strong program implementation skills ... team player ... professional appearance and manner ... 2 yrs. college-level Spanish.

**Strengths**

- planning, implementation and coordination
- decisionmaking and goal setting
- supervisory and leadership
- fundraising and grant writing
- client and victim contact
- training and inservices
- writing and editorial
- document and form design
- budgeting and forecasting

234

**Combination.** *Beverley Drake, Rochester, Minnesota*

A creative format for a creative person. The first page of a two-page resume is like the cover page of a three-page resume but presents the person's name, the objective, and a profile

**MELODIE KIMBER**

17 Spring Road
Milwaukee, Wisconsin 50000

(414) 555-0000

- language proficiency
- program planning and implementation
- writing and public speaking skills
- organizational and time management
- extensive computer background
- high work ethic and attention to detail
- strong problem resolution skills

**HUMAN SERVICE POSITION**

**ACCOMPLISHMENTS AND EXPERIENCE**

**Human Service and Administrative Skills**

- supervision and training of volunteer staff of 10+ for human service agency
- training and certification as victim advocate to provide counseling / assistance in court, hospitals, police stations
- successful initiation and implementation of emergency fundraiser for human service group
- speaker for community groups and agencies regarding human service topics
- assistance in organization of Sudden Infant Death Syndrome statewide conferences
- coordination and verification of data in government contracts; research and assimilation of business information
- responsibility for operational functions and development of policies and procedures for career consulting firm
- performance of needs analyses and implementation of business strategies
- human resource issues, including hiring and development of training programs

**Writing, Editorial, and Media-Related**

- media liaison with radio stations for human service group
- development of corporate marketing portfolio and procedure manual
- writing and setup of brochures, press releases and training manual
- production of prevention skills booklet for Wisconsin State workshops
- re-design, writing and editing of quarterly newsletters with countywide distribution
- co-author of workbook on Child Sexual Abuse

**Technology Expertise**

- self-taught Windows, PageMaker, Lotus, Excel, Quicken, Peachtree, AmiPro, Word, PowerPoint, WordPerfect
- conversion of manual accounting system to computerized system; data base and mailing list setup
- technical support and training to staff

**WORK HISTORY**

| | |
|---|---|
| Business Development Coordinator, Startup Executive Training Corporation, Anytown, Wisconsin | 1996 to present |
| Contract Administrator, Visionary Corporation, Anytown, Illinois | 1992 to 1996 |
| Editor and Victim Advocate, Important Human Service Group, Anytown, Wisconsin | 1993 to 94 |
| Office Administrator, Child Illness Group, Anytown, Illinois | 1991 to 92 |

**EDUCATION, RECOGNITION, AND MEMBERSHIPS**

Bachelor of Arts in Communication—University of Wisconsin—1994
Associate of Arts in Accounting—Oakton Community College—1991
Member: Women in Communication; National Association of Female Executives (NAFE)
Thesis paper on gender bias recognized by Dr. Myra and David Sadker, Washington DC researchers

**REFERENCES AND PORTFOLIO OF WRITING AND DESIGN WORK AVAILABLE**

between a thin-thick line and a following thick-thin line. The shadowed box indicates qualifications and skills. Thickening of the lines calls attention to the centered section headings. Achievements and "energy level" are shown by three main skill groups in a balance of "deep compassion" and drive.

**STAN LASSO**
133 Brook Lane
Troy, Illinois 62294
**(618) 555-0448**

## SUMMARY OF QUALIFICATIONS

Ten years experience managing people, technical projects, and plant operations for Shell Oil Company. Successful track record of optimizing key resources, cost controls, and overall profitability. Earned the company's highest performance ranking for 10 consecutive years. Solid background and bottom-lime accomplishments in:

| | |
|---|---|
| Supply/Trading | Distribution |
| Environmental Health & Safety | Project Engineering/Marketing |
| Budgeting/Inventory Control | Operations Management |
| Regulatory Compliance | Strategic Planning |

## PROFESSIONAL EXPERIENCE

**SUPPLY/TRADING:** Coordinated all light feedstock movements in and out of the Eastern Shell refineries. Oversaw inventory management, movement scheduling, and optimizing feedstock net back to Shell.

- Reduced average MTBE inventory from 1,650 Mbbls in 1993 to 600 Mbbls in 1995. This reduction equates to a savings of $9 million starting in 1995.
- Increased Shell's gasoil export position from 7th in the U.S. in 1993 to 1st in the U.S. in 1994. The international gasoil cargoes averaged an increased net back to Shell over domestic platts of $275,000 (2.5 shipments per month) or $8 million increased annual net back.
- Researched, evaluated and imported foreign and domestic olefin feedstocks that are price and yield advantaged over previously used olefin feed. Net savings in 1994 versus 1993 was $16 million.

**DISTRIBUTION:** Managed a staff of 62 people which included 37 drivers, 14 operators, 4 mechanics, 2 clerks and 5 supervisors. Oversaw budgetary control, safe operation, environmental compliance and productivity of three gasoline distribution plant terminals.

- Reduced plant operating expenses $1.7 million over a two-year period.
- Developed and implemented a plant inspection manual that is now used company wide.
- Managed environmental clean-up of two Massachusetts priority sites (distribution terminals). The recovery systems collected over 300,000 gallons of petroleum products from 1991 - 1993.
- Supervised the safe dismantlement of over 40 tanks and associated pipe while overseeing the construction of a new loading rack, three 120 Mbbl storage tanks, and associated piping.

**ENVIRONMENTAL HEALTH AND SAFETY:** Managed the remediation of over 200 environmental locations in New York, New Jersey, Delaware, Maryland, Washington D.C. and Virginia. Oversaw budgetary control, environmental compliance and remediation of each site.

- Researched and initiated the recycling of gasoline contaminated soil into hot asphalt mix versus the accepted practice of landfilling the soil. The liability savings is immeasurable.
- Successfully finalized the clean-up at 40 environmental sites by obtaining State agency closure.
- Developed and implemented a computerized quarterly review system designed to both enhance regulatory compliance and reduce the number of environmental sites. The system is now used throughout the Eastern Region.
- Supervised the design and installation of 15 permanent recovery systems that include pump and treat, soil venting, air stripping, thermal destruction and carbon adsorption.

**235**

**Combination.** *John A. Suarez, Troy, Illinois*

A combination format as essentially a functional resume with a work history and professional experience that actually is listed chronologically but without dates and with functional titles.

**STAN LASSO** **PAGE 2**

## PROFESSIONAL EXPERIENCE (CONT.)

**PROJECT ENGINEERING/MARKETING:** Managed the renovation and maintenance for 100 Shell service stations in the New Jersey area. Oversaw budgetary control, permit acquisition, and redesign of gasoline service stations.

- Rebuilt 4 service stations ranging in cost from $600,000 to $1.2 million. Designed and obtained permits to rebuild an additional 27 service stations (constructed after my reassignment).
- Developed construction drawings and constructed the district's first car wash.
- Developed construction drawings and constructed the district's first double-wall underground storage tanks.
- Developed and implemented a computer program that tracks the maintenance costs at every station. The program was adopted by all Eastern Marketing Districts.

## WORK HISTORY

SHELL OIL COMPANY 1985 - Present

| | |
|---|---|
| Planning and Economics Coordinator, Wood River IL | (Aug. 1995-Present) |
| Eastern Light Feedstock Coordinator, Houston, TX | (1993) |
| Plant Superintendent, Fall River, MA | (1990) |
| Environmental Engineer, Atlanta, GA | (1988) |
| Construction Engineer, West Orange, NJ | (1985) |

## EDUCATION

Bachelor of Science, Mechanical Engineering, Montana State University

## AWARDS

- 1995 President's Award - Distillate Enhancement Team
- 1995 President's Award - Olefin Feedstock Diversification Team
- 1995 Vice-President's Award - Distillate Enhancement Team
- 1995 Vice-President's Award - Olefin Feedstock Diversification Team
- 1994 Special Recognition Award - Gas Oil Exports
- 1993 Special Recognition Award - Emergency Response to Tank Truck Spill
- 1990 Special Recognition Award - Asphalt Treating Contaminated Soil
- 1988 Special Recognition Award - Design and Installation First Double-Wall Tanks
- 1987 Laurel Society Award - Earned by the leading performer in the Retail Marketing District

REFERENCES AVAILABLE UPON REQUEST

Qualifications in two columns can be altered easily to target the resume to specific job opportunities outside the petroleum industry. For each experience, a brief paragraph indicates responsibilities, and bulleted items show notable achievements. The awards are a strong ending.

# LAURA A. LAULER

4592 Wickham Road
Melbourne, FL 32935
(404) 752-2929

To obtain a position in which I can utilize my leadership skills, and expertise gained as a Project Coordinator and Classroom Instructor.

## WORK HISTORY

| | |
|---|---|
| 1995 | Hiatus - School Board of Orange County |
| 1993-1994 | **Project Coordinator/Resource Teacher** - Magnet Schools for Desegregation |
| 1993 | **Adult Basic Education in English** - Dayton High School |
| 1988-1993 | **Second and Third Grade Teacher** - Ocean Breeze Elementary School |
| 1988 | **Customer Service Clerk** - XYZ Semiconductor, Melbourne, Florida |

## EDUCATION AND TRAINING

**Master of Science in Educational Leadership**, GPA: 3.7
ROLLINS COLLEGE, Winter Park, Florida, 1990

**Bachelor of Science in Elementary Education**, GPA: 3.4
UNIVERSITY OF CENTRAL FLORIDA, Orlando, Florida, 1987

## SUMMARY OF QUALIFICATIONS

**Leadership, Training, and Educating**

- Conducted faculty training on Cooperative Learning Strategies, Problem Solving, and Hands-on Learning. Math Committee Chairperson at Dayton Elementary.
- Conducted presentation on Magnet Schools Development to elementary and middle schools, 1994. Magnet Schools.
- With one week preparation time, conducted presentation for Primary Education Conference: Eliminating Bias in the Classroom/Helping Children Feel Good About Themselves and Others Too, 1994. Primary Education Conference, University of South Florida.
- Developed three-pronged math intervention plan which utilized Cooperative Learning, Modality Teaching, and Problem Solving/Critical Thinking Skills and implemented it at the 2nd grade level, achieving a 9% increase in a 12-week period. Dayton Elementary.
- Planned and implemented staff development programs as needed; researched, developed, implemented, and maintained unified curriculum programs as required. Magnet Schools.

**Communication, Research, and Motivation**

- Successfully performed grant writing, managing a $2 million grant over 2 years, coordinated federal regulations with school district policies, acted as liaison to Washington, negotiating residual funds, monitoring budget, and maintaining accurate audit files. Magnet Schools.
- Outstanding conferencing skills; recruited new schools to Magnet program through presentations to faculty and school improvement committees. Magnet Schools.
- Obtained staff development trainers by recruiting through state universities and coordinating individual school request and needs. Magnet Schools.
- Strong research skills; established professional organization contacts and located resources to promote assistance in Magnet school system. Magnet Schools.

**236**

**Combination.** *Laura A. DeCarlo, Melbourne, Florida*

This person "on hiatus" needed a resume that would "sell her leadership skills while maintaining the approved chronological format of the education field." A traditional format would not have

**Lauler - Resume Page 2**

**CERTIFICATIONS**

Certified, State of Florida, Elementary Education, Grades 1-6

Certified, State of Florida, Educational Leadership, Grades K-12

**PROFESSIONAL MEMBERSHIPS**

Member, Phi Delta Kappa Melbourne Chapter, Professional Education Fraternity

Member, Kappa Delta Pi, International Honor Society in Education

**PROFESSIONAL TRAINING AND SKILLS**

**Continuing Education in Computers and Technology including:**
**Microsoft Word, Works, and Excel; and WordPerfect**, 1991 to Present

**Managing Multiple Workshops, Projects, and Objectives**
SKILLPATH, Inc., Orlando, FL, 1994

**Facilitative Leadership Training**
INTERACTIVE ASSOCIATES, Winter Park, FL, 1994

**IBM Eduquest Technology Training**, Grade: A, Credit: 4.0
UNIVERSITY OF SOUTH FLORIDA, Tampa, FL, 1994

**Magnet Schools Development Conferences**
Washington D.C., Savannah, GA, Tampa, FL, 1993-1994

**Technology Conference**
Phoenix, AZ, 1993-1994

**Leadership Awareness/Effectiveness Training**
SCHOOL BOARD OF ORANGE COUNTY, FL, 1992

**Math Institute**, 60 hours
SCHOOL BOARD OF ORANGE COUNTY, FL, 1992

**VOLUNTEER EXPERIENCE**

Volunteer for "Reaching Out to Touch Young Minds" drug awareness club for young African American males, Orlando Community Center, 1991-1993

**REFERENCES**

Available upon request

sold her skills. The Work History is put "first for reference, then education, then all her leadership-relevant achievements in a functional format." The site of each achievement is indicated. The results: 15 resumes sent, 7 responses, 3 interviews, 3 offers, and 1 job in 62 days.

**BETTY MONTENAGRO**
35 Flats Road
Story Point, New York 00000
**(555) 555-5555**

## CAREER OBJECTIVE:

EXPERIENCED individual seeks a position with advancement opportunities that will utilize acquired skills and knowledge to contribute to organizational success.

## PROFILE SUMMARY:

*A highly knowledgeable professional with proven experience in coordinating and managing all aspects of production planning • Instrumental in increasing profits for employers through innovative problem solving and program development • Possesses a strong base of knowledge and experience which will assist organizations in meeting their objectives.*

## DEMONSTRATED STRENGTHS:

- Utilize computers and maintain data systems to efficiently monitor inventory levels.
- Effectively coordinate the flow of goods through inbound and outbound areas; manage storage operations.
- Negotiate contracts/services with vendors and external shipping sources.
- Proven sourcing, negotiating and procurement skills.
- Knowledgeable of GMP's.

## PROFESSIONAL EXPERIENCE:

**AMERICA B.I.R. & Co.** Mahwah, New Jersey
*Production Coordinator* *1990 - Present*

- Accountable for all production activities for the 3rd largest business travel agency in the United States.
- Generates ticketing, maintains QC records and follows up on delivery of tickets.
- Updates and establishes client profiles in Sabre System.
- Communicates with airline personnel for refunds.
- Interfaces with clients' accounting departments to verify monthly statements.

*Achievements:*

- ♦ *Instrumental in saving the company thousands of dollars by implementing stringent controls.*
- ♦ *Established log sheets for outgoing/incoming tickets to ensure accuracy.*
- ♦ *Generated master listing of reusable non-refundable tickets for clients' accounting reference. Saved clients thousands of dollars monthly on expired, unused tickets.*
- ♦ *Initially hired as a temporary employee and requested as a permanent staff member by upper management.*

237

**Combination.** *Alesia Benedict, Rochelle Park, New Jersey*

Distinctive features in this resume include the double-line page borders; the separator bullet(s) in the Profile Summary, Computer Skills section, and Education section; the double underlining

**BETTY MONTENAGRO** **(555) 555-5555** **- Page Two -**

## PROFESSIONAL EXPERIENCE continued...

**WILLIS AND GEIGER** North Bergen, New Jersey
*Operations Manager* *1988 - 1990*

- Performed production planning and scheduling for raw materials, finished products and the manufacturer of products.
- Controlled and coordinated the manufacturing and shipment of finished goods, from sample stage through completed production.
- Accountable for quality control, purchasing and inventory control.
- Recruited, trained and supervised staff.
- Responsible for product costing and viability; coordinated design requests with contractors, outlining costs.
- Sourced contractors and suppliers.

**JOHN KISS AND SONS** North Bergen, New Jersey
*Assistant Product Manager* *1983 - 1988*

- Managed staff in coordinating raw materials for all aspects of manufacturing to customer shipping.
- Conducted time studies to establish piece work rates.
- Maintained inventory control.

**KRAUSERS** Montvale, New Jersey
*Manager* *1979 - 1981*

- Directed store operations; increased sales by 25%.
- Served as District Training manager and developed personnel's customer service skills.

## COMPUTER SKILLS:

Macintosh • PC's • Excel • Saber System • System One

## EDUCATION:

Manchester College • Manchester, Connecticut
Liberal Arts

under the employers' names; and the diamond bullets for achievements in the Professional Experience section. Italic in the Profile Summary, job titles, dates, and Achievements helps these items stand out. The Education section, which shows neither a degree nor a date, is at the end.

## BARBARA WALTERS, R.N.

**1459 California Avenue Yorktown Heights, NY 10598 (914) 245-1997**

**CAREER SUMMARY**

Health Care Administrator with over twenty years experience in pioneering health care programs, services and technologies. Consistent contributions in increasing patient census, reducing operating costs and increasing net revenues in competitive health care markets. Broad based general management qualifications with particular expertise in improving cost containment and staff retention.

**PROFILE**

- Motivated Management Professional with more than twenty years experience in direct patient care and clinical evaluations.
- ***Proven ability*** to ***ensure quality health*** care while ***containing costs*** within the hospital environment.
- ***Demonstrated capability*** to ***efficiently prioritize*** a broad range of responsibilities; ***possess strong problem resolution skills***.
- ***Skilled in coordinating programs*** and interfacing with professional medical and administrative staff. Able to develop excellent rapport and work effectively with individuals on all levels, maintaining highest levels of professionalism.
- Effective, experienced trainer.
- Certified Childbirth Educator - CCES
- Certified in Intravenous Therapy and Venopuncture.

**AREAS OF EFFECTIVENESS**

**Improve resource utilization.**
**Evaluate Clinical service requirements.**
**Determine equipment and technology needs.**
**Coordinate hospital services for all departments on an on-going basis.**

**EXPERIENCE**

1985 - Present

**MOUNT VERNON HOSPITAL,** Mount Vernon, NY
**Administrative Nurse Coordinator: Maternal Child Health Department**

- Based upon needs assessment, ***developed cross-orientation*** and ***staffing patterns*** to functionally ***utilize all staff from three units.***
- ***Orchestrated community outreach program resulting in a 36% increase in*** the ***unit census.*** Achieved increase in overall patient satisfaction.
- Served as liaison to promote a multidisciplinary approach to patient care.
- Order supplies; ***developed*** monthly ***ordering system*** for standing orders ***which eliminated financial stresses*** and promoted the smooth functioning of the unit.
- Oversee budget. Prepare five year projections.
- ***Coordinate staff*** and ***operations*** of Maternal Child Health Department.
- As nursing instructor, oversaw clinical aspects of obstetrics rotation for second year nursing students in the R.N. program.
- Provided educational programs to elevate level of competency for all staff.
- ***Reviewed and revised policies and procedures*** to reflect Family Centered Care: a facility for patient and significant others to be in a home like environment.
- Promoted Breast Feeding Education
- Serve as Hospital Lactation Consultant.
- Prepared Child Birth Education classes.

1983 - 1985

**BOARD OF COOPERATIVE EDUCATIONAL SERVICES,** Valhalla, NY
**Clinical Nursing Instructor: Secondary Level**

- Provided clinical instruction in Basic Fundamentals of Nursing and Maternal Child Health, to students of Practical Nursing.

**238**

**Combination.** *Mark D. Berkowitz, Yorktown Heights, New York*

This writer likes to boldface significant words to make them stand out. If you read down the two pages quickly and focus on just the bold italic words, you get a quick view of the person's skills,

**BARBARA WALTERS** ***page 2***

1983 - 1985 — **MOUNT VERNON BOARD OF EDUCATION,** Mount Vernon, NY
**Substitute School Nurse**
- Rendered first aid care to students.
- Completed student files for new admissions and transfer students including immunizations and annual physical exams and dental surveys.

1980 - 1983 — **WHITE PLAINS HOSPITAL MEDICAL CENTER,** White Plains, NY
**Head Nurse: Labor and Delivery Unit**
- ***Commended for developing*** an ***effective*** management ***structure*** to ***ensure*** the delivery of the ***highest quality nursing care*** to all patients.
- ***Developed staffing*** pattern to ***maximize utilization of personnel.***
- Trained new personnel, providing ongoing evaluation.
- Formulated and implemented policies of nursing care provided in unit.
- Liaised with department heads, medical staff, hospital management team and served as chairperson to various committees.

1975 - 1980 — **Staff Nurse: Labor and Delivery Unit**
- Oversaw total patient care in labor, delivery, cesarean section, recovery and post partum period.
- Interpreted fetal monitoring data for Non-Stress Tests and Oxytocin Challenge Tests.
- Provided patient care for termination of pregnancy including post-operative counseling.
- Updated policy and procedure manuals.

1972 - 1975 — **BRONX MUNICIPAL HOSPITAL CENTER,** Bronx, NY
**Staff Nurse: Surgical Unit**
- Prepared patients for surgery.
- ***Initiated pre-operative teaching classes*** and rendered all phases of post-operative care.
- Participated in instituting Primary Nursing.

**EDUCATION**

**HERBERT LEHMAN COLLEGE, C.U.N.Y.,** Bronx, NY
**Master of Science Program: *Nursing*** — *in progress*
- Specialization: Maternal Child Health Clinical Specialist

**MERCY COLLEGE,** Dobbs Ferry, NY
**Bachelor of Science: *Behavioral Science*** — 1981
- Specialization: Community Health

**BRONX COMMUNITY COLLEGE,** Bronx, NY
**Associate of Applied Science: *Nursing*** — 1972

**PROFESSIONAL AFFILIATIONS**

**A.S.P.O.**
**N.A.A.C.O.G.**
**C.C.E.S.**

**REFERENCES**

Available upon request.

activities, and achievements. The entire Areas of Effectiveness section is bold. The Experience section shows continual work from 1972 to the present, so dates are put prominently at the left margin. With her master's degree in progress, dates in the Education section are right-aligned.

**JOSEPH R. PARKER**
1015 Blodgett Street
Clio, MI 48430
810-555-9428

**HIGHLIGHTS OF EXPERIENCE**

*Project Management*

- Participate in budget development of street maintenance program.
- Prepare cost estimates for work projects; monitor manpower, capital and materials costs and generate monthly reports.
- Coordinate construction, maintenance and repair of streets, sidewalks, buildings, parks and other city property and facilities; make daily site visits.
- Prepare contingency plans for weather-related and other emergencies.
- Act as Field Operations Supervisor during special events and emergencies.
- Originally developed and continue to complete annual updates of Pavement Maintenance Schedule. Identify and prioritize streets; prepare cost estimates.
- Monitor activities in city's Recycling Depot.

*Supervision*

- Supervise 5 foreman with 20-40 employees (60-70 during emergency situations).
- Determine job assignments, crews and work schedules.
- Collaborate with other supervisors and administrative personnel regarding joint projects, work schedules, policies, procedures and staffing needs.
- Monitor employee relations; participate in employee grievance procedure as necessary.
- Developed and presented several training programs.

*Technical*

- Participate in major sewer projects, including large diameter new sewer construction and repair of existing systems (sanitary and storm).
- Oversee repair of vehicles and equipment.
- Ensure adherence to appropriate safety regulations.
- Operate specialized equipment including pavers, excavators, graders, front-end and backhoe loaders, street sweepers, and trucks.
- Maintain technical expertise in areas of responsibility.
- Possess Class A Commercial Drivers License.

**EMPLOYMENT HISTORY**

CITY OF DEXTER • Dexter, MI (1973-1996)

**Street Maintenance & Construction Coordinator**
**Senior Construction Foreman** and
**Heavy Construction & Maintenance Equipment Operator** (dual position)
**Equipment Operator**
**Asphalt Raker**
**Greenskeeper**
**Truck Driver**
**Sewer Cleaner**
**Laborer**

**EDUCATION AND TRAINING**

BUSINESS & INDUSTRY TRAINING CENTER • Dexter, MI
**First Line Supervision** (1992, 1993, 1995)
**Total Quality Service** (1993)

SAGINAW VALLEY UNIVERSITY • Saginaw, MI
**B.A.S.** (1993) - *Significant Coursework:* Economics, Political Science, Philosophy

WASHTENAW COMMUNITY COLLEGE • Ann Arbor, MI
**Associate in Applied Science - Business Management** (1986) - *With Honors*

*References available on request.*

239

**Combination.** *Janet L. Beckstrom, Flint, Michigan*

After having laborer positions for the same employer for 23 years, this individual took "an early retirement/buyout at age 42." With "managerial potential," he was looking for a supervisory job.

# ROBERT J. ASHER

Playa Del Rey, California
310.555.5555

## PROFILE

Results-driven executive manager with expertise in global operations, distribution, international letters of credit, collections, and cross-cultural film technologies. Strong international and domestic experience.

## SELECTED ACHIEVEMENTS AND QUALIFICATIONS

*ADMINISTRATIVE AND ACCOUNT MANAGEMENT*

- Direct responsibility for the promotional and broadcast delivery of 2200 titles in the libraries of: NOMOLOS, LANAC+ (Paris), SACIS (Rome), Dino de Laurentis, OCLORAC, and Active Entertainment, serving over 220 North American and worldwide TV markets.
- Successfully directed the International Distribution for the 900 title Noiro Pictures library.
- Operated as the distribution Account Executive for Geffen Records and Buena Vista Int'l. (Sidney), primarily servicing Noiro Pictures.
- Secured contract approval for deal memos, processed license agreements and amendments, contract collections and account receivables, including opening and negotiating letters of credit.
- Apprised sales and acquisition's departments on current and future projects.
- Ability to develop rapport and build relationships with customers and clients through attention to detail in defining needs and providing service and solutions to meet those needs.
- Excellent management and leadership skills resulting in top employee performance.
- Strong emphasis on cost containment, production and distribution control.
- Experienced and effective with collections procedures.
- Maintained current status reports between sales, production and distribution departments.

*FILM, PUBLICITY, AND BROADCAST MATERIAL DISTRIBUTION*

- Organized post-production and distribution departments; master tape acquisition and production.
- Responsible for setting and releasing titles based upon rights availability, and maintenance of world-wide bicycling (tapes) schedule.
- Liaison with publicity, post-production and distribution in fulfilling client requirements.
- Demonstrated expertise in comprehensive sound, film, music and effects, dubbing and laboratory requirements, and computerized post-production systems.
- Strong background in International post-production standards and distribution requirements for both major foreign and overseas English language markets.

***Technical Skills*** - expertise with: D-1-SONY DVR2000; D-2-SONY DVR18/28; DIGIBETA-SONY DVW500/P; 1"-SONY BVH 2000; AMPEX VPR6; Betacam-SONY BVW 75/P.

## PROFESSIONAL EXPERIENCE

| | | |
|---|---|---|
| **DIRECTOR** - International Distribution | *NOMOLOS INT'L ENTERPRISES*, Beverly Hills, CA | 1995 to present |
| **DIRECTOR** - International Distribution | *NOIRO PICTURES INTERNATIONAL*, Century City, CA | 1992 to 1995 |
| **DISTRIBUTION MANAGER** | *MIDNITE EXPRESS INTERNATIONAL*, Inglewood, CA | 1991 to 1992 |
| **DIRECTOR** - Licensing and Operations | *THOMAS TRADE GROUP*, Long Beach, CA | 1988 to 1991 |
| **OPERATIONS MANAGER** | *AMERCEP, INCORPORATED*, Los Angeles, CA | 1987 to 1988 |
| **LAW CLERK, DEPT. OF JUSTICE** | *U.S. ATTORNEYS OFFICE*, Portland, OR | 1983 to 1986 |

## EDUCATION

*UNIVERSITY OF CALIFORNIA LOS ANGELES* — Westwood, California
**GRADUATE STUDIES**, 1994 -1996 — Film, Television and Video program

*PORTLAND STATE UNIVERSITY* — Portland, Oregon
**GRADUATE PROGRAM**, 1987 — Pacific Rim International Business

*LEWIS & CLARK COLLEGE* — Portland, Oregon
**B.A., DOUBLE MAJOR**, 1986 — International Affairs and Asian History
Minor: International Business

**240**

**Combination.** *Patricia S. Cash, Prescott, Arizona*

A partial triple line points to the name and enhances the contact information. Bulleted groups emphasize "business acumen and technical expertise in the international and domestic markets."

**ANDREA PARKER SMITH**
1154 Cheyenne Drive
Cocoa Beach, FL 32905
(404) 727-6878

---

Medical Office Manager position utilizing extensive experience in medical administration.

---

**CREDENTIALS**

- **Insurance Billing:** Extensive knowledge especially in Medicare. Knowledge of Managed Care. CPT-4 and ICD-9 Coding. Experienced in electronic medicare transmissions.
  - Successfully reduced accounts receivable from $2.5M to $1.3M in the space of one year for Porter Medical Center.

- **Computers:** Quick learner experienced in WordPerfect and computerized billing software.
  - Successfully created a computerized filing system which reduced referencing time by approximately 50%.

- **Administration/Management:** Extensive experience in shift management, work delegation, hands-on procedures, scheduling, and resolution of customer problems.
  - Created and provided medical education programs for all ages from pre-schoolers through senior citizens at Medical Examiner's Office. Conducted in-service training program for Police and Fire Departments.
  - Wrote, edited, and presented marketing presentations on Porter Medical Center sales and services to various non-profit and profit agencies.

- **Emergency Medical Support:** Certified EMT. Perform emergency medical duties while working on ambulance squad. Proficient in taking medical histories and prioritizing medical emergency workloads.

- **Medical Training/Certifications:** Certified Bereavement Counselor. Certified in First Aid and Basic Life Support. Medical Office Administrator Honor Graduate from Herzing Institute. HIV/AIDS education course.

**PROFESSIONAL PROFILE**

**Billing/Collections Director**, Porter Medical Center, Maitland, Florida, 1994-Present

**EMT Shift Manager**, Portico Aid Squad, Portico, Kansas, 1988-1992

**Account Reservation Manager**, Voyages, 1981-1988
Supervised reservationists and developed custom tour packages for individuals and groups.

**Manager, Law Library**, Dadin, Cooper, and Swinger, New York City, NY, 1979-1981
Hired as Receptionist and promoted to managing the law library.

**Certified Bereavement Counselor**, Medical Examiner's Office, New York City, NY, 1977-1978
Taught in-service courses to New York City Police and Fire Department and counseled parents on the loss of their children.

**EDUCATION**

**Bachelor of Arts** - St. Judes University, Jasmin, NY

**241**

**Combination.** *Laura A. DeCarlo, Melbourne, Florida*

This person wanted a medical office management job. With experience in medical office billing and a diversified background, a functional format best points to her goal. The Profile is a history.

# STEVEN BENSON

101 Roberts Avenue White Plains, NY 10606 (914) 761-1997

**OBJECTIVE**

A position in Industrial Technology which will benefit from my exceptional Quality Control expertise and utilize strong systems analysis and inventory control skills to the fullest.

**PROFILE**

- Well qualified Manufacturing Technology Professional with ***strong Q/C track record*** in ***achieving first piece acceptance***.
- A ***resource person, problem solver, trouble shooter*** and ***creative turn-around manager***.
- Demonstrated ability to efficiently prioritize a broad range of responsibilities and ***consistently meet deadlines***.
- Peak performer; strong record ***innovating procedures*** to ***increase productivity***.
- ***Demonstrated training and development*** abilities, producing peak performing teams.
- ***Certified Manufacturing Technologist***.

**EXPERIENCE**

1993 - Present

**HOLIDAY INN,** Mount Kisco, NY
**Food & Beverage Director**

- Direct staff of 30; manage monthly operating budget in excess of $65k.
- Frequently serve as Manager-on-Duty for entire hotel.
- ***Computerized inventory*** for kitchen and lounge which ***decreased*** liquor ***expenses*** and ***increased sales*** by $3k per month.
- ***Initiated rotating inventory*** to ***move slower selling inventory*** and ***decrease on-premises inventory***.
- Motivated staff into more productive selling mode by initiating incentive plans.

1989 - 1993

**MICHAEL'S TAVERN II,** Tarrytown, NY
**Manager**

- Supervised staff of 17; oversaw payroll.
- Instituted promotional events to increase sales.

1986 - 1990

**PRESTO PLASTICS,** Stamford, CT
**Assistant Quality Control Manager** for this manufacturer of display and packaging products.

- Supervised team of three quality control inspectors.
- Oversaw three satellite assembly locations producing electronic circuit boards and computer monitor turntables in addition to packaging products.
- Improved record keeping on machine settings per piece.
- Worked closely with tool & die team to better assure customers of high quality production levels.

***<u>Significant Achievements</u>***

- ***Instituted procedural changes*** resulting in ***first piece acceptance levels increasing*** from ***70% to 91.7%***.
- Facilitated communication with customers, gaining better input on tolerance specifications which resulted in ***higher profit margins per production run***.

**EDUCATION**

**S.U.N.Y. COLLEGE at BUFFALO,** Buffalo, NY
**Bachelor of Science: <u>Industrial Technology</u>** GPA: 3.0
**NAIT Accredited**
***Certified Manufacturing Technologist***

**REFERENCES**

Available upon request.

242

**Combination.** *Mark D. Berkowitz, Yorktown Heights, New York*

Bold italic calls attention to important words and phrases. Bold, italic, and underlining are used for the Significant Achievements side heading. Left-alignment of dates helps to make white space.

# LINDA A. BURN

999 S. Fourth Street • Preston, MD 00000 • (999) 999-9999 • Fax (111) 111-1111



***Financial management professional with extensive experience and expertise in accounting and grant administration with two leading nonprofit organizations. Strong background in human resource administration. Excellent technical skills with in-depth background in accounting systems and data base management in both Macintosh and Windows environments. Developer and sole proprietor of a successful financial consulting business (Money Matters, Preston, MD) which has provided financial solutions and support to individuals, small businesses and non-profits since 1992.***

**AREAS OF EXPERTISE**

- Accounting for Non-Profits
- Grant Administration
- Data Base Management
- Human Resource Administration
- Financial Management of Small Businesses
- Personal financial planning

**PROFESSIONAL BACKGROUND**

**THE WILKINS INSTITUTE, BALTIMORE, MD**

***Financial Director/Operations Manager*** 12/92 to 8/96

Responsible for the overall financial management of The Global Vision Group, a grant making program of the Lister Charitable Foundation, administered by The Wilkins Institute. Managed the program's $1.3 annual operating budget and monitored $5 million in grants awarded annually through the program.

***Specific duties included:*** Reviewing and approving slating materials from prospective grantees; coordinating the write-up process for grant proposals; developing monitoring plans for projects; monitoring compliance with reporting requirements; reviewing and approving monitoring reports; authorizing grant payments; processing budget modifications and project extensions; managing the operation of the program office which included staffing, etc.; managing the operation of the Macintosh Grant Making Data Base; drafting and monitoring annual operating budget; and preparing interim financial reports for Wilkins Institute and the Lister Charitable Foundation.

**THE WILKINS INSTITUTE, BALTIMORE, MD**

***Accounting Manager*** 4/86 to 12/92

Managed staff of four accounting department employees and assisted with administration of benefits program which included a self-funded health insurance plan.

***Specific duties included:*** Working directly with the Treasurer/Controller in preparing financial statements, budget proposals and specialized financial reports required by grant-funding corporations; overseeing accounts receivable, payable and payroll; assisting with the processing and management of the Institute's investments; working with outside auditors on year-end close and subsequently audited financial reports; serving on the Institutes's Staff Advisory Committee for health and retirement benefits; assisting with the hiring of administrative staff for policy programs; proofreading and editing correspondence from the Treasurer's office.

**SANFORD CORPORATION, QUEENSTOWN, MD**

***Conference Operations Assistant*** 1987 to 1990

**BRINKS'S BANK OF WELLVILLE, WELLVILLE, MD**

***Teller*** 1975 to 1984

**WELLVILLE CHILD DEVELOPMENT CENTER, WELLVILLE, MD**

***Receptionist/Financial Records Clerk*** 1975

**EDUCATION**

**WINDMILL COLLEGE, HOLLYHOCK, MD**

***Associate of Arts, Accounting***

Graduated with Honors, 1990

**JONESTOWN COLLEGE, JONESTOWN, DE**

Currently enrolled in Accounting and Business Management program. Goal: Bachelor of Science, Accounting, 12/97.

**243**

**Combination.** *Thomas E. Spann, Easton, Maryland*

The resume opens with a profile in bold italic, followed by an Areas of Expertise section. The small section headings in the margin make the names and titles to the right seem more dominant.

## LEONA VAN-SMITHERS

1213 Westridge Lane | Seattle, Washington 98776 | Ph: (209) 897-9076

**PROFESSIONAL PROFILE**

Human resource executive with proven track record in managing HR functions for professional employer organizations with multi-site and multi-state locations. Effective communicator with skills in public relations, team building and new business development.

- **Human Resources** - Skilled in recruiting, hiring, interviewing and screening job applicants. Solid experience in candidate selection, new employee orientation, performance evaluation, discipline, counseling, safety management and benefits administration.
- **Training** - Experienced in developing and administering training programs and seminars for staff at all levels. Effective facilitator with well-developed presentation skills.
- **Administration** - Proactive manager with experience in creating a human resource policies, procedures and programs; able to develop budgets and manage HR offices at multiple locations.
- **Legal** - Skilled negotiator with strong legal background and extensive knowledge of local/state/federal regulations and issues related to employment law, sexual harassment, legal liability, Worker's Compensation and risk management.

*Hands-on manager with common-sense approach to problem solving.*

**EXPERIENCE**

OREGON STAFFING SERVICES, INC. - Seattle, Washington

**Human Resources Director** (9/92-Present)

Hired to rebuild HR department for professional employer organization with 3,500 employees in four states. Recruit, interview, screen, hire and train staff. Develop new HR policies, procedures and programs.

- Provide legal advice on issues related to human resources.
- Represent company at unemployment hearings.
- Administer benefit program.
- Set up drug testing program.
- Oversee corporate training.

NORTHWEST BUSINESS SERVICES, INC. - Tigard, Oregon

**Risk Management Specialist** (6/85-7/92)

Coordinated risk management functions for professional employer organization; played an active role in problem solving and conflict resolution.

- Developed safety programs, investigated accidents and set up safety committees.
- Played active role in legislative lobbying; acted as company representative at Bureau of Labor and unemployment hearings.
- Reduced Workers' Compensation costs by $400,000.
- Cut unemployment claims by 50%.
- Created new job application and accident investigation forms.

**EDUCATION**

PORTLAND STATE UNIVERSITY - Portland, Oregon

**Master of Business Administration** (1989)

**244**

**Combination.** *Pat Kendall, Aloha, Oregon*

Contact information within horizontal lines is easy to spot. The four, bold, embedded headings in the Profile section indicate the person's four key skills areas. The job titles are easily seen, too.

**Roberta Henson**
153 Elm Street, Boston, Massachusetts 02111
(617) 555-5153

## Profile

- Health care management professional with demonstrated analytical, problem-solving, and leadership skills complemented by a strong clinical background.
- Key contributor to diverse programs including JCAHO accreditation, computerized tracking and reporting for improved data analysis, policy and procedure writing, and numerous specially assigned management projects.
- Excellent organizational skills and a strong ability to see projects through to completion.

## Professional Experience

FAIRVIEW RETIREMENT COMMUNITY, Boston, Massachusetts 1991-March 1996
**Director, Staff Development**

Managed the provision and coordination of training for 250 health care professionals in a large skilled nursing facility. Contributed to overall facility management in varied capacities.

BUSINESS MANAGEMENT

- Developed computerized inservice tracking spreadsheets for a staff of 250.
- Using computerized spreadsheet, tracked incident statistics and created monthly reports for the Safety Committee; used data from reports to analyze problem areas and recommend solutions.
- Served as the facility's Infection Control Nurse; developed tracking system for infection statistics.
- As a member of the Human Resources committee, addressed issues and created policies.
- Wrote Quality Assurance program and other policies and procedures for the Nursing Department.
- Key member of a committee working to prepare the facility for JCAHO accreditation process.
- As a member of the Management Team for the facility, regularly called upon to utilize excellent organizational, problem-solving and writing skills for a variety of special assignments.

TRAINING/COORDINATION

- Planned, coordinated and presented staff inservice education; recruited additional trainers from both inside and outside the facility.
- Completed Train-the-Trainer training and taught state-approved Nurse Aide classes.
- Implemented the use of the Long Term Care Network for staff training. Tracked and taped training sessions presented via satellite; set up video library for staff use either in the facility or at home; prepared schedules of sessions to be presented and marketed use of the program to staff.

NORTH SHORE HOME FOR THE AGED, Rockport, Massachusetts 1988-1991
**Nurse Manager**

- Included 24-hour responsibility and management of the facility's skilled care unit.

NEW ENGLAND MEMORIAL HOSPITAL, Stoneham, Massachusetts 1980-1988
**Staff Nurse: Emergency Department** (1980-83), **Hemodialysis Unit** (1983-1988)

- Helped initiate kidney retrieval and perfusion program. Played a key coordinating role in transporting and maintaining donated kidneys and coordinating the transplant program with national transplant centers, hospital laboratories, nephrologists, transplant surgeons, patients and families.

## Education/Training/Certification

MA in Gerontology, May 1996 • SALEM STATE COLLEGE, Salem, Massachusetts
Graduate, RN Program, 1980 • DEACONESS HOSPITAL SCHOOL OF NURSING, Boston, Massachusetts
RN License, 1980 (Current status)
Numerous nursing and management education training courses, seminars, and workshops.

**245**

**Combination.** *Louise Kursmark, Cincinnati, Ohio*

This laid-off person thought she could not get a health care management or training position. Managerial achievements and training background are stressed. The person had a job in three weeks.

# Christina Monroe

9856 East Chester Road • Adrian, Michigan 49221
(517) 365-1258

## PROFESSIONAL QUALIFICATIONS

- Portfolio/Money Market Funds Analysis
- Employee Benefits Management
- Operating Budgets Development
- Accounts Payable/Accounts Receivable/Payroll
- Assets/Liability/Credit Analysis
- Project Planning/Management

## PROFESSIONAL EXPERIENCE

ST. THOMAS ACADEMY, Tecumseh, Michigan — June 1991-October 1995
**Director of Finance**

- Developed operating budgets and maintained budgets with monthly and quarterly reports. Handled all delinquent accounts, deposits, taxes, and government forms. Managed a money market fund. Acted as liaison for accounting firms.
- Managed stock portfolio and compiled agendas and financial forms. Bought and sold stocks. Compiled information and presented it to the trustees. Acted as a liaison between trustees and stock broker.
- Handled all day-to-day operations of Academy. Supervised staff of up to 75 employees. Helped develop policies and procedures handbook. Worked on strategic planning, including implementing financial recommendations. Set up new computer system and computerized entire office. Computer programs included: Open Systems, WordPerfect 6.0, Windows, and Lotus 1-2-3. Served on Advisory Board and Safety Board.
- Received and reviewed proposals and bids from health care providers. Presented the best to the Principal of the Academy.
- Developed and sent out scholarship forms. Reviewed and categorized completed forms and recommended families to receive scholarships. Maintained scholarship fund by reviewing payments received.
- Maintained safe operating conditions of building, including capital improvements and day-to-day general maintenance; supervised custodial engineers and maintained Academy guidelines for cleanliness.
- Hired, trained, and supervised cafeteria personnel. Purchased supplies by consulting catalogs and interviewing suppliers to obtain prices. Bought and sold equipment.
- Purchased equipment by consulting catalogs and interviewing suppliers to obtain prices. Obtained information on warrantee and maintenance agreements.

LUKE'S PLASTICS, Tecumseh, Michigan — September 1981-November 1990
**Office Manager**

- Managed accounts receivable, accounts payable, and payroll. Acted as a liaison for accounting firms.
- Received and reviewed proposals and bids from health care providers.
- Hired, trained, and supervised staff of 3 employees and developed new computer system using Open Systems. Purchased all office equipment by consulting catalogs and interviewing suppliers to obtain prices.
- Member of the Lenawee Personnel Association.

## CONTINUING EDUCATION/SEMINARS

*Sponsored by St. Thomas Academy*
- Shortcut To Windows
- Excel
- WordPerfect 6.0 for Windows

*Sponsored by Luke's Plastics*
- Office Management
- Understanding Financial Statements
- How to Supervise People

## EDUCATION

Adrian College, Adrian, Michigan
**General Business Courses**

**246**

**Combination.** *Christina M. Popa, Adrian, Michigan*

The Professional Qualifications section "brings the most important information right to the top." This information in two columns can be altered to target the resume to a specific position.

# REBECCA CALDERWOOD

714 East 9th Street ▪ Astoria, New York ▪ 11222
Phone: (718) 434-7872 ▪ E-mail: RCalderwood@msn.com

## HEALTHCARE ADMINISTRATOR / PROGRAM DIRECTOR

Experienced administrator with a proven ability to run successful programs. Proficient at setting, expecting, and achieving high standards of quality. Currently direct a facility regarded as a model program. Respected leader with excellent team-building, communication, and interpersonal skills.

## EDUCATION

**Master of Science in Health Administration,** Hunter College, New York, NY, 1990
**Bachelor of Arts in Psychology,** Union College, Schenectady, NY, 1984

## EMPLOYMENT

**Heartland Agency,** Woodside, NY
**Director, 1990 to present**
Administer program that serves adults with disabilities. Manage $5 million in funding. Oversee more than 50 management, clinical, and direct care staff members. Devise systems for admission, discharge, organization, and staffing. Monitor all facets of the 20,000 square foot plant and comply with OSHA standards. Ensure compliance with NYS OMRDD Part 690, 633, 635, and 624 policies.

Key Accomplishments:

- Fostered an environment of teamwork and cooperation that boosted staff morale.
- Initiated a recruitment campaign that increased consumer enrollment from 73 to 129.
- Undertook a classroom reorganization project that improved quality services and increased consumer independence.
- Developed a positive relationship with other departments so that all programs work toward common goals.
- Set-up and chair the interagency Human Rights and Informed Consent committees.
- Selected to direct a satellite program for geriatric consumers.

**United Samaritans,** Flushing, NY
**Program Coordinator, 1985 to 1990**
Managed department that received more than $2 million in funding. Hired, supervised, and evaluated professional and support staff. Supervised the work activities of 350 consumers in the Extended Rehabilitation Department. Acted as Director of Rehabilitation in her absence.

Key Accomplishments:

- Secured three new agency programs by responding to Request for Proposals.
- Prepared statistical reports and handled external audits for all programs.
- Devised consumer satisfaction survey that sparked improvements in programming.
- Promoted from Case Manager and maintained a large caseload as Coordinator.

## COMPUTERS

Advanced user of WordPerfect, Microsoft Word, R&R Relational Report Writer, Lotus 1-2-3, SPSS, and Microsoft Publisher. Train colleagues on how to use a computer and provide technical guidance. Experience with installing network systems and computer hardware.

**247**

**Combination.** *Kim Isaacs, Jackson Heights, New York*

"Education is put at the top" because of the importance of the master's degree in Health Administration. The Computers section is "a strong ending" for this health administrator.

# Vincent M. Smithers

One West Croy
Portland, Oregon 97223
503 / 244-4355

**BACKGROUND SUMMARY**

Creative problem solver with broad experience in operations management and troubleshooting; skilled in strategic planning, sales, marketing, budgeting and project management. Capable leader/motivator with well-developed team-building skills; experienced in hiring, training and evaluating employees.

- Able to analyze complex situations, resolve problems and make recommendations to improve efficiency and maximize profitability.
- Solid training and background in engineering; able to understand and interpret technical data and communicate effectively with engineers and staff.
- Computer literate. Experienced in researching and developing custom software for business; thoroughly familiar with applications for billing, tracking, statistical analysis and project management.

**EXPERIENCE**

UNITED SERVICES LTD. - Portland, Oregon

**DIRECTOR OF OPERATIONS** (5/90-Present)

Manage three separate divisions. Involved in day-to-day operations of all businesses, including strategic planning, staffing, budgeting, fiscal management, sales and service. Oversee agent incentive program and coordinate all phases of marketing and new business development.

- Implemented operating procedures that increased weekly gross from $124,000 to $488,000 in 12 months.
- Developed and launched new division that contributed 16% of gross revenue.

ARCO MEDICAL PRODUCTS - Portland, Oregon

**SERVICE MANAGER** (6/82-6/90)

Coordinated service operations and supervised a staff of 11 technicians. Conducted repair seminars and instructed sales staff and customers in technical aspects of equipment operation. Developed programs that reduced inventory, improved service and ensured compliance with preventative maintenance requirements.

**EDUCATION**

PORTLAND STATE UNIVERSITY - Portland, Oregon

**B.S., ELECTRICAL ENGINEERING** (1983)

**References Provided Upon Request**

248

**Combination.** *Pat Kendall, Aloha, Oregon*

The pair of double lines direct attention to the enclosed Background Summary, which mentions the person's most important skills. In the Experience section, bullets point to achievements.

# Marilyn Smith

**2510 Loyanne ♦ Spring, Texas 77373 ♦ (713) 350-2100**

---

**PROFILE:**

**MULTI-UNIT FOOD AND BEVERAGE OPERATIONS MANAGER**

Well-qualified professional with 6 years experience in multi-unit F&B operations and Food Service Management. Expertise includes:

★ Human Resource Training and Administration
★ Purchasing and Inventory Management
★ Multi-Unit Operations Management
★ Customer Service and Client Relations
★ Promotions and Special Events
★ Catering Operations
★ Staff Recruitment and Scheduling
★ Vendor Sourcing and Negotiation

***Contributed to significant cost reductions and revenue/profit growth through efforts in productivity, efficiency and quality improvement.***

**PROFESSIONAL EXPERIENCE:**

**NORTHGATE COUNTRY CLUB**, Houston, TX 1990 - 1996

***Prestigious, private golf and tennis resort community with over 800 members. Fast-track promotion through a series of increasingly responsible management positions. Advanced rapidly based upon consistent improvement in employee morale and productivity, client satisfaction and revenues.***

**FOOD AND BEVERAGE SERVICE DIRECTOR**

Full management responsibility for all F&B service operations at four on-site dining areas and a full service catering department operating year round. Recruited, hired, trained, scheduled and supervised a staff of 22. Negotiated vendor contracts and managed a multi-million dollar purchasing and inventory management program.

- Planned, designed and facilitated service area for the new Cafe Northgate.
- Achieved a 33% cost savings on china through competitive pricing strategies.
- Negotiated a 50% reduction in linen supplies.
- Saved thousands of dollars in paper supplies through vendor sourcing.
- Orchestrated all special events and holiday receptions for up to 450 people, including entertainment, theme planning, and special equipment/accessories.

**INDEPENDENT CONSULTANT** 1983 - 1989

Contracted administrative services to companies, small businesses and individuals. Performed accounting, marketing, and secretarial functions for the medical industry.

***Prior***
Office Manager for Chief Orthopedic Surgeon in Houston. Responsible for scheduling, payroll, collections, insurance and financial reporting.

**EDUCATION:**

University of Southern Louisiana
Lafayette, Louisiana
*General Management* 1976

**249**

**Combination.** *Cheryl A. Harland, The Woodlands, Texas*

This Food and Beverage Service Director did not have a college degree. While raising a family, she had had only several part-time positions. Nevertheless, the writer creates this strong resume.

**ALAN STEVENS**
**123 East 25th Street • New York, NY 10009 • (212) 765-8732**

**PROFESSIONAL SUMMARY**

» Extensive experience in security management with special security assignments for high profile clientele.

» Strong knowledge of state-of-the-art security equipment.

» Proven expertise supervising a wide range of operations.

**SECURITY EXPERIENCE**

*SECURITY DIRECTOR*
**Studio 76**, New York, NY — 1990 - 1992

- Initially hired to revamp entire security operation for 2,000 capacity nightclub.
- Responsible for entire security operation including management consultation, staffing, purchasing/set up of security equipment, money management, and payroll.
- Hired, trained, supervised, and scheduled 18 security personnel.
- Served as personal liaison with NYPD, investigators, and community groups.

**MAJOR ACCOMPLISHMENTS**

- Revamped security system in a high risk environment.
- Implemented new security measures: installed electronic metal detectors, rearranged closed circuit TV cameras, and changed collection points for admission.
- Changed staff assignments from fixed to rotating positions.
- Improved staff training by instituting more formal training procedures.
- Adopted more selective admission policies.
- Substantially decreased serious incidents involving the police department.

*SECURITY SUPERVISOR*
**Hogan Security Corporation,** New York, NY — 1990 - 1991

- Managed security operations for special events at New York City hotels, numerous society parties and corporate events at restaurants and office buildings.
- Served as personal bodyguard to numerous entertainment celebrities.

*POLICE OFFICER* — 1983 - 1990
**New York City Police Department**, New York, NY

- Performed police officer duties in high crime area as an Anti-Crime Officer (plain clothes).
- Chosen as a Training Officer and Property Officer.

*NIGHTCLUB SECURITY SUPERVISOR* — 1979 - 1982
**Various Nightclubs throughout New York City**

- Responsible for client selection and crowd control for top NYC nightclubs.

**OTHER EXPERIENCE**

*INTERNATIONAL PRINTING QUALITY CONTROL MANAGER* — 1992 - Present
**TCD,** New York, NY

- Ensure quality control standards for printing of books and manuals.

**EDUCATION**

1992 - Present — **New York City College,** New York, NY
*Candidate for B.S. in Security Management* (expected graduation date: 1994)

- Courses include: Terrorism; Security Monitoring; Fire Safety

1987 - 1990 — **New York University,** New York, NY

**SKILLS**

Fourth Degree Black Belt - Korean Boxing
Knowledge of security equipment including closed circuit TV

**250**

**Combination.** *Etta Barmann, New York, New York*

This person has considerable experience in security operations. His most recent experience was in another field while he completed his degree. Security Experience is put first; the other, last.

**EMMELINE WHITCOMB**
0000 North West
Anywhere, USA
(000) 000-0000

## EXPERIENCE SUMMARY

**RESULTS-ORIENTED MANAGER** with proven ability to impact operations and increase profit margins for multi-million dollar manufacturer. Experienced in multiple disciplines including:

- Manufacturing
- Production Scheduling
- Warehousing
- Distribution
- Finance
- Accounting

Capable of critically evaluating and responding to diverse organizational needs (procedural enhancement, productivity improvement, inventory management, cost reduction). Computer literate in mainframe and PC environments; knowledge of various software programs with emphasis on Lotus 1-2-3.

## PROFESSIONAL EXPERIENCE

BRITTON MANUFACTURING, Anywhere, USA 6/88-Present

**Director, Manufacturing & Distribution** -- Directly accountable for manufacturing, distribution, and various accounting functions for leading manufacturer/food processor.

***Manufacturing/Distribution:*** Plan production for eight lines (1,500 items), manage raw material and finished goods inventories, coordinate warehousing, and oversee distribution. Develop strategies to improve raw material staging/preparation, plant efficiency, and freight allowance controls.

- Contributed to production increase from 88 to 114 million pounds per year over 3-year period.
- Reduced back order rates below corporate goal to 1.5% and lowered finished goods inventory levels.
- Implemented new JIT purchasing program; experienced in MRP systems.

***General Management:*** Prepare and manage $2.2 million budget for three warehouse facilities. Coordinate sales, production, and accounting functions. Supervise three department managers with indirect supervision of staff of 20. Additionally responsible for production bonus administration, rework control, and analysis and costing activities.

- Instrumental in reduction of production labor from 2.2 cents to 1.6 cents per pound.
- Initiated operational systems and scheduling procedures to achieve overtime savings of approx. 32%.
- Assumed additional responsibility for fiscal and operational management of Illinois plant.

***Finance/Accounting:*** Supervised accounting staff in preparation of general ledger, financial statements, account reconciliations, accounts payable, accounts receivable, production accounting, and costing of raw material usage data for co-packer entities.

- Upgraded computer software to aid in production scheduling, MRP, and process/product costing.
- Prepared cost accounting for as many as 300 new products per year.
- Promoted through positions as Staff Accountant and Senior Accountant.

PRIOR EXPERIENCE: Accounting Analyst, Safeco Insurance Co., Anywhere, USA 1/84-5/88

## EDUCATION

CALIFORNIA STATE UNIVERSITY, LOS ANGELES: **B.S., Business Administration • Option in Finance**
SEMINARS: **Dr. W. Edwards Deming TQM Course • JIT Seminar**

**References Upon Request**

251

**Combination.** *Susan Britton Whitcomb, Fresno, California*

The Experience Summary is a profile that shows this person's abilities, areas of experience, and computer literacy. In the Professional Experience section, bullets signal quantified achievements.

# Joan Wilkerson

3161 West Beach Street
Huntington Beach, CA 92432 **(310) 234-4567**

## Qualifications Summary

Accomplished Marketing/Sales Executive with a stellar track record in diverse business environments . . . envisioned and brought to fruition profitable new ventures, profit centers, products . . . generated new foreign and domestic business . . . intellectually and emotionally equipped to compete in a fast-paced, aggressive sales environment . . . excel in business development, with well-developed prospecting, cold calling, and networking skills . . . persuasive and articulate communicator.

## Business Experience

***Marketing & Management -- Food Service*** 1986-Present

**Director of Marketing**, Hanny's Inc., Huntington Beach, CA
**National Sales**, Venture Manufacturing, Inc., Huntington Beach, CA

As Director of Marketing, guided young organization to achieve steady growth, doubling number of locations and gross sales during three-year tenure. Planned and implemented effective marketing strategies to reach target market. Negotiated and executed franchise contracts as licensed agent in the State of California; purchased and managed local franchise, developing business from start-up to $200,000 in sales. Subsequently recruited by Venture Manufacturing, the world's leading manufacturer of high volume, institutional food service facilities. Perform worldwide technical sales as licensed salesperson; successfully developed new products and multi-million dollar markets.

***Marketing & Sales -- Steel Industry*** 1979-1986

**Manufacturer's Representative**, Noble Company, Inc., Santa Ana, CA
**Vice President of Marketing**, Saudi American Corporation, Dallas, TX and Riyadh, Saudi Arabia
**Senior Salesman**, Kaiser Steel Corporation, Los Angeles, CA

Fifteen years experience in the steel industry, initially with Kaiser Steel as the youngest salesman in the company's history. Opened lucrative territories, developing significant business volume among steel service centers and large manufacturers. Responsibilities involved extensive international travel, at one time living in Saudi Arabia while managing a new venture. Negotiated and administered contracts valued in excess of $5 million; interfaced extensively with representatives from Saudi Arabia, France, Germany, the U.K., and Korea.

***Business Development & Management -- Publishing*** 1969-1978

**Publisher**, *Sea World Magazine*, Sea World, San Diego, CA
**Publisher**, *Journal of Marine Education*, The Marine Corporation, Newport Beach, CA
**Vice President of Marketing**, Educational Properties Incorporated, Costa Mesa, CA
**Director of Advertising**, *Pacific Magazine*, Graphics 2, Inc., Newport Beach, CA

Instrumental in developing and exploiting direct marketing to schools, school districts, and state departments of education. Successful experience in print advertising sales led to involvement in the publishing business. Launched new ventures and was responsible for conceptual development, marketing, production, and world-wide distribution of a well-accepted film series and popular scientific journal. Secured federal funds, as well as corporate support through solicitation of Fortune 50 companies. Approached and enjoyed a long-term collaboration with the Cousteau Group.

**References Upon Request**

**252**

**Combination.** *Susan Britton Whitcomb, Fresno, California*

More than three pages pared down to one. Two or more companies are grouped together under a field subheading to eliminate gaps from closure. Narrative style helps to "meld it all together."

**MEL GIBSON, RRA**

333 Ocean Avenue • Los Angeles, Ohio 55555 • (888) 555-2018

**EXPERTISE**

Experienced **Health Information Management Administrator** able to offer an unusual combination of technical, operational, and human resource management skills in:

- **Managerial and Administrative Systems Analysis**
- **Internal and External Customer Service Delivery**
- **Development of Policies and Procedures**
- **Employee Development and Motivation**

**CERTIFICATIONS**

AMERICAN HEALTH INFORMATION MANAGEMENT ASSOCIATION

- **Registered Records Administrator—October 199x**
- **Accredited Records Technician—September 198x**

**CAREER DEVELOPMENT**

MEDICAL CLASSIFICATION CENTER, Los Angeles, Ohio **199x to Present**

**Health Records Administrator**—May 199x to Present

**Administrative Assistant / Medical Records Administrator**—November 199x to May 199x

- Recruited to position after having served in a consultative capacity, May to November 199x.
- Senior Administrator charged with the:
  - √ Maintenance and modification of Department of Corrections (DOC) inmate health records.
  - √ Planning and managing development and maintenance of Psychiatric hospital health records.
  - √ Overseeing management of DOC Records Repository.
- Execute multiple functions:
  - √ **Direct** QA/CQI program; **advise** clinical and correctional staff on health record documentation practices and chart completion policies; **develop / implement** policies and procedures for storage and retrieval of health, legal and institutional files, and processing of medicolegal documents / correspondence; **project growth** and **implement design changes** to accommodate program expansion; **manage** computer technology relevant to health care information and records program; **oversee** county billing program; **recommend** staffing changes.
- In addition to general administrative duties involving 3 direct staff reports and 1 indirect report at the Iowa State Penitentiary, diverse scope of responsibility involves:
  - √ **Coordinating** court reporting requirements; **serving** as chair of Kirkwood Community College's Medical Records Committee and QI Committee; **acting** as main resource contact to nurse managers at 8 state corrections facilities for legal questions relevant to health records; and **functioning** as Medical Records Consultant / Committee Member to Pharmacy Therapeutics / Health Services Committee, Psychiatric Hospital Utilization & Review Committee, and Management Team for Statewide Telemedicine Project.

*continued ...*

**253**

**Combination.** *Elizabeth J. Axnix, Iowa City, Iowa*

A full horizontal line divides the contact information on this page. Another full line is part of a header on page two. A distinctive feature is a fixed-width, right-aligned partial line for each

**MEL GIBSON, RRA**
*Page Two*

**CAREER DEVELOPMENT**, *cont.*

DEPARTMENT OF VETERANS AFFAIRS MEDICAL CENTER, Los Angeles, Ohio 198x to 199x

**Assistant Chief, Health Information Management Section**—July 199x to November 199x

- √ Ensured compliance with JCAHO standards in directing daily tasks of 23 staff; developed employee performance standards and wrote annual performance evaluations; originated and updated positions descriptions; prepared additional staffing and equipment needs justification.
- √ Coordinated annual patient census and fiscal year close-out; conducted quality improvement monitors on medical record documentation, coding, chart completeness/accuracy, and medicolegal compliance; oversaw coding and submission of Agent Orange and Persian Gulf Registry Programs.

**Supervisor, Medical Records**—February 198x to July 199x

- √ Supervised a staff of 7; wrote annual performance evaluations.
- √ Monitored workflow to Coding and Release of Information units; conducted quality improvement monitors to ensure accuracy and completeness of work.

**Ward Clerk**—July 198x to February 198x

- √ Expedited new admissions records and assembled medical records of discharged patients.
- √ Scheduled laboratory tests, radiology examinations and follow-up appointments.

**Research Technician**—May to July 198x

- √ Analyzed medical records utilizing Intensity of Service/Severity of Illness criteria.

**COMMUNITY COLLEGE INVOLVEMENT**

ANYWHERE COMMUNITY COLLEGE, Rapids, Ohio

**Health Information Technology Advisory Committee**—198x to 198x; 199x to Present

- √ Chair, Medical Records Committee, 199x to Present
- √ Co-Chair, Quality Improvement Committee, 199x to Present
- √ Member, Utilization Review Committee, 199x to Present

ANOTHER COMMUNITY COLLEGE, Rapids, Ohio

**Evening Instructor**—November 199x to January 199x

- √ Instructed Health Care Administration Program students in Medical Record Science.
- √ Prepared lectures and material for class discussion; developed and administered exams to test students on lectures and readings presented.

**Health Information Technology Advisory Committee**—198x to 199x

**EDUCATION**

UNIVERSITY OF OSTEOPATHIC MEDICINE AND HEALTH SERVICES

- **BS—Health Information Management** 199x

ANOTHER COMMUNITY COLLEGE

- **AAS—Medical Record Technology** 198x

**PROFESSIONAL AFFILIATIONS**

OHIO HEALTH INFORMATION MANAGEMENT ASSOC. **198x to Present**
AMERICAN HEALTH INFORMATION MANAGEMENT ASSOC. **198x to Present**

section heading. This resume actually could have been put in other groups: Administrators, Coordinators, Chiefs, Supervisors. It has been put here arbitrarily with Directors on the basis of the first multiple function ("Direct") mentioned in the Career Development section.

**FRANK FRAMPTON**
**117 Wood Ridge Avenue**
**Tampa, Florida 33647**

**(813) 000-0000 (Residence)** **(813) 000-0000 (Office)**

**OPERATIONS / MANAGEMENT / MARKETING**

**Strategic Business Planning ◆ Large-Scale Operations ◆ Financial Management ◆ Human Resources**

***CAREER PROFILE***

**Dynamic management career** encompassing over 20 years experience and accomplishments in progressive leadership positions initiating from midlevel to senior executive status. Tenure blends well-developed business acumen with ability to perform in highly visible roles, capitalize on growth opportunities and deliver strong, sustainable results.

***MANAGEMENT***
-- High-profile managerial experience serving as Director of Operations and Regional Manager. In addition, led the directorship of several governmental programs within the U.S. General Accounting Office.
-- During tenure spearheaded diverse scope of administrative functions; coordinated regional activities in six states, Puerto Rico and the Virgin Islands; pinpointed staffing requirements and managed up to 125 multidisciplined personnel.
-- Introduced total quality management concepts and organizational initiatives focused on maximizing proficiency, performance and team building.

***MARKETING***
-- Fully conversant with sales/marketing of service-oriented products in highly competitive industry.
-- Successfully develop client relations, negotiate contracts, "close the sale" and generate revenues.
-- Focus on providing quality customer service; combine expertise in public relations and professionalism to establish long-term working relationships.

***FINANCIAL MANAGEMENT***
-- Accountable for administering $10 million budget and maintaining effective cost controls.
-- Charged with tracking industry trends, conducting economic evaluations, financial planning, forecasting and budget analyses.

***HUMAN RESOURCES***
-- Demonstrated leadership in utilizing proactive approach to strengthening employee relations, consensus building, identifying issues and executing programmatic solutions to re-engineer work environments and augment policies/procedures.
-- Participated in critiquing, composing text materials and conducting training seminars nationwide.
-- Key role in hiring, training, developing and promoting administrative personnel.

***RELATED SKILLS***
-- Results-oriented exhibiting keen analytical abilities; astute in recognizing areas of improvement, with the vision to develop and institute applicable solutions.
-- Articulate communicator, excellent writing skills and extensive experience in public speaking; frequently called upon to testify before U.S. Congressional Committees to report findings on analyses, audits and evaluations of national and international programs.
-- Prudent decision-maker possessing outstanding record of ability to take charge, define and interpret complex issues, and facilitate directives. Work well under pressure and against deadlines.
-- Computer literate: IBM-PC, Windows, WordPerfect

254

**Combination.** *Diane McGoldrick, Tampa, Florida*

A resume for a member of the "gray population" starting his third career. After the contact information, a thin-thick line and below it a thick-thin line enclose the headline about areas of

**FRANK FRAMPTON** **Page Two**

***EMPLOYMENT HISTORY***

BAY REALTY - Tampa, FL **March 1997 - Present**
**Residential/Commercial Salesperson**

C B REALTY - Tampa, Florida **May 1996 - March 1997**
**Residential Real Estate Salesperson**

U.S. GENERAL ACCOUNTING OFFICE - Washington, D.C. **1974 - 1995**
*Exceptional record of increased responsibilities and successive promotions led to a pivotal role supporting Congressional requests or mandates for independently performed audits and evaluations of governmental programs and activities.*

**Director of Operations, Program Evaluation and Methodology Division** (Washington, D.C.) **(1994-1995)**
Managed total spectrum of human resources and business activities for Washington headquarters; accountable for monitoring $8 million budget.

**Regional Manager, New York Regional Office** (Albany, NY) **(1991-1994)**
Reported directly to Comptroller General of the U.S. Oversaw $10MM budget and expedited large-scale administrative operations comprised of 125 professional staff members located in six states, Puerto Rico and the Virgin Islands.

**Director of Education and Labor Issues** (Washington, D.C.) **(1988-1991)**
Directed and delegated assignments to 110 staff professionals from coast-to-coast; prepared audit and evaluation reports, briefings, and provided testimony at congressional hearings. Spoke before professional education and labor organizations.

**Director of Income Security Issues** (Washington, D.C.) **(1987-1988)**
Conducted planning and execution of due diligence work requisite to formulating reports for congressional committee.

**Midlevel Manager** (Washington, D.C.) **(1974-1987)**
Presided over 15 staff, responsible for researching science and technology, community and economic development, and personnel management.

U.S. AIR FORCE **1954 - 1974**
**Supervising Officer/Management Industrial Engineering Team**
Top Secret Security Clearance. Honorable Discharge. Vietnam Veteran.

***EDUCATION/PROFESSIONAL LICENSURE***

CENTRAL MICHIGAN UNIVERSITY
**M.S. Industrial Management**

PARK COLLEGE - Missouri
**B.S. Economics/Business Administration** (Graduated *Summa Cum Laude*)

HARVARD UNIVERSITY - J.F. KENNEDY SCHOOL OF GOVERNMENT
**Graduate, Senior Fellows Program**

STATE OF FLORIDA - **Salesperson Real Estate License**

***MEMBERSHIPS/AFFILIATIONS***

Tampa Association of Realtors
Greater Tampa Chamber of Commerce
Aircraft Owners and Pilots Association

expertise. The all-uppercase italic subheadings in the Career Profile help to cluster experience. In the Employment History section, you can see his years of service in the Air Force, his career with the U.S. General Accounting Office, and his first couple of years in real estate.

# Angela Ocipoff

(516) 555-5555

64 Cologne Avenue, Apt. B1 • Malverne, NY 55555


## Experienced Marketing and Promotion Professional

High-energy background in all aspects of retail center marketing and promotion with Marketing Property Investors, a leader in major shopping center and commercial real estate ownership, operation and management.

## Summary of Qualifications

- Blend creative and administrative abilities to achieve bottom-line results.
- Excellent rapport with management, vendors, media and agencies.
- Tenacious and resourceful; will always find a way to get project done.
- Team with agencies to edit and design event ads and collateral materials.
- Smithaven Mall newsletter editor and contributor.
- Management and budgetary oversight for staff of twelve.
- Frequent presenter at board of director and mall tenant meetings.
- Experienced with MS Word, WordPerfect, Lotus 123 and Pagemaker.

## Career Highlights

- Produced charity event that helped Seaview Mall continue to develop a strong community presence. Solicited merchant donations, radio coverage, local politicians and community group involvement. Wrote press releases, determined and placed advertising. Event was well attended and received great press.
- Administered production of Seaview Mall's Summer Sidewalk Sale and developed free "Rainy Day Kids" craft center and Summer Concert Series. Advertised throughout thriving summer beach communities, arranged aerial banner pulls, developed radio/newspaper campaign, solicited for tenant participation.
- Planned new customer service kiosk and implemented concierge type customer service at Smithaven. Hired, budgeted and managed staff of twelve. Offered gift certificates, mall information, complaint resolution and special services. Commended by customers for problem resolution.
- Managed all pre-production and production of Seaview Mall's for-profit Women's Health Show. Wrote contracts, obtained permits, planned and placed ads, handled tenant interface.
- Directly involved in planning and production of Smithaven Mall's grand re-opening party with $750,000 budget. Managed administration and follow-up of corporate guest list. Personally distilled numerous press releases into concise brochure profiling new up-scale shops.

## Special Skills

### Event Production and Marketing

themes
budgets
advertising
collateral materials
event coordination
local partnerships
media participation

### Mall/Tenant Communications

program coordination
event promotion
mall shows
advertising tie-ins
vendor ad budgets
sales surveys
consumer profiles
one-on-one interface

### Mall Service Management

concierge service
customer assistance
complaint resolution
certificate promotions
operations budgets
staff administration

**255**

**Combination.** *Deborah Wile Dib, Medford, New York*

A creative resume for "a very young, energetic manager with a background far beyond what would be expected for two years of work experience." If you read the resume from end to

# Angela Ocipoff

page two

## Employment

MARKETING PROPERTY INVESTORS (Fallbrook Operations), New York, NY — 1995 to present

Acting Marketing Director, Seaview Mall, NJ (6/97 to present)

- Conceive, develop and coordinate numerous profit and non-profit special events and mall shows.
- Determine event/show content, solicit media participation, plan and produce advertising and collateral materials.
- Formulate advertising budgets, administer payroll and oversee lease required advertising program.

Marketing Specialist, Smithaven Mall, NY (4/96 to 6/97)

- Developed customer service kiosk and concierge service concepts. Hired, budgeted, scheduled and managed staff of twelve. Reconciled $2.5 million sales accounts.
- Participated in special event planning and implementation logistics. Aided in advertising production and campaigns. Edited advertorials, worked with media for print, television and radio advertising.
- Conducted sales and marketing surveys of customers and tenants to determine shopping patterns, demographics and advertising benefits.

Specialty Leasing Assistant, MPI, New York, NY (1/96 to 4/96)

- Evaluated perspective tenants for kiosk/cart leasing for 20+ nationwide shopping centers. Controlled paperwork; determined product suitability.

Marketing Assistant, Sparksville Center Mall, PA (6/95 to 1/96)

- Created and set-up special programs. Aided fashion coordinator in planning shows and soliciting tenant participation/donations. Implemented surveys for advertising and event follow-up; analyzed and presented results.

## Education

B. A. in English Literature, Hofstra University, Uniondale, NY

- Attended on academic/tennis scholarship
- Achieved Most Valuable Player award
- Won Collegiate Tennis Number One Doubles Championship

## Personal Interests and Volunteer Activities

- Accomplished tennis player and national lifetime member of USTA.
- Taught for two years at USTA Tennis Center at Flushing Meadow.
- Experienced traveler. Studied in Venice. Toured France and England.
- Lived for one month in Kenya to help construct church library.
- Volunteered in patient recovery area of North Shore University Hospital.

beginning, you can sense her whirlwind development. If you read from beginning to end, you can picture her present situation as a launchpad for future successes. The first page is impressive because of the Special Skills column. Remember that skills clustered by fields are alterable for special targeting.

# Blaine K. Wilson

2222 Woodridge Dr. • Milton, MD 00000 • (111) 111-1111

***Senior level business management generalist with extensive and progressive experience in manufacturing operations and human resources administration.***

Areas of Expertise

- All aspects of Human Resource management.
- New business and product development.
- Marketing and sales strategies for existing and pre-venture organizations.
- Internal operating and capital budget administration.
- Procurement and vendor development.
- Process control and state-of-the-art manufacturing technologies.
- Negotiating labor contrcts.
- Self Directed Work Teams and other TQM tools and concepts.

Employment Overview

Data Tech, Inc., Howard, MD
***Director, Operations and Administration*** ***1995 to present***

Responsible for all operational aspects of the Company. Direct reports include Finance, Human Resources, Production and Software Engineering. Works extensively with senior level management in new product development and marketing.

Independent Consultant, Easton, MD ***1991 to 1995***

***Rayweb Corporation***---Provided management consulting for the complete start-up of a new division. Responsibilities included business plan development, marketing plan, product design, building and site development, manufacturing start-up and installation for modular docking components.

***State of Delaware, Department of Economic and Employment Development***---Managed the start-up phase and development of the Professional Outplacement Assistance Center; the first operation of its kind in the country.

***Rayfield Industries***---Complete P&L responsibility for a $10 million, multi-product glass manufacturing facility. Increased manufacturing capacity by 30% through the successful transfer and introduction of new product lines.

Also provided consulting services in the area of business financing and start-up, marketing, human resources, materials and operations management for: ***T.A. O'Rielly Co., Business Trends Inc., Viewdex Corporation, JHU Corporation.***

Worldview Industries, Dayton, OH
***Manager, Human Resources*** ***1985 to 1991***

Recruited in 1985 to spearhead the Human Resources effort for the largest and most state-of-the-art production facility for this Ohio based manufacturer.

**256**

**Combination.** *Thomas E. Spann, Easton, Maryland*

The two bold, italic lines under the contact information are essentially a profile statement. The Areas of Expertise, in bulleted list form, can be modified easily to target the resume to a specific

Page Two

**Blaine K. Wilson** 2222 Woodbridge Dr. • Milton, MD 00000 • (111) 111-1111

Fordham Inc., Defense Electronics Division, Bay Acres, MD

***Manager, Professional Staffing*** ***1983 to 1985***

Directly responsible for recruitment for this DoD, high technology organization including the newly formed Special Technology Center and the Fiber Optics operations. Efforts resulted in an organization that doubled its size in two years.

Maryland Metals Corporation, Towson, MD

***Manufacturing Manager*** ***1969 to 1982***

Twelve years extensive training and experience in all aspects of manufacturing production in the speciality metals industry. Initially employed as a student intern in 1969. Promoted to the position of Manufacturing Manager in 1981.

Education

Wilton College, Stowe, VT

***Bachelor of Science, 1973***

Guest Lecturer

U.S. Naval Academy, Transition Assistance Program

Anne County Economic Development Corporation

United States International Business Commerce Committee

Professional and Civic Associations

Society of Human Resource Management

American Management Association

National Conference of State Legislators

Home Builder Association of Maryland

Maryland Polytechnic Institute Alumni Association

Purchasing Managers Association of Baltimore

employer or job opportunity. Notice where and how small caps are used in this resume. (To create small caps on the fly, choose the small caps feature and type upper- and lowercase text. To make upper- and lowercase text small caps, select the text and choose the small caps feature.)

**MARK MANAGER**
420 Main Street
Newton, MA 02159
(617) 555-1234 (h) (508) 555-5678 (w)

**PROFILE**

Over 16 years of Human Resource Management experience in positions of progressive responsibility in the technology, retail and financial services industries. Responsible for company-wide programs that foster strong employee involvement and facilitate effective communication. Respected decision-maker with a demonstrated ability to build consensus among groups with conflicting interests using experiences developed as a professional mediator. Substantial experience in implementing valuing diversity programs. Consistently recognized for innovation and excellent performance.

**EXPERIENCE**

**Digital Equipment Corporation**, Maynard, MA 1983-Present

**Human Resource Director (Acting)/Human Resource Operation Manager** 1995-Present
Digital Integrated Circuits
**Group Human Resource Planning and Development Manager** 1991-1995
Digital Integrated Circuits
**Manufacturing Team Operations Manager** 1988-1991
Product Development Center
**Human Resource Planning and Development Manager** 1986-1988
Product Development Center
**Management Development Consultant** 1983-1986
Management Training & Development Organization

***Accomplishments***

- Oversee the effective delivery of all human resource management, including compensation, recruitment, HR information systems, and university relations in a worldwide business with almost 4,000 employees and an annual operating budget in excess of $625 million.
- Manage a staff of 40 in a complex technical organization.
- Developed and implemented core human resource programs in performance management and human resource planning that sharpened organizational effectiveness by providing managers with practical tools and critical information.
- Served as Human Resource Manager to 5 headquarters vice presidents.
- Introduced innovative reward program that resulted in the retention of key employees.
- Increased the efficiency of human resources operations through the introduction of PC-based human resource tools.
- Served as Manufacturing Program Manager for several major product introductions.
- Managed the implementation of team-oriented operations that cut costs, built team spirit through shared responsibilities, and reduced time-to-market.
- Implemented an Alternative Dispute Resolution (ADR) program that is expected to save millions of dollars in litigation costs.

***Awards:***

- Digital Achievement Award for Outstanding Contributions to Diversity Work 1994
- Digital Achievement Award for Competitive Benchmarking 1993
- Managerial Excellence Award 1991
- Educational Services Instructor Excellence Award 1985

**257**

**Combination.** *Wendy Gelberg, Needham, Massachusetts*

A resume for "a 'prize' who was kept on the payroll even as the company reduced its workforce by over 50,000." To call attention to this person's "steady progression to higher levels of

**MARK MANAGER** **Page 2**

**RELATED EXPERIENCE**

**State Street Bank**, Boston, MA 1982-1983
**Employee Relations Manager**
Managed the employee relations and work re-design programs in a service industry environment and implemented human resource and organizational development projects throughout the business.

**Eddie Bauer**, Boston, MA 1980-1982
**Training Manager**
Developed retail training programs emphasizing customer relations, return-on-investment, margin management, and merchandising techniques delivered in over 30 stores throughout the US and at corporate headquarters.

**Eastman Kodak Corporation**, Rochester, NY 1978-1980
**Training Consultant**
Managed corporate writing program to improve technical writing and designed communications and assertiveness skills training.

**PRIOR EXPERIENCE**

**Newton Public Schools**, Newton, MA 1973-1978
**American Repertory Theatre**, Cambridge, MA 1972-1973
**Juilliard School**, New York 1972

**EDUCATION**

| | | |
|---|---|---|
| **Certificate** | Mediation and Dispute Resolution, Metropolitan Mediation Services, Brookline, MA | 1994 |
| **MBA** | Executive Program, Suffolk University, Boston, MA | 1984 |
| **BA** | Communications, Speech and English, State University College of New York at Buffalo | 1972 |

**PUBLICATION**

Co-author of *Better Business Communications,* a college text on communications and business writing, D.C. Heath and Company, 1986.

responsibility and his significant number of awards," the writer "clustered all the Digital job titles together under the company name," eliminating some repetition. The writer also combined all the achievements and awards under separate headings, putting the best information on page one.

**BENJAMIN S. HILL**

**1996 North Broadway** **Yonkers, NY 10701** **(914) 963-1997**

**LAW ENFORCEMENT**
**Management - Director of Training**

Dynamic, results-oriented Law Enforcement professional with more than 20 years hands on experience in training and developing high calibre, peak-performing organizations. Possess strong supervisory and management skills. Demonstrated consistent success in trainees placing in top 10% on all security and law enforcement exams.

**PROFILE**

- ***Proven skill*** in ***establishing*** and ***maintaining excellent business relationships*** with diversified civilian clientele and police staff; from community members to management.
- ***Strong*** interpersonal and communication ***skills; demonstrated ability*** to work effectively with individuals on all levels.
- ***Possess strong insights*** into numerous areas of criminal psychology and motivation.
- ***Effective motivator*** of self and others; skillful team builder.
- ***Commended for excellent leadership skills*** with ability to set the tone for ***police professionalism*** and for ability to ***act quickly*** in ***resolving complex*** and ***diversified problems.***

**SIGNIFICANT ACHIEVEMENTS**

- ***Nominated for service*** on the Board of Directors: Essex County Domestic Violence and Criminal Justice Planning Corporation.
- ***Successfully initiated program*** to place and monitor offenders that were sentenced to community service in lieu of imprisonment.
- ***Credited with developing, designing*** and ***instructing*** the ***College's most popular course***, Self Defense & Safety: Spring 1994.
- ***Achieved outstanding training record: 89% passing rate*** on the exam for State Certificate in Security.

**CERTIFICATION**

New York State: Certified Police Instructor — 1977
- ***Fully certified to teach in any of the Police Academies of New York.***

New York State: Primary and Secondary Teaching License — 1971

**PROFESSIONAL EXPERIENCE**

1995 - Present

**BOARD OF COOPERATIVE EDUCATIONAL SERVICES,** Valhalla, NY
**Instructor: Security and Law Enforcement**
- ***Teach highly-regarded program*** in Security and Criminal Justice.
- ***Developed*** and ***implemented*** two year curriculum currently in use.
- Act as ***security advisor*** for all campus affairs.
- ***Assembled active, well-qualified team*** of consultants to advise on continuing program development.

1993 - 1994

**NORTH COUNTRY COMMUNITY COLLEGE,** Saranac Lake, NY
**Instructor: Criminal Justice**
- Taught the following courses: Introduction to Criminal Justice, Juvenile Delinquency, Criminal Investigation, and Self Defense.
- Provided comprehensive academic and career advisement for 56 Criminal Justice majors.
- ***Successfully directed*** a Criminal Justice internship program involving placement, monitoring, teaching, and supervising students at ten internship locations in two counties.
- ***Developed*** a network for Criminal Justice majors to obtain current information on available jobs in the field; acquired information on upcoming civil service tests.

**258**

**Combination.** *Mark D. Berkowitz, Yorktown Heights, New York*

A resume for a high school teacher who became a successful Police Sergeant, then a community college instructor, next an elementary school teacher, and currently a Security and Law

**BENJAMIN S. HILL** *page 2*

**PROFESSIONAL EXPERIENCE** *continued*

1973 - 1993 **YONKERS POLICE DEPARTMENT,** Yonkers, NY
**Police Sergeant**
- Promoted 1989; supervised 22 police officers for Yonkers' ***largest*** and ***busiest precinct***.
- ***Oversaw*** all day-to-day ***precinct operations***.
- Ensured that all assignments and calls were handled in a timely, professional manner.
- Functioned as ***Patrol Supervisor*** with ***authority*** to call in specialized units for emergency, medical, and other situations; ***coordinated*** with Support and Auxiliary Units, as needed.
- Hired police officers to fill vacancies and handle overtime situations.
- Ensured that all policies and procedures were followed and adhered to.

1973 - 1989 **Police Officer**

1994 - 1995 **NEW YORK CITY BOARD OF EDUCATION: I.S. 118,** Bronx, NY
**Teacher of Grades 6 and 7**

1971 - 1973 **BOARD OF EDUCATION,** Yonkers, NY
**High School Teacher**

***HONORS AND AWARDS***

*Commendations For Courageous Actions & Intelligent Work (6)*
*Certificates of Excellent Police Work (11)*
*Police Officer Of The Year (2)*
*Commendation From New York State Assembly*
*Commendation From New Your State Senate*
*Commendation From The House Of Representatives*
*Recipient of Numerous Letters Of Appreciation And Commendation From Civilians*
*Recipient of Pulaski Association Award*

**EDUCATION**

**WESTCHESTER COUNTY LAW ENFORCEMENT AGENCY,** Valhalla, NY
**Professional Certificate: *MPTC Police Supervision*** 1990

**LONG ISLAND UNIVERSITY,** Dobbs Ferry, NY
**Master of Science: *Criminal Justice*** 1977
- ***Graduated with Honors***; GPA: ***3.85***

**LONG ISLAND UNIVERSITY,** Brooklyn, NY
**Bachelor of Science: *Education*** 1977

**CONTINUING EDUCATION**

**YONKERS POLICE DEPARTMENT,** Yonkers, NY 1976 - 1993
**Human & Community Relations For Law Enforcement** (1992 - 1993)
**Problem Oriented Policing (POP)** (1991)
**Advanced Evidence Technical School** (1982)
**Basic Evidence Course** (1981)
**Crime Prevention Course** (1976)

**FEDERAL BUREAU OF INVESTIGATION,** Peekskill, NY
**Certificate: *Criminal Investigation School*** 1980

**REFERENCES** Available upon request.

Enforcement Instructor for a cooperative educational board. His career goal is to be a Director of Training in Law Enforcement. Supportive information for this goal is enclosed within lines. Side headings and boldfacing of keywords ensure visibility of the most important information.

# LAUREN M. MALLOY, R.N.

100 Birch Tree Road
Tampa, Florida 33607
(813) 000-0000

**HEALTH CARE ADMINISTRATION**

**HOSPITALS. . . NURSING HOMES. . . . HOME HEALTH AGENCIES**

**Management ◆ Operations ◆ Quality Assurance ◆ Training**
**Program Development ◆ Strategic Planning ◆ Team Building**

## *PROFESSIONAL PROFILE*

*CAREER OVERVIEW*

-- Senior-level health care administrator with 20-year tenure in progressively responsible positions encompassing a unique combination of professional nursing experience and well-defined, business acumen.

-- Pivotal role as Director of Nursing spearheading administrative, operational and managerial initiatives that augment quality assurance, professional development, standards of patient care and program development.

-- Proven ability to identify, formulate and implement action plans that validate quality assurance programs, increase performance, maximize operational proficiency, and enhance ongoing educational needs.

-- Well-versed in maintaining compliance with State and Federal Governmental Regulations and requirements for Joint Commission for Accreditation of Hospitals and Home Health Agencies.

-- Served as Registered Nurse Specialist conducting investigations and surveillance of Nursing Homes, Home Health Agencies and other related health care facilities in conjunction with complaints alleging non-compliance of state/ federal regulations.

-- Professional nursing background. . .charge and supervision positions in ICU, CCU, ER, open heart surgical unit, and sports/industrial medicine. Represented management in mediating union/management labor disputes at Mount Sinai Hospital, NY.

-- Prior experience includes Columnist and Editorial Writer of national/international issues for Long Island Newspaper; management of commercial/residential real estate office, Long Island, NY.

*RELATED SKILLS*

-- Keen analytical abilities, adept in tracking and forecasting medical industry trends; astute at recognizing areas of need improvement, with the vision to develop and institute programmatic solutions.

-- Pro-active leader with competent decision-making skills; demonstrated record of conceptualizing and facilitating directives that achieve strong/sustainable results.

-- Effective communicator, well-developed organizational, composition, and interpersonal skills; proficiency in hiring /training/motivating personnel and building team concepts.

259

**Combination.** *Diane McGoldrick, Tampa, Florida*

A resume created to help this person market her credentials as a Consultant to Hospitals on Quality Improvement and Risk Management. The parallel lines and the diamond bullets ensure

**LAUREN M. MALLOY, R.N.** Page Two

***EMPLOYMENT HISTORY***

TAMPA BAY NURSING CENTER — Tampa, FL
***Assistant Director of Nursing*** — **December 1995 - March 1996**

COMMUNITY HOSPITAL, Home Health Division — Tampa, FL
***Continuing Quality Improvement Coordinator*** — **July 1995 - October 1995**

HEALTH CARE AGENCY, Division of Health Quality Assurance — Tampa, FL
***Registered Nurse Specialist*** — **June 1990 - June 1995**

DESOTO UNICARE CORPORATION — St. Petersburg, FL
***Director of Nursing*** — **June 1989 - June 1990**

PALM NURSING CENTER — Dade City, FL
***Director of Nursing*** — **May 1988 - June 1989**
- Obtained first deficiency free nursing survey with a superior rating.

WEST SHORE VILLAS — Tampa, FL
***Director of Nursing*** — **March 1986 - May 1988**
- Obtained first superior rating for facility.

WINTERHAVEN HEALTH CARE CENTER — Lakeland, FL
***Director of Nursing*** — **April 1985 - August 1985**
- Obtained first deficiency free nursing survey.

***EDUCATION***

NEW YORK HOSPITAL SCHOOL OF NURSING - New York City, NY
**Registered Nurse (3-year Diploma)**

***PROFESSIONAL TRAINING/CERTIFICATIONS***

-- **State of Florida, *Registered Nurse*,** License #0000000

-- Currently pursuing Certification in Continuing Quality Improvement and Risk Management

-- Certification - National Council on Licensure, Enforcement and Regulation "Clear" (1992)
(University of Missouri - Law Enforcement Institute School of Law)

-- Management Techniques (30 hours) (1986)
(University of Southern California)

-- Certified Medical Hypnotherapist (1984)
(Long Island School of Medical Hypnotherapy)

that the reader will see the areas of expertise. The division of the Professional Profile into Career Overview and Related Skills subsections avoids the repetition that would have occurred if these skills had been mentioned in the History. The person started her business and is doing well.

**JOHN C. JOHNSON**

100 Maple Lane
Burlington, VT 00000

**(800) 555-0000**

**PROFESSIONAL STRENGTHS**

**Track record of accomplishment in organizations that depend on the marketing of intangible products, private sector donations, strong community relations, and the coordination of development programs.**

- **DEVELOPMENT & FUND-RAISING**
- **MARKETING**
- **SPECIAL EVENTS MANAGEMENT**
- **BUSINESS PLANNING**

**EXPERIENCE AND ACCOMPLISHMENTS**

**DIRECTOR, OLYMPIC FUNDRAISING** Aug 1995 - present
**Olympian Bill Smith**, Burlington, VT

Hired to organize and supervise fundraising events for the 1992-93-94 U.S. National Kite Flying Champion to cover expenses for the 1996 Olympic Summer Games in Atlanta.

- Successfully raised funds for Mr. Smith's 1992 Summer Olympics participation on a volunteer basis.

**CONSULTANT** Jun 1994 - May 1995
**New England Promotions**, Burlington, VT

Agent for the Principal of a 600-member sports facility, health club, and restaurant.

- Developed business plan, including marketing plan, revenue forecasts, and management structure.
- Presented business plan to venture capitalist, resulting in initial investment of $750,000.
- Prepared request for bid proposal for eight architecture firms. Interviewed prospective architects and selected the final firm.
- Liaison between company, Burlington Downtown Development Corporation, and city offices.

**DIRECTOR OF DEVELOPMENT / CONSULTANT** Aug 1992 - Jun 1995
**Bishop Jones School** / Order of the Fathers, Portland, OR

Managed a five-person development office charged with targeting and soliciting parent, alumni, and corporate gifts for this private college-preparatory school. Also served as a member of the school's Board of Regents and chaired committees on finance and public relations for school accreditation.

- Developed and executed special events and fund-raising programs including phonathons, direct mail solicitations, grant programs, auctions, raffles, golf tournaments, and sports hall of fame dinners.
- Increased net income of annual alumni giving appeal by 610%, annual parent giving appeal by 90%, corporate appeal by 150%, and a special event by 438% while maintaining zero-based budgeting.
- Addressed development officers at the National Catholic Development Conference on first-time implementation of phonathons and effective telephone solicitation techniques.
- Presented seminar to Portland Diocesan Schools Development Directors on preparation and management of successful capital campaigns.

**260**

**Combination.** *Alan D. Ferrell, Lafayette, Indiana*

This person was "very successful, but relatively young for his ideal job—director of development in university athletics." The writer amplified any development/fund-raising success, called

***Johnson, page 2***
***Experience continued***

**DIRECTOR OF ALUMNI / ASSISTANT CAMPAIGN MANAGER** Apr 1991 - Jul 1992
**The Assisi Institute of Burlington (VT)** / Order of the Fathers

Targeted and solicited all out-of-state major gift prospects for a $7M capital campaign. Organized and supervised class reunions, phonathons, golf tournament, and special events.

- Directed and increased annual alumni giving appeal by $50,000.
- Edited the quarterly alumni newsletter and assisted in completion of the alumni directory.
- Developed marketing plan for student recruitment.
- Established a minority engineering scholarship program between The Assisi Institute, Tufts University, and Digital Equipment Corporation.

**Design Partners Corporation**, Burlington, VT Oct 1990 - Mar 1991
Quoted and purchased all materials and controls for an established design and build company.

**Payroll Advisory Incorporated**, Burlington, VT Jun 1990 - Sep 1990
Established accounts for payroll processing company via telephone contact.

**MAJOR VOLUNTEER CONTRIBUTIONS**

**DIRECTOR**
**The Maple Tree Tournament**, Burlington, VT

Directed annual July 4th beach volleyball tournament from 1990 - 1995. Solicited and secured corporate sponsors, including Spalding, Anheuser Busch, bolle', Oakley, Women's Professional Volleyball Association, Nefas Sportswear, Overkill Sportswear, and Freestyle Watches. Coordinated over 400 teams from 10 states, Canada, and Australia for two-day event.

**CONSULTANT**
**St. Bonaface School**, Salem, OR

Advised administration at economically disadvantaged school on techniques of grant writing, establishing a board of trustees, and defining a long-range financial plan. Executed a plan to provide school with laboratory and sports equipment to improve science and physical education curricula.

**EDUCATION**

**B.S. Business Management,** St. Bonaface College, Salem, OR Aug 1986 - Jun 1990
Education concentration

- St. Bonaface (College Division I) Basketball Team, 1986 - 1987
- St. Bonaface (College Division I) Volleyball Team, 1988 - 1990
- All-West Volleyball selection, 1990

**AFFILIATIONS AND ACTIVITIES**

National Society of Fundraising Executives, 1991 - 1994
National Catholic Development Conference, 1992 - 1994
Winner, The Maple Tree Tournament, Burlington, VT, 1992 and 1994
Condo-Community Association, Burlington, VT, 1991 - 1992
Coached women's varsity basketball, The Assisi Institute. 1991 State Finalist.
President, Maple Valley Volleyball Association, Burlington, VT, 1990 - present

attention to "highly visible responsibilities," and played up "heavy involvement in sports environments." The bulleted items are important especially for showing development skills, but every section of the resume has a role to play in qualifying this person for his targeted goal.

**Richard A. Stevens**

123 Whiteoak Drive • Radcliff, Kentucky 40100 • (502) 555-1111

**PROFESSIONAL SUMMARY**

- Over 20 years of progressively increasing levels of responsibility and documented success in general management, including operations and personnel management, sales and marketing, communications and public relations, training, purchasing, and financial management.
- Adept in start-up and turnaround. Able to rectify problem situations and implement prudent, cost-effective solutions.
- Recognized by superiors, peers, and subordinates as a manager who values diversity, inspiration, and challenges.
- Able to organize and coordinate multiple projects effectively and simultaneously with emphasis on attaining outstanding results.

**PERSONNEL MANAGEMENT**

- Supervised and managed as many as 300 staff members and support employees. Recruited, interviewed, hired, and developed personnel. Wrote performance evaluations and provided counseling. Negotiated with unions to resolve disputes. Directed public relations activities.
- As the Deputy Personnel Director managed all human resource and administrative functions for a large organization. Monitored personnel actions involving more than 7,800 records. Directly managed and supervised 80 employees.
- Took a disjointed staff and molded it into a fine working team:
  - *Situation:* General Manager of an office that was responsible for departments in a five-state area. The staff were not meeting basic goals and quotas; there was a decided lack of team work, low morale, poor performance, and discipline.
  - *Action*: Constantly expressed enthusiasm and a winning attitude. Got personally involved. Mentored and tutored employees; provided additional training. Developed incentives and provided motivation. Whenever they had a problem, helped them solve it "on-the-spot".
  - *Result*: Within one month, took the department from the bottom of the list to number one in the country. During two years of managing the office, it consistently remained in the top ten and five times was ranked number one in the nation. The staff went from meeting only 60% of their quota to 110%.

**SALES, MARKETING, AND PUBLIC RELATIONS**

- Took over general management of a large nightclub/restaurant system that was losing money and within 30 days had the clubs bringing in a profit.
  - Acquired information concerning current and potential market. Took a "make it happen" proactive, dynamic stance and, formed a long-range plan that would also provide immediate revenues. Solicited and obtained financial support. Devised and implemented a comprehensive outreach program and developed a widespread marketing campaign. Improved quality of service / food and ensured reasonable, competitive prices. Increased membership by 60%.
  - Club system was rated one of the best and most profitable in Europe; clubs cleared $1,500+ profit each night.
- While managing six large nightclubs, planned and monitored the construction of another $4 million club. Negotiated with different personnel, vendors, and suppliers to achieve the best possible prices. Designed and implemented management systems, administrative policies, and operational procedures.
- As a Club Management Consultant, provided assistance and suggestions to improve club operations. Consulting service turned around approximately 24 clubs serving six communities and increased club profits by 25%.

**261**

**Combination.** *Connie S. Stevens, Radcliff, Kentucky*

This resume has a thin-thick-thin, triple-line border on both pages. Three different bullet styles are used: filled square bullets in the Professional Summary, filled arrow tips in the remaining

**Richard A. Stevens** **Page 2**

- Developed community relationships with the media and leaders in the public and private sectors. Very articulate speaker. Presented highly effective public presentations.

**FINANCIAL MANAGEMENT**

- Served as Chief Executive Officer of the company which had 53 offices located throughout ten states, as well as Europe and Panama. Managed logistics, advertising, and training. Effectively developed, implemented, and managed an annual operating budget in excess of $38 million.
- Was General Manager of a recruiting office responsible for 257 counties in a five-state area. Programmed and executed a budget of over $2.5 million.
- As Manager of six large nightclubs/restaurants, developed and programmed operating budget of $2.5 million.
- As Manager of Logistics and Services, worked with engineers to develop and implement the $4 million renovation of four nightclubs. Brought the renovations in $150,000 "under budget."
- Directed the plans and implemented the construction of a retail beverage store. Brought automation into the store and $500,000 worth of inventory. Through effective advertising, marketing, and budgeting, cleared over $20,000 profit in the first month of operation.
- Able to "cut corners" and still negotiate cost-effective contracts to add and upgrade office automation and take care of the organization.

**EDUCATION & TRAINING**

- *Kansas State University* • Manhattan, KS
  **Master's Degree** • Degree Conferred 1975
- *Kansas State University* • Manhattan, KS
  **Bachelor of Science** • Degree Conferred 1972
- **Business Process Reengineering** • Executive Seminar Center • 1995
- **Executive Club Management** • Florida International University • 1985
  9 Credit Hour Graduate Course
- **Hospitality and Club Management** • Indianapolis • 1980

**CAREER PATH**

- U.S. Army Recruiting Command • Fort Knox, KY • Jun 95 - Present
  **Deputy Director of Personnel**
- U.S. Army Recruiting Battalion • Des Moines, IA • Mar 93 - May 95
  **General Manager / Recruiting Battalion Commander**
- First Recruiting Brigade • Fort Meade, MD • Aug 91 - Mar 93
  **Chief of Staff**
- U.S. Army Recruiting Battalion • Pittsburgh, PA • Jul 89 - Jun 91
  **Executive Officer**
- Command and General Staff College • Fort Leavenworth, KS • Aug 88 - Jul 89
  **Student**
- Services Division • Fort Myers, VA • Sep 85 - Jul 88
  **Manager / Chief**
- Club System • Kaiserslautern, Germany • Mar 80 - Aug 85
  **Area Club Manager**

sections, and half-filled arrow tips in Personnel Management and Sales, Marketing, and Public Relations sections. Note especially the half-filled bullets in the Personnel Management section. They point to sections of a narrative about an achievement: Situation, Action, and Result.

**Margaret A. Troise**
00000 Gates Lane
Wantagh, NY 00000
(000) 000-0000

**OBJECTIVE:**

Senior level Management position in a dynamic, future oriented healthcare organization geared to maximizing the potential of my skills, experience and interests.

**EXPERIENCE:**

ALLEVA SERVICES INC., Braintree, KY 1995 to 1996
*(A nationally recognized healthcare management company specializing in outsourcing of health information management services.)*
**Consultant/Interim Operations Director**

Position included multiple interim management and consulting assignments for an innovative company offering outsourced health information management and related services to a national client base.

**Major Accomplishments**

- Reengineering of processes to reduce receivables from 4.75 million to under 2 million for a major metropolitan institution recently acquired by Columbia/H.C.A.
- Developed and initiated implementation of an Outcomes Focused Program of Clinical Quality Improvement for a client with 300+ medical staff.
- Conducted a feasibility study for integrating management of radiology film library with health information management operations at a tertiary referral center.
- Developed a formalized process for transitioning interim management of health information departments to full outsourcing (management and staff) under multi-year contracts.
- Conducted initial and subsequent operational assessments of health information departments for use in contract development. This involved immediate process improvements and establishments of interim and ongoing deliverables.
- Conducted process studies focused on "Best Practices" approach to productivity evaluation and development of appropriate staffing plans.

THE VALLEY STREAM MEDICAL CENTER, Hobart, KY 1990 to 1995
**Director of Medical Administrative Services**

Executive management position responsible for strategic planning and operations of Quality, Utilization, Discharge Planning and Infection Control. Promoted from Director of Quality Improvement with responsibilities for Health Information, Social Services, Risk Management and Medical Staff Services/Liaison.

**Major Accomplishments:**

- Successfully coordinated institution wide Total Quality Management Program.
- Restructured and implemented state-of-the-art health information management systems.
- Managed successful focused surveys and subsequent full survey by JCAHO.
- Modified procedures for diagnostic and procedural coding resulting in a 3/4 million reduction in receivables.
- Streamlined and strengthened the medical staff organization by implementing process improvement techniques to modify systems and procedures.
- Initiated the development of clinical practice guidelines to improve the process of care.

**262**

**Chronological.** *Betty Geller, Elmira, New York*

After the contact information, this resume provides a targeted Objective statement and then goes right into indicating work experience chronologically from most recent to least recent.

**Margaret A. Troise** **Page 2**

UNIVERSITY HOSPITAL OF HILLIARD, Hilliard, NY 1988 to 1990

**Administrator for Regulatory Affairs**

Division level management responsibility for a 400 bed university teaching hospital. Strategic and operational responsibilities for Quality Assurance, Risk/Claims Management, Utilization Review, Medical Staff, Health Information. Corporate liaison with all regulatory agencies.

**Major Accomplishments:**

- Design and implementation of microcomputer based Medical Information Systems.
- Implemented institution wide Risk Management Program.
- Responsible for JCAHO survey resulting in three year accreditation.
- Developed management systems for monitoring/follow-up of interactions with N.Y.S. Department of Health.

COOPERS AND LYBRAND, Hilliard Bay, NY 1986 to 1988

**Manager, Clinical Consulting Group**

Managed consulting staff. Responsible for developing new business opportunities and ensuring cost effective completion of contractual engagements. Developed successful and acclaimed programs. Provided interim management services for the University Hospital of Hilliard Bay for Health Information Services.

CENTRAL CITY HOSPITAL, Gordon Stream, KY 1983 to 1986

**Director, Medical Data Systems**

A multi-faceted senior management position. Responsible for implementing major technical and administrative programs. Directed departments of Health Information, Admissions/Registration and Communications.

HOSPITAL AND MEDICAL CENTER, Gordon Stream, KY 1980 to 1983

**Director, Medical Record Services**

Director level responsibility for Quality Assurance, Cancer Registry and Medical Records. Designed and implemented leading edge systems and programs. Managed a staff of 32 employees.

**EDUCATION:**

NEW YORK UNIVERSITY, New York, NY
**Master of Science in Health Care Administration**

CALVARY HILL COLLEGE, Gordon Stream, KY
**Bachelor of Science in Medical Records Management**

Credentialed as Health Information Professional

**PROFESSIONAL ORGANIZATIONS:**

American Health Information Management Association
National Association for Healthcare Quality

No dates are given in either the Education section or the Professional Organizations section. Bullets point to major accomplishments. From 1980 to 1990, the person showed interest in program development. From 1990 on, the person focused on process development with some success.

# JOHN N. THOMPSON

(202) 222-7474
123 East Bay, Fremont, CA 94321


## QUALIFICATIONS

**EXPERIENCED SALES / MANAGEMENT PROFESSIONAL** with over 20 years in the agribusiness industry. Highlights include:

- Domestic and international experience selling and marketing agricultural chemical products of manufacturing companies, **generating over $100 million in sales.**
- 8-year record of opening new markets in Europe, Asia, Eastern Bloc, and Latin America, **developing in excess of $12 million in new business.**
- Management strengths include strategic planning, budgeting, and marketing; history of developing new business through existing distribution channels, as well as creating additional channels.
- Ability to provide innovative input into the process of producing new agricultural-chemical products, improving time-to-market and speeding growth of sales.
- Proven capacity to mentor salespeople in developing more effective sales and management skills.

## PROFESSIONAL EXPERIENCE

CAPIN INDUSTRIES CO. LTD., Hong Kong — 1995 to 1996

**Director of Agricultural Operations**

Directed activities of a large cotton farming development project in the CIS (formerly USSR) for an international textile manufacturing company. Joint ventured with the CIS government to build a series of textile plants in Tajikistan. Projects employed latest in western technology and farming methods as well as western management personnel.

- Managed start-up operations, including recruitment and management of Farm Managers for multiple locations, Head Agronomist, and Manager of Maintenance and Equipment.
- Prepared and executed annual $4.5 million operational budget; developed 5-year capital budget.
- Sourced and negotiated $16.4 million in capital equipment purchases with the US, Europe, and Israel.
- Developed site plans and 5-year operational plans for bringing new land into production (development process, land preparation, water management, agronomics, harvesting, transport).
- Interfaced with local joint venture partners (government officials) on ongoing and planned activities.

AGRIBUSINESS FIRM, Sacramento, CA — 1988 to 1994

**Vice President - Sales and Marketing**

Co-founded start-up manufacturer of bio-rational pesticides, functioning as key member of management team in setting company policy and direction. As Sales/Marketing V.P., led all sales and marketing efforts, supervising and directing sales team of four and market development representative in generating profits for the company in North, South, and Latin America, as well as the Far East. Interfaced with Regulatory Affairs Manager, federal E.P.A., California E.P.A., and other regulatory agencies.

- Grew sales from zero to more than $2 million annually in less than five years.
- Captured 63% of total pheromone-based pesticide sales in southwestern cotton market, despite the presence of two major competitors.

(continued)

263

**Combination.** *Susan Britton Whitcomb, Fresno, California*

The original resume was three pages for this senior management professional, who planned eventually to contact an executive recruitment firm. The writer provided a thorough

## John N. Thompson

Page Two

### Professional Experience

AgriBusiness Firm (continued)

- Originated and implemented "Master Distributor" strategy to circumvent lack of marketplace visibility -- trained personnel in providing technical support to existing distributor salespeople.
- Initiated relationship and negotiated contract with international agricultural-chemical company to distribute products in Mexico.
- Developed and introduced innovative sprayable Pink Bollworm control product into southwestern cotton market in under three years.
- Identified major market opportunity for new Chilean forest industry product and led two years of field development activity.
- Invented and developed new insect-feeding stimulant for use with microbial or I.G.R. insecticides.

Shell Oil Company, Bartlesville, OK 1981 to 1988

**Technical Products Manager**

Directed domestic and international technical pheromone sales for bio-tech subsidiary, one of the world's largest producers of synthetic technical pheromones.

- Grew sales from zero to $400,000 in 1st year.
- Recognized need for company-owned controlled release system for pheromones and convinced upper management of strategy's validity.

### Education

UNIVERSITY OF ARIZONA, TUCSON

- **Bachelor of Science Degree, Business Administration**
- Marketing major
- Economics and Finance minor

### Professional Affiliations

Western Agricultural Chemical Association (Offices included Board of Directors, Finance Committee Chairman, California State Action Committee); Association of Applied Insect Ecologists; California Agricultural Pest-Control Advisors Association; Entomological Society of America, Pacific Branch

### Licenses and Patents

California Department of Food and Agriculture, Pest-Control Advisor's License; certified to make written recommendations in the following categories: Insects, Mites, and Other Invertebrates; Plant Pathogens; Nematodes; Weeds; Defoliation; Plant Growth Regulators

Insect Feeding Stimulant For Use With Microbial Insecticides - U.S. PATENT PENDING

♦ ♦ ♦

Qualifications section because the most recent position was not as related to the individual's prior senior-level sales positions. Bullets for each job experience point to a number of achievements. These are quantified whenever possible. Bold and underlined job titles stand out.

**MARGARET ANN TROISE**

323 West Drive
Elmira, New York 00000

Home: (607) 000-0000
Office: (607) 000-0000

**EXECUTIVE PROFILE**

Highly qualified executive with extensive progressive administrative and management experience in adult education and teaching. Successful consultant and trainer. Proficient in program development and implementation. Interact well with corporate and community organizations. Knowledgeable in budgeting and grant writing. Excellent presentation and communication skills.

**PROFESSIONAL EXPERIENCE:**

ELMIRA CHILDREN'S CENTER, Elmira, New York — 1980 - Present

**PROGRAM DIRECTOR** (1994-Present)

Involved in all phases of the change process in relocating to a larger facility; collaborated with outside consultant, facilitated smooth transition for staff, families and Board of Directors. Supervise 40 professional staff, volunteers, students and paraprofessionals. Handle all intake procedures, enrollment and program implementation. Schedule, evaluate and monitor staff activities.

- Doubled enrollment, tripled staff, and expanded ages of children served.
- Established and maintain excellent rapport with professional and community groups.

**DIRECTOR** (1980-1994)

Managed a new day care center, including program design. Developed and administered $350,000 annual budget. Managed staff of professionals, paraprofessionals, volunteers and student interns. Worked closely with corporate officials, Elmira Inc. Foundation, Board of Directors, community agencies and parents. Represented Elmira, Inc. with media and corporations nationwide.

- Wrote successful grant through Elmira's Work Family Department to develop and present on-site parent education classes to corporate employees.
- Developed plans and procedures for program promotion, recruitment/enrollment, and parent involvement.
- Designed and coordinated a comprehensive seminar on employer-supported child care for Elmira, Inc.

ELMIRA COUNTY PEDS PROGRAM, Elmira, New York — 1979 - 1980

**DIRECTOR**

Administered Parent Education Discussion Series (PEDS) program to train parents and professionals working with families. Selected and supervised training staff. Responsible for community relations and promotion. Developed and administered budget.

- Designed and implemented a training for trainers program.
- Managed contracts with agencies requesting professional consultation and training.

ELMIRA CITY COLLEGE, Elmira, New York — 1977 - 1986

**ADJUNCT PROFESSOR**

Developed and instructed courses in Human Services and Early Childhood Education for the Adult Education Program.

**264**

**Combination.** *Betty Geller, Elmira, New York*

Reading a resume from beginning to end gives you often an overview of the person and a snapshot of his or her best skills and victories to date. Reading a resume from end to beginning gives

**MARGARET ANN TROISE** **Page Two**

---

**EDUCATION:**

STATE UNIVERSITY OF CALIFORNIA - at Los Angeles
**Graduate Certification Program in Education** (30 hrs.) - 1967

UNIVERSITY OF CALIFORNIA - at Berkeley
**Bachelor of Arts in Anthropology/Humanities** - 1965

Courses and Seminars in Management and Supervisory Development, Adult Education, Women in Management, Day Care Administration, Training for Trainers, The Working Parent, and Early Childhood Education through:
Cornell University, Elmira City College, Wheelock College, Gesell Institute, Bank Street College of Education, Effectiveness Training, Inc.

New York State Permanent Teaching Certification (N-6)
State of California Permanent Teaching Certification (N-8)

**CONSULTING/PRESENTATIONS:**

- Interviewed by '20/20' regarding a special television presentation focusing on corporate child care.
- Consulted with Time-Life Books for their new series on parenting, including options for working parents.
- Consulted with Elmira Chemical Corporation (Midland, Michigan) regarding the design of a corporate sponsored child care program.
- Designed and implemented training programs for NYS and PA school administrators and teachers, hospital administrative and medical personnel, human services management and staff.
- Trainer and group facilitator of training for trainers course, sponsored by Cornell University Regional Head Start Training Office.
- Designed and implemented programs utilized by public schools to explore alternative styles of education.
- Conducted presentations on corporate-sponsored day care to: Appalachian Regional Day Care Commission; Broone & Young Management Consultants; Chatham College; Boston University and Wheelock College.

**PUBLICATIONS:**

Book published entitled *Art Through Your Child's Eyes* (1979), written for parents of pre-school children explaining their child's growth and development in art.

**AFFILIATIONS:**

Board of Directors, Chemung City Women's Center
Member, National Association for the Education of Young Children

***- REFERENCES AVAILABLE UPON REQUEST -***

you a sense of development and how it happened that the person is where he or she is now. This is a resume that reads well in either direction. Circular bullets call attention to important achievements; hyphen bullets point to successful consulting projects and presentations.

**Dr. Glen Malone**
49 School Road West
Manalapan, New Jersey 07726
Office: (908) 613-3987 Ext. 549
Residence: (908) 536-7545

**General Statement**

Over twenty-five years in education: last sixteen in a leadership role. Possess an earned doctorate. Have elementary, secondary, and university experience. Strong background in curriculum development, staff supervision, test analysis, public relations, and financial/personnel resource management.

**New Jersey Certification:**

School Administrator Certificate, 1982
Principal/Supervisor Certificate, 1978
Instructional Certificate, French, 1979
Certificate of Eligibility, School Business Administrator, 1992

**Education:**

Teachers College, Columbia University, New York, NY
1979 - Ed.D. - Curriculum and Teaching - Research and Theory

Richmond College (College of Staten Island), Staten Island, NY
1975 - Sixth Year Certificate - Educational Administration and Supervision

New York University, New York, NY
1967 - M.A. - French Language and Literature

Douglass College, Rutgers University, New Brunswick, NJ
1966 - B.A. - French Language and Literature

Université de Paris, Paris, France
1965 - Diplôme Supérieur d'études françaises - French Literature

**Experience Full-Time:**

South River Board of Education, South River, NJ
**Director of Curriculum and Instruction** **1994-Present**

K-12 district, 160 teaching staff members, 45 support personnel. Responsible for district-wide curriculum development, staff in-service, test analysis, federal grants, basic skills and ESL/Bilingual programs. Work with four principals and Director of Special Services on staff supervision, building-level projects, and implementation of current curriculum trends.

Roosevelt Board of Education, Roosevelt, NJ
**Chief School Administrator** **1992-1994**

One-school district, k-6. Fifteen teaching staff members, five support personnel. Nine-member Board of Education, Board Secretary/Business Administrator. Sending-receiving relationship with neighboring district for grades 7-12. Responsible for all programs and services, curriculum development, staff supervision, public relations, budget development, facilities planning.

Milltown Board of Education, Milltown, NJ
Mr. Patrick J. Wilder, Superintendent (retired)
**Principal** **1989-1992**

Supervised twenty-five teaching staff members and nine support personnel. Developed building budget, introduced <u>Here's Looking At You 2000</u> and <u>Social Decision Making</u>. Edited <u>Pandasian Press</u>, <u>Student Handbook</u>, and <u>Parent Information Guide</u>. Was responsible for district's Basic Skills Improvement Program, testing, federal grants, various curriculum development and special project committees.

**265**

**Combination.** *Beverly Baskin, Marlboro, New Jersey*

The General Statement at the beginning is similar to a Profile section, which nudges the format from chronological to combination. Such a judgment is debatable, however, and most writers will

State of New Jersey, Department of Education - Dr. Mary R. Guidette, Middlesex County Superintendent (formerly, Dr. Virginia L. Brinson)
**Educational Planner, Evaluation Specialist,**
**School Program Coordinator** **1981-1989**

Monitored and provided technical assistance to local districts. Special assignment areas included planning objectives, the statewide testing program, program evaluation, and test analysis. Other assignments included graduation requirements, the SRA process, ESL/bilingual programs, ISIP's, basic skills, grant reviews, and multi-district consortia.

Upper Freehold Regional School District, Allentown, NJ
Dr. Stephen L. Sokolow, Superintendent
**Supervisor of Instruction** **1979-1981**

Supervised and evaluated over sixty teaching staff members. Responsible for budget coordination, staff development programs, curriculum and grant proposal development, test analysis, organization for computer use (classroom and office). Established Freshman Learning Community and Foreign Language in the Elementary School (FLES) programs. Created Parents' Newsletter.

New York City Board of Education, Brooklyn, NY
**Teacher** **1970-1975; 1967-1969**

Taught French, Spanish, German, English and reading. Coordinated language laboratory. Advised various clubs, publications, and special event activities.

Venet Advertising, New York, NY
**Director of Marketing Research** **1969-1970**

Researched products and consumer use of products. Prepared and presented reports and financial analyses. (On leave from NYC Board of Education.)

**Experience Part-Time**

New Brunswick Tomorrow, New Brunswick, NJ
**Consultant, Educational Task Force** **1982-1983**
Developed reports, coordinated staff development and public relations projects.

Georgian Court College, Lakewood, NJ
**Adjunct Lecturer** **1979**
Instructed graduate course in curriculum design and development.

Brooklyn College (CUNY), Brooklyn, NY
**Adjunct Instructor** **1978-1979**
Supervised student teachers. Developed ties with receiving schools. Instructed seminars.

Barnard College, Columbia University, New York, NY
**Half-Time Instructor** **1975-1976**
Supervised student teachers. Developed ties with receiving schools. Instructed seminars.

have their own set of criteria for deciding whether a particular resume has a chronological, functional, or combination format. In the field of Education, certification is essential for hiring, so the New Jersey Certification section is put first. Likewise, degrees are necessary for licensing, so Education is put next.

**Publications:** "In Favor of Immersion Programs," Pedagogic Reporter, January, 1983.
"Learning Styles," Pedagogic Reporter, March, 1984.

**Professional Membership:**
Association for Supervision and Curriculum Development (ASCD)
New Jersey Association for Supervision and Curriculum Development (NJASCD)
Phi Delta Kappa

**REFERENCES**

Dr. Mary Regina Guidette
County Superintendent of Schools
State of New Jersey, Department of Education
Middlesex County Office
200 Old Matawan Road
Old Bridge, New Jersey 08857
(908) 390-6000

Mr. Michael Maddaluna
County Superintendent of Schools
State of New Jersey, Department of Education
Monmouth County Office
3435 Highway 9
P. 0. Box 1264
Freehold, New Jersey 07728-1264
(908) 431-7816

Mr. Patrick J. Wilder
Superintendent of Schools (retired)
38 Topaz Lane
Hamilton Township, NJ 08690
Home: (609) 585-2055

Mr. John P. Ord
Former Board of Education President
P.O. Box 223
Roosevelt, New Jersey 08555
Home: (609) 443-1744
Work: (908) 349-8444

Complete placement folder, including course work, background and confidential references, is on file at Teachers College, Columbia University.

The distinction between full-time and part-time experience is useful since many teachers with a master's degree in their field can teach as adjunct faculty at a college or university. Normally, References are not included in a resume, but there are exceptions.

# ROBERT B. GOODMAN

**555 Mansfield Lane**
**Durham, North Carolina 66666**
**(777) 555-9999**

## CAREER PROFILE

**Top-producing Sales Executive** with over 10 years of progressive experience in sales and marketing of waterjet cutting equipment. Significant increase in profit margins and reduction in expenses in highly competitive environments has been attained by strategic growth planning and marketing and sales development, along with comprehensive product knowledge. Successfully established and developed two Regions to multimillion-dollar status in less than two years. Acquired largest-ever sales in division history twice; first Waterjet Division Representative to ever win **"Circle of Excellence" Award**. Instrumental in design and introduction of new products. Initiated first-ever advertising and marketing program and successfully negotiated contract for after-market intensifier parts.

## AREAS OF EXPERTISE

- **Strategic Sales & Market Planning** ♦ **Market Penetration / Development**
- **Key Account Relationship Management**
- **Full P&L Responsibility** ♦ **Budgeting & Forecasting** ♦ **Escalating Profit Margins**
- **Personnel Development / Supervision** ♦ **Competitive New Product Launching**
- **Negotiations / Acquisitions** ♦ **Advertising** ♦ **Pricing / Service Management**
- **Communications / Public Relations / Presentation**

## PROFESSIONAL EXPERIENCE

**SUPERIOR CUTTING SYSTEMS, Durham, North Carolina** **1994 – Present**

**Director of Sales and Marketing / Director of Products Division**

- Recruited to independently establish and develop Product Division; **initiated first-ever advertising and marketing program** with small budget, concurrently with managing all sales functions.
- Analyze customer needs/requirements. Establish competitive price structure of products.
- Penetrated U.S./international markets; **increased market share from zero to 15%** in first year.
- **Doubled company sales first year to $2.3 million** (1995); projected increase for 1996 is 66%.
- **Assisted in machine content design**; introduced two computer-controlled waterjet systems in less than one year (in less than half the normal time).
- **Successfully negotiated contract with Fortune 200 corporation to provide after-market parts** for competitors' intensifiers which Superior will manufacture and market; **project first year sales revenue of $600,000.**

**266**

**Combination.** *Ann Klint, Tyler, Texas*

A resume for a person who was starting a business of his own in which he did the same things he was doing for other companies. He needed this resume to present to a financial institution

**ROBERT B. GOODMAN** **Page Two**

**REMINGTON CORPORATION, Denver, Colorado** **1981 - 1994**

WATERJET CUTTING SYSTEMS DIVISION, Denver, Colorado
**National Sales and Marketing Manager–Industrial** (1991–1994)

Initially promoted within Fortune 200 company to assume responsibility for all sales to North and South America; shortly thereafter, assumed additional responsibility of all domestic marketing, then acquired responsibility for Customer Demonstration Center (CDC)/Job Shop and Telemarketing functions. **Formulated and efficiently administered Sales and Marketing budget of $1 million.**

Significant Achievements

- **Initiated Job Shop operation** which offset all costs associated with CDC operation.
- **Reduced sales expense by 10%; increased bookings an average of 15% per year.**
- **Facilitated successful market introduction of two products.**
- **Substantially reduced expenses and increased domestic sales by 30%** in two years during poor economy and reduction in sales staff.
- **Streamlined operations** (layoff forced by downturn in aerospace industry); personally covered West Coast territory one week each month, maintaining 70% of previous year's sales revenue.
- **Planned, organized, and presided** at trade shows. **Featured Speaker** at multiple industry conventions and SME functions to promote products and technology; established excellent rapport with potential clients (domestic and international).

**Regional Sales Manager - Midwest** - Colorado Springs, Colorado (1989–1991)

Relocated to Denver to learn automotive industry and develop camaraderie with key accounts.

Significant Achievements

- **Within first two months, closed sales of approximately $450,000, generating total of $900,000.**
- **Acquired largest sale in Division history** (to date) with order to General-Mills; **$920,000.**
- **Reestablished General Motors account; generated over $1.5 million** in next 12 months (account was lost for four years prior to reestablishment).
- **Recipient of "Circle of Excellence" award; only Waterjet Division Representative to ever receive this award** (company-wide sales club award).
- **Generated $2.3 million in sales** in 1990; won significant projects with major corporations (General Electric, Lockheed, General Motors, Georgia Pacific, Pratt & Whitney, General Mills).
- **Established, implemented, and conducted sales training program** for new sales engineers.

**Regional Sales Manager - Southeast** - Nashville, Tennessee (1985–1989)

- Moved to Nashville to open up Southeast Regional Sales Office; developed territory to **million-dollar territory in two years.**
- **Acquired largest sales in Division history** (to date) with order to Lockheed-Marietta; **$485,000.**
- **Led Region to Number One Region** despite limited systems capability and no Regional OEM accounts focused in waterjet.

for a loan. The writer felt that the loan officer should have an overview of the person's career, see multiple areas of expertise, and know of all his important accomplishments. This resume is the result. It is longer than a two-page resume because the purpose of the resume was different. As you review this resume, notice the

**ROBERT B. GOODMAN** **Page Three**

**REMINGTON CORPORATION** (Continued)

OIL AND GAS COMPRESSOR DIVISION, Miami, Florida/Oklahoma City, Oklahoma
**Project Manager - Offshore Marketing** (1980–1985)

Began career with Remington in 1980 as **Project Coordinator**; rapidly progressed to **Applications Engineer**, to **Senior Applications Engineer**, to **Technical Sales / Project Manager** responsible for product management of separable gas compressor packages.

- **Instrumental in development of international market** with Peru, Germany, China, Japan, and others.
- Performed detailed thermodynamic compressor analysis for proper sizing of gas compressor stages used for pipeline; **enhanced oil recovery and gas wells.**
- **Efficiently managed multimillion-dollar projects** from conception through design, manufacturing, and installation; **consistently completed projects under budget.**
- In 1983, transferred back to Miami to manage more complex offshore projects.

## EDUCATION / PROFESSIONAL DEVELOPMENT

UNIVERSITY OF ARKANSAS – Fayetteville, Arkansas
**B.B.A. in Marketing** (1980)

UNIVERSITY OF COLORADO - Denver, Colorado
Successfully completed "**Effective Sales Management**" Program

Successfully completed "**Management Assessment**" Program
(Provided by Remington to employees who are "promotable")

~ ~ ***References Furnished On Request*** ~ ~

information that is in boldface. Look at the extra number of items in the Areas of Expertise. Check out the Significant Achievements subsections to see the bold statements that might appeal to a loan officer. If you were the officer, what would *you* do?

# JOEL M. AARON

323 W. 47th Street
Elmira, New York 00000

Home: (607) 000-0000
Office: (607) 000-0000

## OBJECTIVE

A management position that will contribute to the business strategy and profitability of an organization through progressive and innovative leadership of the human resources function.

## EXECUTIVE SUMMARY

Senior level manager with twenty years broad based and progressively responsible experience in management and human resources. **Corporate** and **division** assignments in diverse environments including **growth, start-up, restructuring** and **acquisition**. Proven ability to work with CEO and senior management team to integrate the human resource function within the business, manage start-ups and rapid growth and handle restructuring and downsizing. Strong human resource generalist skill set. Highly effective interpersonal skills at all organizational levels.

## PROFESSIONAL EXPERIENCE

**ELMIRA MARKETING, INC.**, Elmira, New York
*(A $90 million publicly held, direct mail and manufacturing company with more than 900 employees focused on printing, paper and personalization of consumer products.)*

**Corporate Director of Human Resources** **1993 - Present**

Responsible for the development, direction and deployment of all company wide human resources programs with a focus on supporting the profitability and growth goals of the corporation. Functional responsibilities include compensation and benefits, wage and salary administration, employment, employee relations, management development and training, employee communications and safety. Emphasis on operational issues as well as the strategic planning within the business. Report to the President and Chief Operating Officer. Executive management team member.

***Key Accomplishments:***

- Created a new human resources organization, philosophy and program including the recruitment and hiring of a staff and the development of programs and services that support the business.
- Established the human resources organization as a key asset contributing to the profitability and growth of the business.
- Active member of the senior management team participating in operational and strategic decision making impacting the direction of the business.
- Realized annual cost savings of approximately $100,000 while improving the benefit level, through aggressive management of employee health insurance.
- Reduced workers compensation costs by $125,000 by introducing a new loss control program, moving to a new insurance carrier and through employee and manager education.
- Developed and introduced the company's first corporate wide management training program.
- Created an employment function, successfully recruiting employees at all levels of the organization. Recruited and hired two key executives and effectively developed and managed innovative recruitment programs focused on hiring 300 seasonal workers.
- Purchased and installed a human resource information system replacing a manual record-keeping system.
- Developed an executive compensation competitive analysis, identifying inequities, resulting in the implementation of modifications to base salary and bonus levels.

**267**

**Combination.** *Betty Geller, Elmira, New York*

A resume for a Human Resources Director who wanted a targeted Objective, a Summary, and an Experience section with highlighted key accomplishments. On page two, prior experience (1983

**JOEL M. AARON** **Page Two**

**GREAT ATLANTIC INC.** (Formerly Graphic Concepts Inc.), Elmira, New York
*(A $100+ million computer business selling systems to telephone companies.)* **1983 - 1993**

**Director - Employee Relations** 1985 - 1993

Responsible for all employee relations activities of the organization with 1,000 employees. Supervised two managers with a $1M budget. Functional responsibilities included compensation and benefits, employment, employee relations, field employee relations, employee communications and employee services. Reported to Vice President Human Resources.

***Key Accomplishments:***

- Provided leadership within the business for the successful transition of human resource policies and programs following acquisition.
- Developed and implemented an ongoing management communications program including employee meetings, management meetings, CEO luncheons and monthly HR indicators.
- Created an employee relations survey tool used to assess the "pulse" of the organization.
- Led the shutdown of the manufacturing operation including the successful re-deployment of employees and a significant workforce reduction while maintaining productivity.
- Developed an employee relations organization that aligns human resources with the business.
- Managed several significant workforce reductions including selection, administration and outplacement, providing balance between business requirements and legal considerations.
- Created a company newsletter staffed by volunteers.
- Developed an innovative employee wellness program.
- Established an employee assistance program.
- Developed a human resource quality survey tool used to measure the department.

**GRAPHIC CONCEPTS INC.** (Office Systems Division), Albany, Virginia
*(A business unit developing and marketing office automation computer systems.)*

**Manager - Human Resources** 1983 - 1985

Managed the human resource function of this start-up business unit. Developed and organized a human resource department including a staff of two. Focused on staffing, compensation, employee relations. Reported to the General Manager.

***Key Accomplishments:***

- Integrated the human resource function within the business.
- Executed cost effective recruiting programs expanding professional employment levels from a base of 50 employees to 220 in 18 months.

**BROWN INSTRUMENT COMPANY,** Elmira, New York
*(A process control company, division of Albion Corporation.)*

Human Resource positions in compensation and employment **1979 - 1983**

**GEORGETOWN MEMORIAL HOSPITAL,** Georgetown, New York

Positions in operations and human resources **1974 - 1979**

**KINSEY COUNTY HEALTH DEPARTMENT,** Kinsey, New York **1972 - 1974**

**EDUCATION**

**Bachelor of Science,** SUNY Elmira - 1972
**Executive Development Certificate Program,** Baylor Institute of Technology - 1989

**COMMUNITY INVOLVEMENT**

Board of Directors, Private Industry Council
Elmira County Human Resource Association

and earlier) is shortened so that the resume won't be longer than two pages. Important words are made bold to stand out in the Executive Summary. Four of the companies mentioned in the Professional Experience section are explained in italic statements within parentheses.

**CARL J. BURGER** 6804 Garden Cove • Maple, Tennessee 00000 • **(000) 000-0000**

## CAREER GOAL

Seeking to obtain a position in an environmental organization that will utilize a results-oriented career and strong marketing, managerial and leadership skills to positively impact organizational development.

## PROFILE SUMMARY

*A highly successful professional with an accomplished career in the environmental industry. Excellent analytical skills with the ability to assess situations and implement viable solutions. Demonstrated strengths include superior team leadership and staff motivation. Excels at establishing and developing a region to maximum potential. Successfully managed multi-million dollar budgets. Noted in Who's Who Environmental Registry.*

## PROFESSIONAL EXPERIENCE

**ENERGY SYSTEMS SOLUTIONS, INC.** - Memphis, Tennessee **1993 to Present**
*A $30 million national energy service company providing financing, analysis, installation of energy efficiency improvements and full maintenance services for the retail, commercial, institutional and governmental markets. A subsidiary the second largest utility holding company in the United States.*

**Director of Utility Marketing**

- Directly accountable for developing and fostering strategic relationships with electric utilities throughout the U.S.
- Conducts comprehensive research and responds to request for proposals for DSM bidding.
- Serves as a liaison with utilities in service territory and qualifies company to participate in utility rebate programs.
- Represents company at trade shows and conferences throughout the United States.

  - *Successfully responded to DSM Pilot Project request for proposal from Texas Utilities Electric: wrote proposal, negotiated contract and currently coordinating implementation process (contract valued at $20 million).*
  - *Expanded market depth to include retail, commercial, institutional, government, hospital and non-profit organizations.*
  - *Developed hazardous waste disposal policies and procedures.*
  - *Generated training materials for sales and marketing force.*
  - *Designed and implemented effective marketing plans.*

**ENERGY, INC.** - Bergenfield, New Jersey **1986 to 1993**
*An international energy consulting firm with annual revenue exceeding $20 million.*

**Director of Marketing and Operations**

- Directed all functions pertaining to the maintenance and expansion of utility accounts in the Mid-Atlantic Region.
- Provided overall management to 7 East Coast branches, including recruiting, training, and developing a staff exceeding 100 professionals.
- Controlled an annual budget of $8.5 million.

  - *Achieved on target sales plan of $10 million in revenue for 1993.*
  - *Increased sales by 20% over a 3 month period.*
  - *Targeted and negotiated with 3 new clients resulting in additional sales of $3 million.*

**268**

**Combination.** *Alesia Benedict, Rochelle Park, New Jersey*

Italic is used for the Profile Summary, descriptive statements or phrases about each employer mentioned in the Professional Experience section, bulleted achievements, and academic rank at

**CARL J. BURGER** **(901) 754-7082** **- Page Two -**

## PROFESSIONAL EXPERIENCE experienced...

**CONSERVATION MANAGEMENT CORP.** - Union, New Jersey **1984 to 1986**
*An energy consulting company, servicing New Jersey, Pennsylvania, Maryland, and Washington D.C.*

**New Jersey Regional Manager**

- Established energy audit accounts with 4 New Jersey utilities.
- Developed report format for energy audit, established tracking system, and served as a liaison to maintain client relations.
- Managed and developed a staff of 10 employees.

**NEW JERSEY DEPARTMENT of ENERGY** - Newark, New Jersey **1980 to 1984**
*An energy conservation government agency.*

**Energy Conservation Program Manager**

- Designed, implemented and managed 3 statewide demand-side management programs.
- Accountable for coordinating all trade show functions, including booth design and staffing, and composing marketing literature and brochures.
- Promoted energy conservation through speaking engagements.
- Developed standard for certifying energy auditors.

## EDUCATION and CERTIFICATIONS

B.S. (Environmental Science) • B.S. (Business Administration) - Ramapo College, Mahwah, NJ
*Graduated Cum Laude*

Environmental Leadership Training Institute Certification (Tufts University)
Outward Bound Alumni
CPR Certification • First Aid Certification
Certified Energy Manager

## REPORTS and PUBLICATIONS

New Jersey Energy Management Workbook for Not-for-Profit Buildings • New Jersey Energy Management Workbook for Commercial Buildings • New Jersey Energy Management Workbook for Multi-Family Buildings • The Effect of Free Energy Audits for Con Edison's Mid-size Commercial and Industrial Customers, presented at the New York State Demand-Side Management Symposium, May 1988, Albany, New York. Published in proceedings.

## PROFESSIONAL AFFILIATIONS

Association of Energy Engineers
Association of Energy Services Professionals

graduation. Job titles are bold, underlined, and centered. The centering of job titles under centered section headings makes it possible for the eye to travel down the center of each page for a quick overview of the resume. The person "secured a new position (six-figure income) within two weeks."

# JANICE R. CARR, RNC,BS,CDONA

700 BLADES STREET • WESTON, MD 00000• (999) 999-9999

***Proven leadership record in long-term care management and administration.***

***Demonstrated ability to manage nursing care systems and programs to insure optimum occupancy in long term care facilities.***

***Awarded "Director of Nursing of the Year" in Delaware by the National Association of Directors of Nursing Administration.***

***Excellent working knowledge of Medicaid, Medicare and managed care.***

***Team Player--commended by superiors for interdepartmental skills and the ability to work effectively with health care professionals on all levels.***

**Professional Background***

WESTON VILLAGE MANOR, INC., WESTON, MD

***Director of Nursing*** 12/92 to present

Responsible for managing all nursing care services in a 105-bed, long-term care facility, which includes a retirement community of 150 independent residents. Manages a $1.6 million departmental budget and supervises nursing staff of 75 employees. Develops annual goals for the nursing department. Plans, implements and administers numerous programs to meet the medical, emotional and psychological needs of the residents. Serves as Chief in Command in the absence of the Administrator.

*Developed and implemented:*

- In-house training program for certification of Geriatric Nursing Assistants. Results included improved quality care for residents and savings in administrative costs for the facility.
- Improved computerized billing methods which streamlined data entry procedures.
- Salary ceiling program that lowered personnel costs.
- Accident prevention program that improved safety for residents and staff.
- Policies to meet "restraint proper" criteria of federal guidelines.
- IV Therapy program.
- Medication error reduction program.
- Incontinence Reduction and Management program.
- Program to better maintain functional abilities of residents.
- "Wellness Fair" for residents and staff.

***Staff Development Coordinator*** 9/91 to 12/92

Developed and presented in-service staff training programs to meet state requirements. Developed Care Giver Support Group to improve staff morale and lower absenteeism and staff turnover. Supervised nursing care given at the unit level. Assisted with quality assurance projects. Acted as Assistant Director of Nursing in absence of ADON.

SHADY SIDE HOSPITAL AT EASTON

***Relief RN*** 1985 to 1989

***Assistant Head Nurse--Pediatrics*** 5/84 to 9/85

***Licensed Practical Nurse*** 5/80 to 5/84

DR. LEWIS SMITH, DDS, WESTON, MD

***Dental Assistant*** 1/80 to 5/80

LISTER NURSING HOME, DENTON, MD

***Licensed Practical Nurse*** 1979 to 1980

MEADE COUNTY HOSPITAL CENTER, GLENVILLE, MD

***Licensed Practical Nurse*** 1975 to 1979

* Interrupted career from 9/85 to 11/91 to help build family-owned business

## 269

**Combination.** *Thomas E. Spann, Easton, Maryland*

Putting profile, skills, award, knowledge, and work style information in a double-line box at the top just after the contact information says this individual is someone special. The paragraph after

JANICE R. CARR, RNC,BS,CDONA 700 BLADES STREET • WESTON, MD 00000• (999) 999-9999

**Education**

HOYT UNIVERSITY, QUINCY, LA
***Currently enrolled in Master of Science program in Health Services Management***

UNIVERSITY OF DELAWARE,, DOVER, DE
***Bachelor of Science, Gerontology, 1996***

EXXES COMMUNITY COLLEGE, ALLEN, MD
***Associate Degree, Nursing, 1984 Registered Nurse***

PLAINVIEW CITY HOSPITALS, SCHOOL OF PRACTICAL NURSING, PLAINVIEW, MD
***Licensed Practical Nurse, 1975***

**Specialty Certifications/ Licensure**

NATIONAL ASSOCIATION OF DIRECTORS OF NURSING ADMINISTRATION IN LONG-TERM CARE
***Certified Director of Nursing Administration, 1995 (#1007)***

AMERICAN NURSES ASSOCIATION
***Certified in Gerontological Nursing, 1992 (#187019-09)***

REGISTERED NURSE, DELAWARE

**Professional Affiliations**

AMERICAN NURSES ASSOCIATION

DEALWARE NURSES ASSOCIATION, DISTRICT #2
***Member of the Nominating Committee***
***Treasurer***

NATIONAL GERONTOLOGICAL NURSING ASSOCIATION

NATIONAL ASSOCIATION OF DIRECTORS OF NURSING ADMINISTRATION IN LONG-TERM CARE
***Secretary***

ALZHEIMER'S ASSOCIATION

PLAINVIEW LONG-TERM CARE NURSE ADMINISTRATOR'S GROUP
***Secretary***

PLAINVIEW WOMEN'S NETWORK
***Board Member-Past Treasurer***

SOROPTIMIST INTERNATIONAL OF MEADE COUNTY

FOR ALL SEASONS, INC.
***Board Member***

MEADE PARTNERSHIP

**Awards**

NATIONAL ASSOCIATION OF DIRECTORS OF NURSING ADMINISTRATION IN LONG-TERM CARE
***"Director of Nursing of the Year" for the State of Delaware, May 1991***

the current position indicates responsibilities, and bulleted items are achievements. Centering the dates enables the eye to see them quickly without having to travel to the right margin, where they would be if they were right-aligned. The contact information is repeated as a header on page two.

# ROSE MARY ALLEVA

24 Wayside Lane Court
Wantagh, New York 00000
Home: (000) 000-0000
Office: (007) 000-0000


## QUALIFICATIONS

- Organizational, administrative, human resources management and training skills
- Proficient in policy and program development, community organization, recruitment and development of volunteers, grantsmanship, fundraising, marketing and promotion
- Strong communication, analytical and creative abilities

## PROFESSIONAL EXPERIENCE

AMERICAN CANCER SOCIETY
***Director of Service and Rehabilitation*, Elviratown State Division**
Elviratown, New York 1992-Present

- Planning - Developed and implemented goals and action plan for serving 20,000 cancer patients and their families
- Training - Planned and conducted statewide training on patient services and customer service. Conducted national training on serving the socio-economically disadvantaged
- Promotion - Identified and implemented strategies for increasing referrals for patient services. Developed informational, educational and services campaign for prostate cancer
- Fundraising - Identify and solicit project sponsors. Assisted unit in increasing Community Crusade income twelvefold in one year
- Editing - Publishes statewide quarterly breast health newsletter. Produced brochure on employment rights and resources. Compiled 120-page directory of federal and state resources
- Conferences - Planned and managed 5 statewide conferences
- Evaluation - Developed instruments to record or analyze patient services

***Executive Director*, Smalltown County Unit**, Smalltown, New York 1984 - 1992
Served and was accountable to four different populations:

- Public
  - Through electronic and print media, served as a spokesperson to keep public informed about cancer issues, advances in research, available services and programs
  - Received national community demonstration grant to reach the socio-economically disadvantaged
- Donors
  - Increased giving by 142%
  - Developed annual residential campaign to a $.67 per capita giving level, 319% above the state average
- Patients
  - Increased number served by 23%
  - Implemented two new comprehensive service programs
  - Advocated local and systemic changes for medically uninsured people
- Volunteers
  - Increased volunteer base by 40%
  - Developed and implemented programs to motivate, recruit, train, supervise, develop and retain volunteers

Received 19 Achievement Awards in the areas of fundraising, service, education and communications

Received 3 Staff Awards, including the James Leonard Staff Exemplar Award

**270**

**Combination.** *Betty Geller, Elmira, New York*

A resume for a Director's Director, a person who became a director early in her career and has had director positions ever since, supervising other directors in her Executive Director roles.

**Rose Mary Alleva** **Page Two**

***Holiday Valley Area Director*** 1984 - 1988; 1990 - 1992
Concurrently with Executive Director duties, supervised executive directors in 5 other County Units

- In 7 years, total income from the Holiday Valley Area increased 126% to $540,355 annually
- Selected and trained staff, developed and implemented organizational and administrative plans, prepared and monitored budgets, supervised volunteer recruitment and training, and fundraising

SILVER COUNTYWIDE OFFICE FOR THE AGING, Silver, New York
***Director*** 1980 - 1983

- Developed and implemented 10 new service programs
- Established first senior citizens' center in Silver County
- As editor, expanded 8-page senior citizens newsletter to 24-page tabloid and doubled circulation
- Secured foundation and discretionary grants to raise $89,000 for program activities

KANSAS STATE DEPARTMENT OF SOCIAL SERVICES, Division of Adult Residential Care, Kansas, Missouri
***Director, Enforcement Unit*** 1979 - 1980
***Social Services Representative*** 1977 - 1979

COOPERATIVE EXTENSION OF LINDSAY COUNTY, Lindsay, New York
***Community Resources Development Assistant*** 1976

ELMIRA COUNTY BOARD OF ASSISTANCE, Elmira, New York
***Caseworker*** 1973 - 1975

**EDUCATION**

- Master of Social Work, University of Pittsburgh; Concentration: Planning and Community Organization, 1976
- National Institute of Mental Health Fellow, University of Pennsylvania, 1972
- Bachelor of Arts in Psychology, Happy Valley College, 1971
- Institute of European Studies, Barcelona, Spain, 1969-70

**PUBLICATIONS**

- "It's A Kid's World: A Child's Guide To Smalltown County"

**PROFESSIONAL AND COMMUNITY ACTIVITIES**

- Smalltown Rotary Club, 1989-Present; Home Show Chairman, 1992
- Our Little Town Church, 1985-Present; lector, organizer of Youth Mass
- Little Town Elementary School, 1990-Present; volunteer for various school activities

A unique feature in this resume is the use of a category just after a bullet in order to tag the achievement. For example, the achievement of developing and implementing goals and an action plan is tagged as "Planning." The reader can read just the tags and spot quickly an interest area.

**DONALD J. NEWMAN**
40 Conover Court
Belle Mead, New Jersey 08502

Home: (908) 359-0631 Office: (908) 820-3344

Fifteen years of continuous advancement and increased responsibilities as an executive for a Fortune 100 company. Eight years of executive purchasing management, and six years in sales and sales management. Additional experience leading groups in quality and operations. Successfully accomplished these major business challenges:

- Obtained cost reductions of $25 million through contract negotiations.
- Restructured non-productive sales and operating units.
- International sourcing and worldwide equipment leasing.
- Enhanced customer satisfaction levels.
- Directed implementation of Total Quality Management process.
- Increased revenues by $30 million.
- Developed sales and operations software systems.
- Led corporate wide process improvement teams.

B.A. in Business Management from Rutgers College, 1978

## Professional Experience

**SEA-LAND SERVICE, INC. (Subsidiary of the CSX Corporation - 1980-Present)**

**DIRECTOR OF PURCHASING**
**MARINE AND FUEL SERVICES (Elizabeth, NJ - 1992-Present)**

Promoted to this newly created position to lead a staff of 18 in managing international and domestic Marine Service requirements for 90 ships worldwide. Negotiate product, service, and maintenance contracts exceeding $300 million annually. Initially defined organization structure and staffed two offices after benchmarking competition and world class companies. Re-engineered and merged two departments into one; consolidated four offices into two and reduced headcount from 28 to 18. Manage equipment leasing program worldwide. Achieved cost reductions of $8 million in 1994 and $6 million in 1993. Utilized effective strategic planning in contract negotiations, process improvements, and systems development. Assumed responsibility for Europe and Far East Marine Purchasing, and negotiated international source contracts. Chosen as member of the CSX Interunit Purchasing Task Force. Elected to the Management Council of the International Marine Fuel Association. Selected as Leader of the Quality Management Team for Corporate Purchasing and Member of the Corporate Quality Steering Committee. Attended Harvard Business School Program on Negotiations for Executives.

**DIRECTOR OF FUEL PURCHASING (Elizabeth, NJ - 1991-1992)**

Responsible for worldwide procurement of fuel totaling $125 million annually. Working closely with my staff, successfully redesigned the fuel procurement strategy to enhance performance. Headed the team that partnered Microsoft and our Information Resources group to develop a fuel decision and management system. Monitored and tracked performance, analyzed purchases and trend price changes; evaluated suppliers. Benchmarked world class companies including Pepsi, Xerox, Hertz, United Airlines, Norfolk Southern, and AT&T. Member of the International Marine Fuel Association. Participated in Focus Group for CSX Fuel Purchasers. Cost reductions of $3 million achieved in 1992.

**271**

**Combination.** *Beverly Baskin, Marlboro, New Jersey*

An experience-emphasis resume that does not include formal sections about education, affiliations, or other matters. An advantage is that, after an experience summary with bulleted

**DONALD J. NEWMAN**

Page 2

## Professional Experience

**DIRECTOR OF QUALITY (Edison, NJ - 1990-1991)**

Selected for initial staffing of the Corporate Quality Department. Responsible for Total Quality Management (TQM) efforts worldwide. Accomplished trainer and facilitator in all quality tools. Developed training curriculum consisting of courses in Basic Quality Management, Problem Solving, Process Improvement and Re-Engineering, Customer Focus, Supplier Management, and Benchmarking.

**SALES MANAGER (Edison, NJ - 1987-1990)**

Promoted to New Jersey Sales Manager after three years in sales. Managed eight sales associates generating $50 million in revenue contribution. Developed territory enhancement strategy to restructure for increased customer satisfaction and revenue growth of 15% annually. Lead partnership development programs with major customers including Panasonic, K Mart, Toys R Us, and M&M Mars. Headed corporate systems development team, successfully improving our customer profile data base. Selected as outstanding sales manager and assigned to lead a Customer Focus Initiative team on a four week Asia business development trip. Additional sales training: Producing Results From Others (AMA), Effective Sales Management, Select The Best.

**ACCOUNT EXECUTIVE (Pittsburgh, PA - 1985-1987)**

Elevated to head field office in Pittsburgh covering three states. Generated sales of $16 million in 1986 up 33% from previous year. Created telemarketing program piloted by the two person inside support group, subsequently adopted by all field offices nationwide. Selected as top salesperson in 1986.

**SALES REPRESENTATIVE (New York, NY - 1984-1985)**

Transitioned into sales in New York City, increased account base from 75 to 125 active accounts and revenue from $4 to $6 million in 1985. Selected twice as Salesperson of the Quarter. Completed Xerox Professional Selling Skills Training (Intermediate and Advanced).

**PURCHASING MANAGER (Elizabeth, NJ - 1980-1984)**

Joined Sea-Land as Purchasing Manager in charge of equipment procurement. Promoted in 1982 to Group Manager with staff of five, accountable for $40 million in expenditures. Performed nationwide field audits to ensure adherence to contracts and company policy. Reduced costs by $8 million over four years.

**PRUDENTIAL INSURANCE COMPANY OF AMERICA (Newark, NJ - 1978-1980)**

Corporate Training Program graduate, assigned to Corporate Purchasing as a buyer of capital goods.

accomplishments and a one-line indication of a degree, the rest of the two-page resume can be used to describe Professional Experience in greater detail. After a two-year insurance position, the person's career path has been growth and elevation in the same company since 1980.

## *Catherine A. Nottingham*

934 Charles Drive Rochester, Minnesota 55555-5555 (555) 555-5555

**OBJECTIVE:** Directorship of a medium to large urban or suburban library system that will utilize existing skills and experience while offering opportunity for professional advancement.

**PROFESSIONAL EXPERIENCE:**

**HIAWATHA PUBLIC LIBRARY; HIAWATHA, MINNESOTA** **1992 - Present**

**Library Director**

*Executive responsibility for management and operation of suburban library with two branches, 60 employees, annual budget over $1.1 million, and circulation of over 500,000 volumes per year.*

Answer to Library Board and Town Board of Hiawatha.

- Report to Library Board on budgetary and managerial issues.
- Work with Library Board to develop annual budget based on long-range goals.
- Present budget to Town of Hiawatha Board for approval.

Supervise professional staff:

- Implement employee evaluations.
- Establish goals and objectives for professional staff.
- Empower employees by moving responsibility down organizational chain.
- Institute training/development program for library staff.

Serve on committees of Twin Cities Library System:

- Co-Chair Town Library Directors' Council.
- Co-Chair Directors' Advisory Council.
- Automation Policy Committee.

Act as liaison between library and community:

- Serve on local Chamber of Commerce Board.
- Co-chair Town of Hiawatha Internet Committee,
  - Currently developing "Home Page".
  - Launched public access to Internet, September 1995.
- Collaborate with school district on Summer Reading Program with over 1300 children participating.

**MAJOR ACHIEVEMENTS**

Instituted five-year capital improvement campaign (1993-1997) and obtained grants to fund projects. **Campaign objectives realized in four years, one year ahead of schedule**. Campaign includes:

- Installation of new roofs and new carpeting in both branches.
- Installation of new HVAC systems in both branches.
- Construction of new entrances at one branch to comply with Americans with Disabilities Act (ADA) access requirements.

As part of Capital Campaign, developed three-year technology plan to upgrade library automation systems. Secured cooperation with Town of Hiawatha to participate in their equipment leasing plan and connect with their LAN. This innovation resulted in achieving goals **ahead of schedule** and at a **substantial cost savings**. Improvements implemented include:

- Migration from terminals to LAN's and WAN's.
- Migration from GEAC to CARL (Automated library systems handling circulation and O.P.A.C. catalog).
- Implementation of on-line catalog (CARL).
- Automation of office functions.

Increased annual budget by over 33% in three years:

- Justified increases to Town Board at time when budget cuts were proposed.
- Increased materials budget by 42% in three-year span.
- Increased personnel budget by 30% in three-year span.

**272**

**Chronological.** *Arnold G. Boldt, Rochester, New York*

Using small type and wide double-indention, the writer packs much information on two pages and still provides considerable white space. Italic appears after each job title in a description of

*Catherine A. Nottingham* | ***Resume - Page 2***

**ADDITIONAL PROFESSIONAL EXPERIENCE:**

**ST. PAUL PUBLIC LIBRARY; ST. PAUL, MINNESOTA** 1981 - 1992

**Department Head, Interlibrary Loan & Centralized Reserves** 1986 - 1992
*Planned, coordinated, and managed all interlibrary loan and centralized reserves services for the Pioneer Library System, which encompassed over 100 individual branches in a five county region of southern Minnesota. Provided ILL services to Twin Cities Regional Library Council, school library systems, and MSILL on contract basis.*

- Supervised staff of 18 employees.
- Recommended and implemented policy and procedural changes.
- Prepared and monitored departmental budget.
- Represented ILL services at Central Division Heads' meetings.
- Served on regional and state-wide committees relating to interlibrary loan.
- Provided training to member libraries on ILL services.
- Assisted in planning/implementation of automated circulation system.
- Chaired Office Automation Committee for Central Library.

**Special Librarian, Central Library** 1986
*Established and coordinated usage of automated circulation system (GEAC) for Central divisions. Trained staff on use of GEAC and responded to user problems.*

**Science and Technology Reference Librarian** 1981 - 1985
*Selected titles and developed Science and Technology collection. Assisted member libraries with reference and collection development. Supervised pages, library assistants, and interns.*

**HARRIETVILLE PUBLIC LIBRARY; HARRIETVILLE, MINNESOTA** 1978 - 1980

**Acting Director** 1979
*Assumed Director's duties for seven month period shortly after move into new facility with doubled circulation.*

**Adult Services Librarian** 1978 - 1980
*Developed adult, reference, and Audio/Visual collections for large suburban library. Assisted Library Director in planning and management.*

**PROFESSIONAL AFFILIATIONS:**

Minnesota Library Association:
Continuing Education Committee
Interlibrary Loan Committee

American Library Association

**EDUCATION:**

**Master of Library Science**
School of Library and Information Science
State University College at Cuylerville
Cuylerville, New York

**Bachelor of Science, Biology**
Holy Cross College
Worcester, Massachusetts

responsibilities and accomplishments. Information about the current position occupies almost the whole of page one. Clustering duties into four areas makes them easier to grasp. Similarly, grouping major achievements into three groups in a separate subsection makes them easy to see.

**DAVID R. NICHOLS**
1042 Big Bear Lane
Hinsbrook, IL 00000
Phone (708) 555-5555
Fax (708) 555-1111

**PROFILE**

High-caliber HR Director experienced in employment, benefits and compensation, training and organizational development, labor relations, union avoidance, safety, and compliance. Verifiable record of achievements in continuous improvement, team building, and cost containment.

**EXPERIENCE**

8/92 to Date **DIRECTOR - HUMAN RESOURCES**
**ABC Company,** Crete, IL

Direct all human resource activities for this manufacturer of accessories and parts for the automobile after-market ($170M in annual sales, 1,200 employees, 2 plants). Supervise a staff of five; report to the President.

Revamped department, producing improved efficiency with fewer personnel. Commended for upgrading staff.

Implemented managed care networks, giving employees a choice between an HMO and a Point of Service PPO. Generated annual savings of over $500 per employee. Identified $15,000 in fraudulent medical claims.

Outsourced production of Summary Plan Descriptions and Plan Documents. Brought plans into compliance with ERISA and IRS regulations. Outsourced pension plan and EAP administration, eliminating of one staff position.

Produced company training and development needs assessments, working closely with other departments. Set up an on-site literacy training program in conjunction with the Piper Literacy Center.

Implemented substance abuse and harassment policies. Conducted employee awareness seminars on topics such as drugs and alcohol, child care resources, and educational/training programs for career development.

Maintained union-free status following a UAW organizing drive. Administer the employee complaint procedure.

Responsible for resolution of complaints with such agencies as the EEOC, NLRB, and OSHA.

Implemented a human resources information system to meet top management reporting needs. Trained administrative staff in various software packages: Excel, Access, Word.

*continued...*

**273**

**Combination.** *Jennie Dowden, Flossmoor, Illinois*

This individual "wanted a format that was different, but still conservative enough for the business world." The positioning and half-framing of the date to the left of the company name is just

**DAVID R. NICHOLS**
page 2

7/88 to 8/92 — **MANAGER - HUMAN RESOURCES**
**XYZ Company,** Pontiac, IL

Managed the human resource function for this industrial spring manufacturer ($90M in annual sales, 650 employees). Emphasis was on labor relations. Chief Negotiator in contract negotiations with a production/maintenance union and a clerical union. Established new benefit programs and labor agreements with no disruption. Three year agreements provided for no general increases.

Managed employee insurance plans, 401(K), and defined benefit pension plans. Generated savings of $450,000 the first year in health care savings.

Worked closely with line managers in developing a pay-for-performance incentive plan.

6/76 to 7/88 — **INTERN to MANAGER - LABOR RELATIONS**
**Fortune 100 Consumer Products Company,** various locations

Gained diverse knowledge and expertise in such areas as EEO, wage administration, recruiting, labor relations, and contract administration.

Job Progression: Employee Relations Intern, Specialist - Wage Administration, Specialist - Employment, Employment Supervisor, Manager - Labor Relations.

**EDUCATION**

**B.S., INDUSTRIAL RELATIONS,** with honors, 1976
**Illinois University,** Central, IL

**AFFILIATIONS**

Board of Directors, Will Community College
Board Member, United Way of Crete

***References and additional data furnished on request.***

enough of an innovation to make the resume look different. Because the half-frame appears as an extension of the horizontal line, the new element blends with the rest of the resume. The person's early experience as an intern is briefly summarized. Main attention is given to his current job.

**HENRY W. BAKER**
**4000 North Belton Street**
**Center, Wisconsin 55555**
**(999) 333-3333**

## CAREER PROFILE

**Baking Executive** with over 20 years of progressive experience in the baking industry, the past 15 of which have been with a Fortune 400 company, advancing to one of top 25 corporate positions. Experience encompasses all aspects of retail baking and wholesale cake production. Highly proficient in decorating and pastry creations. Expertise in product/sales presentations, advertising, administration. Significant increase in profit margins/market share and reduction in expenses in highly competitive market has been attained through strategic growth/production planning, personnel development/management, and superior customer service.

## AREAS OF EXPERTISE

- **In-Store Management** ♦ **Manufacturing Management** ♦ **Technical Service / Sales**
- **Strategic Growth/Production Planning** ♦ **Design / Creation of Automated Programs**
- **Cost Accounting** ♦ **Budget Preparation/Management** ♦ **Labor / Cost Control**
- **Total Quality Management (TQM)** ♦ **Statistical Process Control (SPC)**
- **Formulation / Development of Signature Bakery Products**

## PROFESSIONAL EXPERIENCE

**WILLIAMS GROCERY COMPANY** — **Center, Wisconsin**

**Director of Bakery Manufacturing** (1990–1996)

Initially directed operation of two commissary plants serving 36 bakeries; expanded to 24-hour, 7 days/week production operation serving 73 bakeries within five-year period.

- Advanced to one of top 25 positions in Fortune 400 company in 9 years due to hard work and perseverance.
- Effectively supervised entire move from 12,000 sq ft bakery to new 17,000 sq ft plant in Shreveport, Louisiana without interruption of service to bakeries.
- **Designed layout of state-of-the-art 84,000 sq ft plant**; selected/successfully negotiated the purchase of $3.5 million bakery equipment (savings of over $500,000). Directed maintenance crew in installation and start up of new equipment; coordinated move of existing equipment in timely manner to eliminate downtime.
- **Streamlined production operations**; quadrupled productivity per manhours; directed supervisory team in training 75 employees in conversion from hand and batch production methods to automated production.
- **Designed and created complex, computerized Production Planning Program**; encompassed 2 mg. memory and over 38,000 formulas; created several spreadsheet programs to plan production, monitor sales, track costs, and report production efficiency. **Devised inventory control systems** that automatically updated costs.
- **Formulated and developed multiple signature products**; established solid foundation of procedures and processes to ensure consistent product quality.
- Produced in-house presentation manuals for custom and wedding cakes.

274

**Combination.** *Ann Klint, Tyler, Texas*

A resume with visual variety from alternation between center-alignment and full justification. The contact information is centered, but the Career Profile is formatted with full justification.

**HENRY W. BAKER** **Page Two**

**WILLIAMS GROCERY COMPANY (Continued)**

**Plant Manager** (1982–1990)

- Managed commissary bakery that encompassed six stores with nine employees and production of full line of retail products; expanded to 20 hour/day, 7 days/week production with 61 employees serving 24 bakeries.
- **Achieved profit six months earlier than forecasted**; maintained consistent profitability.

**Bakery Specialist / Bakery Manager** (1981–1982)

- Managed in-store bakery consisting of combination of scratch/mix production.
- Promoted to Bakery Specialist within six months; instrumental in opening of several in-store bakeries.
- Initiated and launched special projects. Resolved profit problems.
- Taught basic baking and decorating skills to other employees.

## ADDITIONAL EMPLOYMENT EXPERIENCE

**Journeyman Baker / Decorator**, BYERLY FOODS, St. Louis/Park, Minnesota (1979–1980). Produced large variety of products from scratch in an upscale, high-volume bakery.

**Pastry Chef**, NORTHSTAR HOTEL, Minneapolis, Minnesota (1978–1979). Responsible for desserts and pastry for three restaurants and high-profile banquet functions in 4-star hotel.

**Journeyman Baker / Decorator**, McGLYNN BAKERIES, Eden Prairie, Minnesota (1975–1977). Baked and decorated products in Target Stores.

**Crew Leader**, POPPIN' FRESH PIES (Division of Pillsbury), Hopkins, Minnesota (1973–1975). Created gourmet pies in pie commissary; gained knowledge in use of variety of pie processing equipment. Assisted in opening new plant in Elk Grove Village, Illinois.

**In-Store Bakery Manager**, ALBERTSON'S, Dallas, Texas (1970–1973). Produced all items from scratch processing. Recognized as most profitable store in 19-store division.

## EDUCATION / PROFESSIONAL DEVELOPMENT

UNIVERSITY OF MINNESOTA – **Associate Degree in Vocational Education / Art**

DUNWOODY INDUSTRIAL INSTITUTE – **Certified Baker**

AMERICAN INSTITUTE OF BAKING
**Sanitation; Sanitation by Design; Cookie Production; Extending Shelf-Life**

**DALE CARNEGIE • SKILL PATH LEADERSHIP SEMINARS • UNION-FREE WORKSHOPS**

## PROFESSIONAL AFFILIATION

AMERICAN SOCIETY OF BAKERY ENGINEERS

The Areas of Expertise section is center-aligned, but the two Experience sections display full justification. The remaining sections are center-aligned. Saying little about the first 10 years of work experience avoids repetition and provides room for saying more about the last 16 years.

# DANA L. SIMONS

000 N. West • Anywhere, USA
(000) 000-0000

## OPERATIONS MANAGEMENT

**Operating Systems / Organic Food Processing / Quality Assurance**
**Accounting / Finance / Human Resources / Training / Customer Service**

### QUALIFICATIONS SUMMARY

Twenty-year career marked by substantial contributions in the areas of:

- **Operations Management**
  - Profit Improvement/Internal Controls
  - Production Planning
  - Warehouse Management
  - Customer Service
  - Data Systems Management
  - Conflict Resolution
- **Organic Food Processing/Quality Assurance**
  - Assurance of Organic Integrity and Traceability of Raw Materials
  - Pesticide Residue Audit Programs
  - Auditing/Inspection of Co-Pack Operations
  - Industrialization of New Products
  - HACCP Standards
  - IQF Processing
  - Drum Drying - Cereal
  - Thermal Processing
- **Accounting/Finance**
  - Inventory/Manufacturing Accounting
  - Cost Accounting
  - Capital/Operating Budgets
  - Financial Analysis
  - Financial Statements
  - GAAP/Reporting
  - System Conversion/Upgrades
- **Human Resources/Training**
  - Procedure Manuals
  - Design/Implementation of Training Programs
  - Customer Relations
  - Employee/Management Relations
  - Job Descriptions
  - Vision Statement
- **Global Perspective**
  - European Business Relations
  - Japanese Business Culture

### PROFESSIONAL EXPERIENCE

***Director of Raw Materials/Quality Assurance***
Organic Foods, Inc., Anywhere, USA (1989-Present)

Instrumental in success of start-up company, the nation's only processor of "3-year certified organically grown" baby food with nationwide distribution.

Initially performed inventory accounting and human resource functions in corporate New England office; transferred to assist in establishing West Coast food processing operation.

- **Processing Operations:** Insured quality, organic integrity, and traceability of all raw material for 40-item product line. Audited co-pack operations. Coordinated development of raw material specifications. Selected 3rd party lab facilities for testing. Acted as liaison with regulatory agencies. Assisted with production planning and scheduling of plant operations.

  Designed and monitored Pesticide Residue Testing Program (one of the first in the organic food processing industry) which contributed to cost savings of 23%. Directed lab testing in compliance with specifications for joint venture with Japanese company.
- **Human Resources/Staff Development:** Contributed to company's first Employee Handbook and position descriptions. Collaborated in designing and implementing training and staff development programs. Brought harmony to the diverse needs of personnel in east coast, central, and west coast locations.
- **Accounting/Finance:** Developed integrated systems which easily accommodated tenfold growth over 5-year period. Equipped senior management with new exception reports necessary for sound business decisions.

275

**Combination.** *Susan Britton Whitcomb, Fresno, California*

A resume with a two-column format after the contact information and areas of expertise on page one. Thick horizontal and vertical lines help to define the areas of the resume. The vertical line

**DANA L. SIMONS, page two**

***Controller***

JOHNSON COMPANY
Anywhere, USA (1985-1989)

**Accounting:** As first accounting manager in this rapidly expanding organization, designed and implemented formal accounting procedures to support revenue growth from $8 to $13 million during my tenure. Developed accounting systems for capital spending, product cost, and labor reporting. Performed cost analysis and designed procedures to generate management information in the areas of sales analysis, fixed asset, and inventory accounting. Developed telephone monitoring system which reduced telemarketing costs by 12%.

**Human Resources:** Management responsibilities were expanded to include hiring and supervision of Accounting, Warehouse, and Data Systems managers. Organized a full complement of training programs for support, administrative, and executive staff. Significantly improved communications among production, accounting, and marketing departments.

***Cost Accountant***

DECK & DECK
Anywhere, USA (1982-1985)

Generated manufacturing cost reports for major food processing company. Prepared and administered operating and capital budgets. Developed and monitored inventory control systems.

***Cost Accountant***

VERMONT MANUFACTURING
Anywhere, USA (1981-1982)

Performed cost accounting and special projects functions for manufacturer filling government contracts. Analyzed and made recommendations regarding raw material usage, labor distribution, budgeting, and burden expense accounting. Provided leadership in the selection and implementation of a new manufacturing data gathering system; project included soliciting user feedback which led to corporate buy-in.

***Special Projects Accountant***

OAK INDUSTRIES
Anywhere, USA (1977-1981)

Developed replacement cost accounting system and procedures for monitoring and controlling capital expenditures ($22 million); system was subsequently adopted a company-wide model.

Promoted to Controller of Flexible Laminating Division with $12 million in annual sales. Supervised purchasing, cost accounting, and materials handling.

***Assistant to President***

COLGATE COLLEGE
Anywhere, USA (1975-1977)

Provided administrative support to President with responsibilities encompassing speech writing, organizing faculty and trustee meetings, coordinating President's calendar, and liaison work with President's New York law office staff. Promoted from initial position in accounting.

***Prior Experience***

On-Call Hiring Consultant for Petersham Memorial Hospital and Petersham Pottery.

Various management positions in small business environments; responsibilities extended to multi-site operations management, business planning, employee supervision, buying, customer relations.

## EDUCATION

*B.S. MANAGEMENT*
NORTH ADAMS STATE COLLEGE
North Adams, Massachusetts

Coursework focus included Business Management, Accounting, and Human Resources Management

## REFERENCES

Provided upon request.

on page one functions also as a pointer to the areas of expertise. The bulleted qualifications are grouped according to five categories. In the Professional Experience section, bulleted fields introduce achievements in paragraph form. Paragraphs on page two show responsibilities as well.

**PAUL P. PLOCHART**

6422 Grail Court ◆ Dayton, Ohio ◆ 45000

*Office*: (123) 456-7890 ◆ *Home*: (123) 567-8904


**OBJECTIVE:**

Progressive sales management position with a growth-oriented organization in which I can immediately apply my advanced knowledge of marketing-technique development and training, together with my interpersonal and leadership skills, while continuing to develop them to their maximum potential.

**KEY SKILLS PROFILE:**

- A pro-active and creative communicator with a broad, boundaryless perspective, able to disseminate ideas and generate action across all levels of an organization.
- Function effectively as an autonomous, self-motivated individual, cognizant of time and cost constraints in managing multiple projects.
- Able to bring together diverse individuals to form a unified, cross-functional team, and motivate them to identify personally with key objectives. Excellent ability to identify potential interpersonal barriers and communication problems and take the steps necessary to circumvent them. Solid record of team leadership, with the capacity to train, mentor and develop professionals from diverse specialties and different external organizations.
- Customer-oriented, with demonstrated ability to develop an instant rapport and build lasting relationships with new and existing clients, through maximum attention to detail in determining their real needs, then providing service beyond expectation – based on consistent and comprehensive follow-up.
- Track record of delivering effective, informational presentations to prospective clients, showing them the true relative benefits of individual services.
- In-depth knowledge of the features of all available makes and models of automobiles, trucks and vans, as well as of the various methods of financing their acquisition.
- Broad experience in the creation, development and implementation of lease-related, value-added products both for individual and corporate clients.
- In-depth working knowledge of a broad spectrum of accounting and financial operations, including: financial planning, forecasting & analysis; cost & sales accounting; accounts payable/receivable; inventory; and payroll.
- Superior analytical skills, able to extract pertinent information, patterns and trends from a mass of complex data, present concise executive summaries, and devise creative, comprehensive solutions to evolving problems.
- Strong advocate of the need to develop and continuously enhance knowledge of product, processes, and market, as well as for the introduction and structured follow-through of technological and organizational systems to maximize process efficiency.

**EXPERIENCE PROFILE:**

**JOE EINSTEIN LEASING**, Dayton, Ohio **August 1989 - Present**

[One of the top ten lessors in the U.S.A., with over 27,000 lease vehicles nationwide]

***Director of Consumer / Dayton Fleet Leasing***

*Total responsibility for all aspects of leasing cars, trucks and vans at five locations in the Greater Dayton area, with three distinct areas of focus: Consumer Lease, Dayton Fleet Operations, and Renewal Team.*

- **Consumer Lease:**
  - Hire, train, motivate and oversee the day-to-day activities of two to three lease consultants per location, each generating 8 to 12 new vehicle deliveries per month, with an average gross profit per unit of $1,100 over Joe Einstein's purchase price.
  - Responsible for ensuring that each consultant is thoroughly conversant with all the concepts and benefits of leasing relative to buying, *before* any quotes are given.
  - Provide continuous training so that each consultant is capable of pricing out and "building" *any* make or model of car, truck or van available.
  - Ensure that each consultant has in-depth knowledge of quoting and delivering through any finance source, e.g. local and national banks, manufacturer's programs, or Joe Einstein leasing direct.

*...continued*

276

**Combination.** *Barry Hunt, Cincinnati, Ohio*

A resume for a professional baseball player who, within three years of leaving baseball, became a General Sales Manager in automotive sales and three years later was a Director of Fleet Leasing.

**PAUL P. PLOCHART** **Page 2**

**Experience ... contd.**

- **Fleet Operations:**
  - Hire, train, motivate and oversee the day-to-day activities of four Area Managers in the Mid-State region, with a view to maximizing the return from this huge and virtually untapped market.
  - Responsible for ensuring that each manager is fully equipped to make successful calls on small and medium businesses in their area, offering the services of Joe Einstein to handle their corporate / commercial fleet needs; each Area Manager is required to prospect for and generate at least 70 new leases the first year.
  - Train each manager in all aspects of all corporate fleet programs, dealer programs, and consumer lease products.
  - Monitor and approve/disapprove all itineraries, call reports, expense reports, projections and results.
- **Renewal Team:**
  - Oversee a team of three to four highly experienced lease consultants providing lease renewal services, both for their own clients and as a back-up in the absence of the original consultant.
  - Achieved consistent growth in renewals: guaranteed figures go from 900 (1995) through 1,225 (1996) to 1,500 (1997).

**DEFIDEL AUTOMOTIVE GROUP,** Dayton, Ohio **February 1984 - August 1989**

***General Sales Manager*** ***August 1986 - August 1989***

- Responsible for hiring, training, scheduling and overseeing four Sales Managers and up to 40 staff.
- Averaged 250 to 300 new & used units per month — an 18% increase over the previous management team.
- Optimized inventory to ensure maximum dealer profits as well as guaranteeing the best selection and value for the customer.

***Sales Manager*** ***July 1984 - August 1986***

- Assisted in hiring and training own sales staff of up to 10 people.
- Maintained a consistent gross average profit of $1,350 per sale.
- Negotiated and closed deals for the entire sales staff.
- Consistently achieved an excellent customer satisfaction rating.

***Sales Representative*** ***February 1984 - July 1984***

- Demonstrated new and used cars, and wrote up offers for review by Sales management.
- Maintained an average of 14 sales or leases per month, with an average profit of over $1,200 per deal.
- Recognized for maintaining excellent customer relations through consistent follow-up and follow-through.

**CINCINNATI REDS ORGANIZATION,** Cincinnati, Ohio **1980 - 1983**

***Professional Baseball Player***

## EDUCATION:

**UNIVERSITY OF CALIFORNIA AT DAVIS:** B.S., *Sports Medicine*. GPA 3.4. **1977 – 1981**

***REFERENCES AVAILABLE UPON REQUEST***

The half-page-long Key Skills Profile shows the reader the candidate's extensive knowledge and abilities. In the Experience Profile, key responsibilities of the current position are grouped according to three categories. Three job titles organize data about the preceding employer.

**Colin L. Racine** 23 Third Street • Marleton, NY 55555 • (555) 555-5555

**Marketing • Sales • Management • Environmental Capital Equipment**

**Career Profile**

- **Total P&L responsibility for fully autonomous vertical unit of innovative producer of air pollution control equipment. Skilled in domestic and international sales, marketing and production management of sophisticated engineered solutions to industrial environmental pollutants.**
- **Accounts encompass multi-national and Fortune 1000 companies, government agencies, national laboratories, colleges and universities in the United States, Canada, Western Europe, Scandinavia, Mexico, Asia and Australia.**
- **Corporate customers include IBM, DuPont, Siemens, Lucent, Texaco, Westinghouse, Elf Atochem, Hoechst Celanese, Ciba Geigy, and Merck. Representative government and non-profit clients encompass The FDA, The EPA, National Labs (Brookhaven, Oak Ridge and Los Alamos), colleges, universities and medical institutions.**

**Areas of Expertise**

- **High-tech/capital equipment**
- **International/government sales**
- **Account development, OEM sales**
- **Project planning /cost containment**
- **New product development**
- **Meticulous production supervision**
- **Advertising, copywriting, layouts**
- **Marketing strategies**
- **Innovative revenue enhancement**
- **Production scheduling**

**Representative Achievements and Qualifications**

- As Director of Air Pollution Technology for Cleanaire (division of Avionix), produced $1.2 million in sales in 1996 fiscal year, representing $165 thousand in pre-tax profits.
- Increased bookings from $300,000 to $500,000 in two years as Cleanaire Product Manager. Raised bookings from $500,000 to $1.2 million in 5 years as Unit Manager and Director of Air Pollution Technology. Ship 100% of orders.
- Consistently create 15% pre-tax profit—well above pollution control industry average of 5% to 6%. Achieved results by aggressive cost containment, focused marketing to high profit industries, and expansion of product offerings.
- Made biggest wet scrubber sale in Mystaire history—a booking of $312,000 that represented $200,000 gross profit.
- Skilled communicator. Translate complex concepts to simple terms for understanding of clients in cross disciplines with overlapping project parameters. Give understandable presentations to technical and management clients with varying degrees of education and field expertise.
- Expert client/engineer technical liaison; consult with design engineers to meet unique client needs and methodically cover every specification to avoid costly mistakes. Manage multiple projects on deadline while maintaining high quality.
- Hold total Cleanaire advertising/marketing control. Produce exceptional programs on a shoestring budget. Write copy for all brochures, flyers, mailers, postcards, direct mail pieces and press releases. Produce copy/photography for glossy color projects. Most pieces designed in-house; outsource major work.

277

**Combination.** *Deborah Wile Dib, Medford, New York*

A resume which shows that two lines enclosing important information draw the eye to that information. In a sweep of the resume, the reader sees first the fields headline under the contact

**Colin L. Racine** **page 2**

---

**Career Development**

**Avionix, Inc., Long Island City, NY** — **3/89 to present**
**Cleanaire Air Pollution Control Division**

**Director of Air Pollution Technology** — 6/96 to present
**Unit Manager** — 6/91 to 6/96
**Product Manager** — 3/89 to 6/91

Manage entire P&L responsibility for vertical unit of Air Pollution Control Division of major environmental equipment company ($10 million annual sales). Administer entire day-to-day operation encompassing sales, marketing, engineering, drafting, production and customer service. Design, engineer and market sophisticated contaminant scrubbing equipment to major national and international clients. Direct engineers, draftsmen, salespeople, buyers and system production technicians. Supervise staff of nine, indirectly manage 15 support personnel.

- In 1996 fiscal year, produced $1.2 million in sales with $165 thousand in pre-tax profits— a 15% profit rate.

**Cannon, Inc., New York, NY** — **1/87 to 3/89**
**Account Representative**

Sold state-of-the-art micrographic equipment to financial institutions. Hired after completion of rigorous (40% fail-out rate) nationally recognized Cannon, Inc., Marketing Education Center training course.

- Major transactions included $150,000 sale of one of the first automated document retrieval systems to a major New York City based savings bank.

**Rainbow Painting, Buffalo, NY** — **1985 to 1987**
**Owner/Operator**

**Chemco, Corp., Buffalo, NY** — **1984 to 1985**
**Laboratory Chemist**

---

**Computer Skills**

**Hardware:** IBM and MAC platforms with DOS, Windows or Windows '95

**Software:** Microsoft Word, Microsoft Excel, Microsoft Access, various contact management software, File Maker Pro, MacProject Pro

---

**Affiliations**

**Member:** **Air and Waste Management Association**
**Member:** **Semiconductor Safety Association**

**Education**

**1984** **Boston University, Boston, MA**
Bachelor of Science Biology-Chemistry/Pre-Med

**Professional Development**

**1994** **Fred Pryor Seminars**
Sales Motivation Techniques, Project Management

**1993** **Hofstra University, Uniondale, NY**
Business Management

**1987** **Eastman Kodak Co., Rochester, NY**
Marketing Education Center Sales Training Program

information, next the bulleted areas of expertise, and finally the computer skills on page two. The person's career shows tremendous growth from a lab chemist in 1984 to Director of Air Pollution Technology in 1996 with worldwide accounts including some of the largest corporations.

# KAREN L. DeMARRA

**6162 Torrance Court · Whitcomb, NJ 22222 · (555) 555-5555**


## HEALTH CARE ADMINISTRATOR

***· Specializing in Ambulatory Care ·***

Dynamic, innovative, and proactive health care administrator with extensive experience in planning and delivering programs and services consistent with the needs of the community. Strong focus on prevention and a holistic approach to health care. Attuned to industry trends and skilled in adapting to changes in the health care environment. Expertise in strategic planning, program development, grant writing, patient care management, community relations, financial management, and quality improvement.

## PROFESSIONAL ACCOMPLISHMENTS

**Wilmington Ambulatory Care Center, Wilmington, NJ** 1987 - Present
(A division of Wilmington Medical Center and an affiliate of the Clariston Health Care System)

**DIRECTOR** (1989 - Present)

Full responsibility for the planning and management of this free-standing (15,500 sq. ft.) ambulatory care facility providing emergency, laboratory, radiology, and community education services to 20,000 patients annually. Insure the provision of quality, cost-effective health care that meets the changing needs of the community within the parameters of regulatory agencies and reimbursement mechanisms. Develop and administer a $2 million budget. Lead a team of four department supervisors and 35 employees. Collaborate with hospital executives, as part of the executive management team, in program evaluation and expansion. Scope of responsibility includes program development, financial management, patient care management, quality improvement, marketing and public relations, staff training and development, community education, facility management, and human resources.

### Program Development

■ Initiated, developed, and implemented a model clinical geriatric evaluation / management service focused on maintaining independence and enhancing quality of life. Recruited experts to assist with program expansion. Program model is expected to be adapted for use throughout the entire system.

■ Designed and introduced "Corporate Care," an occupational health service for small businesses, offering pre-employment physicals and testing, drug screening, workers' compensation assessments, and OSHA compliance evaluations. Played a key role in promoting services and negotiating contracts with municipal agencies, schools, and local businesses.

■ Collaborated with the Brown County Association for Retarded Citizens in laying the groundwork for the first Brown County clinic for developmentally disabled individuals, which will provide routine medical care for this population that faces tremendous obstacles in obtaining care.

### Community Education

■ Introduced innovative community education programs focusing on the integration of traditional medicine and alternative medicine in helping individuals participate in a holistic approach to health maintenance and prevention.

■ Initiated and developed a unique stress management program based on a model from Harvard Medical School and the New England Deaconess Hospital, which was presented during their seven-day "Symptom Reduction" training program.

■ Oversaw the implementation of traditional disease management seminars on topics related to diabetes, heart disease, hypertension, vision loss, and pulmonary problems.

### Quality Improvement

■ Established quality improvement programs, procedures, and monitoring systems to insure that services, patient care, and facility maintenance are above industry standards.

■ Instituted an advanced certification requirement for ER nurses prior to the state certification mandate, to insure high standards of care.

■ Provided staff with opportunities for continuing education and professional development.

**278**

**Combination.** *Rhoda Kopy, Toms River, New Jersey*

Horizontal lines enclosing the person's job titles enable the reader to see the individual's career path at a glance. Boldfacing plays an important role in this resume, drawing attention to the

**KAREN L. DeMARRA** **Page Two**

## PROFESSIONAL ACCOMPLISHMENTS (continued)

**OPERATIONS SUPERVISOR (1987 - 1989)**

Worked closely with facility director and hospital administrators in developing and implementing start-up plans for this new ambulatory care facility. Managed daily operations, which involved scheduling, staffing, programming, and patient care.

### Facility Start-up

- Played a key role in transforming plans for a comprehensive ambulatory care facility into a reality: Analyzed staffing needs and hired staff; developed job descriptions and benefit / compensation packages; established and documented policies and procedures; determined hours of operation based on community feedback; interacted with regulatory agencies and obtained necessary licenses and certificates; assessed programming needs and developed relevant programs.
- Created a patient-focused environment and recruited staff who could provide quality care in a caring, empathic manner.
- Instituted a 48-hour patient call-back system, later adapted on a system-wide scale, to inquire about patients after their release, answer questions, insure compliance, and assess their impressions regarding care and service.

### Community Relations

- Interacted with municipal police and fire departments and government agencies to increase awareness of the facility's services; successfully encouraged utilization of services.
- Elicited ideas and feedback from the community concerning the facility, services, and programming needs during quarterly meetings with a community board.

**Wilmington Medical Center, Wilmington, NJ** 1982 - 1987
(A 350-bed community hospital)

**ADMINISTRATIVE SUPERVISOR (1985 - 1987)**

Oversaw the operation of the hospital during evening and night shifts. Used knowledge of hospital procedures, regulations, and resources to quickly resolve crises. Scope of responsibility included staffing, scheduling, facility management, patient care management, crisis intervention, disaster management, and community relations.

From 1976 - 1985 held positions as an ER Charge Nurse, and Occupational Health Nurse, and a Trauma Nurse.

## LICENSURE / EDUCATION / PROFESSIONAL DEVELOPMENT

B.A., Health Care Administration (in progress), Strickland College, Stokes, NJ
Registered Nurse, State of New Jersey
R.N. Program, St. Michael's Hospital, New York, NY, 1966
Certified Hypnotherapist, American Board of Hypnotherapists
Attended training programs in Management, Finance, Employee Relations, Gerontology and diverse health care issues.

## PROFESSIONAL AFFILIATIONS

Organization of Nurse Executives • American Association of Ambulatory Care Managers • American Gerontological Society National Association of Counselors and Therapists • Emergency Department Nurses Association • American Board of Hypnotherapists

## ACTIVITIES

Radio Talk Show Host, "To Your Health," WZZB • Emergency Management Council, Manchester Township Commission on the Status of Women in Ocean County • Former President, Lakehurst / Manchester Rotary Club • New Jersey State Leadership Institute for Rotary International • Ocean County Chamber of Commerce • P.A.L., Manchester Township • Board Member, Salvation Army

contact information, the centered heading over the profile information, the section headings and subheadings, and the header on page two. The filled square bullets share the same level of "blackness" with headings. The headings, the header, and the bullets tie together the two pages visually.

# RICHARD A. BARNES

*4566 PRESTON ROAD • MIDVIEW, MD 21980 • (411) 890-4556*

## *HIGHLIGHTS OF QUALIFICATIONS*

- Twenty-seven years experience in propane. Thorough knowledge of the industry.
- Track record of success in propane sales and marketing.
- Six years experience as advertising and marketing chairman of the Southern Propane Gas Association.
- Five years experience as liaison for Tri Gas & Oil with the Bethney Oil Heating Association.
- Networked extensively with the Windmill Builders Association.
- Long term association with the Caroline Poultry Industry.
- Recognized by superiors for skills in employee motivation and staff development.
- Experienced in HVAC sizing and design.

## *INDUSTRY EXPERIENCE*

**SMITH GAS & OIL, CHESTERTOWN, MD** **3/89 TO PRESENT**

*Safety Director/Industrial Propane Engineer (2/91 to present)*

Major Accomplishments

- Increased sales of industrial equipment by 35%.
- Developed new safety inspection program for plant.
- Redesigned several propane bulk plants to meet new code requirements.
- Revised safety manual to incorporate new rules and regulations.
- Implemented new type of accident reporting.
- Redesigned all hazardous materials shipping papers.
- Developed employee training for DOT hazardous material regulations.

*Propane Manger (3/89 to 1/91)*

Major Accomplishments

- Achieved 12% savings in gallons by researching and implementing a new correction factor system.
- Decreased expenditures on tanks by 50% through complete evaluation of correct tank sizing on existing accounts.
- Implemented new computer system in service department to reduce expenses.
- Increased efficiency in service department through restructuring of filing system.
- Developed and implemented performance based pay structure.
- Initiated and developed new training programs.

**SOUTHERN PROPANE GAS ASSOCIATION, WESTON, PA** **1/74 TO 2/89**

*District Manager (3/78 to 2/89)*

Major Accomplishments

- Designed sales and marketing plan which helped secure many new large volume accounts.
- Improved sales by evaluating and reorganizing Yellow Page advertising.
- Increased district sales by 27% and profitability by 35% over a five-year period.
- Consistently ranked among highest of 19 districts in semiannual sales promotions.
- Saved $25,000 in annual costs by placing hydraulic pumps on all transports.
- Reduced accounts receivable by 50% and reduced delinquent rate by an average of 5%.

*Service Manager (1/74 to 3/78)*

- Promoted to this position 30 months sooner than normal.

279

**Combination.** *Thomas E. Spann, Easton, Maryland*

The amount of white space is achieved by some smaller type, ample line spacing before and after section headings, relatively short bulleted lines, and tabbed (not right-aligned) dates. Italic directs

# Richard A. Barnes

4566 Preston Road • Midview, MD 21980 • (411) 890-4556 Page Two

### *Industry Experience* (Continued)

**Big Burner, Inc., WindyHill, MD** **8/75 to 8/76**
*Service Manager*

**River County Gas, Chapel, MD** **1/73 to 12/73 & Summers 1963 to 1968**
*Service/Delivery Man*

### *Education*

**Delvaine College, North Hook, NC**
*B.A., Psychology, 1968*

### *Industry Related Training*

**Western Gas & Electric Co, Rockville, MD**
*Master Gas Fitter Course, 1992*

**Northern Propane Inc., Brunswick, NJ**
*District Management Development Conference, 1988*

**Fan Jet Inc., Wheaton, MD**
*Gas Venting School, 1988*

**American Propane Gas Association,**
*Completed and taught course in Liquified Petroleum Gas Training, 1988*

**Delaware Propane Gas Association, Dover, DE**
*Propane Transportation, 1984*

**Sidney Black, Inc., Philadelphia, PA**
*Commercial Water Heater Sales (Correspondence Course),1983*

**Northern Propane Inc., Brunswick, NJ**
*Management by Objectives, 1979*

### *Computer & Technical Training*

**River Run College, Water Mills, MD**
*Introduction to CADD (Computer assisted design drafting), 1993*
*Introduction to Lotus 1,2,3, (1992)*

**Maryland County Community College, Exton, PA**
*Basic Electricity, 1987*
*Basic Computers, 1986*

### *Other*

**North Stewart University, Wheeling, PA**
*Customer Relations Seminar, 1988*
*Communication Management, 1984*

Holds current Maryland Home Improvement License

***Please respect strict confidentiality***

the eye to the contact information, section headings, job titles, header on page two, education data, and the request for confidentiality. See the use of boldfacing, small caps, and the Major Accomplishments subheadings on page one. Note the space given to additional training.

**BRUCE E. DEPAUL**
606 Hyde Park Drive
Traverse City, Maine 21211
(Residence) 555.555.5117
(Business) 555.555.2322

## CAREER PROFILE

Thirty-one years of outstanding experience working with troubled youth; providing direct care, direct-care supervision, teaching, program management, training, direction, consultation, and delivering speeches.

## SIGNIFICANT ACHIEVEMENTS

- Planned, developed, and implemented a community-based program to teach troubled youth to utilize the resources of the community and to grow and develop independence.
- Researched, designed, and developed a completely secure one-of-a-kind detention center program.
- Lectured on juvenile behavior at Colleges and Universities in several states.
- Valuable experience in open community and secured facility environments.
- Extensive experience in the design of token economy systems.

## EDUCATION AND PROFESSIONAL DEVELOPMENT

*STATE UNIVERSITY* — Maine
**MASTER OF SOCIAL WORK (MSW)**, 1978
Concentration in *Administration*
Undergraduate concentration in *Business Management*

*CORNELL UNIVERSITY* — New York
**CERTIFIED TRAINER** – Therapeutic Crisis Intervention, 1986
**TRAINING OF TRAINERS** – Certification update, 1992

*Seminars/Workshops/Courses included:*

| | |
|---|---|
| Project Management | Total Quality Management |
| Managing Change | Essential Elements of Effective Instruction |
| How To Make Meetings Work | Program Evaluation |
| Gangs | Sexual Harassment |
| Violence In The Workplace | The Leadership Challenge |
| Labor Relations | Grievance Administration |
| Residential Treatment Issues | Child Abuse, Exploitation, and Neglect |
| Expert Witness | AIDS: Separating Facts From Myths |

The Violent Youth Offender: Programs and Techniques
Basic & Advanced Residential Care in Detention
Train the Trainer: NJDA Juvenile Detention Care Giver Curriculum
Changing Direction of 'At Risk' Children
Qualified Video Implementor: Changing Directions

**280**

**Combination.** *Lorie Lebert, Novi, Michigan*

This individual has been a Director of different kinds of youth centers ever since receiving his M.S.W. degree in 1978. The bold, partial line below the name in the contact information

## EXPERIENCE

*STATE OF MAINE* – Family Independent Agency, Office of Delinquency
*(Formerly: Department of Social Services)*

**DIRECTOR – Harrison Bentley Youth Reception Center**, 1988-current
- Executive Director of maximum secure juvenile detention center designed to provide five comprehensive assessments for placement (risk, behavioral family, medical, and educational).
- Personally designed and developed the program, designed the training plan, developed the educational program concept, and developed international operations.
- Work within an $8 million budget.

**DIRECTOR – Vista Monte Assessment Center**, 1987-88
- Executive Director for a campus-based residential center providing temporary care for adolescent males requiring comprehensive assessment for permanent placement.

**DIRECTOR – Grace Residential Care Center**, 1987-1988
- Executive Director, responsible for overall operations of a community-based residential care center for troubled adolescent females designed to provide long-term care.

**DIRECTOR – Monumental Hope Shelter Center**, 1979-87
- Executive Director responsible for the overall operations of a community-based temporary shelter center, designed to provide residential care for fifteen delinquent, neglected and abused youth using the resources of the community (i.e. educational, religious, health, recreational, etc.) to facilitate continuing adolescent development.

**DIRECTOR – Maplegrove Residential Center**, 1978-79
- Managed long-term community residential treatment program for adolescents.

**YOUTH SPECIALIST – Burlington Residential Center**, 1966-78
- Planned, implemented, and evaluated specialized treatment plans adolescents.

## TEACHING

*FIELD INSTRUCTOR FOR:*

Maine State University
Eastern Maine University
Oakmont University
University of Augusta
Maplegrove College
Maine State University

*. . . ongoing lectures and seminars related to the care and treatment of adolescents*

BRUCE E. DEPAUL (RESIDENCE) 555.555.5117 — (BUSINESS) 555.555.2322
606 HYDE PARK DRIVE — TRAVERSE CITY, MAINE 21211

suggests that this person is important and someone worth considering. The Education section is put on the first page because the list of seminars/workshops/courses amounts to an areas-of-expertise section. At the end of page two, contact information is supplied again as a reminder.

# ANDREA KARLSON

1776 Camino Lumbre
Santa Fe, NM 87505
(505) 471-1997

**OBJECTIVE**

A position as Director: Pharmacy Department, in a hospital setting, which will utilize considerable clinical expertise, strong management skills and comprehensive budgeting/purchasing abilities in order to maximize departmental quality and efficiency.

**OVERVIEW**

- Organized, detail-oriented pharmacy professional with successful twelve year track record.
- People person, sensitive and perceptive; able to work effectively with individuals on all levels.
- Demonstrated expertise in the use of all manner of medications with emphasis on those prescribed for psychiatric populations.
- Proficiency using Lotus 1-2-3 for Windows to analyze financial projections.
- Licensed in the states of New Mexico and New York.

**AREAS OF EFFECTIVENESS**

***Consultation:*** Utilizing strong clinical knowledge base, make recommendations to physicians regarding most appropriate medication regimen. Recommend medications that are clinically effective as well as cost effective.

***Computerization:*** was instrumental in selecting and installing the ***"Compute Rx"*** system which accelerated the pharmaceutical ordering process while increasing accuracy, providing better drug interaction data and expediting the patient billing process.

***Monitoring Patients' Medications:*** possess in depth knowledge about a full range of drug interactions. Have demonstrated ability to recommend the most clinically effective combinations while minimizing potential adverse reactions.

**EXPERIENCE**

September 1988 - Present

**FOUR WINDS HOSPITAL,** Katonah, NY (125 beds)
**Assistant Director: Pharmacy Department**

- Promoted to Assistant Director, May 1992, on the basis of clinical expertise and organizational accomplishments.
- Coordinate effective functioning of pharmacy operations with all hospital personnel, both professional and non-professional.
- Develop and implement pharmaceutical service programs based upon the needs of patients.
- Assist in establishing and monitoring data relating to pharmacy activity and productivity.
- Provide significant contribution to the set-up and modifications of the Formulary; establishing specifications for all items and selecting supply sources.
- Provide significant input during drug usage evaluations.
- Oversee Quality Assurance functions: monitor polypharmacy; monitoring of adverse drug reactions.
- Oversaw departmental computerization which resulted in improved cost control.
- Implemented procedures for ordering pharmaceuticals utilizing wholesalers' software packages, thereby simplifying and accelerating purchasing.

**281**

**Combination.** *Mark D. Berkowitz, Yorktown Heights, New York*

A resume for a person who, since her degree in Pharmacy in 1982, has worked her way up to Assistant Director in a hospital Pharmacy Department. She now wants to become the Director of

**ANDREA KARLSON** ***Page 2***

| | |
|---|---|
| September 1988 - May 1992 | **FOUR WINDS HOSPITAL,** Katonah, NY<br>**Staff Pharmacist**<br>• Performed Unit Inspections; researched and presented medical material.<br>• Significant participation in the Pharmacy Quality Assurance Program; monitored records for transcription and procedural errors.<br>• Filled, compounded and dispensed prescriptions. |
| January 1983 - September 1988 | **CVS PHARMACY,** Mahopac, NY<br>**Supervising Pharmacist**<br>• Supervised a staff of three pharmacists.<br>• Ordered all pharmaceuticals utilizing an inventory control system.<br>• Utilized IBM PC to monitor patient prescriptions, histories and drug interactions.<br>• Oversaw all functions of a community pharmacy.<br>• Acted in the capacity of *Preceptor* to pharmacy interns, trained pharmacists and pharmacy technicians.<br>• Performed periodic employee evaluations. |
| May 1982 - January 1983 | **RITE AID PHARMACIES,** Vails Gate, NY<br>**Staff Pharmacist**<br>• Performed all required responsibilities as a community pharmacist.<br>• Filled, compounded and dispensed prescriptions.<br>• Provided consultation to both physicians and patients.<br>• Performed all aspects of the retail process. |
| **EDUCATION** | **ALBANY COLLEGE OF PHARMACY,** Albany, NY<br>**Bachelor of Science: Pharmacy** 1982 |
| **PROFESSIONAL AFFILIATIONS** | **Member: *American Pharmaceutical Association*** |
| **REFERENCES** | Available upon request. |

a Pharmacy Department in another hospital. The Overview is a profile of her experience, "people" skills, professional expertise, computer literacy, and licensing. Boldfacing of three Areas of Effectiveness categories calls attention to her knowledge and a key achievement.

# Lauren J. Rossignol

421 Back Road
Abington, MA 02351

Home: (617) 459-3057
Office: (617) 395-3027

## Professional Profile

Resourceful business manager with recent experience directing inside sales operations for a major publishing company. Talent for serving as diplomatic liaison and "relationship builder" demonstrated throughout several reorganizations and integrations. Leadership style best described as providing tools for success and expecting the most from assigned employees. Principal areas of competency include:

COORDINATING NEGOTIATING WRITING
TRAINING PRESENTING TROUBLESHOOTING

## Accomplishments

- Created and cultivated a 22-member Inside Sales Department to a fully operational state within a four-month period. Hired and trained sales staff, re-designed office space, coordinated installation of phone system, established budgets and sales quotas in conjunction with VP of Sales, and developed compensation structures including incentive programs.
- Developed special sales promotion necessitating selection and training of key sales representatives, set up and implementation of program evaluation criteria, and development of follow- up systems to document customer response. Program's success prompted management to request the organization and introduction of similar promotions.
- Selected by top-level management to participate as a team member charged with shutting down a company and integrating their marketing, customer support, and title maintenance procedures into the remaining company's operations. Conducted intensive research, hired and trained additional staff, and completely redesigned the order plan system.
- Administered a Community Service Award program involving the coordination of an independent judging panel, application review, notification of winners, and awards presentation at the American Library Association national conference.
- Established a complete on-site Business Office requiring extensive communications with payroll and accounting managers, purchasing of computers and office equipment, instituting full accounting systems, and training staff members in all operations.
- Developed a Customer Support Department following a layoff which reduced work force by one-half. This involved establishing inter-state communication systems, developing computerized database management systems for product/customer information, conducting product training, and negotiating extensively with representatives from the merging companies and their distribution facilities.

**282**

**Combination.** *Elizabeth M. Carey, Waterville, Maine*

The writer used a box to direct attention to the skills of this individual who has yet to complete her degree. The following Accomplishments section demonstrates skills mentioned in the box.

# Lauren J. Rossignol

Résumé, Page 2

## Work Experience

ABC Publications, Boston, MA (1986 to Present)
**Director of Inside Sales** (10/94 to present)
— Direct inside sales operations with Sales Quota of $30 million and Expense Budget of $2.5 million
— Hire, train, supervise, and evaluate the supervisor of standing orders, 20 telephone sales representatives, and 5 department coordinators.
— Establish and maintain communication with support staff in Connecticut and New York, regional managers from across the country, and field sales representatives nationwide requiring numerous site visits and telephone conference meetings.

**Business Manager** (10/86 to 10/94)
— Set up and managed business office including responsibility for accounting, human resources, and general "business" matters.
— Served as Human Resource support person to employees providing education on and assistance with workers' compensation, benefits, payroll, insurance, and related H.R. issues.
— Coordinated through telephone interactions with English and Australian company representatives on billing, credit, and shipment issues related to a large print co-publication project.

Abington School Department, Abington, MA (1984 to 1986)
**Secretary to the Superintendent** - 15-town district
— Adapted word processing and spreadsheet programs for various uses including correspondence, board meeting agendas/minutes, student lists, teachers agreements, district employee registry, and budget preparations.
— Maintained district personnel files, sick leave records, and health insurance information. Assisted employees with questions. Filed State reports for auxiliary personnel and substitute teachers.

The Midnight Express, Weymouth, MA (1981 to 1984)
**Business Manager**
— Managed all financial matters including A/R (billing, collections, rental income, distributor payments), A/P (coding, payment schedules, creditor relations), Payroll (salary and commission checks, tracking time, personnel file maintenance, taxes, insurance billing and claims), Accounting Systems (account balances and reporting). Supervised one assistant.

## Education

Boston College, Boston, Massachusetts - Associate of Applied Business program - Four classes remaining

General High School, Princeton, New Jersey - Graduate

Filled arrow bullets help to direct the eye to each accomplishment. The boldfacing of job titles on page two makes them easily seen. Dash bullets on page two do not compete with the filled bullets on page one but nevertheless do their job of pointing to duties, responsibilities, and achievements.

**FRANK FOODMAN**
P.O. Box 1234 • Lynchburg, Virginia 24503 • (804) 384-4600

**MULTI-UNIT FOOD & BEVERAGE OPERATIONS MANAGER**

Well-qualified professional with 14 years experience in multi-site F&B Operations and Food Service Management. Expertise includes:

- Food & Labor Cost Controls
- Management Training & Development
- Staff Recruitment & Scheduling
- Purchasing & Inventory Management
- Catering Sales & Operations
- New Facilities Start-Up
- Capital Acquisitions
- Menu Planning & Pricing
- Kitchen Operations
- Customer Service & Guest Relations

***Contributed to significant cost reductions and revenue/profit growth through efforts in productivity, efficiency and quality improvement.***

**FOOD SERVICE MANAGEMENT EXPERIENCE:**

**WATER THEME PARK**, Lynchburg, Virginia 1986 to 1989

**Director of Food & Beverage**

Full P&L management responsibility for all F&B operations at two large theme parks in Central Virginia. Scope of responsibility included 12 F&B sites and a large catering department operating 110 days annually and generating over $1.6 million in sales. Recruited, hired, trained, scheduled and supervised a staff of four managers and 150 hourly employees.

Directed central kitchen operations, all F&B facilities, a multi-million dollar purchasing and inventory management program, vendor contracts, menu development and pricing, staff planning and scheduling, regulatory compliance, budgeting and labor/food cost controls. Managed the entire catering and special events operation including group sales and event planning, staffing, scheduling and logistics.

- Reengineered and streamlined F&B operations. Reduced costs of sales from 33% to 27% and increased profit return by 8% annually through a series of strategic operational, management and cost reduction initiatives.
- Increased F&B sales revenues by $20,000 despite a 5% decline in park attendance by expanding menu offerings and improving quality of food preparation/service.
- Introduced employee incentives and reduced turnover of seasonal staff.
- Negotiated and administered a cooperative internship program for Hotel and Restaurant Management students at the University of Virginia and Virginia Tech.

**DELI AND CATERING**, Pensacola, Florida 1980 to 1986

**Multi-Unit Operations Manager**

Fast-track promotion from Restaurant Manager to Multi-Unit Manager directing eight high-volume food service operations. Recruited, trained and directed 16 unit managers and over 200 employees. Held full operational responsibility for the entire region including purchasing, inventory planning, staff scheduling, menu pricing, facilities management, local market advertising, special promotions, budgeting and customer service.

- Revitalized operations, introduced service and management training programs, authored corporate policies and procedures, and introduced employee productivity incentives.
- Increased average unit sales by 16% and lowered food costs systemwide by 3.5%. Reduced employee turnover by more than 21%.

283

**Combination.** *Wendy S. Enelow, Lynchburg, Virginia*

A cleverly crafted resume for an individual who must want to return to food and beverage operation. Work experience is arranged *not* by descending chronological order across two pages

**FRANK FOODMAN**

***Page Two***

**FOOD SERVICE SALES & MARKETING MANAGEMENT EXPERIENCE:**

**AMERICAN FOODS**, Lynchburg, Virginia 1992 to Present
*(Manufacturing Subsidiary of Ben & Jerry's Ice Cream)*

**Sales Manager** (1992 to Present)

Plan strategies, develop programs and direct sales/marketing programs for private label and co-packing accounts throughout a 26-state territory. Customer base includes restaurants, institutional accounts, food service companies, casinos and other food manufacturers (e.g., Breyer's, Eddy's, Nestle, Dannon).

- Built revenues from $4.5 million to $9 million. Closed numerous major accounts including Sysco Foods and Target Stores. Led the company's entry into the Las Vegas casino market and built to over $1 million in first year sales.
- Established a regional broker network to manage relationships with local restaurant, food service and institutional accounts.

**National Accounts Manager** (1992 to 1993)

Recruited to direct the start-up of Ben & Jerry's branded products sales and marketing programs into the non-commercial food service sector (e.g., schools, colleges, hospitals). Chosen for assignment based upon extensive hands-on F&B operations management experience. Trained and supervised 24 sales associates.

- Built first year revenues to over $1 million.

**FOOD BROKERS**, Lynchburg, Virginia 1989 to 1992

**Owner/General Manager**

Founded and managed a food brokerage distributing to restaurants, hotels, institutional accounts, food service companies and delis throughout a 7-state region. Recruited and trained a regional broker network to expand sales coverage and increase account base within high-growth markets.

- Increased sales by 308% over a two-year period.

**EDUCATION:**

**Bachelor of Science in Business Administration**, University of Florida, 1988

***References Provided Upon Request***

but by category of experience: food and beverage operation on page one; food service sales and marketing management on page two. For actual descending order, switch the order of the categories. Earlier experience is more relevant to the apparent goal, so that work is put first.

**MARK D. BERKOWITZ**

**1312 Walter Road**
**Yorktown Heights, NY 10598**
**(914) 245-8192**

**OBJECTIVE**

A position Managing a Career Planning & Placement Center, in a college setting, which will utilize extensive Career Counseling/Job Search expertise and teaching experience to assist students and graduates with internship placements and to rapidly find meaningful employment.

**OVERVIEW**

- Twelve year track record in developing, targeting and executing successful assessment/counseling and career planning programs for diverse groups.
- Strong people orientation; experienced in developing successful training programs.
- Exceptional follow through abilities and detail orientation; able to plan and oversee projects from concept to finished product.
- Effective communicator; extensive experience presenting high caliber workshops.
- Extensive one-on-one and group counseling and problem solving exposure.
- Expertise in administering, interpreting and evaluating state-of-the-art assessment tools, both manual and computerized, including: Myers-Briggs Type Indicator; 16 PF; Campbell Interest and Skills Survey; Strong Interest Inventory; Self Directed Search; Career Anchors; SAGE Compute-a-Match Vocational Aptitude Battery.
- Ten years career counseling experience in private practice.
- Seven years experience teaching Industrial Arts and Adult Education.
- **N**ational **C**ertified **C**areer **C**ounselor   **C**ertified **P**rofessional **R**esume **W**riter

**EXPERIENCE**

9/85 - Present

**B.O.C.E.S. SOUTHERN WESTCHESTER,** Valhalla, NY
**Director: Career Assessment & Counseling Center**

- Plan and coordinate all activities of the Career Assessment and Counseling Center. ***Co-Developer*** of the ***Career Development Model adopted by*** the ***New York State Department of Education***'s Gender Equity Center.
- ***Spearheaded Job Shadowing program***, enabling students to progress into internships.
- ***Provide Career Development expertise*** to the Westchester School/Business Partnership.
- ***Provided*** both ***group and individual career counseling*** and job search skills to displaced workers referred by Westchester County Office for Employment and Training.
- ***Present resume writing workshops*** to adults and students, during last year of vocational training. Conduct interviews to gain additional data, digitally typeset and laser print resumes.
- ***Planned and coordinated large scale assessment*** of over seven hundred and forty three prospective employees of General Motors (Tarrytown); selected top twenty six for hiring as trainees.
- ***Developed and ran specialized assessment battery for the U.S. Department of Labor***; identified top twenty candidates for funded Machinist training program.
- ***Implement assessments*** and ***make training program recommendations*** for clients of the White Plains Job Training Partnership Act (JOB TRAC) office as well as for handicapped clients of the White Plains Office of Vocational Rehabilitation (V.E.S.I.D.).
- ***Provide consultation*** in selection of specific assessment instruments and train regional guidance personnel in assessment procedures.
- ***Provide Outplacement services***, upon request, to terminated staff: counseling, resume and cover letter writing, job search coaching, preparing for interviews, and assessment.

8/88 - Present

**COLLEGE OF NEW ROCHELLE,** New Rochelle, NY
**Adjunct Professor**: Graduate School

- Collaborated on development of *The Job Search Process* and co-teach course to professional graduate level students in Counseling and Career Development.
- Develop curriculum and teach course in *Use Of Computers In Career/Life Planning.*
- Develop curriculum and teach course in *Vocational Counseling And Training In The Education Of The Exceptional Child.*

**284**

**Combination.** *Mark D. Berkowitz, Yorktown Heights, New York*

The writer's own resume, included here to show the background and credentials of one of the professional resume writers whose resumes are featured in this Gallery. If you ever wonder who a

Mark D. Berkowitz page 2

9/89 - 7/93 **NETWORK RESUME & CAREER SERVICES,** New York, NY
**Career Development Consultant**
- Developed, coordinated, documented and implemented Assessment/Career Counseling program.
- Planned and ran workshops related to clients' on-going career development needs.

6/90 - 11/90 **AT&T ALLIANCE FOR EMPLOYEE GROWTH AND DEVELOPMENT, INC.,** White Plains, NY
**Outplacement Counselor/Workshop Facilitator**
- ***Facilitated group career change workshops*** for surplussed AT&T employees in career decision making, values clarification, and occupational research.
- ***Provided comprehensive training*** in resume writing and personal marketing/job search techniques.
- ***Administered and interpreted interest*** and ***personality assessment instruments***; provided individual counseling sessions.

9/83 - 6/85 **NEW YORK CITY BOARD of EDUCATION; DIVISION of SPECIAL EDUCATION**
**Vocational Evaluator/Program Coordinator**
- Organized and implemented city wide program in Vocational Evaluation and Career Development.

1/78 - 6/83 **DARIEN HIGH SCHOOL,** Darien, Ct.
**Teacher of Industrial Arts**
- Taught the following courses: Auto Mechanics; Small Engines; Adult Education (Auto Repair); Mechanical Drawing; Engineering Drawing, and Architecture.
- Played a pivotal role in making Industrial Arts classes suitable environments in which students with special needs could be mainstreamed and achieve success.
- Was instrumental in the implementation of school's career planning program; selected materials for the career resource library.

**EDUCATION**

**M.S. CAREER DEVELOPMENT,** 1989
COLLEGE OF NEW ROCHELLE, New Rochelle, NY

**M.S. SPECIAL EDUCATION - LEARNING DISABILITIES,** 1985
HERBERT LEHMAN COLLEGE, Bronx, NY

**BACHELOR OF SCIENCE: INDUSTRIAL ARTS EDUCATION,** 1975
NEW YORK UNIVERSITY, New York, NY

**PROFESSIONAL AFFILIATIONS**

American Counseling Association

American Society for Training and Development

National Board for Certified Counselors

National Career Development Association

Professional Association of Resume Writers
- Certification Board Testing Coordinator (C.P.R.W.)

**REFERENCES** Available upon request.

professional resume writer is, this resume gives you information about one of the leading writers in the United States. In this resume as well, you can see this writer's tendency to use bold italic for significant words and phrases so that *they* get read even if the reader doesn't read every word.

**BARBARA E. ANDERSON**

**11605 Hidden Palm Drive**
**Boco Raton, Florida 00000**
**(813) 000-0000**

**PROFESSIONAL SUMMARY**

Progressive career reflecting comprehensive experience in administration and operation of university library centers and media services. Tenure encompasses eight years as Director and eleven years as Assistant Library Director, as well as a demonstrated record of successive advancement and notable accomplishments. Goal-directed, innovative thinker with proven success in initiating and implementing high-caliber automated information delivery systems. Proven ability to smoothly incorporate and blend traditional library resources with new technologies and formats. Expertise in short/long term strategic planning, team building, budgeting and serving as an academic instructor. Excellent facilitator exhibiting visionary leadership and effective problem-solving, communication, interpersonal, organizational and analytical skills. **Hold MLS and MBA degrees.**

**SELECTED CAREER ACCOMPLISHMENTS**

- Accountable for diversifying/elevating library to current level of state-of-the-art research/educational center offering traditional and computerized resources.
- Initiated and managed rapid growth of facility automation by increasing number of computers from 1 to 80 and establishing remote access to library resources for distance education students throughout the State of Florida.
- Directed installation of NOVELL and UNIX networks, Internet/Web access, E-mail, CD-Rom and multimedia workstations for local and remote access to electronic databases and resources.
- Created full time Library Education Department to teach computer research and instructional technology skills to students, faculty and staff. Eighteen courses have been developed with an annual attendance of over 800.
- Successfully developed and managed a two-year turnaround/improvement plan to increase customer satisfaction and utilization of Media Center services. Increased quality and level of support for faculty utilizing instructional technology in the classroom. Upgraded and automated the audiovisual, graphics, photography, video production and broadcasting departments.
- Designed/supervised construction of new state-of-the-art, open access computer labs and computer education classroom equipped for teleconferencing and virtual library projects.
- Directed extensive remodeling projects involving reconfiguration of library infrastructure, classrooms, amphitheaters, and production studios to support distance education and multimedia courses.
- Augmented and improved document delivery and copy center service resulting in reduced turnaround time and a 20% increase in revenue that led to a total cost recovery operation.
- Devised a highly successful library/media center public relations program to promote and advertise services/resources.
- Responsible for successful selection and implementation of computer systems for purchasing, copy center, circulation, reference and account areas which improved efficiency and service.
- Actively participated in initial planning decisions prior to construction of new medical center library for staffing, equipment, furnishings, lighting, security and supplies.
- Successfully lobbied State of Florida legislature to change the library funding formula. As a result the library materials budget increased more than 50% since 1995.

**285**

**Combination.** *Diane McGoldrick, Tampa, Florida*

Academic resumes, or curriculum vitae, or CVs for short, are the exception to the "no longer than two pages" rule. When applying for positions at other universities, professionals in

**BARBARA E. ANDERSON** Page 2

**EDUCATION**

**MBA** ***(Specialized in management and marketing)*** **1988**
Temple University, Philadelphia, PA

**MS Library Science** **1971**
Boston College - Boston, MA

**BA Anthropology/Archeology** ***(Minor in Education)*** **1970**
University of Pennsylvania - Philadelphia, PA

**EMPLOYMENT HISTORY**

**DIRECTOR, HEALTH SCIENCES CENTER LIBRARY and MEDIA CENTER (Faculty Rank: University Librarian)**
**University of Miami, Miami, FL** **1989 - Present**

- Pivotal role directing all managerial aspects of library (168,000 volumes, 1,600 journal subscriptions) and media center. Provide leadership for policy direction, service planning and program implementation; oversee staffing requirements, budgeting, collection management and integration of technology with instructional programs. Supervise 28 library and 11 media center staff members.

- Formulate and administer $2.5MM operating budget.

- Extensively interact with division heads to identify, develop, promote and trouble shoot services, new programs, technological issues and resource allocations.

- Act as liaison between the Library/Media Center and its peer groups at the local, state and national levels. Establish cooperative agreements for resource sharing to reduce costs and improve access to library collection

**ASSISTANT LIBRARY DIRECTOR**
**University of Massachusetts Medical Center, Worcester, MA** **1978 - 1989**

- Directed daily operations for extensive scientific library (120,000 volumes, 2,500 journal subscriptions). Hired, trained and supervised a staff of 18.

- Developed, promoted and managed cost-effective programs and services to support research, clinical and teaching needs of medical center personnel and affiliated hospitals.

- Upheld strong rapport with faculty, students and research staff to determine and meet their informational needs. Investigated/ instituted new methods of obtaining and delivering information such as CD-Rom and on-line systems.

**PUBLIC SERVICES LIBRARIAN**
**University of Massachusetts Medical Center, Worcester, MA** **1971 - 1978**

- Cultivated programs, policies and procedures for public service areas of library along with directing/participating in public service functions.
- Wrote policy and procedure manuals.

academia usually need to submit extensive documentation of their credentials. Unlike resume readers in the corporate world, academic deans and department heads will read and assess CVs that are four pages or often much longer. In a CV any section might be extra long through more details. A CV might have sections

**BARBARA E. ANDERSON** Page 3

### TEACHING EXPERIENCE

**ADJUNCT FACULTY** **1992 - Present**
**University of Miami, Miami, FL**

Developed and taught Health Science Library course; continue to teach library administration course sections.

**NELINET** ***(New England Library Network)*** **1981 - 1986**
Newton, MA

Designed curriculum, prepared course materials and taught introductory and advanced courses for academic librarians/managers in information retrieval, organization and management.

### EDITORIAL EXPERIENCE

**ASSISTANT TO EDITOR-IN-CHIEF** **1985-1990**
**American Journal of Non-Invasive Cardiology, S. Karger Publishers**

Involved in all phases of start-up for new peer-reviewed medical journal including policy, procedures, public relations, problem-solving and marketing. Developed computer tracking peer review system to ensure timely processing of manuscripts.

### FUNDRAISING EXPERIENCE

Successfully solicited and received over $50,000 in donations to purchase multimedia computer equipment and software.

Active participant in annual University of Miami Scholarship & Library Fund Drive - 1991-Present

**Chair**: United Way Campaign - 1995
**Co-Chair**: United Way Campaign - 1994

Significant participation in several multi-campus, interdisciplinary library grant proposals.

### PROFESSIONAL AFFILIATIONS

Medical Library Association
Southern Chapter Medical Library Association
Florida Health Science Library Association
Florida Library Association
Tampa Bay Professional Womens Association

not found in a corporate resume—for example, Editorial Experience, Publications, Academic & Professional Committee Memberships, Special Lectures Given, Grants, Honors, Sabbaticals, and so forth. With many pages, CVs are hard to "unify." One way to give all the pages a uniform look is to provide a header like the

**BARBARA E. ANDERSON** Page 4

**ACADEMIC & PROFESSIONAL COMMITTEE MEMBERSHIPS**

***University of Miami***

Virtual Library Project - 1996-Present
Distance Learning, Planning and Implementation Committee - 1995-Present
Health Sciences Center Long Range Information Services, Strategic Planning Committee - 1995-Present
Academic Computing Committee - 1993-Present
Curriculum Committee / Colleges of Medicine & Nursing - 1990-Present
Library Directors Group - 1989-Present
Library Council - 1989-Present
Chief Information Officer Search Committee - 1996
National Library of Medicine, Regional Advisory Council - 1993-1996
Library Directors Search Committee - 1991

***Chair***

Media & Audiovisual Service Review Committee - 1993
Faculty Search Committees - 1993-1996
Medical Library Association Nominating Committee - 1996

***Conference Planning***

Chair: 1995 Florida Health Science Libraries Annual Conference, St. Petersburg, Florida
Three day educational conference.

Chair: 1994 Medical Library Association Southern Chapter Annual Conference, Orlando, Florida
Four day conference with 250 attendees.

***University of Massachusetts*** *(Prior Affiliations)*

Special Library Association
Medical Library Association
Small Business Association of New England
Massachusetts Area Health Science Libraries
Worcester Area Chamber of Commerce

***Boards***

Chair: Professional Staff Review Board
New England Online Users Group Board of Directors / Treasurer, 1981-1987
UMASS Voice / Editorial Board

***Chair***

Publicity / North Atlantic Health Science Libraries, Inc.
Worcester Area Cooperating Libraries, Inc.

**MEMBERSHIPS**

Christian Womens Club
American Cancer Society / Tampa Center

one at the top of pages two, three, and four in this resume. The header replicates the triple line under the contact information at the top of page one. Another way is to use boldface and italic consistently.

**Christopher W. Smith**
81 Bailey Drive, Ansonia, Connecticut 06401
(203) 555-8181

## Profile

**Manufacturing management professional** experienced in all phases of the production process and committed to leading a lean, efficient, empowered work force to achieve quality and excellence.

Proven ability to improve production efficiency, analyze and implement new processes, and achieve buy-in by production, management and administrative staff.

Effective problem-solver who enjoys the challenge of achieving goals and accomplishing objectives; career history of consistent advancement based on achievements.

## Professional Experience

**NORTHEAST RAIL CORPORATION,** Bridgeport, Connecticut 1988-Present

**General Foreman** (1993-Present)
Member of the management team with accountability for scheduling, quality, safety, and customer contact. Manage 70 production workers, 1 supervisor and 3 team leaders producing $22 million annually in rail equipment.

- Schedule production work to assure efficient and cost-effective use of labor and materials while meeting customer deadlines.
- Coordinate production activities and maintain an open flow of communication with Shipping/Receiving, Engineering, Purchasing and other company departments.
- Lead a strong focus on quality, conforming to quality requirements of customers, government agencies, and in-house QA Committee.
- Review all drawings before releasing to shop floor for production; work cooperatively with Manufacturing Engineering to resolve difficulties and assure a smooth production process.
- Serve as plant Safety Chairman and as member of corporate Health and Safety Committee.
- Maintain extensive customer contact, providing strong customer service and support.

**KEY ACCOMPLISHMENTS**

- Implemented Lead Man position to replace traditional Supervisor role. Allows workers to develop "ownership" and provide more input into the production process — scheduling tasks, completing jobs, using their experience and intelligence to perform their jobs at a higher level.
- Achieved first-year savings of $250,000 in tooling and labor costs: analyzed data on tool cost and life; conducted cost/use analyses on alternative tooling; selected new tooling that yields greater tool life and a more efficient production system. In addition to tooling savings, eliminated 1 staff position and extensive overtime required by former production process.
- Improved on-time shipments from less than 50% to more than 95%.
- As key member of TQM team, instrumental in creating a Quality Assurance manual and training shop employees in its use.
- Implemented SPC methods to eliminate machine deviations.
- Instituted a strong focus on safety through education and employee empowerment that has resulted in fewer accidents and a more alert and productive work force.

**Second Shift Supervisor** (1991-93)
Charged with setting up entire production operation for newly instituted second shift.

- Selected, hired, and trained 20 production employees.
- Achieved productive, stable, fully operational and highly efficient production force within 3 months.

**286**

**Combination.** *Louise Kursmark, Cincinnati, Ohio*

A resume that presents "the strong skills and accomplishments of a young man who had 'come up through the ranks' and had an impressive list of achievements in only eight years." Because

## Christopher W. Smith

Page 2

**NORTHEAST RAIL CORPORATION** (continued)
**CNC Programmer, Manufacturing Engineering Department** (1989-91)
Supervised 1 assistant in the preparation of programs for shop floor production.

- Improved scheduling and allowed CNC machinists greater control over their work by providing programs for several jobs with increased lead time.
- Moved engineering office to main shop floor to allow greater communication between engineering and production staff and promote a collaborative work environment.
- Instituted record-keeping program to track and record hundreds of CNC programs; this greatly reduced program re-working and provided greater consistency to the production process.

**Machinist,** 1988-89

### Education and Training

**A.S., MANUFACTURING ENGINEERING,** 1993 — Southwestern Connecticut Technical College

- Attended school 1990-93 while working full time.

**CORPORATE REENGINEERING:** 6-month course, 3 days per week, meeting with management peers at corporate headquarters in Boston to learn new management methods and the ramifications of corporate restructuring.

**TQM:** 3-day initial training and numerous 1-day refresher courses.

**OSHA:** 10-hour OSHA card; certified as OSHA trainer.

**COMPUTER PROFICIENCY:** includes AutoCAD, WordPerfect, Windows, Lotus 1-2-3, Excel.

### Professional Affiliations

American Society for Quality Control, member since 1989.

of his many accomplishments, the writer used two pages "to give sufficient weight to his qualifications and position him for an even more responsible position." A partial line pointing to each section heading is a nice touch. Having a separate subheading for key accomplishments is a strong tactic.

**FRANK ENAMEL**

2333 E. Marilyn Street
Dale Heights, IL 60139
708/555-7528

**OBJECTIVE:**

**Production Operations / Management**
A position where technical and leadership skills would be utilized.

**PROFILE:**

- Experience as Foreman, Supervisor and Machinist, including full responsibility for job scheduling and quality control.
- Background in CNC and production line setup; familiar with AS 400 systems for inventory/cost control, purchasing and invoice processing.
- Hire, train and supervise workers in complete product assembly: from parts fabrication to final packing and shipping.
- Determine and meet specific customer needs; handle customer service, problem solving and troubleshooting in a professional manner.

**EMPLOYMENT:**

Wilton Tool Corporation, Palatine, IL — 1/85-6/95
**Production Foreman**
Managed all night shift operations and the production/assembly of tools including square-wheel grinders, vices, c-clamps, band saws and drill presses.
Trained and supervised up to 23 employees in part and product fabrication, stocking, inventory control and all machine shop activities.
Involved in order picking and the processing of all related paperwork for smooth operations.

* Planned and conducted staff meetings to maintain high motivation and worker morale.
* Developed/improved work cells and maintained high product quality.
* Setup machinery and systems, including Fanuc controls and CNC equipment.
* Utilized the corporate computer system for inventory tracking and updating.

Urban Investment & Development Corp., Bloomingdale, IL — 4/81-11/84
**Security Supervisor**
Trained and supervised up to five employees in safety and security for a $500 million inventory at Stratford Square Mall.

International Harvester Company, Melrose Park, IL — 4/63-12/81
**Foreman - Component Division** — 1976-12/81
Responsible for a team of 40 employees in engine machining and the production cylinder heads valued up to $800 each.
Produced flywheel housings, flywheels and various grey iron and aluminum engine parts with more than 150 machine tools, including transfer lines, NC and CNC machine tools.

## 287

**Combination.** *Steven Provenzano, Schaumburg, Illinois*

A resume for a person whose record of employment shows steady growth in responsibility at one company for eighteen years, safety and security work for three years, and night work as

**Frank Enamel** **Page Two**

Controlled more than $1.2 million in process inventory.

* Through cost reduction, lowered inventory to $200,000 with only one percent machining scrap.

**Foreman - Large Crawler Tractor Assembly** 1975-1976

Supervised 20 employees in the assembly of tractors valued up to $195,000 each.
Established and directed a shift operation; accommodated orders for the USSR, Poland and Iran.
Ensured timely off-line production, unit repairs, maintenance, tuning and testing.
Oversaw the shipment of OEM service parts.

**Foreman - Medium Crawler Tractor Assembly** 1974-1975

Managed 18 employees and the production of tractors valued up to $96,000 each.
Worked directly with the General Foreman for prompt off-line production and OEM service part shipments.

**Foreman - Small Crawler Tractor Assembly** 1971-1974

Trained, scheduled, supervised and motivated 35 employees producing tractors valued up to $40,000.
Handled all duties similar to position listed above.

**Foreman - Machining** 1970-1971

Responsible for three shifts in assembly line startup, production checks, packing and shipping of service parts and assembly line procedures.
Supervised 50 employees as Foreman of the Gear Division and Gear Laboratory.

**Sectional Supervisor** 1968-1970

Involved in the cost-effective production of gears and shafts for assembly, service and interworks plants, as well as Rockford Clutch Company.
Trained and supervised 67 employees in absence of supervisor.
Coordinated assembly line and OEM part production schedules and machining requirements.

* Involved in a new tractor line parts startup program; organized follow-up and shipments to assembly lines between production staff and machinists.

**Management Development Program** 1967-1968
**Quality Control - Gear Laboratory** 1963-1967

**EDUCATION:**

Attended courses at Chicago Technical College, Bogan Junior College and Triton Junior College (In-Plant Courses)
Courses included Methods Time Measurement through the MTM Association for Standards and Research First Aid Training, including CPR.

Attended the IH Foreman Development Program at Elmhurst College.
Attended a Communication course and Assertiveness Seminar.

**SALARY:**

Salary at Wilton Tool Company: $32,300. Open to negotiation.

Production Foreman for ten years. Sentences under job titles indicate responsibilities. Items bulleted with asterisks are noteworthy activities and achievements. Underlining the names of employers and colleges helps them stand out. Using boldface for the job titles makes them easily seen as well.

# MARTY GARTHY

23010 N. Chintilly | Chandler, AZ 85000 | [622] 999-1777

## SUMMARY OF QUALIFICATIONS:

- Over 10 years experience in utility construction....gas/water/sewer lines....
- Served as Crew Foreman for over 4 years....
- Provided Customer Service/resolved issues over line construction....
- Tested/purges lines....
- Brought in high percentage of projects under deadlines....
- Familiar with Blue Stake/BS laws/city/county/state construction codes....
- Prepared information for AZ Corporation Commission annual audits....
- Articulate....aggressive....outgoing....professional demeanor....safety conscious....team player....dedicated....loyal....

## EMPLOYMENT HIGHLIGHTS:

ARIZONA PIPELINE CO. - Phoenix, AZ
***Foreman:*** 1992 to present (1989 to present)
- Supervised crew of up to 9....
- Operated equipment/drove trucks/fitted pipes....
- Installed/tract mains/scattered main extensions....replaced ¼ section main/services....
- Replaced scattered steel mains/services....
- Dealt with city/county staff....
- Assisted with pricing/bidding for contracts....
- Operated trenchers/excavators/back hoes/loaders/dozers....

IRONWOOD UNDERGROUND - Pinetop/Lakeside, AZ
***Operator/Pipe Fitter:*** 1987 - 1989
- Tapped utility services....
- Set grade/manholes for sewer/water lines....
- Installed mains....

## EDUCATION:

PIMA COMMUNITY COLLEGE - Tucson, AZ
Major: General Studies

## TRAINING/CERTIFICATION:

- OSHA Excavation
- Certified Welder: Pipe/Joining, PE
- Commercial Drivers License: Class 'A'
- Currently training for Steel Welding

288

**Combination.** *Fran Holsinger. Tempe, Arizona*

A one-page resume from a writer who likes to spread similarly formatted material over two pages and to supply them with a front cover on a folded 11" x 17" sheet of paper. The whole resume looks bold.

# CHRISTOPHER D. ATHLETE

**11092 Runaway Bay**
**Longview, Texas 75600**
**(903) 777-1155**

## HIGHLIGHTS OF QUALIFICATIONS

- **Efficient, enthusiastic Golf Professional** with proficiency in **individual / group golf instruction**, **tournament organization / management**, and **pro shop merchandising / administration**.
- Successfully completed **GPTP Level I**; pursuing Class A designation.
- Astute **financial / accounting manager**; experienced in governmental, not-for-profit, and public auditing, tax preparation, and **cash management**. Accurate with attention to detail.
- Exceptional **public relations**, **communication**, and **interpersonal** skills; quickly establish positive rapport with people of diverse ages, cultures, and personalities. **Customer satisfaction oriented.**
- Computer literate: Windows, Logical Solutions, WordPerfect, MS-Word, Excel, Lacert, Unilink, Fast Advantage, Lotus 1-2-3.
- Outgoing personality. Patient. Highly **career-** and **goal-oriented.**

## EDUCATION

BAYLOR UNIVERSITY – Waco, Texas
**Bachelor of Science Degree, Accounting** (1996)
Graduated Cum Laude with GPA of 3.40; Dean's List; Recipient of academic and athletic scholarships

## PROFESSIONAL EXPERIENCE

PROFESSIONAL GOLF CLUB — Longview, Texas
**Assistant Golf Professional** — January 1997 – Present

- Manage entire 18-hole private golf operation encompassing 480 members, pro shop, and staff of five in the absence of Head Golf Professional; activity approximately 70,000 rounds annually.
- Plan, organize, and execute tournaments and clinics; independently manage tournaments and clinics. Mark course and supervise range; provide assistance to members/guests; resolve member complaints/conflicts.
- Teach golf lessons to individuals and groups; establish excellent rapport with members and guests.
- Pro shop management includes customer service, administration of books, cash management, purchasing, merchandising, displays, inventory control, sales, and club repair.
- **Nominated for "Assistant of the Year"** for the East Texas Chapter of the PGA.

THOMAS & BROWN, L.L.C. — Waco, Texas
**Accountant** — June 1996 – November 1996

- Audited governmental and public entities. Prepared tax returns for corporations and individuals.

BAYLOR GOLF COURSE — Waco, Texas
**Golf Shop Manager** — Summer, 1995

- Managed golf shop; purchased and displayed merchandise; organized tournaments.

EAST TEXAS GOLF WORLD AND DRIVING RANGE — Longview, Texas
**Sales Associate / Range Assistant** — Summer, 1994

- Began as Range Assistant; promoted quickly to Sales Associate due to acquired knowledge and outstanding performance.

## GOLF HONORS / ACADEMIC ACTIVITIES

**Captain of University Golf Team ♦ 10 All-Tournament Teams ♦ Men's Sun Belt All-Conference Team**
**Athletic Advisory Committee ♦ Beta Alpha Psi Accounting Society ♦ Business Students Association**

289

**Combination.** *Ann Klint, Tyler, Texas*

In the absence of a Head Golf Professional, this Assistant Golf Professional was looking for an apprenticeship at an exclusive golf club. His accounting background will be useful in this role.

**Bruce Mullen** PGA PROFESSIONAL *Head Golf Professional*

2169 Beechwood Court
Hanford, California 93230
Telephone (209) 584-2064

Practical experience and training have provided good working knowledge of these key areas:

| | |
|---|---|
| **Golf Shop Operations** | **Membership Services** |
| **Sales & Merchandising** | **Staffing & Management** |
| **Course Maintenance** | **Equipment** |
| **Inventory & Purchasing** | **Lessons, Clinics & Promotions** |

Offer exceptionally broad-based business-operations experience in golfing, including private clubs, public courses and driving ranges. Active participant and top-finisher in Northern California PGA events. Work very effectively with all playing-levels of golfers. Strongly committed to the game and its growth.

**Manager / Head Professional**
17TH GREEN DRIVING RANGE Lemoore, California Jan. 1995 - Present
Joined this stand-alone, self-service driving range with 35 grass tee stations in the summer of 1994 as an instructor and after investigating with the owner the installation of a 20-stall franchise game area, *On Target Golf*, became associated with the five-year old facility full time. Key accomplishments:

- Established a small, 500-sf pro shop that opened in March and has contributed $22,000 in hardgoods sales (20% of total revenue) in six months. In addition to clubs, bags and shoes, sales include $4500 in balls, clothing, and club repairs.
- Average hardgoods inventory is $8500, with an average margin of 31.5 percent.
- Oversaw the start up of the On Target Golf facility.
- Totally upgraded all amenities and equipment, including launching a club repair program and setting up hot and cold snack bar.
- Maintain a robust instruction schedule, which includes range patrons as well as a following from a local private club. Through Aug. 1995: 311 lessons, three each in junior, ladies, and free clinics.
- Reinstated to PGA Class A in June 1995.

---

**Mortgage Banking Industry 1983-94**: Worked with three mortgage brokers in southern California and in last years was managing a three-branch operation that had annual production of over $90 million . More complete details of this very successful career will be provided upon request.

---

**First Asst. Professional**
CALABASSAS COUNTRY CLUB Calabassas, California 1981 - 82
Supported the head pro's annual-buying program in which members of this private club were able to purchase all goods at cost-plus-ten percent.

- Set up a tight purchasing program that brought in the right merchandise, good dating and enabled the pro shop to make three inventory turns a year.
- Increased sales by 55 percent, and provided more lessons that any other first assistant or head pro.
- Taught golf to physically handicapped people, including several confined to wheelchairs.

*Continues...*

**290**

**Combination.** *Ted Bache, Portola Valley, California*

A substantial resume for a Head Golf Professional. Boldfacing stands out nicely in the contact information, the key areas section, the job titles, the Mortgage Banking Industry 1983-84

*Page Two* *Bruce Mullen*

**First Asst. Professional**
OAKMONT COUNTRY CLUB Glendale, California 1979 - 80
Played key role restructuring the inventory and merchandising of the pro shop for this 350-member country club that was one of the more exclusive in the area.

- Created superior merchandise displays and selections that saw the sales volume increase one and a half times and profit margins grow by over 20 percent.
- Launched a 'regripping' winterizing program for members' clubs that was well received and increased the volume of repair business.
- Managed a night driving range that was owned by the Oakmont head professional.
- Gave more lessons than any other assistant.

**Manager & First Asst. Professional**
VALENCIA & VISTA VALENCIA GOLF CLUBS Valencia, California 1977 - 78
Started with the Valencia G.C., a championship course designed by Robert Trent Jones, Jr., and a year later was promoted to manager and first assistant of Vista Valencia, an 18-hole executive course with a nine-hole par-three facility. Both courses were owned by the Newhall Land & Farming Company and the positions included managing pro shop personnel, merchandising, club repairs, and all teaching.

- Considerably improved merchandising operations at both facilities, but especially at Vista Valencia where excessive inventory was reduced from $40,000 to $22,000, brought in sales of $65,000 and a doubling of the average margin to 30 percent.
- Established a successful junior golf program in which over 125 golfers participated. Graduation included a trip to Dodger Stadium which honored five students on the field for the Anthem.

**First Asst. Professional**
KNOLLWOOD GOLF COURSE Granada Hills, California 1976
After six months at this public course that had 300 rounds a day on weekends and was one of the busiest in the area, was given added responsibility for all purchasing and merchandising of pro shop inventory.

- Increased inventory from $20,000 to $30,000 and more than doubled annual sales to $95,000 with an average profit margin of 30 percent.
- Gave more lessons (400-plus annually) than any other assistant professional, and instituted the first and highly successful junior swing class and summer clinic.

---

**PGA Training & Accomplishments**

- Advanced Professional Training School, enrolled for Nov. 1995
- Elected to PGA Jr. Class A - 1981 (reinstated, 1995)
- Playing Exam/Test, passed 1979
- PGA Business School 2, successfully completed Jan. 7-11, 1980
- PGA Business School 1, successfully completed Nov. 13-17, 1978

Member of PGA Northern California section and currently first alternate for the National Club Pro Championship. Personal low round is 64. Since reinstatement, have played in five events: placed tied-for -39th, 21st, 11th, 5th, and 17th. Earlier tournament victories with SCPGA include Mission Hills CC, Calabassas CC, El Cabalero, and Oakmont CC.

---

**BS Degree - Business & Economics**
University of Southern Alabama - 1974

statement enclosed within horizontal lines, the PGA Training & Accomplishment heading (also enclosed within lines), and the academic degree at the end. Bullets point to significant activities and achievements for all of the positions held. A narrative paragraph is given for each workplace.

**STEVEN F. SHADDOX**

**5555 Lake Cameron** **(444) 555-9999 (Home)**
**Bowden, Oklahoma 50000** **(444) 555-8888 (Work)**

**SUMMARY OF QUALIFICATIONS**

- **Class A PGA Head Golf Professional** with progressive, successful experience in **golf instruction** and **management**.
- Thorough knowledge of all aspects of golf: teaching, products, and operations.
- Strong playing ability. Finished 4th in **West Oklahoma Chapter Championship** (1995); competed and placed in both **Tommy Ammour** and **Future Majorz** tours (1996).
- Efficient managerial skills; **increased sales 28%; increased golf shop profits 17%; improved inventory turnover by more than 200%; significantly increased number of lessons taught.**
- Exceptional **communication** and **interpersonal** skills; effectively communicate with people on all levels. Motivate instructors and employees for maximum productivity.

**CERTIFICATIONS**

USGA COURSE AND SLOPE RATING CERTIFIED

CERTIFIED EMERGENCY MEDICAL TECHNICIAN/EMERGENCY CARDIAC CARE

**PROFESSIONAL EXPERIENCE**

**LAKE CAMERON GOLF CLUB** **Bowden, Oklahoma**
**Head Professional** **1991 - Present**

- Recruited as **Assistant Professional**; promoted to **Head Professional** after one year.
- Full responsibility for 27-hole private golf operation; 2,000 members; 650 golf members.
- Hire, train, supervise staff of seven.
- Control merchandising, budgeting, purchasing, advertising, promotions, and inventory.
- Produce computer-generated management reports.
- Manage daily play, tournaments, outings for 55K-60K member rounds, 3,500 guest rounds.
- Organize and direct all junior, senior, ladies clinics; provide group and individual lessons using latest video techniques.
- Write monthly article for Lake Cameron.
- Oversee 15-station range. Manage 100 cart rental fleet.

**Significant Achievements**

- Instrumental in design and layout of new nine-hole course construction in 1995.
- Drastically increase number of lessons each year.
- Consistently increase sales; increased sales $38,000 (28%) during first year as Head Pro.
- Increased golf shop profits 17% in 1993.
- Improved inventory turnover by more than 200%.
- Significantly reduced fleet maintenance, shop overhead, and personnel costs.

**291**

**Combination.** *Ann Klint, Tyler, Texas*

A resume that is easy to grasp because of its centered section headings and center-aligned information on the second page for quick reading down the page. The thin-thick line under the

**STEVEN F. SHADDOX** **Page Two**

**EDUCATION**

PGA BUSINESS SCHOOL I (Top Five Percent)
PGA BUSINESS SCHOOL II (Top Five Percent)

George Alexander Teaching Seminar (1995)
Ping Custom Fitting Seminar (1995)

UNIVERSITY OF KANSAS - Lawrence, Kansas
Major: **Business**

**RECOGNITIONS**

Future Majorz Tour - Finished 4th, Score 70, 72 (1996)
Southern Oklahoma Open - Finished 34th, Score 74, 74, 72 (1995)
West Oklahoma Chapter Championship - Finished 4th (1995)
NTPGA Carbite Apprentice Championship - Finished 5th, Score 72 (1994)
West Oklahoma Pro-Am - Scoring Average 71 (1994)
Low Pro, Three Chapter Pro-Am Events (1994)
Low Pro, Harmony Country Club, Score 70 (1994)
Low Pro, Willowbrook, Score 69 (1994)
PGA WEST, John Deere, 2nd Place, Score 74 (1994)
Qualifier, Texas State Open (1993)
Player's Ability Test (Low Qualifier) (1991)

**MILITARY EXPERIENCE**

**Non-Commissioned Officer**, NATIONAL GUARD (1989-1995)

*~ ~ References Furnished On Request ~ ~*

contact information appears in the header at the top of page two and helps to tie the two pages together visually. Strong diamond bullets and the boldfacing of significant words and phrases lend weight to the Summary of Qualifications. Achievements stand out at the bottom of page one.

**DAVID L. SMITH**

**PGA Golf Professional - Class A**

7701 Par Four Drive • Munster, IN 00000
(111) 555-5555

**PROFILE**

- Career Golf Professional with 20 years of experience - 11 years as Head Golf Pro.
- Dependable, high-energy leadership ability, including setting a high standard for service.
- Strong skills in business planning and management, staff training, and teaching.
- Personable and cordial; relate well to a wide range of personalities in all age groups.

**ACCOMPLISHMENTS AND RESPONSIBILITIES - SHADY LAWN COUNTRY CLUB**

***Administration / Golf Shop / Driving Range***

- Managed all golf activities and programs. Delegated responsibility to Assistant Professionals. Upgraded staff and trained as well as motivated employees.
- Monitored $80K inventory, handled purchasing and bookkeeping, and administered payroll for 14 employees.
- Managed the Golf Shop. Remodeled interior, developed annual merchandising buying plan, and instituted a member program with gift consultation and size file. As a result, sales increased over 250%. Also implemented a yearly sale to liquidate past-season merchandise.
- Supervised Driving Range. Provided preventive maintenance for equipment and <u>new</u> <u>range</u> <u>balls</u> every season. Utilized C.D.G.A. computer handicapping.
- Boosted cart revenues by 50%. Supervised Caddy and Cart Program. Designed cart shed and established cart maintenance schedules. Responsible for a fleet of 60 motorized carts.
- Established procedures and wrote policy manuals for Golf Shop, Club Storage Department (385 golf bags), as well as Caddy and Cart Program. Revised and updated manuals as necessary. Installed a complete Club Repair Department. Experienced in complete golf club construction and repair. Provided dependable, quality repairs - often overnight.
- Coordinated outside outings with Club Manager and Greens Superintendent for added income. Participated in membership marketing by promoting club benefits at various functions.
- Introduced a color-coded marking system that promoted faster play.

***Instruction***

- Promoted a sound lesson program facilitated by the construction of a first-class driving range, including targets and a practice chipping green with sand traps. Provided ample staffing of instructors. Personally taught 250 lessons per season.
- Demonstrated effective and up-to-date teaching skills, including the use of video taping. Average student's handicap dropped 2-4 strokes, and a few dropped 10 strokes. Expanded class schedules to meet the demand for advanced instruction. Provided two Assistant Professionals each season, which enhanced availability of instruction and play with pros.

***Tournaments***

- Revamped club tournament programs, increasing participation by 25% in two years. Also introduced information sheets for all major events. Coordinated logistics with Sports Committee in organizing and running programs. Shot action photos to give to participating members. Served as referee for club championship matches.

- continued -

**292**

**Combination.** *Jennie Dowden, Flossmoor, Illinois*

The thick double line is a strong divider between the contact information and the rest of the page. The line makes a strong header as well at the top of page two. Accomplishments and

**David L. Smith,** page 2

***Programs & Events***

- Enhanced and expanded the Junior Golf Program to include the following:
  - Instruction and competition, eight weeks of the season.
  - Special endeavors to encourage participation.
  - Expansion of Junior privileges on the golf course itself.

  Results: Junior Golfers have won state titles and played on college teams.
- Conducted yearly events:
  - Golf clinic and breakfast for new members.
  - On-going ladies clinics.
  - Twilight Social Tournament - 3:30 PM / 9 holes / BBQ afterwards.

**TOURNAMENT PARTICIPATION**

- Hammond Times Pro-Am, Oak Ridge Country Club - 1st Place
- Community Charities Pro-Am, Briar Ridge Country Club - 1st Place
- Glenwood School Pro-Am, Big Oaks Country Club - 2nd and 4th Place
- Pro-Am Scratch Championship, Woodbridge Country Club - 3rd Place
- Pro-Club Champ Better Ball, Lakeview Country Club - 3 times placed in top 5
- Pro-President, Flosswood Country Club - 1st Place
- Pro-Superintendent, Flosswood Country Club - 2nd and 3rd Place
- J.C.K. Masters, Orion Lake Country Club - 1st and 2nd Place
- **Qualified for every Indiana Open attempted.**

**PGA SCHOOLS / RECENT PGA CONTINUING EDUCATION**

| | |
|---|---|
| PGA School II, 1976<br>Buffalo, NY | PGA School I, 1975<br>West Palm Beach, FL |

- Computerized Operations Workshop
- Training, and Conditioning Education Seminar
- Financial Management Seminar
- Negotiation and Interpersonal Skills Seminar
- Club Repair Seminar - Research and Development
- Advanced Teaching Workshop

**PGA ACTIVITIES**

- Instructor at Junior Golf Clinic at Pine Grove
- Instructor at Star Golf Clinic at Oak Hill
- Instructor at Indianapolis South Golf Expo
- Instructor at IPGA Golf Show at Hanover College
- Member of IPGA Committee
- Author of golfing articles in regional publications

**WORK HISTORY**

SHADY LAWN COUNTRY CLUB, Munster, IN
**PGA Head Professional**, 1985 to 1996
**Teaching Professional**, 1981 to 1985
**Assistant Professional**, 1979 to 1981

WINDING RIVER COUNTRY CLUB, Orlando, FL
**Assistant Professional**, 1977to 1979

SHADY GROVE COUNTRY CLUB, Flosswood, IL
**Assistant Professional**, 1976 to 1977

responsibilities at Shady Lawn Country Club are grouped according to four side subheadings. Private clubs like a Pro who is a good player. The Tournament Participation section tells of his good playing record. The PGA Schools section helps to offset his lack of a college education.

**CARL D. COACH**
21 Seaside Avenue • Kennebunkport, ME • 55555
(207) 555-5555

**Seeking a challenging head coach position utilizing my acquired skills and abilities and where there is an opportunity for personal and professional growth.**

PROFILE

A highly motivated individual who thrives in a challenging sports environment and knowledgeable in all aspects of coaching, club management, smooth operations and profitability. Specific strengths include strong team organizational abilities, excellent coaching skills, and solid playing experience. Adept at all aspects of personnel management, recruiting, training and development. Excellent public relations and marketing abilities.

SUMMARY OF QUALIFICATIONS

- An experienced coach/general manager with the requisite knowledge, work ethic and the competitive spirit and "will" to lead team towards achieving top rank status.
- Highly focused and results oriented with strong organizational and game planning skills.
- Excellent communications, promotions and public relations abilities; able to effectively communicate ideas to others.
- An effective motivator, personable and persuasive, able to relate to diverse individuals and build instant rapport and capable of providing on-going support and motivation to team members.
- Performance driven - capable of analyzing and setting goals, and devising and implementing team strategy to enhance player's abilities.
- Capable of working independently and as a "Team Player," with the self motivation, initiative and savvy necessary to meet the challenges of today's competitive sports environment.

COACHING EXPERIENCE

HOLYOKE TIGERS FOOTBALL CLUB • 1990 to 1992; 1994 - present
Holyoke, Massachusetts
**Owner / Head Coach**
- Directly responsible for all aspects of team management, including fiscal, administrative and personnel matters.
- Successfully coordinated and supervised all special events and promotions.
- Provided motivational training to players with an emphasis on achieving a "team effort" and successfully led team to finish the year with a 9-3 record.

**Director of Player Personnel**
- Demonstrated excellent interpersonal communications skills seeking out and recruiting team players; successfully recruited six College All Americans and six Minor League All Americans.
- Provided motivation and support to team members, assisting team players with locating housing, transportation, etc.
- Successfully initiated a fundraising campaign that raised in excess of $20,000.00.

**Offensive Coordinator**
- Developed and implemented playbook and coordinated and trained players in all aspects of game strategy and motivated team through player / coach team meetings.
- Reviewed play tapes and performed film break down in preparation of coaches meeting.
- Trained players in short yardage offense, inside/outside runs, option passing, goal line and back to the wall offenses, and called plays during game time.

**Special Teams Coordinator**
- Responsible for all aspects of special teams coordination, including kick-off, kick return, punt, punt return, field goals and extra points.
- Utilized excellent analytical and organizational skills preparing game player lists, assigning substitution list, and ensuring all team members were kept informed of their game status.

**Assistant Coach** • 1989
Worcester Jr. High Lions Football Team - Worcester, Massachusetts
- Part-time position coaching running backs, quarterbacks and receivers in effective game strategies.

**293**

**Combination.** *Patricia Martel, Saco, Maine*

A well-organized resume for a Head Coach who was looking for another Head Coach position. His coaching experience with the Holyoke Tigers is grouped according to four categories as

**CARL D. COACH**

21 Seaside Avenue • Kennebunkport, ME • 55555
(207) 555-5555

COACHES CLINICS / WORKSHOPS

RIDDEL COACHES CLINICS • 1991 to Present
Attended weekend seminars held in Burlington, Massachusetts providing training in:

➢ **Northern Arizona's Offensive Program** • 1995
*(Steve Axman - Northern Arizona Head Coach)*

➢ **Auburn's 3 step Quick Dropback Passing Game** • 1994
*(Tommy Bowdon - Auburn Offensive Coordinator)*

➢ **Miami's Kicking Game** • 1993
*(Dave Arnold - Miami Kicking Game Coordinator)*

➢ **Syracuse's "I" Offensive Program and Power "I" Program** • 1993
*(George Deleone - Syracuse Offensive Coordinator)*

➢ **SMU's Run & Shoot Pass Protection and Pass Protection Blocking Techniques** • 1992
*(Billy Kid - SMU Offensive Line Coach)*

➢ **Florida State's "I" Blocking Technique** • 1991
*(Brad Scott - Florida State Offensive Coordinator)*

PLAYING EXPERIENCE:

HOLYOKE TIGERS • **Holyoke, Massachusetts**
- 1992 Eastern Football League (E.F.L.)
- 1991 Continental Interstate Football League
- 1st Team All Conference LF - C.I.F.L.

MASSACHUSETTS RAMS • **Springfield, Massachusetts**
- 1990 Eastern Football League (E.F.L.) - Tail Back/Fullback

TAMPA BAY RAIDERS • **Tampa Bay, Florida**
- 1978 Minor League Football System - Fullback
- 1977 Minor League Football System - Fullback

EDUCATION

**University of Maine** - Orono, Maine • 1981 to 1984
*Major area of study: Business Administration*

**REFERENCES AVAILABLE UPON REQUEST**

subheadings. In the Coaches Clinics/Workshops section, a different kind of bullet points to clinics attended. For each clinic or workshop, the leader's name is in italic and within parentheses. Yet another bullet style is used in the Playing Experience section to show teams and positions played.

**LISA JOHNSON**
20 Moral Road • Belleville, Illinois 62221 • (618) 555-8847

**SUMMARY OF QUALIFICATIONS**

Six years experience as the Head Coach of highly competitive basketball, volleyball, and softball teams for a quality NAIA women's intercollegiate athletic program in the American Midwest Conference (formerly the Show-Me Collegiate Conference). A successful track record for graduating student-athletes (97%), managing athletic programs, recruiting, and developing talent at the high school, junior varsity, and varsity levels. Actively involved in faculty, athletic, and student affairs committees. Proven athletic administration skills include:

| | | |
|---|---|---|
| Budgeting | Travel Planning | Public Relations |
| Staffing/Scheduling | Academic Standards | Recreational Programs |

- Graduated 60 Academic All Conference volleyball and softball players in the last five years. Coached volleyball teams that qualified for post season play each year and softball teams that have finished no less than fourth in the conference, including a regional championship and a 4th place national finish.
- Member of the American Volleyball Coaches Association, National Softball Coaches Association, and National Association of Intercollegiate Athletics.
- Served as the Director of Public Relations for the St. Louis Steamers Soccer Club from 1985-1987. Accustomed to developing a strong rapport with local media contacts.
- Hold an M.A. Degree in Speech Communication from Southern Illinois University at Edwardsville and a B.A. Degree in Communication from St. Louis University. Earned Academic All Conference honors in basketball as an undergraduate. Taught various Physical Education (activities and theory) and Communication courses over the last six years including Public Speaking, Interpersonal Skills, Small Groups, and Persuasion.

**COACHING HIGHLIGHTS/COMMITTEE WORK**

Head Volleyball/Softball Coach, McKendree College, Lebanon, Illinois 1989-Present

- 1995: American Midwest Rating Committee, Volleyball
- 1995: 4th Place, NAIA National Softball Championship, the highest national tournament finish for any athletic team at McKendree College
- 1995: NSCA Exposure Camp Director
- 1995: NAIA Executive Committee, Softball
- 1995: NAIA Midwest Region Champions, Softball
- 1995: NAIA Midwest Region Coach of the Year, Softball
- 1994: NSCA Exposure Camp Staff
- 1993: NAIA District #20 Chair, Softball
- 1992: Show-Me Collegiate Conference Champions, Volleyball
- 1992: Show-Me Collegiate Conference Coach of the Year, Volleyball

| | 1990 | 1991 | 1992 | 1993 | 1994 | 1995 | Totals |
|---|---|---|---|---|---|---|---|
| **SOFTBALL** | | | | | | | |
| Won/Loss | 29-14 | 19-9 | 21-10 | 22-8 | 28-18 | 41-16 | 160-75 (68%) |
| NAIA All Americans | 1 | n/a | n/a | n/a | n/a | 2 | 3 |
| All Conference | 2 | 3 | 3 | 4 | 5 | 5 | 22 |
| Academic All Conference | 1 | 1 | 5 | 7 | 8 | 9 | 31 |
| **VOLLEYBALL** | | | | | | | |
| Won/Loss | 18-10 | 24-20 | 18-11 | 25-13 | 28-13 | 16-21 | 129-88 (60%) |
| NAIA All Americans | n/a | n/a | 1 | 1 | 2 | 2 | 6 |
| All Conference | 2 | 2 | 3 | 4 | 3 | 3 | 17 |
| Academic All Conference | 2 | 2 | 5 | 6 | 7 | 7 | 29 |

294

**Combination.** *John A. Suarez, Troy, Illinois*

A striking resume because of the well-designed table at the bottom of the page. The three columns of skills in the Summary and the Coaching Highlights are also visually appealing.

# Linda R. Jones

4329 Thirsty Court • Indianapolis, Indiana 46224 • (317) 271-4855

## Goal: Assistant Principal

## Education:

- Master in Administration, Butler University, Indianapolis, Indiana; 1989.
- Master Degree, Emotionally Disturbed and Learning Disabilities, Indiana University, Indianapolis; 1981.
- Bachelor of Science, Mental Retardation, Indiana State University, Terre Haute, Indiana; 1973.

## Experience:

**INDIANAPOLIS PUBLIC SCHOOLS** 1973-Present

- Arm Junior High School: 1989-Present

  **Special Education Department Head (1994-Present):** Supervise teaching and support staff, serve as resource person, and oversee structured environment for Special Education Department.
  - Leader and spokesperson for professional meetings and conferences.
  - Liaison between administration, teachers, and students.
  - Teach special education classes.
  - Observe students and set up paperwork for psychological evaluations.

  **Resource Teacher, Arm Inclusion; 1993.**
  **Teacher, L.D. Science and Social Studies; 1989.**

- Easy Corner High School, **Teacher, Special Education Department, L.D. History; 1988.**

- North High School, **Teacher, L.D. Government and Economics; 1985-1988.**
  - School resource/liaison for up-to-date instructional computer materials.
  - School Advisory Committee member.

- Cristmore High School, **Teacher, Mildly Mentally Handicapped students; 1984-1985.**

- Green Manor Junior High, **Teacher, Mildly Mentally Handicapped and Learning Disabled students; 1981-1984.**
  - Cheerleading sponsor, 1981-1983.
  - Special Student Services Team - evaluated students for special education services; 1982.

- School #83, Junior High School Department, **Teacher, Mildly Mentally Handicapped students; 1974-1981.**

- School #33, Junior High School Department, **Teacher, Mildly Mentally Handicapped students; 1973-1974.**

**SUMMER LEADERSHIP EXPERIENCE:**

- **Youth Supervisor,** summer work program sponsored by I.P.S.
- **Site Supervisor,** Parks and Recreation Department, Arsenal Park.
- **Guidance Counselor,** incarcerated youth and young adults, sponsored by Yiles Foundation.

**295**

**Chronological.** *Carole E. Pefley, Indianapolis, Indiana*

A resume for a Special Education Department Head who was looking for an Assistant Principal position to make use of learning received through work on a second master's degree.

**DENNIS M. SEYMOUR**
983 Rosewood Avenue
Romulus, MI 48174
(313) 946-5555

**PROFILE**

**Purchasing Management**

- Diverse background with experience in all management, purchasing, and manufacturing entities.
- Proven record of supplier cost reduction through negotiation, and through coordination of team efforts such as Kaizen programs and Value Analysis/Value Engineering (VA/VE).
- Extensive knowledge of and experience in Japanese lean manufacturing and management/team oriented techniques.
- Strong leadership and decision-making abilities. Excellent troubleshooter; solve problems on a daily basis.
- Extensive experience in developing employee training programs for the division.
- Computer literate in Excel, Word, Access, and purchasing and engineering databases.
- Adaptable – have consistently met challenges of reorganizing and restructuring departments in times of growth or downsizing.

**ACHIEVEMENTS**

**At Ford Motor Company:**

- Department led the division with an annual cost reduction averaging 2.5% per year.
- Negotiated a $3 million annual cost reduction on automotive transmission purchases.
- Helped build and establish purchasing department from the ground floor level, and set up policies and procedures for its growth.
- Completed in-depth training for ISO 9000 Quality System implementation assessment and auditing. Also serve as divisional coordinator.
- As internal Kaizen coordinator for the Purchasing Division, lead team in reducing costs of supplies, and in streamlining/automating procedures to work efficiently with reduced staff.
- Traveled to Europe to assure quality of tooling built in Germany, and to Japan for business and training.

**EXPERIENCE**

11/87-Present

**Ford Motor Company-Dearborn Stamping Plant**, Dearborn, Michigan

*Leader - Administration/New Model Purchasing (2/95-Present)*

Manage New Model Purchasing and Administration Department. Supervise all new model and launch activities within the purchasing division, and coordinate with all outside divisions, parent companies, and suppliers. Oversee all administrative functions within the division, including system improvement and automation. Develop overall purchasing division policies, procedures, and budgets. Coordinate the implementation of all ISO 9000 procedures and systems. Develop and implement all divisional training programs for approximately 65 employees.

*Leader - Purchasing Product Procurement (3/93-2/95)*

Supervised a $750 million annual buy electrical and functional part production procurement department. Approved all sourcing, pricing, and purchase orders. Conducted all high level negotiations and established long-term contracts with suppliers. Developed and implemented short and long-term business plans for the department.

**296**

**Combination.** *Deborah L. Schuster, Newport, Michigan*

"A Profile can replace an Objective," particularly if the target field—in this instance, Purchasing Management—is mentioned as a subheading. "Putting all of the accomplishments in one section

Dennis M. Seymour Resume/2

**EXPERIENCE**
(Continued)

**Ford Motor Company** (Continued)

*Leader - Purchasing Product Procurement (Promotion) (4/91-3/93)*

Supervised a $300 million annual buy interior trim production procurement department.

*Professional / Buyer - Purchasing Product Procurement (Promotion) (11/89-4/91)*
*Specialist / Buyer - Purchasing Product Procurement (5/89-11/89)*

Responsible for sourcing and procurement of interior and exterior trim components for all vehicles from a worldwide supply base. Using detailed cost analysis, negotiated all part and tool pricing from prototype through final production stages. Audited and analyzed all potential suppliers and production readiness through launch phase.

*Specialist - Purchasing Administration (11/87-5/89)*

Developed a system for coordinating, tracking, implementing, and expediting engineering changes for the Purchasing Division. Developed and implemented systems for cost recovery from all local source suppliers for material rejections. Coordinated and implemented supplier training of company purchasing and delivery procedures. Worked directly with procurement departments in investigating, solving, and expediting resolution of local source supplier issues. Developed departmental procedures.

11/83-11/87

**Chrysler Corporation-Trenton Engine Plant**, Trenton, Michigan

*Analyst - Pre Production Purchasing (Promotion) (9/86-11/87)*

*Supervisor - Materials Handling (7/85-8/86)*

*Supervisor - Production (2/85-7/85)*

*Supervisor - Quality Control (Receiving Inspection) (12/84-1/85)*

*Supervisor - Quality Control (11/83-12/84)*

**EDUCATION**

**University of Michigan,** Ann Arbor, Michigan
*Bachelor of Science in Administrative Management (1983)*
*Studies toward Master of Science in Administration (Ongoing)*
*Projected Completion: Spring, 1998*

near the beginning avoids burying some of them on the second page." Putting in the left column all the dates for frequent promotions in a company can look like job hopping, so the dates of *overall* employment are put in the left column, while the dates for each position are put after it.

## Jillian S. Seinfield

27221 Heavensacre
Loyola, Montana 27221
999 555.4321

### Profile

Energetic, organized, and qualified professional. Ten years of experience in technical and management areas of diagnostic imaging.

### Qualifications Summary

*Management*

- Experience with accreditations and state radiation inspections.
- Organized in record management, statistics, and schedules.
- Initiate and apply process improvement strategies to department operations.

*Technical*

- Certified RDMS and RT.
- Experience in sonography includes: abdominal, small parts, neonatal, OB/GYN, vascular, and invasive/interventional procedures.
- Experience in radiography, mammography, and cat scan.
- Provide technical advice to physicians, residents, staff technologists, and students.

### Employment History

*Hope Hospital – The City Medical Center*

**Radiology Services Leader**, 1992 to Present .................... City, State

- Direct day-to-day operation of satellite imaging center.
- Supervise department technical and clerical personnel.
- Coordinate the flow of work through department, based on patient volume.
- Serve as liaison to all hospital departments, public, patients, and physicians.
- Evaluate equipment for purchase.
- Perform sonographic and radiographic procedures.

**Staff Sonographer**, 1990 to 1992 .......................... City, State

- Successfully established a new facility/service including: equipment, supplies, lab organization, and implementation of procedures and protocol.
- Performed sonographic, radiographic, and mammographic procedures.

**Staff Sonographer**, 1987 to 1990 .......................... City, State

- Performed sonographic procedures including vascular studies.

297

**Combination.** *Lorie Lebert, Novi, Michigan*

This individual wanted a higher-level management position, so the resume highlights management and technical experience. For this reason, "Management" and "Technical" are

*Page Two of Résumé for:*

**JILLIAN S. SEINFIELD**

**EMPLOYMENT HISTORY** *(continued)*

*BIOMEDICAL DIAGNOSTIC SERVICES* . . . . . . . . . . . . . . . . . . . . . . . . . . . . . . . City, State
**DIAGNOSTIC IMAGING TECHNOLOGIST**, 1986 to 1987
- Performed sonographic, radiographic, and mammographic procedures.

**EDUCATION**

*POPULAR CITY COLLEGE* . . . . . . . . . . . . . . . . . . . . . . . . . . . . . . . . . . . . . . . City, State
**B.A.S.**, 1991
- *Major:* Diagnostic Medical Sonography

*HOPE HOSPITAL SCHOOL OF RADIOLOGIC TECHNOLOGY* . . . . . . . . . . . . . . . . . City, State
**R.T.**, 1982

**CERTIFICATION**

American Registry of Diagnostic Medical Sonographers, 1986

American Registry of Radiologic Technologists, 1984

*CPR*

**PROFESSIONAL ACTIVITIES**

*Member*, Society of Diagnostic Medical Sonographers

*Member*, State Sonographer Society

*References Available On Request*

subheadings in the Qualifications Summary. The bold triple line is eye-catching and makes the reader see the candidate's last name and the rest of the contact information. Small caps are used for the contact information, headings, subheadings, workplaces, job titles, and education sites.

**STEPHEN WILSON**
**1996 Springhurst Street** **(914) 962-1997**
**Yorktown Heights, NY 10598**

**OBJECTIVE**

A position as Chief of Police, for a mid-sized Police Department, which will utilize my extensive experience in Police operations, strategic planning, and proven managerial expertise.

**PROFILE**

- Effective Law Enforcement Professional with ***proven innovative organizational expertise***, exceptional follow-through abilities and excellent management skills. Able to oversee projects from concept to successful implementation.
- Demonstrated ability to fully ***utilize resources for maximum effect***.
- ***Pro-active Strategist***; able to effectively meet the needs of community while ***maintaining highest levels*** of ***morale***.
- Completed Homicide Investigator's course, June 1995
- Consistently rated Above or ***Well Above Standards*** on evaluations by superiors.

**QUALIFICATIONS**

- In April 1995, was chosen co-presenter at a Human Resource Society workshop/seminar re: creating organizational Vision and Mission statements.
- Selected to participate in the ***Executive Development Program*** of the New York City Leadership Institute, involving key executives representing many branches of city government.
- Two and one half years experience as Precinct Commander in the New York City Police Department.
- Possess both Bachelor and Master of Arts in Sociology.
- More than five years ***command experience*** at rank of Captain; more than twenty years service in the New York City Police Department.

**EXPERIENCE**

May 1995 - Present

**NEW YORK CITY POLICE DEPARTMENT**
**Investigative Coordinator** and **Duty Captain, Detective Borough Manhattan**

- Monitor and direct all criminal investigations of six precinct detective squads in Manhattan North.
- Direct newly developing criminal investigations in the whole Borough of Manhattan and, periodically, the entire City.

January 1995 - May 1995

**NEW YORK CITY POLICE DEPARTMENT**
**Borough Captain, Patrol Borough Manhattan North**

- Interim commanding officer in 34, 26, 20 precincts, while assigned commanders were on extended sick leave or vacation.

September 1992 - December 1994

**NEW YORK CITY POLICE DEPARTMENT**
**Commanding Officer, Tenth Precinct (Captain)**

- Managed 225 person police operation in Manhattan's West Side "*Chelsea*" community, overseeing patrol, investigative and administrative functions.
- Directed procedures for maintaining discipline and training personnel. Due to new procedures, recorded productivity gains and an increase in morale.
- Instituted more effective anti-robbery program utilizing efficient human resource management strategies. During two year tenure, ***effected successive 10% decreases in robberies***.
- In 1994, ***achieved 25 year lows in four of the seven major crime categories***.
- Re-scheduled patrols for higher visibility and providing a more effective theft deterrent.
- Liased with assorted political and community entities in the Chelsea community, receiving several letters of appreciation from them upon completion of assignment. Coordinated with other Police Departments including Port Authority, Housing Police, Transit Police and, on occasion, FBI and DEA.

**298**

**Combination.** *Mark D. Berkowitz, Yorktown Heights, New York*

An impressive resume for a Police Officer with a stellar record of promotion within the New York City Police Department. This writer's tendency to use bold italic for significant words and

Stephen Wilson page 2

May 1990 - September 1992

**NINTH PRECINCT,** NYC
**Executive Officer (Captain)**
- Served as Second in command for one of Manhattan South's busiest commands in the East Village; Acting Commander in CO's absence.
- Supervised crowd control at numerous demonstrations, rallies and protest marches in and around Tompkins Square Park.
- Served as Evening and Night Duty Captain 2-3 times each week.

November 1989 - May 1990

**PATROL BOROUGH MANHATTAN SOUTH**
**Duty Captain and Supervisor of Patrol**
- Oversaw total police operations on both evening and night tours for entire borough.
- Monitored patrol force members within Second division to ensure compliance with Departmental policy

June 1985 - November 1989

**FIELD CONTROL DIVISION/ORGANIZED CRIME CONTROL BUREAU**
**Lieutenant Team Leader**
- Investigated allegations of corruption and major misconduct against members of OCCB assigned to Brooklyn, Queens and Staten Island using confidential informants, undercover operatives, Detectives and a variety of technical equipment to accomplish objectives.
- Organized and mounted pro-active investigations to uncover possible corrupt activities by members of OCCB.

May 1984 - June 1985

**52nd PRECINCT**
**Lieutenant Platoon Commander**
- Oversaw all police operations on precinct platoon assigned.
- Investigated communications and complaints from public.

May 1982 - May 1984

**43rd and 44th PRECINCTS**
**Sergeant Patrol Supervisor**
- Supervised street patrol functions on platoon assigned.

September 1973 - May 1982

**46th PRECINCT**
**Police Officer**
- Four years uniform patrol service; all shifts.
- Five years in anti-crime, plain clothes patrol.
- Personally effected more than 450 arrests, for various offenses (over a nine year period), averaging 50 per year.
- Accumulated ***20 Excellent Police Duty*** and ***3 Meritorious Police Duty*** medals for notable police work.
- Honored as Police Officer of the Month (April 1976) for exceptional performance of duty.

**ADDITIONAL EXPERIENCE**
August 1964 - July 1968

**UNITED STATES ARMY**
- Assigned to Army Security Agency, working with Top Secret clearance.
- Attained rank of Staff Sergeant.
- Served as room supervisor for Top Secret mission.

**EDUCATION**

**NEW YORK UNIVERSITY,** New York, NY
**M.A. SOCIOLOGY** 1975

**ST. VINCENT COLLEGE,** Latrobe, Pa.
B.A. SOCIOLOGY 1970

**REFERENCES**

Available upon request.

phrases serves the candidate well in calling the reader's attention to key traits, skills, experience, and achievements. Although the page border is a thin single line, such a border on each page ties the two pages together visually.

**JOSEPH A. RAPPAPORT**

4162 Bark Lane **(000) 000-0000** Market Fields, New York 00000

## BUSINESS / FINANCIAL MANAGER

**RESULTS ORIENTED** professional with comprehensive experience in all business areas • Utilizes extensive financial management experience to guide organizations to maximum levels of profitability/productivity • Aggressive, persistent and consistent • Demonstrated leadership, time management and problem solving skills with the ability to set priorities to ensure favorable outcomes • Confident decision maker • Thoroughly versed in PC's, IBM AS/400 and numerous software applications.

### DEMONSTRATED STRENGTHS:

- *Fully experienced in all aspects of business operations including P&L management, operations, sales, marketing and staff development.*
- *Providing leadership to multimillion dollar organizations within highly competitive markets.*
- *Skilled in devising and implementing strategic programs to ensure organizational growth.*
- *Experienced with federal standards of cost allocation for professional service firms and governmental agencies.*
- *Versed in governmental contracts at federal and state levels.*

### PROFESSIONAL AFFILIATIONS:

F.R. HAMILL • New York, New York **1993 - Present**

***Unit Financial Officer***

- High profile, senior level financial management position accountable for P&L of 5 nationwide profit centers for a leading engineering design firm. Profit centers account for 50% of firm's annual revenue of $100 million.
- Provides leadership and guidance to each profit center and interfaces closely with profit center managers to develop annual budgets and forecasts.
- Institutes cost reduction efforts to ensure sales and profit goals are achieved.
- Directs all financial functions pertaining to the profit centers, including cash flow, client billing and revenue realization/accruals.
- Reviews and negotiates terms and conditions for client contracts and subcontracts.
- Evaluates profitability on all proposed and existing projects.
- Develops and directly manages a professional staff of project accountants and cash collectors to peak levels of productivity.

***Achievements:***

- ♦ *Significantly increased profitability by developing and implementing improved cash collection tactics.*
- ♦ *Authority to act on behalf of Chief Financial Officer.*
- ♦ *Served as CFO/Controller for a joint venture with annual revenue exceeding $6 million.*
- ♦ *Liaison between profit centers' managers and corporate staff; facilitated communications and developed a synergistic team spirit.*

O'CONNOL & ASSOCIATES • Mountain Lakes, New Jersey **1989 - 1992**

***Administrative Director (consultant)***

- Managed administrative, financial and marketing projects for key clients of a major construction and program management firm.
- Directed MIS operations for all offices within New Jersey, Pennsylvania and the District of Columbia, including state-of-the-art office automation conversion.
- Oversaw staffing of MIS personnel.

***Achievements:***

- ♦ *Developed training and reference manuals pertaining to effective management of major construction projects for the Facilities Division of the U.S. Postal Service.*
- ♦ *Served as Project Manager/Administrator for construction claims litigation projects.*

(continued...)

**299**

**Combination.** *Alesia Benedict, Rochelle Park, New Jersey*

Using all uppercase for RESULTS ORIENTED is attention getting because no other embedded words in the resume are treated that way. The use of a bullet as a separator appears in the

**JOSEPH A. RAPPAPORT**
**(000) 000-0000 • Page Two**

**PROFESSIONAL AFFILIATIONS continued**

ERNST & YOUNG • New York, New York **1980 - 1989**

***Principal***
- Developed and managed strategic marketing tactics, targeting City/State governmental agencies and municipalities in an effort to expand clientele for an international management consulting firm.
- Counseled clients in the areas of financial management of major municipal construction projects, productivity and management studies, computerized systems design and the development of cost allocation plans.
- Delivered effective presentations and negotiated contracts.
- Directed a staff of professional consultants and project managers; ensured quality control, budgets restraints and superior client relations.

***Achievements:***
- ♦ *Managed the largest consulting client for the New York office for 4 consecutive years.*
- ♦ *Instrumental in clients' increasing recovery of federal funds through the preparation of comprehensive cost recovery plans: recovered as much as $60 million in federal grant refunds for one specific client.*
- ♦ *Active member of the Staff Review Committee and the Office Automation Committee.*

N.J. DEPARTMENT of ENVIRONMENTAL PROTECTION • Trenton, New Jersey **1978 - 1980**

***Grants Manager***
- Coordinated the State's Sewerage Construction Grants Program and executed administration of department's federal funds.
- Controlled an annual operating budget of $3 million; accountable for over 50 employees.
- Determined audit conclusions of potential recipients; over $200 million in annual funds were allocated to local municipalities to construct and manage wastewater construction projects.

**EDUCATIONAL BACKGROUND:**

Bachelor of Science in Accounting • LaSalle University • Philadelphia, Pennsylvania

NASD Series 7, 63

opening profile "paragraph," the employer information in the Professional Affiliations section, and the degree information. Double-underlining the name of each employer makes the names easily seen. A centered heading, diamond bullets, and italics make the achievements stand out.

**BERNARD S. GOLDMAN**
1025 Washington Street • Apt. 6H • Hackensack, New Jersey 00000 • **(555) 555-5555**

**PROFESSIONAL OBJECTIVE**

Highly capable and dedicated professional seeks challenging, responsible position within a growth-oriented organization to apply education, training and expertise in:

**Environmental Sciences • Medical Services • Occupational Health & Safety**

**DEMONSTRATED STRENGTHS**

- *Well-qualified, knowledgeable professional integrating education and training in the fields of medicine, biology and chemistry.*
- *Strong background in hazardous waste site assessment and management, environmental analysis and toxicology, risk assessment and site remediation.*
- *Thoroughly versed in all emergency medical care procedures, methods and standards.*
- *Fully trained and experienced in providing medical treatment at hazardous spill sites.*
- *Proven ability to work well in high-pressure and stressful environments, responding efficiently and with expertise in crisis situations.*
- *Effective communicator; relates well with others in both a team and/or individual basis.*

**ACADEMIC CREDENTIALS**

***M.A. in Environmental Sciences***
New Jersey Institute of Technology, Newark, New Jersey

***B.A. in Biology, A.A. in Chemistry, Dean's Honor List***
Quinnipiac College, Hamden, Connecticut

***Certificate in Pre-Medical Postgraduate Studies***
Columbia University, New York, New York

***Certifications and Special Training:***
Certified Pesticide Applicator, Category 3B
CPR Instructor, American Red Cross
Certified Hazardous Material Spill Response Technician
Certified Emergency Medical Technician
Certified Scuba Diver
OSHA/HAZWOPER Training Program
Horticulturist

**PROFESSIONAL EXPERIENCE**

**ROGERS ENVIRONMENTAL MANAGEMENT, INC.** — Rutherford, New Jersey
***Health & Safety Officer*** — 1993-1996
Hired to monitor daily air quality of an 80-acre hazardous waste disposal work site as well as within the surrounding community to ensure health and safety. Experienced in utilizing various portable analyzers and gas chromatography instruments to identify harmful levels of particulates, hydrogen sulfides and volatile organic compounds.

- ♦ *Assumed full authority to recommend work site shut-down in the event that contamination levels reached dangerous peaks jeopardizing personnel safety and health.*
- ♦ *Applied expertise on health and safety issues to provide on-site technical support.*
- ♦ *Played key role as technical consultant during monthly meetings with contractor, various regulatory agencies and local civic groups; provided analysis of samples collected.*
- ♦ *Identified a major problem in the detection capabilities of the chromatography equipment resulting in the development and implementation of new EPA standards for TCA.*
- ♦ *Skilled in the repair and maintenance of extremely sensitive chromatographic instrumentation resulting in considerable cost savings and minimal work flow disruption.*

**300**

**Combination.** *Alesia Benedict, Rochelle Park, New Jersey*

In another resume by the same writer, you can see again the use of a bullet as a separator (in the contact information, the fields at the end of the Professional Objective, and the computer

**BERNARD S. GOLDMAN** **(555) 555-5555** **- Page Two -**

**PROFESSIONAL EXPERIENCE continued...**

**L.A.B., INC.** Ridgefield, New Jersey
***Research Technician*** 1992-1993

Prepared blood and urine samples for chemical analysis and assisted physicians during medical examinations of subjects for an international, independent research firm conducting clinical studies on pharmacological products pending licensing approval.

- ♦ *Skilled in performing phlebotomy and EKG analysis.*
- ♦ *Responsible for observing research participants throughout the clinical study period; prepared charts and files for each participant.*
- ♦ *Served as bio-hazardous waste and inventory control manager to ensure strict compliance to health and safety standards.*

**GROW-LAWN** Hackensack, New Jersey
***Owner/Manager*** 1987-present

Established and manage successful lawn care firm with three full-time employees. Develop residential and commercial business accounts handling sales through scheduling and quality control.

- ♦ *Consistently manage pesticide handling procedures per EPA standards, to minimize employee and public exposure.*
- ♦ *Developed and implemented warehouse safety procedures and the mandatory use of appropriate employee personal protective equipment.*

**ADDITIONAL EXPERIENCE**

**BERGENFIELD AMBULANCE CORP.** Bergenfield, New Jersey
***Emergency Medical Technician*** 1990-present

Advanced to Second Lieutenant. Trained to provide emergency response and medical treatment to variety of patients in crisis situations. Instrumental role in training and supervising a team of 50 health care professionals to provide emergency medical services. Initiated and developed various health education programs presented to the community.

**EXAMINATION MANAGEMENT SERVICES, INC.** Fairfield, New Jersey
***Medical Examiner*** 1996

Coordinated and performed basic medical examinations with clients for a national firm serving the insurance industry. Performed various medical exams including EKGs, lung capacity testing, blood pressure and pulse rate. Collected and analyzed blood and urine samples.

**AFFILIATIONS**

American Society of Safety Engineers
National Association of Underwater Instructors

**COMPUTER SKILLS**

Windows • Excel • WordPerfect

skills at the end) and the use of diamond bullets before important information in italic. Academic credentials important to the targeted fields are put in early and center-aligned to make them stand out. Center-aligning the Affiliations and Computer Skills sections makes them look better.

## RICKY GORDON

123 Whiteoak Drive • Martin, Kentucky 40100 • (502) 555-1111

### OBJECTIVE

A professional position which utilizes my skills and education and allows for future advancement in security, safety, or loss prevention

### SUMMARY OF QUALIFICATIONS

- B.S. degree and six years of experience in security, safety, and loss prevention.
- Good written and oral communication skills. Able to work independently or with a group.
- Dependable, hard-working, and mission-oriented.
- A strategic planner who is able to creatively anticipate the needs of the future while executing current responsibilities.

### PROFESSIONAL EXPERIENCE

CHEMICAL CORPORATION • Martin, KY Jan 91 - Present
**Security and Loss Prevention Officer**

- Developed and implemented safety training programs for plant personnel. Attended outside seminars several times a year to keep up-to-date on current safety methods. Then presented new methods to groups of plant personnel.
- Conducted inspections of facilities and production processes to insure compliance with all corporate and government regulations.
- Certified EMT. Responded to medical, fire/rescue, and hazardous materials emergencies on plant site.
- Implemented security program through site audit, patrols, and electronic surveillance. Audited equipment and "secure areas" and proposed changes to improve security.
- Effectively handled problems by making good decisions and using sound judgment. Developed and wrote standard operating procedures.

MARTIN COUNTY SHERIFF'S DEPARTMENT • Lawrence, KY Jul 89 - Jan 91
**Correctional Officer**

- Provided protection and security for the facility. Insured accountability. Supervised 20 to 60 personnel on a daily basis. Performed patrol and security rounds. Monitored cameras and surveillance equipment. Scheduled and completed projects in a timely manner.

### MILITARY EXPERIENCE

U.S. ARMY TRANSPORTATION CORPS Jun 87 - Jul 89
**Transportation Supervisor** (Second Lieutenant)

- Supervised 30 personnel. Trained and developed new personnel. Wrote performance evaluations. Provided counseling and career development.
- Always brought projects in *on time* and *under budget*.

**301**

**Combination.** *Connie S. Stevens, Radcliff, Kentucky*

A vertical line attached at the left margin to a thin horizontal box is a creative design element. That element and "display type" in the name and headings are repeated on the second page.

## RICKY GORDON

**Page 2**

### EDUCATION & MEMBERSHIPS

- KENTUCKY UNIVERSITY • Martin, KY
  **Bachelor of Science** • June 1987 • *Industrial Security/Loss Prevention Management*
- Member of ASIS since 1988

### CERTIFICATION & TRAINING

- Emergency Medical Technician
- Hazardous Communications
- Confined Space Rescue
- Anzel Fire Training
- Professional Development, American Society for Industrial Security
- Numerous other safety and loss prevention courses. Information available upon request.

### COMPUTER SKILLS

- IBM-Compatible Computer
- Excel
- MS Word
- Harvard Graphics
- WordPerfect
- Lotus 1-2-3

### HONORS

- Academic Excellence in Security and Loss Prevention • 1987
- Presidential Award for Academic Excellence • 1987
- National Society of Scabbard and Blade • 1987
- African-American Male with Highest GPA • 1986 • 1987
- Kentucky University Committee Minority Scholarship Winner • 1986 • 1987

### EXCELLENT REFERENCES AVAILABLE UPON REQUEST

Three kinds of bullets are used for variety. The writer advised the client about networking, and he picked up a number of job leads at a convention in New Orleans. From these he received three job offers and accepted a position with the largest security organization in the United States.

# *AN ACADEMIC*

*1234 East 11th Street • Someplace Nice, State 55555 • (913) 555-1234*

## PROFILE

Experienced **School Administrator** with vast knowledge of effective teaching procedures. Excellent writer and speaker. Seeking administrative position to continue my dedication to innovative education and teacher development.

## PROFESSIONAL EXPERIENCE

*BIGTIME SUBURBAN SCHOOL DISTRICT*, Bigtime, State

**Elementary School Principal** (Dates)

*School 1* (Dates) at-risk population, xxx students K-6
*School 2* (Dates) at-risk population, xxx students K-6
*School 3* (Dates) xxx students K-6

Managed the overall operation of public schools with populations ranging from 360 to 980 students. Developed and executed budgets. Scheduled classes, events and staff; supervised instruction through comprehensive evaluation. Maintained current knowledge of research and innovations in instruction and school management; facilitated staff development. Cultivated in-depth understanding of at-risk populations and Special Education strategies.

**Classroom Teacher** (Dates)

## COMMITTEE INVOLVEMENT

- Coordinating Principal for in-service; district liaison among 12 schools
- State Special Education Compliance Team
- Teacher Evaluation Committee
- Principal Representative for Special Education Curriculum

## EDUCATION

*STATE UNIVERSITY*, Somewhere, State

**M.S. School Administration**
**B.S. Education**

## CERTIFICATION

- State Administrator
- State Teaching Certificate, K-8

**302**

**Combination.** *Linda Morton, Lawrence, Kansas*

This writer's task was to take CV format, "which is basically a list," and make the resume visually interesting "with lines and white space" and "more informative" with the "inclusion of

# An Academic

*Page 2*

## CONTINUING EDUCATION

Teacher Evaluation, *Midwest University*
Theory of Learning, *A College*
Cooperative Learning, *University of Big State*
Reading Workshop, *State University*

## AFFILIATIONS

Phi Delta Kappa
Board of Directors, County Hospital for Retarded Citizens
National Association of Elementary Principals
State Association of Elementary Principals
Local Chapter of Lions Club

## ACHIEVEMENTS

- Instrumental in bringing Effective Schools Program to district.
- Established Cooperative Learning and pilot technology programs.
- Initiated and developed internship program for Japanese teaching Japanese language and culture. Worked directly with Education Department in Japan.
- Developed gifted program for children as a cooperative effort between teachers and parents. Adopted by other district schools.
- Involved teachers in Invent America project working with the U.S. Patent Office. Presented ideas for creative workshop to area schools.
- Improved ratings for two different schools from low to high achievement in five years. One was rated top in effectiveness.

**CREDENTIALS AND REFERENCES ON REQUEST**

achievements." She not only provided double lines that break up the resume into sections but also broke the lines so that they bracket the centered headings. Boldfacing is used for the headings, job titles, degrees, and closing references statement. The Achievements section looks uncluttered.

# Debra Turner

4 Longview Drive | Jackman, ME 04945 | (207) 902-3967

**Principal / Assistant Principal**

*Qualified By*

- *~ 19 years as Classroom Teacher*
- *~ Academic Leadership Experience*
- *~ Completion of Principal Internship*
- *~ Gifted & Talented Programming*
- *~ Requisite Education and Certifications*
- *~ Curriculum Development Success*
- *~ MEA / Learning Results Involvement*
- *~ Special Education Activities*

*Education*

M.S. in Exceptionality, Concentration: Gifted Child Education, 1989
University of Maine, Orono, Maine

B.S. in Early Childhood Education, Human Development Program, 1977
University of Maine, Farmington, Maine

*Certifications*

State of Maine Administrative and Professional (K-8) Certifications

*Experience*

Lincoln Memorial School, Lincoln, Maine

**Grade Four Teacher**, 1977-present
Teach, supervise, and evaluate students; communicate with students, parents, and administrators in promoting the educational development of each student.

**Team Leader**, Grades 3-5, 1993-present
Supervise coordination, scheduling, and documentation of team activities.
Facilitate meetings in reviewing, evaluating, and implementing curriculum goals.

**Intern to Principal**, 1995-96
Training and hands-on experience in following areas:

- ~ budget planning/fiscal management
- ~ personnel management
- ~ program/curriculum development
- ~ student personnel services
- ~ staff development
- ~ school leadership/operations
- ~ teacher supervision/evaluation
- ~ school/community relations
- ~ exceptionality programs
- ~ federal/state laws
- ~ educational philosophy
- ~ instructional strategies

Worked closely with Principal in setting goals and revamping the Chapter I/Title I programs in response to the Improving American Schools Act.

**Additional LMS Involvement:**
Gifted and Talented Volunteer Program Coordinator, 1986-present
Member, Technology and Curriculum (Literacy, Science, and Health) Committees
Past Member, Textbook Selection and Wellness Committees

**303**

**Combination.** *Elizabeth M. Carey, Waterville, Maine*

Because this person "was seeking a position in a highly competitive education field," the writer "chose a unique format with the white on gray side sections emphasizing creativity." The

**Debra Turner**

Résumé Page 2

*Maine Department of Education Participation*

**Maine Education Assessments**, 1993-present
Seminars/Work Sessions attended in relation to:
MEA: Question Development, Writing and Scoring
Learning Results: Formation of L.R. Document and Performance Indicators

~ Follow-up Maine Dept. of Education workshops related to linking Performance Indicators to State and Local Assessments
~ Learning Results Seminar/Work Sessions to rewrite Performance Indicators for *all* areas and develop Health questions for fourth grade MEA's
~ "Teachers Summit #2" of Learning Results to develop Performance Indicators for content area of Health
~ "Journeys for Change" seminar to begin the process of changing Curriculum Assessment Instruction at Lincoln Memorial School
~ Member of initial Committee which developed questions for the Health portion of the MEA's

**Maine Parent-Professional Group**, 1990-present
Meet regularly as a member of this organization whose primary goal is to promote and model collaborative parent-professional partnerships on the state and local levels for the support of children with special needs. Serve as group facilitator during "Parents Encouraging Parents" conferences.

**Healthy Me, Healthy Maine Program**, 1991-94
Co-Coordinator for HM/HM Program Grant; developed and wrote health curriculum for Lincoln Memorial School with monies obtained from grant

*Supporting Statements*

"Ms. Turner's potential as an administrator has been demonstrated in her leadership skills, organizational skills and knowledge of all the duties of a school administrator. She has effectively handled groups with conflicting interests -- teachers in various grade level teams, her own team members and challenging members of the community."
*Principal, LMS*

"Ms. Debra Turner represents all that is good, exciting, and challenging in public education today. She has demonstrated outstanding talent as a teacher, a voracious appetite for growing as a professional, and exceptional potential and promise to be a preeminent administrator."
*Grade Four Teacher, LMS*

"Ms. Turner has spent a good many hours beyond the duties of her classroom working on curriculum development and programs for the professional growth of all staff that have enhanced the quality of education at the elementary school."
*Superintendent of Schools*

integration of horizontal lines with the side section is a plus. Tilde (~) bullets appear with the list of qualifications and in the Experience section. Powerful supporting statements, or testimonials, appear at the end, offering "'proof' of the client's abilities in a number of areas."

# MARTHA L. PRICE

**24 Ridge Road ▪ Katonah, New York 10536 ▪ (914) 555-0000**

## LABORATORY TECHNOLOGIST

### SUMMARY OF QUALIFICATIONS:

**Senior Clinical Laboratory Technologist** with ten years of experience and a record of rapid promotions to progressively responsible positions. Solid background in managing all departmental functions. Expertise in hands-on use of instrumentation for chemical analyses: Hitachi 747-100, Hitachi 747-200 and Kodak Ektachem 700 Analyzers.

### MANAGEMENT PROFILE:

- Enthusiastic team player with history of exceeding standards and expectations.
- Excellent time manager able to handle multiple tasks concurrently.
- Skilled troubleshooter ensuring bottom-line results in a fast-paced environment.
- Consistently awarded more projects than others for ability to manage logistics and attend to detail.
- Effective communicator with strength in motivating, training and developing staff.

### PROFESSIONAL EXPERIENCE:

GOTLIFE LABORATORIES, Bedford, New York 1987–present
**Senior Clinical Laboratory Technologist** 1992–present
Manage Toxicology Screening, Serum Chemistry and Therapeutic Drug Monitoring Departments and supervise staff of 15. Perform all assays utilizing urine chemistry.

- Reduced error rate from 15% to 5% by managing Quality Assurance on over 1,000 specimens daily, completing all primary and secondary testing with same-day results.
- Organized team to run Quality Controls on all tests and prevented out-of-range results.
- Consistently achieve 100% results on blind sample proficiency testing to regulate company for N.Y. State Inspections and College of Applied Pathologists.
- Consolidated departmental functions and saved time by devising formula for analyzers, resulting in new parameters for tests and methodologies.
- Revise critical tasks and standard strategies with collaborative reviews, linking latest technology with processes.
- Developed detailed, 100-page procedure manuals, shortening time and level of training for new hires.
- Train, coach and evaluate staff for improved performance and elimination of repeatable errors.

**Clinical Laboratory Technologist** 1988–1992
Directed fully independent testing in the Toxicology Screening and Immunology Departments.

- Conducted assays on cocaine, nicotine metabolite, thiazides, propranol and micrototal protein in urine chemistry on Hitachi 747-100 analyzers.
- Performed ELISA screens for HIV-1/HIV-2 in serum and dried blood spots, confirming with a Western blot.
- Assayed orinase, nicotine metabolite, thiazides and beta-blockers in urine chemistry on microtiter plates.

**Clinical Laboratory Technician** 1987–1988
Entry-level laboratory position with fast-track promotion.

- Assisted with testing and analysis in the Serum Chemistry Department, completing specialized training on the Kodak Ektachem 700 Analyzer.

**304**

**Combination.** *Phyllis B. Shabad, Ossining, New York*

Some seniors assume managerial roles by virtue of their seniority. This individual *minored* in Chemistry but then chose Chemistry as her main career field. The writer therefore emphasized

**MARTHA L. PRICE** page two

**EDUCATION:**

**Bachelor of Science in Marine Biology** 1987
**Minor in Chemistry**
Connecticut College, New London, Connecticut
Dean's List

**PROFESSIONAL DEVELOPMENT:**

**MANAGEMENT TRAINING**
**SkillPath Seminars**, Mission, Kansas
- Managing Multiple Projects, Objectives and Deadlines–1994
- Managing Negativity in the Workplace–1994

**TECHNICAL TRAINING**
**Currently:**
- Training on the GC-MS (Gas Chromatograph-Mass Spectrometer) for drug abuse combinations, used in clinical, reference and forensic labs.

**Boehringer Manheim Corporation**, Indiana
- Advanced Operator Training: Hitachi 747-100 Analyzer–1994
- Basic Operator Training: Hitachi 747-100 Analyzer–1992

**Toxi-Lab Incorporated**, Massachusetts
- Rapid Drug Detection, using thin-layer chromatography on Toxi-Lab System–1991

**American Association for Clinical Chemistry**, Washington, D.C.
- Laboratory-Based Nutritional Assessment–1995
- Monitoring Glycemia in Diabetes Mellitus–1995
- Meeting CLIA 1988 Requirements: QC, QA, PT
- Laboratory Tests for Diagnosing and Monitoring Cancer–1994
- PSA and Prostate Cancer: Update–1994
- New Laboratory Tests for Diagnosing Heart Disease–1994

**COMPUTER SKILLS**
**Hardware**
- PC/Mac competency

**Software**
- Microsoft Word 7.0, Excel, Access
- Specialized software: Lab Information System; Statistical Software for Analyzer

**CERTIFICATION:**

National Certification Agency for Medical Laboratory Personnel
- **Certification in Clinical Chemistry**–1997

**AFFILIATION:**

American Chemical Society

in the Management Profile the person's managerial skills and stressed in the Professional Experience section the individual's professional development. The writer also devoted much space to the person's post-college training, especially certification for the chemical industry.

# Miriam DeLeon

325 West Broadway
Hicksville, NY 55555

phone ■ (555) 555-5555
E-mail ■ compgeek@aol.com

## Career Profile

Broad experience in all phases of the Project Life Cycle with managerial and technical emphasis in development and implementation. Perform development, project management and technical specialist functions on a wide variety of traditional and cutting-edge systems and software. Think critically, learn quickly, develop expertise and produce immediate contributions. Blend leadership, creative and analytical abilities to produce bottom-line results. Dedicated, responsible and unusually organized. Enjoy a challenge and thrive under the pressure of focused activity.

| | | | |
|---|---|---|---|
| **Hardware** | ■ IBM 3090<br>■ Personal Computers | ■ UNIX<br>■ WANG VS/PC | |
| **Environments** | ■ MVS/ESA<br>■ TSO/ISPF | ■ MS DOS<br>■ OS/2 | ■ Windows 95<br>■ Windows NT |
| **Languages** | ■ MVS/JCL<br>■ IBM COBOL<br>■ IEF/COMPOSER | ■ ASSEMBLER<br>■ QUICK JOB<br>■ EASYTRIEVE | ■ C/C++<br>■ WANG VS COBOL<br>■ BASIC |
| **Software** | ■ MS Word<br>■ MS Publisher<br>■ MS Project<br>■ MAPPS | ■ SPFPC<br>■ Flow Charting<br>■ Banyan E-mail<br>■ Lotus Notes | ■ DB2/2<br>■ Cross Talk<br>■ Paradox<br>■ Excel |
| **Abilities** | ■ project plans<br>■ data modeling<br>■ technical design | ■ coding/testing<br>■ client/server concepts<br>■ work station configuration | ■ product evaluations<br>■ system training<br>■ package retrofits |

## Representative Projects and Highlights

- Cutting-edge IEF/COMPOSER 5.3 DB2 C/COBOL client/server collection payment tracking system for MS WINDOWS platform with IBM mainframe batch processing.
- Development of modifications to an ASSEMBLER variable life insurance administration system.
- In-house modifications and enhancements to a multi-million dollar vendor CICS/IMS COBOL client oriented investment sensitive insurance administration system.
- IMS COBOL batch system to initially load and then provide daily maintenance for over 5 million contracts and 4 million clients from 13 administration systems for a CICS/IMS COBOL client management information system.
- Installation of and enhancements to a vendor's batch COBOL Stock and Bond System onto an IBM mainframe.
- Evaluation of ten state-of-the-art project management software systems. This $360,000 project resulted in the recommendation of one package, coordination of training activities across divisions and achievement of upper management support.
- Modification and enhancements to a WANG VS COBOL and PC BASIC insurance proposal systems for the agency force.

**305**

**Combination.** *Deborah Wile Dib, Medford, New York*

A two-page resume with a third page as an Addendum. The person's name and thick line become part of the header on pages two and three. Under the Career Profile, the first of three

## Miriam DeLeon

page two

### Employment

**METROPOLITAN LIFE, NEW YORK, NY** **1978 to July, 1997**

| | | | |
|---|---|---|---|
| ■ **Senior Technical Specialist** | 1995 to 1997 | ■ **Project Manager** | 1985 to 1986 |
| ■ **Senior Project Manager** | 1991 to 1995 | ■ **Technical Specialist** | 1984 to 1985 |
| ■ **Project Manager** | 1988 to 1991 | ■ **Sr. Programmer/Project Manager** | 1983 to 1984 |
| ■ **Programming Consultant** | 1986 to 1988 | ■ **Senior Programmer/Analyst** | 1979 to 1983 |

**Consultant, technical and programmer functions**

- Participated in data modeling, analysis, technical design, program design/coding, platform cross generation, testing and production implementation tasks.
- Functioned as model administrator for IEF/COMPOSER 5.3 project.
- Performed setup and configuration tasks for both test and production workstation environments.
- Wrote technical and program specifications, production support manuals and user error message procedure manual.
- Installed vendor package retrofits.

**Managerial responsibilities**

- Developed project plans and technical communications for upper management.
- Supervised teams of up to 12 technical professionals.
- Coordinated the development of program modifications and enhancements.
- Oversaw the creation of technical and programming specifications.
- Performed committee representation functions.

### Education

**Over 700 hours of professional development courses in technical, programming, and management skills.**

- Metropolitan Life, Wang, The New School for Social Research, Digital, IBM, Mitchell, Beta Data, TCC, XEROX, Communispond, Learning Tree, Hofstra University, JMAC and Texas Instruments.

**Original Technical Training**

- PSI Institute, COBOL, Assembler, RPGII Programming 1977 to 1978

tables in this resume displays the extent of the person's computer literacy. At the beginning of the Employment section on page two, a second table without lines shows the individual's work history at Metropolitan Life. The third table is the Education and Professional Development Addendum.

# Miriam DeLeon

## Education and Professional Development Addendum

| Course | Institution | Duration | Dates |
|---|---|---|---|
| ■ COBOL, Assembler, RPGII Programming | PSI Institute | 6 months | 6/77-1/78 |
| ■ COBOL Programming Series | Equitable | 8 weeks | 9/78 |
| ■ JCL and Utilities | Equitable | 4 days | 12/78 |
| ■ IMS Overview | Equitable | 1 day | 4/79 |
| ■ Advanced COBOL Programming | Equitable | 4 days | 4/79 |
| ■ MVS Overview | Equitable | 1/2 day | 8/79 |
| ■ Wang Operations/Procedures/COBOL | WANG | 10 days | 2/80 |
| ■ Management and Motivation | Equitable | 2 days | 4/80 |
| ■ Structured Design and Programming | Equitable | 5 days | 8/80 |
| ■ IMS Data Base Programming | Equitable | 3 days | 3/81 |
| ■ IMS Data Base Communications | Equitable | 2 days | 3/81 |
| ■ VM/CMS | Equitable | 3 1/2 days | 4/81 |
| ■ Writing for Impact | Communispond | 1 1/2 days | 3/82 |
| ■ Data Communications Overview | Equitable | 1//2 day | 9/82 |
| ■ Orientation for New Managers | Equitable | 2 days | 2/83 |
| ■ Intro. to the WANG PC | WANG | 1 day | 12/83 |
| ■ Basic Programming for the IBM PC | Equitable | 3 1/2 days | 1/84 |
| ■ dBase | New School | 8 sessions | 3/85 |
| ■ Lotus 1-2-3 | New School | 8 sessions | 3/85 |
| ■ dBase | Digital | 3 days | 7/85 |
| ■ Speaking on Paper | Communispond | 1 day | 10/85 |
| ■ CSP Seminar | IBM | 1 day | 1/86 |
| ■ MAPPS-Management & Project Planning | Mitchell | 5 days | 1986 |
| ■ MAPPS-Micro/Macro Planning | Mitchell | 1 day | 1986 |
| ■ MAPPS-Updating Project Plans | Mitchell | 1 day | 1986 |
| ■ MAPPS-Graf/Plot | Mitchell | 1 day | 1986 |
| ■ MVS/XA Overview | Equitable | 1 day | 4/86 |
| ■ Brainstorming | Equitable | 1 day | 4/86 |
| ■ James Martin Seminar | Technology | 5 days | 6/86 |
| ■ VS COBOL Workbench | Equitable | 1 day | 7/86 |
| ■ RMDS | Equitable | 1/2 day | 10/86 |
| ■ Local Area Networks | Beta Data | 2 days | 10/86 |
| ■ Life 70 Accelerated Education | TCC | 5 days | 2/87 |
| ■ Expert JCL | Technical Com | 2 days | 5/87 |
| ■ VSAM | Technical Com | 3 days | 6/87 |
| ■ PC Configurations | Equitable | 1 day | 10/87 |
| ■ COBOL II | Equitable | 1 day | 1/88 |
| ■ XICS | XEROX | 5 days | 4/88 |
| ■ CCA/IPW Workshop | TCC | 3 weeks | 5/88 |
| ■ Insurance Basics | Equitable | 1 day | 1/90 |
| ■ Time Management | Equitable | 1 day | 1/90 |
| ■ Equitable Products | Equitable | 1 day | 2/90 |
| ■ UNIX | Learning Tree | 4 days | 4/92 |
| ■ C Programming | Hofstra University | 7 sessions | 6/92 |
| ■ Assembler Programming | JMAC/Equitable | 5 days | 7/92 |
| ■ C Programming | JMAC/Equitable | 5 days | 9/92 |
| ■ AXANET Overview | JMAC/Equitable | 1 day | 6/93 |
| ■ DPR Overview | JMAC/Equitable | 1/2 day | 6/93 |
| ■ NSDK | JMAC/Equitable | 2 days | 6/93 |
| ■ Microfocus COBOL | JMAC/Equitable | 1 day | 6/93 |
| ■ Planning for Future Retirement | Equitable | 3 days | 9/93 |
| ■ IEF | Texas Instruments | 2 weeks | 1/94 |
| ■ Paradox | Equitable | 1 day | 11/94 |
| ■ IEF/COMPOSER | Texas Instruments | 5 weeks | 4/95-5/95 |
| ■ IEF Encyclopedia Concepts & Subsetting | Texas Instruments | 4 days | 2/96 |

This table is, in effect, a 56-row, 4-column table without lines. The first row is a heading row in which the column headings are put. The duration of the events ranges from a half-day to six months, and the dates are in ascending order from June 1977 to February 1996.

234 Tea Rose Court
Davenport, FL 33837

# Jane S. Frances, P.E.

(941) 000-0000

## *CAREER PROFILE*

- **Civil/Environmental Engineer** with 11-year tenure reflecting a career path of outstanding performance and progressive advancement to more challenging, leadership roles. Possess well-defined technical ability; proactive project management skills; proven expertise in strategic planning and design from conceptual through completion stages; and keen analytical, problem-solving and troubleshooting skills.

- **Demonstrated strengths** in spearheading Phase I, II and III environmental assessments; conducting audits/investigations/ UST analyses; performing sampling/testing procedures; authoring comprehensive reports/remedial programs; calculating operational/fiscal efficiency; interpreting compliance issues; and developing bid documentation.

- **Effective communicator** with excellent organizational and interpersonal skills. Proficiency in prioritizing duties, working as a team member, and building client relations that achieve long-term sustainable results.

- **Computer Literate:** Working knowledge of computer programming and modeling
  Familiar with several spreadsheet and project management softwares

## *AREAS OF EXPERTISE*

--Hazardous Waste Management
--Solid Waste Management
--Construction Management
--Stormwater Management
--Wastewater Management
--Cost Estimating

## *EDUCATION/PROFESSIONAL LICENSURE*

UNIVERSITY OF CENTRAL FLORIDA
**M.S. Civil Engineering/Construction Management** (1984)
*Publication:* Master's Thesis - ***The Use of Computers in Construction Management*** (included self-written program utilizing CPM and computer graphics to perform resource leveling)

HAITI STATE UNIVERSITY
**B.S. Civil Engineering** (1982)

**State of Florida** - Registered Professional Engineer in Civil/Environmental Engineering (1990)

## *EXPERIENCE*

SOUTHWEST FLORIDA ENVIRONMENTAL ENGINEERING, INC. **1985 - Present**
**Senior Environmental Engineer** (1995-Present)
**Promoted through Engineer Levels IV-VI** (1990-1995)
**Engineer Level III** (1986-1990)
**Resident Engineer** (1985)

Self-motivation, initiative and results-oriented attitude led to successive promotions. Experienced in civil/environmental project management at all levels. Accountable for diverse scope of multi-faceted disciplines involving hazardous waste, stormwater, wastewater, and construction management. Provide strong operating results in productivity/efficiency improvements via implementing innovative methodologies and cost-effective directives. Ensure compliance with all statutory regulations.

** Recipient of **Outstanding Performance Recognition Award** for exceptional work as Project Manager for the Hillsborough County Aviation Authority Property Acquisition Program.

## *PROFESSIONAL AFFILIATIONS*

American Society of Civil Engineers
Water Environment Federation
Women Transportation Seminar Committee

306

**Combination.** *Diane McGoldrick, Tampa, Florida*

A bold line and a triple line enclose the contact information and call attention to it. The Career Profile shows four different kinds of skills. The Areas of Expertise are listed in flexible columns.

**DAVID TAYLOR**
15 Oak Street • Beaumont, TX 77713 • (409) 555-1234

**OBJECTIVE**

To acquire a **Management** position with a security or consulting firm.

**CAREER PROFILE**

A highly dedicated, committed, service-oriented professional whose career includes **28 years experience** in city, county, and state law enforcement. Gained valuable administrative experience serving eight years as Sheriff of Monroe County. Area of expertise includes personnel management, labor union contract negotiations, budget forecasting and development, implementing community programs, as well as all aspects of law enforcement.

**CAREER HISTORY**

1/89 - Present **MONROE COUNTY**, Monroe, Texas
*Sheriff - Accomplishments by skills area includes:*

**Administration**

- Direct and manage all aspects of Sheriff's Office. Directly supervise 156 employees.
- Successfully manage operating budget of $5M - $7M in the "black". Responsible for forecasting budget requirements, preparing budget proposals, submitting and negotiating budget terms with Commissioner's Court.
- Experienced in applying for and receiving federal and state grants. Utilize grants to establish special programs such as Violent Crime, Victim Services, Community Policing, Auto Theft, and D.W.I. Enforcement.
- Negotiate contracts with six local school districts to provide risk intervention officers.
- Indirectly involved in planning and construction phases of new $6,000,000 jail addition which opened February 1996.
- Obtained state license to operate Monroe County Sheriff's Department Training Academy. Work in conjunction with Monroe University Criminal Justice Program and their instructors.
- Key player in winning several major federal and state lawsuits filed by employees and prisoners. Save county millions of dollars by strictly adhering to federal and state court mandated policies, procedures, and methods of operations.
- Maintain professional relationship with local media reporters and keep them apprised of developments in high profile cases.

**Personnel**

- Effectively negotiate union labor contracts with employees on a yearly basis.
- Update and revise personnel polices and procedures manual. Write job descriptions for new positions when required.

**Law Enforcement**

- Supervise all aspects of county jail housing up to 250 inmates. Directly responsible for inmates' well-being.

**307**

**Combination.** *JoAnn Nix, Beaumont, Texas*

A resume for a Sheriff whose managerial success has prompted an interest in a management position with a security or consulting firm. Reading the Career History backward reveals a steady

**David Taylor**, *continued ...*

- Sheriff's Office has seized over $1,750,000 in 'drug' money from criminals which has been used to buy state-of-art equipment, vehicles, K-9, etc. thereby saving tax dollars.
- Directly involved in all aspects of law enforcement such as searching for missing persons, homicides, drug busts, and racial demonstrations.

1984 - 1988 **COOK & TURNER, P.C.**, Houston, Texas
*Legal Investigator*
Interviewed clients and performed initial investigation for personal injury cases.

1981 - 1983 **HOUSTON POLICE DEPARTMENT**, Houston, Texas
*Police Officer*

1981 **MAGNOLIA POLICE DEPARTMENT**, Magnolia, Texas
*Police Officer*

1978 - 1981 **MONTGOMERY COUNTY,** Montgomery, Texas
*Reserve Deputy Constable*

1965 - 1977 **DEPARTMENT OF PUBLIC SAFETY**
*Highway Patrol Trooper in Corpus Christi, Texas (7 years) and Houston, Texas (6 years).*

**EDUCATION**

**Texas Law Enforcement Management Institute**, 1994
*Third Texas Sheriff to graduate (program equivalent to FBI Academy)*
2,500+ Hours of **Advanced Specialized Training**
**Texas Dept. of Public Safety Law Enforcement Academy**, 1965

**CERTIFICATE**

Master Peace Officer Certificate with T.C.L.E.O.S.E.
*Highest level of license a peace officer can achieve*

**PROFESSIONAL AFFILIATIONS**

Sheriffs Association of Texas
National Association of Sheriffs
Texas Jail Association
National Association of Chiefs of Police
Texas Police Association
American Correctional Association

**References Available Upon Request**

record of growth in various areas of law enforcement. Information about the current work site is grouped according to three categories. Administration, the category most relevant to the Objective, is developed the most. The person lacks a college degree but has had much training.

**THOMAS M. TROISE**
**0000 West Indian Road**
**Elmira, NY 00000**
**(000) 000-0000**

**PERSONAL**

Willing to give 100% to a career oriented position. Motivated with a high degree of integrity in personal and professional interaction.

**CAREER GOAL**

To be the Golf Course Superintendent of a highly respected, well managed facility.

**EDUCATION**

The Pennsylvania State University
Certificate Degree in Turfgrsss Management
Graduated with Highest Distinction

University of Wisconsin
Bachelor of Science in Business Administration

**EMPLOYMENT**

**Valley Stream Country Club, Valley Stream, NY**
**Superintendent - March 1994 to Present**

- Responsible for maintenance operations of a private golf course which hosts an annual LPGA tour event "The LPGA Corning Classic".
- Supervise equipment maintenance and repairs including golf cart fleet.

**Honeywell Country Club, Honeywell, NY**
**Superintendent - March 1990 to February 1994**

- Supervised golf course construction including greens, tees, bunkers and irrigation improvements.
- Supervised daily maintenance of hard-tru tennis courts and paddle tennis courts.
- Supervised maintenance crew. Involved hiring, training, daily scheduling as well as ensuring adherence to club policies and course safety rules.

**ADDITIONAL EMPLOYMENT EXPERIENCES**

**Honeywell Country Club, Honeywell, NY** - March 1988 - February 1990

- Assistant Superintendent

**Pine View Golf Club, Pine View, CO** - March 1987 - September 1987

- Responsible for preparation of the course for an annual PGA tour event "The International".

**Montauk Country Club, Montauk Point, NY** - May 1982 - September 1986

**CERTIFICATIONS/MEMBERSHIPS**

- New York Pesticide Applicators License
- Golf Course Superintendents Association of America
- Pennsylvania Turfgrass Council
- United States Golf Association

**References Upon Request**

**308**

**Chronological.** *Betty Geller, Elmira, New York*

A very targeted resume for a Golf Course Superintendent. His education is complemented by professional activities. The writer herself regarded the format as chronological. Note use of bold.

# GARY RAMIREZ

**19 Adams Road • Ellenville, NJ • (555) 222-2222**

## CONSTRUCTION / PROJECT SUPERINTENDENT

**• Available For Out-Of-State Projects •**

Over 15 years of construction management experience with prior surveying background. Excellent track record in supervising a wide range of complex, multimillion dollar projects, including construction and major renovation of hotels, casinos, airports, schools, high-rise buildings, sewerage treatment plants, and industrial facilities. Expertise in interpreting and implementing architectural concepts, and uncovering potential design problems. Reputation for saving substantial time and money through effective blueprint analysis, resource planning, scheduling, and supervision. Strong focus on quality control. Talent for establishing rapport and credibility with local officials, subcontractors, trade unions, and crews. Bilingual (English/Spanish).

## KEY PROJECTS

**NEW YORK TIMES PRODUCTION FACILITIES**, Edison, NJ ($450 million)
Oversaw fast-track project requiring large-scale demolition of an old air conditioning plant and construction of a printing facility within existing structure. Involved extensive interior structural steel construction, substantial concrete and masonry work, and construction of loading docks and footing foundations for printing presses.

**THE ROBERT VAN FOSSAN PLAZA**, Newark, NJ ($3.6 million)
Managed the complex construction of a street-level pedestrian plaza over an existing three-story parking garage. Coordinated interior renovations to existing building during normal working hours. Implemented special construction methods due to weight limitations. Avoided additional project costs and delays by uncovering design problems, and working with architects and engineers to correct them.

**MORRISTOWN DEVELOPMENT PROJECT**, Morristown, NJ ($200 million)
Supervised the construction of an underground, three-story, 2500-car parking garage, two 150,000 sq. ft. nine-story office buildings, and 100,000 sq. ft. of retail commercial space at street level.

**GOVERNMENT SERVICE OFFICES AND PUBLIC LIBRARY**, Atlantic City, NJ ($15 million)
Functioned as project superintendent in the construction of a public library and nine-story structural steel office building with curtain wall fascia. Implemented specialized scheduling and construction techniques because of extensive delays in fabrication and erection of curtain wall system due to design problems.

**WHITEHALL LABORATORY / WAREHOUSE**, Hammonton, NJ ($10 million)
Oversaw extensive renovations to existing pharmaceutical plant and supervised construction of an adjacent 105,000 sq. ft. structural steel warehouse addition requiring heavy masonry work; required strict scheduling to facilitate plant operation during construction.

**BUCKINGHAM TOWERS**, Fort Lee, NJ
Directed the construction layout of a 26-story high-rise condominium project. Uncovered and rectified numerous design problems in cooperation with architects and engineers.

**CONNECTICUT EDUCATION ASSOCIATION BUILDING**, Hartford, CT
Recruited mid-project to troubleshoot diverse scheduling and construction problems with the erection of an eight-story structural steel office building with pre-cast fascia. Successfully got project back on track.

## ADDITIONAL PROJECTS

**Linden Roselle Sewerage Treatment Plant • Newark International Airport • Park Place Hotel & Casino • Harrah's Marina Hotel & Casino • Manchester Elementary School**

## EMPLOYMENT HISTORY

| | | |
|---|---|---|
| **PROJECT SUPERINTENDENT** | T.A.K. Construction Co., Harrison, NJ | 1993 - 1995 |
| **PROJECT SUPERINTENDENT** | Ogren Construction Company, Vineland, NJ | 1991 - 1992 |
| **CONSTRUCTION SUPERINTENDENT** | Morganti, Inc., Ridgefield, CT | 1990 |
| **PROJECT SUPERINTENDENT** | Bergen Engineering Company, E. Rutherford, NJ | 1987 - 1990 |
| **HEAD SURVEY PARTY CHIEF** | Interstate Industrial Corporation, Secaucus, NJ | 1985 - 1986 |
| **PROJECT SUPERINTENDENT** | Mellon Stuart Construction Co., W. Trenton, NJ | 1984 - 1985 |
| **PROJECT SUPERINTENDENT** | Dowling Construction Co., Atlantic City, NJ | 1983 - 1984 |
| **PROJECT SUPERINTENDENT** | First Roc-Jersey, Morristown, NJ | 1981 - 1983 |
| **CONSTRUCTION SUPERINTENDENT** | Perini Corp., Framingham, MA | 1980 - 1981 |
| **CONSTRUCTION SUPERINTENDENT** | Turner Construction Co., New York, NY | 1978 - 1980 |

**309**

**Combination.** *Rhoda Kopy, Toms River, New Jersey*

A pair of thin-thick lines enclose the profile section just under the contact information and draw attention to the person's experience, expertise, and skills. The Key Projects list is impressive.

# NICHOLAS ENMACH

11207 S Bermosan Way Tempe, AZ 55555 [555] 000-0000

## SUMMARY OF QUALIFICATIONS:

- Over 5 years experience as Superintendent/Working Foreman in high voltage electrical construction....
- Scheduled manpower/materials....
- Oversaw multiple jobs simultaneously in: AZ/CA/OR/NY/NM/PA/CT/TX....
- Tracked man hours/material & job costs/weekly & monthly schedules....
- Dealt directly with clients/subcontractors....
- Resolved problems....
- Brought in projects under budget/on time....
- Excellent communication skills....team player....very organized....willing to learn....hard worker....dedicated....decisive....

## EMPLOYMENT HIGHLIGHTS:

PHOENIX POWER CONSTRUCTORS - Chandler, AZ

***Superintendent:*** 1990 to present.

- Began as parts runner....delivered to job sites....
- Promoted to Apprentice Electrician after 6 months....worked on high voltage power construction....
- Operated: cranes/loaders/forklifts....handled piping/welding....
- Promoted to Foreman...supervised 5 - 10 crew members....
- Supervised jobs at power plants/mines/on highways....
- Promoted to Superintendent....Journeyman Electrician....
- Knowledgeable with federal regulations/OSHA/NEMA/NEC standards....
- Managed hydro electric/substation/refinery projects....

MAJOR PROJECTS:

- Bonneville Dam Revamp Project: $40 million
- Los Alamos Lab: $300,000
- Palm Springs Substations: $16 million
- Maxwell, CA: $15 million
- Superstition Freeway
- Army Corps of Engineers Hydro Electric Dam at Fort Peck, MT
- Hohokam Highway: Loop 202

## EDUCATION:

NORTHERN ARIZONA UNIVERSITY - Flagstaff, AZ

ARIZONA STATE UNIVERSITY - Tempe, AZ

Major: Criminal Justice

**310**

**Combination.** *Fran Holsinger, Tempe, Arizona*

A one-page resume from a writer whose specialty is a two-page resume plus a cover. Intense black characters, strong diamond bullets, and concluding ellipses (....) are marks of her style.

# Roger E. Milton

3245 Main Street
Appleton, Wisconsin 54914

Office: (414) 722–7947
Home: (414) 875–1874

## Summary of Qualifications

Results–oriented, profit–driven executive with excellent qualifications in plant management and staff development gained through 20+ years experience. Demonstrated success in implementing processes and building operations which have consistently reduced operating costs, improved production yields, and increased profitability. Strong supervisory and leadership abilities, with a proven capacity to build effective, productive teams.

## Experience

XYZ Corporation, Appleton, Wisconsin — June 1982–Present

**Production Superintendent**, Main Street Plant

- Full P&L responsibility for Manufacturing and Finishing Departments, warehouse and shipping operations.
- Directly supervise 8 salaried shift supervisors and an assistant superintendent. Indirectly supervise 200 union employees and 40 temporary employees working on three shifts.
- Instrumental in the transfer of Finishing operations to Main Street Plant which resulted in increased utilization of direct labor pool and reduced supervisory and staff costs.
- Improved profits through better communications with hourly employees, development of an effective Plant Maintenance Program, and supervisory shift control and reporting.

BYT Company, Inc., Neenah, Wisconsin — April 1979–June 1982

**Production Superintendent**

- Supervised 7 employees directly, and 200 indirectly in this unionized three–shift production facility with an annual inventory valued at $8MM.
- Reduced unfavorable labor and material usage variances through improved communications and reporting procedures, and installation of shop floor controls.

CSZ Corporation, Education Division — October 1973–April 1979

**Operations Manager**, Green Bay, WI (6/77–4/79)

- Full P&L responsibility for three facilities within division. Developed a profit improvement program which increased 1977 profits 22% through staff and administrative cost reductions.

**Procurement and Plant Manager**, Green Bay, WI/Fairfield, MD (1/76–6/77)

- Procured shipping and production supplies as well as items for resale.
- Decreased direct labor cost by 7% while increasing production by 21% at the Fairfield facility.

**Plant Manager**, Green Bay, WI (10/73–1/76)

- Decreased manufacturing expense by 11% while maintaining same rate of production.

## Education

B.A. in Biology — University of Wisconsin–Madison — 1972

Management Seminars and Courses — University of Wisconsin System — 1975–1981

**311**

**Combination.** *Kathy Keshemberg, Appleton, Wisconsin*

This victim of downsizing was looking for a similar job in the same industry. He wanted only a one-page resume, so the writer made a strong Summary and included selected achievements.

# MATTHEW T. ANDREWS

**1608 Cimmarron Trail**
**Tyler, Texas 75703**
**(903) 599-8855**

## AREAS OF EXPERTISE

- **Production / Operations Management**
- **Inventory Control / Management**
- **Plant Maintenance**
- **Mechanical Engineering**
- **TQM • SPC • PLC**
- **Capital Improvement Projects (CIP) Design / Development**
- **Budget Management**
- **OSHA / MSHA / EPA / Safety Training**
- **Lockout / Tagout Procedures**

- 15 years of experience and thorough knowledge of **plant operations**; proven success in **Production**, **Operations**, and **Inventory Management**; **Mechanical Engineering**; and **Plant Maintenance**; consistently maintain **excellent on-time / under-budget record.**
- Cognizant of OSHA, MSHA, EPA, and Lockout/Tagout procedures / regulations. **Safety Instructor**.
- Expertise in **troubleshooting, malfunction identification**, and **problem solving.**
- Outstanding **team development / team building, conflict / dispute resolution, communication**, and **interpersonal** skills; **effective motivator**; expediently and diplomatically resolve conflicts / disputes. Establish positive rapport with people of diverse ethnic backgrounds and personalities. **Team-spirited.**
- **Highly creative / innovative; design / develop / implement capital improvement projects** (up to **$2.5 million**) which **reduce costs, accelerate production**, and **increase profitability**.
- Superb **time management** abilities. **Career-** and **results-oriented.** Held **Top Secret/SBI Clearance.**

## EDUCATION

KELLER GRADUATE SCHOOL OF MANAGEMENT – Phoenix, Arizona
**MBA with Distinction**

UNITED STATES NAVAL ACADEMY – Annapolis, Maryland
**Bachelor of Science in Mechanical Engineering**
Successfully completed **EIT Exam**

## PROFESSIONAL EXPERIENCE

PHILLIPS INTERNATIONAL 1990 – Present

**Maintenance Superintendent**, Tyler, Texas (November 1996–Present)

- Direct, supervise, and motivate team of 17 electricians, pipe fitters, carpenters, and machinists.
- Plan, schedule, and direct maintenance operations; ensure continuity in power/production and mill operations, functionality of equipment, and strategic inventory control to prevent downtime; operate within prescribed annual budget of $1.7 million.
- **Design, develop, and implement capital improvement projects** to **reduce costs** and **improve profitability**.
- **Established/implemented/conducted Employee Training Program; significantly increased personnel knowledge of plant's mechanics** and **safety in the workplace.**

312

**Combination.** *Ann Klint, Tyler, Texas*

This individual was looking for a "plant management position." He had "substantial experience in production and plant maintenance, but limited experience in overall plant maintenance." The

**MATTHEW T. ANDREWS** **Page Two**

PHILLIPS INTERNATIONAL (Continued)

**Maintenance Supervisor**, Superior, Arizona (October 1993–November 1996)

- Supervised maintenance crew of 12; managed production, operations, and inventory of entire plant.
- Established and efficiently managed $2 million annual budget.
- Conducted safety training program; ensured compliance with OSHA, MSHA, EPA regulations.
- **Designed, developed, and implemented pumping system** for solar salt production which **reduced costs by $50,000 per month** and **increased production by 30 tons per hour**.

**Project Engineer**, Superior, Arizona (February 1992–October 1993)

- Designed, developed and installed capital improvement projects.
- Responsible for **complete installation of plastic membrane liners** in solar ponds which **drastically reduced brine costs** and resulted in **$100,000 savings annually**.

**Project Engineer**, Kansas City, Kansas (April 1990–February 1992)

- **Designed, established, and implemented capital improvement projects of up to $2.5 million** from conceptualization through completion.
- **Replaced obsolete steam boilers with state-of-the-art equipment**; resulted in **significant natural gas savings**.

UNITED STATES NAVY 1982 - 1990
**Lieutenant / Warfare Officer / Quality Assurance Officer**

Advanced to rank of **Lieutenant / Antisubmarine Warfare Officer** directly responsible for operation, planning, maintenance, and security of a nuclear-powered attack submarine and training, supervision, and safety of a division with 28 personnel. Served as **Qualified Officer of the Deck / Ship's Duty Officer; assumed total responsibility of ship** during Captain's absence.

- **Devised/implemented Quality Assurance System; authored/implemented QA program** and **safety procedures for the entire ship.**
- **Implemented ship's Radiological Control Program**; managed the chemistry control of the ship's nuclear power plant.
- Directed all mechanical and electrical operations of Sonar, Fire Control, and major mechanical systems (nuclear pumps, valves, turbines, generators, and reactor).

♦ ♦ **Professional References Furnished On Request** ♦ ♦

crucial section is the Areas of Expertise, for it is here that a reader is best able to infer whether the candidate has the skills for the targeted goal. The writer uses boldfacing to call attention to key experience, skills, personal traits, and achievements. Center-alignment points to the MBA.

# Daniel D. Schumm

805 South County Line Road
Hebron, Indiana 46341 (219) 996-6110

## Objective

Production Management position that would utilize my Total Quality Management and self-directed workforces to strengthen a company's operations that values and rewards results.

## Professional Experience

**Production Supervisor/ISO 9001 Certified Internal Auditor** 05/99-Present
*ABC Medical Packaging*, Chicago, Illinois ♦ Responsibilities: Supervise and manage $20^{+}$ nonunion employees for the Lamination, Coating, Printing, Slitting and Converting Departments; Practice ISO 9001, SPC, and TQM to maintain quality standards; Evaluate productivity to determine efficiency and utilization levels (standard vs. actual); Coordinate and implement computerized specifications to maintain constant quality; Review defect summaries; Develop teams to control safety, quality, productivity, and scrap levels; and Screen, hire, train, and terminate employees ♦ Specialized Training: Basic Flexography Seminar, *Fox Valley Technical College*, 05/99; and CPR Training Certificate, Red Cross, 05/99-Present.

**Shipping/Receiving and Production Supervisor** 05/99-05/99
*XYZ Food Service International,* Chicago, Illinois ♦ Responsibilities: Supervised and managed $15^{+}$ union employees; Received, filled, and distributed material orders to internal production departments; Developed and implemented SPC program; Designed and scheduled employees to perform daily cycle count; and Reduced internal material order delivery times by 200%.

**Operations Supervisor/Team Leader** 05/99-05/99
*ABC Foods Corporation,* Chicago, Illinois ♦ Responsibilities: Supervised and managed $20^{+}$ union employees for the Slice Pak Department; Produced daily production schedule; Reviewed inventory levels and properties; Implemented TQM and self-inspection programs to maintain quality standards; Increased finished product levels by 10%; Reduced reject levels by 5%; and Screened, hired, trained, and terminated employees ♦ Specialized Training: Ergonomics Seminar, *Northwestern University*, 05/99; Leading Effective Teams, *ABC Foods Corporation*, 05/99; Manufacturing Process Control, *ABC Foods Corporation*, 05/99; Total Quality Management, *ABC Foods Corporation*, 05/99; and Basic Management, *ABC Foods Corporation*, 05/99.

**Owner** 05/99-05/99
*Painting and Remodeling Services,* Merrillville, Indiana ♦ Responsibilities: Developed and implemented business and financial plan; Marketed sales area; Supervised, trained, and managed $2^{+}$ employees for project sites; and Maintained safety and quality.

## Education

**Bachelor of Science (Industrial Technology)** 05/99-05/99
*Ball State University,* Muncie, Indiana.

**Diploma** 05/99-05/99
*Merrillville High School,* Merrillville, Indiana. Vocation: College Preparatory.

## References

Furnished upon request.

**313**

**Combination.** *Susan K. Schumm, Hebron, Indiana*

Large bold type makes the name, section headings, job titles, and Education information easy to read at a glance. Italic is used for the names of employers and educational institutions.

## JEFFREY J. KUTIN

323 West 47th Street ▪ New York, New York 00000
Phone: (000) 000-0000


**PROFILE:**

Sixteen year career in the Culinary Arts with experience in administrative and management positions. Knowledge of food preparation and food services management. Skills include:

- Restaurant Conceptualization/Design
- Front/Back of the House Operations
- Catering & Banquet Services
- Food & Beverage Control
- Menu Development
- Cost & Inventory Control

**EXPERIENCE:**

**Supervisor** - Shaklee Corporation, New York, NY ▪ 5/95 - Present
Total operational responsibility including P&L, marketing and promotion of full product line, servicing over 100 customers. Provide management training for business builders (distributors). Utilize Windows and Easy Manager for ordering and inventory control applications.

**Executive Chef/Administrator** - Wonderland Garden Cafe, Springfield, NY ▪ 2/94 - 2/95
Conceptualized, opened and oversaw total operations for fine dining facility offering full lunch and dinner service, and catering of special events. Developed restaurant theme, purchased all supplies and developed menu. Managed personnel, ordering and inventory control.

**Executive Chef/Administrator** - Beverly's Cuisine, New York, NY ▪ 12/94 - 5/95
Opened fine dining facility, including kitchen design and operations. Responsible for all front of the house operation.

**PRIOR EMPLOYMENT:**

**Executive Chef** - John Smith's Restaurant, Garden, NY ▪ 4/92 - 2/94

**Kitchen/Restaurant Manager** - The Knotty Garden Restaurant, Harvard, NY ▪ 6/91 - 4/92

**Executive Chef/Sous Chef** - Bailey's Restaurant, Silver Lake, NY ▪ 12/90 - 6/91

**Sous Chef** - Malcom John's Inn, Crystal Lake, NY ▪ 9/88 - 12/90

**Broiler Cook** - The Lodge at Briarcliff, Briarcliff, NY ▪ 10/86 - 9/88

**Kitchen Manager** - The Knotty Garden Restaurant, Harvard, NY ▪ 2/82 - 10/83

**Line Cook** - Irondequoit Town Lounge, Irondequoit, NY ▪ 3/80 - 2/82

**Baker/Doughmaker** - Bentley Bagel Shop, Bentley, NY ▪ 2/80 - 3/81

**EDUCATION:**

Business Management, 1989 - City College of the Finger Lakes, Finger Lakes, NY
Automated Supply Management Certificate, 1984 - US Navy "A" School, Malden, MS
Food Service Program, 1983 - Harrison County BOCES, Harrison, NY
General Education Diploma, 1983 - New Valley High School, New Valley, CT

**MILITARY SERVICE:**

**Storekeeper (Third Class)** - United States Navy, Automated Supply Management, New Valley, CT
Obtained an Honorable Discharge

**- References Furnished Upon Request -**

**314**

**Combination.** *Betty Geller, Elmira, New York*

This Chef/Food Service Professional wanted to move into an executive-level position. The Profile shows his varied skills. Administrative positions he has held are in boldface under Experience.

190 River Drive
Ann Arbor, Michigan 48100
(810) 995-1234

# STEVE J. CHAMBERS

## SUMMARY OF QUALIFICATIONS

- Well organized, results oriented individual
- Developed extensive troubleshooting and problem-solving skills
- Over four years experience as a flight operations specialist
- Proven written and oral communication skills
- Ability to prioritize, delegate, and motivate

## SOFTWARE EXPERIENCE

- WordPerfect
- Lotus 1-2-3
- dBase
- Excel
- DrawPerfect
- Quattro Pro

## PROFESSIONAL EXPERIENCE

- Kept track of flight records for over 600 pilots and provided on-time notification of crews for flights.
- Monitored pilot legality under Part 121 of Federal Aviation regulations.
- Entered records accurately on computer system utilizing Excel computer program.
- Served as liaison between upper management and crew.
- Set up communications network.
- Set up, operated, and maintained communications security system.
- Conducted military courses and evaluated progress.
- Controlled the flow of traffic operations occurring during the day and night by providing clearances and weather reports.
- Compiled and processed log books and flight records quickly and accurately.
- Trained and supervised personnel, emphasizing safety procedures.
- Developed excellent troubleshooting and problem-solving skills.
- Performed data entry duties using dBase and Quattro Pro.
- Organized special projects for the office.

## WORK HISTORY

**Supervisor** 1995-Present
GENERAL INTERNATIONAL AIRWAYS, Ypsilanti, Michigan

**Systems Integration Officer/Second Lieutenant** 1993-Present
NATIONAL GUARD, 134th SIGNAL BATTALION, Shelby, Michigan

**Crew Scheduler** 1994-1995
GENERAL INTERNATIONAL AIRWAYS, Ypsilanti, Michigan

**Flight Operations Specialist** 1989-1993
NATIONAL GUARD, 38th AVIATION REGIMENT, Grand Rapids, Michigan

**Office Assistant** 1988-1993
ACADEMIC AFFAIRS, UPPER MICHIGAN UNIVERSITY, Howell, Michigan

## EDUCATION

SIGNAL OFFICERS BASIC SCHOOL, Atlanta, Georgia
**Graduated** July 1994
*Courses of Note:* Communication Networks/Telecommunications • Automation/Electronics

UPPER MICHIGAN UNIVERSITY, Howel, Michigan
**B.S. in Aviation Management** April 1993
*Courses of Note:* Aircraft Maintenance I & II • Flight Operations I & II • Aviation Law and Insurance • Aviation Ground Instruction • Aircraft Management • Aviation Safety, Accident Investigation, and Training • Aviation Maintenance, Operation, and Management • Aviation Industry Regulations

315

**Combination.** *Christina M. Popa, Adrian, Michigan*

A distinctive feature of this resume for a Supervisor/Flight Operations Specialist is the placement of Summary of Qualifications and Software Experience in parallel columns to save vertical space.

# SARAH Z. GRAINGER

6000 Suite Road
Indianapolis, IN 46202
(600) 222-2222

## JOB TARGET ♦ PRODUCT MANAGEMENT

## PROFESSIONAL HIGHLIGHTS

CREATIVE FOODS UNLIMITED — Prospect, IA

***Quality Assurance Supervisor*** — 1995 - Present

- Oversee and monitor all production and processing phases of a variety of canned vegetable products to meet strict FDA and Company regulatory standards
- Maintain SPC through data bases generated to produce statistical documentation
- Supervise, delegate responsibilities, monitor performance, and participate in performance reviews of Laboratory Technicians and Quality Assurance Assistant

***Purchasing Manager*** — 1995 - Present

- Directly responsible for approving all purchase orders for goods and services
- Act as liaison between suppliers and Director of Purchasing in supplying blanket purchase orders

***Safety Coordinator*** — 1995 - Present

- Promote employee safety through informative meetings with employees on a periodic basis to discuss preventative maintenance techniques
- Update operational manuals based upon OSHA standards, Company regulations, and employee feedback

RESTAURANT FOODS LTD. — Australia

***Professional Intern*** — 1994

- Researched and tested product design and development with modified atmosphere packaging to extend shelf life of perishable/refrigerated products
- Thoroughly researched and determined waste management discrepancies identified through logistics and production departments
- Quickly became acclimated to international surroundings and became familiar with unique forms of communication and lifestyle of citizens

## EDUCATION

*Bachelor of Science in Food Science*
Harbor Bay University • Harbor, IA • May 1995

*Foreign Student Exchange*
Bishop's University • Australia • 1994

## MEMBERSHIPS & HONORS

*Institute of Food Technologists • Member*
*Food Science Club • Alumnus*
National Honor Society
Rotary Club Award • Recipient
Leadership & Service Award • Recipient

*References Available Upon Request*

316

**Chronological.** *Betty Callahan, Kalamazoo, Michigan*

This resume is easy to read because of large bold type in the name, goal, and headings; bold italic for the job titles; and just italic for some Education data and selected Membership data.

**RICHARD S. HASSELL**
14 Dorett Drive
Wappingers Falls, New York 12590
(914) 462-8178

---

**Operations Manager** Oversee the operation and procedural routine of air conditioning/refrigeration supply warehouse in Netherlands Antilles, utilizing over twenty-four years direct experience in the installation and repair of commercial/industrial equipment. Diversified background encompasses inventory control, equipment maintenance, technical training and staff supervision.

***HIGHLIGHTS of QUALIFICATIONS***

* Readily transcend cultural/language barriers; native Dutch Antillian
* Multi-lingual; fluent in English, Dutch and local dialect of Papiomento
* Dependable, self-motivated, mature, focused and persistent
* Ability to oversee large projects and follow through to completion
* Strong initiative in decision-making and assumption of responsibilities

***PROFESSIONAL EXPERIENCE***

**AIR CONDITIONING & REFRIGERATION ENGINEER**
*Johnson Controls,* White Plains, NY (1995-Present)
- Install and service A/C equipment in northern and southern tier Westchester County office buildings
- Provide training on equipment installation and maintenance to refrigeration technicians
- On-call for 24-hour emergency response

**AIR CONDITIONING/REFRIGERATION SUPERVISOR**
*Turbo Associates,* Syosset, NY (1981-1995)
- Supervised the set up and installation of large and small A/C & Refrigeration units
  - Periodically inspected all job site
- Streamlined operation by installing automatic controls to reduce service calls to job site
  - Increased efficiency facilitated reduction in manpower requirements from 3 to 1 technician
  - Effectively reduced labor costs by approximately $100,000 annually
- Maintained stock inventory of parts and materials required for customer service
- Developed proposals of small unit installation jobs (5 to 10 ton units)
- Provided 24-hour on-call emergency response; assessed situations and took necessary remedial action

**SENIOR PLANT SUPERVISOR**
*G.E.B.E. Water Plant,* St. Maarten, Netherlands Antilles (1977-1981)
- Monitored control room of government operated water treatment plant
- Maintained all equipment; repaired condensers; rebuilt pumps
- Implemented emergency response plan during mechanical failures, activated emergency response team

***CERTIFICATION/LICENSES***

Proper Refrigerant Practices (US EPA Program)

***PROFESSIONAL ASSOCIATION***

Refrigeration Service Engineers Society

***EDUCATION/TRAINING***

State University of New York at Farmingdale (1981-1983)
Advanced Air Conditioning & Refrigeration Policies
Basic Thermodynamic Concepts
Refrigeration & Air Conditioning Controls
Elements of Electricity I & II

**317**

**Combination.** *Marian K. Kozlowski, Poughkeepsie, New York*

This person is not a Supervisor now but had this role for 18 years. In his original resume, Education came first. The writer made the profile and Highlights and overhauled everything.

## ARLO HAMBLIN

31 Gerry Drive
Belleville, Illinois 62221
(618) 555-2323

### SUMMARY OF QUALIFICATIONS

Seven years of distinguished military service in law enforcement positions. A Certified Customs Officer with additional training in field operations and security activities for high-profile military functions. Hold a Top Secret SSBI clearance (effective March 1995). Strong knowledge of general police duties including:

| | | |
|---|---|---|
| Individual/Team Movement | Target Detection/Engagement | Challenges/Identification |
| Search Procedures | Evidence Protection | Resource/Protection Programs |
| Traffic Control/Operations | Security/Emergency Response | Defense Management |
| Antiterrorism | Threat Identification | Dispatching |

### PROFESSIONAL EXPERIENCE

United States Air Force, 1988-Present

**ELITE GUARD SUPERVISOR** (1993-Present): Control entry for three centralized headquarters. Lead security response teams in support of a unified command, major command, and a field operating agency. Perform personal security for distinguished visitors and key personnel. Screen and process more than 5000 workers and visitors daily. Provide customer service and headquarters-related information to visiting military and civilian personnel.

- Performed major command-level ceremonies including the visits of the Chief of Staff, French Air Force, and Secretary of Defense.
- Competitively selected to provide ceremonial support during the visit of the Secretary of the Air Force; earned an Air Force Commendation Medal, a Certificate of Appreciation from the security police commander and numerous individual commendations for outstanding job performance.
- Selected to train others on a new automated entry control and alarm system.

**LAW ENFORCEMENT SPECIALIST** (1988): Investigated offenses involving vehicular and pedestrian traffic. Protected personnel, equipment, and facilities. Monitored radio communications and provided routine vehicle patrol. Performed operator maintenance on assigned equipment, materials, and vehicles. Apprehended and detained suspects; accepted custody of military personnel apprehended by other agencies. Dispatched law enforcement and security patrols to incidents involving priority resources.

- Ranked in the top 2% among peers; hand-picked by specific VIP military officials to lead anti-terrorist and security activities at an elite post in Germany. Earned an Air Force Commendation Medal and numerous letters of appreciation from traveling dignitaries.
- Provided convoy security over unsecured roads to ensure successful delivery of critical resources during a vital humanitarian relief effort in the Middle East. Earned an Air Force Achievement medal.

### EDUCATION/SPECIALIZED TRAINING

- B.A. Degree, Management/Communications, Concordia University Wisconsin, Mequon, Wisconsin
- A.A. Degree, Criminal Justice, Community College of the Air Force (pending results of CLEP test)
- Antiterrorist Driving and Surveillance Detection Course, International Training Incorporated
- Distinguished Graduate, Air Base Ground Defense Training, Fort Dix, New Jersey
- CPR/BLS Instructor

REFERENCES AVAILABLE UPON REQUEST

**318**

**Combination.** *John A. Suarez, Troy, Illinois*

Centered headings over a full horizontal line make it easy to size up the design of this resume. The qualifications in columns can be easily altered to adapt this resume to a specific job target.

# CHRISTOPHER S. JADEN

*369 Harborside Drive • Lakeland, Florida 33801 • (941) 555-5555*

## SUMMARY OF QUALIFICATIONS

- Diverse experience in warehouse operations management, truck fleet operations, and personnel management. Knowledge of DOT regulations and safety.
- Comprehensive understanding of design and redesign of manufacturing facilities; industrial operation of kilns and pneumatic discharge systems; hazardous material regulations (including spill recovery); and fleet fuel and preventive maintenance efficiencies.
- Ability to grasp needs in distinct areas of responsibility; exceptional interpersonal skills, including ability to effectively interact with all levels of clientele and staff. Team-oriented management philosophy with emphasis on boosting employee productivity.

## EMPLOYMENT EXPERIENCE

**DEHYDRATION SPECIALIST/SHIFT SUPERVISOR** - The Food Group, Inc., Davenport, Florida *1993-Present*

- Experienced in all aspects of food manufacturing including blending and packaging.
- Develop weekly employee schedules; cover staff shortages as necessary.
- Coordinate training of warehouse personnel in driving tractor/trailers.
- Develop job descriptions for warehouse personnel; assist in the formulation of policies/procedures manual.
- Assist warehouse personnel with cost-saving projects including organizing dispatch and traffic control.
- Request all raw materials from the warehouse for use in the production facility.
- Familiar with the guidelines and procedures of: Good Manufacturing Practices (GMP) and American Institute of Bakers (AIB).

**GENERAL MANAGER** - Pallet Providers, Dundee, Florida *1990-1993*

- Directly supervised all facets of the facility's operation.
- Oversaw all phases of the manufacturing process; formulated bids for large orders.
- Managed existing customer base and acquisitioned new accounts; led division through account acquisition from leading competitor.
- Accountable for all profit and loss variances.

**DRIVER TRAINER/EMERGENCY RESPONSE COORDINATOR** - ACH Transport, Dundee, Florida *1985-1990*

- Worked on team to determine specifications of tractors and trailers to be purchased.
- Coordinated Emergency Response Team activities including accident and air bag recovery.
- Developed new customer base in field.
- Organized accident follow-up procedures regarding retrieval of equipment and damage control.
- Coordinated mobile dispatch operations; trained inexperienced new tractor drivers.

**ASSISTANT STORE MANAGER** - One-Stop Convenience Corporation, Dundee, Florida *1985*

**PRODUCTION SUPERVISOR** - Pronto Manufacturing, Tampa, Florida *1982-1985*

## EDUCATION

Bachelor of Science - Business Administration and Management, University of Florida *1983*

## LICENSES AND CERTIFICATES

Operations Management/Supervision (80-hour course), University of South Florida *1986*
Class A CDL, All Endorcements
Certified in Forklift Operations and as a Front-End Loader

**319**

**Combination.** *E. René Hart, Lakeland, Florida*

Small type with adequate white space between sections and subsections makes the design easy to comprehend. Bold capital letters for the job titles in the Experience section also are "friendly."

# JEFFREY JONES

**4321 Bach Avenue – Portage, MI 49002**
**(616) 555-0101**

**QUALIFICATIONS:**

- ✔ Nine years successful supervisory and management experience.
- ✔ Strong interpersonal communication abilities, as well as highly-developed writing skills.
- ✔ Highly effective in promoting productive work environments with strong emphasis on team building, quality, and safety.
- ✔ Able to set and achieve short- and long-term goals while meeting strict deadlines.
- ✔ Proven commitment and vision with a sincere dedication to continuous improvement.
- ✔ Computer literate, including Microsoft Word, Excel, Word Perfect, and Lotus.

**EDUCATION:**

**BBA, General Business / Communications, 1995**
Davenport College, Kalamazoo, Michigan

Financed **100%** of my college education through part-time employment and loans.

**Additional Training:** Management by Objective (Certified); Hazardous Materials Management (Certified); Employee Relations and the Law; Sexual Harassment; Total Quality Management; Safety.

**EMPLOYMENT:**
8/87–Present

UNITED PARCEL SERVICE - Kalamazoo, Michigan
**Preload Supervisor** (Portage Center) - Train, schedule, and supervise second-shift preload team members. Act as liaison with dispatch operations personnel (6/93–Present). Selected achievements:

- Reduced misload frequency by **65%**, saving **$60,000** annually.
- Increased stop count by **15%**, generating annual savings of **$30,000.**
- Decreased start-up time by **30%** and saved **400+** work hours with new dispatch procedure idea.
- Selected from among 20 supervisors to act as **first respondent** to a hazardous material spill.

**Primary Supervisor** (Oshtemo Center) - Responsible for training, motivating, and delegating team members, as well as maintaining a safe work environment (6/91–5/93). Significant highlights:

- Reduced loading **3 hours per day**, producing **$32,000** in annual savings, by revamping system.
- Created safe awareness programs resulting in **100,000+** safe work days.
- Awarded **"Most Improved Center in the District."**

**Preload Supervisor** (Oshtemo Center) - Same as present (8/88–5/91). Selected accomplishments:

- Initiated new employee incentives which substantially **decreased tardiness** and **absences,** while concurrently **increasing motivation** and **team morale.**
- Selected as **1** of **40** professionals to act as **Information Guide** to internal and external VIPs.
- Led team to **lowest turnover rate** in the district.

4/89–6/93

**Varsity Baseball Coach** – Plainwell High School, Plainwell, Michigan
Responsible for teaching mechanics and developing players' capabilities. Notable achievements:

- Trained and led team to accomplish **3** conference and **1** district championship wins.

**320**

**Combination.** *Mary Roberts, Tarpon Springs, Florida*

Achievements in this resume are quantified whenever possible, but the quantities are made bold for emphasis. "The recently earned BBA degree is listed before 'Employment' also for emphasis."

**Jeffrey A. Geller RPh**
00000 Chestnut Ridge Road ▪ Elmira, New York 10000-0000
Phone: (000) 000-0000 ▪ Fax: (000) 000-0000

**PROFESSIONAL QUALIFICATIONS**

Well-qualified Supervising Pharmacist with a strong background in a retail environment. Proficient in establishing and maintaining excellent customer rapport. Knowledgeable in third-party billing (low rejection rate). Outstanding track record of contributions and achievements. Highlights include:

- Accurate/High-Volume Dispensing
- Advertising & Promotions
- Nursing Home/Hospice
- Budget Administration
- Inventory Control
- Computer Literacy

**EXPERIENCE**

**Supervising Pharmacist/Pharmacy Manager**
Kmart Corp., Anywhere, NY • 6/93-Present

Oversee Pharmacy Department including dispensing of prescriptions quickly and accurately without auxiliary staff, managing third-party plans (Medicaid/Medicare), ordering, maintaining appropriate inventory levels of prescription products, and interacting with wholesale drug companies. Create highly successful, no budget advertising for promotional purposes. Service Bentley Township Hospice Plan.

- Negotiated for and established four new third-party plans; one program implemented state-wide in all Kmart Stores.
- Set up and implemented District's first Computerized Accounts Receivable System.
- Consistently received Outstanding Performance Evaluations.
- Recipient of numerous Customer Care Awards.

**Supervising Pharmacist/Staff Pharmacist**
Fay's Drugs, Wantagh, NY • 9/90-6/93

Managed Pharmacy and dispensed approximately 400 prescriptions per day. Provided service to nursing homes and hospice care.

- Successfully maintained Store Level Accounts Receivable System.

**Registered Pharmacist**
Harry's Pharmacy, Bailey, NY • 9/88-12/89

Prepared, compounded and dispensed drugs and therapeutic devices from written or oral prescriptions.

**Post-Graduate Pharmacy Intern**
Fay's Pharmacy, Albany, NY • 3/88-8/88

**Full-Time Pharmacy Intern**
Jamestown Hospital, Jamestown, NY • 9/86-12/86

Prepared unit-dose medications, IV's/IV admixtures, mini-bags, TPN's, chemotherapy and oncologic drugs.

**Undergraduate Work Study**
Green Medical Center Hospital, Green, NY • 12/84-5/85

Nuclear Medicine Department. Extensive exposure to Radiopharmacy.

**EDUCATION/CREDENTIALS**

**Bachelor of Science in Pharmacy**
Hudson College of Pharmacy, Carmody, NY • 12/87

On-going Continuing Education in all phases of Pharmacology

New York State Licensed/Registered Pharmacist

**321**

**Combination.** *Betty Geller, Elmira, New York*

Bulleted qualifications emphasize areas of expertise. Apart from the separator bullets, bullets in the Experience section point to specific job achievements. Centered job titles are a snap to read.

# SALLY JEAN SEIVERS

5550 Montego Way #202
Indialantic, FL 32901
(407) 555-1212

## OBJECTIVE:

Reservationist/Customer Service position

## QUALIFICATIONS SUMMARY:

- Over 8 years experience in Hospitality field.
- Quick learner; promoted twice in 9 months at Hilton Suites Hotel.
- Computer literate utilizing WordPerfect, Lotus 1-2-3, and Computel Systems. Accurate 10-key numerics.

## EDUCATION:

**Bachelor of Science in Hospitality Management**, 4/90
University of Tampa, Tampa, Florida

## PROFESSIONAL PROFILE:

**Reservation Supervisor and Group Coordinator**, 1993 to 1995
Hilton Rialto Hotel, Melbourne, Florida

- Promoted from Front Desk Clerk to Front Office Supervisor in only three months.
- Promoted again from Front Office Supervisor to Reservation Supervisor in an additional six months.
- Perform guest check in and check out, handle cash and provide front office supervision.
- Assist guests and resolve all complaints and problems.
- Input future reservations and assemble group files.

**Front Desk Clerk**, Marriott Hotel, Bradenton, Florida, 1993

- Provide excellent guest services and ensure the upkeep of hotel as needed.

**Front Desk Clerk**, Holiday Inn, Tampa, Florida, 1992 to 1993

- Provide fast, friendly service, guest pick up, and prompt message relay.
- Maintain logs of guest Complementary breakfasts.

**Hospitality Internship**, Holiday Inn, Venice, Florida, 1990

- Hands on training in all hotel positions including: Housekeeper, Cook, Dishwasher, Bartender, Waitress, Cashier, Laundry, Front Desk Clerk, Night Audit, Shipping and Receiving.

**322**

**Combination.** *Laura A. DeCarlo, Melbourne, Florida*

The person in hospitality needed a resume fast. The writer stressed bullets, a large font, and some achievements. The person got an interview and from it a job as Assistant Hotel Manager.

## MITCH R. SMITHERS

1434 Hobart Avenue
Tigard, Oregon 97224

Home: (503) 599-3244
Work: (503) 344-9077

**OBJECTIVE**

Leadership position in a team-oriented manufacturing environment.

**PROFILE**

Twenty years of increasing responsibility as a front-line supervisor in high tech environments, including wafer fabrication, electro-mechanical assembly, test and cleanroom operations.

- Thoroughly familiar with TQM, JIT and ISO certification requirements.
- Demonstrated ability to facilitate improvements in quality, cost and customer relationships.
- Computer literate (Excel, Lotus 1-2-3, Word, Windows).
- Strong advocate of empowerment concepts.

**EXPERIENCE**

ADVO COMPUTER PRODUCTS OF AMERICA - Beaverton, Oregon

**SUPERVISOR II** (1992-Present)

Supervise manufacturing activities for multiple product lines and direct a labor force of 16 assemblers and technicians in an ISO 9002 certified facility. Build effective teams that work together to meet internal and external customer needs. Actively facilitate improvements in quality, cost control, safety and training.

- Achieved a "3" quality rating (on scale of 0-3) from a major customer for a period of three years.
- Successfully integrated TQM concepts by encouraging operators to understand and meet customer needs.
- Charter member of ISO 9002 plant team.
- Directed implementation of new product manufacturing and start-up operations.

MENCO CORPORATION - Aloha, Oregon

**MANUFACTURING SUPERVISOR** (1985-1992)

Supervised cleanroom (with 12-35 employees) in a wafer fab facility. Tracked quality, schedules and efficiency in the Wet Masking, Thin Films, Spin, Develop Check and Dry Mask areas.

- Built a highly productive manufacturing team.
- Reduced dummy wafer costs and increased yield in the Wet Masking area.
- Charter member of JIT team.

DELCO CORPORATION - Mountain View, California

**PRODUCTION SUPERVISOR / PRODUCTION LEAD** (1979-1985)

Supervised production crew of 12 and oversaw the manufacturing of audio recorders for radio and television studios. Provided operator training and ordered all needed parts.

- Worked closely with engineering staff to pilot new products.
- Consistently exceeded quality and production goals.

**SPECIAL TRAINING**

Zenger-Miller Frontline Leadership . . . Just-In-Time . . . ISO 9000 / 9002 . . . Quality Action Teams . . . General Business Management . . . Circle Facilitator Class . . . Problem Solving . . . Staff Supervision and Motivation.

**REFERENCES**

Provided upon request.

## 323

**Combination.** *Pat Kendall, Aloha, Oregon*

The pair of lines makes the contact information stand out. The Profile indicates knowledge, ability, computer literacy, and orientation toward helping others who can be helped.

# John Phillips

498 West North Street
Elmira, NY 00000
**(000) 000-0000**

**Objective:** Position in **Restaurant/Bar Management.**

**Experience:**

VIRGIN LEGEND ELKS CLUB — 1992 to Present
**Bar Supervisor**
Responsible for inventory ordering and control. In charge of booking and arrangements for banquets of up to 250 guests. Supervise 4 employees.

VALLEY CREEK COLLECTION AGENCY — 1991 to 1992
**Owner/Operator**
Performed personal collections. Established new accounts, handled all accounting/bookkeeping functions including billing. Handled marketing/P.R. requirements.

**Independent Broker** — 1990 to 1991
Brokered new and used electronic manufacturing equipment. Solicited new accounts, serviced new and existing international customer base.

BRADLEY'S HOMETOWN HOAGIES — 1989 to 1990
**Owner/Operator**
Handled all ordering, inventory, bookkeeping/payroll, marketing and advertising. Supervised 15 part-time employees.

BARRACUDA MANUFACTURING — 1987 to 1989
**General Manager**
Oversaw production, manufacturing, accounting, sales, and advertising for company specializing in brokerage of used/refurbished electronic manufacturing equipment. Supervised 30 employees.

DENNY'S RESTAURANTS — 1983 to 1987
**Manager/Training Manager**
Responsible for food/liquor inventory control, bookkeeping, ordering, sanitation control, and cash control. Supervised 55 employees and trained new employees.

BENTLEY CREEK, INC. — 1978 to 1980
**Internal Auditor**
Audited books and procedures of airport and municipal parking lots throughout the United States. Performed employee performance surveillance.

**Education:**

Valley Area Community College, Valley Port, NY
**Associates Degree in Accounting**

Penn State University, State College, PA
**Bachelors Degree in Business Administration**
Recipient, **Outstanding Leadership Award** - Penn State Student Government Association

**Affiliations:**

Board of Directors, VALLEY PORT MULTIPLE SCLEROSIS SOCIETY
**Secretary** - 1988 to 1990
**President** - 1990 to 1992

**References Available Upon Request**

**324**

**Chronological.** *Betty Geller, Elmira, New York*

This classic chronological format for an older worker begins with an objective and targets the "employment goal." The positions held are then indicated in descending chronological order.

# JUSTIN M. BROWNING

400000 Carol Dr.
Coffer, AL 00000
(000) 000-0000

**JOB TARGET ♦ PRODUCTION SUPERVISION**

## SUMMARY

- Over 18 Years Hands-On Experience in Welding Environment
- Strong Leadership and Supervisory Skills, Complimented by Mid-Western Work Ethic and Ability to Work Well With Others
- Knowledgeable of Production Data Entry (MRP)
- Experienced in Collaborating with Engineering, Production, Materials, and Purchasing Departments
- Proven Ability to Perform in an Efficient Manner in Diversified Settings to Complete Tasks in a Timely Manner

## PROFESSIONAL EXPERIENCE

**COLLECTION CORPORATION** — USA

*PRODUCTION WELDER* — *1992 - Present*

- Provide highest quality performance through various welding processes

*FABRICATION SUPERVISOR* — *1985 - 1992*

- Supervised, hired, trained, delegated responsibilities, and monitored performance of up to 20 welders and machine operators
- Managed six figure departmental supply budget on an annual basis
- Responsible for the purchase of all production machinery, including arranging for outside contractors to maintain equipment for optimum production
- Operated all machinery common to structural and plate steel fabrication

*CERTIFIED WELDER / ASSISTANT FOREMAN* — *1980 - 1985*

**QUALITY COMPANY** — Holland, MI

*PRODUCTION WELDER* — *1977 - 1979*

## CERTIFICATION & LICENSURE

*ANSI / AWS D1.1-94*
*ASME*
*Licensed Fork-Lift Operator*

## CONTINUED EDUCATION

*Employee Relations on a Supervisory Level*
*Welding Applications & Processes* • *Fabricators & Manufacturers Association*
*LAKE SUPERIOR COLLEGE* • Lake Superior, MI
*Engineering Technology Honor Student* • *1 Year Curriculum*

*References Available Upon Request*

**325**

**Combination.** *Betty Callahan, Kalamazoo, Michigan*

A resume for a past blue-collar Supervisor. It is friendly to read because of large, dark type; diamond bullets; uppercase letters; underlined headings; and center-aligned text toward the end.

# Terrence D. Townsend

5432 Concourse Street • Lodi, California 95240 • (209) 555-1212

***OBJECTIVE*** A position as Maintenance Supervisor.

***SUMMARY***
- Strong background in production-line maintenance supervision.
- Goal oriented with excellent oral and written communication skills.
- Formulate and deliver new ways to increase quality, productivity and reduce costs.
- Skilled on WordPerfect, Windows, CC Mail, VAX 3.1, knowledge of Lotus 1-2-3.

***EXPERIENCE AND ACCOMPLISHMENTS***

**SUPERVISION**
- Pro-actively supervised and motivated up to 50 maintenance employees.
  - Encouraged team efforts and collaboration to attain goals and objectives.
- Monitored mechanical job progress adhering to specifications and completion deadlines.
- Developed and implemented Corrective Active Teams to **improve run efficiencies** and raw material waste on All Bran line by 18%.
- Redesigned machinery to **decrease overweights** on individual line by 24%.
- Prepared, planned and scheduled preventative maintenance during equipment downtime to maximize personnel work hours.

**MECHANICAL WELDING AND FABRICATION**
- Fabricated and converted upgraded custom conveyance system from 100% mechanical machine to PLC controlled package feeder and idler.
  - **Saved over $60,000 annually** in down time on one machine alone.
- Reduced consumer complaints by designing and fabricating parts to run new wax liner.
  - **Saved over $1 million** by eliminating wax purchase and increasing sales.
- Headed task force to brainstorm methods of increasing maintenance efficiency.
- Installed and removed machinery, operated cranes and heavy-duty forklifts.

**SAFETY**
- Trained in confined space entry and rescue, fire prevention and fighting, hazardous waste material handling and disposal, first aid CPR, and blood bourne pathogens.
- **Reduced lost-time accidents by 50%** in 1994 utilizing DuPont STOP Program.

***EMPLOYMENT HISTORY***

1981-present **KELLOGG COMPANY**, San Leandro

**Maintenance Supervisor** 1992-1995
Coordinate and supervise activities of maintenance personnel to assure preventive maintenance, breakdown repair, construction jobs, instrumentation and calibration are completed within budget.

**A-Level Maintenance Mechanic** 1981-1992
Acted as sole maintenance mechanic on night shift for this cereal manufacturer.

1980-1981 **Maintenance Mechanic • COCA COLA**, Oakland
Repaired, maintained, and troubleshot production facility equipment, utilizing welding, machining, blueprint reading, pipefitting, rigging, and fabricating skills.

***EDUCATION***
College of Alameda - Psychology, Alameda
San Leandro Adult Vocational School—Welding, Machine Technology, San Leandro

***ADDITIONAL TRAINING***
Alan Bradley —PLC 5 Basic Troubleshooting and Programming, Hayward
Zenger/Miller—Front Line Leadership, Kellogg's
American Management Association
- Management Skills for First Line Supervisors,
- Grievance and Communication Handling Skills, Sacramento

**326**

**Combination.** *Nancy Karvonen, Willits, California*

The parallel lines enclose part of the contact information, the Objective, and the Summary, clustering these items visually. Experience and Achievements are grouped under three categories.

# MATILDE KHAN

**114 Meadows Drive • Brooklyn, New York • 02222**
**Phone: (718) 222-4243 • E-mail: BMatt1@aol.com**

**SUMMARY**

- Nine years of hands-on and supervisory experience in the jewelry industry.
- Expertise in design, product development, appraisal, sales, and buying.
- Creative and artistic with superior attention to detail.
- Results-oriented leader; Self-motivated to produce high-level work.
- Extensive experience with gemstones and a talent for discerning quality.

**EMPLOYMENT**

**1991 to present**

**Parker Fine Jewelry Company,** East Islip, NY
**Product Development Supervisor**
- Develop new programs for national home shopping television shows.
- Coordinate product development for department that produces 75 to 100 designs per month.
- Supervise 5 Jewelry Designers and 3 Stone Setters.
- Selected to head seven member Color Product Development team.
- Use leadership role to encourage creativity among team members.
- Facilitate departmental communication and assist team with product-line decisions.
- Review artist designs to determine feasibility for production.
- Create new designs and present specifications to designers.
- Implement cost-cutting measures while maintaining quality products.

**1988 to 1991**

**Midtown Jewelry,** New York, NY
**Manager, Colored Stone Division,** Precious Gems Department
- Supervised and evaluated a team of 12 Lapidaries.
- Coordinated work flow between Lapidaries and Stone Setters.
- Negotiated prices and purchased colored stones.
- Used organizational methods that doubled the department's output.

*Previous Positions/Promotions:* Assistant to Diamond and Colored Stones Buyer, Assistant Shop Supervisor, Jeweler's Apprentice
- Crafted fine jewelry in 18 karat gold and platinum.
- Evaluated newly cut stones for proper shape and color quality.
- Estimated size, weight, and color specifications based on designer drawings and customer request.

**COMPUTERS**

- Proficient in Microsoft Word, Excel, Access, and PowerPoint.
- Knowledge of Lotus 1-2-3 and WordPerfect.
- Experience using commercial on-line services and the Internet.

**EDUCATION**

**Bachelor of Business Administration,** Major in Marketing
Brooklyn College, Brooklyn, New York, 1987

*Professional Courses:*

- Stone Setting - Polishing - Design - Casting - Identifying Gems

**327**

**Combination.** *Kim Isaacs, Jackson Heights, New York*

The writer made this resume as a 5-row, 3-column table without vertical lines. The first column is shaded; the third column has the main information. The second is the thin space between.

# Charles W. Xavier

000 Chicago Ave.
Chicago, IL 00000
(000) 000-0000

**Qualifications & Strengths**

Strong Communication Skills
Positive Rapport with Clients
Client Care Management
Supervisory Abilities
Detailed Documentation
TBI Injury

**Education**

APPLE VALLEY COMMUNITY COLLEGE
Apple Valley, IL
*Associate Degree of Nursing, May 1991*
*Practical Nurse Certification, May 1990*

**Employment**

APPLE VALLEY NURSING HOME, Apple Valley, IL
May 1991 - Present
***Nursing Supervisor/RN***
Supervise the residential care of up to 247 middle-age through elderly clients. Develop, coordinate, and implement client care management. Prepare and educate client for successful discharge from facility. Monitor, assess, and communicate client progress to attending physician on a periodic basis. Participate and collaborate in care planning meetings with departmental advisors, client, and family members. Traumatic Brain Injury Unit. Train, delegate responsibilities, and evaluate performance of 31 CNAs at variable times.

ELDERLY CARE CENTER
Blossom Village, IL, May 1989 - May 1991
***LPN***
Provided direct client care and maintained personal hygiene and safety of up to 12 diverse client caseloads. Supervised, delegated responsibilities, and monitored performance of up to 7 CNAs. Oversaw all phases of client care management.

MONOPOLY STORES
Apple Valley, IL, August 1985 - May 1989
***Supervisor/Customer Service Representative***
Responsible for the daily business operations including scheduling, training, and monitoring performance of service employees, cashiers, and baggers. Balanced and documented cash drawers on a nightly basis. Established positive relationships with customers to ensure satisfaction and encourage repetitive business.

**References**

Available Upon Request

**328**

**Combination.** *Betty Callahan, Kalamazoo, Michigan*

The information below the contact information either was or could be formatted in a 1-row, 3-column table. A vertical line is in the second column. Pressing Enter pushes the row downward.

**HARRIET R. JALETTE**
3333 Biloxi Boulevard
Biloxi, MI 00000
(000) 000–0000

**SUMMARY:**
Sixteen years experience in transportation with varied responsibilities including supervision/scheduling of drivers and dispatchers, and maintaining high quality customer service operations.

**PROFESSIONAL EXPERIENCE:**
Biloxi County Transit, Biloxi, MI — 1991–present
**Supervisor/Dispatcher**
- Hire, train, supervise and schedule drivers.
- Assure on-time performance of buses.
- Process reports and documentation.
- Troubleshoot driver and customer problems and concerns.
- Work closely with maintenance department.
- Establish and maintain excellent working relationships with local police departments, U. Miss. Transit, and the surrounding community.
- Recommend schedule adjustments.

Happy Trails Bus Lines, Tuscaloosa, AL — 1979–91
**Dispatcher** (1986–91)
**School Bus Trainer** (1987–91)
**School Bus Driver** (1979–91)
- Dispatched and trained school bus, transit and coach drivers.
- Operated mainframe computer system to post and update schedules and personnel data.
- Concurrently operated two-base radio station and telephone.
- Organized learning sessions for 60 drivers to obtain commercial licenses.
- Generated timely reports and documentation.

Triboro Bike Racers, Inc., Tuscaloosa, AL — 1982 & 83
- Responsible for creation and all aspects of operation of a BMX bicycle race track.

Parker's Department Store, Jacksonville, FL — 1960–65
**Head of Personnel**
**Advertising Bookkeeper**
- Managed all bookkeeping for the advertising departments of three separate stores.
- Hired and scheduled, processed time cards for one hundred employees.
- Coordinated store markdowns; entered inventory information on stock ledger.
- Operated PBX switchboard and teletype machines.
- Secretary to the Store Manager, all duties inclusive.

**ADDITIONAL EXPERIENCE:**
Held various secretarial and retail jobs while raising a family. — 1965–79

**EDUCATION:**
A.S. in Business, Jacksonville Commercial College, Jacksonville, FL — 1960
**Additional Training/Licensure:**
- Commercial Divers License with Passenger and Air Brake Endorsement.
- School Bus Trainer License
- Alcohol and Drug Testing Training for Supervisors
- MARTA, Passenger Assistance Techniques
- Understanding Issues of Sexual Harassment

**MEMBERSHIPS/ACTIVITIES:**
Treasurer, Alabama Association for National Bicycle League — 1984–91
Thirty years, Sunday School Teacher, Biloxi/Tuscaloosa/Jacksonville Baptist Churches

**329**

**Combination.** *Shel Horowitz, Northampton, Massachusetts*

Boldfacing aids the eye in spotting the name at the top, the section headings, the job titles, and the subheading, "Additional Training/Licensure." Grouping job titles avoids repetition of duties.

**MARY DUNN-HOWARD**

5643 S.W. Birch Lane | Tigard, Oregon 97223 | Ph: (503) 455-9077

**PROFESSIONAL PROFILE**

Qualified production supervisor with seven years of experience working in a high volume manufacturing environment. Pecple-oriented manager with ability to motivate, coach and build highly effective teams that *consistently exceed manufacturing goals.*

Broad experience in:

- Production crew hiring, training, discipline and performance evaluation
- Development of training programs; classroom and one-on-one training
- Safety and OSHA compliance issues
- Quality control and quality management circles

COMPUTER SKILLS - Microsoft Windows, Microsoft Publisher, Microsoft Office (Excel, Lotus 1-2-3, WordPerfect, Word and Access)

**EDUCATION**

PORTLAND STATE UNIVERSITY - Portland, Oregon
**Graduate, Supervisory Development Program** (1988)

TEXTRONIX TRAINING - Comprehensive training in employee supervision and production production management (44 classes)

**RELEVANT EXPERIENCE**

TEKTRONIX CORPORATION - Beaverton, Oregon (Seven years; 1980-88)
**Production Supervisor / Lead Trainer / Operator - Wafer Fab**
Hired as operator and gained promotions to trainer, lead trainer and production supervisor. *As production supervisor:*

- Directed production operations in the wafer fab area.
- Hired, trained, supervised, motivated and disciplined 18-27 employees.
- Led a Quality Circle group.
- Produced training manuals and provided training for operators and engineering technicians.
- Acted as head of Safety Committee and taught safety awareness courses.
- Received superior performance reviews in all areas.
- Consistently met or exceeded all production goals.

AUTO BODY PLUS - Hillsboro, Oregon (Seven years; 1990-Present)
**Business Manager**
Manage business operations of auto collision repair business and handle all decision-making related to financial management, accounting, budgeting and capital equipment expenditures.

- Supervise clerical and detail staff; hire, discipline and terminate employees.
- Ensure company compliance with all OSHA and DEQ requirements.
- Function as liaison between SAIF Corporation and OACA to facilitate staff education in loss prevention and safety awareness.

**REFERENCES**

Provided upon request.

**330**

**Combination.** *Pat Kendall, Aloha, Oregon*

A scannable resume that is not ugly. A resume for scanning should not have bold characters because they "touch." Extra letter spacing was added to bold job titles to make them scannable.

# CLARK M. SMITHERS

One Maynard Avenue • Portland, Oregon 97256 • (503) 246-5555

***Production Supervision / Production Planning***
***Materials & Inventory Management***

**PROFESSIONAL PROFILE**

Over 13 years of combined experience in production supervision, team building, inventory control, production planning, forecasting and quality management. Hands-on experience in estimating job costs, planning projects for manufacturing, and scheduling/troubleshooting job shop operations.

- Extensive experience in traffic management, including domestic heavy haul and air/ocean exporting.
- Analytical problem solver with strong mechanical aptitude.
- Thoroughly familiar with Just-In-Time principles.
- Fair-minded supervisor with good sense of humor.

**EXPERIENCE**

KINGSTON MANUFACTURING - Hillsboro, Oregon
*Sawmill equipment manufacturer*

**PRODUCTION SUPERVISOR** (7/90-Present)

Coordinate production operations; supervise employees, prioritize production requirements and manage inventory. Hire, train, motivate and evaluate production crews. Provide inventory forecasts and estimate inventory requirements. Work closely with staff in the engineering, manufacturing, purchasing, sales and accounting departments.

Additionally responsible for all traffic management functions; negotiate rates and schedule truck shipping and exporting (including shipments to Germany, South America, Australia and New Zealand). Developed in-house system for paperwork processing.

- Created programs to streamline purchasing, inventory control, warehousing and shipping/receiving.
- Reduced department overhead, while successfully maintaining previous production levels.
- Set up product mix spreadsheets that reduced inventory requirements and substantially cut delivery times.
- Improved department morale by promoting a positive work environment.

**PRODUCTION PLANNER** (8/81-7/90)

Estimated labor and material requirements. Requisitioned materials and maintained inventory records. Worked with master scheduler to coordinate MRP functions. Responsible for monitoring and troubleshooting individual production projects.

**EDUCATION**

PORTLAND COMMUNITY COLLEGE - Portland, Oregon
Associate of Arts (1981)

CONTINUING EDUCATION
- MRP
- Computer Operations
- Supervisory Skills

**AFFILIATIONS**

Member, APICS

331

**Combination.** *Pat Kendall, Aloha, Oregon*

An easy-to-read resume because of ample white space, lines enclosing the contact information, centered areas of expertise, underlined side headings, bold job titles, and controlled line spacing.

**STUART CLEMENSON**
**70 Hartley Court**
**Smithley, NJ 00000**
**(111) 111-1111**

## PROCESSING SUPERVISOR

Highly skilled, resourceful processing supervisor with eight years of experience in the processing field. Reputation for "can-do" attitude, expert problem-solving abilities, and commitment to producing quality results. Background includes compound preparation for high-profile products, including Clorox 2 Liquid Detergent; Colgate, Aim, and Arm & Hammer Toothpaste; and Rave Hair Conditioners. Extensive experience includes:

- New Product Line Batching and Start-Ups
- Chemicals / Reactions / Potential Dangers
- Mathematical Calculations / Conversions
- Chemical Pre-Weighing / CAS Numbers
- Laboratory Skills
- Computer Batching
- Equipment Operation and Repair
- Inventory Control
- Staff Supervision and Training
- Safety Requirements

## PROFESSIONAL EXPERIENCE

**Q.R.S. PHARMACEUTICAL**, Smithley, NJ — 1986 - Present

**PROCESSING SUPERVISOR** (1990 - Present)

Presently manage two 12-hour compound processing shifts for this major contract packer. Selected to oversee all functions related to production of Clorox 2 liquid detergent, including operation and maintenance of six 10,000 gallon storage tanks, two 10,000 gallon mixing tanks, and four 10,000 gallon chemical tanks.

***Production***
Regularly reviewed production schedules with plant manager, scheduling manager, and mechanics supervisor. Obtained all required materials and produced bleach in 10,000 gallon batches (up to 100,000 gallons daily) by deadline.

***Set-Up and Modifications***
Played critical role in developing processing systems and designing equipment layout for production of new Clorox product. Received recognition from Clorox for role in successful start-up. Assisted with two other formulation changes, and resolved major foaming problem by uncovering formulation error and making adjustments.

***Client Relations***
Viewed as key liaison with Clorox for eight years. Established credibility and developed high level of trust, negating the need for company representatives to be on-site. Maintained daily contact with Clorox representatives regarding production and scheduling issues.

***Inventory***
Maintained responsibility for safely storing 80,000 gallons of liquid chemicals and 50,000 lb. of dry chemicals. Ordered materials and scheduled up to five weekly deliveries.

***Supervision / Training***
Supervised three chemical compounders, insuring accuracy and productivity. Conducted regular evaluations. Oriented and trained new hires on an individual basis and provided on-going instruction on processing changes.

***Equipment Operation, Maintenance, and Repair***
Operated, maintained, and repaired positive displacement pumps, centrifugal pumps, stick pumps, eductors, air-operated and manual valves, and mixers. Rebuilt / repaired $40,000-$50,000 pumps and mixer motors.

**FORMER POSITIONS at Q.R.S. Pharmaceutical included:**

**CHEMICAL COMPOUNDER** (1988 - 1990)
**ASSISTANT WAREHOUSE CONTROLLER / FORKLIFT OPERATOR** (1987 - 1988)
**LABORER** (1986 - 1987)

## ACTIVITIES

Racing Crew Chief (NASCAR modified cars), Sands Township, NJ
Racing Manager, Shore Metric Car Care, Lewiston, NJ

332

**Combination.** *Rhoda Kopy, Toms River, New Jersey*

This resume has the "look" of an executive resume because of smaller print, narrower margins, more skills to indicate, more experience to list, and an upward career path within a company.

**Evelyn King** *(304) 555-0444 - Work*

*1234 First Avenue • Belle, WV 25015 • (304) 555-8883 - Home*

**SKILLS OVERVIEW**

- Ten years' experience in information systems management
- Over 20 years' experience with computer operations, including:
  - » IBM AS/400 Model D70 » IBM PCs and Applications
  - » IBM 4341-2 operating under CICS, NCP, VTAM, OS/VS
- Highly skilled at streamlining information processing operations, reducing administrative costs, and increasing reporting efficiency
- Results oriented with a reputation for reliably meeting deadlines
- Excellent at coordinating projects from inception through implementation
- Self-disciplined team player with outstanding organizational skills
- Highly ethical, consistently productive, and even-tempered

**EMPLOYMENT HISTORY**

***Data Center Supervisor*** 1986-Present

WEST SERVICES, INC., Belle, West Virginia

*Responsibilities*:
- Manage systems to ensure quality and timely distribution of reports
- Troubleshoot and monitor computer operations to reduce downtime
- Manage time-sensitive check runs of over $1 million weekly
- Hire, train, and supervise computer operators and data entry personnel

*Accomplishments:*
- Developed and maintain procedure manuals and training models, detailing steps necessary for accurate completion of 10-15 separate processes
- Initiated centralization of data processing from three regional offices
- Separated data entry and operations, markedly increasing efficiency

***Account Manager*** 1983-1985

DATA SYSTEMS Corporation, St. Albans, West Virginia
- Trained new users of Medic 80 software and Wordstar word processing
- Provided ongoing customer support to numerous medical office employees
- Position required excellent problem-solving and interpersonal skills

***System Operator*** 1968-1983

WALKER & COMPANY, Columbus, Ohio
- Began in data entry position and promoted to supervisor of 7 operators
- Processed payroll for 300, requiring a high degree of confidentiality
- Prepared and distributed daily, weekly, and monthly operations reports

**EDUCATION**

West Virginia Unviersity, Morgantown, West Virginia
Computer Science and Management major, with course work in systems analysis, programming, and COBOL.

IBM Shortcourse, Atlanta, Georgia
Data Processing Operations Management — In-depth course featuring hands-on applications through case studies.

**333**

**Combination.** *Barbie Dallmann, Charleston, West Virginia*

This person was going to move to another state, lacked a degree, and feared she couldn't get a comparable job. The writer stressed experience, skills, and achievements and put Education last.

**HOWARD T. HAMMER**
**116 Princess Lane • Barlow, NJ 66666**
**(555) 555-5555**

**MAINTENANCE TECHNICIAN / SUPERVISOR**
***Carpentry • Plumbing • Electric • Painting • Landscaping • Pool Maintenance***

Conscientious, energetic "go-getter" with extensive experience in all aspects of building maintenance. Repeatedly selected to rectify serious problems resulting from neglect. Excellent time management and interpersonal skills. Ability to prioritize, schedule, delegate, and supervise work. Reputation for being able to accomplish a large volume of work with minimal manpower.

***Committed to high standards of workmanship.***

## SKILLS

| | | |
|---|---|---|
| Interior / Exterior Painting | Bathroom / Kitchen Renovations | Flooring (Tile / Carpet) |
| Hot Water Heater Maintenance | Window / Door Replacements | Fuel / Oil Boiler Maintenance |
| Deck Construction | Parking Lot Maintenance | Fuse Panel Work |
| Landscaping / Lawn Care | Lock Rekeying / Key Cutting | Complete C.O. Preparation |

## EXPERIENCE

**MAINTENANCE TECHNICIAN / SUPERVISOR, Gary Galen Associates, Barlow, NJ** **1986 - Present**

Full responsibility for the maintenance of apartment complexes with 80-280 units. Schedule and perform preventive maintenance and repairs, and respond promptly to emergency situations. On call 24 hours a day, seven days a week. Promoted within two months to maintenance supervisor from maintenance apprentice.

**Diamond Club Apartments, Barlow, NJ (1990 - Present)**

Selected to initiate extensive repairs and renovations on a poorly-maintained 4-building, 80-unit complex of one and two bedroom upscale apartments. Supervise one laborer and effectively maintain a complex which would normally require a maintenance staff of four. Complete all work orders within 24 hours.

- Rebuilt 26 severely deteriorated decks within one year and performed major renovations on apartments: replacement of kitchen floors/subfloors and cabinets; bathroom remodeling, including sheetrocking and tile/tub replacement; and installation of new windows and entry doors.
- Increased occupancy rate to 98% by closely monitoring facility needs, immediately making repairs, and performing preventive maintenance.
- Reduced apartment turnover time from 4 days to 1-1/2 days, through effective scheduling and time management.
- Maintained 16 25,000 BTU boilers and drained heating system annually; maintained an Olympic-size pool (water testing, addition of chemicals, annual openings/closings).
- Drastically reduced the need for police intervention at complex through close monitoring.

**Golden Gardens, Stranton, NJ (1989 - 1990)**

Challenged to rectify serious safety and health hazards at this 4-building, 120-unit low-income complex.

- Dug up and resealed foundation, and installed all new plumbing on bottom floors to avoid further problems with flooding and leakage.
- Significantly improved appearance of property: performed landscaping, painted signs, and added courtyard lights.
- Assisted in resolving major roach infestation; worked closely with exterminating company to control problem.
- Maintained an Olympic-size pool.

**Cedar Apartments, Gordon, MD (1986 - 1989)**

Maintained a 280-unit, 5-building apartment complex. Developed a solid foundation in performing building maintenance and repairs, and gained customer service skills.

**OWNER / MANAGER, H. H. Painting, Dasto, MD** **1985 - 1989**

Established and built a busy part-time residential painting business, offering house painting (interior/exterior), driveway painting, and lawn painting. (Concurrently worked as a maintenance technician for Gary Galen Associates.)

- Earned an excellent reputation for quality work and developed a high repeat business.

**334**

**Combination.** *Rhoda Kopy, Toms River, New Jersey*

The parallel lines enclose and therefore call attention to areas of expertise and a profile. As items listed in columns, the skills selection can be altered to target the resume to a specific job opening.

**Jeffrey Mitchell**
252 Doremus Avenue
Teaneck, NJ 55555
Phone: (000) 000-0000 Pager: (000) 000-0000

---

**Job Objective:** Private chauffeur for a corporation, chief executive officer and/or family.

**Qualifications:**

- Available for on-call assignments 24 hours a day.
- Understanding of the protocols and diplomacy associated with a chauffeur's position.
- Confident working in stressful, often unpredictable or potentially dangerous situations.
- Safe driving record; trained in offensive and defensive driving techniques.

**Licenses:**

- Class A commercial driver's license
- New Jersey State handgun carry permit #10569327

**Employment:**

RYAN INVESTIGATIVE SERVICES, INC., Hackensack, NJ (1987 to present)
**Field Supervisor**, accountable for the protective transportation of corporate executives, precious metals, and large sums of currency.

EAGLE DETECTIVE AGENCY, Rochelle Park, NJ (1983 to 1987)
(Company merged with Ryan Investigative Services in 1987)
**Supervisor**, in charge of uniformed and plain clothes armed officers.

PRESTIGE LIMOUSINE SERVICE INC., Secaucus, NJ (1982 to present)
**Chauffeur** (part-time) for VIPs and special assignments. Clients included CEOs from Exxon, IBM, and Warner Communications as well as several television, stage and sports celebrities.

**Achievements:**

- Under New Jersey State cabinet clearance, handled entire perimeter traffic security for Governor Florio's inaugural ball, January 1990.
- Acted as security chauffeur under U.S. Secret Service clearance for Walter Mondale/Geraldine Ferraro presidential campaign in New Jersey, 1988.
- Awarded numerous commendations for outstanding performance in the tactful, quick and effective extinguishment of problems interfering with service or well-being to the client.

**Community Service:**

- Special Deputy Sheriff, Bergen County
- Deputy Constable, Hudson County

**Education:** Graduate of Parsippany High School (1980)
On-the-job training over eleven years in investigative work.

**Military:** U.S. Marine Corps Reserves (1986 to present). Status - Inactive.

335

**Combination.** *Melanie A. Noonan, West Paterson, New Jersey*

A resume for a Supervisor who is only a high school grad. However, with experience as a Marine and with executives and celebrities as clients, this Security Chauffeur has a fascinating career.

## GARRY LOGGINS

124 W. Crown
Mt. Vernon, Illinois 62864
Home: (618) 555-9444
Work: (618) 555-8999

### QUALIFICATIONS SUMMARY

- Ten years experience supervising human resources, customer service, and administrative support functions for a major utility company. Managed overlapping duties with strong results.
- Solid track record of developing cost-saving procedures and increasing internal and external customer satisfaction. Strive to maintain a cutting-edge knowledge of customer service issues.
- A dynamic leader and team development specialist who empowers staff to raise their own performance standards. Successfully coached rapidly changing departments facing redesigned work processes without interruption or decrease in quality.
- Actively involved in daily HR functions: training, recruitment, career development, compensation and benefits, personnel management, labor/community relations, and health/safety issues.

### PROFESSIONAL EXPERIENCE

ILLINOIS POWER, Mt. Vernon, IL 1985-Present

**CUSTOMER SERVICE SUPERVISOR/HR GENERALIST**, Mt. Vernon, IL (1990-Present)
Maintain a $350,000-$600,000 budget and personnel records for 90 employees via HRIS system. Review and forward EEO compliance reports. Coordinate employee drug testing and benefits administration. Test, screen, and interview entry-level applicants. Serve as local media liaison.

- Organized the first southern division meter reading workshop, leading to improved morale and overall performance.
- Guided the department to a top 10% company ranking in productivity and efficiency.

**CUSTOMER SERVICE SUPERVISOR**, Jacksonville, IL (1989)
Managed a staff of eight employees and a budget of more than $300,000.

- Redesigned meter reading routes; reduced the number of readers while increasing the number of meters read per hour by 20%, saving the company more than $50,000 per year.
- Designed a model program whereby employees would call and ask customers to rate or evaluate their work. This program was copied and used by many other officers.

**ASSISTANT CUSTOMER SERVICE SUPERVISOR**, Decatur, IL (1985)
Supervised bargaining unit personnel within the confines of a budget and union contract.

- Wrote a manual to standardize credit techniques, rules and policies for customer service reps.
- Redesigned meter reading routes; reduced the number of readers while increasing the number of meters read per hour by 20%, saving the company more than $100,000 per year.

### EDUCATION

- M.S. Degree, Industrial/Organizational Psychology, Radford University, Radford, VA (1984)
- B.S. Degree, Psychology, Southern Illinois University at Edwardsville (1982)

### CIVIC INVOLVEMENT

Member, Board of Directors, United Way; Past President of the Mt. Vernon Lions Club; Member of the Mt. Vernon Economic Development Commission; Member of the Chamber of Commerce; YMCA Coach; Boy Scout Pack Leader

REFERENCES AVAILABLE UPON REQUEST

**336**

**Combination.** *John A. Suarez, Troy, Illinois*

This person had done many Human Resources tasks but never had job titles that showed this experience, so the writer used HR buzzwords extensively in the Summary and job descriptions.

**ROBERT A. MAYES**
**4350 Ashley Drive**
**Tampa, Florida 33613**
**(813) 000-0000**

### *CAREER PROFILE*

***Former Baseball Professional*** with diverse background and extensive experience in the areas of **recruiting/scouting** professional players for major league baseball teams; **teaching, administration and coaching** at college and secondary school levels; and **product-oriented sales, marketing, and account management.** Offer progressive track record; excellent academic credentials; and demonstrated skills in public relations, supervision and written/oral communications. Highlights of qualifications include:

- Proven ability to assume challenging roles, perform in highly visible positions, work under pressure to meet deadlines, and produce strong sustainable results.
- Proactive leader with strengths in formulating and implementing administrative policies/procedures; establishing and achieving goals; identifying and resolving problem issues; and exercising prudent judgment.
- Excellent strategic planning and organizational skills; extremely conversant with directing/supervising staff, developmental programs, and promotional activities.
- Articulate communicator, adept in public speaking; able to captivate and impact large audiences of all people levels. Dynamic skill sets in recruiting, sales, and contract negotiations.
- Professional, conscientious work ethic and team player attitude; successful in motivating others and consensus building.
- Computer knowledge: DOS, Windows and Microsoft software.

### *EDUCATION / LICENSURE*

**M. Ed. Degree - Administration and Supervision** FLORIDA ATLANTIC UNIVERSITY - Boca Raton, FL

**B.S. Degree - Education** UNIVERSITY OF MISSOURI - Columbia, MO
Major: Physical Education / Minor: Physiology *Graduated with honors*

***Post Graduate Courses***

**Principles of Guidance** UNIVERSITY OF ILLINOIS - Champaign, IL
**Student Behavior and Control Seminar** BRADLEY UNIVERSITY - Peoria, IL

***Licensure***

State of Florida Teaching Certification (Inactive)
State of Florida Certification in Administration and Supervision (Jr. College/University level)

### *PROFESSIONAL EXPERIENCE*

**PROFESSIONAL MAJOR LEAGUE SPORTS**

***SCOUTING SUPERVISOR***
**Chicago White Sox / Central and Northern Florida**
**Oakland Athletics / State of Florida**
**Cleveland Indians / Florida, Georgia, Alabama**

Charged with scouting amateur baseball talent from colleges/universities, junior colleges and high schools. Acted as a liaison between professional teams and potential prospects, their parents and coaches. Key role in conducting contract negotiations and finalizing documentation for execution.

***Scouting Achievements***
→ Kurt Smith (initially Oakland A's; currently playing for Florida Marlins)
→ John Doe (pitcher - Oakland A's)
→ Mike Jones (major leagues pitcher - Cleveland, Chicago Cubs and Detroit Tigers)

337

**Combination.** *Diane McGoldrick, Tampa, Florida*

Dates in this resume were intentionally left out. The candidate was "part of the gray population" looking for employment and was four years from being eligible for Social Security. The writer

## ROBERT A. MAYES

**Page Two**

### *PROFESSIONAL EXPERIENCE* *(continued)*

**COLLEGE AND SECONDARY SCHOOL EDUCATOR / ADMINISTRATOR / COACHING**

***ASSISTANT PROFESSOR / HEAD BASEBALL COACH***
**Birmingham Southern College** - Birmingham, AL
**St. Leo College** - St. Leo, FL

Tenure at both colleges encompassed similar scope of responsibilities. Positions held included: ***Assistant Professor*** for undergraduate Professional Teacher Training Programs (taught courses in education and physical education), ***Student Academic Advisor***, ***Recruiter, Continuing Education Instructor*** (taught courses in administration and supervision), ***Interim Director of Student Housing*** and ***Head Baseball Coach***. Established outstanding coaching record at each college (Birmingham Southern: 224 Wins/59 Losses; St. Leo: 169 Wins/98 Losses).

***Achievements***
→ Spearheaded successful implementation and certification of physical education major program at St. Leo College
→ Southern States Conference Baseball Coach of the Year - 5 consecutive years (1979-1983) (Birmingham Southern)
→ Featured speaker Medalist Hall of Fame National Clinic (1980, 1981) (Birmingham Southern)
→ NAIA World Series / Ranked #4 in NAIA Final National Poll (Birmingham Southern - 1982)
→ NAIA World Series / Ranked #3 in NAIA Final National Poll (Birmingham Southern - 1979)
→ Pioneered first baseball team in history of St. Leo College to compete in NCAA Division II Post-Season Championships
→ Led St. Leo's baseball team to top ten rankings in the NCAA Division II for five consecutive years

***DIRECTOR OF TECHNICAL STUDIES***
**Peace Corps Venezuela at University of South Florida (Bayboro Campus)**

Trained Peace Corps volunteers for positions in teaching and coaching.

***DEAN OF STUDENTS***
**Lincoln-Way Community High School** - New Lenox, IL

Directed and coordinated policies and procedures related to student misconduct, discipline and control. Provided counseling and recommendations to ensure conformity to school regulations.

**SALES/MARKETING**

***ACCOUNT REPRESENTATIVE***
**Medalist Industries** - Milwaukee, WI

Handled account management combined with sales of sports equipment and athletic uniforms to sporting goods dealers, high schools and colleges/universities.

### *MILITARY*

U.S. Army - Honorable Discharge

### *PROFESSIONAL ORGANIZATIONS*

Florida Diamond Club
American Association of Professional Baseball Players

uses boldfacing to grab attention and sustain interest. Special right-arrow bullets point to achievements, which are clustered under separate subheadings. This is one of those resumes that should be read backward as well as forward to gain a sense of the individual's career path.

**DONNA M. GRANT, RN**
21212 Harrison Court SW
Port Ludlow, Washington 00000
RN# 00000000

**555-555-5555 Home** **555-555-5555 Work**

**OBJECTIVE**

A position in nursing where I can use my education and experience to improve the quality of life for patients, regardless of the circumstances of their illnesses or injuries.

**SUMMARY OF QUALIFICATIONS**

- More than 15 years of experience as a Registered Nurse working in nursing and health-related fields.
- Home Health Nursing Supervisor, Staff Nurse and Case Manager.
- Comprehensive knowledge of Medicare and Medicaid regulations and charting requirements.
- Charge Nurse in Alzheimer facility.
- Trained and experienced in the special needs of terminal patients.
- Active advocate for, and participant in, community education on health issues.
- Bilingual - Excellent oral and written communications skills in English and Spanish.
- Extensive experience working with people of diverse cultural backgrounds.

**PROFESSIONAL EXPERIENCE**

Compassionate Care, Port Townsend, Washington ***1991 - Present***
***Nursing Supervisor***

Manage daily operations of regional office serving Jefferson, Kitsap and Mason Counties. Oversee Nurse Case Manager, Certified Nursing Assistants, Physical, Occupational and Speech Therapists, and M.S.W. counselor. Evaluate patient care based on nursing notes, initial assessments and other documentation for Medicare appropriateness and outcome-based analysis. Organize and facilitate interdisciplinary team conferences. Participate in hiring, evaluation and termination of staff. Assist in the promotion and marketing of services to health care providers, including physicians' offices, clinics and hospitals.

Golden Years Care Center, Port Angeles, Washington ***1991 - 1994***
***Charge Nurse***

Assisted Alzheimer and mentally challenged residents with medications and treatments. Using the concepts of the Gentle Care Program, encouraged residents to take greater control of their needs and everyday activities. Performed documentation in compliance with Medicare/Medicaid requirements. Held Scheduled Care Conferences with residents and family members to review plans of care and set new goals. Monitored residents for effects of psychotropic medications. Supervised team of LPNs and CNAs.

International Travel - Sabbatical ***1989 - 1991***
***Nursing Volunteer***

Traveled throughout Mexico, French Polynesia, Cook Islands, Tonga and New Zealand providing informal assistance at local health clinics.

**338**

**Combination.** *Lonnie L. Swanson, Poulsbo, Washington*

This person was worried about the time she had taken off from work during 1989-1991. While interviewing the client about how she had spent her time during those years, the writer realized

DONNA M. GRANT, RN — Page 2

AIDS/ARC Support Group, Grays Harbor County, Washington — ***1986 - 1989***
***Community Coordinator***
Developed and implemented pilot program in Grays Harbor County to provide emotional, medical and financial assistance to individuals with AIDS/HIV. Worked with families and companions in hospice-type settings. Offered emotional and spiritual support. Participated in community education.

Media Marketing, Seattle, Washington — ***1983 - 1986***
***President/Owner***
Managed the day-to-day operation of a small software company which developed products used in informational displays serving markets in public access cable TV, advertising, hospitals, airports, hotels, etc.

Citrus Grove Center, Orange County, California — ***1981 - 1983***
***Staff Nurse***
Worked in emergency room, medical and surgical, and labor and delivery services. Assisted in location of and liaison with community resources for medically indigent populations from Mexico and South East Asia.

National Council of Churches, San Marcos, California — ***1972 - 1981***
***Migrant Ministry***
Participated in various social action programs involving migrant workers, including pesticide legislation; community advocacy; nutrition; health issues; and employment. Funded by the Council of Churches and the Campaign for Human Development.

## EDUCATION

**Bachelor of Science in Nursing** - Pending 1996
Regents College, New York, New York
All undergraduate work completed. Currently completing Nursing Clinical Examination.

**Associates Degree in Nursing** - 1980
Bakersfield College, Bakersfield, California

**Bachelor of Science in Biology** - 1972 - Unpetitioned
California State University, Northridge, California

### Certifications and Continuing Education

CPR - Basic Life Support Certification - 1996
IV Certification - 1996
Nurse Delegation - Rules & Regulations
Dermal Wound Management
Pain Management
Infection Control
HIV/AIDS Clinical & Ethical Issues
Life After Loss
OSHA/WISHA Requirements

## ACTIVITIES AND AFFILIATIONS

Quality Improvement Committee
Medicine Wheel Spiritual Group - Natural and Alternative Medicine
Soup Kitchen Volunteer
Volunteer for Parish Nursing in the Local Community

that the individual had, in effect, taken a sabbatical. That concept was put into the resume, and the "gap" was no longer a gap. Reference to a sabbatical actually strengthens the resume and shows that the candidate is "a very appealing applicant" with exotic travel experience.

# Roger Rogers

37 Allison Way
Grays, Indiana 55555
(555) 555-5555

***SUMMARY OF QUALIFICATIONS***

- ✓ Large volume warehouse management experience in all aspects including both shipping and receiving ends for catalog and wholesale companies
- ✓ Known for initiative and excellent communication and organizational skills
- ✓ Managerial skills include inventory control and personnel supervision
- ✓ Leadership skills demonstrated through interpersonal skills, positive motivation and example and creating team efforts with goals of superior customer satisfaction
- ✓ Enjoy project concept, design, implementation and follow through

***EMPLOYMENT HISTORY***

***Receiving Supervisor***
LLT Commodities, Inc., Brandon, Indiana — 1991 - present

**Personnel**
- ✓ Interview and hire full time employees, currently 15
- ✓ Train group leaders, assistants, and clerical support
- ✓ Set up requirements for temporary work force of 100 employees
- ✓ Supervise seasonal two shift operation from September through December

**Unloading**
- ✓ New receipt reconciliation to packing lists and purchase orders, location selection, input and inventory tracking
- ✓ Accountable for support of shipping requirements, cross dock, and customer back orders
- ✓ Oversee an average of 50 truck loads per day, seasonally, with 70% floorloads and 30% skidded
- ✓ Design and implement current policies and procedures with goal of paperless system

**Traffic**
- ✓ Routing and scheduling of domestic LTL and TL (15/day)
- ✓ Rate negotiations of FAK and increased discount reducing overall freight costs with increased tonnage from 1991 to present more than 4 Million pounds per year (3,500# average shipment)
- ✓ Continuous tracking of overseas shipments including scheduling and terminations (1,700/per year)

**Warehouse**
- ✓ Operation procedures for safety, security, and sanitation
- ✓ Design and implementation of a new locator system to reduce errors and increase productivity
- ✓ Procedures and system support coordination for bi-annual inventory
- ✓ Power equipment selection for lease, rent and purchase

**Public Warehouse**
- ✓ Responsible for selection of site and coordination of four facilities
- ✓ Schedule outbound and inbound truck loads and request stock needs for shipments to customers
- ✓ Leased tractor/trailers with drivers (15 truckloads daily over 2 shifts)
- ✓ Assisted in the design and implementation of new public warehouse computer inventory system

**339**

**Combination.** *Patricia L. Nieboer, Fremont, Michigan*

A resume on colored "decorator" paper. The contact information is repeated on page two. An informal font is used throughout the resume for a "different" look. The use of bold italic for the

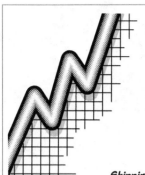

# Roger Rogers

37 Allison Way
Grays, Indiana 55555
(555) 555-5555

***Shipping Manager***
<u>The Factory</u>, Lake Forest, Indiana 1988 - 1991

- ✓ Hire, train, and motivation of temporary and full time work force
- ✓ Responsible for multiple warehouse layout, safety, security, sanitation, storage, and distribution
- ✓ Assisted with support of multiple factory stores
- ✓ Handled layout and replenishment of a multi-seasonal pick belt and package bundling time
- ✓ Herbie recognition and training
- ✓ Accountable for budgets of staff, supplies, overhead, and transportation needs
- ✓ Scheduled inbound and outbound traffic including company owned and leased vehicles
- ✓ Routing of LTL and trailer load shipments for consumer and wholesale accounts
- ✓ Dealt with Federal Express powership plus participation
- ✓ Controlled UPS manifesting, zone skipping, and hundred weight programs
- ✓ Implemented and modified computer reports for shipping labels and bar coding

***Dispatcher and Tractor/Trailer Driver***
<u>Hoffman Brother's Cartage</u>, Citytown, Indiana 1980 - 1988

***EDUCATION AND TRAINING***

*Management and Control of Freight Costs and Shipping Operations*, American Management Association 1995
*Successfully Managing People*, American Management Association 1994
*Supervisory Development*, LLT Commodities, Inc. 1991
*Frontline Leadership*, College of Lake County, The Factory 1990
*Supervisory Development*, Northern Indiana Business Association 1988, 1989, 1990

***AFFILIATIONS***

Building Chairman Sanctuary and Educational Center 1988 - 1990
Self-employed Landscape Design and Installation 1968 - present

*Professional References Available Upon Request*

section headings and job titles makes them easy to spot. Underlining makes it easy to see the names of employers if you want to look for them at a glance. Check marks for bullets contribute to the different look. Subheadings under the current position make responsibilities easier to see.

# Sondra Sanchez

**5555 First Avenue • North Woods, California 50005 • (555) 500-5000**

**SUMMARY OF QUALIFICATIONS**

- **Over 17 years experience in all phases of procurement**, for both military and commercial sectors, including 5 years as Purchasing Supervisor.
- Demonstrated ability to work well under pressure, promptly and effectively handling multiple tasks simultaneously.
- Self motivated with a track record of pro-active problem solving. Works well independently or as part of a productive team.
- Possesses a strong work ethic with attention to detail.
- A quick learner who takes direction well.
- Superior communication skills; interacts effectively with all level of co-workers and outside vendors.

**HIGHLIGHTS/ACCOMPLISHMENTS**

- **Reduced cost 25%** on major product lines.
- Consolidated supplier base resulting in **15% savings.**
- Established and developed strong sub-contract vendor relations, **increasing productivity and reducing labor cost by 30%.**
- **Avoided production delays** by developing alternative sources for hard-to-find or obsolete products.
- **Improved receiving procedures by 20%** through implementation of procedures for early deliveries and overshipments.
- Corrected material inventory availability and delivery problems **resulting in meeting production deadlines with cost reductions of 25%.**
- Assisted Production Control department in **implementation of bar coding and MRP.**

***Recognition:***

- Recognized by DCMAO for outstanding achievement
- Honored as Employee of the Month.

**EXPERIENCE**

*As Buyer for major designer/manufacturer of electronic systems and subsystems and international distributor of electronic components:*

- Purchased/procured electronic components, printed circuit boards, raw materials, fabricated parts, tools, cable assemblies, etc., including vendor negotiations and research, sourcing and inspection of facilities.
- Obtained and evaluated competitive bids; negotiated and finalized contracts.
- Interfaced extensively with other corporate departments including Engineering, Production, Marketing and Sales.
- Utilized thorough knowledge of Small Business Plan System.
- Supervised and trained departmental personnel.
- Maintained all rental, leasing and blanket agreements for supplies and services.
- Negotiated contracts for sheet metal, PCB's, machined parts and electronic assemblies per B/P Specification, Source control dwg's and military specs.

**340**

**Combination.** *Vivian Van Lier, Van Nuys, California*

This Purchasing Supervisor worked for the same company for 17 years until it closed. She learned her job "by advancing through the ranks." The writer wanted to show how the person

**SONDRA SANCHEZ** **Resume • Page 2**

**HISTORY**

ELECTRONIC SYSTEMS INC., North Woods, CA • 1978 to 1995

*Superior job performance resulted in fast-track promotion through series of progressively more responsible positions.*

| | |
|---|---|
| **Purchasing Supervisor/Buyer** | 1990 to 1995 |
| **Buyer** | 1990 |
| **Jr. Buyer** | 1989 to 1990 |
| **MIS System Operator** | 1989 |
| **Material Analyst** | 1985 to 1989 |
| **Purchasing Administrator** | 1982 to 1985 |
| **Customer Service Administrator** | 1981 to 1982 |
| **Shipping/Receiving Clerk** | 1979 to 1981 |
| **Assembler** | 1978 to 1979 |

**COMPUTER SKILLS**

- Software: WordPerfect (DOS and Windows), Microsoft Word, Lotus 1-2-3, Excel.
- Order entry, IBM MAPICS 34 & 36, IBM System 36 Marcam (Purchasing), Query.

**LANGUAGE SKILLS:** Bilingual English/Spanish

**EDUCATION/TRAINING**

"Winning at Negotiations" — Simon Sayz
Advanced Purchasing — California State University, North Woods, CA
Integrated Overview of Production and Inventory Control (APICS), — California State University, North Woods, CA
Inventory Control System (APICS) — California State University, North Woods, CA

**Seminars:** *High Impact Communication Skills, How to Supervise, JIT, TQM, IBM System 34 & 36, MAPICS software.*

***References Available Upon Request***

influenced the bottom line and "was able to meet increasingly challenging positions." The Summary of Qualifications is also a profile. Indicating her achievements in one section has more impact than listing them under her various roles. Italic is used to focus the reader's attention.

Paula A. Gold

PO Box 25, Coram, NY 55555 • 555-555-5555 H, 555-555-5555 Fax

*"...Mrs. Gold is one of the most organized people...often developing methodologies to enhance the work flow...If a project must be completed, she is the person you want in charge. She strives for solutions and can achieve whatever she sets out to do..."*

James F. Tierney
Center Manager
Suffolk County Dept.
of Social Services

*"...Prompt attention by especially observant Center staff averted a major statewide problem...(that) would have affected every Social Services district in the state. Staff responsible for timely reporting of potential problem was Supervisor Pat Gold..."*

Eugene F. Durney
Director
Policy and Procedures
Suffolk County Dept.
of Social Services

## Professional Profile

- Twenty six years progressive advancement in the Suffolk County, New York Civil Service system's Department of Social Services. Currently functioning as Social Services Supervisor (grade 23), managing a staff of twenty-three and carrying case loads of 2,000 income maintenance clients or weekly client application loads of 350 cases.
- Deeply committed to the exceptional performance of professional responsibilities. Consistently commended by superiors for initiative, organization, and ability to accurately perform multiple tasks. Cool-headed and effective under pressure. Interact well with all levels of staff and clients; diffuse crisis situations on a daily basis.

## Achievements and Qualifications

### Leadership and Administration

- Consistently and calmly manage intense pressure situations, with staff and clients often in crisis. Easily adjust to changing priorities, deadlines, and multiple client/staff demands.
- Anticipate and institute corrective action for problems; "protect" superiors by diffusing conditions before they reach crisis stage. Commended by County Executive for independent leadership role in Center emergency situation.
- Received State Commendation for discovery and immediate notification of a computer problem that would have crashed the entire New York State data system if not corrected by end of business day.
- Highly organized and analytical. Prepare complex budgets. Maintain statistics on every key function of department for administration comparisons, legal brief preparations, and request, regulation and decision justifications.
- Knowledgeable in all departmental systems through inquisitive and self-motivated learning. Quickly master new regulations and procedures.

### Communication, Training and Development

- Meet with clients, court staff, legal representatives, advocates and Social Services' staff in often agitated or tense situations.
- Compose internal and external reports/correspondence. Write legal briefs for hearings on departmental client decisions. Deliver clear and concise presentations to staff and public.
- Function as technical/regulatory resource for multiple Social Services centers. Simplify complex laws and regulations for staff training.
- Often called upon to thoroughly train new staff in limited time.

341

**Combination.** *Deborah Wile Dib, Medford, New York*

This Supervisor was a retiree moving to the South but with the "goal of starting a second civil service career in a new location." First-column testimonials demonstrate her capabilities and

## Paula A. Gold

page two

*"...Your job performance at the Coram Health Center would be commendable on any given day...however, due to extremely adverse conditions, your performance could better be described as noble...it is reassuring to know that devoted workers like yourself can be counted upon to perform the necessary functions of our county government."*

Letter of Commendation
Robert T. Gaffney
Suffolk County Executive

*"...Mrs. Gold...does an excellent job responding to the pressures of the unit...works side-by-side with her staff frequently filling in as QC, clerk, receptionist and examiner...I have met few individuals with the commitment and leadership qualities that Mrs. Gold displays."*

Paul Robinson
Suffolk County Dept.
of Social Services

### Career Development

**SUFFOLK COUNTY CIVIL SERVICE, NEW YORK** — **1973 to present**

**Suffolk County Department of Social Services**

S.S. Examiner III, Supervisor (grade 23) — 1987 to 1997

S.S. Examiner II, Quality Control and Training Coordinator (grade 17) — 1977 to 1987

S.S. Examiner I (grade 13) — 1973 to 1977

Control a unit of twenty-three staff members. Maintain unit work flow; keep log down to five days by law. Plot vacations and flex schedules. Write staff evaluations. Approve major financial and law decisions. Interface with clients, lawyers, and advocates. Prepare legal briefs to support positions in "fair hearings". Master federal, state and local regulations.

Meet with clients directly; often diffuse disruptive or difficult situations. Clear lobby of hundreds of people by closing; find shelter for homeless, battered women, etc. Deal with a staff overloaded with daily crisis.

**Suffolk County Data Processing**
Magnetic Tape Librarian (grade 9) — 1972 to 1973

**Suffolk County Children's Shelter**
Clerk/Typist (grade 5) — 1971 to 1972

### Computer Skills

Windows, Microsoft Word, New York State system interfaced with Social Services Software, courses in data processing and B.A.S.I.C.

### Continuing Professional Education

- **Supervisory Management:** Dun & Bradstreet
- **Managing Multiple Priorities:** Dun & Bradstreet
- **Corrective Action Planning:** Maximus, Inc.
- **Business Communications:** Dowling College
- **Sociology:** Suffolk County Community College
- **Introduction to Data Processing:** Empire State College
- **Programming in B.A.S.I.C.:** SUNY Stony Brook

### Education

**B.A. in Sociology With High Honors (concentration: Marketing)**
State University of New York at Oneonta

show that she "had a high level of potential to jump into a new position and make an immediate impact." Grouping achievements and qualifications under subheadings is an effective way to handle a long list of items. Note the use of bold in the Continuing Professional Education section.

# Joanna T. Nolan

6130 N. Islandia Circle
Glendale, Arizona 87520

**602/431-1211**


**Objective & Capabilities**

To use more than 20 years hands-on accounting experience in an active office environment seeking a hardworking individual with abilities in:

| | |
|---|---|
| **Payroll - ADP System** | **WordPerfect** |
| **Accounts Payable/Receivable** | **Lotus 1-2-3** |
| **Typing (55-60 wpm)** | **10-Key by Touch** |

- Learns quickly. Rapidly developed overall knowledge of business operation and PC software applications.
- Effective use of strong mathematical aptitude; noted for accuracy and ability to complete projects on time.
- Exceptionally well organized and detail oriented with the well-developed prioritization skills to coordinate complex assignments.
- Flexible and cooperative. Considered a productive team member.
- Utilizes professional discretion in handling confidential matters.

**Experience**

7/85 - 9/95

***St. Martin Acquisitions, Limited Partnership***
***dba MasterCrafters*** Glendale, Arizona
**SUPERVISOR: PAYROLL & PAYABLES**

Long-term association with this manufacturing company in a multi-functional capacity demanding proficiency in communications, computer use, accounting and interpersonal relations.

- Preparation of weekly and semi-monthly payroll for 125 to 200 employees and executives at 7 locations in four states.
- Proficient with *ADP Payroll System,* on PC with modem, to organize and record payroll data, generate a variety of reports and provide top level management with the necessary information to make executive decisions.
- Developed and implemented highly effective debit memo system that significantly improved cash flow and increased annual income by $30/$40,000.
- Extensive interaction with purchasing agents to verify invoices, make necessary adjustments to reflect actual prices/quantities.
- Consistently commended for accuracy.

1972 - 1984

***Mega Bank of North Dakota*** Fargo, North Dakota
**HEAD NOTE TELLER**

Twelve years productive association in the Commercial Loan Department, providing supervision and training to *Assistant Note Teller.*

- Provided support to commercial loan officers; accepted notes and collateral; processed payments and payoffs; returned collateral for satisfied debts; responsible for daily transaction balance subject to internal, state and federal audits.
- Initiated tickler system for UCC to track renewals which improved renewal rate.
- Designed daily worksheet for newly installed computer system.
- Attention to detail resulted in discovery of three forgeries, which could have caused major problems for the bank.

**Personal**

References and additional information available upon request.



**342**

**Combination.** *Brooke Andrews, Mesa, Arizona*

This individual over 50 had no degree but did want a job with higher wages. The writer's task was to make clear the person's skills, responsibilities, and successes. She found a job in one month.

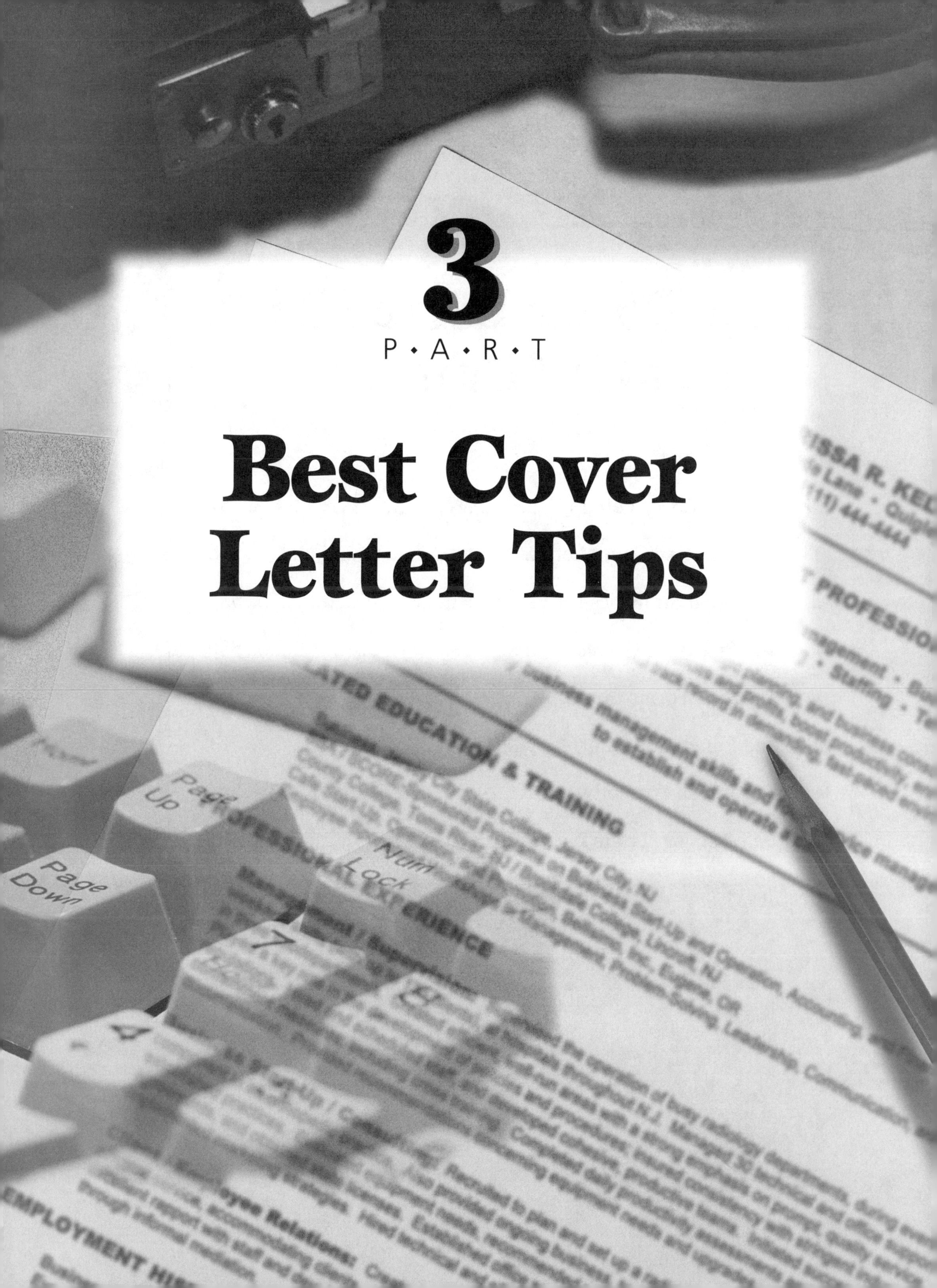

# 3
# P•A•R•T

# Best Cover Letter Tips

# Best Cover Letter Tips at a Glance

# Best Cover Letter Tips

In an active job search, your cover letter and resume should complement one another. Both are tailored to a particular reader you have contacted or to a specific job target. To help you create the "best" cover letters for your resumes, this part of the book mentions some common myths about cover letters and presents tips for polishing the letters you write.

## Myths about Cover Letters

1. **Resumes and cover letters are two separate documents that have little relation to each other.** The resume and cover letter work together in presenting you effectively to a prospective employer. The cover letter should mention the resume and call attention to some important aspect of it.

2. **The main purpose of the cover letter is to establish friendly rapport with the reader.** Resumes show that you *can* do the work required. Cover letters express that you *want* to do the work required. But it doesn't hurt to display enthusiasm in your resumes and refer to your abilities in your cover letters.

3. **You can use the same cover letter for each reader of your resume.** Modify your cover letter for each reader so that it sounds fresh rather than canned. Chances are that in an active job search, you have already talked with the person who will interview you. Your cover letter should reflect that conversation and build on it.

4. **In a cover letter, you should mention any negative things about your life experience, work experience, health, or education in order to prepare the reader in advance of an interview.** This is not the purpose of the cover letter. You might bring up these topics in the first or second interview, but only after the interviewer has shown interest in you or offered you a job. Even then, if you feel that you must mention something negative about your past, present it in a positive way, perhaps by saying how that experience has strengthened your resolve to work hard at any new job.

5. **It is more important to remove errors from a resume than from a cover letter, because the resume is more important than the cover letter.** Both your resume and your cover letter should be free of errors. The cover letter is usually the first document a prospective employer sees. The first impression is often the most important one. If your cover letter has an embarrassing error in it, the chances are good that the reader may not bother to read your resume or may read it with less interest.

6. **To make certain that your cover letter has no errors, all you need to do is proofread it or ask a friend to "proof" it.** Trying to proofread your own cover letter is risky, even if you are good at grammar and writing. Once a document is typewritten or printed, it has an aura about it that may make it seem better written than it is. For this reason, you are likely to miss typos or other kinds of errors.

   Relying on someone else is risky too. If your friend is not good at grammar and writing, that person may not see any mistakes either. Try to find a proofreader, a professional editor, an English teacher, a professional writer, or an experienced secretary who can point out any errors you may have missed.

7. **After someone has proofread your letter, you can make a few changes to it and not have it looked at again.** More errors creep into a document this way than you would think possible. The reason is that such changes are often done hastily, and haste can waste an error-free document. If you make *any* change to a document, ask someone to proofread it a final time just to make sure that you haven't introduced an error during the last stage of composition. If you can't find someone to help you, the next section gives you advice on how to eliminate common mistakes in cover letters.

# Tips for Polishing Cover Letters

You might spend several days working on your resume, getting it "just right" and free of errors. But if you send it with a cover letter that is written quickly and contains even one conspicuous error, all of your good effort may be wasted. That error could be just the kind of mistake the reader is looking for to screen you out.

You can prevent this kind of tragedy by polishing your cover letter so that it is free of all errors. The following tips can help you avoid or eliminate common errors in cover letters. If you become aware of these kinds of errors and know how to fix them, you can be more confident about the cover letters you send with your resumes.

## *Using Good Strategies for Letters*

1. **Use the postal abbreviation for the state in your mailing address.** See best resume writing strategy 1 in Part 1.

2. **Make certain that the letter is addressed to a specific person and that you use this person's name in the salutation.** Avoid using such general salutations as Dear Sir or Madam, To Whom It May Concern, Dear Administrator, Dear Prospective Employer, and Dear Committee. In an active job search, you should do everything possible to send your cover letter and resume to a particular individual, preferably someone you've already talked with in person or by phone, and with whom you have arranged an interview. If you have not been able to make a personal contact, at least do everything possible to find out the name of the person who will read your letter and resume. Then address the letter to that person.

3. **Adjust the margins for a short letter.** If your cover letter is 300 words or longer, use left, right, top, and bottom margins of one inch. If the letter is

shorter, the width of the margins should increase. How much they increase is a matter of personal taste. One way to take care of the width of the top and bottom margins is to center a shorter letter vertically on the page. A maximum width for a short cover letter of 100 words or fewer might be two-inch left and right margins. As the number of words increases by 50 words, you might decrease the width of the left and right margins by two-tenths of an inch.

4. **If you write your letter with word processing or desktop publishing software, use left-justification to ensure that the lines of text are readable with fixed spacing between words.** The letter will have a "ragged right" look along the right margin, but the words will be evenly spaced horizontally. Don't use full justification in an attempt to give a letter a printed look. Unless you do other typesetting procedures, like kerning and hyphenating words at the end of some lines, full justification can make your letter look worse with some extra wide spaces between words.

## *Using Pronouns Correctly*

5. **Use *I* and *My* sparingly.** When most of the sentences in a cover letter begin with *I* or *My*, the writer may appear self-absorbed, self-centered, or egotistical. If the reader of the letter is turned off by this kind of impression (even if it is a false one for you), you could be screened out without ever having an interview. Of course, you will need to use these first-person pronouns because most of the information you put in your cover letter will be personal. But try to avoid using *I* and *My* at the beginnings of sentences and paragraphs.

6. **Refer to a business, company, corporation, or organization as "it" rather than "they."** Members of the Board may be referred to as "they," but a company is a singular subject requiring a singular verb. Note this example:

   New Products, Inc., was established in 1980. It grossed over a million dollars in sales during its first year.

7. **If you start a sentence with *This*, be sure that what *This* refers to is clear.** If the reference is not clear, insert some word or phrase to clarify what *This* means. Compare the following lines:

   My revised application for the new position will be faxed to you by noon on Friday. You indicated by phone that *this* is acceptable to you.

   My revised application for the new position will be faxed to you by noon on Friday. You indicated by phone that this *method of sending the application* is acceptable to you.

   A reader of the first sentence wouldn't know what *This* refers to. Friday? By noon on Friday? The revised application for the new position? The insertion after *This* in the second sentence, however, tells the reader that *This* refers to the use of faxing.

8. **Use *as follows* after a singular subject.** Literally, *as follows* means *as it follows*, so the phrase is illogical after a plural subject. Compare the following lines:

| | |
|---|---|
| Incorrect: | My plans for the day of the interview are as follows: |
| Fixed: | My plans for the day of the interview are these: |
| Correct: | My plan for the day of the interview is as follows: |
| Better: | Here is my plan for the day of the interview: |

In the second set, the improved version avoids a hidden reference problem—the possible association of the silent "it" with *interview*. Whenever you want to use *as follows*, check to see whether the subject that precedes *as follows* is plural. If it is, don't use this phrase.

## Using Verb Forms Correctly

**9. Make certain that subjects and verbs agree in number.** Plural subjects require plural forms of verbs. Singular subjects require singular verb forms. Most writers know these things, but problems arise when subject and verb agreement gets tricky. Compare the following lines:

| | |
|---|---|
| Incorrect: | My education and experience has prepared me . . . . |
| Correct: | My education and experience have prepared me . . . . |
| Incorrect: | Making plans plus scheduling conferences were . . . . |
| Correct: | Making plans plus scheduling conferences was . . . . |

In the first set, *education* and *experience* are two things (you can have one without the other) and require a plural verb. A hasty writer might lump them together and use a singular verb. When you reread what you have written, look out for this kind of improper agreement between a plural subject and a singular verb.

In the second set, *making plans* is the subject. It is singular, so the verb must be singular. The misleading part of this sentence is the phrase *plus scheduling conferences*. It may seem to make the subject plural, but it doesn't. In English, phrases that begin with such words as *plus*, *together with*, *in addition to*, *along with*, and *as well as* usually don't make a singular subject plural.

**10. Whenever possible, use active forms of verbs rather than passive forms.** Compare these lines:

| | |
|---|---|
| Passive: | My report will be sent by my assistant tomorrow. |
| Active: | My assistant will send my report tomorrow. |
| Passive: | Your interest is appreciated. |
| Active: | I appreciate your interest. |
| Passive: | Your letter was received yesterday. |
| Active: | I received your letter yesterday. |

Sentences with passive verbs are usually longer and clumsier than sentences with active verbs. Spot passive verbs by looking for some form of the verb *to be* (such as *be*, *will be*, *have been*, *is*, *was*, and *were*) used with another verb.

A trade-off in using active verbs is the frequent introduction of the pronouns *I* and *My*. To solve one problem, you might create another (see Tip 5 in this list). The task then becomes one of finding some other way to start a sentence.

11. **Be sure that present and past participles are grammatically parallel in a list.** See Tip 62 in Part 1. What is true about parallel forms in resumes is true also in cover letters. Present participles are action words ending in *-ing*, such as *creating*, *testing*, and *implementing*. Past participles are action words usually ending in *-ed*, such as *created*, *tested*, and *implemented*. These are called *verbals* because they are derived from verbs but are not strong enough to function as verbs in a sentence. When you use a string of verbals, control them by keeping them parallel.

12. **Use split infinitives only when *not* splitting them is misleading or awkward.** An *infinitive* is a verb preceded by the preposition *to*, as in *to create*, *to test*, and *to implement*. You split an infinitive when you insert an adverb between the preposition and the verb, as in *to quickly create*, *to repeatedly test*, and *to slowly implement*. About 50 years ago, split infinitives were considered grammatical errors, but opinion about them has changed. Many grammar handbooks now recommend that you split your infinitives to avoid awkward or misleading sentences. Compare the following lines:

| | |
|---|---|
| Split infinitive: | I plan to periodically send updated reports on my progress in school. |
| Misleading: | I plan periodically to send updated reports on my progress in school. |
| Misleading: | I plan to send periodically updated reports on my progress in school. |

The first example is clear enough, but the second and third examples may be misleading. If you are uncomfortable with split infinitives, one solution is to move *periodically* further into the sentence: "I plan to send updated reports periodically on my progress in school."

Most handbooks that allow split infinitives also recommend that they not be split by more than one word, as in *to quickly and easily write*. A gold medal for splitting an infinitive should go to Lowell Schmalz, an Archie Bunker prototype in "The Man Who Knew Coolidge" by Sinclair Lewis. Schmalz, who thought that Coolidge was one of America's greatest presidents, split an infinitive this way: "*to instantly and without the least loss of time or effort find* . . . ."[1]

## Using Punctuation Correctly

13. **Punctuate a compound sentence with a comma.** A compound sentence is one that contains two main clauses joined by one of seven conjunctions (*and*, *but*, *or*, *nor*, *for*, *yet*, and *so*). In English, a comma is customarily put before the conjunction if the sentence isn't unusually short. Here is an example of a compound sentence punctuated correctly:

[1] Sinclair Lewis, "The Man Who Knew Coolidge," *The Man Who Knew Coolidge* (New York: Books for Libraries Press, 1956), p. 29.

I plan to arrive at O'Hare at 9:35 a.m. on Thursday, and my trip by cab to your office should take no longer than 40 minutes.

The comma is important because it signals that a new grammatical subject (*trip*, the subject of the second main clause) is about to be expressed. If you use this kind of comma consistently, the reader will rely on your punctuation and be on the lookout for the next subject in a compound sentence.

14. **Be certain not to put a comma between compound verbs.** When a sentence has two verbs joined by the conjunction *and*, these verbs are called *compound verbs*. Usually, they should not be separated by a comma before the conjunction. Note the following examples:

    I *started* the letter last night *and finished* it this morning.

    I *am sending* my resume separately *and would like* you to keep the information confidential.

    Both examples are simple sentences containing compound verbs. Therefore, no comma appears before *and*. In either case, a comma would send a wrong signal that a new subject in another main clause is coming, but no such subject exists.

    *Note:* In a sentence with a series of three or more verbs, use commas between the verbs. The comma before the last verb is called the *serial comma*. For more information on using the serial comma, see resume writing style Tip 64 in Part 1.

15. **Avoid using *as well as* for *and* in a series.** Compare the following lines:

    Incorrect: Your company is impressive because it has offices in Canada, Mexico, as well as the United States.

    Correct: Your company is impressive because it has offices in Canada and Mexico, as well as in the United States.

    Usually, what is considered exceptional precedes *as well as*, and what is considered customary follows it. Note this example:

    Your company is impressive because its managerial openings are filled by women as well as men.

16. **Put a comma after the year when it appears after the month.** Similarly, put a comma after the state when it appears after the city. Compare the following pairs of lines:

    Incorrect: In January, 1998 I was promoted to senior analyst.
    Correct: In January, 1998, I was promoted to senior analyst.

    Incorrect: I worked in Chicago, Illinois before moving to Dallas.
    Correct: I worked in Chicago, Illinois, before moving to Dallas.

17. **Put a comma after an opening dependent clause.** Compare the following lines:

| | |
|---|---|
| Incorrect: | If you have any questions you may contact me by phone or fax. |
| Correct: | If you have any questions, you may contact me by phone or fax. |

Actually, many writers of fiction and nonfiction don't use this kind of comma. The comma is useful, though, because it signals where the main clause begins. If you glance at the example with the comma, you can tell where the main clause is without even reading the opening clause. For a step up in clarity and readability, use this comma. It can give you a "feel" for a sentence even before you begin to read the words.

18. **Use semicolons when they are needed.** See resume writing style Tip 78 in Part 1 for the use of semicolons between items in a series. Semicolons are used also to separate main clauses when the second clause starts with a *conjunctive adverb* like *however*, *moreover*, and *therefore*. Compare the following lines:

| | |
|---|---|
| Incorrect: | Your position in sales looks interesting, however, I would like more information about it. |
| Correct: | Your position in sales looks interesting; however, I would like more information about it. |

The first example is incorrect because the comma before *however* is a *comma splice*, which is a comma that joins two sentences. It's like putting a comma instead of a period at the end of the first sentence and then starting the second sentence. A comma may be a small punctuation mark, but a comma splice is a huge grammatical mistake. What are your chances for getting hired if your cover letter tells your reader that you don't recognize where a sentence ends, especially if a requirement for the job is good communication skills? Yes, you could be screened out because of one little comma!

19. **Avoid putting a colon after a verb or a preposition to introduce information.** The reason is that the colon interrupts a continuing clause. Compare the following lines:

| | |
|---|---|
| Incorrect: | My interests in your company *are:* its reputation, the review of salary after six months, and your personal desire to hire handicapped persons. |
| Correct: | My interests in your company *are these:* its reputation, the review of salary after six months, and your personal desire to hire handicapped persons. |
| Incorrect: | In my interview with you, I would like *to:* learn how your company was started, get your reaction to my updated portfolio, and discuss your department's plans to move to a new building. |
| Correct: | In my interview with you, I would like to discuss *these issues:* how your company was started, what you think of my updated portfolio, and when your department may move to a new building. |

Although some people may say that it is OK to put a colon after a verb like *include* if the list of information is long, it is better to be consistent and avoid colons after verbs altogether.

20. **Understand colons clearly.** People often associate colons with semicolons because they sound alike, but colons and semicolons have nothing to do with each other. Colons are the opposite of dashes. Dashes look backward (see resume writing style Tip 80 in Part 1), and colons usually look forward to information about to be delivered. One common use of the colon does look backward, however. Here are two examples:

    My experience with computers is limited: I have had only one course on programming, and I don't own a computer.

    I must make a decision by Monday: that is the deadline for renewing the lease for my apartment.

    In each example, what follows the colon explains what was said before the colon. Using a colon this way in a cover letter can impress a knowledgeable reader who is looking for evidence of writing skills.

21. **Use slashes correctly.** Information about slashes is sometimes hard to find because *slash* often is listed under a different name, such as *virgule* or *solidus*. If you are not familiar with these terms, your hunt for advice on slashes may lead to nothing.

    At least know that one important meaning of a slash is *or*. For this reason, you often see a slash in an expression like ON/OFF. This means that a condition or state, like that of electricity activated by a switch, is either ON or OFF but never ON and OFF at the same time. As you saw in resume writing style Tip 75 in Part 1, this condition may be one in which a change means going from the current state to the opposite (or alternate) state. If the current state is ON and there is a change, the next state will be OFF, and vice versa. With this understanding, you can recognize the logic behind the following examples:

    | | |
    |---|---|
    | Incorrect: | ON-OFF switch (on and off at the same time!) |
    | Correct: | ON/OFF switch (on or off at any time) |
    | Incorrect: | his-her clothes (unisex clothes, worn by both sexes) |
    | Correct: | his/her clothes (each sex had different clothes) |

    *Note:* Although the slash is correct in *his/her* and is one way to avoid sexism, many people consider this expression clumsy. Consider some other wording, such as "clothes that both men and women wear" or "unisex clothes."

22. **Think twice about using *and/or*.** This stilted expression is commonly misunderstood to mean *two* alternatives, but it literally means *three*. Look at the following example:

    If you don't hear from me by Friday, please phone and/or fax me the information on Monday.

What is the person at the other end to do? The sentence really states three alternatives: just phone, just fax, or phone *and* fax the information by Monday. For better clarity, use the connectives *and* or *or* whenever possible.

23. **Use punctuation correctly with quotation marks.** A common misconception is that commas and periods should be placed outside closing quotation marks, but the opposite is true. Compare the following lines:

| | |
|---|---|
| Incorrect: | Your company certainly has the "leading edge", which means that its razor blades are the best on the market. |
| Correct: | Your company certainly has the "leading edge," which means that its razor blades are the best on the market. |
| Incorrect: | In the engineering department, my classmates referred to me as "the guru in pigtails". I was the youngest expert in programming languages on campus. |
| Correct: | In the engineering department, my classmates referred to me as "the guru in pigtails." I was the youngest expert in programming languages on campus. |

Unlike commas and periods, colons and semicolons go *outside* double quotation marks.

## *Using Words Correctly*

24. **Avoid using lofty language in your cover letter.** A real turn-off in a cover letter is the use of elevated diction (high-sounding words and phrases) as a bid to seem important. Note the following examples, along with their straight-talk translations:

| | |
|---|---|
| Elevated: | My background has afforded me experience in. . . . |
| Better: | In my previous jobs, I. . . . |
| Elevated: | Prior to that term of employment. . . . |
| Better: | Before I worked at. . . . |
| Elevated: | I am someone with a results-driven profit orientation. |
| Better: | I want to make your company more profitable. |
| Elevated: | I hope to utilize my qualifications. . . . |
| Better: | I want to use my skills. . . . |

In letter writing, the shortest distance between the writer and the reader is the most direct idea.

25. **Check your sentences for an excessive use of compounds joined by *and*.** A cheap way to make your letters longer is to join words with *and* and do this repeatedly. Note the following wordy sentence:

> Because of my background and preparation for work and advancement with your company and new enterprise, I have a concern and commitment to implement and put into effect my skills and abilities for new solutions and achievements above and beyond your dreams and expectations. [44 words]

Just one inflated sentence like that would drive a reader to say, "No way!" The writer of the inflated sentence has said only this:

> Because of my background and skills, I want to contribute to your new venture. [14 words]

If, during rereading, you eliminate the wordiness caused by this common writing weakness, your letter will have a better chance of being read completely.

**26. Avoid using abstract nouns excessively.** Look again at the inflated sentence of the preceding tip, but this time with the abstract nouns in italic:

> Because of my *background* and *preparation* for *work* and *advancement* with your *company* and new *enterprise*, I have a *concern* and *commitment* to implement and put into *effect* my skills and *abilities* for new *solutions* and *achievements* above and beyond your *dreams* and *expectations.*

Try picturing in your mind any of the words in italic. You can't because they are *abstract nouns*, which means that they are ideas and not images of things you can see, taste, hear, smell, or touch. One certain way to turn off the reader of your cover letter is to load it with abstract nouns. The following sentence, containing some images, has a better chance of capturing the reader's attention:

> Having created seven multimedia tutorials with my videocamera and Gateway Pentium computer, I now want to create some breakthrough adult-learning packages so that your company, New Century Instructional Technologies, Inc., will exceed $50,000,000 in contracts by 1995.

Compare this sentence with the one loaded with abstract nouns. The one with images is obviously the better attention grabber.

**27. Avoid wordy expressions in your cover letters.** Note the following examples:

> at the location of (at)
> for the reason that (because)
> in a short time (soon)
> in a timely manner (on time)
> in spite of everything to the contrary (nevertheless)
> in the event of (if)
> in the proximity of (near)
> now and then (occasionally)
> on a daily basis (daily)
> on a regular basis (regularly)
> on account of (because)

one day from now (tomorrow)
would you be so kind as to (please)

After each of these phrases is a suitable substitute in parentheses. Trim the fat wherever you can, and your reader will appreciate the leanness of your cover letter.

28. **At the end of your cover letter, don't make a statement that the reader can use to reject you.** For example, suppose that you close your letter with this statement:

    If you wish to discuss this matter further, please call me at (555) 555-5555.

    This statement gives the reader a chance to think, "I don't wish it, so I don't have to call." Here is another example:

    If you know of the right opportunity for me, please call me at (555) 555-5555.

    The reader may think, "I don't know of any such opportunity. How would I know what is right for you?" Avoid questions that prompt yes or no answers, such as, "Do you want to discuss this matter further?" If you ask this kind of a question, you give the reader a chance to say no. Instead, make a closing statement that indicates your optimism about a positive response from the reader. Such a statement might begin with one of the following:

    I am confident that . . . .
    I look forward to . . . .

    In this way, you invite the reader to say yes to further consideration.

## Exhibit of Cover Letters

The following Exhibit contains sample cover letters that were prepared by professional resume writers to accompany resumes submitted for this book. In most cases, the names, addresses, and facts have been changed to ensure the confidentiality of the original sender and receiver of the letter. For each letter, however, the essential substance of the original remains intact.

Use the Exhibit of cover letters as a reference whenever you need to write a cover letter for your resume. If you have trouble starting and ending letters, look at the beginnings and ends of the letters. If you need help on writing about your work experience, describing your abilities and skills, or mentioning some of your best achievements, look at the middle paragraph(s). Search for features that will give you ideas for making your own cover letters more effective. As you examine the Exhibit, consider the following questions:

1. **Does the person show a genuine interest in the reader?** One way to tell is to count the number of times the pronouns *you* or *your* appear in the letter. Then count next the number of times the pronouns *I*, *me*, and *my* occur in the letter. Although this method is simplistic, it nevertheless helps you see where the writer's interests lie. When you write a cover letter, make your first paragraph *you*-centered rather than *I*-centered. See also Tip 5 earlier in Part 3.

2. **Where does the cover letter mention the resume specifically?** The purpose of a cover letter is to call attention to the resume. If the letter fails to mention the resume, the letter has not fulfilled its purpose. Besides mentioning the resume, the cover letter might direct the reader's attention to one or more parts of the resume, increasing the chances that the most important part(s) will be seen by the reader. It is not a good idea, however, to put a lot of resume facts in the cover letter. Let each document do its own job. The job of the cover letter is to point to the resume.

3. **Where and how does the letter express interest in an interview?** The immediate purpose of a cover letter is to call attention to the resume, but the *ultimate* purpose of both the cover letter and the resume is to help you get an interview with the person who can hire you. If the letter doesn't display your interest in getting an interview, the letter has not fulfilled its ultimate purpose.

4. **How decisive is the person's language?** This question is closely related to the preceding question. Is interest in an interview expressed directly or indirectly? Does the person specifically request an interview on a date when the writer will be in the reader's vicinity, or does the person only hint at a desire to "meet" the reader some day? When you write your own cover letters, be sure to be direct and convincing in expressing your interest for an interview. Avoid being timid or wishy-washy.

5. **How does the person display self-confidence?** As you look through the Exhibit, notice the cover letters in which the phrase "I am confident that . . ." (or a similar expression) appears. Self-confidence is a sign of management ability but also of essential job-worthiness. Many of the letters display self-confidence or self-assertiveness in various ways.

6. **Does a letter indicate whether the person is a team player?** From an employer's point of view, an employee who is self-assertive but not a team player can spell T-R-O-U-B-L-E. As you look at the cover letters in the Exhibit, notice whether any letter mentions the word *team*.

7. **How does the letter make the person stand out?** As you read the letters in the Exhibit, do some letters present the person more vividly than other letters? If so, what does the trick? The middle paragraphs or the opening and closing paragraphs? The paragraphs or the bulleted lists? Use what you learn here to help you write distinctive cover letters.

8. **How familiar is the person with the reader?** In a passive job search, the reader will most likely be a total stranger. In an active job search, the chances are good that the writer will have had at least one conversation with the reader by phone or in person. As you look through the cover letters in the Exhibit, see whether you can spot any letter which indicates that the writer has already talked with the reader.

After you have examined the cover letters in the Exhibit, you will be better able to write an attention-getting letter—one that leads the reader to your resume and to scheduling an interview with you.

**Roberta Henson**
153 Elm Street, Boston, Massachusetts 02111
(617) 555-5153

Sheila Robbins, RN
Director of Patient Services
South Shore Home Care
850 Providence Highway, Suite 250
Dedham, MA 02026

Dear Ms. Robbins:

I am responding with a great deal of interest and enthusiasm to your recent advertisement for a Nurse/Branch Manager. My qualifications, as described in the enclosed resume, appear to be an excellent match for the requirements of this position.

I have well-developed administrative skills complemented by a strong clinical background. In my most recent position, I provided both administrative/management services and direct inservice education. I am comfortable giving group presentations and have a down-to-earth yet compassionate approach to potentially difficult issues. I enjoy diverse job responsibilities and am able to work well both independently and with a team. One of my strengths is developing and maintaining cooperative working relationships with diverse individuals.

At this point in my career I am seeking a position with an organization that values hard work, strong nursing and management skills, and the desire to excel. May we schedule an appointment to further discuss my qualifications for this position?

Thank you for your consideration.

Sincerely,

Roberta Henson

enclosure

1

**For Resume 245.** *Louise Kursmark, Cincinnati, Ohio*

A four-paragraph letter with a Purpose, Qualifications, Interview Request, and Thanks pattern. The first paragraph refers to the resume, which is an expected task of a cover letter for a resume.

**John N. Thompson**
(202) 222-7474
123 East Bay, Fremont, CA 94321

Dear _______________:

As a senior executive, I would like to enlist your firm's assistance in exploring professional opportunities in the biotech field. My background encompasses a 20-year career in the agricultural chemical field, with a particular emphasis most recently in the area of agricultural biotechnology.

You'll note that my résumé evidences significant experience in the fields of marketing as well as product development. This background includes considerable experience in the international marketplace, having worked in Europe, the Pacific Rim countries, South America, and Mexico. It is my conviction that these areas are primed for growth in the coming years, particularly the Pacific Rim and Latin American countries. Should the right opportunity present itself, I am available for relocation, including an overseas posting.

Specific career highlights relating to my interest in biotechnology center around my efforts which helped establish AgriBusiness Corp. in 1988, a company which developed biopesticides through a joint venture between two Fortune 100 companies, Shell Oil and Dow Corning Corporation. As V.P. of Sales and Marketing/Field Product Development, I am quite proud of the fact that we were able to start with no product base and ultimately generate over $2MM in product sales in five years time.

Should my qualifications coincide with any engagements you currently need to fill, I would appreciate your consideration.

Sincerely,

John N. Thompson

Enclosure: Résumé

2

**For Resume 263.** *Susan Britton Whitcomb, Fresno, California*

A networking letter for help in exploring job possibilities. The letter is therefore not part of an application for a specific job. The second paragraph refers to the resume and plays up experience.

**CHRISTOPHER S. JADEN**

369 Harborside Drive
Lakeland, Florida 33810
(941) 555-5555

July 15, 1996

Stephen Jones
Human Resources Director
Any Company
Post Office Box 4367
Tampa, FL 33650

Dear Mr. Jones:

I am writing to express an interest in potential senior sales/marketing management positions with your organization. As my enclosed résumé notes, I have extensive experience in the sales, marketing and promotion of multi-locational residential communities, and my accomplishments reflect a proven ability to perform in diverse and varied functions of considerable responsibility.

Currently, I am seeking a new association with a company that can benefit from my expertise as a highly productive, dynamic, profit-oriented manager with a proven record of achievement in sales, marketing and sales/marketing management. Additionally, I have a consistent record for achieving sales goals, expanding market share, reducing costs, and increasing profits.

In summary, I am a diligent and motivated sales and marketing executive who offers you an extensive background of experience and accomplishments. Given the opportunity, I believe that I would be a valuable asset to your organization.

Thank you for taking the time to review my résumé. I enthusiastically await the opportunity to further discuss my qualifications with you in an interview.

Sincerely,

Christopher S. Jaden

*Enclosure*



**For Resume 61.** *E. René Hart, Lakeland, Florida*

Experience, Expertise, a Profile, and Thanks in anticipation of an interview are the topics in turn in this four-paragraph letter. The first paragraph calls attention to experience and achievements.

BRADLEY BOSSLE

1100 W. Lancaster Way #1-105 Tempe, AZ 55555 [555] 000-0000

September 11, 1996

Mr. Stanley D. Hockle
Director AVSECH Services
PO Box 555
Wichita, KS 55555

Dear Mr. Hockle:

I am very interested in the Aircraft Management positions you Advertised in the *Arizona Republic*. The enclose Professional Profile will provide you with information regarding my background and experience.

As my Profile indicates, I have had extensive experience in management and customer service. Most recently I was the service manager for Cintas Corporation in Tampa, FL. In this capacity I increased and maintained a full one-third of the customer base of $80,000/week. We were able to consistently exceed our sales goals and reduced the loss of accounts to less than 4%. Prior to that time I owned and operated an Insurance office in Apache Junction, AZ. As a Captain in the Air Force, my responsibilities were extensive. There I supervised a staff of 32, provided complete support services for the American Community in Germany, implemented innovative management initiatives as well as training over 180 flight crew members. The development and administration of a budget is something I am well versed in. I believe that my experience will enable me to quickly become a valuable asset to your organization.

I would appreciate a personal interview, at your convenience, so that we may discuss in greater detail how my background will benefit your firm.

I look forward to hearing from you.

Sincerely,

Bradley Bossle

Encl: 1

4

**For Resume 194.** *Fran Holsinger, Tempe, Arizona*

A scan of the original decorator paper is included to show how the layout of the text and triple lines has been integrated with the paper's design. Note that the resume is called a Profile.

**_Quincy P. Evans_**

***9872 Town Court North***
***Lawrenceville, New Jersey 08648***
***Residence: (609) 799-2998***
***Business: (609) 799-5409***

Dear Sir/Madam:

As a **veteran manager**, I understand that success depends on a strong commitment to *customer satisfaction* and a constant focus on the *bottom*. Executing the basics and finding new solutions and business opportunities are the key to increasing performance and market share. I believe that my background in **district operations, financial reporting, and supervisory Management** reflect a commitment and an ability to find solutions to these challenges.

My career in management began in 1985 with the Foot Locker organization. I have received increasing responsibilities and promotions to Manager Trainer, and I am currently responsible for a group of stores in Southern New Jersey as well as operating my own $2.5 million unit. I am involved in district management and weekly/monthly projections relating to sales reporting. I have developed excellent supervisory skills and serve as a troubleshooter, taking on many regional assignments. As part of my duties, I am responsible for conducting presentations at managers' meetings.

Throughout my career, I have approached my work with a strong sense of urgency, working well under pressure and change. I am considered a forward thinker and a team player who has a strong commitment to my people and the organization I work for.

I look forward to speaking with you personally so that we may discuss my qualifications in greater detail. In the interim, thank you for your consideration, attention, and forthcoming response.

Sincerely,

Quincy P. Evans

Enclosure

**For Resume 210.** *Beverly Baskin, Marlboro, New Jersey*

The writer boldfaces important terms to make them stand out. The four paragraphs show in turn areas of expertise, responsibilities and skills, a profile, and interest in an interview—with thanks.

**Robert L. Norwood**
3220 Mountain Ridge Road
Montgomery, Alabama 36100
[334] 555 -1575 Residence [334] 555 -1066 Cellular

October 3, 1998

Mr. John Carmody
President
Four Hills Country Club
1520 Tramway Boulevard, NE
Albuquerque, New Mexico 87112

Dear Mr. Carmody:

My club sought me out to guide them through a $2,000,000 renovation and expansion. Now that the project is nearly finished, I want to make the same kind of contribution to another club. That is why I am exploring — very confidentially — opportunities in Albuquerque.

My specialty is constantly finding what club members want, then giving them more than they expect. Of course, members must have more than extraordinary service in gracious settings. They want confidence that their club will *always* be the best. I deliver that reassurance. If adding a General Manager with that personal standard appeals to Four Hills, we should talk.

I will seek out *anyone* whose ideas will help make my club shine. Sometimes that person is on the board, very often it is a member. But I go beyond the obvious sources to talk with employees and suppliers. I am as comfortable walking with the president as I am in talking with the janitor.

Not infrequently there are tangible payoffs: cutting supply costs by $35,000 in a single year while *improving* the service we offered. At times the results are intangible: the pride in our members' eyes after a garden party for the Secretary of Defense.

As a first step in putting my drive and energy to work for you, I have enclosed my résumé. It can only hint at my track record. Because words on paper cannot replace personal conversations, I encourage you to test me for yourself in a telephone interview soon.

Sincerely,

Robert L. Norwood

One enclosure: Résumé

6

**For Resume 93.** *Donald P. Orlando, Montgomery, Alabama*

This letter avoids all the clichés commonly found in cover letters. The five paragraphs indicate in turn the applicant's goal, specialty, methods, achievements (payoffs), and interest in an interview.

**JANE B. DOE**
555 Main Street
Anytown, USA 00000
(000) 000-0000

April 18, 1994

Mr. John Smith
Coffees & More
500 Lockwood Avenue
Anytown, USA 00000

Dear Mr. Smith:

As a coffee lover, I am writing regarding my interest in career opportunities within Coffees & More. With its outstanding reputation, your organization is one in which I would like to invest my education and experience. My resume, therefore, is enclosed for your consideration.

My interest in specialty coffee started during my employment in 1988 with Coffee Unlimited, a roaster-retailer located in Anytown, USA. After learning the basics of blending, flavoring, and roasting, I became fascinated with these processes and their diverse results. Since then, I have been "hooked" on the coffee industry and have continued my independent research of coffee and all of its related topics.

Currently, I am the Store Manager at Gift Baskets Galore. We prepare creative and unique gift baskets of gourmet food, liquors, and specialty coffees. Because of my extensive knowledge of specialty coffees, I serve as a chief information source to our customers. While I have been most satisfied with my job thus far, I am more interested in pursuing a career in the coffee industry.

I would welcome the opportunity of a personal interview to discuss how I can contribute to the success of Coffees & More. I will contact you within the next few weeks to see if a meeting can be arranged. In the meantime, if you have any questions, I may be reached at the above-named telephone number.

Thank you very much for your time and consideration. I look forward to speaking with you.

Sincerely,

Jane B. Doe

Resume enclosed.

**For Resume 204.** *Joellyn Wittenstein, Buffalo Grove, Illinois*

The cup graphic in the resume and cover letter links the two visually. The five paragraphs show in turn the person's purpose, motivation, knowledge and interest, follow-up plans, and thanks.

7

**ROSA A. WATERS**

156 Main Court
Virginia Beach, Virginia 23466
804 • 604 • 3058

June 20, 1995

Mainstay Human Health Division
Sales - NV, Box 58
493 Baindaid Street
Philadelphia, Pennsylvania 19100

Please accept this letter as an application for a sales career with Mainstay & Co., Inc. advertised in The Star Pilot. My confidential résumé is enclosed for review and consideration. I believe you will find me well qualified.

Detailed on my résumé is a solid successful background in the health care field with more than 12 years in pharmaceutical sales. My credentials and achievements are a matter of record. I have expertise in institutional sales, development of key physicians and pharmacy supporters. I am a leader in product launches, territory management, and customer service. As a goal oriented team player, took responsibility for my actions and gave my work that extra effort to exceed objectives.

I understand that Mainstay & Co., has developed a new, non-estrogen product for the treatment of osteoporosis. While working with Rich Laboratories, I received excellent education and training in many fields including orthopaedics, gerontology, and cardiology.

My departure from Rich Laboratories was due to marriage and relocation. Now settled in Virginia, I am anxious to focus on new and exciting challenges for a leader in the drug industry. My compensation at Rich Laboratories ranged from $24,900 to $57,000. Current salary requirements range from mid-to-high $30Ks with flexible and negotiable specifics dependent on benefit structure, responsibility, and advancement opportunities.

I feel particularly well qualified to provide the skills you require for a dynamic career with Mainstay & Co. The opportunity to meet with you to explore the contributions I can make will be most welcome. I now look forward to hearing from you.

Sincerely,

Rosa A. Waters
enclosure

8

**For Resume 180.** *Anne G. Kramer, Virginia Beach, Virginia*

The second paragraph covers the applicant's background, achievements, areas of expertise, and a profile so that the other paragraphs can indicate other specifics and interest in an interview.

**WILLIAM PENNINGTON**

0000 N. West Avenue
Anywhere, USA

(000) 000-0000
Available for Relocation

August 24, 1996

Mayor William Fentino
City Hall
0000 City Hall Street
Anywhere, USA

Dear Mayor Fentino:

As President of The Men's Shop, I have had the opportunity to meet you on several occasions. Without exception, I have been impressed with your straightforwardness and commitment to doing what is best for the city of Anywhere.

Today I read with great interest your new plan to lure international business to the city. Having held senior management positions with both Fortune 500 companies and closely-held business firms, I am well-versed in diverse and international business development strategies.

As an example, while with The Best Retailers (one of the nation's largest manufacturers and retailers based in Chicago), I envisioned the concept for, negotiated the structuring of, and directed the successful opening of 60 joint venture stores in the Orient and 12 stores in Europe (a first in the retailing industry). As such, I have knowledge of the business and social protocol required to conduct business with the Pacific Rim and, more importantly, am focused and tenacious in accomplishing planned goals.

Recently I successfully completed my temporary assignment with The Men's Shop. The timing of your project appears fortuitous, and I would be most interested in a position as Project Leader for this complex task.

Should you have need of an individual with extensive experience in strategic planning, high profile leadership, and the diplomacy required to gain consensus among divergent interests, I would welcome an opportunity to meet with you.

In advance, thank you for your time. I look forward to hearing from you.

Sincere regards,

William Pennington

Enclosure (résumé)

9

**For Resume 12.** *Susan Britton Whitcomb, Fresno, California*

A common cover letter fault is the display of self-interest and preoccupation with oneself, but this letter shows—through the ample use of *you* and *your*—evident interest in the reader of the letter.

**PAUL P. PLOCHART**
6422 Grail Court ◆ Dayton, Ohio ◆ 45000
*Office*: (123) 456-7890 ◆ *Home*: (123) 567-8904

September 16, 1994

*Attention*: Mr. George Jones
*Vice President*
GRAND PRIX LEASING
1234 Liverpool Avenue
Chicago, IL 99999

Dear Mr. Jones:

While recognized for consistently exceeding the requirements of my present position, and accordingly in receipt of consistently good performance reviews, I find recent changes in corporate structure appear to have limited the potential for both corporate and personal growth, relative to what they previously were. Consequently I am feeling progressively less fulfilled in addressing my career aspirations, and wish to embark on a fresh course.

I am now actively seeking an executive position with a dynamic, growth-oriented organization, in which my career can continue to flourish and develop to its maximum potential. Your organization has attracted my attention as one which may be able to offer the type of challenge I am pursuing. My strong desire is to obtain a leadership position within your organization. I am enclosing for your initial review my résumé outlining my career to date.

At the present time, I am the *Director of Consumer / Dayton Fleet Leasing* at *Joe Einstein Leasing, Inc.* My responsibilities cover a broad spectrum of management functions. Some of the principal areas of capability and experience are indicated in my résumé.

I believe that I can make an immediate and effective contribution to your organization. I would very much welcome the opportunity of a personal appointment in the near future, during which I can learn more about the aims and culture of your establishment, and you can assess at first hand the qualities I could bring to it.

Either you can reach me at the telephone numbers given above, or I will call you in the near future to set up an appointment at our mutual convenience. In view of my present position with Joe Einstein, I would greatly appreciate your exercising utmost confidentiality in this matter.

Thank you for your consideration.

Sincerely yours,

Paul P. Plochart

*Enclosure:* Résumé

10

**For Resume 276.** *Barry Hunt, Cincinnati, Ohio*

In this six-paragraph letter, the first paragraph indicates why the applicant wants to leave his current job, and the second paragraph explains why he is interested in the target organization.

**Meredith Lee**

98 Seaview Avenue, Revere, MA 02151 • (617) 555-9821

Ellen Smith, President
Village Green Management Company
800 Middlesex Avenue
Lexington, MA 02173

Dear Ms. Smith:

As a Revolutionary War buff, I moved to Boston six years ago excited at the prospect of visiting the famous battle sites of Lexington and Concord and observing how they have evolved to the present day. And I have not been disappointed — I have long been an admirer, in particular, of Lexington's combination of reverence for the past with respect for the business and commercial needs of its residents today. I would greatly enjoy contributing to the strong business climate in Lexington and therefore am responding to your recent advertisement for a Property Manager.

I am an experienced property manager with a strong finance and project management background. Specific accomplishments include:

- Maintaining low vacancy rates by ensuring well-managed and well-maintained properties and a high level of service to tenants. As well, I conduct thorough screening of prospective tenants to ensure a good fit with the available property.
- Controlling costs and closely monitoring budgets and expenditures while at the same time making appropriate investments in construction and maintenance to assure safety, quality, and an excellent appearance.
- Meeting the challenge of achieving profitability for newly purchased properties in a short time frame.

I am a highly motivated, goal-oriented manager with strong communication skills and the ability to work well with diverse individuals. I am seeking an opportunity with a company that values solid management skills, a strong work ethic, and the desire to excel. If you would like to learn more about my background, accomplishments, and management philosophy, then please contact me for an interview at your convenience.

Sincerely,

Meredith Lee

enclosure



**For Resume 164.** *Louise Kursmark, Cincinnati, Ohio*

This is the first of eight cover letters with bulleted items. In this letter the bullets are in the second paragraph and point to accomplishments. Present participles make the items parallel.

**DELILAH BRAN**

0000 North West Circle
Anywhere, USA
(000) 000-0000

November 14, 1995

The Cooking Palace
0000 North West
Anywhere 00000

Attn: District Manager

I love to cook. I also love to sell. I do both equally well and believe the combination would be a perfect fit for your new store in Minneapolis.

The enclosed résumé outlines my experience and talents. Briefly, my background includes:

- **Sales** -- whether in commission sales of stoves or as waitperson for a 4★★★★ restaurant, consistently set new sales records and earned highest ticket average ... remembered names and faces ... always used the "golden rule" when serving customers.
- **Retail Management** -- experienced in new store layout, fixtures, displays, merchandising ... marketing, promotions, advertising ... buying, pricing ... in six years with a consignment business, enjoyed significant and consistent annual growth.
- **Cooking** -- experienced caterer with a flair for presentation ... from elegant, intimate dinner parties to gala events ... entertained some of the city's finest!

Your store is much anticipated and long-awaited by many in the area who appreciate quality products and the art of cookery. I would be interested in any position which would best use my talents and look forward to learning more about plans for this new store.

Sincerely,

Delilah Bran

Enclosure

12

**For Resume 231.** *Susan Britton Whitcomb, Fresno, California*

The crossed horizontal and vertical lines match those of Resume 231. In the second paragraph the right-pointing bullets call attention to achievements, areas of expertise, and experience.

**Matthew K. Taylor**

(513) 555-2323
8752 Elm Street, Cincinnati, Ohio 45202

Mr. James Smith, President
Recycled Products, Inc.
1111 Main Street
Dayton, Ohio 45401

Dear Mr. Smith:

Having accepted an early retirement opportunity following a long and successful career with Cincinnati Gasket Company, I find myself at the age of 52 seeking a new challenge that will allow me to contribute my considerable management skill and experience in an environment that promises a great deal of personal satisfaction. I view your company, with its focus on recycling consumer waste, as just such an opportunity.

My accomplishments demonstrate my skills as a manager and my ability to improve operations while ensuring a stable, cooperative work force. Specific achievements include:

- Gaining the support and cooperation of plant workers to implement improved processes by soliciting their input, valuing their contributions, and respecting their work.
- Establishing new administrative departments (human resources, engineering) and assisting them to develop into productive work units whose efforts improved company efficiency.
- Building and maintaining consistently positive relationships with union representatives over 25 years representing the company in all negotiations and communications.

I would appreciate the opportunity to meet with you to explore how my management skills and solid experience can make a difference to your operations.

Thank you for your consideration.

Sincerely,

Matthew K. Taylor

enclosure

13

**For Resume 53.** *Louise Kursmark, Cincinnati, Ohio*

In this four-paragraph letter, the bullets in the second paragraph direct attention to specific achievements. As in Cover Letter 11, opening present participles make the items parallel.

**ALAN A. ALADIN**

0000 N. West Avenue
Anywhere, USA

Residence (000) 000-0000
Cellular (000) 000-0000

As an experienced **Economic Development Specialist,** I am writing to inquire of opportunities which might be available on a full-time or contract basis with your firm. The enclosed résumé outlines my 20-year history with the City of Bilton and the County of Attowa.

Strengths and experiences which may be of particular interest to you include:

- Sourced, negotiated, and secured over $255 million in new commercial/industrial development for the City of Bilton, an achievement which created $57 million in new single-family and multi-family construction and more than doubled population growth during my tenure.
- A creative problem-solving approach to financing, including experience with public/private sector partnerships, creation of assessment districts, and bond financing (as well as traditional financing methods) which enabled the city to underwrite over $28 million in new public works projects.
- Numerous contacts within, and ability to service, a broad client base including state, county and city agencies, lending institutions, and varied business interests representing utility, retail, and manufacturing concerns.
- Proactive leader with the ability to inspire cooperation, communication, and consensus among varied interests (public agencies, private sector, support staff, media, and the community-at-large).

Should you have need for an individual with my skills and experience, I would appreciate an opportunity to meet with you to explore our mutual interests. I will be in touch.

Sincerely,

Alan A. Aladin

Enclosure

14

**For Resume 80.** *Susan Britton Whitcomb, Fresno, California*

Four bulleted items in the second paragraph point to strengths and experiences of possible particular interest to the reader. The final sentence enables the person to control the next step.

**PAUL PETERSON**
5555 Sandy Hill Drive
Anytown, U.S.A. 55555
(000) 000-0000

October 17, 1995

Any Corporation
Mr. Lance Viper
55 Corporate Lane
Anytown, U.S.A. 55555

Dear Mr. Viper:

**Results are the only true measure of success...**

Throughout my career, I have committed myself to a high standard of "Results-Oriented" leadership. By adhering to a work ethic that respects hard work and expects exceptional quality, I have successfully contributed to the productivity and profitability of each organization I have worked for.

A summary of my qualifications and achievements is included on the accompanying resume. Some of my responsibilities have included:

- Directing the activities of 150+ employees at sites throughout the U.S.
- Managing the successful launch of a new product.
- Developing and implementing processes and procedures to increase efficiency.
- Recruiting, training and supervising personnel.

I am knowledgeable in control and compliance as required by Good Manufacturing Practices and am accustomed to profit and loss responsibilities.

I am confident in my ability to make an immediate and long-term contribution to your organization. I would welcome the opportunity to meet with you to discuss my qualifications in further detail.

Thank you for your consideration. I look forward to hearing from you.

Sincerely,

Paul Peterson

Enclosure



**For Resume 147.** *Sheryl Wilde, San Diego, California*

After a statement that links results with success, the first paragraph affirms that the candidate is a results-oriented leader. The four bulleted items in this cover letter are key responsibilities.

**Charles M. Downer**

2114 Pitt Street
Alexandria, Virginia, 23100

[703] 555-5555 (Home)
[703] 555-6666 (Office)

October 9, 1995

Mr. Charles W. Morgan
Chairman
Coleman County Board of Education
2315 Wesley Street
Coleman, Georgia 30243

Dear Mr. Morgan:

Whenever I speak with colleagues in educational leadership, the conversation often focuses on measuring the value of what we do. But now, after some 26 years of administering educational programs, I am persuaded that *who* does the measuring is as important as the measures themselves. Simply put, I am happiest - and therefore most successful - helping teachers and principals and, most important, students succeed. If that approach appeals to the Coleman County Board of Education, I would like to explore joining your team as your Chief Executive Officer.

My curriculum vitæ should help you learn about my background. I have even included a very small sampling of the successes I helped obtain. However, such documents cannot explain *how* I made progress for my organizations. In everything I do I hold to these principles:

- I must show that I care about the mission through deeds, not words,
- I reward the extra time it takes for staff members to make themselves visible and accessible,
- My organization's mission is ultimately measured in the success of the community from which my students come,
- I reward taking prudent risks if the goal is to further the mission, and
- I do not care who gets the credit as long as objective measures show we are doing our mission very well.

I am employed by an organization that values my services. However, I want to return to the field I love most. And so I am "testing the waters" with this confidential application. May I call in a few days to explore the possibility of an interview?

Sincerely,

Charles M. Downer

One enclosure: Résumé



**For Resume 21.** *Donald P. Orlando, Montgomery, Alabama*

In this confidential letter to a board of education, bullets point to principles related to the applicant's preferred "mission" of helping principals, teachers, and students succeed.

**Linda R. Jones**

4329 Thirsty Court • Indianapolis, Indiana 46224 • (317) 271-4855

July 10, 1995

Mr. Joe Rene, Director of Personnel
Metropolitan School District
of What Township
Administrative Service Center
200 East 83rd Street
Indianapolis, Indiana 46240

Dear Mr. Rene:

I read with interest the Coordination of Special Education position as advertised in the Employment Bulletin of University Career Center. I feel my experience reflects a person who is dedicated, a great communicator with excellent administrative and leadership skills, and talented in resolving concerns and issues within a school environment. My resume is enclosed for your consideration.

I would like to highlight the following characteristics of my experience:

- Proficient in organizing daily activities; able to focus on immediate concerns.
- Realize cost effectiveness of maintaining accurate student count.
- Extensive experience in communicating with special education students.
- Very directed toward the needs of the school; stay abreast of new policies and procedures.
- Familiar with outside service agencies and professionals to facilitate student learning. Knowledge of handicap conditions.
- Strong personal interaction with students and parents.
- Assist with interviewing and hiring of new staff.
- Physically hand schedule special education students.

I would welcome the opportunity to sit down and discuss the needs or goals of your school, and how my knowledge and expertise in school administration could be mutually beneficial. Thank you for your assistance in this matter, and I look forward to hearing from you soon.

Sincerely,

Linda R. Jones



**For Resume 295.** *Carole E. Pefley, Indianapolis, Indiana*

This cover letter has eight bulleted items, which attest to the individual's skills, experience, profile information, knowledge, interpersonal relationships, and special education work.

**JOHN C. JOHNSON**

100 Maple Lane
Burlington, VT 00000

**(800) 555-0000**

September 25, 1995

Ms. Darlene Abbott
Department of Athletics
University of Portland
Portland, OR 00000

**RE: Director of Annual Giving for Athletics**

Dear Ms. Abbott:

Please accept the enclosed resume as my expression of strong interest in your advertised position, Director of Annual Giving for Athletics.

My development and fund-raising experience includes all facets of the profession in an academic environment and a very significant sports orientation. The resume amplifies the following:

- Strategic fund-raising utilizing personal appeal, direct mail, phone solicitation, and special events
- Proven ability to increase net income in all categories of appeal
- Director of Development and Board member for a private school in Oregon, targeting parent, alumni, and corporate gifts
- Director of Alumni for a private school, targeting major gift prospects
- Olympic fund-raising for a U.S. National Champion
- Planning and marketing a 600-member sports facility
- Leadership through coaching and personal sports participation
- Experienced instructor on telephone solicitation and managing capital campaigns

I am in the process of relocating / returning to the Portland Area and would be delighted to have an interview opportunity.

Thank you for your consideration.

Sincerely,

John C. Johnson

18

**For Resume 260.** *Alan D. Ferrell. Lafayette, Indiana*

Nine bulleted statements make up most of this cover letter. The focus of the statements is to show how the resume presents the applicant's experience, skills, and positions held.

A•P•P•E•N•D•I•X

# List of Contributors

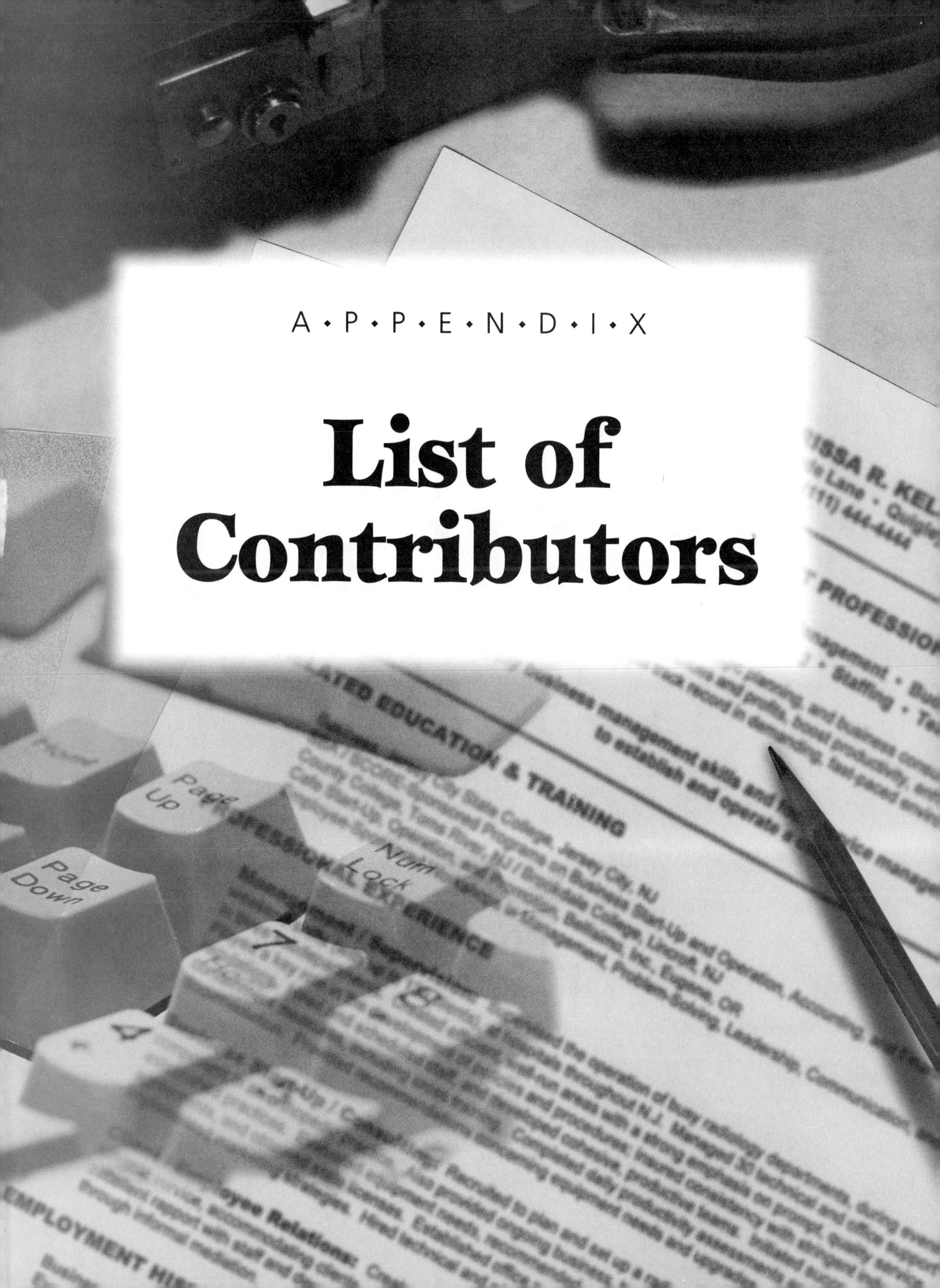

# List of Contributors

The following persons are the contributors of the resumes and cover letters in this book. All of the contributors are professional resume writers. To include in this Appendix the names of these writers and information about their business is to acknowledge with appreciation their voluntary submissions and the insights expressed in the letters that accompanied the submissions. Resume and cover letter numbers after a writer's contact information are the numbers of the writer's resumes and cover letters included in this book, not page numbers.

## Alabama

### *Montgomery*

*Donald Orlando*
*The McLean Group*
640 South McDonough
Montgomery, AL 36104
Phone: (334) 264-2020
Fax: (334) 264-9227
Member: NRWA, PARW
Certification: NCRW, CPRW
Resumes: 21, 81, 93, 186, 227
Cover letters: 6, 16

## Arizona

### *Mesa*

*Brooke Andrews*
*A New Beginning: Business Communications & Résumés*
258 West Second Street
Mesa, AZ 85201
Phone: (602) 844-2300
Fax: (602) 844-2301
E-mail: brooke@amug.org
Member: PARW
Certification: CPRW
Resume: 342

### *Prescott*

*Patricia S. Cash*
*Résumés for Results*
P.O. Box 2806
Prescott, AZ 86302
Phone: (520) 771-8127
Fax: (520) 771-1229
E-mail: geow@goodnet.com
Member: PARW
Certification: CPRW
Resumes: 28, 50, 89, 150, 240

### *Tempe*

*Fran Holsinger*
*Career Profiles*
1726 East Southern, Suite 8
Tempe, AZ 85282
Phone: (602) 413-9383
Fax: (602) 413-1753
E-mail: fholsinger@aol.com
Member: PARW, RWCA
Resumes: 17, 107, 159, 194, 288, 310
Cover letter: 4

## California

### *Campbell*

*Georgia Adamson*
*Adept Business Services*
180-A West Rincon Avenue
Campbell, CA 95008
Phone: (408) 866-6859
Fax: (408) 866-8915
E-mail: peach2000@aol.com
Member: NRWA, PARW
Certification: CPRW
Resume: 101

### *Fort Bragg*

*Nancy Karvonen*
*A Better Word and Résumé*
15850 Hwy. 20
Fort Bragg, 95437
Phone: (707) 964-1140
Fax: (707) 964-3423
E-mail: abetterword@saber.net
Member: PARW
Certification: CPRW
Resumes: 105, 326

### *Fresno*

*Susan Britton Whitcomb*
*Alpha Omega Résumé Services*
1255 West Shaw, #101A
Fresno, CA 93711
Phone: (209) 222-7474
Fax: (209) 222-9538
E-mail: SUS1RESUME@aol.com
Member: NRWA, PARW
Certification: NCRW, CPRW
Resumes: 1, 6, 12, 34, 35, 60, 80, 86, 129, 130, 188, 223, 225, 231, 251, 252, 263, 275
Cover letters: 2, 9, 12, 14

### *Orange*

*Christine Edick*
*Action Résumés*
1740 West Katell Avenue, Suite J
Orange, CA 92867
Phone: (714) 639-0942
Fax: (714) 639-3262
E-mail: yourtype@cruznet.net
Member: NRWA, PARW
Resume: 94

### *Portola Valley*

*Ted Bache*
*Kingston-Bache Résumés*
3130 Alpine Road, Suite 200-B
Portola Valley, CA 94028
Phone: (650) 854-8594
Fax: (650) 854-8594
Resumes: 18, 290

### *San Diego*

*Sheryl Wilde*
*The Wilde Writer*
10876 Whitehall Road
San Diego, CA 92126
Phone: (760) 632-1972
Resume: 147
Cover letter: 15

### *San Jose*

*Gary Watkins*
*Watkins Communications Group*
4970 Cherry Avenue, #22
San Jose, CA 95118
Phone: (408) 267-1094
E-mail: gawa+kim@hotmail.com
Resume: 100

### *Van Nuys*

*Vivian Van Lier*
*Advantage Business & Career Services*
6701 Murietta Aveue
Van Nuys, CA 91405
Phone: (818) 994-6655
Fax: (818) 994-6620
E-mail: vvanlier@aol.com
Member: PARW
Certification: CPRW
Resume: 340

## Florida

### *Fort Lauderdale*

*Shelley M. Nachum*
*Career Development Services*
4801 South University Dr., Suite 201
Ft. Lauderdale, FL 33328
Phone: (954) 434-0989
Fax: (954) 434-4284
E-mail: cardevsv@safari.net
Member: PARW
Resume: 92

### *Indian Rocks Beach*

*Jean F. West*
*Impact Résumé & Career Services*
207 10th Avenue
Indian Rocks Beach, FL 33785
Phone: (813) 593-2548
Fax: (813) 593-7386
E-mail: ImpactRes@aol.com
Member: NRWA, PARW
Certification: CPRW
Resume: 87

### *Lakeland*

*E. René Hart*
*First Impressions Résumé &*
*Career Development Services*
7100 Pebble Pass Loop
Lakeland, FL 33810
Phone: (941) 858-6989
Fax: (941) 859-9718
E-mail: ReneHart@aol.com
Member: PARW
Certification: CPRW
Resumes: 61, 134, 145, 319
Cover letter: 3

### *Melbourne*

*Laura A. DeCarlo*
*Competitive Edge Career Service*
1600 West Eau Gallie Blvd., Ste. 201
Melbourne, FL 32935
Phone: (800) 715-3442
Fax: (407) 752-7513
E-mail: lauraads@aol.com
Web site: www.acompetitiveedge.com
Member: NRWA, PARW
Certification: CPRW, ICCC
Resumes: 79, 226, 236, 241, 322

### *Tampa*

*M. Carol Heider*
*Heider's Secretarial Service, Inc.*
4860 W. Kennedy Blvd.
Tampa, FL 33609
Phone: (813) 282-0011
Fax: (813) 639-9288
E-mail: hssheider@aol.com
Member: PARW, NASS
Certification: CPRW
Resumes: 2, 185, 197, 208

*Diane McGoldrick*
*Business Services of Tampa Bay*
2803 West Busch Blvd., Suite 103
Tampa, FL 33618
Phone: (813) 935-2700
Fax: (813) 935-4777
E-mail: mcgoldrik@ix.netcom.com
Member: PARW
Resumes: 11, 24, 58, 83, 140, 191, 192, 254, 259, 285, 306, 337

### *Tarpon Springs*

*Mary Roberts*
*The Write Source Business & Career Center*
25400 US Highway 19 N, Suite 296
Clearwater, FL 34623
Phone: (813) 797-8973
Fax: (813) 725-0190
E-mail: WORDS2SELL@aol.com
[***Last known contact information***]
Member: PARW
Certification: CPRW
Resumes: 75, 108, 216, 320

## Georgia

### *Savannah*

*Carol Lawrence*
*A Better Resume*
P.O. Box 9826
Savannah, GA 31412
Phone: (888) 278-1096
Fax: (912) 832-4385
Member: PARW
Certification: CPRW
Resumes: 37, 184

## Illinois

### *Buffalo Grove*

*Joellyn Wittenstein*
*A-1 Quality Résumés & Career Marketing Services*
1220 Mill Creek Drive
Buffalo Grove, IL 60089
Phone: (888) 563-5596
(847) 255-1686
Fax: (847) 255-7224
E-mail: joellyn@interaccess.com
Web site: a-1qualityresumes.com
Member: NRWA, PARW
Certification: CPRW
Resume: 19
Cover letter: 7

### *Elmhurst*

*Georgia Veith*
*ABC Résumé Services*
135 Addison Avenue, Suite 224
Elmhurst, IL 60126
Phone: (708) 782-1222
Fax: (708) 279-5599
[***Last known contact information***]
Member: PARW
Certification: CPRW
Resumes: 148, 153

### *Flossmoor*

*Jennie R. Dowden*
*Jenn's Résumé Service*
3115 Heather Hill Court
Flossmoor, IL 60422
Phone: (708) 957-5976
Fax: (708) 957-5976
E-mail: cpd@wwa.com
Member: PARW
Certification: CPRW
Resumes: 20, 124, 174, 273, 292

### *Schaumburg*

*Steven A. Provenzano*
*A Advanced Resume Service, Inc.*
1900 East Golf Road, Suite M100
Schaumburg, IL 60173
Phone: (847) 517-1088
Fax: (847) 517-1126
E-mail: ADVRESUMES@aol.com
Member: PARW
Certification: CPRW
Resumes: 168, 287

### *Troy*

*John A. Suarez*
*Executive Career Fitness*
519 Nottingham
Troy, IL 62294
Phone: (888) 521-3483
E-mail: JASuarez@aol.com
Member: PARW
Certification: CPRW
Resumes: 26, 102, 111, 132, 133, 143, 235, 294, 318, 336

## Indiana

### *Anderson*

*Jon C. Shafer*
*Gaslight Communications*
212 Historic West 8th Street
Anderson, IN 46016
Phone: (765) 640-1511
Fax: (765) 640-1488
[***Last known contact information***]
Resumes: 57, 74, 114, 117, 121, 176, 201, 205, 232

### *Bloomington*

*John D. King*
*John D. King & Associates*
205 North College Avenue, Suite 614
Bloomington, IN 47404
Phone: (812) 332-3888
Member: NCDA (National Career Development Association)
Resume: 171

### *Hebron*

*Susan K. Schumm*
*The Printed Page*
805 South County Line Road
Hebron, IN 46341
Phone: (219) 996-6110
Fax: (219) 996-6110 (voice first fax)
E-mail: schumm@netnitco.net
Web site: http://2.netnitco.net/users/schumm/schumm.html
Resumes: 233, 313

### *Indianapolis*

*Carole E. Pefley*
*TESS, Inc.*
5661 Madison Avenue
Indianapolis, IN 46227
Phone: (317) 788-8377
Fax: (317) 788-8378
Member: PARW
Certification: CPRW
Resumes: 144, 295
Cover letter: 17

### *Lafayette*

*Alan D. Ferrell*
*ADF Professional Résumés*
1001 Salem Street
Lafayette, IN 47904
Phone: (765) 423-1858
Fax: (765) 494-6385
E-mail: ferrell@mgmt.purdue.edu
Resumes: 98, 163, 260
Cover letter: 18

### *Zionsville*

*Mary Ann Finch Vandivier*
*Finch Vandivier Writing Service*
65 E. Cedar, Suite C
Zionsville, IN 46077
Phone: (317) 873-3189
Fax: (317) 733-0885
E-mail: FINVAN@aol.com
resumecounselor:finchvandivierwritingservices
Member: PARW
Resume: 126

## Iowa

### *Iowa City*

*Elizabeth J. Axnix*
*Quality Word Processing*
329 East Court Street
Iowa City, IA 52240
Phone: (319) 354-7822
Fax: (319) 354-2220
E-mail: axnix@earthlink.net
Member: PARW
Certification: CPRW
Resumes: 5, 32, 46, 253

## Kansas

### *Lawrence*

*Linda Morton*
*Transcriptions*
1012 Massachusetts, Suite 201
Lawrence, KS 66044
Phone: (785) 842-4619
Fax: (785) 842-2846
E-mail: morton_sscm@compuserve.com
Member: PARW
Certification: CPRW
Resume: 302

## Kentucky

### *Radcliff*

*Connie S. Stevens*
*A-to-Z Résumé & Career Service*
1138A North Hill Street
Radcliff, KY 40160
Phone: (502) 352-4323
Fax: (502) 352-4336
E-mail: ConnieSS@aol.com
Member: NRWA, PARW
Resumes: 4, 99, 113, 261, 301

## Louisiana

### *West Monroe*

*Melanie Douthit*
*A First Impression*
309 Somerville Lane
West Monroe, LA 70503
Phone: (318) 396-7571
Fax: (318) 396-7571
E-mail: meladou@aol.com
[***Last known contact information***]
Member: PARW
Resume: 26

## Maine

### *Bangor*

*Joan M. Roberts*
*CareerMasters*
61 Main Street, Suite 55
Bangor, ME 04401
Phone: (207) 990-2102
Fax: (207) 990-1197
E-mail: jobsrch@aol.com
Member: PARW
Certification: CAGS, CPRW
Resumes: 62, 123, 169, 189

### *Saco*

*Patricia Martel*
*Saco Bay Business Services*
263 Ferry Road
Saco, ME 04072
Phone: (207) 284-4960
Fax: (207) 284-5937
E-mail: sbbs@ime.net
Member: PARW
Resumes: 84, 230, 293

### *Waterville*

*Elizabeth M. Carey*
62 Vidette Ave.
Waterville, ME 04901
Phone: (207) 872-2879
Member: PARW
Certification: CPRW
Resumes: 30, 213, 282, 303

*Becky J. Davis*
*Connections Secretarial Services*
6 Boutelle Avenue
Waterville, ME 04901
Phone: (207) 872-5999
Fax: (207) 872-5999
E-mail: RezWriter@aol.com
Member: PARW
Certification: PLS, CPRW
Resumes: 207, 214

## Maryland

### *Easton*

*Thomas E. Spann*
*Lee Edward Associates*
7605 Dover Woods Road
Easton, MD 21601
Phone: (410) 822-4459
Fax: (410) 820-4981
E-mail: resumes@skipjack.bluecrab.org
Web site: http://www.bluecrab.org/members/resumes
Member: PARW
Resumes: 23, 161, 200, 243, 256, 269, 279

## Massachuetts

### *Needham*

*Wendy Gelberg*
*Advantage Résumé*
21 Hawthorn Avenue
Needham, MA 02192
Phone: (781) 444-0778
Fax: (781) 444-2778
E-mail: wgelberg@aol.com
Member: NRWA, PARW
Certification: CPRW
Resumes: 54, 257

### *Northampton*

*Shel Horowitz, Director*
*D. Dina Friedman, Co-Director*
*Accurate Writing & More*
P.O. Box 1164
Northampton, MA 01061
Phone: (800) 683-WORD or
(413) 586-2388
Fax: (617) 249-0153
E-mail: info@frugalfun.com
Resume: 329

### *Northboro*

*Steven Green*
*CareerPath*
242 Brewer Street
Northboro, MA 01532
Phone: (508) 393-5548
Fax: (508) 393-6120
E-mail: steven@workingsmart.com
Member: NRWA, PARW
Certification: CPRW
Resume: 48

## Michigan

### *Adrian*

*Christina M. Popa*
*Executive Business Services*
3203 Moore Road
Adrian, MI 49221
Phone: (517) 263-6976
Fax: (517) 265-8385
E-mail: ebs@ini.net
Member: PARW
Certification: CPRW
Resumes: 88, 109, 142, 179, 246, 315

### *Flint*

*Janet L. Beckstrom*
*Word Crafter, Inc.*
1717 Montclair Avenue
Flint, MI 48503
Phone: (800) 351-9818
(810) 232-9257
Fax: (810) 232-9257
E-mail: wordcrafter@voyager.com
Member: PARW
Resumes: 3, 76, 122, 137, 172, 198, 228, 229, 239

### *Fremont*

*Patricia L. Nieboer*
*The Office*
Post Office Box 86
Fremont, MI 49412
Phone: (616) 924-4867
Fax: (616) 924-4867
Certification: CPRW, CPS
Resumes: 316, 325, 328

### *Kalamazoo*

*Betty A. Callahan*
*Professional Results*
2415 South Rose Street
Kalamazoo, MI 49001
Phone: (616) 382-2122
Fax: (616) 381-4584
Member: PARW
Certification: CPRW
Resumes: 316, 325, 328

### *Newport*

*Deborah L. Schuster*
*The Lettersmith*
P.O. Box 202
Newport, MI 48166
Phone: (734) 586-3335
Fax: (734) 586-2766
E-mail: lettersmith@foxberry.net
Member: PARW
Certification: CPRW
Resumes: 139, 167, 193, 209, 218, 220, 296

### *Novi*

*Lorie Lebert*
*Résumés for Results*
P.O. Box 267
Novi, MI 48376
Phone: (248) 380-6101
Fax: (248) 380-0169
E-mail: llebert@aol.com
Member: PARW, *Who's Who for Entrepreneurs*
Certification: CPRW
Resumes: 15, 95, 110, 175, 280, 297

### *Parchment*

*Randall S. Clair*
*JOBQUEST Resume Writing & Design*
P.O. Box 125
Parchment, MI 49004
Phone: (616) 344-5559
Fax: (616) 344-5559
Certification: CPRW
Resumes: 105, 154, 155, 199

## Minnesota

### *Rochester*

*Beverley Drake*
*CareerVision Resume & Job Search Systems*
3936 Highway 52N, #224
Rochester, MN 55901
Phone: (507) 252-9825
Fax: (507) 252-1525
E-mail: bdcprw@aol.com
Member: PARW, NAJST
Certification: CPRW
Resume: 234

## New Jersey

### *Fair Lawn*

*Vivian Belen*
*The Job Search Specialist*
1102 Bellair Avenue
Fair Lawn, NJ 07410
Phone: (201) 797-2883
Fax: (201) 797-5566
E-mail: vivbel@erols.com
Member: NRWA, PARW, Five O'clock Club Speakers Bureau
Certification: NCRW, CPRW
Resumes: 68, 96, 116, 131, 224

### *Marlboro*

*Beverly Baskin*
*Baskin Business & Career Services*
6 Alberta Drive
Marlboro, NJ 07746
Other offices: Princeton, NJ
Woodbridge, NJ
Phone: (800) 300-4079
Fax: (732) 972-8846
E-mail: BBCS@skyweb.net
Member: NRWA, PARW
Certification: NCC, CPRW
Resumes: 22, 210, 265
Cover letter: 5

### Rochelle Park

*Alesia Benedict*
*Career Objectives*
151 West Passaic Street
Rochelle Park, NJ 07662
Phone: (800) 206-5353
Fax: (800) 206-5454
E-mail: Careerobj@aol.com
Member: PARW
Certification: CPRW
Resumes: 8, 45, 82, 112, 221, 222, 237, 268, 299, 300

### Toms River

*Rhoda Kopy*
*A HIRE IMAGE*
26 Main Street, Suite E
Toms River, NJ 08753
Phone: (732) 505-9515
Member: NRWA, PARW
Certification: CPRW
Resumes: 14, 19, 72, 178, 278, 309, 332, 334

### Waldwick

*Fran Kelley*
*The Résumé Works*
71 Highwood Avenue
Waldwick, NJ 07463
Phone: (201) 670-9643
Fax: (201) 670-9643
E-mail: twofreespirits@worldnet.att.net
Member: NRWA, PARW
Certification: CPRW, SPHR
Resume: 71

### West Paterson

*Melanie A. Noonan*
*Peripheral Pro*
560 Lackawanna Avenue
West Paterson, NJ 07424
Phone: (973) 785-3011
Fax: (973) 785-3071
(973) 256-6285
E-mail: peripro1@aol.com
Member: NRWA, PARW
Certification: CPS
Resumes: 63, 69, 138, 187, 335

## New York

### Elmira

*Betty Geller*
*Apple Résumé & Typing Service*
456 W. Water Street, Suite 1
Elmira, NY 14905
Phone: (607) 734-2090
Fax: (607) 734-2090
Member: NRWA, PARW
Certification: CPRW
Resumes: 97, 115, 151, 165, 202, 262, 264, 267, 270, 308, 314, 321, 324

### Jackson Heights

*Kim Isaacs*
*Advanced Career Systems*
34-41 85th Street, Suite 6-G
Jackson Heights, NY 11372
Phone: (718) 565-8016
Fax: (718) 565-8016
E-mail: CareerSys@aol.com
Member: NRWA, PARW
Certification: NCRW, CPRW
Resumes: 85, 127, 149, 183, 195, 247, 327

### Medford

*Deborah Wile Dib*
*Advantage Résumés of New York*
77 Buffalo Avenue
Medford, NY 11763
Phone: (516) 475-8153
Fax: (516) 475-8153
E-mail: gethired@advantageresumes.com
Web site: http://www.advantageresumes.com
Member: NRWA, PARW, NAJST
Certification: CPRW
Resumes: 7, 13, 27, 29, 65, 66, 157, 255, 277, 305, 341

### New York

*Etta Barmann*
*Compu-Craft Business Services, Inc.*
124 East 40th Street, Suite 403
New York, New York 10016
Phone: (212) 697-4005
Fax: (212) 697-6475
Member: PARW
Certification: CSW, CPRW
Resumes: 144, 215

*David Feurst*
*Compu-Craft Business Services, Inc.*
124 East 40th Street, Suite 403
New York, New York 10016
Phone: (212) 697-4005
Fax: (212) 697-6475
Member: PARW
Certification: CPRW
Resumes: 16, 196

*Martin Weitzman*
*Gilbert Career Résumés, Ltd.*
275 Madison Avenue
New York, NY 10016
Phone: (212) 661-6878
Fax: (212) 661-7595
E-mail: gilcareer@aol.com
Member: NRWA (President)
Certification: NCRW, CPRW
Resume: 173

### Ossining

*Phyllis B. Shabad*
*CareerMasters*
95 Woods Brooke Circle
Ossining, NY 10562
Phone: (914) 944-9577
E-mail: careermasters@cyburban.com
Member: NRWA, PARW
Certification: NCRW
Resumes: 135, 152, 304

### Poughkeepsie

*Marian K. Kozlowski*
*MKK Resume Consulting Service*
47 South Gate Drive
Poughkeepsie, NY 12601
Phone: (914) 462-0654
Fax: (914) 462-0654
Member: PARW
Resumes: 118, 119, 158, 215, 217, 317

### Rochester

*Arnold G. Boldt*
*Arnold-Smith Associates*
625 Panorama Trail, Bdg 2, Suite 200
Rochester, NY 14625
Phone: (716) 383-0350
Fax: (716) 387-0516
Member: PARW
Certification: CPRW
Resume: 272

### Scotia

*Barbara M. Beaulieu*
*Academic Concepts*
214 Second Street
Scotia, NY 12302
Phone: (518) 377-1080
Fax: (518) 346-5763
E-mail: acresume@global2000.net
Member: PARW
Certification: CPRW
Resume: 136

### Yorktown Heights

*Mark D. Berkowitz*
*Career Development Resources*
1312 Walter Road
Yorktown Heights, NY 10598
Phone: (888) 277-9778
(914) 962-1548
Fax: (914) 962-0325
E-mail: cardevres@aol.com
Member: NRWA, PARW
Certification: CPRW, NCCC
Resumes: 70, 238, 242, 258, 281, 284, 298

## North Carolina

### Charlotte

*Deborah C. Sherrie*
*Market Yourself Services*
710 Jefferson Drive
Charlotte, NC 28270
Phone: (704) 366-9337
Fax: (704) 365-1317
E-mail: dsherrie@mindspring.com
Member: PARW
Certification: CPRW
Resume: 170

### Wilmington

*Sandy Adcox Saburn*
*C$^3$ Resources*
3329 Wrightsville Avenue, Suite L
Wilmington, NC 28403
Phone: (910) 395-5500
Fax: (910) 395-6653
E-mail: c3@wilmington.net
Member: PARW
Certification: CPRW
Resumes: 103, 146

## Ohio

### *Cincinnati*

*Barry Hunt*
*KeyWords*
7265 Kenwood Road, Suite 160
Cincinnati, OH 45236
Phone: (513) 984-1362
Fax: (513) 984-2921
[***Last known contact information***]
Resumes: 90, 276
Cover letter: 10

*Louise M. Kursmark*
*Best Impression*
9847 Catalpa Woods Court
Cincinnati, OH 45242
Phone: (888) 792-0030
Fax: (513) 792-0961
E-mail: lk@yourbestimpression.com
Web site: www.yourbestimpression.com
Member: NRWA, PARW
Certification: CPRW
Resumes: 53, 164, 182, 245, 286
Cover letters: 1, 11, 13

### *Grove City*

*Susan D. Higgins*
*Q Résumé Services*
3368 Independence Street
Grove City, OH 43123
Phone: (614) 873-3123
Fax: (614) 873-3123
E-mail: SusanQ@aol.com
Certification: CPRW
Resume: 44

## Oregon

### *Aloha*

*Pat Kendall*
*Advanced Résumé Concepts*
18580 SW Rosa Road
Aloha, OR 97007
Phone: (503) 591-9143
Fax: (503) 642-2535
E-mail: reslady@aol.com
Member: NRWA, PARW
Certification: NCRW, CPRW
Resumes: 38, 47, 56, 73, 91, 211, 212, 244, 248, 323, 330, 331

## Tennessee

### *Hendersonville*

*Carolyn S. Braden*
*Braden Résumé & Secretarial*
108 La Plaza Drive
Hendersonville, TN 37075
Phone: (615) 822-3317
Fax: (615) 826-9611
Member: PARW
Certification: CPRW
Resumes: 39, 162

### *Murfreesboro*

*Tracy Bumpus*
*First Impressions Career and Résumé Services*
P.O. Box 895
Murfreesboro, TN 37133-0895
Phone: (615) 890-3273
Fax: (615) 890-8532
E-mail: tbumpus@rezamaze.com
Web site: www.rezamaze.com
Member: PARW
Certification: CPRW
Resume: 141

## Texas

### *Beaumont*

*JoAnn Nix*
*Beaumont Résumé Service*
7825 Fox Cove
Beaumont, TX 77713
Phone: (409) 899-1932
Fax: (409) 924-0019
E-mail: Brsnixtx@aol.com
Web site: http://members.aol.com\TXResumes
Member: PARW
Certification: CPRW
Resume: 307

### *Tyler*

*Ann Klint*
*Ann's Professional Résumé Service*
1608 Cimmarron Trail
Tyler, TX 75703
Phone: (903) 509-8333
Fax: (903) 509-8333
E-mail: Resumes-Ann@tyler.net
Member: PARW
Certification: CPRW
Resumes: 31, 160, 190, 219, 266, 274, 289, 291, 312

### *The Woodlands*

*Cheryl Ann Harland*
*Résumés by Design*
25227 Grogan's Mill Road, Suite 125
The Woodlands, TX 77380
Phone: (281) 296-1659
(888) 213-1650
Fax: (281) 296-1601
E-mail: ios@neosoft.com
Member: PARW
Certification: CPRW
Resumes: 51, 78, 249

## Virginia

### *Lynchburg*

Wendy S. Enelow
The Advantage, Inc.
119 Old Stable Road
Lynchburg, VA 24503
Phone: (804) 384-4600
Fax: (804) 384-4700
E-mail: wenelow@inmind.com
Web site: http://crm21.com\theadvantage
Member: PARW
Certification: CPRW
Resumes: 9, 10, 59, 64, 283

### *Virginia Beach*

*Anne G. Kramer*
*Alpha Bits*
P.O. Box 61876
Virginia Beach, VA 23455
Phone: (757) 464-1914
E-mail:akramer@livenet.net
Member: NRWA, PARW
Certification: CPRW
Resume: 180
Cover letter: 8

## Washington

### *Poulsbo*

*Lonnie L. Swanson*
*A Career Advantage*
21590 Clear Creek Road NW
Poulsbo, WA 98370
Phone: (360) 779-2877
Fax: (360) 779-2877
E-mail: resumewriter@silverlink.net
Member: PARW
Certification: CPRW
Resume: 338

## West Virginia

### *Charleston*

*Barbie Dallmann*
*Happy Fingers Word Processing & Résumé Service*
1205 Wilkie Drive
Charleston, WV 25314
Phone: (304) 345-4495
Fax: (304) 343-2017
E-mail: BarbieDall@Prodigy.Com
Member: NRWA, PARW
Certification: CPRW
Resumes: 25, 52, 55, 125, 128, 156, 333

## Wisconsin

### *Appleton*

*Kathy Keshemberg*
*A Career Advantage*
302 East Murray Avenue
Appleton, WI 54915
Phone: (920) 731-5167
Fax: (920) 739-6471
E-mail: kathyKC@aol.com
Member: NRWA, PARW
Certification: CPRW
Resumes: 49, 177, 311

For those who would like to contact the Professional Association of Resume Writers, its address is as follows:

Professional Association of Resume Writers
3637 Fourth Street North, Suite 330
St. Petersburg, FL 33704
Phone: (813) 821-2274
Fax: (813) 894-1277

For those who would like to contact the National Résumé Writers' Association, write to Ms. Phyllis Shabad, Secretary NRWA, CareerMasters, 95 Woods Broke Circle, Ossining, NY 10562

# Occupational Index

## *Current or Last Position*

**Note:** Numbers are resume numbers in the Gallery, not page numbers.

# D



# E

## F



## G



## H



## I



## J



## L



## M

## N



## O

**See us on the World Wide Web: www.jist.com**

## *America's Top 300 Jobs,* Seventh Edition

**A Complete Career Handbook**

*Based on information from the U.S. Department of Labor and other sources*

This book includes all job descriptions from the *Occupational Outlook Handbook,* plus Mike Farr's *The Quick Job Search.* Well-written narrative with many charts and photos. Job descriptions cover the nature of the work, working conditions, training needed, earnings, and more. A complete career exploration handbook for students, job seekers, career changers, and others. Part of America's Top Jobs® series.

ISBN 1-56370-717-9 / Order Code LP-J7179 / **$18.95**

## *Career Guide to Industries,* 2000-2001 Edition

**A Companion Reference to the *Occupational Outlook Handbook***

*U.S. Department of Labor*

This information-packed review of 42 top industries discusses careers from an industry perspective and covers employment trends, earnings, types of jobs available, working conditions, training required, and more. Includes cross-references to jobs in the *Occupational Outlook Handbook.*

ISBN 1-56370-804-3 / Order Code LP-J8043 / **$16.95**

## *America's Top Military Careers,* Third Edition

*Based on information from the Department of Defense*

This accurate, up-to-date reference helps people make the transition into and out of the armed forces. It describes military occupations, including information on working conditions, physical demands, advancement opportunities, duty locations, pay, benefits, and more. It also shows how military experience relates to civilian jobs. Ideal for those considering military careers; active military personnel developing long-term goals; former military personnel seeking civilian jobs; career counselors; and others.

ISBN 1-56370-706-3 / Order Code LP-J7063 / **$19.95**

**Call 1-800-648-JIST or Fax 1-800-JIST-FAX**

**See us on the World Wide Web: www.jist.com**

## America's Top Jobs for People Without a Four-Year Degree, Fifth Edition

*By J. Michael Farr*

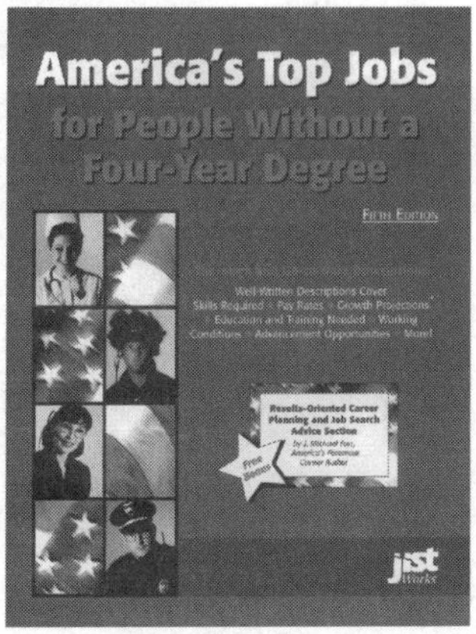


Many of today's good jobs don't require a four-year degree. This book identifies and describes jobs in all major occupations and industries that can be learned on the job or through training programs. The descriptions are based on the latest *Occupational Outlook Handbook* and include details on job responsibilities, working conditions, skills required, training required, growth projections, average earnings, and more. A special section helps you find a job fast.

ISBN 1-56370-722-5 / Order Code LP-J7225 / **$16.95**

## America's Fastest Growing Jobs, Sixth Edition

*By J. Michael Farr*

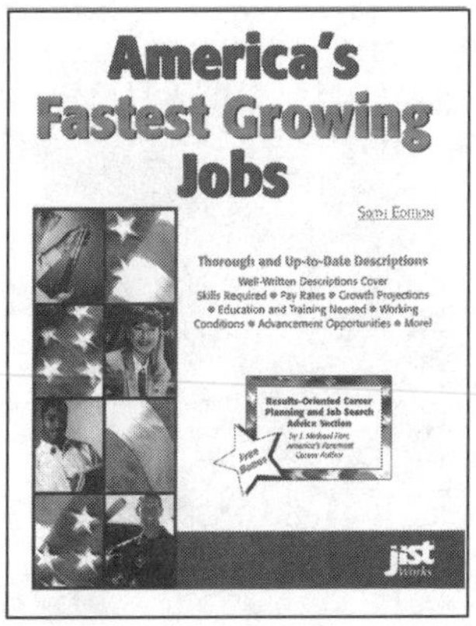


Get thorough descriptions of the fastest growing jobs in our economy, plus a bonus section with job search advice. Job descriptions are based on the latest data in the *Occupational Outlook Handbook.* Ideal for students, career changers, counselors, and job seekers of all ages.

ISBN 1-56370-718-7 / Order Code LP-J7187 / **$16.95**

## America's Top Jobs for College Graduates, Fourth Edition

*By J. Michael Farr*

Discover the major jobs that require a four-year degree and offer the greatest potential for growth and earnings. The job descriptions in this book explain working conditions, skills required, growth potential, education required, typical earnings, and other facts. The data is based on the newest *Occupational Outlook Handbook,* and other sections provide information on labor market trends, effective job search techniques, and the benefits of a college degree.

ISBN 1-56370-720-9 / Order Code LP-J7209 / **$16.95**

**Call 1-800-648-JIST or Fax 1-800-JIST-FAX**

See us on the World Wide Web: www.jist.com

## America's Top Medical, Education, & Human Services Jobs, Fifth Edition

*By J. Michael Farr*

This is an indispensable reference for anyone interested in three large, fast-growing fields. It describes major medical, education and human services jobs and includes details on skills needed, education and training required, growth opportunities, salary ranges, and more. Descriptions are based on the lastest data from the *Occupational Outlook Handbook.* Extra sections cover the most effective job search techniques, industry trends, and sources of additional information.

ISBN 1-56370-721-7 / Order Code LP-J7217 / **$16.95**

## America's Top White-Collar Jobs, Fifth Edition

*By J. Michael Farr*

This information-packed review of 42 top industries discusses careers from an industry perspective and covers employment trends, earnings, types of jobs available, working conditions, training required, and more. Includes cross-references to jobs in the *Occupational Outlook Handbook.*

ISBN 1-56370-719-5 / Order Code LP-J7195 / **$16.95**

## Guide to America's Federal Jobs, Second Edition

**How to Find a Government Job**

*By the Editors at JIST*

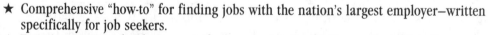

Hundreds of thousands of job seekers need the information in this book!

★ Comprehensive "how-to" for finding jobs with the nation's largest employer–written specifically for job seekers.
★ Functions as "two books in one"–first as a guide for finding and applying for government positions; second as a reference providing valuable information on all major federal agencies.
★ Federal job opportunities exist in virtually all occupations throughout the country–employing almost three million people!

ISBN 1-56370-526-5 / Order Code LP-J5265 / **$18.95**

Call 1-800-648-JIST or Fax 1-800-JIST-FAX

**See us on the World Wide Web: www.jist.com**

## *The Resume Solution,* Second Edition

**How to Write (and Use) a Resume That Gets Results**

*By J. Michael Farr*

*The Resume Solution* is written in a powerful style with tips that make great looking–and reading–resumes. Advice is offered in short, to-the-point sentences; exactly the style for resumes.

This book uses a step-by-step approach, offers solid advice on how to use a resume to secure more interviews and offers, gives information on electronic job seeking, and provides numerous examples and worksheets.

ISBN 1-56370-180-4 / Order Code LP-J1804 / **$12.95**

## *The Federal Resume Guidebook,* Second Edition

**How to Write a Winning Federal Resume**

*By Kathryn K. Troutman*

The second edition of *The Federal Resume Guidebook* leads you through the complexities of finding and analyzing job announcements; writing federal resumes for both human and scanner "eyes"; and packaging your resume to meet both federal and vacancy announcement criteria. Whether you're seeking your first federal job or a federal promotion, *The Federal Resume Guidebook* is an essential resource.

ISBN 1-56370-545-1 / Order Code LP-J5451 / **$21.95**

## *The Quick Resume & Cover Letter Book,* Second Edition

**Write and Use an Effective Resume in Only One Day**

*By J. Michael Farr*

This unique book will help you write a solid resume in just a few hours and improve it later, in stages, as you have time. This edition features over 90 sample resumes from professional resume writers, plus notes on the resumes highlighting easy-to-imitate techniques. Special sections cover career planning, other correspondence, and the most effective job search techniques.

ISBN 1-56370-634-2 / Order Code LP-J6342 / **$14.95**

**Call 1-800-648-JIST or Fax 1-800-JIST-FAX**

## More Good Books from JIST Works

### The Very Quick Job Search, Second Edition
*Get a Better Job in Half the Time!*
*By J. Michael Farr*

A major revision of the most thorough career planning and job search book on the market, this is a "must have" for job seekers and career counselors! Major topics include interviewing, resumes, time use, and trends.

ISBN: 1-56370-181-2
**$16.95** / Order Code: LP-J1812

### Young Person's Guide to Getting & Keeping a Good Job, Second Edition
*By J. Michael Farr, Marie Pavlicko, & Gayle MacDonald*

The best job search book ever for high school students.

- ✶ Easy-to-read narrative sections
- ✶ Lots of in-the-book activities
- ✶ Entertaining graphics to enhance learning
- ✶ Excellent career planning and job search advice
- ✶ Easy-to-use instructional aids

ISBN: 1-56370-555-9
**$9.95** / Order Code: LP-J5559

### Getting the Job You Really Want, Third Edition
*A Step-by-Step Guide*
*By J. Michael Farr*

A complete revision of a best-seller with great advice on identifying skills, defining the ideal job, getting a job in less time, and surviving on the job. Lots of in-the-book activities. Instructor's Guide available.

Instructor's Guide:
ISBN: 1-56370-196-0
**$14.95** / Order Code: LP-RWRIG

ISBN: 1-56370-092-1
**$12.95** / Order Code: LP-RWR

### How to Get a Job NOW!
*Six Easy Steps to Getting a Better Job*
*By J. Michael Farr*

Covers major job search topics:

- ✶ Identify key skills
- ✶ Define your ideal job
- ✶ Get two interviews a day
- ✶ Do a good job in the interview
- ✶ Follow up on all contacts

ISBN: 1-56370-290-8
**$7.95** / Order Code: LP-J2908

### The Right Job for You! Second Edition
*An Interactive Career Planning Guide*
*By J. Michael Farr*

This book presents solid career planning principles that have worked for thousands of people. It is easy to read and use, with frequent in-the-book exercises, case studies, and examples.

ISBN: 1-56370-286-X
**$9.95** / Order Code: LP-J286X

### The Quick Interview & Salary Negotiation Book
*Dramatically Improve Your Interviewing Skills and Pay in Just a Few Hours*
*By J. Michael Farr*

Mike Farr, America's leading author of job search books, shares simple, fast, effective techniques for:

- ✶ Improving interviewing skills
- ✶ Handling unusual and difficult interview situations
- ✶ Negotiating salaries and pay increases

ISBN: 1-56370-162-6
**$12.95** / Order Code: LP-J1626

**Call 1-800-648-JIST or Fax 1-800-JIST-FAX**

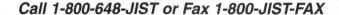

# JIST Ordering Information

JIST specializes in publishing the very best results-oriented career and self-directed job search material. Since 1981 we have been a leading publisher in career assessment devices, books, videos, and software. We continue to strive to make our materials the best there are, so that people can stay abreast of what's happening in the labor market, and so they can clarify and articulate their skills and experiences for themselves as well as for prospective employers. **Our products are widely available through your local bookstores, wholesalers, and distributors.**

## The World Wide Web

For more occupational or book information, get online and see our Web site at **www.jist.com**. Advance information about new products, services, and training events is continually updated.

## Quantity Discounts Available!

Quantity discounts are available for businesses, schools, and other organizations.

## The JIST Guarantee

We want you to be happy with everything you buy from JIST. If you aren't satisfied with a product, return it to us within 30 days of purchase along with the reason for the return. Please include a copy of the packing list or invoice to guarantee quick credit to your order.

## How to Order

For your convenience, the last page of this book contains an order form.

**24-Hour Consumer Order Line:**
Call toll free 1-800-648-JIST
Please have your credit card (VISA, MC, or AMEX) information ready!

**Mail your order to:**

**JIST Publishing, Inc.**
8902 Otis Avenue
Indianapolis, IN 46216-1033
**Fax:** Toll free 1-800-JIST-FAX

**Key Code: LP**

# JIST Order and Catalog Request Form

Purchase Order #: ______________ (Required by some organizations)

Please copy this form if you need more lines for your order.

**Billing Information**

Organization Name: ______________

Accounting Contact: ______________

Street Address: ______________

City, State, Zip: ______________

Phone Number: (     ) ______________

**Phone: 1-800-648-JIST**
**Fax: 1-800-JIST-FAX**
**World Wide Web Address:**
**http://www.jist.com**

**Shipping Information with Street Address (If Different from Above)**

Organization Name: ______________

Contact: ______________

Street Address: (We *cannot* ship to P.O. boxes) ______________

City, State, Zip: ______________

Phone Number: (     ) ______________

Credit Card Purchases: VISA____ MC____ AMEX____

Card Number: ______________

Exp. Date: ______________

Name As on Card: ______________

Signature: ______________

| Quantity | Order Code | Product Title | Unit Price | Total |
|---|---|---|---|---|
| | ——— | **Free JIST Catalog** | **Free** | ——— |
| | | | | |
| | | | | |
| | | | | |
| | | | | |
| | | | | |
| | | | | |
| | | | | |
| | | | | |
| | | | | |

| | |
|---|---|
| Subtotal | |
| +5% Sales Tax *Indiana Residents* | |
| +Shipping / Handling / Ins. (See left) | |
| TOTAL | |


*jist Publishing*
**8902 Otis Avenue**
**Indianapolis, IN 46216**


## Shipping / Handling / Insurance Fees

**In the continental U.S.** add 7% of subtotal:

- Minimum amount charged = $4.00
- Maximum amount charged = $100.00
- FREE shipping and handling on any prepaid orders over $40.00

Above pricing is for regular ground shipment only. For rush or special delivery, call JIST Customer Service at 1-800-648-JIST for the correct shipping fee.

**Outside the continental U.S.** call JIST Customer Service at 1-800-648-JIST for an estimate of these fees.

**Payment in U.S. funds only!**

**JIST thanks you for your order!**